THE LITERARY THEORY HANDBOOK

Blackwell Literature Handbooks

This new series offers the student thorough and lively introductions to literary periods, movements, and, in some instances, authors and genres, from Anglo-Saxon to the Postmodern. Each volume is written by a leading specialist to be invitingly accessible and informative. Chapters are devoted to the coverage of cultural context, the provision of brief but detailed biographical essays on the authors concerned, critical coverage of key works, and surveys of themes and topics, together with bibliographies of selected further reading. Students new to a period of study or to a period genre will discover all they need to know to orientate and ground themselves in their studies, in volumes that are as stimulating to read as they are convenient to use.

Published

The Science Fiction Handbook
M. Keith Booker and Anne-Marie Thomas

The Seventeenth-Century Literature Handbook
Marshall Grossman

The Twentieth-Century American Fiction Handbook
Christopher MacGowan

The British and Irish Short Story Handbook
David Malcolm

The Crime Fiction Handbook
Peter Messent

The Literary Theory Handbook
Gregory Castle

GREGORY CASTLE

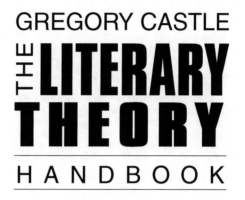

THE LITERARY THEORY
HANDBOOK

WILEY Blackwell

This edition first published 2013
© 2013 John Wiley & Sons, Ltd

Wiley-Blackwell is an imprint of John Wiley & Sons, formed by the merger of Wiley's global Scientific, Technical and Medical business with Blackwell Publishing.

Registered Office
John Wiley & Sons, Ltd, The Atrium, Southern Gate, Chichester, West Sussex, PO19 8SQ, UK

Editorial Offices
350 Main Street, Malden, MA 02148-5020, USA
9600 Garsington Road, Oxford, OX4 2DQ, UK
The Atrium, Southern Gate, Chichester, West Sussex, PO19 8SQ, UK

For details of our global editorial offices, for customer services, and for information about how to apply for permission to reuse the copyright material in this book please see our website at www.wiley.com/wiley-blackwell.

The right of Gregory Castle to be identified as the author of this work has been asserted in accordance with the UK Copyright, Designs and Patents Act 1988.

Library of Congress Cataloging-in-Publication Data

Castle, Gregory.
 The literary theory handbook / Gregory Castle.
   pages cm. – (Blackwell Literature Handbooks)
 Includes bibliographical references and index.
 ISBN 978-0-470-67195-5 (Pbk. : alk. paper) 1. Criticism–History–Handbooks, manuals, etc.
2. Literature–History and criticism–Theory, etc.–Handbooks, manuals, etc. I. Title.
 PN86.C35 2013
 801′.9509–dc23
                                        2012050374
A catalogue record for this book is available from the British Library.

Cover image: Wyndham Lewis, *Workshop*, *c.*1914–15, oil on canvas, 765 × 610 mm. Tate, London. © Tate, London 2013.
Cover design: Richard Boxall Design Associates.

Set in 10/12.5pt Sabon by SPi Publisher Services, Pondicherry, India

1   2013

For Ralph and Donna Castle,
whose encouragement and support come without condition

and

Camille Angeles-Castle,
who continues to teach me the theory of love

Contents

Acknowledgments

The Literary Theory Handbook was first published in 2007 under the title *The Guide to Literary Theory*. Since publishing the first edition, I have taught a number of literary theory courses and participated on panels and roundtables at international conferences; I also talked with many friends and colleagues about various issues and problems in literary theory. Over those six years, a number of theories and theorists were becoming more prominent and it seemed to me that the time was ripe for another edition, one that would not only include these new directions and new thinkers but also expand and refine the existing material. To all the people involved in these various conversations I owe more than I can say. I am grateful for the opportunity to teach literary theory and thereby discover at first hand what sort of things readers at all levels might require. I thank especially the graduate students at ASU who were instrumental in advancing my own understanding of the myriad theories discussed in this *Handbook*. I want to single out for special thanks Ian Murphy, who served as a research assistant in the final phase of this project, and Kristi Van Stechelman Perkins, a former student and dear friend who has talked with me for hours over the years about theory and literature and life and to her I owe a debt of affection and gratitude. I want also to thank my colleagues in the Department of English, particularly Patrick Bixby, Ron Broglio, Joni Adamson, Mark Lussier, Claudia Sadowski-Smith, and Dan Bivona, for bearing with me when I asked them about their own approach to theory or engaged them in discussions of particular theoretical problems.

I want to thank Professor Gerardine Meaney, director of the Humanities Institute at University College, Dublin, for providing me with office space and library access so that I might work on this book. And to Ruth Black, I give thanks for being such a good host and providing me with a comfortable environment in which to work. Ruby, the boxer, whose contemplative mood rivaled that of any philosopher I have read, kept me company on many rainy afternoons. Finally, I am deeply grateful for the patience and kind attentions of Alyssha Nelson, who watched over the final stages of this book.

I would like to thank the following friends and colleagues for their advice and counsel: Joseph Valente, David Lloyd, James Phelan, Stephen Ross, Margot Backus, Nicholas Allen, Enda Duffy, and Gregory Dobbins. My dear friend Chouki El Hamel, a brilliant historian and critical thinker, bore with me for many hours as I hashed out various theoretical problems and offered sound advice and often led me to new insights. Another dear friend and mentor, John Paul Riquelme, has been a sounding board and guide for more years than I can remember (or will confess to) and has helped me understand the suppleness and nuances of theoretical approaches to literature. But more than that, he and his partner, Marie-Anne Verougstraete, have opened up their home to me on more than one occasion and it was in the third floor aerie of their home in Boston that I was able to finish this book on time. Finally, I want to thank Michael Ryan, with whom I worked on the *Blackwell Encyclopedia of Literary and Cultural Theory*. Over four years of working together, I received what amounted to a master-class in theory. Without his sound judgment and often impassioned advocacy for this or that idea, this *Handbook* would have been a poorer thing.

Any academic book, but especially one of this nature that covers so much ground, involves a number of people who make it possible. I am grateful for the unstinting support of the Hayden Library at ASU, especially the kindness and expertise of Henry Stevens, Library Supervisor, who provided resources and good humor. The folks at Wiley-Blackwell have been wonderful to work with, particularly Ben Thatcher, Project Editor, and Bridget Jennings, Senior Editorial Assistant, who were patient and supportive at every stage of this project. Brigitte Lee Messenger worked patiently with me through copy-editing and proofing, and proved, by her careful work, that none of us are fallible. There are not enough superlatives to describe Emma Bennett, Executive Editor, who shepherded the first edition through production and who helped me plan this new edition. Without her encouragement and support, I may well have thrown in the towel. All writers should be so fortunate as to have an editor so singularly committed to an author's success and well-being.

It may be unconventional to thank the musicians who have filled the air while working on an academic book, but I am part of a generation for whom music is more than the soundtrack of a life. Music is a vital part of all of my work, for without it my thoughts would lack lyricism, they would have stumbled without grace or rhythm. So, to Radiohead and Miles Davis, to Thelonious Monk, Brad Mehldau and Eno, I raise a glass. To the folks at Constellation Records in Montréal, particularly the crew of Godspeed You! Black Emperor, I lift my fist.

Alphabetical Listing of Key Movements and Theories

Introduction

> And the end of our exploring
> Will be to arrive where we started
> And know the place for the first time.
> T. S. Eliot, *Four Quartets*

Nearly a century ago, the English literary critic, I. A. Richards, spoke of a "chaos of critical theories," an assessment that would not be wide of the mark in the early years of the twenty-first century. The student of literature today is confronted with an array of theoretical approaches that touch on nearly every facet of human experience, from language and history to sexuality and gender, from cognitive science to the environment. How is one to choose? *The Literary Theory Handbook* is designed to help readers find their way through the chaos of theory by providing in-depth overviews of the leading approaches. Most of the theorists discussed in these pages assume that literary texts – and not just books, but other kinds of texts, like film and other works of art – give us pleasure and help us understand the world around us. Some recent theoretical fields, like posthumanism, are profoundly concerned with what it means to be human and what our relation ought to be with the *non-human*. This new emphasis is, in some respects, a return to the humanism that for centuries defined literary and cultural study – but with an important difference. For the posthumanism we find today has learned the lessons of theoretical reflection on humanism, anti-humanism, and a host of other perspectives. My point is that not only does *literature matter* but theory matters too, and not simply because it helps us understand literature. Theory has its own claim on our attention because it seeks, like literature has always done, to make the world come alive in our imaginations. Theory can be hard sometimes, especially when a specialized vocabulary is involved. But any theory worth its salt is finally about human experience and how

The Literary Theory Handbook, First Edition. Gregory Castle.
© 2013 John Wiley & Sons, Ltd. Published 2013 by John Wiley & Sons, Ltd.

to make it better. Matthew Arnold, a nineteenth-century English poet and critic, once said that "literature is a criticism of life." I would like to add that theory, at its best, is always trying *to get at the life of literature*. The reader of this *Handbook* is invited to explore in its pages how literature can come alive with a little help from theory.

Since at least 1980, a number of introductory texts have emerged that seek to explain the tenets of the main theoretical trends. *The Literary Theory Handbook* differs in a number of ways. First, it includes a brief history of theory that gives a broad overview from the classical era to the present, with an emphasis on the twentieth and twenty-first centuries; this is a unique feature. Another feature not found in similar texts is a chapter that includes short biographies of literary theorists, which emphasize the major works and accomplishments of over forty key figures. Many guides and introductions provide discussions of the major theories, but few provide the kind of detailed coverage of a wide range of theories that the reader will find in this *Handbook*. Each section of chapter two goes into sufficient detail about each theory, including explanations, quotations, and examples, so that the reader gets a good foundation for further reading. Moreover, the sections are organized under broad categories that help the reader to see the interrelations between and among theoretical approaches. Finally, the *Handbook* offers sample readings (in chapter four) that give the reader a sense of how theoretical analysis works. No other similar book – be it a guide or an introduction – offers all of these features.

The Nature of Literary Theory

The rise of "high theory" in the 1960s and 1970s (think, for example, of deconstruction and feminism) and its popularity in the human and social sciences has changed fundamentally the way we read literature. But theory has been with us since the time of the ancient Greeks, when Aristotle set down his theory of poetics, which was an attempt to understand how tragic drama worked and how it affected its audiences. His *Poetics*, like so many studies after it, focused on the relationship between literature and life and, even when it related the most terrible events, celebrated life and all of its mysteries. Since Aristotle, literary theory has gone through many changes, sometimes circling back on itself to reclaim an earlier idea, other times leaping ahead according to a new paradigm for understanding language or the human experience. The notion of theory that dominates the humanities and social sciences today really begins with theories of form and structure in the 1920s and 1930s, though some theories (like Marxism, psychoanalysis, and feminism) have roots that go back further into the nineteenth century. The 1960s saw a groundswell of theoretical innovation (and, at times, renovation) that has continued, despite alarming talk of the "death of theory," until the present day.

Theory is a way of thinking. In fact, one could say that thinking theoretically is a paradigm for thought itself, at least that form of thought used to understand concepts and ideas and to combine them meaningfully. Broadly speaking, theory is deductive or inductive: in the first, the theorist begins with a general idea and then investigates individual instances of it (literary texts) in order to prove its validity; in the second, the study of individual instances leads to the formation of general ideas based on them. Inductive reasoning is more common in the sciences, though Aristotle's theory of tragedy and some formalist approaches rely on it. By and large, literary theory is deductive, in that a general idea governs our analysis of individual texts. In deduction, knowledge is built up through generalizations that test the limits of what can be included in general categories. Deductive reasoning, particularly in literary analysis, assumes the possibility of alternative viewpoints and thus requires the power of persuasion to make an argument based on a general idea, because other general ideas could account equally well for the same individual texts. Despite this openness to alternatives, the thought process in literary theory remains the same in large part because we are always moving from general principles to particular instances, from general ideas to individual texts. Even theories that attack generalization are grounded on the general principle that generalities ought to be avoided.

One reason literary theory appears so forbidding or impenetrable to so many readers is that it asks us to manage multiple general ideas and devise multiple strategies of interpretation. The tendency toward theoretical collaboration – for example, postcolonial feminism, Marxist deconstruction, posthumanism – has enriched our sense of how theory can be used but it also challenges us to juggle multiple analytical strategies and technical vocabularies. The good news is that the difficulty is one of degree rather than kind, for theoretical thought functions in the same way no matter how many ideas we juggle. *The Literary Theory Handbook* seeks to make this theoretical juggling easier by showing how complex ideas work singly and in combination. Of course, literary theory neither seeks nor can achieve the kind of stability, uniformity, consistency, and UNIVERSALITY that is the aim of scientific inquiry. While scientists cannot ignore such things as ideology, social changes, and political pressures, the scientific method insures that, in the proper conditions, objectivity can be achieved. With literary theory, aspects of society and politics are often the focus of analysis. This does not mean that theory is free of norms and rules or that it is totally subjective; the point is rather that the norms and principles of theory are constructed precisely in order to take the measure of social and political influences on literature. While literary theory involves a subjective element, traditions of practice have made possible a certain consistency that enables readers and theorists alike to share their experience with literary texts. It also allows teachers and writers like myself to communicate fundamental theoretical ideas, concepts, and methods. Literary theory therefore resembles the literary text because the very fact that the latter is a product of a particular person or persons in a particular society and culture at a particular time is vitally important.

In the sciences, a new theory can displace an old one, relegating the older theory to the history of science. This rarely happens in literary theory. We might find that a particular theory (say, formalism) falls out of fashion, but in the humanities, there is always a chance that an "outdated" theory will be revived, often in connection with new ideas (as when narrative theorists use formalist concepts). Another thing that distinguishes literary theory is its openness to a wide variety of disciplines, including anthropology, architecture, biology, communications, design, economics, history, international relations, linguistics, mathematics, music, philosophy, physics, political science, psychology, semiotics, sociology, and theatre. Because literature, and the human experience it both represents and creates, is rich and various, literary theory has found it both useful and invigorating to borrow methods and ideas from these disciplines. In a world that has become increasingly specialized, in which our own experience is often limited to our workplace and own small field of expertise, literary theory makes other forms of expertise available to us and reminds us, by virtue of its openness and adaptability, of the wider world in which we each play our small but significant role.

This leads me to address two problem areas in literary theory that, for some readers, can be a stumbling block: terminology and style. Some theories – for example, deconstruction, Lacanian psychoanalysis, Marxist theory, phenomenology, postcolonial theory, narrative theory – could be faulted for stylistic extravagance, for having a specialized vocabulary, or for close adherence to a specific doctrine. There are sound reasons for each of these qualities, particularly if a given theory (say, Marxism or postcolonial theory) seeks to question conventional modes of writing, thinking, or organizing knowledge. In fact, many contemporary literary theorists seek to subvert or challenge Enlightenment thought, which is typically characterized by a stable and unified subject of knowledge, and a belief in the primacy of reason and in concepts like universality. The style and vocabulary of Jacques Derrida's deconstructionist criticism is in part designed to circumvent easy answers to complex questions about language, just as the difficulties of Luce Irigaray's feminist psychoanalysis are the result of her avoidance of traditional notions of gender, sexuality, and psychology. To be sure, some theorists use obscure terminology or affect a difficult style to mask a trivial or incoherent argument. In these cases, readers are not to be faulted for complaining about jargon or obscurantism.

What is Literature?

An important question needs to be raised at this point, one that is often felt, by readers of all kinds, to be self-evident: what is the object of literary theory? The obvious answer is *literature*. But this obvious answer fails to satisfy readers, especially those who have been engaged in teaching and writing about it for years! So it is worthwhile asking, what do we mean when we use terms like *literature* and *literary*? From the time of Aristotle to the present, philosophers have recognized the preeminence of literature, particularly poetry, in aesthetic theory. "Poetry," writes G. W. F. Hegel, "is adequate to all forms of the beautiful and extends over all of them, because its proper element is the beautiful imagination, and imagination is indispensable for every beautiful production, no matter to what form of art it belongs" (1: 90). Hegel was pretty sure he knew what literature was, as were most critics and readers until the modernist era, when novelists, poets, and playwrights began to experiment with traditional literary forms and raised all sorts of questions about what constitutes a specifically *literary* work. Postmodernism and cultural studies have only made these questions more urgent by expanding our conception of what constitutes a *literary* object (that is, one that can be *read*) to include television shows, advertisements, video games, internet sites, musical compositions, newspapers, cookbooks, and so much more.

Despite a long tradition of regarding literature as a fine art and despite the consensus in previous historical eras that literature is *imaginative* writing – a consensus based on Aristotle's distinction between history and poetry: "the former relates things that have happened, the latter things that may happen" (12) – literary theory has, throughout the twentieth century, called into question the special status of both fine art and literature. Anyone who has read a major anthology of literature will notice that a substantial amount of the material in it is not literary in the sense of poems or fictional stories. One is as likely to find political, historical, or scientific writings as poetry, fiction, and drama. And many of these works are "imaginative" in the sense that they use language in "artistic" ways (that is, they rely on the *connotative* or suggestive meanings as often as the *denotative* or specific meanings of a word). All sorts of fine writing qualifies as literary, which is why we find works by John Stuart Mill, Cotton Mather, Margaret Fuller, and Charles Darwin in literature anthologies. We cannot stop here, however, for the criterion of "fine" or "imaginative" writing has changed over the years and not everyone agrees about how to make judgments about such writing, other than to say it is literary, which brings us back to the original question: but *why* is this kind of writing literary?

If we cannot rely on a special or "fine" use of language or specifically literary genres (e.g., fiction, poetry, drama) as a foundation for defining literature, perhaps we could find what we are looking for by asking whether an author *intended* to create literature. But this, too, is untenable, for it presupposes that we can know such intentions reliably enough to provide a basis for theoretical analysis; in any case, there is no good reason to think that literary authors have any special authority on this matter.

For many readers, literature is that which has stood the test of time, the "classics." But this criterion is unsatisfactory, for one of the reasons a text becomes a "classic" is that it has been kept in print and in the classroom. And until very recently, this meant a process of selection and exclusion by cultural elites (publishers, professors, editors, agents) who created CANONS of literature that reflect their values and vision of the world. Ralph Rader, a Chicago School Neo-Aristotelian critic, puts the case strongly: "writers and works" are "ruthlessly winnowed by the collective judgment and the survivors arranged in a relatively fixed honorific hierarchy of status and value (247). This kind of thinking tends to keep literature cordoned off in privileged spaces (e.g., universities, art schools, literary societies, coteries, and the like) where it is explained by experts (hence, Harold Bloom's idea that literary critics are a kind of secular clergy). Common sense tells us that literature is not restricted to a certain kind of reader, though an English major might have an advantage by virtue of spending a lot of time reading literature and literary criticism. But this advantage does not change the nature of the books she might read, for it is simply a means of *access* to literature. Few readers, though, will be happy with a definition of literature that is grounded in the marketplace or on admissions standards at universities. Nor will they be happy with a definition that limits literature to fiction, poetry, and drama. After all, today's newspaper may be tomorrow's literature, as was the case with Joseph Addison and Richard Steele's essays in the eighteenth-century periodical *The Spectator*. Or it may remain, as most journalistic writing remains, ephemeral, useful primarily to historians. By the same token, what is considered the highest literary achievement today may become a classic; but it is just as likely (if not more so) to be forgotten tomorrow. This is a problem of genre as well, for literary history reveals a complex web of influences in which we see the ascendancy now of poetry, now of the novel as the paradigmatic form for "literature" for a given age. The contemporaries of Addison and Steele did not regard their works as literature, nor were their works written in the forms great literature typically took for their age. Saying this is saying nothing about the quality of their work, its popularity, or its influence. That we *do* tend to value their work *now* as literature, however, says a great deal about twenty-first-century reading habits.

So we are back to our question, which we might answer by considering a definition of literature that emphasizes perennial themes and subject matter. Fair enough, but who is to decide what the important subjects and themes are? Even a cursory glance at literary history shows that themes and subjects change constantly; and while some themes and subjects are consistently treated over the years, they are rarely treated in the same way. Would John Milton's *Paradise Lost*, which deals with the theme of humankind's fall from heavenly grace, be more "literary" than Tony Kushner's *Angels in America*, which focuses on AIDS and the nature of gay experience in late twentieth-century United States? As with the problem of defining what "fine writing" is, so with this problem: there is simply no way to define a *truly literary* theme.

These unsatisfactory answers to our question share one thing in common: they presuppose that literature is separate from other forms of representation, protected by its AUTONOMY from the corrosive effects of social and political life. On this view, the literary text is an AUTONOMOUS text, an idea that has its roots in German idealist philosophy, particularly Immanuel Kant's notion of the art-object as self-contained and self-governing But we might well ask how autonomy can be realized if the art-object – in the present context, the literary text – is so bound up with publishing, marketing, reviewing, and teaching? Even if we argue that literature is autonomous in the sense that it works according to its own inner laws and principles, we must contend with the objection that authors and readers are inextricably caught up in complex ideological and cultural ideas that have powerful effects on how they read and write. One of the most profound achievements of literary theory has been to challenge this idea of autonomy by analyzing ideology, culture, politics, and other elements that we once confidently thought lay outside the sphere of art. Let's go so far as to grant that literature is "relatively" autonomous, that literary language does more than merely serve as a mode of communication in or reference to the external world. What would be the limits of such an autonomy? Who or what would set those limits? In the end, the argument that literature is radically separate from other spheres of life violates good sense as well as logic.

One answer to our question, *what is literature*, does not seem to go away, no matter how hard literary theorists try to disprove it. For some people would have us believe that literature is "high-brow," that it somehow transcends the interests and concerns of the majority of people. If we believed this, we would have to see *literature* at the top of a hierarchy, below which would be popular forms of writing (low- or middle-brow writing, so-called genre fiction, song lyrics, graphic novels, and the like). If we look at literary history, we see that such a distinction falls apart, for it is at bottom a distinction dependent on fluctuations of taste and the nature of textual production. The example of Addison and Steele illustrates this. So too does a novelist like Charles Dickens, whose work was once regarded as "popular" rather than "literary," but is now regarded as one of the great literary giants of the nineteenth century. These criteria having to do with the *value* of literature – that it is *better* (morally, aesthetically, or socially) than other forms of writing – are often unconsciously assumed by the same readers and teachers who might consciously condemn them.

Even if we could agree what "good" and "bad" corresponded to and could agree further that such judgments were worth making, how do we select our criteria: those that existed at the time of publication or those in place at the time of the critic's judgment? Are such criteria, no matter where they originate, a function of purely aesthetic elements, like style and form, or are they a function of social or political ideas? As Friedrich Nietzsche has argued, values are never intrinsic to a work or an action, nor do they come to us from a transcendent source and nor are they universal in character. Our literary values, like our moral ones, are developed in order to preserve our sense of cultural and personal well-being; our judgments are therefore partial and interested, contingent on historically conditioned aesthetic, social, and political attitudes. For some people, this realization leads to the conclusion that all values are relative, and to a point, that is the case. Yet, some values seem to prevail over others and some works inspire the same sense of value in a given community (say, among English majors or among members of a book club). So how do we determine if a book is valuable *as literature*? What makes us so confident, generation after generation, that some works (for example, Shakespeare's plays, Emily Dickinson's poems, Herman Melville's *Moby Dick*, or James Joyce's *Ulysses*) are clearly literature while others (the mass of out of print and forgotten books languishing in secondhand book shops) are clearly not? Part of the reason is that readers recognize in such works the innovation and creativity, the love of language and exuberance in its use, and for these reasons want to continue reading and talking about them. These readers have not necessarily judged these features *good* or *bad*, but they do seem to have consistently found in them a certain kind of pleasure, have regarded them as part of a tradition that includes novels, poems, and plays, but also histories, sermons, essays, and other forms of writing. Readers keep coming back to this tradition and the pleasures it offers, even if what they find is not quite the same as what a prior generation found. Readers who love dramatic characters who speak well of life's joys and vicissitudes are as likely to appreciate Oscar Wilde as Shakespeare, as likely to find Virginia Woolf as compelling as Nathaniel Hawthorne.

Literature, then, might well be that form of writing that engages with life in the most exciting, innovative, creative, and mind-altering ways. It is a way of seeing and being in the world that we find so attractive because it allows us to see the world in a new way. Literature is, as Wolfgang Iser has noted, a kind of anthropological investigation, for it goes into areas of life that are left unexplored by science, philosophy, religion, or politics. Literature, then, is the most fully human way of seeing and understanding the world.

The Practice of Theory

Even if we accept this definition of literature, we are left with the question of how to interpret it, for like our experience with the world, our reading practices vary from person to person. Theoretically, we could have a different reading of a given text for every reader, but what we more often find are common modes of interpretation used by multiple readers who share reading experiences. Stanley Fish, a pragmatist and reader-response theorist, calls these "interpretive communities." Though we often think of such communities in connection with schools, they exist at all levels of society; they exist even when we are not made aware of them, as when readers of crime fiction respond in similar ways to generic conventions. A chemistry textbook, a novel by Virginia Woolf, a cookbook, Kant's philosophy, a Volkswagen manual, the *LA Times*, a back issue of *Star!* magazine: these all require certain conventions of reading and understanding. In each case, the generic expectations of a certain kind of text will be more or less apparent to readers of it, though the communities that read Kant and Woolf will often be more formal, and the members of it more likely to communicate with each other (through criticism, reviews, discussion, and so on). And while such communities have the virtue of creating shared habits of reading, they can run the danger of assuming that their mode of reading is a natural one, even the "best" or "authorized" one (the latter is often the case with respect to sacred texts). Literary theory, particularly in the late twentieth century, seeks to avert this danger and to celebrate the multiplicity of reading standpoints and interpretive communities.

Interpreting literature is a way of raising questions about it. The more questions raised, and the more difficult they are to answer, the more likely we are going to be tempted to want some kind of "toolkit," and theory provides just the variety of tools that readers can employ to answer the questions that literature raise. These questions can be about the form or genre of a text, or about the way gender and sexuality are represented, or about how language works to communicate emotion and states of consciousness, or about how political ideas and ideology are reflected or produced by the text. The range of questions corresponds very closely to the range of our experiences in the world. Formalist and structuralist theorists tend to emphasize a predictable relationship between the reader and the language of literature because individual readers, as Roland Barthes has pointed out, "cannot by [themselves] either create or modify" language, for "it is essentially a collective contract which one must accept in its entirety if one wishes to communicate" (14). At the same time, as poststructuralists emphasize, language can be slippery and unstable, because the *signifiers* (the words in the text) lack a clear and direct relation to what we think (or hope) are the *signifieds* (the ideas or concepts) to which they refer. For some of these theorists, language refers only to itself (that is, signifiers refer to other signifiers), which means that, theoretically, meaning can proliferate endlessly. Both of these positions are valid and valuable ways of reading literature; they respond to different perspectives on the world, on language, and on reading practices. *The Literary Theory Handbook* explores these and myriad other theoretical positions and emphasizes their coexistence not their exclusive authority.

The practice of literary theory is, therefore, not a matter of following an orthodoxy, but of finding the best way to open the text to the questions we want to ask about it. The literary critic who uses theory (either explicitly or implicitly) is free to be creative, to express herself and her own values in the process of answering the questions she poses about the text. Oscar Wilde understood this well when he linked the artist and the critic in terms of their shared creation of a new aesthetic experience. For him, the best criticism treats the work of art "as a starting point for a new creation" and, further, the highest criticism "fills with wonder a form which the artist may have left void, or not understood, or understood incompletely" (150). Wilde's insight is very close to that of hermeneutical critics, who devised techniques for reading sacred and historical texts, for both insist that the reader must listen to what the text has to tell us.

If there is "truth" to be had from literature, it is very much bound up with our ways of reading, which are not all that different from our ways of understanding the world around us. The "special" status of the literary text, then, is attributable not to its essential qualities but rather to the reader's own reading practices and experiences. The task of the critical reader is not to pass judgment on the text but to enjoy the reading process in a disciplined way and to share that pleasure with others.

How to Use the *Handbook*

The Literary Theory Handbook is designed to help readers with this task. One can begin with the historical overview in chapter one, "The Rise of Literary Theory," in order to get a sense of how theory has developed and the relations between and among theories. Another strategy is to consult individual theoretical fields in chapter two, "The Scope of Literary Theory," either by reading a single entry or the entries clustered in one of the six parts. Chapter three, "Key Figures in Literary Theory," and the "Recommendations for Further Reading" are research tools designed to provide biographical and bibliographical information in a quick and accessible fashion. The "Glossary" is a valuable resource that can accompany just about any reading task in literary criticism and theory. Finally, readers who wish to see how theory is used in literary analysis can consult the sample interpretations in chapter four, "Reading with Literary Theory." *The Literary Theory Handbook* provides multiple points of entry for readers of all kinds and for every stage of the process of learning about and enjoying the experience of theory.

To make the *Handbook* a more effective reference tool, I have used a system of cross-referencing. SMALL CAPITALS are used to indicate terms that can be found listed in the glossary. **Boldface type** is used to indicate that a theorist is treated at length in chapter three, "Key Figures in Literary Theory." Generally, I cross-reference the first use of a name or term in any given section. A similar system of cross-referencing terms and concepts is employed in the glossary and index. In chapter two, parenthetical cross-references refer to relevant discussions of a given topic, figure, or concept elsewhere in the *Handbook*, while the "note" at the end of each section points the reader to related sections in the chapter.

Note on Sources

Throughout this *Handbook*, I have supplied the date of first publication in the original language; for texts not originally written in English, I have supplied the title used for the first English translation. Bibliographies, including both works cited and recommend readings, follow each entry on a theory or theorist. For more titles, and a list of anthologies and general collections of literary theory, see the "Recommendations for Further Reading."

Works Cited

Aristotle. *Poetics*. Trans. Richard Janko. Indianapolis: Hackett, 1987.

Barthes, Roland. *Elements of Semiology*. Trans. Annette Lavers and Colin Smith. New York: Hill and Wang, 1973.

Fish, Stanley. *Is There a Text in This Class? The Authority of Interpretive Communities*. Cambridge, MA: Harvard University Press, 1980.

Hegel, G. W. F. *Aesthetics: Lectures on Fine Art*. 2 vols. Trans. T. M. Knox. Oxford: Clarendon Press, 1975.

Rader, Ralph. "Fact, Theory, and Literary Explanation." *Critical Inquiry* 1.2 (December 1974): 245–72.

Wilde, Oscar. "The Critic as Artist." In *Intentions and the Soul of Man*. Vol. 8 of *The First Collected Edition of the Works of Oscar Wilde*. Ed. Robert Ross. London: Methuen, 1908. 99–224.

1

The Rise of Literary Theory

The one duty we owe to history is to rewrite it.

Oscar Wilde, "The Critic as Artist"

The historical life of ideas is neither straightforward nor causal. Ideas from one era are revived and revised for a new generation of thinkers, while new ones emerge from both predictable and surprising sources. This is certainly the case with the history of literary theory. As the twentieth century unfolded, literary theory took on a momentum that might be called progressive, each movement or trend building on the blind spots and logical flaws in those that had come before. But there was also a fair amount of recursive movement – doubling back to pick up a forgotten or misunderstood idea – as well as lateral forays into new terrain. Throughout this history, we find instances of innovation, both new combinations of existing theoretical ideas (for example, Marxist deconstruction) or the emergence of new areas of study (for example, cognitive studies); we also find projects of renovation, in which prior theoretical models (for example, materialist criticism or psychoanalysis) were given a new lease on life. These various modes of historical change were often happening simultaneously, so that we find clusters of intense growth and activity in key periods, especially in the modernist period (1920s and 1930s), the era of "high theory" (the 1960s and 1970s), and the posthumanist revolution that began to gain ground in the 1990s.

From the era of formalism and critical theory to the mid-century flourishing of poststructuralism and feminism to the rise of cultural studies, postcolonial studies, and myriad theories under the banner of posthumanism, we see a rich and complex historical development. One cannot help but notice that from mid-century, the variety of theories increases dramatically, which means that this development is difficult to chart chronologically. For that reason, this history will attempt to

The Literary Theory Handbook, First Edition. Gregory Castle.
© 2013 John Wiley & Sons, Ltd. Published 2013 by John Wiley & Sons, Ltd.

illustrate the simultaneity as well as the progression of theoretical change and renewal. It will also draw attention to recursive tendencies, those moments when theoretical development appears to turn back on itself to reclaim earlier modes of thought and methodologies (as we see in the 1990s with a reinvigorated Marxist theory). Indeed, the game-changing ideas in the posthumanist movement frequently take us back to Friedrich Nietzsche and Charles Darwin, those nineteenth-century "prolegomenal thinkers," as Margo Norris calls them (6), who were products of their time but also, paradoxically, way ahead of it. This temporal paradox defines a good deal of literary theory and serves as a reminder of the importance of *untimely* experience, which Nietzsche describes as "acting counter to our time and thereby acting on our time and, let us hope, for the benefit of a time to come" ("On the Uses" 60).

Early Developments in Literary Theory

Literary theory has its roots in Greek and Roman philosophy, principally Plato's ideas on mimesis and Aristotle's *Poetics*, though there were many competing Athenian thinkers until the time of the Romans. Of special note among the latter is Pseudo-Longinus, whose *On the Sublime* (first century CE) put forward the idea of an aesthetic experience that we might today call "the beautiful" and thereby marked the beginning of AESTHETIC theory. Ideas about art and literature changed little until the Renaissance era, though medieval refinements, like anagogical and allegorical modes of interpretation, were to prove important for hermeneutics and for various schools of formalist and archetypal criticism. The period from the sixteenth through the eighteenth centuries produced a number of important treatises on literary art. Sir Philip Sidney's *Defence of Poesie* (1595) was instrumental in establishing the importance of the literary artist as an "inventor" or "maker," while John Dryden, in his *Essay on Dramatic Poesy* (1668), followed the lead of Pierre Corneille, whose *Of the Three Unities of Action, Time, and Place* (1660) established the principles of a neoclassical theory of drama and thereby formalized modern dramatic art. English neoclassicism reached its height in Alexander Pope's *Essay on Criticism* (1711), which articulates a view of the critic who aspires toward the perfection of "Unerring NATURE," a "clear, unchang'd universal light." For Pope, the task of the critic is to follow the guidelines of those who have come before, for "Those RULES of old, discover'd, not devis'd, / Are Nature still, but Nature Methodiz'd" (ll.70–1, 88–9). The balanced and measured harmony of Pope's couplets give a pleasing aesthetic form to a general neoclassical view of art as an improvement upon nature, a view that in the eighteenth century conformed to the Enlightenment principle of human perfectibility.

In the last quarter of the eighteenth century, English and German Romantic literature challenged the neoclassical vision of art by giving voice to human striving for what lay beyond measure and balance, beyond formal perfection. At the same time, German idealist philosophy developed new theories of aesthetics. Most commentators today regard Alexander Baumgarten's *Aesthetica* (1750) as the starting point of modern aesthetic theories. Baumgarten's task was to find a way to bridge the gap between sensation and reason, a bridge he found in *aesthetics*, which is derived from the Greek αἰσθητός, "sensible, perceptible" [*OED*]). The first major work in this new field was Edmund Burke's *A Philosophical Enquiry into the Origin of Our Ideas of the Sublime and Beautiful* (1757), which sought to establish the general outlines of a theory of *taste* and aesthetic judgment. Burke uses the term "taste" to mean "that faculty, or those faculties of the mind which are affected with, or which form a judgment of the works of imagination and the elegant arts" (6). Like Baumgarten, Burke proceeds from the assumption that taste is bound up with sensation; but he is not content with establishing aesthetics as an inferior kind of cognition. The faculty of imagination becomes an important feature of aesthetic judgment, for "the mind of man possesses a sort of creative power of its own" separate from sensation, "either in representing at pleasure the images of things in the order and manner in which they were received by the sense, or in combining those images in a new manner, according to a different order" (15–16). Burke was able to link empiricism and aesthetics in a systematic way, and his theories of art, particularly of the sublime, which emphasized affective states like terror and pain, were to prove immensely influential. Some years later, Immanuel Kant's *Critique of Judgment* (1790) moved away from the English empirical tradition and Burkean aesthetic sensibility and established the importance of cognition in aesthetic judgments. For Kant, aesthetic judgments, though a "freer" form of ordinary cognition, are grounded in an *a priori* concept of taste that is analogous to the concepts that govern understanding and moral judgment. For Kant, aesthetic judgment *resembles* moral judgment, in that both have to take place outside the determinate CONCEPT, which is essential to reason. We know things because we have concepts for them, categories of understanding, but art, Kant says, does not become known in this conceptual way. All aesthetic judgments are reflective, not cognitive, and are deeply grounded in subjectivity; they are also singular because they cannot be defined under a general concept. An aesthetic idea "cannot become cognition because it is an *intuition* (of the imagination) for which an adequate concept can never be found" (215). But Kant required a universal ground or common sense (*sensus communis*) for artistic judgment. He found it in the idea of an *indeterminate* concept of Beauty (one that has the quality of a concept without being determined by reason), which allowed him to posit a "supersensible substrate of humanity" that grants aesthetic judgment universal validity. It is a necessary illusion, Kant admits, "the best we can do" (213). Kant's theory of the sublime attempted to move past the emphasis on feeling in Burke's philosophy. For both thinkers, the sublime defies the imagination's power to conceive of an object or experience, but Kant tried to show how this failure of the imagination can be overcome by reason. The aesthetic judgment of the sublime, he argued, involves the judgment not of an object but of the relationship between an object's overwhelming presence or force and the ability of the imagination to invoke a concept of "absolute freedom" or "absolute totality" that could assimilate it. When imagination is overwhelmed by perceptions (typically, natural and of the sort Burke describes as terrifying or awesome), reason steps in and "cognizes" what imagination has failed to grasp and thus shows its power over nature. This triumph of reason generates the sublime effect.

The concept of the beautiful is central to Kantian and neo-Kantian aesthetics, according to which judgments of the beautiful are disinterested, universal, and necessary; they present the beautiful object as possessing "purposiveness without purpose" – that is, it appears to have a purpose, it is driven by *seeming to possess* the quality of purposiveness, but it has no *determinate* purpose, no *telos* or goal, and it corresponds to no determinate concept. Friedrich Schiller's *On the Aesthetic Education of Man* (1795) departs from Kant's aesthetics by sidestepping the problem of the concept and concentrating on the DIALECTICAL interplay of reason and imagination. He thus develops the Kantian idea of "play" well beyond where Kant himself wished to take it. In fine art, Kant notes, "the purposiveness in its form must seem as free from all constraint of chosen rules as if it were a product of mere nature" – a free *play* that is also purposive – and it must not "seem intentional; i.e., fine art must have the *look* of nature even though we are conscious of it as art: it must not appear painstaking" (16). Schiller develops the idea of a "play impulse," a state in which artistic play, rather than serving the function of a paradoxical purposiveness without purpose, mediates between sense and reason. By reconciling "becoming with absolute being, of variation with identity," the play-drive mediates the sense-drive and form-drive, by enabling both to "act in concert" and thereby "introduce form into matter and reality into form" (97–9). Schiller's thought was influential among German and English Romantic writers and artists who sought to bring together the material realm of the sensible and the spiritual realm of pure thought. Indeed, the concept of play enabled a new way of "distributing the sensible," as **Jacques Rancière** puts it. "Minimally defined," he writes, "play is any activity that has no end other than itself, that does not intend to gain any effective power over things or persons." The "inactive activity" of the "player" (as opposed to, say, the worker) is a suspension of both the "cognitive power of understanding" and the "sensibility that requires an object of desire" (30). Kant and Schiller remain important among post-Marxist theorists, especially Rancière who argues that their work articulates "the new and paradoxical regime for identifying what is recognizable as art ... the aesthetic regime" (*Aesthetics* 8), one which persists in framing our contemporary discussions of art and aesthetics. (On the aesthetic regime, see Post-Marxist Theory 114–15.)

G. W. F. Hegel answers what he considers to be the key questions confronting Kant and Schiller: Can we speak of universal assent to any aesthetic judgment without a concept of the beautiful or of the artwork? Can art be its own concept? Hegel thought that it could and developed a concept of art that is both true and necessary but that emerges in the same temporal and dialectical process as thought itself. Art aspires to the highest form of Spirit, for "the loftiness and excellence of art in attaining a reality adequate to its Concept will depend on the degree of inwardness and unity in which Idea and shape appear fused in one" (1: 72). Romantic art best exemplifies this notion of the artistic concept as part of the general process of Spirit (or Reason): rather than the "undivided unity of classical art" (a "unity of divine and human nature," which is realized in a "sensuous immediate existence"), we find in Romantic art the "*inwardness of self-consciousness*" that "celebrates its triumph over the external and manifests its victory in and on the external itself, whereby what is apparent to the senses alone sinks into worthlessness" (1: 80–1).

The German idealist tradition exerted a powerful influence on English Romanticism, which in its turn inaugurated a tradition of critical reflection on literature and culture that influenced much of twentieth-century literary theory. One of the chief "conductors" of German aesthetic theory was Samuel Taylor Coleridge, whose *Biographia Literaria* (1817) successfully translated German aesthetics into English terms. The division of imagination into primary and secondary modes and the distinction between imagination and fancy are two of the most famous propositions in that volume, and both are grounded in the aesthetics of Kant, Schiller, and Friedrich Schelling. For Coleridge, the primary imagination is "the living Power and prime Agent of all human Perception, and as a repetition in the finite mind of the eternal act of creation in the infinite I AM" (295–6). The secondary imagination is an "echo" of this primary form, differing only in degree "and in the *mode* of its operation." *Fancy* differs by virtue of its "play" within "fixities and definites," a "mode of Memory emancipated from the order of time and space" (296). William Wordsworth was also influenced by Schiller, particularly his theory of aesthetic "play," and in the distinction he drew between naïve and sentimental poetry, the latter characterized by reflective and skeptical self-consciousness, the former by "natural genius" and spontaneous, *un*selfconsciousness. The preface to *Lyrical Ballads* (co-authored by Wordsworth and Coleridge, 1800) expounds on the nature and function of literary art and the role of the artist in society; it also rejects neoclassical theories of poetic practice and turns to the "natural genius" of the "rustic" man as a model for the poet's aesthetic sensibility. For Wordsworth, the poet is a hypersensitive individual, one "who rejoices more than other men in the spirit of life that is in him" and who is "affected more than other men by absent things as if they were present" (xxviii). The poet finds in the "the native and naked dignity of man" and in divine Nature the "grand elementary principle of pleasure, by which he knows, and feels, and lives, and moves" (xxxiii–xxxiv). The poem written by such a sensitive individual is the product of "emotion recollected in tranquility." Percy Shelley's *Defense of Poetry* puts forward a similar view of the poet as a sensitive participant in an "unremitting interchange" ("Mont Blanc") with the natural world. For Shelley, poets "are the unacknowledged legislators of the world," for they produce an aesthetic object that "is the very image of life expressed in its eternal truth" (46, 10). A more radical statement of poetic sensitivity at the time was John Keats' "negative capability," which refers to the imaginative absorption in the world outside of oneself, a capacity for surrendering one's personality in the contemplation of an object.

Romantic notions of art and the beautiful persisted throughout the nineteenth century and constituted a kind of secular spiritualism in the arts that reached a high point in the poetry of Alfred Lord Tennyson, Walt Whitman, and Emily Dickinson. However, not all writers of the era appreciated the Romantic emphasis on feeling and striving for the infinite. The critic and poet Matthew Arnold was ambivalent about Wordsworth, for example, though he admired him as he did the other major Romantics. As Michael O'Neill notes, Arnold "democratizes Romantic longing, presenting it as an all-pervasive emotion [in which] the special fate of the artist merges into [a] depiction of a general lot" (111). In fact, one of the problems for the Romantics was that they "did not know enough": they "lacked 'materials and a basis; a thorough interpretation of the world was necessarily denied to it" (Arnold 262–3). He believed that poetry, indeed all of literature, could serve an important function as a stabilizing influence in a society that was becoming increasingly less reliant on the church as the source of moral and ethical principles. His "post-Romanticism" may have as much to do with the turmoil of mid-century Europe – marked by the wave of revolutions of 1848 – as with aesthetic concerns. Though much maligned for his cultural conservatism, Arnold may well have been the first literary theorist to recognize the deep connections between aesthetics and culture and, more important, between the critic and society. However, Arnold's privileged position in nineteenth-century English society (his father was headmaster at Rugby School) gave him a somewhat restricted view of how literature could improve social conditions. His influential *Culture and Anarchy* (1869) considers the threat to society in class terms and offers what had become, by the late nineteenth century, a quintessentially liberal humanist solution to the problem. On the one hand, education, redesigned along humanist lines, should provide the kind of cultural knowledge necessary for a rapidly evolving industrial society; on the other hand, criticism should perform the function of recognizing and preserving "the best that is known and thought in the world" (268). Arnold held that "the critical power is of lower rank than the creative," but he also held that criticism (along with philosophy) created "an intellectual situation of which the creative power can profitably avail itself" (260–1). Criticism should be free of Romantic emotionalism, for its chief endeavor is "to see the object as in itself it really is" (258). In order to do this, it must be informed by the "disinterested love of a free play of the mind on all subjects, for its own sake" (268). In a sense, Arnold rewrites Schiller's idea of "play" in a way that resolves the paradox at its heart by making it a function of critical clear-sightedness.

According to Linda Dowling, Arnold and his contemporaries in the mid-nineteenth century, especially writers like John Ruskin and William Morris, embraced a form of artistic democracy, that she calls "Whig aesthetics," rooted in the moral philosophy of the Earl of Shaftesbury and the aesthetics of Schiller. Whig aesthetics promoted the social and ethical utility of art but it also led to its putative opposite, the AESTHETICISM of the *fin de siècle*. For Dowling, Whig aestheticism encompasses such late nineteenth-century figures as Walter Pater and Oscar Wilde. Pater, an Oxford professor who made his reputation as an art historian and critic, had a powerful effect on young artists and writers in the late nineteenth and early twentieth centuries. His *Studies in the Renaissance* calls our attention to the "passage and dissolution of impressions, images, sensations" and argues for a perspective toward experience that is immediate and vital. But the aestheticism he advocates is not entirely a withdrawal from the world into the rarified realm of art – the usual meaning attached to the infamous "Conclusion," in which Pater argues that art proposes to give us nothing "but the highest quality to [our] moments as they pass, and simply for those moments' sake" (190). In fact, Dowling argues that some Victorian readers would not have seen a break in continuity between Pater and his contemporaries, for they saw "an identical impulse toward restored community" rather than an "Aestheticist withdrawal into art." In short, Pater too was motivated by "the liberal spirit of Victorian culture" (xi).

Far more radical were Wilde, Pater's student at Oxford, and Friedrich Nietzsche, who in very similar ways point decisively toward the main concerns of twentieth-century literary theory. Nietzsche and Wilde were great shatterers of tradition; they warned us to go beyond the mere reversal of conventional values ("the last shall be first," Matt. 19:30) and even beyond a critique of those values themselves. For them, as for the modernists who followed, the goal was to interrogate the *value of value itself*, to learn its genealogy, its historical provenance, and to put forward entirely new modes of valuation. In Nietzsche's thought, this *transvaluation* revealed, among other things, a recognition that aesthetics is a fundamental element of our value-making capacity, up to and including the value of truth. The concept *truth* is nothing more than the life-preserving consequence of our *drive toward truth*, not a transcendental, absolute, or universal idea; and we articulate this consequence, whether in the realm of science or morality, in the aesthetic dimension of language. Because language, in conceiving concepts for the things and ideas in the world, is not able adequately to convey the meaning of the multiplicitous and polymorphous nature of the world, truth becomes "a moveable host of metaphors, metonymies, and anthropomorphisms … illusions that we have forgotten are illusions" ("Truth" 84). What is required is to break through the illusion and embrace our status as creative beings – that is, in Wilde's sense of the word, *liars*. In *The Birth of Tragedy*, his most sustained meditation on art, Nietzsche avers that "the aesthetically sensitive man stands in the same relation to the reality of dreams as the philosopher does to the reality of existence; he is a close and willing observer, for these images afford him an interpretation of life, and by reflecting on these processes he trains himself for life" (34). Because we are "aesthetically creating subjects," we are able to correspond to our experience and intuitions, but only "by shattering and mocking the old conceptual barriers" ("Truth" 86, 90). Nietzsche's understanding of the *Übermensch* and the tragic hero confirms the aesthetic nature of human being, for the "one thing needful" is "to give style to one's character," to maintain the "artist's faith." In the "experiments with himself" performed by the "free spirit," "all nature ceases and becomes art" (*Gay Science* 232, 303).

Wilde understood this element of Nietzsche's thought instinctively. While writing *The Picture of Dorian Gray*, both a defense of aestheticism and a cautionary tale of its excesses, he noted that "to become a work of art is the object of living" (Ellmann 311). Like Nietzsche, Wilde believed that life is in many ways a form of aestheticized will or desire. He claimed that the "spirit of transcendentalism is alien to the spirit of art. For the artist can accept no sphere of life in exchange for life itself. For him there is no escape from the bondage of the earth: there is not even the desire of escape" ("English" 248). But this bondage is merely that, a kind of imprisonment, if it is not trumped by art, for one does not go to life for "our fulfillment or our experience," one goes to art, because "Art does not hurt us" (*Intentions* 174). Wilde's approach to art not only sustained the idealist tradition of aesthetics but also broadened its reach: "all the arts are fine arts," he claimed, "and all the arts decorative arts" ("Arts" 301). In *Intentions* (1891), he makes the essentially Nietzschean point that "Truth is entirely and absolutely a matter of style" (30), that the artist's lie (or "untruth") gets us closer to what is "true" about life. In the dialogue "The Critic as Artist," Wilde makes the provocative claim that criticism is a creative act, not a set of principles that guarantee the truth about art. When Ernest conveys the conventional Arnoldian belief that "the creative faculty is higher than the critical," Gilbert delivers the *coup de grace*: "Without the critical faculty, there is no artistic creation at all" (125). Taking his cue from Pater, Wilde believed that the critic's own impressions were the foundation of criticism. Against Arnold's claim that the critic's responsibility is to see the object as it really is, Wilde counters that the "primary aim of the critic is to see the object as in itself it really is *not*" (150). Whereas Arnold constructs a theory in which criticism serves an important, if secondary, role with respect to artistic creation, Wilde insists on the fundamentally *creative* nature of criticism: the critic is not only capable of creation but in fact completes the project of the artist, a radical idea that anticipates the phenomenological aesthetics of Jean-Paul Sartre and Emmanuel Levinas who argue that philosophical criticism can relieve art of its "estrangement" from the world of lived experience.

The revolutionary thought of Wilde and Nietzsche is echoed in the work of Sigmund Freud, whose theories of the mind and its engagement with the world introduced the possibility of an internal estrangement. The idea of the unconscious, the logic of dreams, and the work of transference so central to psychoanalytic therapy, not only reshaped our conceptions of human identity and sexuality, but influenced our understanding of how literary language, indeed language *as such*, worked. If Nietzsche and Wilde transformed the classical aesthetic tradition by redefining the relation of art to life, Freud, like Marx and Darwin before him, redefined the relation of the individual to life. Marx's ONTOLOGY of "species-being," like Freud's theory of the mind, uprooted the notion that the individual was somehow able to transcend her environment by taking a transcendentalist position rooted in philosophy or religion or by assuming an irreducible core of selfhood that remained untouched by social and historical forces. Charles Darwin's theory of evolution further eroded the foundations of Renaissance and Enlightenment humanism. All of these developments would come to have profound implications for literary theory in the twentieth century in large part because they helped to answer the questions posed by artists and writers beginning with the modernists and their most pressing query: what constitutes authentic human experience and how does art faithfully represent it? If the modernists hoped to recover or recreate such an experience, the postmodernists, beginning in the 1950s, threw into radical doubt not only the possibility of representing authentic human experience but also the authenticity of the human, indeed the very criterion of authenticity itself.

Modernism and Formalism, 1890s–1940s

Modernism was a dynamic project that influenced nearly every facet of artistic and cultural life in Europe, England, Ireland, and the United States, and thrived to varying degrees throughout the rest of the world. It unfolded at a time (ca. 1890–1950) of profound social and political turbulence, and took the form of unparalleled aesthetic innovation. In classic dialectical fashion, this innovative trend was paralleled by a fierce but dynamic cultural conservatism that sought not the preservation of tradition, unsullied by modernity, but a new orientation toward both. This is what Ezra Pound meant when he proclaimed the motto of modernism – *make it new* – which captures the creative and recursive temporality at work in modernist aesthetics. If modernist innovation differs from the innovation of past artistic movements, the difference is due primarily to the fact of a *break* with tradition that inaugurates it on a new foundation. We see this double movement of break and refounding – building continuities out of discontinuities – at every stage of the modernist epoch, in which innovation is always a kind of renovation.

This double movement is evident in the work of early modernists like T. S. Eliot, Ezra Pound, T. E. Hulme, and Wyndham Lewis, who announced a decisive break with the aesthetic and literary conventions of the nineteenth century, particularly realism in fiction and romanticism in poetry, while retaining the Arnoldian criterion of "high seriousness" and the idea of a literary tradition marked by canonical "touchstones." Some of them were skeptical, if not dismissive, of mass culture and democracy and mourned the passing of integrated, organic societies in which fine art and artistic vision had a high social value and conferred prestige upon artist and patron alike. Hulme, Eliot, and Pound called for a new classicism in poetry, which Hulme described as "a holding back, a reservation. The classical poet never forgets this finiteness, this limit of man." Hulme's main concern was to avoid the "spilt religion" of Romanticism, with its longing for the infinite, and the political philosophy associated with Jean-Jacques Rousseau and the French Revolution (71). Pound and Lewis founded and promoted the Imagist and Vorticist movements, which provided the aesthetic foundation for this new classical standpoint. In *BLAST*, a short-lived literary journal edited by Lewis, the sculptor Henri Gaudier Brzeska described "vortex" as a transhistoric "driving power … life in the absolute": "VORTEX IS POINT ONE AND INDIVISIBLE" (Lewis 155–6). In the same issue, Pound defines it as an anti-historical form of temporality: all experience rushes into the vortex. "All the energized past, all the past that is living and worthy to live … All the past that is vital, all the past that is capable of living into the future, is pregnant in the vortex, NOW" (Lewis 153). Pound's *Cantos* and Eliot's *The Waste Land* – through strategies of citation, quotation, allusion, pastiche, and other techniques – exemplify the temporal layering of Vorticism: "Ply over ply of life still wraps the earth here" (*Personae*, "Canto II," l. 72). The recursive sense of the past so evident in these works is theorized in Yeats's *A Vision* and novelized in Joyce's *Ulysses*. It is one of the dominant strands of literary theory as it was consolidated in the modernist epoch.

After World War I, aesthetic innovations, in linguistic style, narrative form, and subject matter, increased sharply, peaking in the 1920s and 1930s, the era of high modernism. High modernist aesthetics were complex and at times contradictory. Many writers privileged SUBJECTIVE states and stream of consciousness points of view, which suggests the preeminence of the individual person or personality; yet Eliot's doctrine of depersonalization – "The progress of an artist is a continual self-sacrifice, a continual extinction of personality" (7) – would seem to suggest the preeminence of the work itself (Joyce's Stephen Dedalus, in *A Portrait of the Artist as Young Man*, in a similar way argues for the disappearance of the artist). According to Eliot, the literary work does not reproduce personal emotions but rather produces a form of depersonalized "structural emotion" that expresses "feelings which are not in actual emotions at all" (10). The extinction of emotion or affect is evident throughout modernism and can be achieved through a variety of new techniques – including unreliable and multiple narrative points of view, non-mimetic styles, open poetic forms, esoteric symbolism, and non-linear or non-causal temporalities. One of the most important techniques for effacing the writer's presence was the creation of a *persona* or mask, the preparation, as Eliot puts it in "The Love Song of J. Alfred Prufrock", of "a face to meet the faces that you meet." These artistic techniques were given over to new themes, including what was once forbidden or whitewashed: sexuality and gender relations, non-Western religion and culture, anti-colonialism and racism. In modernist art, we see a dialectical movement between emotion and aesthetics, between personality and style, between a sensitive and vibrant subjectivity and the exorbitant if cool style of the artist as a kind of "spiritual-heroic refrigerating apparatus" (Joyce 223). What appears to be a contradiction is, in fact, a necessary component in a critique of traditional aesthetics. (On Eliot and modernism, see New Criticism 59–60.)

The modernist movement challenged the aesthetic traditions of the nineteenth century, and in the process not only renovated Romantic notions of poetry and poetics, but forged a new theoretical discourse on the novel. Innovation in the modernist novel began with a tactical redeployment of nineteenth-century realist styles (like those found in the work of Charles Dickens, George Eliot, and Balzac). Joseph Conrad and Henry James wrote prefaces to their works that developed some of the earliest theories of how the novel functions. Conrad's preface to *The Nigger of the "Narcissus"* advocates a form of narrative *impressionism* that relies on "magic suggestiveness," which is necessary for a mimetic style that remains faithful to the reality of one's subjective impressions of the world. The absolute subjectivity of the artist and the absolute uniqueness of the modernist work of art both derive from this impressionism, which is testimony not so much to the failure of language to represent the world objectively but rather to the isolation that characterizes our subjective perceptions. "It seems to me I am trying to tell you a dream," Marlow tells his listeners, in *Heart of Darkness*, in words that sum up the narrative dilemma of so many modernist storytellers, who are confronted with "that commingling of absurdity, surprise, and bewilderment in a tremor of struggling revolt, that notion of being captured by the incredible which is of the very essence of dreams" (27). The confusion of author, character, and narrator calls into question the concept of the subject as stable and self-identical, differentiated from both other subjects and other *objects* in the world. Henry James, in the prefaces to his novels, explores the function and authority of narrative point of view; he was among the first to practice and theorize about the technique of narrative focalization by which the novel achieves the effect of a specific *voice*. Their critical reflections were developed further by critics like Percy Lubbock, whose *Craft of Fiction* elaborated on Jamesian ideas and inaugurated a tradition of novel theory concerned with the interrelationship of form and reading practices. From James to E. M. Forster to the early D. H. Lawrence and Joyce, the early modernists created substantial and singular styles that maintained clear lines of affiliation with nineteenth-century novel forms like the *Bildungsroman* and with the empirical style of realism that Ian Watt argued was the basis for the rise of the novel in the eighteenth century and that was still favored by late Victorian and Edwardian novelists like John Galsworthy and Arnold Bennett. (On the novel, see Theory of the Novel.)

The anti-mimetic strand of modernism that we begin to see in the 1920s with Joyce's *Ulysses* and the work of Kafka, Virginia Woolf, and Gertrude Stein, does not reject realist styles so much as the valuation of mimesis as an aesthetic and communicative norm and thus as a mode of social and political legitimation; it also gives priority to modes of analogy and resemblance that evade traditional realism while incorporating elements of the concrete material world into their anti-mimetic narratives. Novelists sought to go as far as possible beyond a conventional realism primarily concerned with the accurate presentation of detail. Woolf famously critiqued this desire for "a series of gig-lamps symmetrically arranged" and called for novelists to move beyond or stretch realism's narrow stylistic range, to unveil life "as it really is" – "a luminous halo, a semi-transparent envelope surrounding us from beginning of consciousness to the end" (Woolf 160). As Wilde, George Bernard Shaw, Bertolt Brecht and, later Beckett, demonstrate in their drama, an aesthetics grounded on mimesis, in which the artist can be assured of a stable relationship between the artwork and the world in which it is produced and received by its audience, no longer suffices because the relationship between art and the world had changed.

Woolf was among a generation of modernist writers who succeeded in breaking down an aesthetic orthodoxy that was profoundly male-dominated and in which women and their thought were primarily represented by male writers. This thesis, conveyed in her polemical *A Room of One's Own* (1929), authorized aesthetic renovation in the service of representing women's authentic experience. Woolf was far from alone. Writers as diverse as Stein and Djuna Barnes in fiction and Mina Loy and H.D. in poetry challenged dominant narrative and verse paradigms. H.D.'s rewriting of mythology from a feminist perspective constitutes both a critique and an appropriation of masculinist cultural traditions, and paved the way for later writers like Adrienne Rich and Angela Carter. Stein's intensely fractured narratives put pressure on the very basis of narrative, the sentence. This kind of radical departure from a realist norm is matched in renovative energy by William Faulkner, whose rich linguistic excesses, shifting points of view, and recursive and multiple temporalities called into question the historical and causal basis of novelistic narrative. Stein and Faulkner's experimental fictions, Marcel Proust's *À la Recherche du Temps Perdu*, and Joyce's *Ulysses*, test the limits of narrative form and characterization and foreground the role played by style in constructing the world of the novel. Temporality, both historical time and memory, is broken up into a chain of intense moments or distorted (telescoped, elongated); multiple timeframes intersect and overlap. Such experiments with narrative form not only challenged aesthetic orthodoxies, they helped to create new ones. Beginning in the 1930s we see increasingly more provocative innovations whose legibility is largely dependent on the new aesthetics illustrated by the works themselves, such as Woolf's late novels, Joyce's *Finnegans Wake*, and Beckett's trilogy (*Molloy*, *Malone Dies*, and *The Unnamable*). These late modernist texts served as litmus tests and tempted critics to announce the death of the novel, announcements that have proven to have missed the point.

We see a similar development in modernist poetry, particularly in the position of the speaker, whose function in lyric poetry had long been to express a coherent and consistent point of view. We can still discern such speakers in early modernist poetry, particularly in W. B. Yeats and Thomas Hardy. But by the 1920s, the poetic speaker is displaced by the diffident and abstract *personae* of such poems as Eliot's "The Love Song of J. Alfred Prufrock" and Pound's *Hugh Selwyn Mauberley*. By the mid-1920s Eliot's *The Waste Land* and Pound's *Cantos* were showing that the poetic traditions that had enabled artistic expression were not only implausible in the twentieth century but inadequate to the aesthetic demands of the modernist artist confronted with new social and political realities. The associational or pastiche style of high modernism (with its mixing of linguistic and rhetorical styles and hybrid genres) manipulates multiple voices and temporal frameworks (which Pound called "ply over ply") in a disjunctive mode of ironic self-reflexiveness. The modernist poem often foregrounds style in a way that deconstructs the relationship between form and content. Pound's early writings on Imagism insist on the role of style as a liberating feature of modernist poetry:

> An "Image" is that which presents an intellectual and emotional complex in an instant to time … It is the presentation of such "complex" instances instantaneously which gives the sense of sudden liberation; the sense of freedom from time and space limits; that sense of sudden growth, which we experience in the presence of the greatest works of art. (*Literary* 4)

Complexity, liberation, new temporalities, new forms of artistic growth – Pound's prescription for the Imagist poet might well stand for modernism generally. Like Eliot's "objective correlative" and Yeats's automatic writing, Pound's Imagism is a sign of how poetic meaning is tied to the style (linguistic and rhetorical) of the poem. As Gwendolyn says in Wilde's *The Importance of Being Earnest*: "In matters of grave importance, style, not sincerity is the vital thing" (150). Neither Gwendolyn nor Wilde is joking. For modernists generally, artistic style was not an affectation; nor was it a more or less excessive ornamentation. In line with other contemporary artistic practices and anticipating French phenomenology and poststructuralism, modernist writers began to see language as the proper *object* as well as the medium of aesthetic production.

   Literary theory owes much to the proclamations and enigmas of the modernists. Of special importance were Eliot's critical essays, which modeled modernist innovation by providing a new and rigorous basis for literary analysis and judgment. Foundational for him was *tradition*, which he regarded as being in dialectical relation with each new individual artist. Such a model of tradition implied a refined historical sense, "which is a sense of the timeless as well as of the temporal and of the timeless and of the temporal together, is what makes a writer traditional. And it is at the same time what makes a writer most acutely conscious of his place in time, of his contemporaneity" (4). Eliot attempted to make a virtue of the "dissociated sensibility" that he believed had "set in" in the seventeenth century and made it impossible to "devour any kind of experience" (247). The classical rigors of the metaphysical poets and Jacobean tragedians provided a hedge against this dissociation and allowed the development of an aesthetic in which sensation and sensibility were unified in an aesthetics of depersonalization. Connected to this willful self-alienation in the service of art is a vision of temporality that accommodates the disjunctive relation of the artist to the social world. Eliot's revolutionary approach to history reflects a general attitude among modernists, one that is reflected in their interest in non-traditional historical thinking. Pound and Yeats were interested in cyclical theories of history, and Joyce famously adapted Giambattista Vico's theory of history as a form of *ricorso* (or recurring phases). T. E. Hulme and Woolf advocated a sense of time that drew on Henri Bergson's notion of duration (*la durée*), in which time is freed of causality and the simultaneity of experiences counters a vision of time as chronological and measured by the clock and calendar. Like Vorticism, modernist historicism breaks down or reconfigures the boundaries between past and present, memory and history and, in the most radical experiments, transforms history into pure duration, an infinitely extensive and differentiated moment.

Literary modernism was accompanied by a revolution in linguistics that saw the rise of a structuralist theory of language. The Swiss linguist Ferdinand de Saussure argued, in *Course in General Linguistics* (1916), that language is grounded in the structural differences between phonemes, very basic sound units, rather than in the mimetic relation of the sign to an external referent. Unlike theories of language that posit a direct and verifiable correspondence between a word and an object or concept in the world, Saussure's structuralism is based on the idea that language functions as a system (*langue*) that determines the meaning of specific statements (*parole*) within it. Words function as SIGNS, which contain both a material SIGNIFIER (which corresponds to what Saussure called a "signal") and a SIGNIFIED (a concept or "signification"). For him, language was primarily a system of internal differences between signifiers, or *phonemes*, rather than the natural or predictable relations between signifiers and signifieds. These relations, he argued, were at bottom arbitrary, the work of convention within the language system.

Beginning in the 1920s, the basic insights of Saussurean linguistics were being adopted by various schools of formalism and structuralism, related disciplines that focused, respectively, on literary and cultural forms. In some cases, as in the work of Vladimir Propp, it is difficult to disentangle the structuralist and formalist elements. His study of folktales, for example, uncovers the structural coherence across cultural boundaries of narrative and character types and provides a formalist taxonomy of folktales. Roman Jakobson typifies the formalist approach to literature, which entails primarily a negotiation between metaphoric and metonymic language functions. Literature tends to be metaphoric, while non-literary texts tend to be metonymic; however, he understood that the functions of language are not so easily separated. In fact, he argued that poetry functions precisely by "projection" of the two levels of language into each other: "The poetic function projects the principle of equivalence from the axis of selection into the axis of combination" ("Closing Statement" 358). Formalism is less interested in the universal character of language as a structure than in how language is used to create different forms of DISCOURSE. Viktor Shklovsky, like Jakobson associated with the Moscow Circle of linguists, argues, in *Theory of Prose* (1925), that literary texts actually reveal or "lay bare" their own form through processes of *estrangement* and *defamiliarization*. These techniques make possible a revaluation of literary language and narrative forms to the extent that these formal processes determine or become themselves the meaning of the text.

Linked to these schools of thought is the New Criticism, a practical formalism that owes a tremendous debt to the criticism and poetics of T. S. Eliot. The New Criticism flourished from the 1920s through the 1940s and was primarily concerned with poetry and poetic form. But whereas Russian formalism grew out of the science of linguistics and provided a theoretical basis for innovation in a wide variety of other disciplines, the New Criticism emerged out of literary modernism as a set of interpretive strategies that did not have a wide impact outside literary studies. These strategies were grounded in large part on the practice and theoretical insights of modernist poet-critics, like Eliot (who edited *Criterion*), Robert Penn Warren (who co-edited the *Southern Review*), and Allen Tate (associated with the *Sewanee Review*). These writers, and the contributors and readers of the "little magazines," were instrumental in promoting the new critical doctrines in England and the United States.

The New Criticism, which privileged the kind of esoteric and erudite poetry that invited close reading and that was eminently suited both to the teacher in the classroom and to the professional critic, was crucial to this development. It encompassed a variety of interpretive methods that shared certain key elements, the most important of which was the notion of the literary work as AUTONOMOUS and self-contained – a "verbal icon," as W. K. Wimsatt and Monroe C. Beardsley famously put it. For I. A. Richards, this autonomy was a form of affective unity. Referring to the difficulty of Eliot's poetry, he asserts that the various elements of his work "are united by the accord, contrast, and interaction of their emotional effects" (290). In Richards' view the formal unity of a literary text is a function of the subjectivity of the critic, who must not ascribe "peculiar, unique and mystic virtues to forms in themselves," since the effects of form are bound up with the mental effects that literary works excite in readers (173). Richards' approach was unique, however, since most New Critics, especially in the United States, downplayed the psychological dimension of the reader and stressed the verbal and rhetorical dimensions of the literary work.

The Chicago School of neo-Aristotelian formalism, which grew around R. S. Crane beginning in the 1930s, opposed the New Critics in part because of their lack of discipline in rhetorical traditions and what was perceived to be their subjective approach to interpretation. Nevertheless, the New Critical methodology and pedagogy dominated in the classroom. The growing importance of English departments in US universities helped to create a class of professionally trained academic critics, many of whom embraced the formalist methods outlined above. A crucial result of this new professional elite was the creation of college textbooks focusing on poetry and fiction – including Brooks and Warren's *Understanding Poetry: An Anthology for College Students* (1938) and *Understanding Fiction* (1959) – in which new formalist modes of interpretation were made available as practical tools in the classroom. It is hard to underestimate both the CANON-forming impetus behind the New Criticism and the extent to which it and other formalist methods transformed the nature of scholarship and teaching. Though its theoretical influence was relatively slight, its effect on practical criticism has been widespread and continues to influence how literature is discussed in the classroom and in scholarly journals.

Cultural and Critical Theory, 1930s–1960s

The emergence of formalism was answered dialectically by the rise of Marxist-oriented critical theory. While aesthetic formalism was to be avoided, as V. I. Lenin insisted in the early twentieth century (see Jay 173), formalism in general represented a movement within a dialectical criticism. "Although inadequate in itself," Martin

Jay writes, "formalism provided a vital safeguard, which substantive rationality, whether legal or logical, ignored at its peril. Formalism, in short, was a genuine moment of the dialectical totality, which ought not to be simply negated" (145). Leon Trotsky has written that formalism "opens a path – one of several paths – to the artist's feeling for the world" and to the nature of relations between the individual artist and the "social environment" (139). However, the main emphasis in Marxian critical theory remains the materialist analysis of society and culture. One of the most significant early figures was Georg Lukács, a vocal critic of the modernist novel and a champion of "critical realism." In 1920, in exile after the failure of the Hungarian Soviet Republic, Lukács published *Theory of the Novel*, a study strongly influenced by Hegel. He describes the novel as a "problematic" genre in that it remains anchored to an ideal of unity and fullness that is incommensurate with social conditions: "The novel is the epic of an age in which the extensive TOTALITY of life is no longer directly given, in which the immanence of meaning in life has become a problem, yet which still thinks in terms of totality" (56).

The same problems that preoccupied Lukács also determined the nature and direction of the social theory coming out of the Institute for Social Research, founded by Felix Weil and incorporated into Frankfurt University in 1923 under the directorship of Carl Grünsberg, who made Marxism its theoretical basis. Max Horkheimer became director in 1930, and the Institute relocated, in the wake of Hitler's rise to power, to Geneva in 1933 and shortly thereafter to New York, where it was affiliated with Columbia University until it was reestablished in Germany after the war. These geopolitical developments were largely responsible for the shift of focus, in the late 1930s and 1940s, from economics and the modes of production to culture and IDEOLOGY. In the postwar period, a wide variety of methods were adopted by Institute members, with Friedrich Pollock joining Horkheimer in the Marxist analysis of state capitalism and Herbert Marcuse joining Erich Fromm in exploring psychoanalytical approaches to society and its institutions; Fromm's theory of "social psychology" was particularly influential. What linked these disparate projects was a commitment to *critical* theory. Unlike *traditional* theory, which is grounded in scientific research and social development under capitalism, critical theory, as Horkheimer described it, entailed a dialectical overcoming of the tension between the individual and society and the abolition of "the opposition between the individual's purposefulness, spontaneity, and rationality, and those work–process relationships on which society is built" (210). Despite differences in methodology and objects of study, the Institute theorists shared a common goal: the systematic investigation of totalitarian and authoritarian ideology (specifically fascism and Nazism), anti-Semitism, and mass commodity culture. **Theodor Adorno**'s collaboration with Horkheimer resulted in arguably the single most influential text to emerge from the Institute, *Dialectic of Enlightenment* (1944). In a dialectical critique of the Enlightenment project of MODERNITY, they demonstrate how rationality produced both the "culture industry" – Adorno's term for the concentrated efforts of media corporations to convert cultural products into COMMODITIES – and the totalitarianism that swept through Europe beginning in the 1920s. From their viewpoint, the lost autonomy of the authentic subject is compensated for only by an empty and abstract individualism promoted by the culture industry.

Another fascinating relationship, which did not result in formal collaboration, was that between Adorno and **Walter Benjamin**. Though not formally a member of the Institute, Benjamin shared many of its concerns and, through his correspondence with him, engaged with Adorno's ideas in a provocative way. He had wide-ranging interests, including music, film, religion, literature, fashion, politics, urban geography, and the Parisian arcades. Like other Institute theorists, his work is characterized by a dialectical method; but unlike them, his understanding of history was influenced by thinkers in the Jewish Kabbalistic tradition. His emphasis on messianism led to the innovative conception of "dialectics at a standstill," which transpires in "now-time" (*Jetztzeit*), a moment of critical historical reflection that enables the redemption of the past. Benjamin also departed from the main line of Institute theory by according the subject a high degree of freedom within capitalist society. Granted, freedom was compromised from the start by the commodified world in which the individual moved; but this "fallen world" was the only one in which humanity could strive for freedom and recover something of a lost wholeness (an idea he borrowed from Kabbalistic thought). The *flâneur*, whose inauthentic subjectivity can be mobilized for progressive points of view, even in the commodified market-world of late capitalism, is the emblem of this freedom. Benjamin's tragic fate – certain that Hitler's Gestapo was on his trail, he committed suicide at the Spanish frontier on September 26, 1940 – stands as a sobering reminder of the price paid by the individual who resists totalitarianism.

The Institute returned to Frankfurt in 1953, and Adorno and Horkheimer became co-directors in 1955. Adorno's death in 1969 and Horkheimer's in 1973 marked the passing of the first generation of critical theorists, though Marcuse would remain influential throughout the 1960s and early 1970s as an intellectual mentor of anti-war activists in Europe and the United States. Beginning in the 1960s, Jürgen Habermas emerged as the leading figure of the next generation. His key works in the 1960s, *The Structural Transformation of the Public Sphere* and *Legitimation Crisis*, were concerned primarily with the problem of achieving political consensus through "communicative rationality" and with resolving the crisis of ideological legitimacy through a reaffirmation of reason and the project of Enlightenment. Like his predecessors, Habermas critiqued capitalism but from a new standpoint, one in which rationality could be reconciled with a genuine form of participatory democracy. By the 1980s, critical theory had moved beyond the institutional parameters of the Frankfurt School, in part due to the rise of post-Marxist theory.

At about the same time that Habermas was reconfiguring Frankfurt School critical theory, British Marxism was finding new expression in cultural studies. After World War II, Britain changed dramatically, in part because of the shift from economic austerity to post-industrial affluence and in part because of the break up of the colonies after the partitioning of India in 1948 (this process arguably began in 1922 with the establishment of the Irish Free State). One response to these transitions and transformations was the rise of CULTURAL MATERIALISM, a form of analysis that sought in concrete social conditions the meaning of cultural movements and aesthetic works and practices. Primarily associated with historians like E. P. Thompson and Eric Hobsbawm, cultural materialism ultimately drove a wide array of theoretical projects. In the early years, Richard Hoggart and **Raymond Williams** brought materialist and sociological methods of analysis to bear on the study of mass culture and literature. Writing in 1982 about his landmark study *Culture and Society: 1780–1950* (1958), Williams remarked that he wrote it "in the post-1945 crisis of belief and affiliation" as an attempt "to understand and act in contemporary society, necessarily through its history, which had delivered this strange, unsettling, world to us" (xii). The Centre for Contemporary Cultural Studies at the University of Birmingham (UK) was established in 1964 in order to understand this new unsettling world.

Broadly speaking, British cultural studies focused on literary and cultural traditions, new media technologies, and marginalized social groups and "subcultures." Hoggart's work on literacy and **Stuart Hall**'s on politics and the police exemplify the sociological tenor of early work at the Birmingham Centre. Of signal importance to thinkers like Hall, Tony Bennett, Colin Mercer, and Janet Woollacott was the Italian Marxist Antonio Gramsci, who was active in the Italian Communist Party throughout the 1920s, until he was imprisoned in 1926 by Mussolini's fascist government under the "Exceptional Laws." Gramsci's *Prison Notebooks*, written in a coded fashion to evade censorship, critiqued the structure of complex capitalist societies and argued that dominant social classes exercise power primarily through HEGEMONY. From the time of Lenin, hegemony was associated with the proletariat and its political control after the revolution; for Gramsci, it came to signify modes of governance associated with any dominant class. It is achieved through modes of indirect and "spontaneous" consensus, and takes the form of DOMINATION in those "moments of crisis of command and direction when spontaneous consent has failed" (12). In his theory of the SUPERSTRUCTURE, hegemony functions as consensus within the civil sphere and as domination in the political sphere. However, as Graeme Turner has noted, the so-called "Gramscian turn" toward the study of ideology and hegemony limited the capacity "to theorize the forms of political conflict and relations specific to the functioning of particular cultural technologies." This was due in part to the limitations of Marxist materialism, which some British cultural studies theorists sought to remedy by turning to the work of thinkers like **Michel Foucault**, whose theory of POWER/KNOWLEDGE expanded the critical potential of Marxist critique so that theorists might "work with" ideology rather than "write it off" as a producer of false consciousness (Turner 31). Though Foucault's work was important for many of the Centre theorists, there was a general reluctance to embrace French poststructuralism, which, by the early 1970s, had become the dominant theoretical movement in the human sciences in the Western world.

The Poststructuralist Turn, 1960s–1970s

The "poststructuralist turn" in literary theory began in France in the early 1960s and was made manifest by October 1966 in a landmark symposium on "The Languages of Criticism and the Sciences of Man" at the Johns Hopkins University Humanities Center. Among those attending were René Girard, Georges Poulet, Tzvetan Todorov, Jean Hyppolite, **Roland Barthes, Jacques Lacan,** and **Jacques Derrida**. The majority of speakers were French and their innovative theoretical work reflected the heady times of the Trente Glorieuses, a postwar period of growth and national renewal that spread through every sector of French society. The provocative challenge to academic traditions issued by these thinkers, particularly Barthes, Lacan, and Derrida, was greeted with enthusiasm by students and teachers in the humanities who sought an alternative to formalist and materialist methodologies.

Like most developments in literary theory, poststructuralism was less a coherent movement than a series of departures from tradition that used similar tactics to achieve sometimes quite different ends. Unlike postmodernism, which tends to bypass or dismiss the importance of structure, poststructuralism remains rooted in the problematic of structure itself, and particularly the *a priori* and transcendent logic by which structures and systems remain coherent and centered. It emerged in the 1960s during the peak period of structuralism and effectively supplanted it with an emphasis on TEXTUALITY as the means by which individuals come to know their experience of and their being in the world. As a response and a critique to structuralism, poststructuralist theorists are indebted not only to Saussure's groundbreaking insights into the structure of language but also to Claude Lévi-Strauss's use of them in the analysis of cultural practices and myths. Drawing on Saussure as well as on the formalism of Roman Jakobson, Lévi-Strauss argued, in *Structural Anthropology* (1958), that elements of culture, like kinship systems, rituals, myths, even common practices like food preparation, could be understood according to structures analogous to those found in language. Moreover, these structures could account for similarities among cultures widely separated geographically. In a sense, structural anthropology confirmed what Freud had theorized in psychoanalytic terms: that some features of human culture, like the prohibition against incest, were not only universal but could be understood and analyzed using a single method. The idea that culture could be studied as coherent and stable signifying systems and that these systems operated in a similar fashion in diverse societies had a galvanizing effect on Barthes, whose *Mythologies* (1957) analyzed aspects of everyday life – like laundry detergent, magazine covers, fashion, and sports – according to their structural dynamics. For him, "mythology" was everywhere in culture, functioning as a "second order" language (i.e., a metalanguage) that transformed the signifying power of objects, images, and everyday language.

Another key area in which structuralism made inroads was the study of narrative. Barthes' "Introduction to the Structural Analysis of Narrative" (1966), one of the earliest and most influential works in the field, argued that meaning in narrative was a function of the distribution or integration of "units" along the lines of linguistic structure. "Structurally, narrative shares the characteristics of the sentence without ever being reducible to the simple sum of its sentences: a narrative is a long sentence, just as every constative sentence is in a way the rough outline of a short narrative" (84). Like Lévi-Strauss's analysis of myth, which also functioned in a sentence-like manner, Barthes' analysis challenged our assumptions not only about narrative but also about the actors and narrators within it. Gérard Genette at about the same time began his multi-volume project *Figures* in the same vein, refining the structural categories of narrative form and exploring in new ways the function of point of view, which until this time was largely understood in very loose terms as a kind of affective distance (for example, the intimacy of first person over against the more disinterested third person). Wayne Booth accomplished much the same thing in his *Rhetoric of Fiction* (1961), in which he sought to define point of view in terms of the rhetorical "implication" or stance taken by a narrator. In all of these cases, as in the structural semantics of A. J. Greimas, narrative emerged as a set of rhetorical or formal *functions* grounded in linguistic structure and difference.

Structuralism helped prepare the ground for poststructuralism, but so too did phenomenology, a branch of philosophy concerned with the problems of consciousness and of ontology (the study of being), particularly the question of what it means to exist, *to be* in the world. From Martin Heidegger to Maurice Merleau-Ponty, phenomenologists had struggled with metaphysical ideas and concepts – dichotomies like subject/object and presence/absence, transcendental ideas, dialectical closure, absolute being – in an attempt to grasp the reality of being outside the confines of an idealist philosophy that posits being as existing prior to our experience of it. In the 1950s and 1960s, phenomenological criticism, from Merleau-Ponty to Bachelard and Poulet, focused on how language mediated being in the world; like earlier thinkers, they struggled with the subject/object, mind/body dualities that plague metaphysics and ontology. One important development in this tradition was reader-response theory. Some of the earliest work in this field was done in the 1930s by the phenomenologist Roman Ingarden, who influenced later thinkers, such as Umberto Eco, Hans Robert Jauss, and **Wolfgang Iser**. Iser's *The Act of Reading: A Theory of Aesthetic Response* (1978) created the foundation for a theory of reading that explained how texts are constructed or completed by the active response of the reader to the challenges issued by them. In the United States, **Stanley Fish** introduced the concept of "affective stylistics," which is grounded in the reader's response to and construction of the literary text. His most popular and influential work, *Is There a Text in This Class?* (1980), combined the aesthetic dimension of Hans Robert Jauss's reception theory with an interest in the way that academic and other social institutions created "interpretive communities" that could account both for shared reading experiences among diverse individuals and for divergent interpretations of the same text. These theories of reading complement and extend the theories of the author and textual authority advanced by Barthes and Foucault in the 1960s. As Barthes put it, the birth of the author takes place "at the cost of the death of the Author" (*Image* 148).

At the heart of poststructuralism is Jacques Derrida's theory of deconstruction, which took aim at the stabilizing and CENTERING constructs in structuralism and on the idea of presence, particularly in the form of a TRANSCENDENTAL SIGNIFIED, that dominated metaphysical philosophy (see *Of Grammatology*, lxv). Following Heidegger, he formulated a critique of PRESENCE in which the "being there" of things, their essence, is revealed to be nothing more than an absence, the deferral of meaning in a process of endless signification. Of the many terms Derrida used to refer to this process, the most important is DIFFÉRANCE, which refers both to the DEFERRAL of meaning and the *difference* that characterizes meaning in language (i.e., the difference between signifiers within language understood as a system). Language is haunted by this absent presence, in which meaning is decoupled from reference, and the signified of any sign is constantly deferred or SUPPLEMENTED (by signifiers) along a signifying chain. It is not that the referent is "missing" but that its absence is crucial to signification. Derrida decisively announced this aspect of the poststructuralist project in his essay "Structure, Sign and Play in the Discourse of the Humanities," in which he critiqued the structuralist anthropology of Lévi-Strauss and concluded that structuralism must follow philosophy into its own deconstruction. The "circle" of "destructive discourses," from Nietzsche to Freud to Heidegger, links the history of metaphysics with is destruction. "*There is no sense,*" he writes, "in doing without the concepts of metaphysics in order to attack metaphysics" (*Grammatology* 250).

Though French forms of deconstruction dominated in the 1970s, there were several noteworthy developments in the United States, particularly in the work of **Paul de Man** and **J. Hillis Miller**. De Man argues for a form of rhetorical analysis that lays bare the "literariness" of the text, its essentially allegorical structure, which is paradoxically bound up with a constitutive blindness to the gaps, contradictions, and aporias that destabilize logical and grammatical understanding. Miller's deconstructionist method is grounded in a phenomenology of reading (influenced by Georges Poulet) that marks the text itself as a phenomenal other. In both De Man and Miller duplicity and its aesthetic and ethical effects – its ironies, doubleness, blindness, and "parasitism" – are located in narrative, in rhetoric, in the very temporality of language, in which the reader and writer confront the limits of human experience *in* language. Joseph Riddel sees in deconstructionist theory a form of "negative humanism" (82) exemplified by Derrida's critique of metaphysics and De Man's insistence on the purely rhetorical function of language. If language is internally differentiated and if it does not refer directly to an object outside of itself, then it becomes self-referential.

The general critique of metaphysics and elaboration of the concept of *différance* resulted in new theories of TEXTUALITY and semiotics and new strategies of interpretation. Preeminent in this regard was the concept of INTERTEXTUALITY, the complex and self-reflexive relations between and among texts within discourse networks (e.g., the novel) that are not necessarily deliberately created by the author (in the sense of influence) but are rather a function of the network itself. The linguist, poststructuralist, and psychoanalyst **Julia Kristeva** pioneered a form of intertextuality that drew on the work of the Russian theorist **M. M. Bakhtin**. Bakhtin emphasized the DIALOGIC structure of literary discourse, particularly the novel, and its openness to language forms of any kind. His theory of HETEROGLOSSIA, though first published in the 1930s, did not have a pronounced effect in European theory until Kristeva and others began to use his work. The idea that the language of the novel was stratified with different ideologically encoded styles, that a dominant monological novelistic voice often suppressed other potential voices, led many theorists to argue that intertextuality was not simply a potential for connection between texts but was in fact the very condition of textual communication as such. It is fair to say that Bakhtin was poststructuralist *avant la lettre*.

Kristeva's work on intertextuality together with Barthes' later theories of writing and textuality speak to a concern with discourse as a system in which language is organized according to the kinds of statements it makes. Michel Foucault's work is crucial to the task of grasping this idea of a DISCOURSE FORMATION. In *Archaeology of Knowledge*, he takes as a "starting-point whatever unities are already given," not in order to study them (for they are "dubious"), but to "make use of them just long enough to ask myself what unities they form; by what right they can claim a field that specifies them in space and a continuity that individualizes them in time; according to what laws they are formed." He will accept "the groupings that history suggests only to subject them at once to interrogation" (26). This tactical maneuver, which he uses to analyze the discursive unities behind medicine, justice, history, psychiatry, and other fields, is not unlike deconstruction: it accepts the existence of unities, but refuses to accept their essential or universal character. In formulating a theory of discourse formations and an ARCHAEOLOGICAL mode of analyzing them, Foucault moves beyond the poststructuralist project, however, for in his work, as in that of the postmodern philosopher Gilles Deleuze, we find concepts of dispersion and the event that in some ways leave the very idea of structure behind. But this does not mean that we leave behind the subject of power, which the late Foucault sees as possessing a kind of tactical AGENCY. This is why his project, and that of other poststructuralists, cannot help but engage in a "critique of our historical era" ("What" 42).

Another exemplary figure in this regard is the French psychoanalyst **Jacques Lacan,** who offers a critique of the subject grounded in structuralist linguistics and Freudian psychoanalysis. At issue for Lacan is the status of the SUBJECT and the nature of language in psychoanalysis. Lacan began writing in the late 1930s and held his first public seminar on psychoanalysis at Sainte-Anne hospital in Paris in 1953. Dissatisfied with the tendencies of ego-psychology, which he believed simplified the nature and role of the ego in the subject, he called for a "return to Freud" from the perspective of structural linguistics and poststructuralist theories of desire, the sacred, the body, and death. Of signal importance for Lacan was the function of language in the formation of the unconscious, which Freud had touched on in his discussion of the dream-work in *The Interpretation of Dreams*. In a 1957 lecture, Lacan famously remarked that "It is the whole structure of language that psychoanalytic experience discovers in the unconscious" (139), and he drew on Saussure's theory of the signifier/signified relation to demonstrate his point. The emphasis on language and signification puts Lacan squarely in the structuralist camp, though his development of Saussurean ideas is clearly poststructuralist. One indication of Lacan's movement away from structuralism is his theory of the orders of human experience. Lacan argued that the individual begins by being immersed in an IMAGINARY order of fantasy, linked indivisibly to the maternal body with no differentiation between self and other. The Oedipal crisis forces the individual to sever the connection to the maternal body and enter the SYMBOLIC order (the Name-of-the-Father, as Lacan puts it). In neither case is the individual able to experience the unmediated material existence that Lacan calls the REAL. The Symbolic order is of particular importance to Lacan, for it is the locus not only of law and reason, the traditional authorities behind PATRIARCHAL power, but also of the "big OTHER," which corresponds to the unconscious, that space in which we hear the voice of our own subjectivity ("I") calling to us from outside of ourselves and fashioning our ego ("me") in an endless circuit of unattainable desires held out to us in the form of the *other* (*objet petit a*). The immersion in the language of the unconscious presents with "a fading or eclipse of the subject" (301).

Lacanian psychoanalysis, together with the strategy of deconstructing binary oppositions and the structures they support, revolutionized feminist theory, which critiqued gender difference and interrogated the patriarchal foundations of philosophy, psychoanalysis, and rationality. The use and abuse of Lacan by feminists like Jane Gallop, **Teresa de Lauretis**, and Laura Mulvey illustrates an important feature of poststructuralist thought, for feminism's response to Lacan was to go even further in the direction of acclaiming the Other, the negative component in the dialectics of psychoanalysis. This appropriation of Lacan leads to a radical FORECLOSURE of the phallic order (i.e., the Name-of-the-Father) that is at the same time an opening in and for the Other. Alice Jardine, writing in 1985, speaks of "a reincorporation and reconceptualization of that which has been the master narratives' own 'nonknowledge,' what has eluded them, what has engulfed them" (25). This nonknowledge is an ambivalent state of subjectivity achievable only outside dialectical closure, in a persistently negative relation to dominant discourses. Feminist poststructuralism is grounded in this kind of negative critique, particularly in France, where Simone de Beauvoir's *The Second Sex* (1949) had already pioneered a dialectical analysis of gender and sexuality and insisted that woman's alienation within a patriarchal order could be overcome only by linking identity to a critique of the philosophical presuppositions of that order. Beauvoir articulated in philosophical terms some of the same issues raised by Virginia Woolf and later by Betty Friedan (in *The Feminine Mystique*, 1963), Kate Millett (in *Sexual Politics*, 1970), and Germaine Greer (in *The Female Eunuch*, 1970). She was to enjoy tremendous influence among French feminist thinkers in the 1960s and 1970s. As Millett's book plainly shows, the politics of gender difference are at the core of this second wave of feminism (the first having crested in the suffragette movement and in the work of modernists like Woolf and H.D.). In the United States, a certain pragmatism prevailed in the feminist approach to equal rights, which is noted too in the work of **Elaine Showalter, Sandra Gilbert,** and **Susan Gubar**. For these critics, the representation of women in literature indexes social attitudes, and the aim of the critic is not only to critique a canon formed and defended by men but also to recognize and promote a canon formed by women.

A significant turn in feminism occurred in the mid-1970s, when the philosopher and psychoanalyst Luce Irigaray challenged the phallogocentrism of psychoanalysis and "speculative" philosophy since Plato, all of which was founded on the reduction of women to the *speculum*, an object that exists solely to constitute another's subjectivity (in the representation of desire). It is a form of existence without essence: "Subjectivity denied to woman: indisputably this provides the financial backing for every irreducible constitution of an object: of representation, of discourse, of desire. Once imagine that woman imagines and the object loses its fixed, obsessional character" (133). In contrast to US feminism, French feminism is oriented toward philosophy, linguistics, psychoanalysis, and politics. **Hélène Cixous'** "The Laugh of the Medusa" (1975) and **Luce Irigaray's** *Speculum of the Other Woman* were critical challenges to patriarchal and masculinist discourse, specifically to the "sex/gender system" that "traffics in women" for the economic benefit of men (see Rubin). This feminist critique of social and cultural institutions is grounded in poststructuralist theories of language and representation. In some cases, as in the work of Irigaray and Cixous, we find that the critique extends to reason and rationality, indeed to the entire edifice of Western philosophy. This critique yielded a practice, ÉCRITURE FÉMININE (literally, "feminine writing" but typically translated as "writing the body"), that was indebted to Lacan even as it posited an alternative to his work. The interdisciplinary character of this practice is illustrated well in Julia Kristeva's work, in which linguistics, SEMIOTICS, psychoanalysis, and Bakhtinian DIALOGISM create what she calls "semanalysis." One of the outcomes of this deconstruction of masculinist and patriarchal discourse is a new focus on questions of gender identity and difference, for both identity and difference are formed in the context of linguistic and social performance. These questions constellate in SOCIAL CONSTRUCTIONISM, which holds that one's identity is neither essential nor immutable but is rather the outcome of multiple social institutions, discourses, relationships, and interactions. As Beauvoir said of women, one is made not born.

Culture, Gender, and History, 1980s–1990s

In 1981, **Fredric Jameson**, one of the most influential Marxist critics in the United States, declared, "Always historicize!" He meant to galvanize late twentieth-century Marxism against postmodernist attacks on history, but his call is echoed in new work across the theoretical spectrum. New historicism, cultural studies, gender theory, postmodernism, postcolonial studies, transnational studies – all of these theoretical fields are noted for their use of historiographic methods to theorize DIFFERENCE. Of course, the desire to theorize difference – including cultural, ethnic, sexual, gender, and other forms of difference – has its roots in the general concept of linguistic difference theorized by Saussure and the poststructuralists. But it is plain that for these new theorists, difference is a function of specific social, cultural, and historical pressures and forces. It is important to emphasize that the historicization of difference does not constitute a departure from or break with poststructuralism; on the contrary, it testifies to the continued relevance of poststructuralist innovations.

This historicization of difference is nowhere more apparent than in postcolonial studies, which is rooted in the Négritude movement in former British and French colonies and in the work of Aimé Césaire, **Frantz Fanon**, and Albert Memmi. This first generation of postcolonial theory consists largely in a dialectical critique of colonial power and nationalism, but Fanon stands out for his psychological insights into violence and the relationship between the individual and the nation. We see in this early anti-colonial discourse a pedagogical impulse, a need to educate the people about the historical conditions of their own existence. However, anti-colonial nationalists often had no alternative but the historical discourse created in Europe *for Europeans* (a point not lost on Jean-Paul Sartre, who championed Fanon and Memmi in their struggle against French colonialism in the Maghreb). The field of postcolonial studies was transformed by **Edward Said**'s *Orientalism* (1978), which drew on poststructuralist theories of difference and discourse to critique the ethnocentric historical vision of empire. This pivotal work exemplifies the archaeological approach developed by Foucault, which allowed Said to map the discourse formation of Orientalism, a vast structure of Western knowledge that effectively created the East *as Orientalized*. The "cultural strength" of the West, Said argued, led to an assumption "that the Orient and everything in it was, if not patently inferior to, then in need of corrective study by the West" (41). Some theorists have criticized Said for not representing the reverse process – representations of the West produced by colonial and postcolonial intellectuals and artists – but we should not let such criticism prevent us from seeing that Said pointed the way for those who, in the 1980s, began "writing back" to the empire.

In part as a response to Said's work, a number of important new theorists began to emerge, and in them we can discern a coherent field of study taking shape. South Asian thinkers took the lead in the early 1980s. Ashis Nandy's *The Intimate Enemy* (1983), and the Subaltern Studies Group, especially the work of **Gayatri Chakravorty Spivak** and Ranajit Guha, revealed both the nature of the effects of colonial discourse in India and the outlines of a nativist and revisionist historiography that could counter dominant narratives about Indian history and its people. The ambivalence of colonial power is in some ways the contradiction at the heart of the nation itself, a contradiction between the needs of the abstract universal idea of the nation and the objective particularity of everyday life. For **Homi Bhabha**, this ambivalence produces a disjunction in which "the invention of historicity, mastery, mimesis" (the core of colonial power) and the "'other scene' *Entstellung*, displacement, fantasy, psychic defense, and an 'open' textuality" (the space of colonial mimicry) (*Location* 107–8). This ambivalence is doubly problematic when we consider issues of gender, for Western feminism, in its attempt to theorize the status of women, too often neglects the social specificity of women's experience in colonial and postcolonial locations. Theorists like Spivak, Chandra Talpade Mohanty, Sara Suleri, and Ania Loomba have challenged the authority of patriarchal imperial power and a dominant Western vision of feminism and social change. In some cases, as in Spivak's "Can the Subaltern Speak?" (1988), theory itself is called into question, particularly its assumption that the social conditions of the non-Western subject can be grasped by an analytical methodology grounded in Western philosophical traditions.

From the mid-1980s, important work appeared by Peter Hulme and Antonio Benitez-Rojo on the encounters between European explorers and indigenous peoples in the Caribbean. In the 1990s, scholars like V. Y. Mudimbe and Achille Mbembe were establishing a standpoint for African critique of postcolonial modernity. Former and current British Commonwealth countries – especially Australia, whose colonial development was complicated by the penal colonies established in the eighteenth century – have their own peculiar postcolonial conditions. Work by Helen Tiffin, Bob Hodge, Vijay Mishra, and Graham Huggan has been especially important since 1990 for drawing our attention to the problems faced by Aboriginal peoples and to the impact of large-scale immigration and SETTLER COLONIZATION. In a similar manner, Irish studies has forged its own brand of postcolonial inquiry which emphasizes Ireland's character as a METROCOLONY and its long history of intimate mismanagement by the British Parliament and the Anglo-Irish ruling class. Because of its close proximity to the center of Empire, Ireland experienced colonialism in a unique fashion. In this regard, it resembled India, where the English language and English political and cultural traditions had become entrenched after centuries of colonial administration. As Luke Gibbons, Declan Kiberd, Joe Cleary, and David Lloyd have pointed out, Ireland's metrocolonial status did not immunize it against the problems faced by other colonial and postcolonial territories. The rise of Irish studies coincides roughly with the accelerated interest in the Asian world beyond

South Asia and the Islamic world. In the twenty-first century, postcolonial theory has increasingly been used to talk about native and indigenous experience in the Americas and to analyze transnationalism throughout the world. We might therefore regard transnationalism as a late development that encompasses the postcolonial world within a vast and complex global environment. Benedict Anderson, Immanuel Wallerstein, Pheng Cheah, and David Palumbo-Lui have explored the implications of a transnational perspective that situates colonial and postcolonial experiences within global networks of trade, communication, and domination and offered a new arena for the dialectical expression of colonial modernity.

Postcolonial and transnational approaches are implicitly forms of historical revisionism and therefore share a set of common concerns with New Historicism, preeminently in the work of US scholars like **Stephen Greenblatt**, Catherine Gallagher, and Walter Benn Michaels. Rooted in Marxist theory and poststructuralist theories of TEXTUALITY and DISCOURSE, New Historicism developed a method for reading literary texts deep within their social and cultural contexts. For example, as Greenblatt has noted, the historical analysis of cultural discourse in the sixteenth century made possible new contexts and new readings of Shakespeare's plays. By virtue of this deep style contextualization, indebted in part to Clifford Geertz's ethnographic technique of "deep description," the New Historicist critic could open up points of contact between the text and its milieu as well as between the reader and the text itself. New Historicists were therefore very attuned to the multiple determinations that constitute the cultural text and thus to historical stratifications that are best understood in non-linear or non-causal ways. Foucault's theories of archaeology and discourse formation were a significant influence on New Historicism, for they provided the framework for mapping historical fields and a model for analysis that gave historical description a qualitative value. If we occasionally find a critic overemphasizing context at the expense of a literary analysis, we just as often discover fresh perspectives that allow us to hear more clearly what the cultural text, distant from us in time, has to say.

The presupposition of historical context and awareness, of a critical eye toward the past and its injustices – in everyday life, in politics, in representations – is the starting point for a critique of race and ethnicity that is, in certain particulars, allied to postcolonial studies. We see this beginning to happen in the work of W. E. B. Du Bois who, in 1903, put forward the idea of "double consciousness." This was a provocative idea, one that emphasized not only a consciousness of racial DIFFERENCE but also a sense of radical internal division, a sense of "two-ness" that Du Bois understood in terms of a doubling of the soul, of the struggle to be human in America. This double consciousness is grounded in the slave trade, which reduced the value of the African subject over against the European. Like the pernicious sexual inequalities that Barbara Smith and bell hooks unmask, it is foundational and systematic. The identity of the African American, like that of other immigrant Americans, is internally split: "an American, a Negro; two souls, two thoughts, two unreconciled strivings" (9). From the time of the Harlem Renaissance to the Civil Rights era of the 1950s and 1960s, a discourse of African American experience flourished. By the 1980s, Smith, Houston Baker, and **Henry Louis Gates** had defined the initial parameters of an African American literary criticism. In *The*

Signifying Monkey: A Theory of Afro-American Literary Criticism (1988), Gates explores the complex and dialectical interplay of native traditions, like the "signifying monkey" motif found in African and early slave literatures, and how native traditions intersect with poststructuralist theories of language and signification.

If Gates offered a way to syncretize Western and African approaches to literary theory, the Afrocentrism of Martin Bernal and Molefi K. Asante advocated the reinstatement of Africa and African culture at the center of Western cultural and intellectual history. Their revisionist histories realigned the discussion of race and slavery in the United States while calling into question the place of Africa in the Western imaginary. At the turn of the twenty-first century, the idea of the "black Atlantic" became popular as transnationalist and transatlantic approaches in Anglo-American and postcolonial studies were establishing new models for understanding the patterns of movement underlying not only the slave trade but all forms of immigration to the United States. In many respects, African American studies found a new global context in which to situate the unique *national* experience of African Americans. Ethnic and indigenous studies, in rethinking localism, have contributed new perspectives to the transnational project of deconstructing oppressive binary concepts and forms associated with nationalism. In some cases, as in US indigenous literatures, figures of the *other* (the trickster and the coyote, for example) become powerful allies in forming authentic individual and group identities that offer credible alternatives to a dominant national culture. But the *other* also comes in the form of a conquering culture, an implacable opponent in an undialectical contest in which all is at stake. (In this, the US indigenous experience duplicates that of colonial oppression, which is the freezing or forfeiture of the dialectic in the colonizer's favor.) This double experience of ALTERITY, like the "double consciousness" described by Du Bois, situates identity at a crossroads and makes it impossible to choose decisively to remain on one side only of a boundary line. This is particularly evident in Chicano/a studies, which grew out of the politics of the United Farm Workers' struggle of the late 1960s. A keynote text is Gloria Anzaldúa's *Borderlands/La Frontera: The New Mestiza* (1987), which announced a radical break with monolingual theoretical discourse, in which the *other* is the object of reflection, and challenged the border between creative and critical writing. In Chicano/a literatures we see a further dimension of the paradox, for at the borderline, where existence is fluid and the social *other* is a familiar, even intimate, presence, the threshold is also a halting point (but not a cessation), where identity is shaped in a process of geographical and cultural reciprocity. Like African American studies at this time, Chicano/a studies was in the avant-garde when it came to theorizing race, ethnicity, and cultural difference. Moraga, Sonia Saldívar-Hull, and others have diversified the theoretical base of Chicano/a studies with work on the legal system, feminism, bicultural experience, and the status of race in the twenty-first century.

The field of Asian American studies, which was emerging at this time, pursued some of the same theoretical issues and addressed some of the same social and political problems. Of particular interest were the linked ideas of immigration and assimilation. Important work in fiction and memoir by Maine Hong Kingston was followed by theoretical projects by such figures as Lisa Lowe, Gail Ching-Liang Low, and David Palumbo-Liu. Palumbo-Liu's description of how Asian America is conceived in the US imaginary might well apply to other similar experiences of assimilation and difference in the United Kingdom and Europe. He considers the 1930s, when immigration, politics (nationalist and fascist), and war created transformations of populations by new flows of immigrants, refugees, and "displaced persons": "the mixture of foreign with the domestic and the various possibilities of interracial and interethnic connections presented a new set of concerns" (40). The United States tried to regulate this flow, but inevitably the US imaginary is "rescripted" by immigration and, even more so, the processes of assimilation and resistance that persist in the generations after first arrival.

Allied in many ways with Chicano/a and Asian American studies, Native American studies has had a long history of resistance to the social and cultural institutions responsible for the decimation and displacement of native peoples. Landmark early works include Vine Deloria's *Custer Died for Your Sins* (1969) and Dee Brown's *Bury My Heart at Wounded Knee* (1970), which critiqued the anthropological representation and social repression of native peoples and offered a revisionist history of the United States. Subsequent work, mostly in the late 1980s and 1990s, contextualized Native American experience within the broader framework of cultural diversity in the United States and created greater awareness of native intellectual thought. Of special importance from the 1980s was the work of Gerald Vizenor, who combined a deep knowledge of native literatures with an interest in Western theoretical discourse, including the concerns of poststructuralism and postmodernism. Of special interest is the critique of the US government's colonialist relations with native peoples, which has led critics like Kevin Bruyneel to explore the possibilities of "the third space of sovereignty." These issues of race, ethnicity, and culture identity have become part of a larger conversation about globalization and transnational development. Central to this conversation are issues of assimilation and social integration in a world system in which national borders and identities are less important for local politics and personal identity. Palumbo-Liu, along with Pheng Cheah and Bruce Robbins, have argued for a world-systems approach to the global history of nationalism and capitalism in which a new cosmopolitanism remakes international cultural connections on the model of global capital flows and trends.

At the heart of this new emphasis on cosmopolitanism and global world systems is a renewed consideration of culture, particularly forms of so-called popular culture that tend to find worldwide distribution and consumption. In this regard, cultural studies, especially in the United States and the United Kingdom, has learned much from post-Marxist, postcolonial, and transnational theories of culture. By the 1990s, nearly every facet of culture was explored, primarily via a deconstruction of the high/low cultural divide, an opposition rooted in the modernism/mass culture distinction that has managed to remain firmly in place despite the concerted attempt by critical theory to dislodge it. Angela McRobbie and Janice Radway, for example, have shown how popular music and literature, youth culture, and middle-class literary tastes serve as vital barometers for larger social and cultural transformations and problems. This trend in cultural studies has reinvigorated film and media studies. **Slavoj Žižek**'s work in film studies, especially his Lacanian readings of Hitchcock, has transformed the field by introducing a theoretical model that conjoined Hegelian critical theory and psychoanalysis. Feminist film theorists like Teresa de Lauretis and Laura Mulvey have critiqued the gendered dynamics of representation, particularly the *gaze* that is doubly represented in film, once by the filmmaker, whose gaze constructs or composes human actors as objects in a visual medium, and again by the viewer whose own gaze reduplicates the filmmaker's. Their work demonstrates the power of a deconstructionist approach to the "determining male gaze" of film and other media forms.

Of course, the challenge to culture is not a new one; we see it in early critical theory and in Derrida's deconstruction of structuralist anthropology. Certainly it is the challenge issued by Lacan, Foucault, and French philosophical feminists, all of whom offered new methods of mapping and interpreting the discourse formations that communicate cultural knowledge and competence. This is the chief importance for literary theory of the French sociologist **Pierre Bourdieu**, whose conception of the SOCIAL FIELD has provided us with innovative paradigms for understanding how "cultural capital" circulates and how individuals negotiate increasingly complex societies. His theory of HABITUS attempts to account for the "socialized subjectivity" of an active agent in the world whose *dispositions* (skills and competences acquired in a given social field) are the mark of social status and *distinction*. The limits and rules that structure the social field, in which the social agent achieves distinction, are neither arbitrary nor external but are constituted by the aggregate of successful social experiences (or "moves") that constitute the field. Foucault's theories of discourse and power and **Judith Butler**'s work on PERFORMATIVITY have been especially influential in developing modes of SOCIAL CONSTRUCTIONISM in which ESSENTIALIST notions of sexual and gender identity are revealed as ideological constructs masquerading as "natural." These constructs play a profound role in the personal choices made by men and women in concrete social situations. Butler's *Gender Trouble* (1990) has been enormously influential in describing the social constructionist thesis and in illustrating the social and political implications of the passive performance of traditional gender roles and of upsetting such roles in self-aware and subversive forms of performativity. Butler was also instrumental in pointing out that there is no common enemy, no "universal or hegemonic structure of patriarchy or masculine domination" (*Gender Trouble* 3). The problem is in the cultural systems at large, particularly in repressive norms of identity, sexual orientation, and social belonging that restrict individual and collective freedoms. This line of theoretical investigation was followed by Anne Fausto-Sterling, Susan Bordo, and **Elizabeth Grosz**, whose work on the body, on the link between science and gender, and on the very idea of a "natural" fact has transformed not only our conceptions of culture but of the natural world that is typically opposed to it. We see in this important work the wide-ranging influence of feminism, which has become fundamental to every discipline in the human and social sciences.

To some extent we see in this emphasis on gender and sexuality a legacy of the poststructuralist critique of difference, particularly of binary structures of knowledge and power. Nowhere is this more evident than in new theories of sexual difference and the critique of compulsory heterosexuality that characterizes societies throughout the world. In the mid-1970s, Monique Wittig, Jeffner Allen, Sarah Hoagland, and Adrienne Rich brought the lesbian body and lesbian sexuality out of the closet and fashioned a theoretical and artistic style that forcefully countered patriarchal power and masculinist intellectual traditions. In fact, it is possible to argue that the feminist critique of gender and sexuality made possible a similar critical "outing" of male homoeroticism and homosexuality. We see this most clearly in **Eve Kosofsky Sedgwick**'s pioneering study, *Between Men: English Literature and Male Homosocial Desire* (1985). Sedgwick builds on Gayle Rubin's theory of "sex/gender systems" and René Gerard's conception of "triangular desire" in her development of two key ideas: homosocial desire and homosexual panic. According to Sedgwick, in the structures of triangular desire, women mediate the desire of men, which is thereby constituted as a form of HOMOSOCIALITY that enables relations of power among men while simultaneously displacing the disruptive homoerotic desire that might spring up between men without such mediation.

Sedgwick's work is unquestionably foundational for the field of queer theory, which offers a critique of the sex/gender system, specifically of the structural homophobia that leads to pernicious forms of homosocial desire (like homosexual panic). It also valorizes (by revaluing) the very condition of being "queer," which includes a range of homosexual and homoerotic positions and ultimately encompasses drag and "female masculinity." Sara Ahmed's work on "queer phenomenology" seeks to understand this otherness as a function of orientation within broader categories, like race and gender, for she hopes "to offer a new way of thinking about the spatiality of sexuality, gender, and race." As in gay and lesbian studies and so many other literary theories, the body becomes a location for meaning, an object in the world, but also a meaningful object, whose impression on us "is dependent on past histories" (1–2). The affective and existential dimension of queer theory links it with other theories of sexual identity, such as masculinity studies, and also with a posthumanist discourse that seeks to move beyond patriarchy, compulsory heterosexuality, and the sex/gender system.

The tendency in these theories of culture, identity, sexuality, and historical revisionism is to rethink the possibilities of human agency in a way that refuses to foreclose participation of any group or individual on the basis of invidious stereotypes or categories of social and cultural exclusion. In the latter decades of the twentieth century, this tendency became especially notable in the refinements of postmodernist critique and in a resurgence of Marxist approaches to culture and politics. If in 1980 Jameson felt the need to declare "always historicize," by the turn of the century one could greet such a call only by saying, "as opposed to what?"

Postmodernism and Post-Marxism, 1980s–2000s

In the era of high theory, from the 1970s to the 1990s, the crucial questions of gender, identity, class and race were raised in theoretical terms that presupposed the legitimacy of theory (of philosophical reflection and analysis) and the very possibility of cultural analysis. But we see in this period, particularly after 1990, new directions in postmodernism and post-Marxism that call into question the assurances of theory but in a way that rejuvenates the theory project by sharpening its self-critical dimension, thereby giving it greater powers of social and cultural critique. Though some might feel that postmodernist and Marxist approaches are antithetical (based on misconceptions that postmodernism rejects history and politics), it is the case that the two intellectual currents, especially by the late twentieth century, are deeply entwined. In fact, many seminal postmodernists, like **Jean-François Lyotard** and **Jean Baudrillard**, began writing from Marxist and socialist perspectives. And the postmodern philosopher Jean-Luc Nancy remains deeply interested in Hegel and the "restlessness of the negative"; his work exemplifies the affinity between postmodernism and the dialectical tradition that inspired Marx. The post-Marxist could not help but concede the reality of postmodernity as a phase of late capitalist development, and the postmodernist cannot help but confirm a materialist approach to society, culture, and aesthetics. Both approaches can be understood as part of a general critique of modernity, with roots in Marxist theory, critical theory, and the modernist movements in Europe, the United Kingdom, and the United States. And while, in the 1970s, the postmodernist Lyotard debated the critical theorist Habermas about whether the project of Enlightenment was finished or still in progress, the fact is that both sides were concerned with the same problem: the value and destiny of an intellectual tradition that was, in the late twentieth century, in crisis. That their answers differed should surprise no one who has even a basic understanding of the history of literary theory.

The "post" in postmodernism can thus be understood as the temporal space of a critique of modernity. Postmodernism rejects any discourse that legitimizes or perpetuates universal truths in the form of ideology and or that advocates a conception of history as dialectical movement toward an absolute end (i.e., in the State). It is profoundly opposed to literary or cultural forms that take solace in mimetic representations that falsify human experience in the service of outmoded conventions or national traditions. Lyotard's *Postmodern Condition* (1979), one of the most important postmodernist critiques, points to the loss of social and political legitimacy that was once conferred upon society by the grand myths of human progress and technological modernity, the MASTER NARRATIVES that explain, justify, and thereby sustain universal truth, historical destiny, and the meaning and value of the past. As Theodor Adorno and other critical theorists well understood, the narratives of enlightenment are essentially narratives of domination in which social inequalities and injustices are normalized. Lyotard argues that master narratives, or *les grands récits*, need to be supplanted by *les petits récits*, local narratives, indigenous ethnographies, paralogy, language games – in short, a "pragmatics of knowledge" (Lyotard *Postmodern* 61). Opposed to idealist totalities, the postmodernist is likely to promote non-teleological and hierarchical networks and ASSEMBLAGES. In *Anti-Oedipus* (1972) and *Thousand Plateaus* (1980), **Gilles Deleuze and Félix Guattari** seek to bypass through critique the dialectical relation between capital and the subject, understood as the *subject of* a neurotic discourse and of commodified desire. The "schizoid" subject escapes self-identity in the vertiginous and unregulated terrain of non-identity. Over against cathexis (the expenditure of psychic energy or *libido*) and sublimation, Deleuze and Guattari offer flows and intensities of desire; they describe desiring machines that subvert the patriarchal family ("Mommy, Daddy and Me") and the repressive logic of capitalism in order to RETERRITORIALIZE SOCIAL FORMATIONS ("bodies without organs"). This conception of desire displaces the Freudian concept of desire as lack – i.e., the

Oedipus complex – and introduces the "schizoid" subject who escapes domination and repressive forms of centered, normative subjectivity. In the vertiginous and unregulated terrain of non-identity, desire is grounded in mobility, expenditure, and (re)distribution, while knowledge is multiplied and dispersed across overlapping and integrated networks. In this postmodern frame of reference, totality gives way to aggregation and multiples, to the kinds of complex wholes found in the RHIZOMATIC structures of communications networks, transnational power, and the internet. It is possible that these alternatives can answer Georges Bataille's call for a "sum of all possibles" in philosophy (258), a form of totality that can include and account for all forms of human experience, including death, the erotic, and the sacred.

Subsequent work by all these thinkers through the early 1990s constituted an aesthetics of affects and absences, of perverse images that confuse our relation to the real – an aesthetics in which the sublime finally emerges not as the struggle to comprehend the incomprehensible but rather as the very incomprehensibility of language itself, the abyss that makes all knowledge possible. Repeating a gesture that goes back to Kant, postmodernists find in aesthetics the mediating point of human thought and the sensuous real. But whereas Kant bypassed the real with the non-concept of a "supersensible substrate of humanity," postmodernists embrace the real in the only forms possible for our perception: the absolute privation of the "thing-in-itself" and the endless precession of simulations that stand in for it. The classic tradition of aesthetics wished to mediate the realms of sense and reason, while the postmodernist tends to collapse them, so that reason takes on the vitalist character of an "immaterial materialism" or, as Baudrillard puts it, the sensuousness of "demon images." The post-Marxist theorist **Jacques Rancière** sees, in postmodernism, a complex disengagement from modernism's uneasy complicity with the aesthetic regime, which amounts to the attainment of a "specificity of art" that comes at the cost of the very regime that identified aesthetics as a way of making art possible (68f).

From Samuel Beckett and Eugène Ionesco during and after World War II to Don Delillo, John Barth, and Thomas Pynchon in the 1960s and 1970s, postmodernist literature depicts a world bereft of legitimation (narrative and otherwise), a world in which progress had reached the dead ends of alienation and narcissism. Indeed, as many theorists have argued, the postmodernist literary text is not interested in the world at all, for its main concern appears to be to represent its own operations. Paul Ricoeur speaks, not approvingly, of the "ideology of the absolute text," in which the referential function (that is, the way literature talks about the world in which we live) is suspended, and there arises in its place seemingly endless self-referentiality, the sublime abyss of language. Robert Scholes and Linda Hutcheon, who have developed theories of FABULATION and METAFICTION, respectively, argue that postmodern fiction tends to comment on and thematize its own linguistic and narrative practices. There are certainly precedents in modernist and avant-garde art for this form of self-referentiality, but postmodernism has brought it to the forefront in new and stimulating ways.

The postmodernist engagement with modernist aesthetics is mirrored in the post-Marxist critique of capitalism in postmodernity, for here too we find roots in modernist critical theory. For example, Adorno's analysis of the culture industry might well qualify as an inaugural post-Marxist project, save for his reluctance to part with the category of the authentic subject, dialectical methods, and the idea of an autonomous art, free of reason's conceptual reductions and the alienating influence of a commodity market. For some scholars, the initial point of emergence lies in the 1930s with Antonio Gramsci's work on hegemony; for others, **Louis Althusser**'s work in the 1960s marks a decisive moment, for his development of certain key concepts – particularly IDEOLOGY and structural causality – redefines the way we regard the relation between BASE and SUPERSTRUCTURE and thus constitutes a significant revision of classical Marxism. Still others would locate the turning point in the 1980s, with the work of Fredric Jameson, who revolutionized Marxist literary criticism with the idea of the "political unconscious" and who revitalized the analysis of postmodern art and culture. By most estimations, Post-Marxism was securely established with the publication of Ernesto Laclau and Chantal Mouffe's *Hegemony and Socialist Strategy* (1985). What is common to all of these figures is the understanding that late capitalism distributes power in new ways. For one thing, because global capital has reached such a degree of rational interconnection and interdependence, nationalism ceases to be a viable point of departure for critique and political action. And while the nation-state does not disappear from view, its modes of legitimation have shifted from narratives of origin that are, at bottom, local mythologies to the disjunctive relations of the nation-state within a geopolitical arena in which multiple and overlapping polygonal connections override the old interstate rivalries of the imperial age (which came to a head in the Cold War period of the mid-twentieth century). What to a postmodernist might seem aleatory and governed by "flows" of information, to a post-Marxist, especially someone like Wallerstein, might seem a densely and intricately articulated global politics mediated by elite interests (the military–industrial–financial complex) that no longer pledge allegiance to a national power.

An important development running coevally with post-Marxism and postmodernism is critical theory, particularly the critique of modernity in the work of Anthony Giddens, Habermas, and Selya Benhabib. For these thinkers, the crisis of modernity is not that the project of Enlightenment is exhausted or no longer relevant to a postmodern world, but rather that it is unfinished. Giddens, for example, counters Adorno's and the early Foucault's skepticism about the subject's agency with respect to POWER/KNOWLEDGE by focusing on "the self-reflexive project of the self" (215), which can serve as a safeguard against a capitalist world in which the subject is commodified and loses all vestiges of freedom. For Giddens, the subject is able to negotiate and "construct" her own identity amid often antagonistic social forces. The idea that social constructionism could evade the recourse to ideological interpellation resonates also in the work of Habermas and his successors who respond to the crisis of legitimacy in the West with new forms of collectivity grounded not in revolutionary political action but rather in rational communication and consensus. One might call this a form of humanist Marxism (directly counter to Althusser's anti-humanism). This is especially the case in the work of Seyla Benhabib, who confronts the problem of global capitalism with a form of transnational cosmopolitanism, which she defines as "a normative philosophy for carrying the universalistic norms of discourse ethics beyond the confines of the nation-state" (18). Her idea of a "discourse ethics," in which interlocutors are "moral conversation partners," resituates Habermas's "communicative rationality" in a social totality defined by diversity and transnational interrelation. In this context, the concerns of critical theory intersect with those of transnationalism and postcolonial theory that seek models of community and sociality beyond the concept of the nation-state. Like the "cosmopolitics" put forward by Cheah and Bruce Robbins and Wallerstein's world-systems theory, Benhabib's cosmopolitanism seeks to redefine the basis and structure of *community* in terms of an openness to gender and ethnic difference but also to new visions of society and the distribution of power and resources. Wallerstein's work has been particularly influential, for it offers a historical approach to complex, interconnected world economies that uses Marxist theory to investigate complex new forms of global capitalism. His "world historical sociology," which started to gain ground among literary theorists in the 1990s, criticizes modernization theory for retaining an outmoded conception of the nation and its role in capitalist development. It offers instead an analytical method that can account for multicultural social formations, global markets, and transnational movements of people and language.

From the early 1990s, Benhabib, along with Judith Butler and Drucilla Cornell, began to use critical theory to address social and political issues concerning women outside the traditional framework of Western feminism. Questions about the possibility of social activism and identity politics became increasingly important in a post-Cold War era in which the subject of postmodernity was threatened with irrelevance. According to Jennifer Wicke, feminism needed "to catch up to a reality we barely have a name for, the postmodern situation of a theory of identity that seeks to overcome the limitations of fixed, immutable, and hierarchical identities, with a feminism still involved in a straightforward identity politics" (33). Fundamental aspects of social life – the legal status of women, the ethics of reproduction, intellectual and aesthetic life, class and racial identity – continue to be the focus of a postmodern feminist theory that appropriates materialist analysis to subvert the dominant discourse of identity that runs from Descartes to poststructuralism. Postmodern feminists, like post-Marxists, pose urgent questions about major transformations in the nature of modernization, knowledge formation, and technical progress that marked both the enduring legacy of the Enlightenment and the limits of its traditional modes of understanding the world.

Post-Marxism, postmodernism, feminism, and critical theorists converge on a number of points, particularly on the importance of Kant and Hegel, whose conceptions of UNIVERSALITY and TOTALITY undergo an immanent critique that makes them available in new ways as tactics in critical analysis (for example, of gender, sexuality, the subject, the state, political actions, and so on). From Jean-François Lyotard's Kantian postmodernism to Slavoj Žižek's twenty-first-century Hegelianism, we are reminded of the continued relevance of dialectics, aesthetics, and the category of the universal. Žižek, Butler, and Laclau have put forward new theories of "provisional totality" and "contingent universality" that can serve tactically as the ground of collective political action (see Butler et al.). Thus, Žižek can claim that "Kantian formalism and radical historicism are not really opposites, but two sides of the same coin" (Butler et al. 111). These forms of "postfoundationalism" remind us of the continuing relevance of idealist philosophy, but they also underscore the importance of innovation and renovation in theoretical traditions.

By the turn of the twenty-first century, the post-Marxist critique of culture had effectively eclipsed the postmodernist project, which is a way of saying that it drew it into dialectical collaboration. But it has also developed something like a post-dialectical standpoint, which has resulted in new theories of the One (Deleuze) and the multiple (Alain Badiou) and new paradigms for political agency and political aesthetics (Rancière), all of which enables an ironic return to the very center of humanism and humanist philosophy: the nexus of reason and sensation in the self-governing realm of art. For the post-Marxist, the capitalist mode of production and the fetishistic culture it (re)enforces must be overcome; however, as Adorno illustrates so well, this overcoming must itself be overcome. In an administered society, even immanent critique, "tarrying with the negative" (as Žižek puts it), can end up affirming the dialectical domination of a master narrative that thrives on opportunities to optimize its own evolution by managing crisis, as both Habermas and Claus Offe have demonstrated. Culture critique, the first moment of overcoming a reified daily life, must itself be subjected to a clarifying revision, a struggle down to the basic units of argument. Adorno's style, like that of Deleuze, Lyotard, Badiou, and so many others, exemplifies this struggle both with and in dialectics, a victory sought over the very thing that triumphs. In a sense, these theorists write from a posthumanist perspective, one that seeks to move beyond the idea of human being *as such*. This perspective takes literary theory in new directions; it opens up the possibility of altering the human presence in this negotiation, to resituate the human in a natural world, not in order to dominate it but to see it from the standpoint of *other beings*.

Posthumanism: Theory at the *Fin de Siècle*

At the turn of the millennium, we now speak of the posthuman, and by doing so, we invoke the humanism that it is at the heart of intellectual development in the West for hundreds of years. In a sense, posthumanism is implicit in the concept of humanism itself, for we can discern it in the works of the great nineteenth-century explorers of the human – Marx, Darwin, Nietzsche, and Freud – who each delivered a tremendous blow to the self-assurance and preeminence of humanism. At the same time, each tends to reinscribe its majesty in the alternative, a dialectical outcome summed up succinctly in Nietzsche's concept of the *Übermensch* ("overman"). For poststructuralists like Foucault and Barthes and philosophers like Bataille, the primacy of "man" was challenged and the homocentric nature of our knowledge and perceptions (the anthropomorphism of all things) was unveiled as an arrogant and shortsighted standpoint. Since Heidegger's *Letter on Humanism* (1947), it has grown increasingly difficult to maintain the position that the concept *human* and the order of knowledge that we designate *humanism* can provide a stable foundation upon which to confront our present situation, to understand the meaning of the past and to build toward a viable, *humane* future.

In the dialectics of identity that characterizes so much discourse on humanism, subjectivity is bound up with mastering the *other*: to be human is *not to be something else*, and that "something else" is typically designated *non-human*. It is, as Nietzsche put it, to take "man as measure of the world" ("On Truth and Lies" 86). However, as phenomenology has revealed, our "apartness" is only a function of perspective. If we learn to see and feel differently, as Merleau-Ponty and others urge us to do, if we can acknowledge that the thing/object gazes at us from its standpoint (its being), we can enter into a kind of communion with that which we can never actually *be*. This cooperative and critical non-identity is an openness to the gaze of the *other* and to the possibility of an *other* intention toward or orientation to the world. Foucault's work is enormously important to posthumanism, particularly his genealogical method, which is ideally suited to the theorist who wishes to challenge all things whose value rests on the basis of their emergence *for human being*. In the very late work on sexuality and the subject of power, Foucault clears the ground for a Nietzschean overcoming of human limits – posthuman, but in the sense that human being becomes more open and multiple, less constrained by ideology and conformist cultural codes.

The posthumanist subject is dethroned, but not dialectically cancelled or SUBLATED; its being is conceded, along with that of other objects, in an ontology that revalues and realigns the human among an expanded order of beings. The first stage of the posthumanist project is the recognition that while all our philosophies are built upon human thought, speculation, imagination, and writing, there is being beyond the human. Shakespeare, at the heart of the Renaissance humanist moment, foresaw this "beyond": "There are more things in heaven and earth, Horatio, / Than are dreamt of in your philosophy" (*Hamlet* I.v.66–7). For the posthumanist, this "something more" is not TRANSCENDENT but profoundly IMMANENT. Understood in terms of immanent being in the world, human beings share a condition with other forms of being. Thus **Donna Haraway** redefines the relationship between nature and culture, in part by exploring the role of non-human actors, such as cyborgs and animals, while **N. Katherine Hayles** explores the interface between human and technological being and advocates a greater sensitivity toward hybrid modes of existence (e.g., the coupling of consciousness to "smart" prosthetic devices). The non-human, which is removed from us from the start by being designated as the absence of human being, is nevertheless caught up *in its own being* and perhaps its own unknowable way of knowing the world. This presupposition underlies a good deal of the writing that I consider under the rubric *posthuman*. From animal studies and ecocriticism, to disability studies and cognitive theory, posthumanism announces, in Bruno Latour's memorable phrase, the "birth of 'non-humanity'" (13).

We may feel more comfortable nowadays talking about science and culture together, in part because we have learned to speak about complex scientific ideas in a "vernacular" fashion, even if we do not always follow the mathematics involved. Indeed, C. P. Snow's "two cultures" idea (put forward in 1959) – that there was a radical break or schism between scientific and humanist cultures – would be untenable to a posthumanist, who would find the terms themselves unstable and tendentious and the idea of a break difficult to entertain. Habermasian critical theory advocates an integration of these cultures, along with the sphere of ethics, but a posthumanist would see them not as separate spheres needing better articulation but as knowledge domains caught up in reciprocal processes of legitimation and innovation. In these processes, the spheres of science and literature and the humanities are impossible to separate for analysis. Interdisciplinary research and study testifies also to this tendency toward an imbrication or collation of different domains (here we see the influence of Foucault and Bourdieu) as well as to a critical component in the reciprocal interchange. On this view, the trend toward collaboration between the humanities and the life sciences is not a resolution of the old "two cultures" debate but a more provocative reopening of it, for the current interdisciplinary formations have done nothing if not allowed both science and the humanities to ask searching questions about the other's status, each one exploring in different ways a landscape in which the human is no longer the "crown of creation." Posthumanism constitutes not simply a further elaboration of cultural studies (as some critics aver) but an interrogation of what is "given" in culture critique: *nature*. It unveils the myth of this givenness and reveals it as a product of human labor and perception, at the same time that it challenges the separation of culture from the "given" world in which cultural experience unfolds and from which it acquires its materials.

This unveiling is itself the object of new ontologies of the *non-human*. This is not a return to the Romantic tradition of *Naturphilosophie* (the total knowledge of nature) but rather a radical rethinking of what constitutes nature and our knowledge of it, a knowledge that can never be total. These new ontologies are grounded in Heidegger's phenomenology but they also challenge the very basis of his work: human Da-sein, that form of being that makes possible and accommodates all other forms of being. These "object-oriented ontologies" all ask, in one form or another, the same question: how can we know the being of another *non*-human being? For Ian Bogost, what is required is a form of "alien phenomenology," governed by new forms of ontology ("tiny," "flat," "object-oriented"), that seeks even more rigorously than in previous phenomenological projects to move beyond a homocentric perspective. Ideas as much as things, plants as much as sentient beasts are, for these theorists, beings of equal status: the smallest object or thing contains a universe, and its relation to other objects or things is the central philosophical dilemma. Thus the idea of the "alien," far from designating an extraterrestrial being, designates *all beings in their interrelation*: "The alien is anything – and everything ... The true alien recedes interminably even as it surrounds us completely. It is not hidden in the darkness of the outer cosmos or in the deep-sea shelf but in plain sight, everywhere, in everything" (Bogost 34). As Graham Harman writes, "every object is both a substance and a complex of relations" – "lemon meringue, popsicles, Ajax Amsterdam, reggae bands, grains of sand. Each of these things remains a unitary substance beyond its impact on others" (19, 85). The smallest object is an autonomous form, a world unto itself, much as Romantic poets like William Blake and Walt Whitman have noted. But the new ontologists approach this insight with the fervor of scientists who hope to get at and describe the being of objects. As other theorists, like Gerald Bruns, are quick to point out, the posthumanist world is made up of "zones of indistinction." This idea, which goes back to the insights of Baruch Spinoza and other philosophers, is meant to underscore the radical decentering of a dualistic perspective that privileges a knowing subject over the object that is known. A perspective, in short, that is ground precisely in the capacity to make distinctions.

In posthumanism at large, the question is both ethical in a traditional way – what is my responsibility to other beings? – and aesthetic in a way that is traceable to Nietzsche and modernists like Wilde – what is my responsibility in the representation of things, of the *beautiful thing*? In one sense, the posthumanist project is a grand *ricorso*, for it embraces the Nietzschean possibility of humanity overcoming itself. In quite another sense, it overcomes this desire to overcome humanity by posing the question of humanity itself. But this questioning too is in the spirit of Nietzsche, who knew all-too-well about the posthumous nature of the truly free spirit, that most profound of contradictions: the philosopher who can laugh at his own humanity from the perspective of his self-overcoming.

Conclusion

Since the 1980s, the death of literary theory has been announced with a dispiriting regularity. In the twenty-first century, this announcement has taken the form of a "meta-theory" about the institutions and sociopolitical conditions that produce theoretical ideas and discourse. Indicative of this trend is an article, published in 2012, in which Jeffrey Williams writes that "Critical University Studies has succeeded literary theory as a nexus of intellectual energy" (B7). There is no doubt that writing about the university, especially in the United States, is a strong new theoretical trend, as is new work being done on the rise of the global university and online/distance learning. However, this brief history shows that literary theory cannot be succeeded in this way (if anything, critical university studies is yet another development of the materialist–historical trend that begins with Hegel). It is in no danger of suffering yet another premature death. *The Literary Theory Handbook* puts forward the evidence of scholars and theorists, artists and critics, all of whom point toward the general good health and robust spirit of theory. In fact, one is tempted to see the last twenty years, since 1990 or so, as a period of revival, during which the two main strands of theory – the formalist/structuralist, which emphasizes language and textuality, and the materialist/historical, which emphasizes culture and ideology – come together in multiple and nuanced ways. While one pathway or another might dominate the course of theory in any given epoch, the two main strands are by and large interdependent. This is nowhere more evident than in the account of theory in the posthumanist epoch, during which formalism and historicism interacted and imbricated with one another, producing exciting new combinations and raising new and controversial questions about the subject, language, identity, textuality, race, gender, and a host of other topics. If anything remains constant in this variegated history, it is the impulse to understand how literary and cultural texts create meaning and how we, as readers, can understand the value and variety of human experience in the world. In this, I believe we are the anticipated heirs, Nietzsche's true peers: "We children of the future, how *could* we be at home in this today!" (*Gay Science* §377). Posthumanism, like so many theories of the twenty-first century, prepares us for the future by offering both trenchant criticism of the human condition and a pathway that inspires hope for what lies beyond our human being.

Works Cited

Adorno, Theodor W. *Minima Moralia: Reflections from Damaged Life*. 1951. Trans. E. F. N. Jephcott. London: Verso, 1974.

Ahmed, Sara. *Queer Phenomenology: Orientations, Objects, Others*. Durham, NC: Duke University Press, 2006.

Althusser, Louis. *Lenin and Philosophy, and Other Essays*. Trans. Ben Brewster. London: New Left Books, 1971.

Arnold, Matthew. "The Function of Criticism at the Present Time." In *Lectures and Essays in Criticism*. Vol. 3 of *Complete Prose Works*. Ed. R. H. Super. 11 vols. Ann Arbor: University of Michigan Press, 1960–77. 258–85.

Barthes, Roland. *Image-Music-Text*. Trans. Stephen Heath. New York: Hill and Wang, 1977.

Barthes, Roland. "Introduction to the Structural Analysis of Narrative." 1966. In *Image-Music-Text*. Trans. Stephen Heath. New York: Hill and Wang, 1977. 79–124.

Bataille, Georges. *Eroticism, Death and Sensuality*. 1962. Trans. Mary Dalwood. San Francisco: City Lights Books, 1986.

Benhabib, Seyla. *Another Cosmopolitanism*. Oxford: Oxford University Press, 2006.

Benjamin, Walter. *Illuminations*. Ed. Hannah Arendt. Trans. Harry Zohn. New York: Harcourt, Brace and World, 1968.

Bennett, Jane. *Vibrant Matter: A Political Ecology of Things*. Durham, NC: Duke University Press, 2010.

Bhabha, Homi. *Locations of Culture*. London: Routledge, 1994.

Bogost, Ian. *Alien Phenomenology, Or What It's Like To Be a Thing*. Minneapolis: University of Minnesota Press, 2012.

Burke, Edmund. *A Philosophical Enquiry into the Origin of Our Ideas of the Sublime and Beautiful*. London: J. Dodsley, 1767.

Butler, Judith. *Gender Trouble: Feminism and the Subversion of Identity*. New York: Routledge, 1990.

Butler, Judith, Ernesto Laclau, and Slavoj Žižek. *Contingency, Hegemony, Universality: Contemporary Dialogues on the Left*. London: Verso, 2000.

Coleridge, Samuel Taylor. *Biographia Literaria, or Biographical Studies of My Literary Life and Opinions*. Vol. 1. London: Rest Fenner, 1817.

Conrad, Joseph. *Heart of Darkness*. 4th ed. Ed. Paul B. Armstrong. New York: Norton, 2006.

Deleuze, Gilles and Félix Guattari. *What is Philosophy?* Trans. Hugh Tomlinson and Graham Burchell. New York: Columbia University Press, 1994.

Derrida, Jacques. *Of Grammatology*. Trans. Gayatri Chakravorty Spivak. Baltimore: Johns Hopkins University Press, 1976.

Derrida, Jacques. "Structure, Sign and Play in the Discourse of the Humanities." In *Writing and Difference*. Trans. Alan Bass. Chicago: University of Chicago Press, 1978. 278–93.

Dowling, Linda. *The Vulgarization of Art: The Victorians and Aesthetic Democracy*. Charlottesville: University Press of Virginia, 1996.

Du Bois, W. E. B. *The Souls of Black Folk*. New York: Vintage Books/Library of America, 1990.

Eliot, T. S. *Selected Essays, 1917–1932*. New York: Harcourt, Brace, 1932.

Ellmann, Richard. *Oscar Wilde*. New York: Knopf, 1988.

Foucault, Michel. *The Archaeology of Knowledge and the Discourse on Language*. 1969, 1971. Trans. A. M. Sheridan Smith. New York: Pantheon, 1972.

Foucault, Michel. "What is Enlightenment?" [*Qu'est-ce que les Lumières?*]. In *Michel Foucault: Beyond Structuralism and Hermeneutics*. Ed. Herbert L. Dreyfus and Paul Rabinow. Chicago: University of Chicago Press, 1984. 32–50.

Giddens, Anthony. *Modernity and Self-Identity: Self and Society in the Late Modern Age*. Stanford: Stanford University Press, 1991.

Gramsci, Antonio. *Selections from the Prison Notebooks of Antonio Gramsci*. Ed. and Trans. Quintin Hoare and Geoffrey Nowell Smith. New York: International Publishers, 1971.

Grosz, Elizabeth. *Volatile Bodies: Toward a Corporeal Feminism*. Bloomington: Indiana University Press, 1994.

Harman, Graham. *Guerrilla Metaphysics: Phenomenology and the Carpentry of Things*. Chicago: Open Court, 2005.

Hegel, G. W. F. *Aesthetics: Lectures on Fine Art*. 2 vols. Trans. T. M. Knox. Oxford: Clarendon Press, 1975.

Horkheimer, Max. "Traditional and Critical Theory." 1937. In *Critical Theory: Selected Essays*. Trans. Matthew J. O'Connell et al. New York: Continuum, 1999. 188–243.

Hulme, T. E. "Romanticism and Classicism." In *Selected Writings*. Ed. Patrick McGuinness. Manchester: Carcanet, 1998. 68–83.

Irigaray, Luce. *Speculum of the Other Woman*. Trans. Gilliam C. Gill. Ithaca: Cornell University Press, 1985.

Jakobson, Roman. "Closing Statement: Linguistics and Poetics." In *Style in Language*. Ed. Thomas A. Sebeok. Cambridge, MA: MIT Press, 1960. 350–77.

Jardine, Alice. *Gynesis: Configurations of Women and Modernity*. Ithaca: Cornell University Press, 1985.

Jay, Martin. *The Dialectical Imagination: A History of the Frankfurt School and the Institute of Social Research*. Boston: Little Brown, 1973.

Joyce, James. *A Portrait of the Artist as a Young Man*. Ed. John Paul Riquelme. New York: Norton, 2007.

Kant, Immanuel. *Critique of Judgment*. 1790. Trans. Werner S. Pluhar. Indianapolis: Hackett, 1987.

Lacan, Jacques. *Écrits: A Selection*. Trans. Bruce Fink. New York: Norton, 2002.

Latour, Bruno. *We Have Never Been Modern*. 1991. Trans. Catherine Porter. Cambridge, MA: Harvard University Press, 1993.

Lewis, Wyndham, ed. *BLAST 1*. 1914. Rpt. Santa Rosa: Black Sparrow Press, 1997.

Lukács, Georg. *The Theory of the Novel*. 1920. Trans. Anna Bostock. Cambridge, MA: MIT Press, 1971.

Lyotard, Jean-François. *The Postmodern Condition: A Report on Knowledge*. Trans. Geoff Bennington and Brian Massumi. Minneapolis: University of Minnesota Press, 1984.

Nietzsche, Friedrich. *The Birth of Tragedy and The Case of Wagner*. Trans. Walter Kaufmann. New York: Vintage, 1967.

Nietzsche, Friedrich. *The Gay Science*. Trans. Walter Kaufmann. New York: Vintage, 1974.

Nietzsche, Friedrich. "On the Uses and Disadvantages of History for Life." In *Untimely Meditations*. Ed. Daniel Breazeale. Trans. R. J. Hollingdale. Cambridge: Cambridge University Press, 1997. 47–123.

Nietzsche, Friedrich. "On Truth and Lies in a Nonmoral Sense." In *Philosophy and Truth: Selections from Nietzsche's Notebooks of the Early 1870s*. Ed. and trans. Daniel Breazeale. Atlantic Highlands: Humanities Press, 1979. 79–91.

Norris, Margot. *Beasts of the Imagination: Darwin, Nietzsche, Kafka, Ernst and Lawrence*. Baltimore: Johns Hopkins University Press, 1985.

O'Neill, Michael. "'The Burden of Ourselves': Arnold as a Post-Romantic Poet." *Yearbook of English Studies* 36.2 (2006): 109–24.

Palumbo-Liu, David. *Asian/American: Historical Crossings of a Racial Frontier*. Stanford: Stanford University Press, 1999.

Pater, Walter. *The Renaissance: Studies in Art and Poetry*. Ed. Donald L. Hill. Berkeley: University of California Press, 1980.

Pope, Alexander. *The Major Works*. Ed. Pat Rogers. Oxford: Oxford University Press, 2009.

Pound, Ezra. *Literary Essays*. New York: New Directions, 1968.

Pound, Ezra. *Personae: The Shorter Poems*. 1926. Rev. ed. Ed. Lea Baechler and A. Walton Litz. New York: New Directions, 1990.

Rancière, Jacques. *Aesthetics and Its Discontents*. Trans. Steven Corcoran. Cambridge: Polity, 2009.

Richards, I. A. *Principles of Literary Criticism*. New York: Harcourt, Brace; London: K. Paul Trench, Trubner, 1924, 1926.

Ricoeur, Paul. "What is a Text? Explanation and Understanding." In *Hermeneutics and the Human Sciences: Essays on Language, Action and Interpretation*. Ed. and trans. John B. Thompson. Cambridge: Cambridge University Press, 1981. 145–64.

Riddel, Joseph. "Coup de Man, or The Uses and Abuses of Semiotics." *Cultural Critique* 4 (Fall 1986): 81–109.

Rubin, Gayle. "The Traffic in Women: Notes on the 'Political Economy' of Sex." In *Toward an Anthropology of Women*. Ed. Rayna R. Reitor. New York: Monthly Review Press, 1975. 157–210.

Said, Edward. *Orientalism*. 1979. London: Penguin, 1985.

Schiller, Friedrich. *On the Aesthetic Education of Man, in a Series of Letters*. Ed. and Trans. Elizabeth M. Wilkinson and L. A. Willoughby. Oxford: Clarendon Press, 1967.

Shelley, Percy Bysshe. *Defense of Poetry*. Ed. Albert S. Cook. Boston: Ginn, 1890.

Trotsky, Leon. *Literature and Revolution*. Ed. William Keach. Chicago: Haymarket Books, 2000.

Turner, Graeme. *British Cultural Studies*. London: Routledge, 1996.

Wicke, Jennifer. "Postmodern Identities and the Politics of the (Legal) Subject." In *Feminism and Postmodernism*. Ed. Margaret Ferguson and Jennifer Wicke. Durham, NC: Duke University Press, 1994. 10–33.

Wilde, Oscar. "Arts and the Handicraftsman." In *The First Collected Edition of the Works of Oscar Wilde*. Ed. Robert Ross. Vol. 14. London: Methuen, 1908. 293–308.

Wilde, Oscar. "The Critic as Artist." In *Intentions and the Soul of Man*. Vol. 8 of *The First Collected Edition of the Works of Oscar Wilde*. Ed. Robert Ross. London: Methuen, 1908. 99–224.

Wilde, Oscar. "The English Renaissance of Art." In *The First Collected Edition of the Works of Oscar Wilde*. Ed. Robert Ross. Vol. 14. London: Methuen, 1908. 243–77.

Wilde, Oscar. *The Importance of Being Earnest*. In *The First Collected Edition of the Works of Oscar Wilde*. Ed. Robert Ross. Vol. 6. London: Methuen, 1908.

Williams, Jeffrey. "Deconstructing Academe: The Birth of Critical University Studies." *Chronicle of Higher Education* (February 19, 2012): B7–8.

Williams, Raymond. *Culture and Society: 1780–1950*. 1958. Rpt. New York: Columbia University Press, 1983.

Woolf, Virginia. "Modern Fiction." In *The Essays of Virginia Woolf. Vol. 6, 1925–28*. Ed. Andrew McNeillie. London: Hogarth, 1986. 157–65.

Wordsworth, William. *Lyrical Ballads, with Pastoral and Other Poems*. Vol. 1. 3rd ed. London: Longman and Rees, 1802.

2

The Scope of Literary Theory

> One couldn't carry on life comfortably without a little blindness to the fact that everything has been said better than we can put it ourselves.
>
> George Eliot, *Daniel Deronda*

In this chapter the reader will find discussions of major theoretical schools and trends grouped under six rubrics:

Form/Structure/Narrative/Genre
Ideology/Philosophy/History/Aesthetics
Language/Systems/Texts/Readers
Mind/Body/Gender/Identity
Culture/Ethnicities/Nations/Locations
People/Places/Bodies/Things

One could argue that some of the theories herein discussed could be placed under a different rubric (for example, disability studies could be located in the Mind/Body/Gender/Identity section). This possibility can in itself become a fruitful way of understanding theory and the relationship between different theoretical perspectives. My intention is to offer something other than an alphabetical or strictly historical arrangement (the reader can use the alternative alphabetical table of contents for easy reference). Still, there is a historical movement here, a double movement actually: the chapter begins with formalism and ends with posthumanism, but within each of the six sections, there is another historical order, so that in section two, the movement is from Marxism to postmodernism, while in section four, it is from psychoanalysis to trauma studies. Each section maps concurrent developments within the broader historical progression of literary theory.

The Literary Theory Handbook, First Edition. Gregory Castle.
© 2013 John Wiley & Sons, Ltd. Published 2013 by John Wiley & Sons, Ltd.

Note on Cross-Referencing

Boldface type throughout indicates that a relevant biography exists in chapter three, "Key Figures in Literary Theory." SMALL CAPITALS indicate an entry in the glossary. I use parenthetical references to alert the reader to relevant discussions of a given topic, figure, or concept elsewhere in the *Handbook*. Pursuing these cross-references can provide a better sense of the variety and complexity of individual theories as well as the potentiality for combining them. A note at the end of each section refers readers to other relevant sections of the chapter. For additional references, see "Recommendations for Further Reading" (383–91).

1   Form/Structure/Narrative/Genre

Formalism and Structuralism

Though formalism and structuralism are highly differentiated theoretical fields, they share a starting point in the structural linguistics of Ferdinand de Saussure, whose *Course in General Linguistics* (1916) outlines a theory of the sign that transformed not only linguistics, but nearly every branch of the humanities and the social sciences. To some degree the relation between formalism and structuralism is historical, for it is possible to discern a progression from formalist studies of language and literature to structuralist studies of discourse, culture, and society. Though formalist and structuralist thought has been criticized for being inflexible, especially by those who take the Saussurean paradigm in a rigid and doctrinaire fashion, the notions of *form* and *structure* are actually quite elastic and capable of myriad formulations.

Ancient and early modern linguistics had concentrated on the study of grammar and prosody, often in connection with interpreting sacred texts. By the eighteenth century, historical forms of study had evolved, which in the nineteenth century led to the rise of modern philology, which emphasized the origins and historical development of languages. Structural linguistics opened up an entirely new area of study that focused not on grammar or history, but on the internal dynamics of language systems. Saussure differentiated language as such (*langage*), the human ability to communicate with signs, from language as a system (*langue*) and both of these from individual instances of speech (*parole*). His work is mainly concerned with the difference between *langue* and *parole*, a difference, he argues, that enables us to distinguish "what is social from what is individual and … what is essential from what is ancillary and more or less accidental." *Langue* constitutes a system separate from the individual, "the product passively registered" without "premeditation" and without any reflection (except, of course, that of the linguist) (13–14). It is an institution that maintains a "series of phonetic differences matched with a series of conceptual differences" (118). By contrast, *parole* "is an individual act of the will and the intelligence," but also "the sum total of what people say," particular usages that comprise "individual combinations of words" and "acts of phonation" (14, 19).

For Saussure, language was both "an institution in the present and a product of the past" (9). The social element of language, indeed of all sign-making practices, constitutes the field of semiology, which he defined as the study of signs and their function in society. Though the terms SEMIOLOGY and SEMIOTICS are often used interchangeably, there are some significant differences. *Semiotics* refers to the general science of signs pioneered in the 1880s by Charles Sanders Peirce. In Peircean semiotics the focus is on the sign as a mark of reference to or representation of an object. Saussure, however, is less interested in reference than in DIFFERENCE. In Saussurean semiology, the SIGN does not designate a mimetic relation between a word and an object or external referent (this aspect of the way language works is purely conventional). Rather, it is a complex unity of a *concept* in the mind and a *sound pattern* that corresponds with it. The latter is not simply the vocalization of the concept. "A sound pattern is the hearer's psychological impression of a sound, as given to him by the evidence of his senses" (66). Saussure calls the sound pattern a *signal* (or SIGNIFIER) and the concept a *signification* (or SIGNIFIED), reserving the term *sign* for the combined operation of the two.

Saussure has famously noted that the linguistic sign is arbitrary "in relation to its signification, with which it has no natural connexion in reality" (69). This is not to say that it is unfixed or free-floating or that the link between signal and signification is the "free choice" of the individual speaker, for "the individual has no power to alter a sign in any respect once it has become established in a linguistic community" (68). By the same token, the fact that language is "something in which everyone participates all the time" means that "it is open to the influence of all." It is finally the community's "natural inertia" that guarantees a conservative influence and makes it impossible for a "linguistic revolution" to take place (73–4), though long-term innovative usage can and does alter convention. Language, however, is not a static institution, for the signifier itself has a temporal aspect and produces a diachronic signifying chain. DIACHRONY refers to the linear and sequential relation of words in an utterance, while SYNCHRONY refers to a systematic whole (i.e., *langue*) existing at a given time. The combinations derived from relations of sequential interdependence Saussure called SYNTAGMATIC – "almost all linguistic units depend either on what precedes or follows in the spoken sequence" (126) – while the relations within the system as a whole are PARADIGMATIC – i.e., "flexional paradigms" (133), the system of inflections, declensions, synonyms, and so on that are both inferred and displaced by words in syntagmatic combinations. This picture of language, at once systematic and individual, existing as a whole entity of relations but also as linear and sequential differences, revolutionized linguistics and became the basis for structuralist theories of anthropology, psychoanalysis, narrative, and sociology.

Russian formalism was the first and most influential outgrowth of Saussurean linguistics. Generally speaking, it focuses on "the sphere of literary phenomena as an autonomous domain with laws and regularities peculiar to it alone" (Petrov 188). The chief theorists were Boris Tomashevsky, Roman Jakobson, Yuri Tynyanov, and Boris Eichenbaum, who were associated with the Moscow Linguistic Circle. Formalists were interested in literature, particularly poetry, and how language functions within literary forms. Jakobson outlined the stages of formalist research: "(1) analysis of the sound aspects of a literary work; (2) problems of meaning within the framework of poetics; (3) integration of sound and meaning into an inseparable whole" ("Dominant" 82). The formalist study of poetics exists within the more general study of language, which Jakobson characterized in terms of six functions: the *addresser* (*emotive* function) and *addressee* (*conative* function); falling in between these are a complex set of determinants that include *context* (*referential* function), *message*, *contact* (*phatic* function: "a physical channel and psychological connection between the addresser and addressee"), and a *code* (*metalingual* function) known to both addresser and addressee ("Closing Statement" 353–7). Jakobson emphasized the poetic function of language, the "focus on the message for its own sake." However, it is an oversimplification to reduce all "verbal art" to a poetic function, which tends to be the "dominant, determining function" and serves, in other contexts "as a subsidiary, accessory constituent" ("Closing Statement" 356). Jakobson defines the *dominant* as the "focusing component of a work of art," which can include such things as rhyme, syllabic scheme, or metrical pattern; it "guarantees the integrity of the structure" ("Dominant" 82). In part as a reaction against Saussure's theory of synchronic (or paradigmatic) and diachronic (or syntagmatic) aspects of language systems, Jakobson identified two axes or levels of meaning in poetry: the *metaphoric* and selective (or substitutive) and the *metonymic* and combinative. "The poetic function projects the principle of equivalence from the axis of selection into the axis of combination" ("Closing Statement" 358). By this Jakobson means that in poetry, selections made on the level of metaphor are transposed onto the level of metonymy where they are combined with other words to create poetic effects. Thus, if I write "my daughter blossoms," I am substituting "blossom" for a similar concept (grows, develops) and then combining it with "daughter" to suggest a flower-like opening up of young beauty. This form of projection "imparts to poetry its thoroughgoing symbolic, multiplex, polysemantic essence" ("Closing Statement" 370). Though the poetic function tends to draw out the latent metonymic quality of metaphor (and vice versa), the metaphoric pole tends to characterize poetry of a certain kind (e.g., Romantic and symbolist trends), while metonymy tends to characterize realistic forms (Jakobson and Halle 90ff).

Viktor Shklovsky's work on formal literary devices, particularly his *Theory of Prose* (1925), seeks as Jakobson's had done to demonstrate the formal operations of art by trying to distinguish literary from "ordinary" language. Like **M. M. Bakhtin**, who also wrote on prose forms, he emphasized what was implicit in formalist analysis: the interrelation of literature and the social world. Shklovsky held that literary devices were unique to literary texts (so in that sense, the literary text is autonomous in Petrov's sense), but these devices also enable literature to serve as a form of resistance to social "automatization." This meant that art's formal properties could have a disruptive and subversive effect in the world. His earliest work, "Art as Technique" (1917), introduced the concept of *ostranenie* ("making strange") or *defamiliarization*, one of the "devices" that constitutes the work of art. Defamiliarization challenges novelistic realism by drawing the reader's attention to the strangeness of what is most familiar and thus calling into question the referential function of language. Another device that defamiliarizes the objects of representation is the "laying bare" of the author's techniques. Shklovsky points to Laurence Sterne's *Tristram Shandy*, a novel that self-consciously addresses the reader and exposes the devices by which the author creates his effects.

Like so many other formalists, Shklovsky conducted his intellectual life on the periphery of the Communist Party. He was an exile in Berlin for a while after World War I (at one time hiding out in Jakobson's house), and was one of many social revolutionaries to evade arrest by the Bolsheviks in the early 1920s. His resistance to the Party line on matters of aesthetics led to intense criticism from Marxist literary critics, and he eventually capitulated to orthodox Marxism with the publication of *A Monument to Scientific Error* (1930).

As a movement, formalism encompassed a wide range of methodologies, from the linguistic formalism of Jakobson, Eichenbaum, and others in the Moscow Circle, to figures like Vladimir Propp and Bakhtin, who were not strictly speaking formalists, but whose work focused on problems of form in relation to narrative and social function. Propp's *Morphology of the Folktale* (1928) analyzes the formal properties of folktales in order to identify their specific narrative functions, particularly with respect to characters and their relations to action. This conjunction of formal components with significant function differed considerably from Jakobson's strictly linguistic functions (on Propp, see Narrative Theory/Narratology 69–70). Bakhtin was similarly anomalous among Russian formalists for being primarily concerned with the relations between ideology and literary forms, specifically the novel. His *Problems of Dostoevsky's Poetics* (1929), and the MATERIALIST formalism that it showcases, was well regarded, and he and his circle flourished in Belarus and Leningrad throughout the 1920s. His essays of the 1930s and 1940s, published in 1981 under the title *Dialogic Imagination*, went well beyond the limits of formalism and postulated a new vocabulary for novelistic narrative. The convergence in his work of structural linguistics, poetics, and ideology critique points to the underlying connections between literary forms and devices and the social world. He was attuned to the subtle shifts and differences between dialects, jargons, and so-called standard speech as they were used in narrative representations of daily life. He was particularly interested in novelists like Charles Dickens and Fyodor Dostoevsky whose works employed techniques of *polyphony*: "A plurality of independent and unmerged voices and consciousnesses" (*Problems* 6). For Bakhtin, the object of formalist analysis is to identify the "authoritative ideological positions" in the novel and how these positions are challenged through other voices, especially idiomatic forms of oral discourse (*skaz*). Bakhtin and his circle were not interested in language in the abstract, formal sense studied by linguists but rather in DISCOURSE, language understood "in its concrete living totality" (181). V. N. Volosinov, for example, insisted that "every sign is subject to the criteria of ideological evaluation (i.e., whether it is true, false, correct, fair, good, etc.). The domain of ideology coincides with the domain of signs ... *Everything ideological possesses semiotic value*" (*Marxism* 10). This perspective on the function of the sign accords with DIALOGISM, Bakhtin's term for the dynamic totality of linguistic possibilities that conditions individual utterances. Dialogized discourse has a "double-voiced" character: oriented both to the "referential object of speech" and to "*another's discourse*, toward *someone else's speech*" (*Problems* 185). Bakhtin describes two predominant forms of double-voiced discourse: *stylization*, in which another's discourse is appropriated to serve new ends, and *parody*, in which a similar appropriation takes place: "but, in contrast to stylization, parody introduces into that discourse a semantic intention that is directly opposed to the original one." The study of language must be conducted within its dialogic context "where discourse lives an authentic life" (*Problems* 193, 202). Bakhtin's term for this context is dialogized HETEROGLOSSIA, "the authentic environment of an utterance, the environment in which it lives and takes shape" (*Dialogic* 272). This environment is characterized by multiple and overlapping historical, cultural, and geographical "idiolects" that stratify and HYBRIDIZE linguistic expression.

Bakhtin's theories of language and discourse introduced an element of socio-historical embeddedness and critique that was missing from formalism. Similar qualities can be found in the *functional structuralism* of the Prague Linguistic Circle, which was also influenced by Jakobson, one of the founding members and vice-chairman. Functional structuralism, unlike formalism, is primarily concerned with language as it is manifested in social contexts. It moves beyond the positivist orientation of formalism, with its reliance on linguistic concepts and methodologies, and emphasizes instead a semiotics of social codes. "The semiotic concept of the literary work," writes Peter Steiner, "rendered it a social fact (i.e., a sign understood by the members of a given collectivity) and enabled the structuralists to relate the developmental changes in literary history to all other aspects of human culture." Steiner also points to the movement in Prague structuralism from poetics to aesthetics, a shift "from a concern with verbal art alone to a concern with all the arts and with extra-artistic aesthetics as well" (177). This shift underscored the difference between the two movements with regard to the norms and values attached to language. For the formalist, all that matters are the facts of language, while for the structuralist "function (as crucial a concept as that of the sign) was inseparable from norms and values" (204).

The shift in emphasis among many European intellectuals paved the way for structuralist approaches across the human and social sciences. Claude Lévi-Strauss, in his groundbreaking *Structural Anthropology* (1958), emphasized the ways in which structural linguistics permitted the study of the "*unconscious* infrastructure" of language. He expanded on Saussure's insights that language was concerned primarily with "relations between terms" and that one could discover the "general laws" of linguistic systems (33). More than any other theorist at the time, Lévi-Strauss demonstrated how structural linguistics could play a "renovating role" (33) in the humanities and social sciences by providing a principled scientific method of analyzing literary and cultural texts. For him, structure is "a model meeting with several requirements," principally that no single element of it can change without effecting other elements, that the transformations in different models are such that they can form "a group of models of the same type." Such models are structurally predictable and their "observed fact" are "immediately intelligible" (279). His study of kinship systems and mythology illuminates the specific ways that structuralism can be applied to symbolic social systems, in which the "arbitrary character of the linguistic sign" is provisional, that is, until its function, in cognitive and linguistic structures, becomes fixed and explicit (94). Structuralism is especially useful in studying mythology, where meaning inheres in the organization of *mythemes*, the "gross constituent units" that make up the whole myth and that correspond to the phonemes, morphemes, and sememes found in linguistics. Unlike these linguistic units, however, which operate on the level of the word or the sound, mythemes operate on the level of the sentence. To understand the structure of a myth, the critic must "break down its story into the shortest possible sentences" and then determine the function of each sentence and its relation to other sentences. Though myths function like languages, the language of myth "exhibits specific properties" and belongs to a "higher and more complex order" (210–11).

Lévi-Strauss's work had a profound effect on intellectual trends in the 1960s, especially in France. It stands behind such diverse developments as **Louis Althusser**'s structuralist Marxism, **Jacques Lacan**'s structuralist psychoanalysis, and Northrop Frye's rhetorical formalism. The object of structural analysis in literary studies, according to Tzvetan Todorov, "is the literary discourse rather than works of literature, literature that is virtual rather than real." It does not offer a paraphrase or "a rational résumé of the concrete work," but presents "a spectrum of literary possibilities, in such a manner that the existing works of literature appear as particular instances that have been realized" (436–7). One of the most prominent structuralists, certainly the most influential for literary theory, was **Roland Barthes,** whose first major work, *Mythologies* (1957), takes Lévi-Strauss's insights about the structural function of mythology and applies them to modern culture. He confesses to being impatient "at the sight of the 'naturalness' with which newspapers, art and common sense constantly dress up a reality which, even though it is the one we live in, is undoubtedly determined by history" (11). His provocative approach reveals how historical forces transform magazine covers, Latin grammar, detergent, toys, ornamental cookery, Greta Garbo, plastic, and a variety of other phenomena into mythologies. He posited a "second order" language (i.e., a metalanguage) that incorporates the *linguistic* sign (i.e., the SIGNIFIER/SIGNIFIED relation taken together) as a new signifier for a *mythic* sign whose signified tends to be ideological in character. The original meaning of the linguistic sign, both its structure and its history of use, undergoes a dialectical process of *deformation* when it is appropriated for mythic signification. The meaning of the linguistic sign is emptied of its history in order to provide a shallow, easily filled form (a Latin sentence, a "Negro" soldier saluting on the cover of *Paris-Match*). This new form will in its turn be given new content (the signified), in the form of concepts that rehistoricize the sign in the mythic context: "this history which drains out of the form will be wholly absorbed by the concept," which "implants" in the mythic sign "a whole new history" (119). And while the creation of the mythic concept entails distortion of the original linguistic function, "this distortion is not an obliteration": "The concept, literally, deforms, but does not abolish the meaning; a word can perfectly render this contradiction: it alienates it" (122–3).

Though structural linguistics played a leading role in the development of semiology and semiotics, the latter are concerned with more than just language, as we have seen in Barthes' *Mythologies*. Indeed, semiotics in the 1960s and 1970s was transformed in the work of Umberto Eco, **Julia Kristeva**, and A. J. Greimas. These developments pushed the field closer to structural semantics and structuralist narratology. For example, in his "Introduction to the Structural Analysis of Narrative" (1966), Barthes investigates the "functional syntax" of narrative structures. Echoing Lévi-Strauss's theory of myths, he argues that narrative is structured like a sentence and that the relations between the various parts of a narrative have a syntactical form and value. "Structurally, narrative shares the characteristics of the sentence without ever being reducible to the simple sum of its sentences: a narrative is a long sentence, just as every constative sentence is in a way the rough outline of a short narrative" (*Image* 84). The multiple levels of narrative organize minimal structural units, character functions, and the acts of narration and reading. These levels "are bound together according to a mode of progressive integration" (88).

Though Barthes' structuralist theories are highly complex and employ a technical formalist vocabulary, he does not ignore context. Indeed, like Bakhtin and the Prague school theorists, he believed that structural systems existed *in the world*. Lévi-Strauss's structuralist anthropology is grounded on this fact, and Barthes' structuralism is always aware of its historical moment: it "does not withdraw history from the world" (*Critical Essays* 219). The fact that narrative does not function MIMETICALLY – nothing takes place "from the referential (reality) point of view" (*Image* 124) – does not mean that narrative is detached from historical conditions. When Barthes claims that "it may be that men ceaselessly re-inject into narrative what they have known, what they have experienced" (*Image* 124), he reaffirms one of Saussure's principal points about language: that it is historically embedded. "Language," Saussure reminds us, "has an individual aspect and a social aspect. One is not conceivable without the other" (*Course* 9). Contrary to popular misconceptions, structuralism does not posit an autonomous or transcendent realm of pure structure, but rather a coherent, internally stable and centered organization of elements in complex interrelations. Structuralism is the study of these interrelations and the knowledge that they afford of the structures they constitute itself.

Note
On formalism and narrative, see Narrative Theory/Narratology; on semiotics, see Poststructuralism.

Works Cited

Bakhtin, M. M. *The Dialogic Imagination: Four essays*. Ed. M. Holquist Trans. C. Emerson and M. Holquist. Austin: University of Texas Press, 1981.

Bakhtin, M. M. *Problems of Dostoevsky's Poetics*. Ed. and trans. Caryl Emerson. Minneapolis: University of Minnesota Press, 1984.

Barthes, Roland. *Critical Essays*. Trans. Richard Howard. Evanston: Northwestern University Press, 1972.

Barthes, Roland. *Image-Music-Text*. Trans. Stephen Heath. New York: Hill and Wang, 1977.

Barthes, Roland. *Mythologies*. 1957. Selected and Trans. Annette Lavers. New York: Hill and Wang, 1972.

Jakobson, Roman. "Closing Statement: Linguistics and Poetics." In *Style in Language*. Ed. Thomas A. Sebeok. Cambridge, MA: MIT Press, 1960. 350–77.

Jakobson, Roman. "Dominant." In *Readings in Russian Poetics*. Ed. Ladislav Matejka, and Krystyna Pomorska. Ann Arbor: Michigan Slavic Publications, 1978. 82–7.

Jakobson, Roman and Morris Halle. *Fundamentals of Language*. 1956. 4th ed. The Hague: Mouton, 1980.

Lévi-Strauss, Claude. *Structural Anthropology*. Trans. Claire Jacobson and Brooke Grundfest Schoepf. New York: Basic Books, 1963.

Petrov, Petre. "Formalism." In *The Blackwell Encyclopedia of Literary and Cultural Theory*. Vol. 1. Ed. Gregory Castle. Oxford: Blackwell, 2011. 188–97.

Saussure, Ferdinand de. *Course in General Linguistics*. Ed. Charles Bally and Albert Sechehaye. Trans. Wade Baskin. New York: McGraw-Hill, 1966.

Steiner, Peter, ed. *The Prague School: Selected Writings, 1929–1946*. Trans. John Burbank, Olga Hasty, Manfred Jacobson, Bruce Kochis, and Wendy Steiner. Austin: University of Texas Press, 1982.

Todorov, Tzvetan. "Structural Analysis in Narrative." In *Modern Literary Criticism, 1900–1970*. Ed. Lawrence I. Lipking and A. Walton Litz. New York: Atheneum, 1972. 436–41.

Voloshinov, V. N. *Marxism and the Philosophy of Language*. Trans. Ladislav Matejka and I. R. Titunik. New York: Seminar Press, 1973.

New Criticism

The New Criticism is an Anglo-American variety of formalism that emerged in the early decades of the twentieth century and dominated teaching and scholarship until the early 1960s. It is less a coherent literary theory than a congeries of critical and theoretical approaches all of which are grounded on the idea that the literary work is AUTONOMOUS, that its unity and meaning are constituted primarily by formal and rhetorical features that take precedence over social, political, and biographical contexts. According to Ewa Thompson, the New Critics were interested in "the symbolic function of language" and "repudiated the attempts to 'scientifize' the literary commentary in its entirety, whereas the Russian Formalists finally accepted these attempts wholeheartedly" (Thompson 87). New Critical practice strongly favors poetic texts, in large part because they exemplify to a greater degree than other literary forms the key elements of ambiguity, irony, and PARADOX. The New Critics were influenced by modernist poets/critics like T. E. Hulme and T. S. Eliot, whose poetry and criticism emphasized the importance of the internal dynamics of poetic form. Eliot believed that "poets in our civilization, as it exists at present, must be *difficult*" (248), and it is just this difficulty that the New Critics sought to explain in their practices of explication (i.e., "close reading").

Before the rise of the New Criticism, historical, philological, and biographical methods predominated, as did *belle lettristic* criticism, which focused on aesthetics in a way that lacked method and discipline. For Eliot, in the period just after World War I, criticism of poetry was little more than "opinion or fancy" unconnected to technical and rhetorical accomplishments. He decried the state of criticism in the early 1920s, which consisted "in reconciling, in hushing up, in patting down, in squeezing in, in glozing over, in concocting pleasant sedatives" (14) – that is, in doing everything but agreeing on the critic's aim. In part, this was due to the lingering influence of nineteenth-century modes of moral and biographical criticism. Modernist poets were experimenting with form and language, and their work could no longer be judged according to the aesthetic criteria of their predecessors. According to Eliot, the critic's task was to understand and explain the "new combinations" of feeling that poetry was capable of expressing. The only legitimate context in which to judge a literary work was the tradition in which it emerged, the "organic wholes" of literature itself, "systems in relation to which, and only in relation to which, individual works of literary art, and the works of individual artists, have their significance." This does not mean that literature cannot serve ends outside of itself, only that "art is not required to be aware of these ends, and indeed performs its function, whatever that may be, according to various theories of value, much better by indifference to them" (12–13). Though art is best understood as existing autonomously (or, to use Eliot's word, "autotelically"), criticism must rely on shared principles. Instead of "narcotic fancies" and "nebulous" appreciation, Eliot advocated a form of practical criticism that could transform the apparently nebulous into "something precise, tractable, under control." The practical critic "is dealing with facts, and he can help us do the same" (20).

At the foundations of the New Criticism, which encompassed a wide variety of formalist approaches, was the idea of the critic as a kind of technician, whose specialized knowledge and skills enabled a form of close reading of literary texts that found meaning and value in form. I. A. Richards, one of the earliest critics associated with this new approach to criticism, was less concerned with formalism than with "rhetoric as a science of the meaning of meaning" (Booth 38). Richards was interested in how created literary values emerged in the act of reading. In *Principles of Literary Criticism* (1924), for example, he explores the psychology of reading and the relationship between emotional responses to literature and the values that literature articulates as a record of our experience. Richards' comment in the Preface – "A book is a machine to think with" (1) – neatly sums up the autonomous self-sufficiency of the literary text. But we should not assume that a book is a mere formal mechanism, for it is capable of "satisfying feeling and desire in various ways" (47). Like Eliot, Richards rejects the vague sort of sentiments that earlier critics substituted for analysis, and advocated a scientific approach to the "mental events" that governed the act of reading. He is most interested in the attitudes created by emotional responses, the "imaginal and incipient activities or tendencies to action" that come into play whenever one is aroused by a work of art (112). The value of criticism, therefore, lies in the "total mental effect" produced by the relations of elements within the work of art (174). The "standard experience" against which a poem is judged is that of the poet "when contemplating the completed composition," and the most effective critics are those "whose experience approximates in this degree to the standard experience" (226–7). Like Eliot's depersonalized poet, Richards' ideal reader must be disinterested and detached, open to many "channels of interest," a standpoint that paradoxically increases the reader's involvement in the text, for "to say that we are *impersonal* is merely a curious way of saying that our personality is more *completely* involved" (251–2). The reader must also be prepared to confront difficult texts, the various elements of which "are united by the accord, contrast, and interaction of their emotional effects" in "the right reader" (290).

The ideal of unity and the assumption that a "right" kind of reader of such poetry actually exists reflects the abiding values of the New Criticism, particularly in the work of the English critic William Empson and the US critics – chiefly Cleanth Brooks, John Crowe Ransom, Allen Tate, and Robert Penn Warren – associated with the

Agrarian-Fugitive movement at Vanderbilt University. All of these critics were interested in developing techniques of close reading that would be sensitive to how irony, paradox, ambiguity, and other rhetorical features constitute the internal dynamics of the literary work. Formal unity, therefore, was a fundamental component of what a poem means and was inseparable from its content. One of Brooks' "articles of faith" was "that the primary concern of criticism is with the problem of unity – the kind of whole which the literary work forms or fails to form, and the relation of the various parts to each other in building up this whole" ("My Credo" 72). Like other New Critics, Brooks emphasized paradox as a constitutive feature of poetic language. He believed that the greatest poems are "built around paradoxes," which are not "some sort of frill or trimming" external to the work, but rather "spring from the very nature of the poet's language ... in which the connotations play as great a part as the denotations" (*Well-Wrought Urn* 194, 8). Whereas previous critics might have detected only "mere decoration" or "sensuous pictures," the New Critic finds "meaningful symbolism," purposeful ironies and ambiguities (142). Brooks agrees with Richards that the poem is an "organic thing," but he does not believe that poetry serves primarily to communicate an emotional experience. "The poem, if it be a true poem is a simulacrum of reality – in this sense, at least, it is an 'imitation' – by *being* an experience rather than any mere statement about experience or any mere abstraction from experience" (194). A poem is a created object, a unity of rhetorical effects, quite different from the unity of responses that Richards describes. Like the "well-wrought urn" in John Keats's "Ode on a Grecian Urn," the poem is entirely self-contained and irreducible to any meaning not located in its structure. The "principle of unity" that informs poetry "seems to be one of balancing and harmonizing connotations, attitudes and meanings" which are all "subordinated to a total and governing attitude" (178, 189). Any attempt to capture this attitude by means of an interpretive summary constitutes what Brooks calls the "heresy of paraphrase."

Irony, ambiguity, and paradox are also the predominant elements in Empson's *Seven Types of Ambiguity*, which echoes Brooks' claim that ambiguity is a vital element of the unity of a literary work. *Ambiguity* is itself an ambiguous term, one that can lead the critic in a number of directions: it "can mean an indecision as to what you mean, an intention to mean several things, a probability that one or other or both of two things has been meant, and the fact that a statement has several meanings" (5–6). Though ambiguity constitutes the literary work as a situational unity or TOTALITY, the "forces" that hold such a unity together may originate "in the poet's mind" and can be discerned only in the context of specific rhetorical contradictions and tensions. "An ambiguity, then, is not satisfying in itself, nor is it, considered as a device on its own, a thing to be attempted; it must in each case arise from, and be justified by, the peculiar requirements of the situation" (235). The only way for a writer to impress upon the reader a conception of unity is to present a "total meaning" in the form of a "compound," so that the reader "can only feel satisfied if he is bearing all the elements in mind at the movement of conviction" (238–9). The influence of Richards' practical criticism is apparent in Empson's emphasis on the reader's role in constructing meaning and in his willingness to attribute ambiguity to the author's intentions, as opposed to the inevitable effects of literary language.

The different and often conflicting strands of the New Criticism are considered in W. K. Wimsatt and Monroe C. Beardsley's *The Verbal Icon* (1954). The authors are critical of romantic IDEALISM and the sort of "practical affective rhetoric" found in Richards and neo-Aristotelian critics of the Chicago School (201–2). They expose two fundamental errors in literary criticism: the *intentional fallacy* and the *affective fallacy*. The intentional fallacy, a form of the genetic fallacy found in philosophy, refers to the common assumption that the meaning of a work corresponds with the author's intentions. "The design or intention of the author is neither available nor desirable as a standard for judging the success of a work of literary art" (3). Only objective criticism can arrive at a sense of a work's value, "which enables us to distinguish between a skillful murder and a skillful poem" (6). This is not to say that authors do not *intend* a meaning, only that their intentions are not identical to the meanings their works might have for readers (including the authors themselves *as* readers). To assume that intention and meaning are identical is thus a fallacy. Modernism challenged the easy identification of authors and their works, notably in the narrative frames of Conrad's *Lord Jim* and *Heart of Darkness*, the modulated, shifting styles of Woolf's and Faulkner's later novels, and even in blatantly autobiographical texts, such as Joyce's *A Portrait of the Artist as a Young Man*. Even if we could gain access to the author's intentions, through archival sources or personal communication, the results would be of no use for criticism, for "critical inquiries are not settled by consulting the oracle" (18). The affective fallacy refers to a category mistake, "a confusion between the poem and its results" (21). Poetry does not acquire its meaning by producing a particular kind of result in the reader (as Richards avers), but rather by simply existing as a verbal object. "A poem should not mean but be" (81), they claim, a view similar to Brooks' that a poem is a "simulacrum of reality." For Wimsatt and Beardsley, a poem exists by virtue of its linguistic and rhetorical materiality; it is a *thing*, and it is this physical character that is the sole object of criticism. The only value the critic need uphold is the autonomy of a dynamic and self-regulating "verbal icon," a "positive and structural complexity, the varied fabric of organic unity" (269). If poetry is also "a fusion of ideas with material" (115), it is not because it is somehow less than verbal, nor because it bears an intimate relation to its referents in the external world, but because of its very "hyperverbal" "counter-logical" nature. The New Critic, enjoined to be aware of "the ambiguous or polysemous nature of verbal discourse" (268), ironically anticipates the poststructuralist, whose vision of language and literature is often regarded as the antithesis of New Critical formalism.

Works Cited

Booth, Wayne. *Critical Understanding: The Powers and Limits of Pluralism*. Chicago: University of Chicago Press, 1979.

Brooks, Cleanth. "My Credo." *Kenyon Review* 13.1 (1951): 72–81.

Brooks, Cleanth. *The Well-Wrought Urn*. New York: Harcourt, Brace and World, 1947.

Eliot, T. S. *Selected Essays 1917–1932*. New York: Harcourt Brace Jovanovich, 1932.

Empson, William. *Seven Types of Ambiguity*. London: Chatto and Windus, 1947.

Richards, I. A. *Principles of Literary Criticism*. New York: Harcourt, Brace; London: K. Paul Trench, Trubner, 1924.

Thompson, Ewa Majewska. *Russian Formalism and Anglo-American New Criticism: A Comparative Study*. The Hague: Mouton, 1971.

Wimsatt, W. K. and Monroe C. Beardsley. *The Verbal Icon: Studies in the Meaning of Poetry*. Louisville: University Press of Kentucky, 1954.

Chicago School Neo-Aristotelian Theory

The Neo-Aristotelian critics of the University of Chicago, beginning in the 1950s, sought to counter the New Criticism by developing a more rigorous formalist methodology. They were less interested in celebrating ambiguity and paradox than in creating the rhetorical tools necessary for a rigorous formalist critical method. Critics like R. S. Crane followed a neo-Aristotelian line and envisioned "a general critique of literary criticism" that would "yield objective criteria for interpreting the diversities and oppositions among critics and for judging the comparative merits of rival critical schools." For Crane, as for the Chicago School at large, pluralism is a reassertion of the Aristotelian notion that "poetry exhibits a multiplicity of structures not capable of reduction to any single type" (*Critics* 5). Beginning in the early 1950s, Elder Olson, Crane's colleague at the University of Chicago, pursued the implications of an Aristotelian approach to rhetoric and to the analysis of English literature. For both thinkers, Aristotle's *Poetics* is the starting point for rhetorical theory, though Olson avers that it has been largely misunderstood, especially by those who regard Aristotle as a final authority on critical methodology. Chicago School critics advocate a form of critical pluralism in which Aristotle's thought can acquire its proper place and authority, "as one among many possible systems; but the meaning assigned to it will be its own" (Olson, "Introduction" xix).

For Olson, Aristotle's relevance hinges on the fact that the *Poetics* offers a durable "science of art," one which rhetorical criticism ought to follow in its analytical practice. The "making" of a poetic work, which always tends toward the work as an end in itself, begins with a process of *reasoning* that "proceeds from the form to be produced to the first thing which can be produced" – that is, *form* as such. Poetic analysis then works backwards from form to the parts that constitute it as a *whole* ("Poetic Method" 180–1). The function of MIMESIS in rhetorical theory is not to imitate a specific object but to take on the natural character of imitation as such. Aristotle argues that "the arts imitate nature," which for Olson means "that the causes and productive process of artificial objects resemble those which nature would have evolved had the products been natural and not artificial" (187). Richard McKeon concurs, noting that "art and nature are both adaptations of means to ends in accordance with reason or formulae (ἄλογον)" (216). Plot is of special importance for "imitative forms" because it "actualizes and completes" all the other parts of the work; it is an "activity of a certain moral quality, such that it produces a particular emotional effect" and engages characters in moral choices (Olson, "Poetic Method" 188). As the function of plot indicates, neo-Aristotelian formalism refuses to divorce form from the matter that it entails, for "the products of the poetic arts are ... composites of form and matter," and their "organic unity must be found in the fact that their existence is due, not to nature, but to art" (Olson, "Introduction" xvi).

Unlike the formal unities of the New Criticism, the organic unity described by Olson is the product of a set of causes: the *material cause* (the means of artistic production), the *formal cause* (the object imitated), the *efficient cause* (the manner of the imitation), and the *final cause* ("that for the sake of which [the object] is imitated") (xvi; see also "Poetic Method" 182–3). Olson and McKeon emphasize that all four causes are involved in the "productive science" of rhetorical analysis, which involves a double movement: "inductive reasoning toward its principle, and deductive reasoning from its principle" (Olson, "Poetic Method" 181). Form *precedes* the matter that constitutes it specifically as an *art* form, and one can move back from the art form to the initial material and formal causes.

The emphasis on plot as a form of moral persuasion yielded, in the work of later Chicago School critics, a richly nuanced rhetorical theory of narrative. Ralph Rader follows closely on the lines laid out by Crane, Olson, and McKeon when he employs a deductive method to account not only for literary form but also for the historical particularities that shape form at a given moment in time. For example, borrowing from Crane and Sheldon Sacks the idea of "represented action," Rader identifies what he calls "deductive models" that are "meant to define the most general differentiating principle of a work's form in such a way that its more particular aspects can be rigorously deduced from it" (174). Rader's deductive method proceeds "by strict logical extension of the initial premises" and is necessarily inflexible for otherwise it would "not risk refutation because it could always be confirmed" (32). Thus, the "general action" (or "action-fantasy") model of a work like Samuel Richardson's *Pamela*, "specifies works of fiction designed to develop and maximize concern for character (or characters) along a line of development" that emphasizes the reader's sense of the character's fate, both what happens and what we *want to happen*. By contrast, Defoe's *Moll Flanders* cannot be read effectively according to this model, in large part because it is "an imitation of a real autobiography" (174, 177). Literary language, even in pseudofactual forms, consists of "dramatic propositions," some of which can be false, but we continue to believe in them, even if they are "an impossibility." Though impossible, they fit "the intuited form of the story as constructed," which produces a quantum of pleasure (37).

David Richter and Sacks, both contemporaries of Rader, depart from a strictly deductive method, but retain an interest in formal analysis and formal unities along Aristotelian lines. Thus Sacks can speak of genre in terms of "variant principles of organization" that establish parameters for the embodiment of "ethical beliefs, opinions or prejudices." Such forms as satire, for example, orient all their various parts toward the end of ridicule; these parts "can only be understood *as* parts of a whole" (7). Other forms, like the "apologue," have a different "informing principle"; for example, an apologue like Samuel Johnson's *Rasselas* is "organized as a fictional example of the truth of a formulable statement or closely related set of such statements" (8). From the point of view of their "informing principles," satire and apologue are "mutually exclusive forms" (10). Perhaps the most prominent class of fiction is the novel of "represented action," in which "characters about whose fate we are made to care are introduced in unstable relationships which are then further complicated until the complications are finally resolved by the complete removal of the represented instability" (15). The Aristotelian notion of "organic unity" is evident in what Sacks calls a "grammar of types" that accommodates a variety of forms, including comic, tragic, and "serious" actions (21–2). Richter, following Crane, pursues a similar line and distinguishes between plots of character and plots of action (i.e., Sacks' "represented action"). While the latter resolves conflict, the former leaves development open-ended within the confines of a single subjectivity. In this, Richter follows Aristotle's injunction that the aesthetic object, to be expressive, must be "whole, complete, and of sufficient magnitude" (*Poetics* 6:1449b, 25; qtd. in Richter 4). This is as true of Woolf or Joyce as it is of conventional realist representations of character. Richter posits a third plot form, characteristic of the "novel of thought," that he calls "rhetorical fictions" (including forms like the apologue), which are not stories told "for their own sake" – that is, they are not, to use Rader's terms, "pseudofactual" or "simular" – but are "exemplary of the real world" (16). Modern apologue forms, like William Golding's *Lord of the Flies* or Thomas Pynchon's *V*, are characterized by a "pattern of action and character that makes the reader intuit the novel's form as rhetorical" (18). Such texts are *potentially* "open" in the sense that they cannot be exhausted, for "there are an infinite number of situations, characters, and actions which could be used to exemplify a given theme" (19). This does not mean that modern novels of this rhetorical type are open because modern experience is unbounded but because "new forms of completeness and closure" arise that are linked to a governing thesis outside the novel.

By far the most influential figure to emerge from the Chicago School was Wayne C. Booth, whose *The Rhetoric of Fiction* (1961) provided a template for a rhetorical understanding of novelistic narrative that goes beyond the limits of the Aristotelianism so evident in writers like Olson, Sacks, and Richter. As Walter Jost puts it, *The Rhetoric of Fiction* "remains justly famous" for developing "the notion of the author's 'second self,' or what he called the 'implied author,' and of the unreliable narrator" (7). These developments are founded in Booth's sense of rhetoric as a mode of "telling," in contrast to the norm at the time that fiction was primarily the art of "showing." For many critics, influenced by the New Criticism's dictum that the literary work of art is autonomous, free of authorial intent, "telling" amounted to authorial intrusiveness, a blatantly rhetorical use of language that calls attention to the fictiveness of the text. Indeed, by rethinking the rhetorical element of narrative fiction, Booth seeks to move beyond the "telling–showing distinction," in order to make sense of the multiplicity of voices in fiction, which for him are the indelible sign of the "author's manipulating presence" (*Rhetoric of Fiction* 16, 19). His main concern is that early critics of the novel tended to consider diverse literary problems in terms of the same criterion: "a novel should be made dramatic" (24). He criticizes the tendency of critics to generalize in an arbitrary way about such criteria as works, authors, and readers; and while he acknowledges that such criteria are "clearly distinct," he also claims that "all authors are disloyal, at one point or another, to the general standards they profess" and willingly sacrifice the coherence of elements of form "in the name of one or another of the three types of criteria" (39).

Booth's general critical method – which Jost characterizes as a "listening-rhetoric" – moves well beyond the neo-Aristotelianism of Crane, Olson, and McKeon, though it remains rooted in the pluralism and rhetorical formalism found in these early thinkers. The distinction he makes between the "real" author, the implied author, and the different forms of narration hinges on a rhetorical conception of narrative literature, in which "the subject is thought of as *something that can be made public*, something that can be made into a communicated work" (105). What he would later come to call "rhetorology" encompasses a far greater field of inquiry than usually associated with rhetoric, for it covers "the entire range of resources that human beings share for producing effects on one another ... It is the entire range of our use of 'signs' for communicating, effectively or sloppily, ethically or immorally" (*Rhetoric of Rhetoric* xi). Implicit in Booth's *rhetoric of rhetoric* is a multiplicity of rhetorical methods and attitudes, and a certain freedom from "rule-bound mode[s] of analysis." Rhetoric is not merely persuasion but a complex attitude toward discourse and the world, "a full embrace of more than one critical method without reducing pluralities to one (a supreme monism), or multiplying them to a vague or meaningless infinity, or canceling them out into zero" (*Critical* 25). For Booth, a "pluralism of modes" does not result in relativism because the critic does not work "in relation to" something outside the activity of criticism; when we consider other critical approaches alongside our own we assess them in terms of the nature and quality of their inquiries within the general field of criticism (26–7).

Pluralism, in Booth's understanding, is bound up with an "ethics of telling and listening" (*Company* 7). Such approaches to literature tend to fall into three categories: pragmatic and rhetorical ethics (associated with Booth and Martha Nussbaum); an "ethics of alterity" (associated with Emmanuel Levinas); and political ethics (associated with trauma theory and postcolonial theory) (Altes 143–5). Booth's "rigorously pluralistic ethical criticism" (*Company* 350) avoids the extremes of reductionism and skepticism so often found in contemporary ethics primarily by using rhetoric to understand and to express our relations with others in the world. If there are limits to pluralism, they do not originate in an external authority (an ideology, a discipline, a political position), but rather in the practice of "rhetorology," the "search for what we share beneath our differences of expression" (*Essential* 333). Booth's chief successors, James Phelan and Peter Rabinowitz, have explored the implications of this ethical pluralism. In line with the neo-Aristotelianism of Crane, they argue for the idea of narrative as a rhetorical act that creates the conditions for the shared experience of reading. The central problem is to "to contribute to our own self-understanding and to an understanding of how our positions and practices relate to those of others in our critical community. In so doing, we miss the opportunity to transform the grounds of self-understanding" (8). Their "metatheoretical claim about the nature of literary criticism" is grounded in a "double attention, to interpretation and to the grounds of interpretation" (11, 8). Deeply indebted to Booth's rhetorical method, Phelan regards narrative "as a distinctive and powerful means for an author to communicate knowledge, feelings, values, and beliefs to an audience" (*Narrative* 18). His "rhetorical poetics" is inseparable from ethics, and judgments made of both the ethical and aesthetic dimension of narrative require an "inside out ... two-step process of reconstruction and evaluation" (*Experiencing* 133). A reconstruction of the narrative project leads inevitably to an evaluation of its formal effects. Narrative progression, as experienced by the reader, is the locus of the interpretive and ethical judgments that make possible the synthesis of "textual dynamics and readerly dynamics." First- and second-order aesthetic judgments – of technique and the overall experience of reading – are "co-extensive with the concept of reading narrative rhetorically" (134). Because the reader's experience is bound up with the structure of narrative, the ethical response to that narrative is a function of narrative, and not of an outside (or HETERONOMOUS) source of moral values. Rhetorical interpretation seeks to "tighten the connection between experience and interpretation" (92) and therefore to draw our attention to the particulars of narrative. Like other theorists of narrative ethics, Phelan stresses the ability "to explore the ethical dimensions of human behavior through the concrete particulars of characters in action." Rhetorical poetics avoids abstractions and reductive thinking in order to get at the "complexities and nuances of ethical choices within the detailed contexts of human lives" (93–4). (On the ethics of reading, see Reader-Response Theory 157–8.)

The emphasis on the reader's experience marks, for Phelan, the principal difference between cultural studies (which, like the New Criticism, is concerned with "generating thematic interpretations" [88]) and rhetorical poetics, which is concerned with the affective, rhetorical, and aesthetic dimensions of the text – dimensions of the "literary experience" in which the reader plays a constitutive role. This does not mean that rhetorical poetics neglects thematic interpretation; on the contrary, Phelan's pluralism would disallow any such exclusion on principle. Rhetorical poetics "does not assume that thematizing is at the center of the interpretive enterprise"; instead, it places thematic approaches alongside its own. "Consequently, the relation between rhetorical poetics and cultural thematics is not one of direct rivalry or perfect complementarity" (91). The relation between the two is determined, finally, by the form of the text and the reader's experience.

The concerns of the Chicago School are echoed in a somewhat idiosyncratic fashion in the work of Kenneth Burke, whose approach to literature borrows insights from anthropology, sociology, semantics, and other areas of study. According to Burke, poetic meanings "cannot be disposed of on the true-or-false basis," which is the case with what he calls "semantic meanings," but exist in relation to each other in terms of "progressive *encompassment*," as in a set of concentric circles (144). Like other rhetorical critics, Burke departs from the New Criticism, but his rhetorical standpoint is less neo-Aristotelian than performative. He regards literature as a form of "symbolic action" that extends beyond the confines of the literary work's formal structure to touch upon the experiences of writing and reading. In his theory of "dramatism," he defines five levels of meaning production in literary works: act, agent, scene, agency, and purpose. Though Burke's emphasis on rhetoric and the special role of poetic language situates him within a tradition of structuralism and formalism, his interest in human behavior and motivation and his desire to see human actions as essentially symbolic are rooted in sociology and psychology.

Works Cited

Altes, Liesbeth Korthals. "Ethical Turn." In *Routledge Encyclopedia of Narrative Theory*. Ed. David Herman, Manfred Jahn, and Marie-Laure Ryan. London: Routledge, 2005. 141–6.

Booth, Wayne. *The Company We Keep: An Ethics of Fiction*. Berkeley: University of California Press, 1988.

Booth, Wayne. *Critical Understanding: The Powers and Limits of Pluralism.* Chicago: University of Chicago Press, 1979.

Booth, Wayne. *The Essential Wayne Booth.* Ed. Walter Jost. Chicago: University of Chicago Press, 2006.

Booth, Wayne. *The Rhetoric of Fiction.* 1961. 2nd ed. Chicago: University of Chicago Press, 1983.

Booth, Wayne. *The Rhetoric of Rhetoric: The Quest for Effective Communication.* Oxford: Blackwell, 2004.

Burke, Kenneth. *The Philosophy of Literary Form: Studies in Symbolic Action.* 1941. 2nd ed. Baton Rouge: Louisiana State University Press, 1967.

Crane, R. S., ed. *Critics and Criticism: Ancient and Modern.* Chicago: University of Chicago Press, 1952.

Crane, R. S. *The Language of Criticism and the Structure of Poetry.* Toronto: University of Toronto Press, 1953.

Jost, Walter. "Introduction." In Wayne Booth, *The Essential Wayne Booth.* Ed. Walter Jost. Chicago: University of Chicago Press, 2006. 1–20.

McKeon, Richard. "Rhetoric and Poetic in the Philosophy of Aristotle." In *Aristotle's Poetics and English Literature: A Collection of Critical Essays.* Ed. Elder Olson. Chicago: University of Chicago Press, 1965. 201–36.

Olson, Elder. "Introduction." In *Aristotle's Poetics and English Literature: A Collection of Critical Essays.* Ed. Elder Olson. Chicago: University of Chicago Press, 1965. ix–xxviii.

Olson, Elder. "The Poetic Method of Aristotle." In *Aristotle's Poetics and English Literature: A Collection of Critical Essays.* Ed. Elder Olson. Chicago: University of Chicago Press, 1965. 175–91.

Phelan, James. *Experiencing Fiction: Judgments, Progressions and the Rhetorical Theory of Narrative.* Columbus: Ohio State University Press, 2007.

Phelan, James. *Narrative as Rhetoric: Technique, Audiences, Ethics, Ideology.* Columbus: Ohio State University Press, 1996.

Phelan, James and Peter J. Rabinowitz. "Introduction: Understanding Narrative." In *Understanding Narrative.* Ed. James Phelan and Peter J. Rabinowitz. Columbus: Ohio State University Press, 1994. 1–15.

Rader, Ralph. *Fact, Fiction and Form: Selected Essays.* Ed. James Phelan and David H. Richter. Columbus: Ohio State University Press, 2011.

Richter, David H., ed. *Falling Into Theory: Conflicting Views on Reading Literature.* 2nd ed. Boston: Bedford/St. Martin's Press, 2000.

Sacks, Sheldon. *Fiction and the Shape of Belief: A Study of Henry Fielding, with Glances at Swift, Johnson and Richardson.* Berkeley: University of California Press, 1964.

Narrative Theory/Narratology

Narrative theory (or, as it is often called, narratology), is concerned with how narrative form functions to produce meaning. Rooted in formalism, narrative theory developed, by the 1960s, into a structuralist method applicable to a wide array of forms, including literature, film, drama, folklore, historiography, psychology, and social theory. Despite this range of applications, narrative theory has remained remarkably stable, its development in the last century marked less by dramatic paradigm shifts than by the refinement of key concepts.

Perhaps the most important of these concepts are *sjuzhet* and *fabula*. According to Petre Petrov, "*sjuzhet* is best understood as plot construction (or emplotment), viewed formally, while *fabula* should be grasped as the sequence of events making up a story (or storyline), but viewed outside the artistic process of narration." These concepts provided Russian formalists interested in narrative with "the conceptual means for bringing the essential topics of 'deformation,' 'perceptibility,' and 'defamiliarization' outside the initial sphere of poetic language and extending their applicability to the narrative genres of literature" (175). This binomial starting point, which is by no means reducible to the "form/content" dualism that drives the New Criticism, offers two fundamentally different ways of accounting for the same events – both as a story and as a way of telling it – and two different temporalities that engage the reader in a complex fictional structure. For Viktor Shklovsky, as Wolf Schmid points out, "the *sjuzhet* as an act of formation meant a defamiliarizing deformation of the *fabula*" (177). This practice of deformation is designed to "lay bear" the literary devices that "motivate" narrative fiction. Both Shklovsky and Tomashevsky developed the idea of "motivation" in order to distinguish the "indications of time" and "indications of cause" from the merely descriptive feature of narrative (Tomashevsky 164). In stories, "causal–temporal relationships exist between the thematic elements," and these elements are themselves reducible to increasingly smaller "particles of thematic material: 'evening comes,' 'Raskolnikov kills the old woman'" and so on. The theme of the smallest, irreducible particle is a *motif*, which is either bound or free, the former being required by the story, the latter capable of being omitted "without disturbing the whole causal–chronological course of events" (165–6). Motifs perform particular functions; for example, *dynamic* motifs are those that change the *situation* constituted by interrelationships between characters and are essential to the story, while *static* motifs (like most descriptions) are ancillary and can be removed or altered. Harmony and tension are created through the deployment of motifs within situations; of vital importance is *exposition*, the "presentation of circumstances determining the initial cast of characters and their interrelationships" that is required for the formation of a plot (168). Exposition can be immediate or delayed, the latter being a common mode of articulating what has already transpired in a story that begins *in medias res* (in the middle of things). Artistic unity, for Tomashevsky, depends on the complex structure of motivation, which operates on multiple levels (e.g., compositional, realistic, artistic). These are not universal structures, for "devices are born, live, grow old, and die." Indeed, "renovated devices with new functions and new meanings" are required to maintain their defamiliarizing function (177). (On defamiliarization, see Formalism and Structuralism 54.)

One of the most fruitful, though idiosyncratic, formalist renovations was Vladimir Propp's work on folktales. In *Morphology of the Folktale* (1928), Propp argues that folktales are made up of specific narrative functions (leaving home, confronting danger at the hands of a villain, the realization of a lack, combat between hero and villain, marriage of the hero, and so on). "Function is understood as an act of a character," writes Propp, "defined from the point of view of its significance for the course of the action" (21). There are thirty-one possible functions, all or some of which may appear in a given tale and invariably in the same order. They are stable and independent of the particular character who fulfills them. The "dramatis personae" of the folktale consist of seven different character types: villain, donor (provider), helper, princess ("a sought-for person"), dispatcher, hero, false hero (Propp 79–80). This limited number of characters and narrative situations permits an astonishing number of story possibilities. In the 1960s, A. J. Greimas modified Propp's structuralist model, refining the typology of functions, which he called *actants*, and the articulation of *actors* (Propp's "characters"). "The result," writes Greimas, "is that if the actors can be established within a tale-occurrence, the actants, which are classifications of actors, can be established only from the corpus of all the tales: an articulation of actors constitutes a particular *tale*; an articulation of actants constitutes a *genre*" (200). Greimas' renovation of Propp's categories moves in the direction of a science of *semantics* concerned with the meaning of the functions of binary pairs: subject v. object, sender v. receiver, and helper v. opponent. These actantial relationships do not operate on the primary level of action ("to be able to do," "to do") but rather express a "specialized relationship of 'desire' … which transforms itself at the level of the manifested functions into 'quest'" (207). Greimas gives the example, greatly simplified, of a "learned philosopher of the classical age" who desires knowledge; his story would be a "drama of knowledge" in which the subject is "philosopher" and the object "world"; the sender "God" and the receiver "mankind"; the opponent "matter" and the helper "mind" (209–10). Any number of actors might be employed in a narrative, depending on the genre, to fulfill these actantial functions.

As Greimas and the early structuralists demonstrate, the form of a given narrative does not necessarily follow the sequence of events that constitute the story it tells. In fact, literature and film often depend on the tensions created between the expected temporal ordering of the story and the actual structure of narrative. Structuralist narratology has theorized these different levels of narration in a number of different ways – as *fabula/sjuzhet*, story/discourse, *histoire/récit* – but in each case, the same drive for a narrative logic is maintained. For example, Claude Bremond, in "The Logic of Narrative Possibilities" (1966), argues for the need to "draw a map of the logical possibilities of narrative as a preliminary to any description of a specific literary genre." A "rigorous method" of the sort he proposes would enable a "classification of narrative based on structural characteristics as precise as those which help botanists and biologists to define the aims of their studies" (387). He asserts, following Propp, that the "basic unit, the narrative atom," is *function* and that an initial grouping of three functions creates an *elementary sequence*: an opening, an actual act or event, and closure. Unlike Propp, however, he argues there is no necessary order in the relation of functions, so that the narrator can choose when and if to "actualize" an act or event. In the end, Bremond claims to arrive at a taxonomy of narrative situations, "a tableau of model sequences, much less numerous than one might imagine and from among which the storyteller must necessarily choose" (389). Ideally, the structuralist approach will enable "a clear characterization and indisputable classification of the events of the narrative" (407).

Roland Barthes' "Introduction to the Structural Analysis of Narrative" (1966) develops a similar method of structural analysis that is less concerned with classification than with developing a *functional syntax* for narrative. For Barthes, narratives function like sentences, but they function on multiple levels and within multiple relations. There are two primary relations: "distributional (if the relations are situated on the same level) and integrational (if they are grasped from one level to the next)" (86). Narrative elements are arranged according to a "hierarchy of instances" – units, action, narration – that are predictable and stable within the limits of a narrative syntax or grammar. At the "atomic" level, *units* perform distributional functions, ordering elements around "hinge-points" of the narrative while at the integrational level they connect and order the relations of character and narration. These units are often fairly minor elements of the story (Barthes offers the example of a cigarette lighter in a James Bond film); but they can serve important functions by linking or "distributing" narrative elements in a causal chain or by integrating different aspects of the narrative across temporal and spatial coordinates. The level of *action* is dominated by character, which is not a "being" in the psychological sense, but a "participant" that enacts a function within a specific sequence: "every character (even secondary) is the hero of his own sequence" (106). Finally, the level of *narration* (often called "point of view") concerns the specific structure of linguistic presentation and the site of reading. At this level, we see a shift from the story being told to the structure of narrative itself, which is understood as a "succession of tightly interlocking mediate and intermediate elements"; narrative "moves along," with "a sort of structural 'limping,' a constant interplay of potentials" (122). The mechanisms of conventional realism – a straightforward and transparent means of referring to the external world – do not apply at this level. For Barthes insist that the "function of narrative is not to 'represent'; it is to constitute a spectacle still very enigmatic for us but in any case not of a MIMETIC order" (124).

Throughout the 1970s and 1980s, Gérard Genette and Mieke Bal further extended the possibilities of narrative and narrativity by complicating the binary relation between *sjuzhet* and *fabula* developed by the Russian formalists and the showing/telling distinction in what Genette calls the "Jamesian tradition" of reflection on the novel. For Genette, narrative exhibits three distinct levels of operation: the *story* (*diegesis*, the level of the signified or narrative content), the *narrative* (the level of the signifier, discourse or narrative text), and *narrating* (the level of the "narrative situation or its instance" [31], including narration and narrators). These three levels correspond to three functions: *narrative* (where the emphasis is on telling a story); *directing* (where the emphasis is on the narrative text; a metanarrative function); and *communication* (where the emphasis is on the relation between narrator and reader). The third function underscores the differences between a *narratee* within the text and the reader or implied reader outside of it. "The reader of a fiction," writes Gerald Prince, "be it in prose or in verse, should not be mistaken for the narratee. The one is real the other fictive" (9). The primary functions of the narratee are to mediate between narrator and reader and between author and reader; but the narratee also "characterizes the narrator," establishes a "narrative framework," articulates themes and develops plotlines and serves as a "spokesman for the moral of the work" (23).

As Prince's theory of the narratee illustrates, the focus on function in narratology permits not only a description of the *form* of narrative but also of the *relations* within it – relations that come together in the "narrative situation" through the technique of *focalization*, which permits the kind of discriminations that Genette regards as crucial for understanding modern fiction. Following Tzvetan Todorov, Genette describes three levels of narrative focalization: *zero* focalization (which is a "classic" narrative form in which "the narrator knows more than the character"); *internal focalization* (in which "the narrator says only what a given character knows"), which can be either fixed (as in Joyce's *Portrait*), variable (as in *Madame Bovary* or Woolf's *Mrs. Dalloway*), or multiple (as in the epistolary novel); and *external focalization* ("in which 'the narrator says less than the character knows,' as in Hemingway's "The Killers") (189–90). Thus *internal focalization* is associated with character and *external focalization* with "an anonymous agent, situated outside the fabula," that is, a "non-character-bound focalizer" (152). Though the idea of focalization is widely accepted, some critics, like Monika Fludernik, find the "most commonly accepted models of focalization [to be] very confusing." Rather than speak of zero, internal, variable, or multiple focalizations – i.e., limitations on perspectives – Fludernik distinguishes between external (extradiegetic) and internal (diegetic) focalization, but does not consider in her theory the idea that Mieke Bal has put forward that "limited perspective" is a "restriction of perspective"; instead, she locates the kinds of limited access that Bal describes on the side of the "extradiegetic" level, for "the ability to see into other people's minds is possible only from an external vantage point" (37–8).

By and large, Bal follows Genette in postulating a tripartite structure of narrative but lays a far greater emphasis on the *fabula/sjuzhet* relation theorized by Russian formalists. For Bal, the *story*, which is the content of the text, produces a distinctive "coloring" of the plot (or *fabula*), which is "a series of logically and chronologically related events that are caused or experienced by actors" (5). The *fabula* orders the elements of a particular medium, in this case a narrative text, and the result is the story (or *sjuzhet*). The three elements – *fabula*, *sjuzhet*, and narrative text – are entwined with one another. Narrative texts differ in the way that they manage the treatment of story, in the way that the story is conveyed to the reader, even if the same *fabula* is used. The *fabula* is the narrative space in which actors, as "agents of action," motivate (or are motivated by) an event, which "always takes time" – not the actual time of actions in the world but that of events as related in the *fabula*. Together with place, the events, actors, and time constitute the *elements* of the *fabula* which are ordered in the *story* (7–8). Bal believes that the world outside the text provides a "universal model" for the *fabula*, which, in most cases, follows a "human 'logic of events'" (182–4). The reader connects with the narrative text on the basis of this logic, which is that of the *fabula* organized by the story, a process in which "every event can also be called a process or, at least, part of a process" (195–6).

Much of the complexities having to do with focalization and the distinctions between *fabula* and *sjuzhet* and between diegetic and extradiegetic narrators hinge on the question of *standpoint*, roughly equivalent to grammatical person. For example, third-person narration differentiates into an array of positions, from total to selective omniscience, from the tightly "focalized" viewpoint of a main character to multiple focalizations that give the reader access to multiple points of view. But as Genette and Bal make clear, the question is not so much one of distance but of *disposition*. Multiple terms have been devised to describe this disposition of narrative perspective. Most theorists agree on the meaning of *tense*, which is the expression of the "relation between the time of the story and the time of the discourse." Theorists tend to differ on how to explain the narrator's perception of a story and on the "the type of discourse used by the narrator" (Genette 29). Genette's solution is to group the narrator's perception and discourse (which Todorov calls *aspect* and *mood*, respectively) under the general category of *mood*, which he defines as "the modalities of representation or the degrees of mimesis." He also adds a new term, *voice*, which he prefers to the psychologically loaded term "person," to designate how "narrating" is itself implicated in "the narrative situation or its instance" (30–1). The category *voice* is meant to help us answer the question, "who is the narrator?" (186). The main problem, for Genette, is that theorists tend to confuse mood and voice, the *who* with the *how* of narration. The difference between a narrative relayed by a character (as in Fitzgerald's *The Great Gatsby*) or one in which the narrative is "focalized" through a character's point of view (as in Joyce's *A Portrait of the Artist as a Young Man*) is not a difference in point of view or *mood* but in voice, in *who is telling the story*. The "single category of 'point of view'" ignores the different "modal determinations" in narratives that appear to operate from the same focal point (187–8).

Of special interest to narrative theorists are the concepts of *person* and *tense*. As we have seen, Genette does not use the term *person*, but other theorists, like Dorrit Cohn, retain the term precisely for the correspondence with grammar (not to mention the very psychological elements Genette wished to avoid). For Cohn, narration is all about presenting the consciousness of characters. For example, in her discussion of third-person narration, she distinguishes among *psycho-narration* (in which mental life is reported by the narrator), *quoted monologue* (also known as "interior monologue," in which mental life appears as a direct expression of the character), and *narrated monologue* (also know as "free-indirect style" or "free indirect speech," in which mental life is refracted through narrative indirectly) (see 10ff). The latter characterizes a good deal of modern fiction and is capable of fine nuances and ambiguities in large part because it "casts a peculiarly penumbral light on the figural consciousness, suspending it on the threshold of verbalization in a manner that cannot be achieved by direct quotation" (103). The distinctions between these various levels are often grounded in *tense*, especially with respect to narrated monologue, whose existential immediacy is conveyed through a form of *reported* thought typically embedded within a past tense or through what is called the "historical present" (that is, a use of the present tense to refer to a past event). Most theorists agree that the present cannot be narrated *in the present*, but James Phelan has argued for just this possibility, which he calls the "homodiegetic simultaneous present" (223). And while this tense violates the mimetic standard – i.e., that "knowledge alters perception," or, as Cohn puts it, "live now, tell later" (qt. in Phelan 227–8) – it does so only if we define mimesis narrowly as "a product of faithful imitation of the real." Not only does this simultaneous present create unique textual effects – such as depicting the "shock accompanying the suddenness of [a character's] understanding" (228) – it also reinforces an ethical imperative on the part of the reader, who is enjoined by such narratives to examine her own assumptions governing character and action.

The principles adduced by narrative theory are widely applicable, in large measure because narrative is a well-nigh universal form of expression that crops up whenever people are asked or required to order their experience in a representation. The widespread interest in "narrativity" throughout the humanities testifies to its efficacy as both an object of study and an analytical technique. Film theory has borrowed many of the concepts developed by narratologists, particularly the *sjuzhet/fabula* relation, which Seymour Chatman reworks in terms of story and discourse. Hayden White and Paul Ricoeur have written extensively on the function of narrativity and its relation to temporality and the shared foundation in mimesis of both historical and fictional narrative. In these fields and many others, narratology continues to refine basic concepts and methodologies and to open up new areas of application, while the more general idea of "narrative knowledge" has become a vital component of nearly every theoretical approach imaginable. Jan Alber and Fludernik, in describing "postclassical narratology," refer to "a large transdisciplinary project that consists of various heterogeneous approaches" in history, film studies, fine arts, art history, cognitive psychology, psychoanalysis, social and political science, sociolinguistics, disability studies, and new media. They also include "transmedial" approaches that "seek to rebuild narratology so that it can handle new genres and storytelling practices across a wide spectrum of media" (8). The trend toward a narratology of "unnatural narratives" – "anti-mimetic narratives that challenge and move beyond real-world understandings of identity, time and space" (14) – indexes both the variety of and necessity for narrative understanding in a rapidly changing world.

Note
On the reader, see Reader-Response Theory; on the novel, see Theory of the Novel and Chicago School Neo-Aristotelian Theory.

Works Cited

Alber, Jan and Monika Fludernik, eds. *Postclassical Narratology: Approaches and Analyses.* Columbus: Ohio State University Press, 2010.

Bal, Mieke. *Narratology: Introduction to the Theory of Narrative.* 1980. 3rd ed. Toronto: University of Toronto Press, 2009.

Barthes, Roland. "Introduction to the Structural Analysis of Narrative." 1966. In *Image-Music-Text.* Trans. Stephen Heath. New York: Hill and Wang, 1977. 79–124.

Bremond, Claude. "The Logic of Narrative Possibilities." 1966. Trans. Elaine D. Cancalon. *New Literary History* 11 (1980): 387–411.

Cohn, Dorrit. *Transparent Minds: Narrative Modes for Presenting Consciusness in Fiction.* Princeton: Princeton University Press, 1978.

Genette, Gérard. *Narrative Discourse.* 1972. Trans. Jane E. Lewin. Ithaca: Cornell University Press, 1980.

Greimas, A. J. *Structural Semantics: An Attempt at a Method.* 1966. Trans. Daniele McDowell, Ronald Schleifer, and Alan Velie. Lincoln: University of Nebraska Press, 1983.

Petrov, Petre. "Fabula/Sjuzhet." In *The Blackwell Encyclopedia of Literary and Cultural Theory.* Vol. 1. Ed. Gregory Castle. Oxford: Blackwell, 2011. 175–9.

Phelan, James. *Narrative as Rhetoric: Technique, Audiences, Ethics, Ideology.* Columbus: Ohio State University Press, 1996.

Prince, Gerald. "Introduction to the Study of the Narratee." In *Reader-Response Criticism: From Formalism to Post-Structuralism.* Ed. Jane Tompkins. Baltimore: Johns Hopkins University Press, 1980. 7–25.

Propp, Vladimir. *Morphology of the Folktale*. 1928. Trans. Laurence Scott. 2nd rev. ed. Austin: University of Texas Press, 1968.

Schmid, Wolf. *Narratology: An Introduction*. New York: De Gruyter, 2010.

Todorov, Tzvetan. "Structural Analysis in Narrative." In *Modern Literary Criticism, 1900–1970*. Ed. Lawrence I. Lipking and A. Walton Litz. New York: Atheneum, 1972. 436–41.

Tomashevsky, Boris. "Story, Plot, and Motivation." In *Narrative Dynamics: Essays on Plot, Time, Closure and Frames*. Ed. Brian Richardson. Columbus: Ohio State University Press, 2002. 164–78.

Theory of the Novel

As the preceding sections have indicated, the novel is an important point of reference in formalist, rhetorical, and narrative theories, but none of them adequately cover the range of issues that have arisen around the study of the novel, especially since the 1950s. Even in the modernist period, when formalism was emerging as a discipline, we find a number of developments that are not covered by formalist approaches, particularly those associated with moral, ethical, and aesthetic dimensions of the novel genre. Joseph Conrad, in the preface to *The Nigger of the "Narcissus,"* provides one of the earliest formulations of novel theory:

> Fiction – if it at all aspires to be art – appeals to temperament. And in truth it must be, like painting, like music, like all art, the appeal of one temperament to all other innumerable temperaments whose subtle and resistless power endows passing events with their true meaning, and creates the moral, the emotional atmosphere of the place and time. (146)

The novel, for Conrad as for many other modernists, is a form of impressionism; as such, it should possess the "magical suggestiveness of music," which can be accomplished only by an "unswerving devotion to the perfect blending of form and substance" (146). The emphasis on impressions was taken up by Henry James, who argues that "a novel is in its broadest definition a personal, a direct impression of life: that, to begin with, constitutes its value, which is greater or less according to the intensity of the impression" (9–10). The author's freedom of expression must not be limited by *a priori* formal considerations. Form "is to be appreciated after the fact," for it evolves out of the author's intense and personal impression of life (10). James uses the image of the "house of fiction" to describe the interrelations of literary form (the window), the "choice of subject" (the perspective from the window of "the spreading field, the human scene") and the "consciousness of artist" ("the posted presence of the watcher") (51). The dominant note in this early development is the idea of consciousness and the problem of conveying impressions.

Early theorists in the Anglo-American tradition, like Percy Lubbock and F. R. Leavis, favored novelistic realism as the most effective way to explore human consciousness and the motivations that lead to moral action. Lubbock's *The Craft of Fiction*, like James' prefaces, is concerned with how the novelist creates a literary form out of experience. He uses the word "craft" in order to describe what holds the reader "fast to the matter in hand, to the thing that has been made and the manner of its making" (v). The "elements of the novelist's method," which Lubbock finds to be "few and simple, but infinite in their possibilities," are arranged uniquely for each theme the novelist encounters, with dramatic action and description alternating or blended together. "Method tends to be laid upon method, so that we get, as it were, layers and stratifications in the treatment of a story." The relation between story and method is based on decorum, on the appropriateness of the relation, for the story that occurs to the novelist "will be that which asks for the kind of treatment congenial to his hand; and so his method will be a part of himself, and will tell us about the quality of his imagination" (75–6). This is another way of putting James' point that the novel is a "direct impression of life," but we should note that Lubbock anticipates reader-response theory in his emphasis on the reader as mirroring the novelist. The reader, he argues, is "the maker of a book … for which he must take his own share of the responsibility." Lubbock grants the critical reader a decisive role, but it is less creative than analytical, for the author as "craftsman" creates a work, and the "critic must overtake him at his work and see how the book was made" (274). Reading is thus the discovery of the formal design of the work.

Lubbock's conception of the novel as a contradiction between "the thing carved in the stuff of thought" and "the passing movement of life" (15) persisted in a variety of forms through the 1960s. Modernists writing in the 1920s tended to view it as a problem in the *realist* novel and experimented with style and narrative form in order to overcome it. The emblematic modernist expression of this viewpoint is Virginia Woolf's "Modern Fiction" (1919), which urges novelists to capture life as it is: "a luminous halo, a semi-transparent envelope surrounding us from the beginning of consciousness to the end" (160–1). E. M. Forster's *Aspects of the Novel* (1927), like Woolf's essay, rejects a mimetic basis for modern fiction and the "demon of chronology" associated with realism (14). Like so many other modernists, Forster insisted on the humanity of the novel: "The intensely, stifling human quality of the novel is not to be avoided"; otherwise, we are left with little "but a bunch of words" (24). He is not interested in impressionism, however, for authors share a "common state" of inspiration. "All through history writers while writing have felt more or less the same," for they exist together in an abstract present in which they "work together in a circular room" (21, 14). Rather than "craft," Forster emphasizes the components or "aspects" of the novel used in common by those writers in the circular room. He devotes chapters to "the story," "plot," "pattern and rhythm," "people," and it is perhaps the latter that has proven most influential, particularly his distinction between "flat" and "round" characters: the former, types or caricatures; the latter, psychologically realistic and "more highly organized" (75).

Developments in Marxist literary theory were moving in a quite different direction. The Marxist critic Georg Lukács, in *The Theory of the Novel* (1920), expressed skepticism about the novel's ability to create an "embracing design" or to give anything like a pattern or rhythm that can authentically organize social life or represent human experience. Over against the epic, which provides a totalizing view of a given society, the novel stands as "the epic of an age in which the extensive totality of life is no longer directly given, in which the immanence of meaning in life has become a problem, yet which still thinks in terms of totality" (56). TOTALITY in the novel is at best purely formal, for it "excludes completeness only so far as content is concerned." But even formally, the novel can at best establish "a fluctuating yet firm balance between becoming and being" (73). At the heart of the novel is the individual's problematic *Bildung*, characterized by a persistent conflict "between what is and what should be." The "immanence of meaning" which the novel form requires, consists primarily in a "glimpse" that cannot possibly capture the hero's "commitment of an entire life." The materials of the novel are "discreet [and] unlimited," in stark contrast to the "continuum-like infinity" of the epic. "This lack of limits in the novel," Lukács writes, "has a 'bad' infinity about it." This is why he favored "biographical forms," for they alone could overcome the temporal lack in the novel and represent "the only essential segment of life" – that is, the experience of the "central problem" confronting the individual in society (80–1). Lukács also favored realism, which in the nineteenth century was the dominant modality of biographical forms like the *Bildungsroman*. He argued that the realist tradition was politically more progressive than the experimentalism of modernist and avant-garde writers, whom he regarded as decadent and bourgeois, incapable of addressing what he believed to be the "central aesthetic problem of realism" – "the adequate presentation of the complete human personality" (*Studies* 7). Referring to Balzac, Lukács describes the "essence of true realism" to be the "great writer's thirst for truth, his fanatic striving for reality – or expressed in terms of ethics: the writer's sincerity and probity" (11). The "organic unity" of nineteenth-century realism and "popular humanism" was, in effect, the response to a "basic problem": "a society so contradictory in its nature that it on the one hand gave birth to the ideal of the complete human personality and on the other destroyed it in practice" (13). Writers like Balzac, Johann von Goethe, and Thomas Mann, however much their own worldview conflicted with reality, were capable of grappling with "the great universal problems of their time" and were harbingers of a "great realist literature" that could help bring about the "democratic rebirth of nations" (13, 19).

Ideologically and aesthetically opposed to Lukács' Marxist theory of the novel was the English critic F. R. Leavis' notion of a "great tradition," founded less on formal than on ethical and moral grounds. In this regard, Leavis, who edited the influential journal *Scrutiny* (1932–53), follows a line of thought associated with Matthew Arnold, the nineteenth-century critic who believed literature ought to aspire to a condition of high seriousness so that it might serve as the basis for a secular morality. Leavis disapproved of modernist writes like Joyce, though on different grounds from those advanced by Lukács. Leavis felt that Joyce lacked the kind of formal integrity and unity that he found in the realist tradition that included George Eliot, Henry James, Joseph Conrad, Charles Dickens, and D. H. Lawrence. In *The Great Tradition* (1948), Leavis notes that these "great novelists" are "very much concerned with 'form'; they are all very original technically, having turned their genius to the working out of their own appropriate methods and procedures" (7). Unlike novelists who embraced AESTHETICISM, Leavis' favorites were concerned with a "formal perfection" that did not come at the expense of "the moral preoccupations that characterize the novelist's peculiar interest in life" (8). James Joyce does not qualify as "great" in part because his work possesses "no organic principle determining, informing, and controlling into a vital whole … the extraordinary variety of technical devices"; it is rather a "pointer to disintegration" (25–6).

Alternatives to this view of the novel – for example, Edmund Wilson's more sympathetic judgments of Joyce's *Ulysses* and other modernist experiments in symbolic narrative – sought to widen the critical focus and, in the process, abandoned a moral for a purely aesthetic point of view. By the 1950s, however, we see a resurgence of interest in realism, precipitated in part by Erich Auerbach's *Mimesis* (1946), which focuses on the art of literary imitation from Homer to Virginia Woolf. Auerbach argues that the "modern consciousness of reality began to find literary form" in the work of the nineteenth-century novelist Stendhal (459). The "merciless objectivity of his realistic power" transcends the realism of earlier periods in that "he always feels and experiences the reality of his period as a resistance" (465). This gives his style a certain energy and lends to his heroes a tragic aspect missing in later realists like Balzac and Flaubert. Balzac's "atmospheric realism," like the Romantic "atmospheric Historism" of his era, lends an almost organic unity to his narrative. In Flaubert's work, like that of his predecessors, we find the two chief elements of modern realism: (1) "real everyday occurrences in a low social stratum … are taken seriously" and (2) "everyday occurrences are accurately and profoundly set in a definite period of contemporary history" (484). The difference is that Flaubert withdraws narratorial comment: "His opinion of his characters and events remains unspoken" (486). Between Flaubert and the modernists, he argues, we find the "mixed styles" of the aesthetic novel (e.g., the work of Edmond and Jules de Goncourt, Walter Pater, and Oscar Wilde), the naturalism of Theodore Dreiser, and the Russian realists. With the modernists, objectivity is entirely displaced by impressionism, and representation turns away from external reality to focus on the consciousness of the characters themselves. Mimesis would seem to have no role in such high modernist experimentation, which is "marked by multipersonal representation of consciousness, time strata, disintegration of the continuity of exterior events, shifting of the narrative viewpoint," and so on (546).

Auerbach's historical treatment situates the novel in a long tradition of mimetic representation; it is the history of an idea rather than of a form. A few years later, Ian Watt, in *The Rise of the Novel* (1957), attempts a history of the form that, despite its limitations (it focuses only on the English novel), nevertheless has had a profound impact on how we think about the realist novel and its influence on later forms. While the novel focuses on human experience – in fact, Watt emphasizes that it "attempts to portray all the varieties" of it – the realism it employs "does not reside in the kind of life it represents, but in the way it presents it" (11). Unlike James and Lubbock, Watt downplays form, in part because he believes the "absence of formal conventions" to be "the price [the novel] must pay for its realism" (13). What he calls "formal realism" – a set of narrative procedures commonly found in the novel – is the "narrative embodiment" of a premise implicit in the form, for if the novel is meant to give "a full and authentic report of human experience," it must use a referential language appropriate to that intention. The term *realism* therefore "does not here refer to any special literary doctrine or purpose, but only to a set of narrative procedures" that provide a "circumstantial view of life" (32). Perhaps more important for subsequent developments was Watt's emphasis on "the nature and organization of the reading public" in the eighteenth century, particularly the development of "non-proprietary or circulating libraries" (35, 42). Equally important was the "distribution of leisure" and the rise of the periodical press, which was accompanied by the "decline of literary patronage by the court and the nobility." The resulting vacuum "between the author and his readers" was filled by those working in the emergent literary marketplace (43, 52). Watt's analyses of works by Daniel Defoe, Samuel Richardson, and Henry Fielding trace a social history of attitudes – about individualism and private experience, about social mobility and the relations between social classes, about the literary marketplace itself – that identifies the novel as the premier genre of modernity.

The 1960s saw one of the most important developments in the theory of the novel, Wayne Booth's *The Rhetoric of Fiction* (1961). Though Booth is associated with neo-Aristotelian formalism, his approach to the novel was critical of theories that focused exclusively on form at the expense of the audience and that privileged realism as a "normative" style. In *The Rhetoric of Fiction*, Booth deepens our understanding of how mimesis works in the novel by pointing out that realist styles are a matter of the author's and the reader's attitudes toward "three variables": "subject matter, structure, and technique." In fact, he knows of "no inherent reason why a realistic structure should require any particular form of realistic *narrative technique*" (57). The variety of such techniques – from Henry James' psychological realism to the naturalism of Thomas Hardy and Émile Zola – testifies to the openness of realist structures to narrative experimentation. The idea of authorial objectivity, another of the general criteria that, like realism, characterizes modern fiction, is also far more complex in Booth's view. "However impersonal he may try to be," he writes, the reader "will inevitably construct a picture of the official scribe who writes … and of course that official scribe will never be neutral toward all values" (71). The author's "second self," the "implied author" is the figure with whom the reader engages and, in many fictions (Booth instances Hemingway's "The Killers"), the narrator and the implied author are one and the same. This is the case with the "undramatized" narrator, who creates the false impression that the story comes to the reader in an unmediated fashion; this is the familiar illusion produced by an "omniscient narrator," and is characteristic of realist fiction. Here, too, the implied author and the narrator collapse into one another. This is not the case with first-person "dramatized narrators," who appear as both a character *and* a teller in the narrated story (think of Nick Carraway in F. Scott Fitzgerald's *The Great Gatsby* or the unnamed narrator in the "Cyclops" episode of *Ulysses*). Such a narrator "is often radically different from the implied author who creates him." The dramatized narrator is often called upon for very specific tasks. Thus Rochester, in *Jane Eyre*, disguises himself as a gypsy in order to convey aspects of Jane's character that Jane herself, as a first-person narrator, could not credibly narrate. Sophisticated forms of this narrative position, which James called "centers of consciousness," tend to focus the narrative through the experience of a single character. Since Flaubert, this has been a dominant feature of modern fiction and is characterized by a form of "free-indirect style" that renders permeable the boundary between character and narrator. Of course the function of a dramatized narrator leaves open the question of reliability. For Booth, an *unreliable* narrator can create obstacles for the reader to overcome, a form of narrative irony that is directed not at the reader but the source of the unreliability itself: "The author and the reader are secretly in collusion," Booth writes of such narrative scenarios, "behind the speaker's back, agreeing upon the standard by which he is found wanting" (304). Booth's rhetorical method, which privileges interpretive pluralism over dogmatism and arid formalism, raises questions concerning the ethics of reading. David Parker has noted that philosophical reflections on ethics point toward a road not yet traveled, but which "literary studies in the end must take." Moral philosophers, like Martha Nussbaum, offer a "variety of new meta-discursive insights and possibilities from which a theoretically self-aware ethical criticism" can proceed in response to poststructuralism (as is the case with the work of **J. Hillis Miller**). In this regard, Parker follows Booth (though not Leavis) in seeking to reestablish "the evaluative criticism of particular texts as an important part of what literary studies are about" (4).

M. M. Bakhtin's theory of the novel invites us to consider another link between the social aspect of literary representation and formal problems of narration, point of view, and voice. Booth has written that Bakhtin "woke him up," in part by showing him that the novel was "capable of a kind of justice to the inherent polyphonies of life," its "inescapably dialogic quality" ("How" 150). For Booth, reading Bakhtin takes us beyond "the question of how we read a novel or even how we evaluate it," for Bakhtin rejects the "false report" of the monological voice, the "essentially egoistical distortion" that follows upon the reduction of multiple worlds to a single author's commanding point of view (152). Bakhtin wrote his major texts in the 1920s and 1930s, during the Stalin era, but it was not until the 1970s that they were introduced to the West, primarily by Tzvetan Todorov and **Julia Kristeva**. As his translator Caryl Emerson argues, *Problems of Dostoevsky's Poetics* (1929) followed Viktor Shklovsky in examining fictional "devices" that created the "aesthetic distance" between "the observing self" and "what it perceives" that makes art possible (640). While for Shklovsky, distance is a function of the reader's "estrangement" from a *thing*, for Bakhtin it is largely a function of a relation "between one person and another person, between two distinct living centers of consciousness" (656). The concept of the "carnivalesque," a mode of discourse or ritual in which traditional hierarchies are turned upside down, suggests one form this relation can take within highly stratified, hierarchical societies, which are destabilized when the subject stages a symbolic emancipation from political and religious authorities.

Bakhtin argues that novelistic narrative is multi-voiced or polyphonic; it is characterized by a condition of HETEROGLOSSIA, his term for the stratification of discourses in novelist narrative, which can range across an array of styles, from the monologic "voice" that we associate with traditional omniscient narrators, to the interpolated dialogue of characters, with their idiolects, professional jargons, street argot, and so on. Each utterance belongs uniquely to a specific context, determined by multiple historical, social, cultural, and economic conditions. Context is inseparable from text, and the heteroglossia that emerges from each discrete social or cultural situation evinces a specific form of DIALOGISM, the dynamic totality of linguistic possibilities that conditions individual utterances within discourse. The stratification of voices in the heteroglossic text, which reflects social differences through the prism of linguistic usage, is accompanied by the distribution of time and space in *chronotopes* ("time-space"), "the intrinsic connectedness of temporal and spatial relationships that are artistically expressed in literature." The chronotope fuses "spatial and temporal indicators" into a single "carefully thought-out, concrete whole"; they define genre and, at bottom, the "image of man, which is "always intrinsically chronotopic" (Bakhtin 84–5). Chronotopes have specific narrative functions; thus the chronotope of meeting "can serve as an opening, sometimes as a culmination, even a denouement (a finale) of the plot," while in the chronotope of the road, "the unity of time and space markers is exhibited with exceptional precision and clarity" (98). The pure form of the epic, with its absolute past and "monolithic and closed world" (29), stands in stark contrast to the novel, which is open and hybrid, appropriating to its biographical, chronological core a multitude of other genres and story forms (e.g., the diary, the letter, the fable, the newspaper). Unlike Lukács, who saw in the novel a failure of the ability to totalize human experience in artistic form, Bakhtin celebrated the openness of the novel. The epic singer and his audience are radically cut off from "the represented world of the heroes … on an utterly different and inaccessible time-and-value plane, separated by epic distance. The space between them is filled with national tradition" (14). The novel, which arises precisely in this national space, touches down on the contemporary moment and thereby attains its "internal social dialogism." His method of "sociological stylistics" reveals this dialogism "as the force that determines [the novel's] entire stylistic structure, its 'form' and its 'content,' determining it not from without, but from within." Form and content cannot be taken separately, for "social dialogue reverberates in all aspects of discourse" (300).

Bakhtin's work was translated and disseminated at a time when historicist modes of analysis were reshaping our understanding of the novel form and its place in literary history. Preeminent in this respect were feminist literary histories – e.g., Elaine Showalter's *A Literature of Their Own* (1976) and Sandra M. Gilbert and Susan Gubar's *The Madwoman in the Attic* (1979) – which demonstrate the importance of novels by women within an alternative history of the novel form. By the 1980s, studies influenced by **Michel Foucault**'s work – particularly *Discipline and Punish*, which analyzes the discourse formation that constitutes discipline as a form of social control and punishment – were drawing our attention to how the novel both represents and, at times, replicates social power. For instance, D. A. Miller, in *The Novel and the Police* (1988), draws on Foucault in order to identify modes of discipline inscribed in the nineteenth-century novel, which depicts "disciplinary practices" and "normalizing sanctions" characteristic of modern modes of "social surveillance" (18–19). Because to some degree "the genre of the novel *belongs* to the disciplinary field that it portrays," it becomes necessary for the critic to focus on the "'micro-politics' of novelist convention" (21). This attention to what **Fredric Jameson** calls the "political unconscious," enables us to reread critically the prevalence of certain tropes (e.g., secrecy, surveillance, punishment) and to experience "the police" as something more than a character or function, to experience the "spatial extension of its networks and the temporal deployment of its intrigues" (23). Thus policing generates plot, and it becomes difficult, Miller concedes, "to distinguish the omniscience [of the narration] from the social control it parallels" (27). Nancy Armstrong's *Desire and Domestic Fiction: A Political History of the Novel* also draws on Foucault to make a quite different argument about nineteenth-century fiction, which, for her, is a space in which women's social position can be rewritten and their subjectivity liberated. She argues that novelists were able to rewrite past domestic practices (including intimate relations) in a way that made possible a new interpretation of social institutions and their value for women's personal development. Despite the outward appearance of respectability and propriety, nineteenth-century British and American fiction was frequently an arena for experimenting with the representation of sexuality and desire. Following Foucault's analysis of the discourse of sexuality in *The History of Sexuality*, Armstrong argues that sexual repression serves at once "as a rhetorical figure and as a means of producing desire" (13). For her, the disciplinary structure of sexuality enables the novel to say "what made a woman desirable" and thereby takes "a decisive step in producing the densely interwoven fabric of common sense and sentimentality that even today ensures the ubiquity of middle-class power" (5). In line with Showalter, Gilbert, and Gubar, she argues that "the history of the novel cannot be understood apart from the history of sexuality" (9).

Critics like Miller and Armstrong demonstrate the double-edged quality of the novel, which both represents and contests the historical conditions it relates. Realism in this respect is duplicitous to the extent that the world represented in the novel, however faithfully, is also brought to the bar of judgment precisely through the power of mimesis to imitate forms of social power in narrative form. Jameson's *The Political Unconscious* (1981) pursues this thesis by way of **Louis Althusser**'s rereading of Marxist theories of BASE/SUPERSTRUCTURE in order to uncover the novel's peculiar modes of narrative articulation and totality. He is particularly interested in "those narrative frames or containment strategies which seek to endow their objects of representation with formal unity" (39). The political unconscious of the novel is discernible in "traces" of the "uninterrupted narrative" of history, specifically, of "the collective struggle to wrest a realm of Freedom from a realm of Necessity" (3). Marxist analysis restores "to the surface of the text the repressed and buried reality of this fundamental history" (19–20), and it does so primarily by using the limitations of tradition in order to expose social contradictions that tradition represses. Once the text is revealed as a politically "symbolic act," it can be situated within "the organizing categories" of social class (69).

As I have suggested, these historical approaches presuppose a kind of mimesis that works "unconsciously," whereby the novel reduplicates the social forces that shape narrative and that narrative in turn strives to critique. George Levine offers another, more traditional, perspective on mimesis and realist styles in *The Realistic Imagination* (1981), which challenges poststructuralist skepticism about generic categories. "Victorian realism," he writes, ought to be regarded as "an astonishing effort both of moral energy and of art, and one that must not be diminished by the historical distortions of contemporary critical method or by the Whiggish view of history ... that we know better now" (4). Levine is reacting in part to critics like Ihab Hassan, Robert Scholes, and Linda Hutcheon and other postmodernist theorists who were turning away from realism and focusing on renovative forms like METAFICTION, which in a curious instance of recursivity, reaches back to formalism to retrieve the idea of "defamiliarization." Metafiction is "fiction about fiction" that draws attention to its own devices by bringing "to the reader's attention those formal elements of which, through over-familiarization, he has become unaware." There is also an affinity in such works with rhetorical approaches to the novel, for this postmodernist defamiliarization creates "new demands for attention and active involvement [that] are brought to bear on the act of reading" (Hutcheon 24). Parody, a predominant mode in metafictional texts, "does not necessarily involve a movement away from *mimesis*," for metafiction "parodies and imitates as a way to a new form which is just as serious and valid, as a synthesis, as the form it dialectically attempts to surpass" (25).

The theory of the novel inevitably circles back to first principles – genre, narrative form, strategies of narration, thematic concerns, social context – and the turn of the twenty-first century makes this recursive condition plainly evident. Genre study has tackled all of these principles, as is evident by renewed attention to the *Bildungsroman*, the *roman à clef*, and the historical novel. New theoretical work on so-called "genre fiction" (e.g., detective novels, science fiction, fantasy and romance) has contributed to a renewed understanding of our assumptions about what constitutes a "literary" text. This kind of critical investigation also challenges our assumptions about class and reading habits, as Janice Radway has shown in her analysis of "readerly desire." What readers like is complicated by the contexts of marketing and "belonging" created by institutions like the Book of the Month Club, which recognize "that reading is an extraordinarily complex and variegated social activity and thus a practice to which different readers bring different tastes and evaluative criteria" (56). This new attention to genre has enabled postcolonial theorists to take a new view of the novel as part of a process of cultural translation in which the novel is transformed under new social and cultural conditions. Jed Esty and I have analyzed the *Bildungsroman* as it emerges in postcolonial locations, while Peter Hitchcock has examined the ways in which the "serial novel" (i.e., trilogies, quartets, and so on) interrogates nationalism and creates new forms of novelistic space that in some cases sustain "the work of decolonization by transnationalizing the time/space of its possibility" (43). Franco Moretti's massive five-volume collection of essays, *Il Romanzo* (The Novel) (2001–3) and Pascale Casanova's *The World Republic of Letters* (2007), which explores global literary production as an orchestrated movement from the metropolis to the periphery, have, in the twentieth century, redefined the concept of world literature, the simultaneous traversal and transcendence of national literary traditions. (On aesthetics, see chapter one, "The Rise of Literary Theory" 12–24, Post-Marxism 114–17.)

These new developments testify to the shortsightedness of twentieth-century critics who, in response to the work of postmodernist novelists like Samuel Beckett, John Barth, and Thomas Pynchon, declared that the novel was an exhausted form. Far from exhausted, the novel continues to innovate formally and thematically, and theorists of the novel continue to claim our attention by reminding us of its ability to represent and shape human experience of all kinds.

Works Cited

Armstrong, Nancy. *Desire and Domestic Fiction: A Political History of the Novel*. New York: Oxford University Press, 1987.

Auerbach, Eric. *Mimesis*. 1946. Princeton: Princeton University Press, 1953.

Bakhtin, M. M. *The Dialogic Imagination: Four Essays*. Ed. M. Holquist Trans. C. Emerson and M. Holquist. Austin: University of Texas Press, 1981.

Booth, Wayne. "How Bakhtin Woke Me Up." In *The Essential Wayne Booth*. Ed. Walter Jost. Chicago: University of Chicago Press, 2006. 140–53.

Booth, Wayne. *The Rhetoric of Fiction*. 1961. 2nd ed. Chicago: University of Chicago Press, 1983.

Conrad, Joseph. *The Nigger of the "Narcissus."* 1897. Ed. R. Kimbrough. New York: Norton, 1979.

Eliot, T. S. *The Use of Poetry and the Use of Criticism*. 1933. London: Faber and Faber, 1964.

Emerson, Caryl. "Shklovsky's *ostranenie*, Bakhtin's *vnenakhodimost*" (How Distance Serves an Aesthetics of Arousal Differently from an Aesthetics Based on Pain). *Poetics Today* 26.4 (Winter 2005): 637–64.

Forster, E. M. *Aspects of the Novel*. 1927. New York: Harvester/HBJ, 1955.

Gilbert Sandra M. and Gubar, Susan. *The Madwoman in the Attic: The Woman Writer and the Nineteenth-Century Literary Imagination*. New Haven: Yale University Press, 1979.

Hassan, Ihab. *The Dismemberment of Orpheus: Toward a Postmodern Literature*. New York: Oxford University Press, 1971.

Hitchcock, Peter. *The Long Space: Transnationalism and Postcolonial Form*. Stanford: Stanford University Press, 2009.

Hutcheon, Linda. *Narcissistic Narrative: The Metafictional Paradox*. Waterloo, ON: Wilfred Laurier University Press, 1980.

James, Henry. *The Future of the Novel*. Ed. L. Edel. New York: Vintage, 1956.

Jameson, Fredric. *The Political Unconscious: Narrative as a Socially Symbolic Act*. Ithaca: Cornell University Press, 1981.

Latham, Sean. *The Art of Scandal: Modernism, Libel Law, and the Roman à Clef*. Oxford: Oxford University Press, 2009.

Leavis, F. R. *The Great Tradition: George Eliot, Henry James, Joseph Conrad*. 1948. New York: New York University Press, 1963.

Levine, George. *The Realistic Imagination: English Fiction from Frankenstein to Lady Chatterley*. Chicago: University of Chicago Press, 1981.

Lubbock, Percy. *The Craft of Fiction*. 1923. New York: Scribner, 1955.

Lukács, Georg. "Realism in the Balance." Trans. Rodney Livingstone. In Ernst Bloch et al. *Aesthetics and Politics*. London: Verso, 1980. 28–59.

Lukács, Georg. *Studies in European Realism*. 1948. New York: Grosset and Dunlap, 1964.

Lukács, Georg. *The Theory of the Novel*. 1920. Trans. A. Bostock. Cambridge, MA: MIT Press, 1971.

Miller, D. A. *The Novel and the Police*. Berkeley: University of California Press, 1988.

Parker, David. *Ethics, Theory and the Novel*. New York: Cambridge University Press, 1994.

Radway, Janice. *A Feeling for Books: The Book-of-the-Month Club, Literary Taste, and Middle-Class Desire*. Chapel Hill: University of North Carolina Press, 1997.

Watt, Ian. *The Rise of the Novel*. 1957. 2nd ed. Berkeley: University of California Press, 2001.

Woolf, Virginia. "Modern Fiction." In *The Essays of Virginia Woolf. Vol. 4, 1925–28*. Ed. Andrew McNeillie. London: Hogarth, 1986. 157–65.

2   Ideology/Philosophy/History/Aesthetics

Marxist Theory

Marxism is both a theory of economics and a theory of history. Its origins lie in Hegelian philosophy and social theory, specifically, in Karl Marx's critique of the Left Hegelians, nineteenth-century thinkers who pursued the radical social and political implications of Hegel's work. Marx's position is forcefully stated in his "Theses on Feuerbach." Ludwig Feuerbach, a leading Left Hegelian, was critical of idealist philosophy and tried to apply a "transformative" method to Hegel's thought, especially about religion. Marx admired this method, seeing it as his chief contribution to philosophy. Like Feuerbach, he borrowed the concept of alienation from the Hegelian tradition, which he used, in the *Economic and Philosophical Manuscripts* (1844), to describe the worker's relation "to the *product of his labor*," which in capitalism takes the form of "an *alien* object" (Marx and Engels 72). Later, in *Capital*, he would see both "labor-power" and the products of labor as equally alienated, for they both take on the form of commodities. It is not a matter of workers being alienated from the objective world (i.e., from the natural world that provides the raw material for labor) but of their having sold their labor to the capitalist, for whom it becomes a source of profit (i.e., surplus value). This shift in attitude is in part a direct response to the Young Hegelian conception of objectification, which tends to celebrate "sensuous contemplation" at the expense of social experience, which for Marx is a "practical, human-sensuous activity," an "*objective* activity" that humanity has the power to effect and change (143). As is clear from *Capital* and other later works, the realm of the *objective* cannot be located in the space of alienation, since it is the object world upon which human beings work in order to create out of nature the means of their subsistence through labor. This means that labor in the object world is a crucial part of human experience. As he put it in the *Economic and Philosophical Manuscripts*, "man is a species being, not only because in practice and in theory he adopts the species as his object ... but also because he treats himself as the actual, living species; because he treats himself as a *universal* and therefore a free being" (75).

Marx's "break" with the Hegelian tradition, summed up in the last of his "Theses on Feuerbach" – "The philosophers have only *interpreted* the world, in various ways; the point, however, is to *change* it" (145) – is worked out in detail in Marx and Engels' *The German Ideology*. By limiting their critique to interpretation, the Young Hegelians merely substitute one interpretation of reality with another, so that, "in spite of their allegedly 'world-shattering' statements," they remain "the staunchest of conservatives" (149). The incomplete inversion of Hegel that they glimpsed in Young Hegelians like Feuerbach failed to grasp the materialist basis of both human life and history. It therefore amounts to little more than ideology, a distortion of consciousness by which "men and their relations appear upside-down as in a *camera obscura*" (154). The "production of life," which transforms given nature into objects of use, is for them a profoundly *social* relationship. Idealist philosophy masks this relationship by inverting the crucial terms of consciousness and life. "Life is not determined by consciousness," Marx and Engels write, "but consciousness by life" (155).

Only by understanding the actual mode of life can one come to understand history and the individual's place in it. The "first premise of all human existence and, therefore, of all history" is that "man must be in a position to live in order to be able to 'make history'" (155–6). This premise grounds Marxist theories of HISTORICAL MATERIALISM, which hold that humanity is the subject of history. Human life is a web of social relations between the individual and nature and between individuals within a community. This means that all social realities are fundamentally material, in that they have their origin and being in specific forms of labor and production. History is therefore the history of the transformations in relations and modes of production, which are themselves transformations in the way labor power is distributed. "Men make their own history," Marx writes in "The Eighteenth Brumaire of Louis Bonaparte," but they do not make it just as they please; they do not make it under circumstances chosen by themselves, but under circumstances directly found, given and transmitted from the past" (595). This may help us understand why the various modes of production were *necessary* stages of development toward a classless society. The past may take the form of "dead generations" that weigh "like a nightmare on the brain of the living" (595), but it is a nightmare through which we must pass in order to arrive at a higher stage of social development. However much Marx regarded history as working dialectically through the transformations in society, he stopped short of insisting that these were anything like *natural laws* whose determinations were utterly disconnected from human activity (though Engels and the Russian Marxist Georgi Plekhanov would later develop this idea in theories of DIALECTICAL MATERIALISM). Indeed, such a disconnection would frustrate the revolutionary critical practice that Marx advocated and modeled in his own work.

The German Ideology briefly sketches the history of the modes of production, which move through stages of development from the medieval guilds and professional associations to early forms of manufacture. The shift from the era of manufacture (roughly the mid-sixteenth to the late-eighteenth centuries) to that of industry led to the consolidation of capital in bourgeois modes of production (207f). But, as Marx notes in *The Grundrisse* ("the foundation," early unpublished writings on political economy), the era of capitalism appears *"sporadically, alongside* the old modes of production, while exploding them little by little everywhere" (274).

At this time of transition, near the end of the period of manufacture, *money* and *monetary* wealth emerged as a COMMODITY in its own right, and soon played a crucial role in the marketplace where it was used as an equivalent value for other commodities. The emergent capitalist money economy displaced modes of production that focused on use-values (i.e., feudal forms of payment like quit-rent-corn and the tithe-corn), along with pre-capitalist forms of property, and "pushe[d] forward towards the making of the *labor market*" (272). Drawing upon a long tradition of reflection on value, Marx distinguishes between *use-value* and *exchange-value* (the latter often referred to as value *as such*). Use-values "constitute the substance of all wealth," no matter what form it takes, but they "become a reality only by use or consumption" (303). When I make or barter for a shirt and subsequently wear it, I consume its value in use; if instead I sell it to someone else then a new value accrues to the shirt: it becomes valuable insofar as it can be exchanged for an equivalent value in *money*. Use-values, therefore, are potentially "material depositories of exchange-value" (304). It is only when this potential is realized in a system of exchange that the use-value is transformed into a commodity. To become a commodity, the products of labor must differ *qualitatively*, while retaining an equivalence in value in terms of relative *quantity* (to use Marx's example, 10 yards of linen = one coat). Because the kinds of labor differ for each of the commodities exchanged, there arises a "complex system, a social division of labour," which leads to specialization and, under conditions of large-scale manufacture (e.g., cooperation of labor power), to a "crippling of body and mind." This is, for Marx, perhaps the most pernicious aspect of capitalism, for the "subdivision of labour is the assassination of a people" (399).

Because the commodity possesses an exchange-value that is totally abstracted from use-value and from its physical form and the material relations involved in its production, it takes on the "fantastic" form of the *fetish*. Marx calls it a "mysterious thing" because "in it the social character of men's labour appears to them as an objective character stamped upon the product of that labour; because the relation of the producers to the sum total of their own labour is presented to them as a social relation, existing not between themselves, but between the products of their labour" (320). The "fetishism of commodities" arises when a social relation is abstracted from the actual conditions of production; such relations can take place *only* in the marketplace, in the circulation and exchange of commodities. Georg Lukács uses the term REIFICATION to describe the mysterious process by which social practices are converted into abstractions and objectified in commodities. The "veil of reification," he argues, cannot be penetrated until the commodity form itself becomes "the universal category of society as a whole." For only then can we understand the "objective evolution of society" and the stance of men and women who must attempt either "to comprehend the process or to rebel against its disastrous effects and liberate themselves from servitude to the 'second nature' so created" (*History* 86).

What is less mysterious is the process by which labor-power can produce profit for the capitalist, for the "consumption of labour-power is at one and the same time the production of commodities and of surplus-value" (343). Surplus-value accrues from the difference between the cost of labor-power and the uses to which it is put. From the capitalist viewpoint, the object is not to exchange equivalent commodities (x hours of labor-power $= x$ number of shirts) but to extract more value from the labor than it contained when it was purchased. For Marx, surplus-value is both credit (for workers sell their labor for payment later) and profit (i.e., "production as the creation of value"). The capitalist creates *new* value by exploiting the "social labor" (i.e., the value associated with maintaining the worker's health and skills to work another day) that is absorbed into the cost of producing commodities. If it takes six hours of labor (the figure used by Marx) to sustain a worker for a single day, the capitalist must increase the hours spent in labor in order to extract extra value from production. Hence, "the value of labour-power, and the value which that labour-power creates in the labour-process, are two entirely different magnitudes." The use-value of the worker thus becomes "a source not only of value, but of more value than it has itself" (357). This is why the duration of the work day is so important for Marx, for in it *extra* value resides. Though workers freely sell their labor in the marketplace at a set value, the work day itself, decoupled from the inherent value of labor-power, becomes an opportunity for exploitation by the capitalist who consumes surplus-labor and converts it into abstract value. "Capital is dead labour," Marx writes, "that, vampire like, only lives by sucking living labour, and lives the more, the more labour it sucks" (363).

The division of labor within the workshop, during the early period of manufacture, facilitated this development by making labor-power more efficient, but the "detail labor" performed there had not yet taken the form of a commodity; this can happen only in the "common product of all the detail labourers," which is the result of a *social* division of labor, which disperses the means of production "among many independent producers of commodities" (395). The introduction of machinery in the period of industrial production (particularly in the nineteenth century) transformed the conditions of production, creating specializations that sapped the workers' humanity even as it appeared to "lighten" their labor, for even this lightening "becomes a sort of torture, since the machine does not free the labourer from work, but deprives the work of all interest" (409). The modern factory, which introduces changes not only in the factory itself but "revolutionizes the division of labour within the society, incessantly launches masses of capital and of workpeople from one branch of production to another" (412–13). The contradiction between an ossified division of labor in the factory and a continuously changing social division of labor produces antagonisms that make the life of workers increasingly unbearable. The revolutionary task is to transform the "crippled" worker into a "fully developed individual" who can work at a variety of tasks and, by virtue of this variety, give "free scope to his own natural and acquired powers" (413–14).

The modes of production described above constitute only part of the social TOTALITY. "The sum total of [the] relations of production," Marx writes, "constitutes the economic structure of society, the real foundation, on which rises a legal and political superstructure and to which correspond definite forms of social consciousness" (4). One of the most important components of twentieth-century Marxist theory is the category of the SUPERSTRUCTURE and its interrelation with the BASE (i.e., productive forces). Broadly speaking, IDEOLOGY refers to the social and cultural institutions and forms of consciousness that arise from this interrelation. It typically designates the standpoint and values of a dominant class (e.g., the bourgeoisie) and constitutes a form of distortion, a misrecognition of the productive forces of society. Lukács was instrumental in developing the concept of ideology, particularly in relation to class consciousness. In *History and Class Consciousness* (1923) he argues that materialist analysis must concern itself with society grasped "*as a concrete totality*, the system of production at a given point in history and the resulting division of society into classes." Only when this sense of historical totality is established "does the consciousness of their existence that men have at any given time emerge in all its essential characteristics" (50). Ideology takes the form of *false consciousness* whenever the subjective consciousness of a specific class (typically, the ruling class) is taken to be the objective consciousness of society at large. This ideological "second nature" is the direct outcome of reification, the "transformation of the commodity relation into a thing of 'ghostly objectivity'" that cannot "content itself with the reduction of all objects for the gratification of human needs to commodities. It stamps its imprint upon the whole consciousness of man" (100). The condition of reification is the mark of a specific historical situation, that of "bourgeois man in the capitalist production process," in which the individual "confronts a reality 'made' by himself (as a class) which appears to him to be a natural phenomenon alien to himself; he is wholly at the mercy of its 'laws.'" He is, in short, "the object and not the subject of events" (135). The *immediacy* of life is precisely the same for both proletariat and bourgeois, but the "specific categories of MEDIATION by means of which both classes raise this immediacy to the level of consciousness" are radically different (150). This difference is determined by the relative position of each class within the economic process, with the proletariat feeling the full brunt of a false consciousness in terms of oppression and exploitation, and the bourgeois feeling the same mediated reality as truly *objective* reality. The difference is that only the proletariat can rejoin history as its rightful home, for "the historical knowledge of the proletariat begins ... with the self-knowledge of its own social situation and with the elucidation of its necessity (i.e., its genesis)." Theorizing ideology and class consciousness in this way – that is, as a dialectical interaction between subject and object within a social process – is, as Lukács himself admits, an attempt to "out-Hegel Hegel" (xxiii). But we might also see here, as Max Horkheimer did, a failure to get beyond the Hegelian goal of dialectical totality (on Horkheimer's critique of Lukács, see Jay 46ff).

In addition to his work on ideology, reification, and class consciousness, Lukács also inaugurated a tradition of Marxist literary theory with his *Theory of the Novel* (1920), which diagnoses the problem of the modern novel in terms of its failure to capture an authentic social totality. He also promoted realism, especially as found in the nineteenth-century novel, believing it to be the most appropriate style for representing the condition of consciousness within a given historical epoch and in a given society. For Lukács, realism is best suited to offer a vision of totality, whether of the "complete human personality" or of "the faithful portrayal of the world [the author] sees" (*Studies* 7, 13). What is at issue, for the literary artist, is not a representation of the world but an account, as Leon Trotsky puts it, of "the artist's feeling for the world" as well as the nature of relations between the individual artist and the "social environment" (139). But, as later theorists have made clear, literature is not an "expressive" form; it does not reflect ideology in the manner of a neutral instrument, for the literary text is both a product and mode of production. For Pierre Macherey, literature is less about the production of a text than about the *re*production of textuality, or to be more precise, of *the literary*: "literature is constituted from texts which, within the limits that specify them, bear within them ... the marks leading to their reinscription in new texts." It is a complex process that knits together the "labour of writing and the labour of its reproduction" (49–50). (On realism and the novel, see Theory of the Novel 75–9, 82.)

Aesthetic forms are highly sensitive sites of social, political, even economic conflict; as such, they can reveal contradictions in social conditions and foster a standpoint for a materialist critique of them. As Louis Althusser has pointed out, ideology and art are two different modes of conceiving reality. Ideology is associated with the scientific production and legitimation of knowledge; and while art has "a quite particular and specific relationship with ideology," that relationship is ultimately one that encourages the disarticulation of art from ideology. Art manages this precisely by permitting us to see, perceive, or feel "the *ideology* from which it is born, in which it bathes, from which it detaches itself as art and to which if *alludes*" (203–4). According to Luke Ferretter, "what Althusser calls 'real' or 'authentic' art, through a kind of internal dislocation, allows us an objective view of ideological discourse as such" (96). Ferretter also points out that Althusser's Marxist aesthetic ultimately fails to overcome its own indebtedness to bourgeois theories of art (97–8). The reason for this lies in the deep interconnection between aesthetics and the idealist tradition from which Marxism emerged. From the mid-eighteenth century, aesthetics has attempted to mediate the opposed realms of sensuousness and reason and all-too-often did so only at the expense of an authentic connection with "practical, human-sensuous activity" (Marx 143). As Terry Eagleton has pointed out, aesthetics models a kind of power that brings the body and its affects, sentiments, habits, and so on, into play. Like the aesthetic artifact, the subject is a law unto itself, "at one with immediate experience, finding its freedom in necessity" (20). But such freedom ultimately turns into a kind of benign intersubjective delusion, an imaginary realm in which real social relations are misrecognized as utopian. "Aesthetic intersubjectivity adumbrates a utopian community of subjects," Eagleton writes. It throws into relief "the ghostly outline of a non-dominative social order" that mystifies and legitimizes "actual dominative social relations" (97). Not everyone agrees that aesthetics can be so easily collapsed into ideology, but it is certainly the case that the articulation of these two categories has proven problematic for Marxist theory precisely because it indexes the resilience of idealist thinking.

The nature of those questions and the precise ways in which literary texts raise them is the chief problem for post-Marxists like Raymond Williams, who sees literature and literary criticism as productive forms of "class specialization and control of a general social practice, and of a class limitation of the questions which it might raise" (49). Fredric Jameson makes much the same point when he argues that "the aesthetic act is itself ideological" and that aesthetic and narrative forms, as ideological acts, perform the function of "inventing imaginary or formal 'solutions' to irresolvable social contradictions" (79). These issues, together with new developments in Marxist theory, will be explored in the next two sections: "Critical Theory," which focuses primarily on the Frankfurt School thinkers and "Post-Marxism," which examines the developments in Marxist thought beginning with Antonio Gramsci and concluding with new theories of globalization. The reader should consult these entries for further discussion of ideology, hegemony, reification, and the Marxist critique of capitalist institutions and the state.

Works Cited

Althusser, Louis. *Lenin and Philosophy, and Other Essays*. 1971. Trans. Ben Brewster. New York: Monthly Review Press, 2001.

Eagleton, Terry. *The Ideology of the Aesthetic*. Oxford: Blackwell, 1990.

Engels, Friedrich. *Dialectics of Nature*. Ed. and trans. Clemens Dutt. New York: International Publishers, 1940.

Ferretter, Luke. *Louis Althusser*. London: Routledge, 2006.

Jameson, Fredric. *The Political Unconscious: Narrative as a Socially Symbolic Act*. Ithaca: Cornell University Press, 1981.

Jay, Martin. *The Dialectical Imagination: A History of the Frankfurt School and the Institute of Social Research*. Boston: Little Brown, 1973.

Lukács, Georg. *History and Class Consciousness: Studies in Marxist Dialectics*. 1923. Trans. Rodney Livingstone. Cambridge, MA: MIT Press, 1983.

Lukács, Georg. *Studies in European Realism*. 1948. New York: Grosset and Dunlap, 1964.

Macherey, Pierre. *In a Material Way: Selected Essays by Pierre Macherey*. Ed. Warren Montag. Trans. Ted Stolze. London: Verso, 1998.

Marx, Karl and Fredrick Engels. *The Marx–Engels Reader*. Ed. Robert C. Tucker. 2nd ed. New York: Norton, 1978.

Trotsky, Leon. *Literature and Revolution*. Ed. William Keach. Chicago: Haymarket Books, 2000.

Williams, Raymond. *Marxism and Literature*. Oxford: Oxford University Press, 1977.

Critical Theory

The term *critical theory* covers a wide variety of social, political, and aesthetic theories, mainly rooted in German idealist philosophy. The most influential of these emerged out of the Institute for Social Research, which was founded by Felix Weil in the years following World War I and was formally granted institute status by the German Education Ministry in 1923. The "Frankfurt School" is a common designation for the first generation of theorists associated with the Institute, including, preeminently, Max Horkheimer, Theodor Adorno, Herbert Marcuse, Erich Fromm, Leo Lowenthal, and Friedrich Pollock. Though strongly influenced by Marx and his successors, they were also indebted, as Martin Jay suggests, to the tradition of "Left Hegelianism" that emerged in the 1840s and culminated in Marx's work. Like the Left Hegelians, the Frankfurt School theorists were concerned with "the integration of philosophy and social analysis. They likewise were concerned with the dialectical method devised by Hegel and sought, like their predecessors, to turn it in a materialist direction." Crucially, they were concerned with the transformation of society through "human *praxis*" (Jay 42). Though rooted in Hegelian or Kantian traditions, Frankfurt School theorists were critical of the concepts of UNIVERSALITY and TOTALITY (in social, political, historical, and aesthetic spheres) associated with these two philosophers. In this respect, the Frankfurt School theorists were opposed to grand philosophical systems and theories of society, and therefore tended to emphasize the essay and the aphorism (in this, they follow Nietzsche's example).

The critical distinction for the Frankfurt School was between *traditional* and *critical* theory. According to Horkheimer, the former is "based on scientific activity as carried on within the division of labor at a particular stage" of capital development, while the latter "considers the overall framework which is conditioned by the blind interaction of individual activities (that is, the existent division of labor and the class distinctions) to be a function which originates in human action and therefore is a possible object of planful decision and rational determination of goals" (207). Critical theory acknowledges the importance of human AGENCY and social action and the experiential basis of critical forms of knowledge, but Horkheimer insists that "no corresponding concrete perception of it" can be known until "it actually comes about." Thus, the "proof of the pudding," as it were, "is still in the future" (220–1). The point here is that critical theory resists dogmatic knowledge cut off from material existence and is especially skeptical of political ideologies that use traditional forms of knowledge, including scientific theories of history and society, to support oppressive regimes.

This skepticism came reflexively to an intellectual circle that arose at the same time as the emergence of totalitarianism. The rise to power of Hitler's National

Socialist Party led to a period of forced exile (1933 to the early 1950s), when the Institute was relocated first to Geneva and then to New York and Columbia University, with some members, like Horkheimer, Adorno, and Marcuse, moving on to California. According to Jay, the Institute underwent significant changes in direction and emphasis during this time; on the one hand, there was a general rhetorical shift that muted the Marxist tenor of works published by the Institute's members; on the other hand, and more important, there was a gradual "loss of that basic confidence, which Marxists had traditionally felt, in the revolutionary potential of the proletariat" (44). Generally speaking, the critical theorists of the Institute, particularly in the second phase after the emigration, were skeptical of doctrinal Marxism, and were more inclined (especially under the influence of US sociology) to incorporate empirical methods and to avoid the "scienticism" that characterized the work of Engels and V. I. Lenin. Marxism, particularly dialectical methodologies, continued to ground much of the Institute's work, though, as Göran Therborn has pointed out, "the dialectic of critical theory developed beyond the Marxian critique of political economy" (72, 77–8). New targets of critique included fascism, anti-Semitism (which many of the Institute theorists saw as an organic outgrowth of fascism), aesthetics, and social and cultural institutions. In all of these themes we can discern an emphasis on MEDIATION, that is, on the material conditions that construct human consciousness and on the impossibility of an *immediate* identity between that consciousness and the object world.

The aim of the Institute was to develop a comprehensive social theory that would both describe relations of power and domination *and* facilitate and encourage radical social transformations; and while abstract idealist philosophies were rejected, the underlying affirmation of Reason in them was by and large retained (see Jay 60–5). "Reason represents the highest potentiality of man and of existence," Marcuse wrote in 1937. "For when reason is accorded the status of substance, this means that at its highest level, as authentic reality, the world no longer stands opposed to the rational thought of men as mere material objectivity." But if reason is to overcome the limitations of idealism, it must constitute a "critical philosophy as well." And if, as is true in the "philosophy of the bourgeois era," reason is "the form of rational subjectivity," then it must of necessity contain the concept of freedom" (*Negations* 100–1). For Marcuse, the preservation of happiness and leisure, and the pleasures of authentic aesthetic experience, were fundamental to individual freedom. Indeed, they were the proper objects of an "administered society" as Marcuse understood it, one in which "the social life-process [is] administered in a manner which brings into harmony the freedom of individuals and the preservation of the whole on the basis of given objective historical and natural conditions" (145). Marcuse's interest in psychoanalysis and "social psychology," like Fromm's, grew out of a desire to make materialist practices more effective in achieving this goal. Marcuse and Fromm approached Freud's work quite differently. For example, Fromm, himself a clinician, regarded "metapsychological" theories like the Oedipus complex to be unsuited to materialist critique; but, for Marcuse, who believed that the "experience of domination [is] symbolized by the primal father – the extreme Oedipus situation" (*Eros* 58; see Jay ch. 3) – Freudian psychoanalysis enabled the critical analysis of human experience under the pressure of social and political forces.

Central to critical theory is the question of domination, particularly as it is manifested in Enlightenment traditions and institutions whose origins lie in the fight against domination. Horkheimer and Adorno's *Dialectic of Enlightenment* (1944) uncovers the dialectical logic of this contradiction. The Enlightenment, they argue, is dialectically entwined with the very mythology it seeks to overcome. "Mythology itself sets off the unending process of enlightenment," and "just as the myths already realize enlightenment, so enlightenment with every step becomes more deeply engulfed in mythology" (11–12). This dialectical complicity is already at work in Homer, whose epic organization is at variance with mythic reality: "The venerable cosmos of the meaningful Homeric world is shown to be the achievement of regulative reason, which destroys myth by virtue of the same rational order in which it reflects it" (44). As J. M. Bernstein puts it, the "mythic dominated origin of culture and civilization is a posit of enlightenment rationality itself" (85). The disenchantment of the mythic unity of nature ultimately led to the alienated SUBJECTIVITY of modernity and the rationalization and COMMODIFICATION of culture, which were both the effects of the "culture industry," the "monstrous machinery of amusement" (Adorno, *Minima* 139) that functions primarily to guarantee the general pacification of the masses in an "administered" society quite different from what Marcuse envisioned. The society dominated by the culture industry reduces all human potential and transcendence to the limited domain of capitalist material production – it is, as Marcuse argued, a "one-dimensional" world in which freedom withers in the face of an instrumentalized reason bent on efficiency and social control. The technologies of popular culture (radio, television, films, advertising, the music and book industries) dominate through apparently innocuous transformations in mood, attitude, and lifestyle that transform the free individual into a consumer with an abstract and alienated relation to the social world around her. In such a world, REIFICATION has become total, so that even our attempts at subjective experience have become radically objectified. Adorno's critique of jazz, which he rejected as commercialized and debased, indicates the extent to which even marginal cultural forms reproduce dominant values and tastes. In a capitalist society, competition and the logic of the marketplace infiltrate all levels of social, cultural, and political practice. Consumer culture is, therefore, "not a luxury but rather the simple extension of production" (Adorno, *Prisms* 26).

While it is easy to see that modern entertainment culture commodifies desire, Adorno reminds us that "so-called entertainment" has always performed the same function: that is, to persuade us to refuse to recognize the "universal injustice" of human experience by accepting a mutilated version of ourselves (147). This tendency simply quickens and becomes general under conditions of modern industrial capitalism, so much so that we comprehend all too well our real social existence as alienated. In a radical contradiction, our incomprehension is suborned by our comprehension. This is the "bad conscience of high culture," for "culture no longer impotently drags its despised opponent [i.e., kitsch] behind it, but is taking it under its direction. In administering the whole of mankind, it administers also the breach between man and culture." In administered societies, Adorno suggests, we live with "less self" than we desire, but we learn through a "playful excess of self-loss that to live in earnest without a self could be easier, not more difficult" (139). Aesthetic subjectivity masks the dislocating loss of self by taking the form of a standardized consciousness. What is at work here is a "kind of reification, technification of the inward as such." The more an artist "masterfully expresses himself, the less he has to 'be' what he expresses" (214). This is not a matter of psychology (i.e., the opening of the self "discovered" by Freud) but a historical tendency – it is the outcome of a capitalist mode of production that commodifies culture all the way down to the inner life of the subject. Harmonious self-development (*Bildung*) no longer stands even as an aspiration because the totality it promises, in its reified form, stands only for the self as a commodity, something that can be exchanged in the vast marketplace of pleasures and entertainments. "The saleable," Adorno notes, "is itself subjectivity administrated by subjectivity" (215).

In "The Work of Art in the Age of Its Technological Reproducibility," **Walter Benjamin** illustrates Adorno's argument about the reification of culture. New art forms like film embody the dislocations of capitalist production, severing the artist and the spectator from a traditional world in which the "aura" of an artwork signals the possibility of aesthetic authenticity. But there is revolutionary potential in this severance. The aura of an artwork originates in its "cultic" function in ritual and thus belongs to a privileged social stratum of rulers and priests. The rise of photography ("the first truly revolutionary means of reproduction" [256]) and other forms of mechanical reproduction represents freedom from "cult values" and the emergence of a new "exhibition value" that makes art and culture, through its very reproducibility, widely available. Once the artwork is severed from its cult function, "all semblance of art's autonomy disappeared forever" (257–8). Film and other new art forms have the capacity to create an emancipatory popular culture in which the once-sacred artwork is "de-sacralized" and "de-aestheticized," its infinite reproducibility making it both more democratic and less bound up with mystifying ritual: "for the first time in world history, mechanical reproduction emancipates the work of art from its parasitical dependence on ritual" (256). With the loss of aura came the loss of the idea that the work of art belongs to a past era, cut off from the requirements of the present. Whereas painting encouraged a "reactionary attitude," film encourages a "progressive reaction … characterized by an immediate, intimate fusion of pleasure – pleasure in seeing and experiencing – with an attitude of expert appraisal" (264). But the very same technologies are used in a quite different way by fascism, which says "Fiat ars – pereat mundus" (let art be created though the world shall perish) and this, Benjamin argues, is the "consummation of '*l'art pour l'art*.'" The self-alienation of humankind "has reached the point where it can experience its own annihilation as a supreme aesthetic pleasure. *Such is the aestheticizing of politics, as practiced by fascism. Communism replies by politicizing art*" (270).

Benjamin's interest in how art gets politicized stands in contrast to Adorno's belief in the autonomy of art – an autonomy that paradoxically guarantees nothing less than the "fracturing" of art and of aesthetic experience. For Adorno, art exists in a state of non-communication because it "seeks, blissfully or unhappily, to seclude itself form the world" (*Aesthetic Theory* 7). However, "aesthetic relations of production," like other productive relations, are subject to "a dialectical tension between nature and domination of nature." The curious autonomy of art consists primarily in its retention of the original estate of humanity, its connection to concrete materiality, which is made possible by casting as "immanent problems of artistic form" the "unresolved antagonisms of reality" (7–8). Without this "heterogeneous moment," art cannot be autonomous; indeed, the "moment of unreality and non-existence in art" – the moment when it appears to transcend the conditions of its emergence and consumption – is precisely when art "point[s] back to the real other" (10). Because Adorno understands the work of art as "both a process and an instant," he must confront the inevitability of reification, which is a "necessary condition of aesthetic autonomy." This accounts for the precarious balance of the artwork between its "thing-like" aspect (what is open to our gaze) and the "inner structure" that "follows the work's immanent logic" (146–7). The peculiar "fragmented transcendence" of works of art are not mysteries (for the transcendence is not "really present" in them) but riddles "precisely because they are fragments disclaiming to be wholes, even though wholes is what they really want to be." Franz Kafka's "damaged parables," like the work of Samuel Beckett and Arnold Schönberg, exemplify this fragile and fragmented artistic autonomy (184).

The concept of the "non-existent" in art, which brings into view the "question of the truth of art ... when a non-existent is seen to rise as if it were real" (122), corresponds to the "non-identical" in Adorno's theory of NEGATIVE DIALECTICS, one of the most important tools for analyzing social and cultural problems without becoming entrapped in a conception of identity that negates the *other* in a dialectical sublation (a process that is essential to IDENTITY understood as self-identity). The concept of "non-identity" answers to a worldview that had been distorted by totalitarianism, anti-Semitism, and the instrumentalization of reason. Non-identity is a "something" without which conceptualization could not take place. As "a cogitatively indispensable substrate of any concept, including the concept of Being," this "something" is the "utmost abstraction of the subject matter that is not identical with thinking" (135). It is a condition for thinking that is eliminated in the act of thought (it is *non-identical* to thought), just as error and misrecognition are foundational for truth. "Without 'something' there is no thinkable formal logic," which means that "something" is not only non-identical, but non-conceptual, the "ontical element at which the purity claimants shudder, the element which, trembling with hauteur, they cede to the special sciences" (138).

To give conceptual thinking a "turn toward non-identity" is "the hinge of negative dialectics" (12). What is more, this "disenchantment with the concept is the antidote of philosophy" (13), for a philosophy guided by concepts like identity is incapable of knowing the world in anything but an abstract manner. Thus, negative dialectics preserves the "negativity" of the NEGATIVE, which resists being appropriated by the positive term of a dialectical process. It is not a reversal of standard dialectical operations. As Adorno warns, "a purely formal reversal" of the formula "identity in non-identity" merely reinscribes conventional dialectical relations (154). Negative dialectics avoids such a reversal by rescuing non-identity from a totalizing process that would subsume it in the production of identity. Nevertheless, in a contradiction that cannot be avoided, the process of rescue remains tied "to the supreme categories of identitarian philosophy as its point of departure" (147).

The deep distrust of identity theory that we see in the work of Horkheimer and Adorno is an expression of a general problematic in critical theory, namely, the alienation of the individual from the material conditions of her existence. Some theorists, like Marcuse, sought reconciliation through sexual and affective liberation. As Douglas Kellner states it, Marcuse sought to revise our views of gratification – that is, to revise the Freudian "reality principle" in the light of a "non-repressive sublimation, a diffusion of sexuality throughout one's activities" (176). Benjamin's messianism sought something similar, though his touchstone was the Kabbalistic tradition rather than psychoanalysis. Still, the result was a similar hope for a reconciliation of the individual with the world. His theory of language and translation makes this point in the context of the individual's relation to God's divine name-giving power. In the act of naming, the "mental being of man communicates itself to God" (*Reflections* 318). While human experience may represent a degraded form of this divine naming, the very structure of language as "coextensive … with absolutely everything" (314) suggests a promise of reconciliation. This idea is developed further in the late essay "On the Concept of History," in which Benjamin claims that the past, regarded by the historical materialist, "carries with it a secret index by which it is referred to redemption." The past pervades our present like a breath, a "*weak* messianic power … on which the past has a claim." And because the true image flits by, like a fugitive breath, it can be "seized only as an image that flashes up at the moment of its recognizability" (390). Benjamin's conception of HISTORICAL MATERIALISM is quite different from that of a doctrinal Marxist's, for whom it refers to the determination of history by the forces of production. In Benjamin's view, the historical materialist seeks to redeem the past by virtue of his critical interpretation of it. Like the "angel of history," he confronts the past as a "single catastrophe" that "drives him irresistibly into the future" (391–2). And in this confrontation, the past is redeemed, "blasted out of the continuum of history" and "filled full by now-time [*Jetztzeit*]" (394–5). The historical materialist constructs a "dialectical image," a temporal CONSTELLATION in which the present becomes "shot through with splinters of messianic time" (397). This process is not a matter of grasping the present caught in the light of the past, nor the past seen from the perspective of the present. Rather, the image "is that wherein what has been comes together in a flash with the now to form a constellation. In other words: image is dialectics at a standstill" (*Arcades* 463).

Hannah Arendt noted that Benjamin was "the most peculiar Marxist ever produced" by critical theory (qtd. in Benjamin, *Illuminations* 10). His messianic hope for a time of reconciliation is in part motivated by his belief that tradition, like the autonomy of art in Adorno, is "damaged" or "fractured," incapable of being transmitted in an age of information. If what is transmissible is the truth of language, the inevitable failure of transmission in modern literature becomes a kind of negative authenticity. "It is the strategic significance of the attempt to translate the experience of modernity into the language of tradition – and its failure – that makes Kafka's work so central to Benjamin's thought" (Osborne 71). A similar problem crops up in Benjamin's reading of Charles Baudelaire's poetry, which, like film, registers "the shocks of consciousness" that remain "subterranean" (*Illuminations* 164–5). There is a conjunction here with technology – especially the camera, which gives "the moment a posthumous shock, as it were" – and life in the big city, where the individual is involved in a "series of shocks and collisions" (175). The person best suited to negotiate such a world is the *flâneur*, the quintessential figure of modernity, adrift in the city, in thrall to a constant barrage of people, objects, and commodities. Benjamin's most challenging and provocative work, the *Arcades Project*, is in many ways devoted to the *flâneur* and the urban environment required for the practice of *flânerie*. In Paris, "the capital of the nineteenth century," Benjamin discovered the new shopping areas known as "arcades," which could arise only on the heels of the textile trade and iron construction (15), world exhibitions ("places of pilgrimage to the commodity fetish" [71]), the interior space of the private individual and collector ("the asylum where art takes refuge" [19]), the boulevards and barricades. In the midst of all this he found the *flâneur*, who is led into "a vanished time ... all the more spellbinding because it is not his own, not private" (416). The city becomes a landscape that splits a "dialectic of *flânerie*: on one side, the man who feels himself viewed by all and sundry as a true suspect and, on the other side, the man who is utterly undiscoverable, the hidden man" (420). Though the idleness of the *flâneur* is "a demonstration against the division of labor," it is for all that still a labor performed in and for capital. "The *flâneur* is the observer of the marketplace. His knowledge is akin to the occult science of industrial fluctuations. He is a spy for the capitalists, on assignment in the realm of consumers" (427). Benjamin's sense that the individual could find some sort of reconciliation with the world in the very technologies that threaten individuality is in stark contrast to his friend Adorno's view that subjective experience has become radically objectivized and abstract. Where Benjamin sees the promise of redemption, Adorno sees only the partial resistance and the reconciliation afforded by a "damaged life."

Benjamin did not survive World War II. Convinced that Hitler's Gestapo were closing in, he committed suicide while trying to escape into Spain. His tragic and untimely death in some ways marked the end of a phase of critical theory in which reconciliation was theoretically possible. Adorno's work during and just after the war provides us with ample evidence of this loss of faith in the project of Enlightenment that, in some ways, subtended the early work of the Institute. By the 1960s, this faith had been revived by Horkheimer's successor as director of the Institute, Jürgen Habermas. Unlike Adorno, who was highly skeptical of the benign force of reason, Habermas believed in the emancipatory potential of the "unfulfilled" project of Enlightenment. The shift of emphasis from class struggle to the larger "conflict between man and nature" that we see in the early decades of the Institute was in part due to the fact that "the possibility of a historical subject capable of ushering in the revolutionary age disappeared" (Jay 279). Adorno had written, in his last major work, that "philosophy, which once seemed obsolete, lives on because the moment to realize it was missed" (*Negative* 3). Habermas takes up the challenge implicit in Adorno's conclusion by analyzing what he believes is the signal difficulty: a misunderstanding of the relation between theory and practice, which, if properly understood, could make philosophy relevant again. He argues that theoretical analysis and the discourse it creates is fundamentally different from practice. The relation between theory and practice can only be grasped if we distinguish between three functions: the creation of "critical theorems"; the "organization of processes of enlightenment" (both the testing of theorems and education about their uses); and, finally, the field of action (in which strategies and "tactical questions" are addressed, in the service of "political struggle") (*Theory* 32). The relation of theory to the processes of enlightenment is different from its relationship with action; in the former relation, the emphasis falls on self-reflection and "changes in attitude" (a pedagogical function), while in the latter case, the product of self-reflection guides strategy. It is important also to distinguish between action and DISCOURSE. In discourse, "facts are transformed into states of affairs" and "norms are transformed into recommendations and warnings" (19). Action can take place only if it is oriented and guided by discourse. The result is what Habermas called *communicative action*, a recuperation of reason and rationality that is non-instrumental and non-coercive and that creates the conditions of consensus and dialogue among all participants of a SOCIAL FORMATION. For it to succeed, participants must "orient their actions to intersubjectively recognized validity norms" (*Communicative* 14). The formation of norms, and the legitimacy they confer on political structures, should not be confused with the repressive norms and bogus legitimation produced by apologists of capitalism; rather, they should be understood in the context of a rational society whose goal is the emancipation of human potentiality within "the good, happy, and rational life," one in which "reason itself draws *its* life from the courage to be rational" (*Theory* 253, 257; my emphasis). Communicative rationality, then, requires a public sphere in which the "unconstrained, unifying, consensus-bringing force of argumentative speech" permits the overcoming of "merely subjective views" and the coordination and fulfillment of mutually agreed-upon norms. This mode of action, guided by theory and mediated by discourse, situates theory and praxis within a context of emancipation that makes possible "both the unity of the objective world and the intersubjectivity of their lifeworld" (*Communicative* 10).

Habermas's critical theory advocates a more active and engaged social consensus, provided that there is the technology and political will to overcome obstacles to access. Something of Benjamin's faith in new cultural technologies is evident in Habermas's belief that communicative rationality could provide a means of achieving social and political consensus and genuine emancipation. In the late 1970s, Habermas defended his position against the postmodernism of **Jean-François Lyotard**, who argued, in *The Postmodern Condition* (1979), that the project of modernity was indeed finished and a new one had already begun. Habermas regarded postmodernism as a retreat from reason and a cynical denial of the responsibilities of the social subject and of the possibility, in a progressive politics, for the "rational organization of everyday social life" ("Modernity" 9). The reification of "everyday praxis" can be combated only by "creating unconstrained interaction of the cognitive with the moral–practical and the aesthetic–expressive elements" of social life (11). Habermas's claim that the "project of modernity has not yet been fulfilled" (12) can be regarded as an expression of critical theory's renewed optimism with respect to modernity. His position, and that of his followers, can be distinguished, according to Seyla Benhabib, by its "emphatic *normative* dimension," by which "critical theory preserves the intentions of practical philosophy to rationally articulate a more adequate form of human existence and to enlighten them in its attainment." Benhabib reaffirms the philosophical ground of critical theory in "the Kantian teaching of autonomy" and the "Hegelian–Marxist transformation of practical philosophy into a philosophy of historical praxis" (5). Her goal is to clarify the "normative foundations" of critical theory by analyzing its "Hegelian legacy" (8–9). Following Habermas, she calls for a "paradigm shift" from "production to communicative action, from the politics of the philosophy of the subject to the politics of radical intersubjectivity" (12). The warrant of critical theory is to critique and, as we see preeminently in Habermas's work, reestablish norms on the solid ground of emancipatory reason. But Benhabib also posits a "politics of transformation," which takes on the task of recognizing "new needs, social relations and modes of association, which burst open the utopian potential within the old" (13).

At the turn of the twenty-first century, questions of rationality, normativity, and the value of enlightenment still remain vital, as does the necessity to ground such questions in reason. What is to be done, asks Wendy Brown, when the "constitutive narratives of modernity" are "tattered," when challenges to such concepts as "progress, right, sovereignty, free will, moral truth, reason" have not yielded any alternatives? (3–4). One response to this question is a greater openness to postmodernist and poststructuralist theories and to ideas coming from feminism, Lacanian psychoanalysis, deconstruction, postcolonial studies, and cultural studies. In 2000, Ernesto Laclau, **Judith Butler**, and **Slavoj Žižek** published a volume of essays that explored Kantian and Hegelian solutions to intractable social problems. This was not a return to idealist philosophy but a tactical deployment of the poststructuralist notion of the "quasi-transcendental." Speaking of **Jacques Derrida**'s use of quasi-transcendentals, Hugh Silverman writes that they are "no longer *simply* transcendentals" because they are neither *a priori* nor bound up in a Heideggerian notion of Being. They are, rather, "the conditions of possibility and impossibility concerning the very conceptualization difference between subject and object"; they are neither finite nor infinite, but exist "at the border of the space of the organized contamination which they open up" (189–90). The "irreducible erratic contingency" (190) that characterizes these quasi-transcendentals, far from disrupting or discounting critical efficacy are the guarantee of such efficacy, for they are the discursive signs of what is possible (and impossible) within a given framework of knowledge. In this way, according to Žižek, contingency (the condition of existing *in time*, of finitude) can "account for the enigmatic emergence of the space of UNIVERSALITY itself" ("Class" 104). Much of Žižek's work is committed to demonstrating that Hegel's concept of the universal realizes itself "only in impure, deformed, corrupted forms; if we want to remove these deformations to grasp the Universal in its intact purity, we obtain its very opposite" (*Sublime Object* 148). To some extent, Žižek follows Adorno in highlighting the negative moment in the Hegelian dialectic, the obstacle or errancy whose misrecognition is constitutive of the whole process. Thus, in the Hegelian "negation of the negation," "what first appears as an external obstacle reveals itself to be an inherent hindrance, i.e., an outside force turns into an inner compulsion" and the negative, the obstacle, is "not annihilated in itself"; in fact, such faith in the negative is, in a way, "magical" (*Tarrying* 25, 135). In Žižek's critique of Hegel, the compulsion to resist sublation (the paradoxical state of annihilation and preservation of the negative term) becomes the sign of a subversive positivity and productivity "proper to misrecognition": "not only is the misrecognition an immanent condition of the final advent of the truth, but it already possesses in itself, so to speak, a positive ontological dimension: it founds, it renders possible a certain positive entity" (*Sublime Object* 64). In a similar way, Butler tries to account for Hegel's idea of universality by noting its temporal character. For her, universality is "developed through a reiterative textual strategy"; it undergoes "revision in time" and "its successive revisions and dissolutions are essential to what it 'is'" (24). What must be avoided is the elevation of particulars (the thought of a single school, the position of a single party) to the status of absolute universality. This alternative, a dynamic and contingent, historically articulated vision of "contingent universality" drives social theory paradoxically back to its origins in idealist philosophy in order that it may leap forward into an unknown future. Reassessing the Hegelian legacy provides a foundation for theoretical models appropriate to a globalized world in which capital has become decoupled from nation-state formations and in which the struggle for existence – for emancipation from oppression and, as a consequence, the attainment of happiness – has increasingly migrated from the realm of politics and the state to the marketplace. It is this new world that post-Marxism arose to confront and critique.

Note

On globalization, see Transnationalism; on Žižek, see Cultural Studies, Psychoanalysis; on Butler, see Feminist Theory, Gender Studies; on aesthetics, see chapter one, "The Rise of Literary Theory."

Works Cited

Adorno, Theodor. *Aesthetic Theory*. 1970. Ed. Gretel Adorno and Rolf Tiedemann. Trans. C. Lenhardt. London: Routledge and Kegan Paul, 1984.

Adorno, Theodor. *Minima Moralia: Reflections from Damaged Life*. 1951. Trans. E. F. N. Jephcott. London: Verso, 1974.

Adorno, Theodor. *Negative Dialectics*. Trans. E. B. Ashton. New York: Seabury Press, 1973.

Adorno, Theodor. *Prisms*. Trans. Samuel and Shierry Weber. Cambridge, MA: MIT Press, 1981.

Benhabib, Seyla. *Critique, Norm, and Utopia: A Study of the Foundations of Critical Theory*. New York: Columbia University Press, 1986.

Benjamin, Walter. *The Arcades Project*. Trans. Howard Eiland and Kevin McLaughlin. Cambridge, MA and London: Belknap Press, 1999.

Benjamin, Walter. *Illuminations*. Ed. Hannah Arendt. Trans. Harry Zohn. New York: Harcourt, Brace and World, 1968.

Benjamin, Walter. "On the Concept of History." In *Selected Writings*. Ed. Marcus Bullock and Michael W. Jennings. Vol. 4. Cambridge, MA: Belknap-Harvard University Press, 1996. 389–411.

Benjamin, Walter. *Reflections: Essays, Aphorisms and Autobiographical Writing*. 1978. Ed. Peter Demetz. Trans. Edmund Jephcott. New York: Schocken, 1986.

Benjamin, Walter. "The Work of Art in the Age of Its Technological Reproducibility." In *Selected Writings*. Ed. Marcus Bullock and Michael W. Jennings. Vol. 4. Cambridge, MA: Belknap-Harvard University Press, 1996. 251–83.

Bernstein, J. M. *Adorno: Disenchantment and Ethics*. Cambridge: Cambridge University Press, 2001.

Brown, Wendy. *Politics Out of History*. Princeton: Princeton University Press, 2001.

Butler, Judith. "Restaging the Universal: Hegemony and the Limits of Formalism." In *Contingency, Hegemony, Universality: Contemporary Dialogues on the Left*. Ed. Judith Butler, Ernesto Laclau, and Slavoj Žižek. London: Verso, 2000. 11–43.

Habermas, Jürgen. "Modernity versus Postmodernity." Trans. Seyla Benhabib. *New German Critique* 22 (Winter 1981): 3–14.

Habermas, Jürgen. *The Theory of Communicative Action*. 1981. Vol. 1 Trans. Thomas McCarthy. Boston: Beacon Press, 1984.

Habermas, Jürgen. *Theory and Practice*. Trans. John Viertel. Boston: Beacon Press, 1974.

Horkheimer, Max. "Traditional and Critical Theory." 1937. In *Critical Theory: Selected Essays*. Trans. Matthew J. O'Connell et al. New York: Continuum 1999. 188–243.

Horkheimer, Max and Theodor Adorno. *Dialectic of Enlightenment: Philosophical Fragments*. Ed. Gunzelin Schmid Noerr. Trans. Edmund Jephcott. Stanford: Stanford University Press, 2002.

Jay, Martin. *The Dialectical Imagination: A History of the Frankfurt School and the Institute of Social Research*. Boston: Little Brown, 1973.

Kellner, Douglas. *Herbert Marcuse and the Crisis of Marxism*. Berkeley: University of California Press, 1984.

Laclau, Ernesto and Chantal Mouffe. *Hegemony and Socialist Strategy: Towards a Radical Democratic Politics*. London: Verso, 2001.

Marcuse, Herbert. *Eros and Civilization: A Philosophical Inquiry into Freud*. 1956. London: Routledge and Kegan Paul, 1987.

Marcuse, Herbert. *Negations: Essays in Critical Theory*. 1968. Trans. Jeremy J. Shapiro. London: Mayfly, 2009.

Osborne, Peter. "Small-Scale Victories, Large-Scale Defeats: Walter Benjamin's Politics of Time." In *Walter Benjamin's Philosophy: Destruction and Experience*. Ed. Andrew Benjamin and Peter Osborne. London: Routledge, 1994. 59–109.

Silverman, Hugh J. and Don Ihde, eds. *Hermeneutics and Deconstruction*. Albany: SUNY Press, 1985.

Snyder, Joel. "Benjamin on Reproducibility and Aura: A Reading of 'The Work of Art in the Age of its Technical Reproducibility.'" In *Benjamin: Philosophy, History, Aesthetics*. Ed. Gary Smith. Chicago: University of Chicago Press, 1989. 158–74.

Therborn, Göran. *From Marxism to Post-Marxism?* London: Verso, 2008.

Žižek, Slavoj. "Class Struggle or Postmodernism? Yes, Please!" In *Contingency, Hegemony, Universality: Contemporary Dialogues on the Left*. Ed. Judith Butler, Ernesto Laclau, and Slavoj Žižek. London: Verso, 2000. 90–135.

Žižek, Slavoj. *The Sublime Object of Ideology*. London: Verso, 1989.

Žižek, Slavoj. *Tarrying with the Negative: Kant, Hegel, and the Critique of Ideology*. Durham, NC: Duke University Press, 1993.

Post-Marxist Theory

One of the lessons of critical theory, which began as an institution devoted to "Marxism as a scientific methodology" (Jay 11), is that classical Marxism could not weather the transition of capital into the advanced forms it took in the twentieth century without significant theoretical modifications. Critical theory approached this problem in such a way as to constitute itself as a post-Marxist development, for its main concerns and methods, while still bearing the earmarks of Marxist theory (dialectical methods, a focus on ideology, the state, and bourgeois society), were increasingly decoupled from the revolutionary class struggle (particularly as it was playing out in Soviet Russia) and the aspirations of orthodox (or "classical") Marxists. In their analysis of instrumental rationality, the culture industry, and the links between fascism and capitalism, the theorists of the Frankfurt Institute uncovered entirely new areas of study, new and decisive problems confronting the critical theorist. Their efforts point up two important dimensions of post-Marxist innovation generally. On the one hand, we find the need for increasingly nuanced and complex methodologies for analyzing advanced capitalist societies, particularly the social democracies that evolved in Europe after World War II and the phenomenon of the welfare state; these developments cannot be separated from the rise of global capitalist expansion, which exacerbated both colonial and neocolonial relations between European states and undeveloped or developing regions throughout the world. On the other hand, we find, across the spectrum of thinkers, that the hope for emancipation from oppressive capitalist regimes fades in direct proportion to the sense that freedom has been purchased at the expense of any kind of authentic individuality. What we call freedom, that which is championed by the French Revolution, the US Bill of Rights, and the entire edifice of Enlightenment thinking about the individual, is really an elegant mechanism by which the authentically free subject is annihilated: "Freedom from society," writes **Theodor Adorno**, "robs [the individual] of the strength for freedom" (*Minima* 149). This lack of faith in the subject of emancipation underwrites the pessimism exhibited by Max Horkheimer and Adorno about the possibility of political action. Even Jürgen Habermas, who reenergizes critical theory by recalling the question of the proper relation of theory to practice, must admit that achieving the conditions necessary for truly effective social and political action is not only a difficult but perhaps interminable task.

Perry Anderson has noted that, "from 1924 to 1968, Marxism did not 'stop,' as Sartre was later to claim; but it advanced via an unending detour from any revolutionary political practice. The divorce between the two was determined by the whole historical epoch" (42) – an epoch that, as I have indicated in the previous section on critical theory, was characterized largely by theoretical reflection. For Anderson, this period of Marxism is marked as "a product of *defeat*," specifically "the failure of the socialist revolution to spread outside Russia" (42). In a sense, this period "paradoxically inverted the trajectory of Marx's own development," for while Marx moved from philosophy to politics, later theorists appear to move from politics back to philosophy (52). Western Marxism or, to use the more common term, post-Marxism, attempts to respond to the challenge implicit in these developments by developing new modes of analyzing complex capitalist societies and rethinking the conditions of possibility for free individuals in a world in which contingency and crises of legitimation threaten the very ground of freedom. Thus we find new theories of DETERMINATION and HEGEMONY that are crucial for understanding the increasingly technologized superstructures of advanced capitalism and new theories of communication and aesthetics that help us understand the increasingly complex relation between art and the social world in which it is created and consumed. Many of these new theories take the form of a *negative* dialectics in which the material freedoms of non-identity are preserved against the abstract freedom of conventional dialectical synthesis. Indeed, it is just this freedom that emerges so often in post-Marxist discourse as the *only* freedom available to us in the twenty-first century.

Recent commentaries regard Ernesto Laclau and Chantal Mouffe's *Hegemony and Socialist Strategy* (1985) as a touchstone, if not an origin, of post-Marxist thought. But they also regard the half-decade or so that preceded its publication as the ground of post-Marxist development. Stuart Sim, for example, argues that Georg Lukács, Rosa Luxemburg, the theorists of the Frankfurt Institute, Sartre and "somewhat unwittingly," **Louis Althusser**, all belong to a strand of "post-Marxism at work *within* classical Marxism" (2). He also regards the work of **Antonio Gramsci** as a necessary precondition for Laclau and Mouffe's rethinking of the problem of class as a function of "articulations" within the base/superstructure relation (Sim 17). This is a plausible genealogy, as is Göran Therborn's, which includes Herbert Marcuse, phenomenologists like Maurice Merleau-Ponty, and Habermas (79). While such thinkers may disavow any "continuing Marxist commitment," their disavowal is not "tantamount to ex-Marxism, nor does it include denunciation or renegacy; development and new desires, yes, maybe even divorce, but only on amicable terms" (165).

The metaphor of marriage and amicable divorce says much about the continuity in Marxist thinking. The emphasis on scientific methods (e.g., Althusser), Hegelian frameworks (e.g., Slavoj Žižek), political action (e.g., Alain Badiou), and the theme of emancipation (e.g., Jacques Rancière) indicates that post-Marxism is recursive in its forward development, reaching back to maintain contact with early Marxist problems and methods, while freely modifying both for a critique of contemporary social conditions. If we take critical theory as the first major post-Marxist trend, a second must be noted as simultaneous with it, one that begins with Gramsci and leads us to the cultural theory of **Raymond Williams** and the structuralist Marxism of Althusser. Laclau and Mouffe would thus mark a third moment, one in which poststructuralism emerges more fully as an allied discourse, one that allows post-Marxism to rethink the problem of historical contingency outside the framework of a totalizing theory. This moment includes the work of French post-Marxists generally, who emerged in the 1960s, and the "neo-Marxism" of **Antonio Negri** and Michael Hardt. It also includes Badiou, who was influenced by Mao as well as Lacan and whose quarrel with postmodernism underscores the imbrication of these two lines of thought, particularly on matters pertaining to the political implications of language, discourse, textuality, and sign systems. Finally, we must account for the recent interest in the work of Immanuel Wallerstein, whose world-systems theory has renewed interest in Marxian historiography and offered new ways to look at the interrelated phenomena of globalization, transnationalism, and neocolonialism.

Lukács insisted that the Marxist critic must "understand reification as a *general* phenomenon constitutive of the *whole* of bourgeois society" (210). It is this understanding that we see manifested in Gramsci's theory of HEGEMONY. The term was originally used with reference to ancient Greek city-states and later adopted by historians to describe the German Confederation of states established in 1815 (see *OED* s.v. "hegemony"). In classical Marxist usage, particularly in the work of V. I. Lenin, hegemony was associated with the triumph of the proletariat, which took the form of a "centralized yet mass-based party" (Adamson 100). Gramsci used the term in more nuanced ways to talk about the power wielded by the state and, in an alternative form, by the working class. Bourgeois hegemony can be characterized in two ways, corresponding to two forms of social organization: "civil society" ("private"), which corresponds to "the function of hegemony which the dominant group exercises throughout society," and "political society" (the state), which corresponds to "'direct' domination or command exercised through the state and 'juridical' government. The functions in question are precisely organizational and connective" (Gramsci 12). For Terry Eagleton, following Gramsci, hegemony is "a rule which operates more through the consensual life of civil society than through the coercive instruments of the state" (27). This "consensual life" takes place in and through institutions (e.g., universities, political parties, state bureaucracies, corporations) and can be regarded as a form of "'spontaneous' consent given by the great masses of the population to the general direction imposed on social life by the dominant fundamental group" (i.e., the ruling class) (Gramsci 12). The goal for this class is to achieve hegemony by extending its ideology – its values, beliefs, and ideals – to every level of society, where it becomes part of the lived texture of everyday life. "Gramsci's hegemony is not a static concept," writes Walter Adamson, "but a process of continuous creation which, given its massive scale, is bound to be uneven in the degree of legitimacy it commands and to leave some room for antagonistic cultural expressions to develop" (174).

For Gramsci, education is decisive for creating and maintaining hegemony, which can be regarded as a form of "educative pressure" on individuals "so as to obtain their consent and their collaboration, turning necessity and coercion into 'freedom'" (Gramsci 242). This so-called freedom – which, as Adorno and others have indicated, is based on the replacement of authentic human experience with abstract subjectivity – is freedom *for* capital; the educative mission in the capitalist state is not directed toward the improvement of the worker but rather of production. Intellectuals are therefore vital in creating and maintaining hegemony, for they serve as "the dominant group's 'deputies' exercising the SUBALTERN functions of social hegemony and political government" (12). Gramsci describes two distinct groups: *traditional* intellectuals (the clergy, professors, writers, artists, and others), who enjoy relative AUTONOMY, and *organic* intellectuals, the "specialists" that "every new class creates alongside itself" (6). Both work within and sustain existing social conditions. Organic intellectuals in capitalist societies are mostly ineffective and "standardized," willing promoters of the dominant class. Traditional intellectuals, like "ecclesiasts" or "medical men," belong to professions and guilds and "put themselves forward as autonomous and independent of the dominant social group" (7). The need for the development of organic intellectuals in the working classes led Gramsci to a radical reconception of "intellectual activity": "Each man, finally, outside his professional activity, carries on some form of intellectual activity, that is, he is a 'philosopher,' an artist, a man of taste, he participates in a particular conception of the world, has a conscious line of moral conduct, and therefore contributes to sustain a conception of the world or to modify it, that is, to bring into being new modes of thought" (9).

The process of building hegemony through intellectual labor is an important part of ideology, certainly for the dominant class, but for subaltern groups as well. For Raymond Williams, ideology is a complex and multivalent phenomenon that refers not only to "a system of beliefs characteristic of a particular class or group" but also to "a system of illusory beliefs" (Lukács called this "false consciousness") in contrast with "true or scientific reality," the discovery of which is the function of MATERIALIST criticism. In bourgeois ideology, these two meanings tend to coincide. To further complicate matters, Williams adds a third possibility: ideology is "the general process of the production of meanings and ideas" (55). He concludes that despite the difficulties in forming a singular definition, it is necessary to arrive at a general term "to describe not only the products but the processes of signification, including the signification of values." Following V. N. Volosinov, he advocates using the terms "ideological" and "ideology" to refer to the production of signs and "the dimension of social experience in which meanings and values are produced" (70). Ideology in this sense empowers hegemony to extend beyond domination. According to Williams, Gramsci understood that "rule" (*dominio*) could never be anything more than a partial response to social and political antagonisms: the reaction to crisis "'by direct or effective coercion.'" Hegemony is "the more normal situation, [which] is a complex interlocking of political, social and cultural forces." It incorporates and goes beyond both culture – the "'whole social process,'" that shapes our lives – and ideology – the "system of meanings and values" that expresses a "particular class interest" (108). Hegemony encompasses both "class outlook" and the social totality, thereby saturating every facet of life with "relations of domination and subordination" (110).

Opposition to hegemony takes the form of rearticulating the various elements of the BASE/SUPERSTRUCTURE complex that have formed under a dominant class. It is, Gramsci writes, an ARTICULATION, "a process of differentiation and change in the relative weight that the elements of the old ideologies used to possess" (109). According to Colin Mercer, rearticulating ideological components allows us "to counter the concepts of reflection and expression" that dominate the correspondence model of truth and of representation (313). For Antonio Negri, writing in the 1960s and 1970s amid a context of radical politics in Italy, this process of rearticulation makes possible the *autonomy* of the working class, which is constructed on the basis of a realization that the crisis state of overdetermination characteristic of advanced multinational capitalism is precisely the basis of the free and unconstrained productive power of the working class (and hence of communism as such) (see Ryan). As Negri points out, "the working class is completely within the organization of capital, which is the organization of society" (Hardt and Negri, *Labor* 60). Thus, capitalist hegemony includes the working class. Antagonisms between the "collective capitalist and the collective worker" tend to be trapped within this social organization, in which crisis is managed in such a way that it produces an artificial harmony between the classes. Indeed, as Michael Ryan points out in a discussion of Negri's early work, this harmony or equilibrium is an "accident" and "'normal' development is in fact the anormal possibility of crisis" (192, 194). The "crisis state" is a "planned" state, one that manages "capitalist socialization" (adjusting wages, prices, production, and so on); and since this socialization is itself the management of a "relationship of exploitation," crisis signals not a revolutionary shift in power (or in Negri's terms *potentia*, the potential for power) but a flexibility intrinsic to capital itself. The means taken by the state to achieve harmony – e.g., the creation of surplus-value, administrative rationality, systems of legitimation – ultimately run up against "continually stronger critical contradictions, which are determined on the level of the planned structure of the state and which determine there an implacable series of failures" (Hardt and Negri, *Labor* 161). These failures drive the resistance of the working classes, for their only recourse is to strike at points of crisis and contradiction in order to rearticulate social elements in the service of working-class autonomy. In this way capitalist crisis becomes a form of "communist production" insofar as it opens the opportunity for the "fully developed social individual and an end to the necessity of wage work" (Ryan 197).

The tendency to see terms like hegemony used primarily to describe the function of the dominant class led in the 1960s to a rereading of Marx's work in an attempt to overcome the "objectification of categories in *Capital*" (Negri 8). Thus Marx's *Foundations of the Critique of Political Economy* (usually called the *Grundrisse*) is for Negri nothing less than "a text dedicated to revolutionary subjectivity," one in which the "theory of surplus value breaks down … antagonism into a microphysics of power." In short, it "opens up on the totality of practice" (14, 18). One result of this new reading of Marx was to foreground the Marxist critique of "generic humanism," that "orgy of totality, rebirth and plenitude to which we give ourselves over" (154). Althusser was central to this critique of humanism. He stressed that, for Marx, humanism is "an *ideology*, a conditional necessity," but also that "revolutionary humanism could only be a 'class humanism,' 'proletarian humanism'" (*For Marx* 231, 221). His structural (or scientific) Marxism is, in some respects, an attempt to fashion a more authentic humanism, one that is grounded on a vision of Marxist dialectic as a form of theoretical practice forming part of "a *new* science: the science of history" (*Lenin* 19; see *For Marx* 174–5). Althusser's reading of *Capital*, in part influenced by **Michel Foucault**, is based on a double reading in which Marx engages critically with his own reading of his predecessors. Just as Marx's theory of dialectics is only available in a "practical state," so his reading of his predecessors can be retrieved only be attending to an "invisible" text "articulated with the lapses in the first [i.e., visible] text." This constitutes a kind of production in itself (the "practical state" of dialectics), "the *production* of the *fleeting presence of an aspect* of its invisible field within the visible field of the existing problematic." To read this invisible field, we need an "*informed* gaze, a new gaze, which is itself a product of that field (Althusser and Balibar 28). Like Negri's reading of the *Grundrisse* in terms of revolutionary subjectivity, Althusser's reading of *Capital* yields a theory of practice by way of a willful misrecognition that yields "the concept of the effectivity of a structure on its elements." This curious absent presence allows us to discern a more sophisticated theory of the relation between base and superstructure than is usually found in *Capital*. Althusser describes a structural causality that refuses a singular relation between base and superstructure and emphasizes multiple articulations throughout the social field, for "*the whole existence of the structure consists in its effects*" (Althusser and Balibar 208; see Jameson, *Political* 25ff). What matters is not a direct economic or material relation between modes of production and the social and political spheres but rather the structure of relations, not always readily discernible, between these modes and spheres *and* across the spectrum of social and cultural institutions.

Inevitably, social relations entail contradictions (between capital and labor), the intensification of which result in *overdeterminations* in the system; for example, the "ruptural unity" of accumulated "circumstances" and "currents" that lead to revolutionary action are, as Althusser argues, in excess of the "pure phenomena" of the constitutive contradiction between capital and labor, which in this ruptural unity, is both determined (at "various levels and instances") and determining (*For Marx* 100). This form of Marxist contradiction differs from Hegel's logical form, which is always internal to a totality; therefore, the complex determinations at play in Hegelian dialectics only appear to be overdetermined. If they are part and parcel of a synthetic totality (that is, if they have been overcome in the process of SUBLATION), then contradiction cannot be *over* with respect to what totalizes it. In Althusser's usage, overdetermination marks the effects of contradiction in social practice and between such practices and the SOCIAL FORMATION in which they take place; and it is "thinkable" once the "real existence of the forms of the superstructure of the national and international conjuncture has been recognized" (113). Thus, in Marx, *all* contradictions are overdetermined, and the question then turns on their *content* and their tendency, either toward "historical inhibition" or "revolutionary rupture" (106–7; see also 252–3). The HISTORICAL MATERIALISM on evidence in this reading of structural causality, as Étienne Balibar demonstrates, concerns the transformations of the forms taken by productive forces within "the structure of the mode of production." The various connections within this structure (e.g., between labor and the "elements of the mode of production") are *a history without a locatable subject*," because the "real subject of each component history [i.e., each connection or aspect of the structure of production] is the *combination* on which depend the elements and their relations, i.e., it is *something which is not a subject*" (Althusser and Balibar 279–80).

This understanding of contradiction and structural causality refocuses attention on articulation across social fields and suggests that the *reproduction* of social relations is just as important as the productive forces at the economic base. Ideology is central to reproduction both of the subject and of dominant social structures, which Althusser calls "ideological state apparatuses," into which "individuals are always-already interpellated by ideology as subjects." Ideology thus "'recruits' subjects among the individuals (it recruits them all), or 'transforms' the individuals into subjects (it transforms them all) by that very precise operation which I have called *interpellation* or hailing and which can be imagined along the lines of the most commonplace everyday police (or other) hailing: 'Hey, you there!'" (*Lenin* 174). This "imaginary misrecognition of the 'ego'" (219) is the first and foremost ideological function of the capitalist state. In this context, Lacan's influence is evident. For, as Lacan says, objectification is the "natural" state of ego development: "The structure of systematic misrecognition and objectification that characterizes ego formation" (*Écrits* 94; see also 123). Following Lacan, Althusser argues that false consciousness is an imaginary construction: "Ideology represents the imaginary relationship of individuals to their real conditions of existence" (*Lenin* 109). Althusser here refers to the Lacanian IMAGINARY, which corresponds to the pre-Oedipal phase of development when the individual has not yet experienced differentiation from the mother, a space of fantasy formations, of resistance to mimesis, reason, rationality, the entire order of the SYMBOLIC. According to Althusser, the "ideological formations that govern paternity, maternity, conjugality and childhood" (211) produce a double distortion of reality: they substitute for the REAL we cannot know and they disguise the real nature of social relations (i.e., the Symbolic order). The displaced real represents a *potential* for critique of and intervention into the Symbolic order of ideology.

Althusserian Marxism dominated the radical left in the 1960s and 1970s, but it did not go unchallenged. Alain Badiou, among others, took issue with Althusserian Marxism, preferring the Maoist approach that was gaining ground in French communist circles in the late 1960s. The revolutionary potential of *les Maoïstes* was put to the test in May 1968, when months of protest against the university system and the war in Vietnam culminated in an uprising of students and workers, which led to a general strike that immobilized France. Much of the intellectual activity surrounding these debates took place in or around the University of Paris VIII in Vincennes, which was established in 1969 in direct response to the student protests the previous year. Foucault was charged with building and then heading the philosophy department which became one of the centers of French post-Marxism after Althusser.

It is in this light that we might read the work of **Jacques Rancière**, a student of Althusser, who later criticized his mentor for his failure to revolutionize pedagogy in line with a truly emancipatory practice. His first book, written expressly as a reflection on May 1968 from the perspective of the "morning after," articulates his sense of disappointment: "A discourse that allows one to speak for others, that cancels out the place and subject of its own speech: such is the mechanism that has found its paradigmatic form in Althusserian discourse, founded as it is on the denial of the place from which it speaks, of what it speaks about, and of who it speaks to" (*Althusser's Lesson* 122). By the mid-1980s, Rancière was an outspoken critic of the educational policies of the French government under François Mitterrand, who sought to impose reforms on the university system that would reinforce, and thereby continue to reproduce, the class inequalities of the society at large. Over against the "stultification" and subordination that characterized conventional pedagogy, Rancière, in *The Ignorant Schoolmaster* (1987), proposed a practice by which educators assumed the equality of intelligence among all people rather than the hierarchical structure of knowledge that subordinates student to teacher. True emancipation comes only when traditional pedagogy is ruptured and the equality of intelligence becomes the presupposition rather than the aim of education. The theorist who does not challenge traditional pedagogical practices cannot help but remain within an institution that confirms and reproduces social inequality. Rather than *speak for* the people, the theorist needs to discover and celebrate the equality of intelligence and aesthetic feeling that is the birthright of all human beings (see, for example, Rancière's *The Nights of Labor*).

The movement away from a Marxism that paradoxically reinscribes the conditions of intellectual and material inequality is notable in Ernesto Laclau and Chantal Mouffe's *Hegemony and Socialist Strategy* (1985). Laclau and Mouffe take Gramsci's concept of hegemony as a starting point for a critique that reveals, behind the concept, something in excess of a "political relation *complementary* to the basic categories of Marxist theory." As Stuart Sim has noted, despite the advances of Gramsci and Althusser, combating the "purity of theory" – which "the spectre of *real* contingency kept at bay" – was the primary aim in the "elaboration of the concept of hegemony" (16–17). It is this specter that Laclau and Mouffe attempt to raise in their critique of hegemony and the "logic of the social" introduced by it. This logic is "incompatible" with Marxist categories in part because it is the logic of a "field of contingent operations," a field of activity and practice that cannot be adequately organized under a "category of 'historical necessity'" (3). Echoing Hardt and Negri, who also placed crisis and contingency at the forefront of critical analysis, Laclau and Mouffe seek a theory of hegemony responsive to contingency and critical of the tendency of bourgeois hegemony to ground itself on inauthentic totalities – that is to say, the particular and limited interests of a dominant group represented as the universal foundation for justice, morality, and politics. The "recomposition" of hegemony for "socialist political practice" requires that we "break with the view that democratic tasks are bonded to a bourgeois stage" of development. This form of "counter-hegemony would permit a true "articulation between socialism and democracy" (58). It is this possibility of articulation that, for Laclau and Mouffe, Gramsci failed to comprehend, for the working class needs "to transform its identity by articulating to it a plurality of struggles and democratic demands" (70).

This does not mean that hegemony is merely a "transitional" concept, for the incomplete "suturing" of hegemonic formations is intrinsic "to every political practice and, strictly speaking, every social practice." This is why Althusser's reliance on "an abstract universal object, the 'economy,' which produces concrete effects" will inevitably fail to account for the complex web of articulations and determinations in the social field (99). Neither "absolute fixity" or "absolute nonfixity" is possible in the social field (111), for articulation takes the form of partially fixed nodal points (or, in Lacan's language, POINTS DE CAPITON, literally "quilting points"), around which signification CONSTELLATES. These points, which can crop up anywhere or at any time, are by their nature partial, for they are determined by the "openness of the social" within an infinite "field of discursivity" (113). Antagonism, particularly between classes but also within them, emerges as a "witness of the impossibility of a final suture," and it has a curiously external relation to the social field, which cannot constitute itself as a totality precisely because of the limits imposed by that antagonism. "Society never manages fully to be society, because everything in it is penetrated by its limits" (127). If counter-hegemony is to be made available as a social strategy, it must not only recognize the discursivity of the field of articulations but also the inevitability of antagonisms – not in the sense that they become the pretense for reform and management of capitalist modes of production (as in classic crisis theory), but in the sense that they remain unfixed and contingent, as the grounds for a strategy that opposes capital. The aim of radical politics is a form of *counter*-hegemony that exploits the inherent instability of every hegemonic position, of recognizing that society is necessarily constituted by "social division and antagonism" and that contingency and disorder can only be partially "fixed" (193).

As we have seen, discourse is vital for hegemonic projects, a point made from a different standpoint by **Jean Baudrillard**, whose early work explores the implications of reification for a theory of production and *re*production of signifying systems. Charles Levin, in an attempt to distinguish Baudrillard from structuralist Marxists like Althusser, describes the former's project as a "phenomenology of reification," of consumption itself, one whose horizon is the limit of capitalist codes of discourse production (11). Baudrillard argues in *The Consumer Society* (1970) that consumption is itself a kind of labor and that "the general climatization of life [and] of social relations represents the perfected, 'consummated' stage of evolution," which moves from abundance to total social condition and finally to the "systematic organization of ambience, which is characteristic of the drugstores, shopping malls, modern airports in our futuristic cities" (*Selected* 36). The "contemporary profusion of sign objects" signal a new mode of consumption that effectively hides the "the *total constraint of the code* that governs social value" (*Critique* 65–6). We forget that our lives are governed by the exchange of signs that replicate the exchange of commodities; indeed, signs become the most durable of commodities. To comprehend this new function of signs we require "a theory of the ideological concept of need," which, Baudrillard argues, is no longer bound up with the "chimerical dialectic of being and appearance" (79–80). The object of need and the subject who needs are confounded in a system of signs in which both terms circulate freely and are distributed across vast discourse formations. Capitalist "mobilization of needs" leads to "controlled desublimation," which entails "the deconstruction of the *ego* functions," and the "'liberation' of the id and the super-ego as factors of integration, participation and consumption" (85). The "pleasure principle" that for Freud must be moderated by the "reality principle" becomes, in the consumer society theorized by Baudrillard, a mechanism of social control and planning. This vision of society (seconded by **Jean-François Lyotard** and Guy Debord and others in the *Socialisme ou Barbarie* group in the 1960s) requires a new analysis of production, one sensitive to the way social relations and needs become determined by the circulation and exchange of signs.

Baudrillard's analysis of an "unconscious social logic that must be retrieved beneath the consecrated ideology of consumption" (*Critique* 63) is echoed in the work of **Fredric Jameson**, whose orientation was both postmodernist and post-Marxist. For Jameson, the analysis of class struggle and the problems of commodity production, which was well suited to the era of industrial capitalism and the initial formation of modern classes, does not adequately account for the way ideology determines social relations in a postmodernist era of "late capitalism." In postmodernity, the "rhetoric of the market" has become the site of radical struggle, the "struggle for the legitimation or delegitimation of left discourse" (*Postmodernism* 263). In part this is due to the market serving, in the place of the state or a class formation, as a "model of social totality." Unfortunately, "market ideology" not only instills a "profound disillusionment with political praxis," it also makes socialism impossible because, by its very nature, markets ensure all too effectively the suppression of human freedom (272–4). As a "displacement from production to circulation," this model offers the advantage of providing – through the fusion of two social codes, the media and the market – a new order of representation, which Jameson associates with the media "in its largest contemporary and global sense." The identification of the commodity with its image signals the erosion of social relations in a physical marketplace, and this abstraction leads ultimately to an "indifferentiation of levels" (between thing and concept, economics and culture, base and superstructure) (275). Everything becomes a sign in circulation, available for consumption, a process that blurs the line between production and consumption to the point of radical indifferentiation and threatens the systems of articulation that for Negri, Hardt, Laclau, and Mouffe enable effective social practice.

This crisis in Marxist theory is the starting point for Hardt and Negri's controversial rereading of our current global environment, in which capital expands on its ability to diversify production and reproduction through the technologies of marketing, management, and organization. For Hardt and Negri, these technologies are used to understand the "constant process of hierarchization" in "the contemporary realization of the world market" (*Empire* 152, 154). Marxist theory needs to rethink not only the structure and impact of global capital but also the nation-states that, in the imperial era, defined globalization in terms of interstate antagonisms. Poststructuralist and postmodernist thought can be of use in this renovation of radical critique. For example, Hardt and Negri argue that the theory of "biopower" put forward by Foucault prepares "the terrain for … an investigation of the material functioning of imperial rule" (*Empire* 22). It allows us to rethink global capital as a form of virtual totality in which "the whole social body is comprised by power's machine" (24). The shift from the era of imperialism to that of Empire constitutes a passage from an era of discipline to one of control, which means that theory must move away from an emphasis on "unidimensional" processes (i.e., on economic or cultural aspects of society) and focus on the "social *bios*" (25). Gilles Deleuze and Félix Guattari offer a more radical reading of biopower. In their view, the social relations of all kinds are at bottom the function of "desiring machines," sites of anti-production, that function only when they are "broken." At the beginning of *Anti-Oedipus*, they write, "what a mistake to have ever said *the* id. Everywhere *it* is machines – real ones, not figurative ones: machines driving other machines, machines being driven by other machines, with all the necessary couplings and connections" (1). If desire is decoupled from the subject (or the *ego* which exists in part to keep the *id* at bay), it is free to play along the surface of the body (both the human body and the social body), which they redefine as a "body without organs" that "presents its smooth, slippery, opaque, taut surface as a barrier" (9). For example, capital is "the body without organs of the capitalist," and it is here, on this sterile site, that surplus-value is produced (10–11). This body without organs "couples production with antiproduction" – it is in fact "produced as antiproduction" (9, 16). Deleuze and Guattari point out that there is no clear distinction between "the social production of reality" and a "desiring-production that is mere fantasy" (30). The parallelism between the "capitalist triangle" (capitalist control over the modes of production, the worker, profits) and the "Oedipal triangle" ("father–mother–me" [385]) is a sterile and ultimately abstract distinction. For, the "truth of the mater is that *social production is purely and simply desiring production itself under determinate conditions*." That is to say, the "social field" is a "historically determined product of desire" (31), whether that desire be "irrational" or entirely within the precincts of instrumental reason. Desire, they imply, is simply desire, and it circulates in varying intensities throughout the social field, constituting it as a fluid and contingent totality.

Hardt and Negri grant the utility of this view of desire and the social body but ultimately find the "radical ONTOLOGY" behind it to be superficial and ephemeral, "a chaotic, indeterminate horizon marked by the ungraspable event" (*Empire* 28). Their own analysis moves beyond this starting point by focusing on "the ontology of production," specifically on how social production is mapped on imperial, colonial, and postcolonial spaces, following the outlines not of "ideal forms," but of the "dense complex of experience" (30). Thus they examine imperialism in terms of its legitimation by communication industries and regard Empire as a vast and virtual "high tech machine ... built to control the marginal event" and to intervene at times of crisis (33, 39). By seeing the imperial "body" in this way, Hardt and Negri hope to avoid the abstract formulations they find in Deleuze and Guattari and to grasp the "figure of immaterial labor power" that drives media and communications and includes "affective labor" (e.g., health services) (53, 292–3). Biopower, therefore, is less concerned with coercive or repressive mechanisms of social control than with systems of classification and regulation that produce increasingly smaller and isolated categories of social subjects. In such a context, the intensity of experience compensates for "incommunicability" (i.e., social struggle is often isolated or of short duration). We find this incommunicability in many modern social struggles – e.g., Tiananmen Square in 1989, the Gulf wars, the uprisings in Tunisia, Egypt, and Syria – with the result that contradiction and crisis are revealed as the norm in a post-Cold War and postcolonial global environment.

This perspective enables Hardt and Negri to investigate the vexed problem of nationalism and sovereignty. The problem with the nation-state is that, once it is expanded into an imperial domain, it suffers a split: internally, it speaks of the "purity of the people," but externally, "the nation-state is a machine that produces Others, creates racial difference, and raises boundaries that delimit and support the modern subject of sovereignty" (114). Imperial sovereignty in fact turns out to signal the end of colonialism and the movement away from the "paradigm of modern sovereignty" (137). And while postmodernist and postcolonial theory can help us understand the mechanisms by which otherness is produced – and it must be borne in mind that this form of production entails slavery as a *mode of production* – they remain fixated on old forms of power and liberation (145–6). The dialectic of inside/outside, of power understood as belonging *by right* to a sovereign (inside) who dominates those without it (outside), is "replaced by a play of degrees and intensities, of hybridity and artificiality" (187–8). In postmodernity, industry gives way to other forms of production (informatics, service, management, consulting, and so on), which leads to new segmentations of both labor and productive forces that further the decentralization and deregulation of transnational capital and further fragment the social body, making imperial administration more complex and inscrutable and resistance harder and harder to consolidate. In a sense, because "Empire is defined by crisis," its decline "has always already begun, and that consequently every line of antagonism leads toward the event and singularity" – that is to say, antagonisms take the form of a matrix of differences and ruptures rather than an isolated part of a totality managed by the techniques of equilibrium. The crises of transnational capital are precisely "immanent to and indistinguishable from Empire" (386).

Liberalism and totalitarianism equally founder in this world of virtual spaces and information, and only a critical focus attuned to the dynamics of biopower can harness intensities and flows of POWER/KNOWLEDGE (to use Foucault's term for the conjunction of discourse and domination) for radical social action. In the new regimes of production (characterized by decentralized transnational capital, affective and immaterial labor, new forms of surplus-labor, and new means of extracting value), the goal is not to overthrow a world driven by market forces, but to deterritorialize it, to move within it and against it, to push at its limits. "Globalization must be met with a counter-globalization, Empire with a counter-Empire" (207). The modes of social action and change associated with an era of industrial capitalism (i.e., *sabotage*, resistance within the productive force) give way to *desertion* and *nomadism*, to resistance on the borders of different forces and in the spaces constituted by their singular imbrications (212).

Deleuze, Guattari, Hardt, and Negri all provide powerful responses to the questions raised by globalization and transnationalism. A quite different response comes from Immanuel Wallerstein, whose world-systems approach to history uses Marxian concepts and a materialist methodology in combination with the French historian Ferdinand Braudel's concept of the *longue durée* (the "long view") to analyze the "long sixteenth century" (ca. 1450–1640). "The new historical materialism embodied in the world system approach," writes Barry Gills, looks at "the history of capital accumulation" throughout the premodern world economy. Wallerstein's historical method is not a materialist science (as it might be for Marxists like Georgi Plekhanov or Althusser), but a discipline on the pathway toward science. "Modern history, history as written in the nineteenth and twentieth centuries," Wallerstein argues, "was the child of this scientific passion. History, *wie es eigentlich gewesen ist* ["to show what actually happened" (Otto Rank)], refused to accept revealed truth, speculation, fiction – that is, magic – as meaningful categories of reality. They were illusions. Thus it is that, for two centuries at least, history has been in search of science" (*Uncertainties* 111). Wallerstein's position makes historiography credible for a Marxist analysis by granting its aspiration for scientific validity at the same time that it insists on what are, properly speaking, speculative modes of validation, since the real world outside, which "is not a fantasy of our mind," is only "*partially* knowable empirically"; at best, we can "summarize this knowledge in heuristic theorizing" (13). In the twenty-first century, we find ourselves at a "critical juncture of our contemporary world system," and the course of action is not to abandon the pursuit of science in history, but to decouple scientific analysis from an oppressive scientific method: "The question is whether we can offer scientific analyses that are not scientistic about the historical choices before us" (14–15).

World-systems theorists have been criticized, as Wallerstein notes, for misunderstanding the "core–peripheral axis of the division of labor" and for privileging a "circulationist" (i.e., concerned with superstructure) over a "productionist" (i.e., concerned with base) explanation of class struggle (*World* 20). As in post-Marxism generally, we find here a breaking down of boundaries between society and the productive forces native to it, between "so-called culture" at the level of the superstructure and the material forces of the base. Taking the world system as the "unit of analysis" – "something other than the modern nation-state" – enables Wallerstein's understanding of a global division of labor defined, though not exclusively, by core–periphery relations of power. If we understand the world system as a "structural TimeSpace," one in which the historical system has a kind of organic life and death, we can see more clearly the "linked compounds" that structure historical development on a world scale and "remain the same over time yet are never the same from one minute to the next" (*World* 22).

Wallerstein's world-systems approach, which aspires to scientific validity even as it embraces "heuristic theorizing," reminds us of the fundamental contradictions and fissures in Marxist theory, which **Jacques Derrida** has described as an "interminable self-critique." The deconstructive "spirit of Marxism" can be interpreted in two ways: on the one hand, it will have "to remain indefinitely necessary in order to denounce and reduce the gap *as much as possible*, in order to adjust 'reality' to the 'ideal' in the course of a necessarily infinite process"; on the other hand, it can be employed in a new round of questioning of "the very concept of the said ideal" (86–7). If, as Derrida believes, deconstruction is the preeminent form of post-Marxist critique, radical philosophy becomes crucial to uncovering the "truth" of such concepts as equality and emancipation. According to Alain Badiou, the philosopher's task, broadly speaking, is to clarify "fundamental choices of thought" and "the value of exception, of the event, and of rupture" (*Polemics* 8). If concepts like equality and emancipation are measured by the capacity to be human, it follows that they are a function of thought (the capacity specific to being human). And if thought is nothing less than the space in which truth marks its passing, then equality is a goal of truth, but it is not an *objective* goal. "Equality is subjective," Badiou argues; it is not "an objective for action" but rather "an axiom of action" (*Infinite* 71–2). Justice emerges when philosophy "seizes" the axiom in a given "political sequence," so that it ceases to be an "Idea" and becomes part of a *situation* of thought, subjectivized and singular, that points not to a "category of state or social order," but to "rupture and disorder." Categories like "justice" must be aligned not with ideals but with singular statements. Indeed, political statements "bearing truth" arise precisely because of the *lack* of order in the state (and the State) that the "true" maxim exposes (74). Philosophy is, at bottom, not a true discourse, but one that facilitates the truths of politics (as it does of science, art, and love). Its imperative is "to seize the event of truths, their newness, and their precarious trajectory" but to seize too, perhaps entirely, "extreme moments of inconsistency" (75, 77). (On Badiou, see Posthumanism 274–6.)

"All too Kantian," is Žižek's verdict of Badiou's theory of the miraculous event, which "disturbs the finite life of the human animal" (825–6), by which I think he means that Badiou's conception of the event – a space in which truths reveal themselves in the "subtraction" of elements that alone constitutes the site of a true situation – is, at bottom, a new theory of the "thing in itself." We glimpse something of this in Badiou's aesthetics. Aesthetic truths, like those in other realms, are subject to this *evental* logic. The work of art emerges within a specific artistic configuration that founds the events possible within it. "Works compose a truth within the post-evental dimension that institutes the *constraint of an artistic configuration*." The configuration is "not an art form, a genre, or an 'objective' period in the history of art, nor is it a 'technical' *dispositif*. Rather it is an identifiable sequence, initiated by an event, comprising a virtually infinite complex of works" (*Inaesthetics* 12–13). In the aesthetic event the trope of *subtraction* constitutes the community of the "multiple" on the basis of its theoretical impossibility: that is, those elements which belong to the multiple but are not presented in it. Rancière, echoing Žižek, sees Badiou's aesthetics as "Platonic in the modern manner," for the "Idea's Platonic eternity transpire[s] within a radicalized notion of anti-*mimesis*" (Rancière, *Aesthetics* 71). In a sense, this means that Badiou's aesthetics remains caught up in an idealist aesthetic regime even as it registers its discontent with it. This discontent has fueled an anti-aesthetic trend that runs from Friedrich Schiller to Nietzsche and Wilde and then to Adorno, one that is concerned primarily with the "discordant relation" that aesthetics itself puts into play by breaking up the classic "order of fine arts." This order had once mediated *poeisis* and *aisthesis* (making and sensing) through *mimesis* (resemblance, imitation). When *mimesis* performs its "legislative" function, art emerges in a "representative regime." In the aesthetic regime, by contrast, this function is suspended and *poiesis* and *aisthesis* "stand in immediate relation to each other." Thus aesthetics emerges not as a "discipline" – though from the time of Kant it has been a key component of philosophy – but as the designation of "a specific regime for the identification of art" (*Aesthetics* 8). Aesthetic discontent is therefore at the heart of the Kantian aesthetic regime, which no longer grants to *mimesis* its legislative function.

By the modernist era, this discontent and disorder had become the chief characteristics of art. According to Rancière, the modernists wanted to hold on to the power of identification belonging to the aesthetic regime, but also wanted to disavow the products of that identification, that is, the disordered forms of *disidentification*. Modernist anti-aesthetics thus becomes a perverse attempt through the mode of identification (aesthetics as anti-aesthetics) to keep disorder in place. As a result of the identification of art with what it is not, the sensible quality of the artwork is invested with the abstract quality of its negation. The arts become increasingly specified, as the forms of disidentification take on the sensible contours of the materials they use; indeed, material becomes all important as the expression of art's specificity (e.g., words on the page, fragments of newsprint in a collage, found objects in sculpture, field recordings and other random sounds in music), which points to a particular order within the aesthetic field. The identity of art with its complete *dis*identification, of art with *non-art*, leads ultimately, in postmodernism, to the defensive torquing of this anti-aesthetic in its "unremitting" attempt "to exorcize from 'its' version of the 'specificity of art' that aesthetic regime of art which brings art into being, but only at the price of disappropriating it" (Rancière, *Aesthetics* 68–9). In some cases, as in Badiou's *Inaesthetics*, this "torsion" grounds the disappearance of the Idea of art, an incomplete ground that is also a founding power, a strife (to use Heidegger's term) that becomes the situation of the aesthetic event.

As Rancière suggests, contemporary post-Marxist aesthetics is characterized by a paradoxical investment in idealist philosophy, particularly Plato's *Republic* and *Protagoras*, which deal with the ideal state and the corruptive power of language (specifically "sophistic" rhetoric) when used mimetically. The injunction in the *Republic* against the imitative capacity of poetry, according to Badiou and Rancière, is levied in order to maintain order in the *polis*. Language creates excitement and disorder, and these need to be controlled. Badiou feels the problem goes deeper than *mimesis*, for it points to the cancellation of thought and the "unnamable" site of its opening up (*Inaesthetics* 26). He reads Plato through the lens of Stéphane Mallarmé's modernism which, like Beckett's postmodernism, enables a philosophical meditation on artistic truth, on an event that takes place or "comes to pass" in a moment of "dissemblance" in which *truth* emerges out of the absolute negation of itself by the logical and ontological possibility of *non-truth*. The poem is "a nonthought that presents itself via the linguistic power of a thought"; it is "the opposite of mimesis" (*Inaesthetics* 18, 21), so it is divorced from an aesthetic regime in which imitation reproduces relations of power in the realm of the sensible (that of history, as Badiou understands it). Like every other truth, an aesthetic truth is a power, manifested as "the song of language" in its capacity to present "the pure notion of the 'there is' (*il y a*) at the same moment that its 'empirical objectivity'" is effaced (22). The poem is thus "an unthinkable thought," a mode of saying that is a silence, and is categorically different from mathematics, which is "a thought that is immediately written as thought" (19). (On aesthetics, see chapter one, "The Rise of Literary Theory" 12–24, Marxist Theory, 89–90 and Postmodernism 128–34.)

The primordial antagonism between the sensible and the spiritual, the purity of thought and the materiality of *not*-thought, is a founding rupture or, conversely, a suture, the point at which mimetic desire is fulfilled by a discourse that redistributes the sensible, placing both the artwork and the subject (as objects) in a newly conceived material space. Badiou's *inaesthetics* replicates the anti-aestheticism of the modernists precisely by installing the disorder and "disidentification" that are the negative essence of modernism's will to formalize as the foundation of the aesthetic regime (Rancière, *Aesthetics* 67ff). Rancière distinguishes between this reinstatement of modernism's anti-aesthetics, which includes Lyotard's theory of the sublime, and a "relational aesthetics," which entails the "despecification" of the different arts and their distribution in space. However different from each other these relational approaches might appear, they converge when they assign to art the same *communitarian* function: "that of constructing a specific world space, a new form of dividing up the common world," a new form of politics devoted to the "distribution of the sensible," which Rancière describes as "the system of self-evident facts of sense perception that simultaneously discloses the existence of something in common and the delimitations that define the respective parts and positions within it." We find in politics as in aesthetics "a distribution of spaces, times and forms of activity that determines the very manner in which something in common lends itself to participation and in what way various individuals have a part in this distribution" (*Politics* 12). In the aesthetic regime, we find the distribution of the sensible and the *in*sensible Idea, which is marked in the sublime as the "passing" of the Idea into the sensible matter of art, of art into *non-art*. In relational aesthetics, on the other hand, the artwork is *always already* latent in every conceivable sensible object, leaving only the installation of a specific set of relations (between artist and material, between both and the space of the work, between all these elements and the spectator, curator, dealer, and so on) to make manifest what is established theoretically: that the specificity of art, its distance from other spheres, is bound up with its purchase on the materiality of what is common, general, generic – in a word *not art*. A sublime aesthetics leans toward Plato and Kant and invests the sensible world with the potential for transcendence; a relational aesthetics (e.g., Deleuze's) leans toward Aristotle and Spinoza, and sees the potential to reform a dynamic whole that has been dispersed. It is responsible, Rancière argues, for the functions of archiving and bearing witness to a common world" and for restoring lost meaning to that world and repairing "the cracks in the social bond" (*Dissensus* 122).

What Badiou and the curators and galleries at the heart of the relational school fail to pursue is the full value of *dissensus*, "the rupture of a certain agreement between thought and the sensible." Rancière has located this dissensus at the core not only of "aesthetic agreement and repose" but of our common sense as well, which no longer tolerates the "everlastingness of a human subject rent in two," but rather moves toward "the restoration of its integrity" (*Dissensus* 98–100). The principle of dissensus is at the heart of politics: it "is not a confrontation between interests or opinions," but the manifestation of a "gap in the sensible" (38). In Rancière's view, common sense – that which constitutes the sense of the common – creates a community of "political subjects" with the "capacity for staging scenes of dissensus" (69). The emancipation sought here is not founded on the Habermasian model of communicative action, which presupposes equal partners and an "explicable" discourse community (38–9). The goal of politics lies not in a proper discourse, but in the struggle for the right to speak, that is to say, for the "equality of intelligence" (*Emancipated* 10). In Rancière's formulation, post-Marxist theory is part of a contemporary effort to overcome the administered society critiqued by the Frankfurt School and the hegemonic formations that were the target of theorists from Gramsci to Jameson. In the undifferentiated theoretical field envisioned by thinkers like Rancière and Hardt and Negri, a materialist critique about society and the social function of art might seem like an impossible task, since in this field the "material" would be ontologically identical with the "non-material." The task of theory becomes one with the task of material practice, for both are equally bound up with the new modes of domination, of discursive power and commodification. Post-Marxism in the twenty-first century illustrates the complex articulations – in aesthetics, politics, and pedagogy – through which emancipation from domination is now thought. It confronts a new world, but one whose contradictions and crises are more readily recognized as constitutive of the very freedom they would seem to disallow.

Note

On Jameson's critique of postmodern art and society, see Postmodernism; on globalization, see Transnationalism; on Foucault, see Poststructuralism; on Lyotard, Deleuze, and Guattari, see Postmodernism.

Works Cited

Adamson, Walter L. *Hegemony and Revolution: A Study of Antonio Gramsci's Political and Cultural Theory*. Berkeley: University of California Press, 1980.

Adorno, Theodor. *Minima Moralia: Reflections from Damaged Life*. 1951. Trans. E. F. N. Jephcott. London: Verso, 1974.

Althusser, Louis. *For Marx*. Trans. Ben Brewster. New York: Pantheon, 1969.

Althusser, Louis. *Lenin and Philosophy, and Other Essays*. 1971. Trans. Ben Brewster. New York: Monthly Review Press, 2001.

Althusser, Louis and Étienne Balibar. *Reading "Capital."* Trans. Ben Brewster. 1968. London: NLB, 1970.

Anderson, Perry. *Considerations on Western Marxism*. London: New Left Books, 1976.

Badiou, Alain. *Handbook of Inaesthetics*. Trans. Alberto Toscano. Stanford: Stanford University Press, 2005.

Badiou, Alain. *Infinite Thought: Truth and the Return to Philosophy*. Ed. and trans. Oliver Feltham and Justin Clemens. London: Continuum, 2003.

Badiou, Alain. *Polemics*. Trans. Steve Corcoran. London and New York: Verso, 2006.

Baudrillard, Jean. *For a Critique of the Political Economy of the Sign*. Trans. Charles Levin. St. Louis: Telos Press, 1981.

Baudrillard, Jean. *Selected Writings*. Ed. Mark Poster. 1988. 2nd ed. Cambridge: Polity, 2001.

Butler, Judith, Ernesto Laclau, and Slavoj Žižek. *Contingency, Hegemony, Universality: Contemporary Dialogues on the Left*. London: Verso, 2000.

Deleuze, Gilles and Félix Guattari. *Anti-Oedipus: Capitalism and Schizophrenia*. 1977. Trans. Robert Hurley, Mark Seem, and Helen R. Lane. Minneapolis: University of Minnesota Press, 1983.

Derrida, Jacques. *Specters of Marx: The State of the Debt, the Work of Mourning and the New International*. New York: Routledge, 1993.

Eagleton, Terry. *Heathcliff and the Great Hunger: Studies in Irish Culture*. London: Verso, 1995.

Ferretter, Luke. *Louis Althusser*. London: Routledge, 2006.

Gills, Barry K. "Capital and Power in the Processes of World History." In *Civilizations and World Systems: Studying World-Historical Change*. Ed. Stephen K. Sanderson. Walnut Creek: Altamira Press, 1995. 136–62.

Gramsci, Antonio. *Selections from the Prison Notebooks of Antonio Gramsci*. Ed. and trans. Quintin Hoare and Geoffrey Nowell Smith. New York: International Publishers, 1971.

Hardt, Michael and Antonio Negri. *Empire*. Cambridge, MA: Harvard University Press, 2000.

Hardt, Michael and Antonio Negri. *Labor of Dionysus: A Critique of the state-Form*. Minneapolis: University of Minnesota Press, 1994.

Jameson, Fredric. *The Political Unconscious: Narrative as a Socially Symbolic Act*. Ithaca: Cornell University Press, 1981.

Jameson, Fredric. *Postmodernism, or, The Cultural Logic of Late Capitalism*. Durham, NC: Duke University Press, 1991.

Jay, Martin. *Marxism and Totality: The Adventures of a Concept from Lukács to Habermas*. Berkeley: University of California Press, 1984.

Lacan, Jacques. *Écrits: A Selection*. Trans. Bruce Fink. New York: Norton, 2002.

Laclau, Ernesto and Chantal Mouffe. *Hegemony and Socialist Strategy: Towards a Radical Democratic Politics*. London: Verso, 1985, 2001.

Levin, Charles. "Introduction." *For a Critique of the Political Economy of the Sign*. By Jean Baudrillard. Trans. Charles Levin. St. Louis: Telos Press, 1981. 5–28.

Lukács, Georg. *History and Class Consciousness: Studies in Marxist Dialectics*. 1923. Trans. Rodney Livingstone. Cambridge, MA: MIT Press, 1983.

Marx, Karl. *A Contribution to the Critique of Political Economy*. Ed. Maurice Dobb. Trans. S. W. Ryazanskaya. 1859. New York: International Publishers, 1970.

Marx, Karl and Fredrick Engels. *The Marx–Engels Reader*. Ed. Robert C. Tucker. 2nd ed. New York: Norton, 1978.

Mercer, Colin. "After Gramsci." In *Antonio Gramsci: Critical Assessments of Leading Political Philosophers*. Ed. James Martin. London: Routledge, 2002. 310–23.

Negri, Antonio. *Marx Beyond Marx: Lessons on the Grundrisse*. 1979. Ed. Jim Fleming. Trans. Harry Cleaver, Michael Ryan, and Maurizio Vianno. South Hadley: Bergin and Garvey, 1984.

Rancière, Jacques. *Aesthetics and Its Discontents*. Trans. Steven Corcoran. Cambridge: Polity, 2009.

Rancière, Jacques. *Althusser's Lesson*. Trans. Emiliano Battista. London: Continuum, 2011.

Rancière, Jacques. *Dissensus: On Politics and Aesthetics*. Ed. and trans. Steven Corcoran. London: Continuum, 2010.

Rancière, Jacques. *The Emancipated Spectator*. 2008. Trans. Gregory Elliott. London: Verso, 2010.

Rancière, Jacques. *The Politics of Aesthetics: The Distribution of the Sensible*. Trans. Gabriel Rockhill. London: Continuum, 2004.

Ryan, Michael. "Epilogue." In Antonio Negri, *Marx Beyond Marx: Lessons on the Grundrisse.* Ed. Jim Fleming. Trans. Harry Cleaver, Michael Ryan, and Maurizio Vianno. South Hadley: Bergin and Garvey, 1984. 191–221.

Sim, Stuart. *Post-Marxism: An Intellectual History.* New York: Routledge, 2000.

Therborn, Göran. *From Marxism to Post-Marxism?* London: Verso, 2008.

Wallerstein, Immanuel. *The Uncertainties of Knowledge.* Philadelphia: Temple University Press, 2004.

Wallerstein, Immanuel. *World Systems Analysis: An Introduction.* Durham, NC: Duke University Press, 2004.

Williams, Raymond. *Marxism and Literature.* Oxford: Oxford University Press, 1977.

Žižek, Slavoj. *Less Than Nothing: Hegel and the Shadow of Dialectical Materialism.* London: Verso, 2012.

New Historicism/Cultural Poetics

New Historicism, which flourished in the 1980s and early 1990s, was part of a general tendency toward historical approaches to criticism. The key figures in the movement are grounded in the Marxist tradition of social theory and draw on the critical historiography that begins with Georg Lukács and extends into the post-Marxist era. But they reject orthodox dialectical materialism because it either misses or dialectically SUBLATES the contingent and unpredictable aspects of culture, that which, for the New Historicists, determines the contexts in which literary texts are produced and read. H. Aram Veeser has compiled a list of five key assumptions underlying it: (1) "every expressive act is embedded in a network of material practices"; (2) every critique inevitably "uses the tools it condemns and risks falling prey to the practice it exposes"; (3) literary and non-literary texts "circulate inseparably"; (4) no discourse "gives access to unchanging truths" nor "expresses inalterable human nature"; and (5) critical methods under capitalism "participate in the economy they describe" (xi).

This historically inflected mode of reading, strongly influenced by poststructuralist theories of language and TEXTUALITY, makes possible a form of "cultural poetics" that strives for the "thick description" described by the anthropologist Clifford Geertz. For Geertz, culture is a complex formation of intersecting discourses and practices that require an ethnographic imagination that can move beyond the Eurocentric and quasi-scientific assumptions of traditional anthropology. As an "interpretive science," ethnography ought not to rest on the distinction between description and evaluation but rather on the distinction between thick description (a mode of inscription) and diagnosis (a mode of specification) – a distinction, in other words, "between setting down the meaning particular social actions have for the actors whose actions they are, and stating, as explicitly as we can manage, what the knowledge thus attained demonstrates about the society in which it is found and, beyond that, about social life as such" (27). Geertz's semiotic approach to culture, which attempts to read the enigmatic surface of "social expressions" (5), provided New Historicists with a methodology that combines empirical observation with textual interpretation. Even when no direct debt appears to be owed to Geertz's methodology, the general framework of interpretation (an inscription followed by a diagnosis) corresponds to what we find in most New Historicist writing.

For the New Historicist, history is an unstable, largely textual, ideologically riven and contested space; it is not the causal, chronological trajectory through "empty, homogeneous time" that, for **Walter Benjamin**, constitutes conventional historical narrative (395). Nor can the New Historian rest assured that the source documents used in historical analysis tell the truth about the past in a way that can substantiate and legitimize the narratives we create to explain the past. This skepticism about history and historical truth is rooted in Friedrich Nietzsche's critique of history. In "On the Uses and Disadvantages of History for Life" (1878), Nietzsche rejects two dominant modes of historiography, the antiquarian and the monumental, and calls for a new kind of *critical* historian: one who has the strength "to break up and dissolve a part of the past" by bringing it to the bar of judgment, where it is "scrupulously examined" before being condemned. Interpretation must grasp this double moment of judgment and condemnation if it is to come close to the meaning of the past and its importance for the life in the present, "that dark, driving power that insatiably thirsts for itself" (75–6). In his later work, Nietzsche developed a theory of GENEALOGY that traces the progress of human values as they are interpreted and reinterpreted in different contexts and with different aims: "the whole history of a thing, an organ, a custom, becomes a continuous *chain* of reinterpretations and rearrangements, which need not be causally connected among themselves, which may simply follow one another" (*Genealogy* 210). The genealogical challenge to the dominant modes of moral philosophy created the conditions for a "transvaluation" of values and valuation. Nietzsche's critique of morality in *Genealogy of Morals* shows decisively that moral values are not the effect or manifestation of timeless, transcendent ideas but the products of specific *human* practices at specific times. Far from reassuring us about our relation to the past, genealogy marks the points of rupture in convention and tradition, nodal points in history of power and domination. Nietzsche shows that a morality "beyond good and evil" was the result of a decisive cultural shift in how we value human actions: an archaic distinction between *good* and *bad* was overturned and redefined when the resentment of the bad devalues the noble good and the bad itself becomes the good, and *evil* is installed as a new target of resentment. The priest of this "slave morality" stands in opposition to the philosopher who strives to pierce the veil of mythology that hangs over this all-too-human spectacle of domination and submission. The idea that the history of values progresses predictably through causation of some kind (transcendent "prime mover" or immanent "inner core") is exploded in a genealogy that reveals not progress but rupture and setback, not predictability but inconsistency and delay. The genealogist explores these events not in order to uncover the truth of history but rather to show that truth (of any kind, but certainly of history) has a history of its own, bound up with human needs and desires.

Michel Foucault's elaboration of Nietzschean genealogy has had a tremendous influence on the New Historicism. In his reading of Nietzsche, Foucault argues that genealogy is a fundamentally interpretive attitude toward the past. It does not "pretend to go back in time to restore an unbroken continuity that operates beyond the dispersal of forgotten things" ("Nietzsche" 146). He therefore seeks something other than the melancholy "angel of history," that for Benjamin serves as the allegory of our own "*weak* messianic power … on which the past has a claim" and which forms a "secret agreement between past generations and the present" (390). Nor in Foucault's view does genealogy "resemble the evolution of a species" or "map the destiny of a people" ("Nietzsche" 146). The historian must be a kind of archaeologist in order to comprehend the spatial dimension of time, which lies outside the framework of a temporal sequence projected backward by the historian. Of particular importance is his analytical method, which abandons conventional ideas about historical sequence, diachronic consistency, causality, and origin. A good example of the ARCHAEOLOGICAL method is *Discipline and Punish* (1975), which describes relations of POWER/KNOWLEDGE and how they shape human experience through the creation of values and the forms of discipline that regulate them. Foucault shows how those that mete out punishment are in the service of power, in its instrumental sense, not timeless religious beliefs or philosophical ideas. In other words, discipline "produces subjected and practised bodies, 'docile' bodies." It "dissociates power from the body" by turning it into an "'aptitude,' a 'capacity,' which it seeks to increase" and by "revers[ing] the course of the energy, the power, that might result from it, and turn[ing] it into a relation of strict subjection" (*Discipline* 138). The "political autonomy" that arises from the invention of discipline leads to ever more refined technologies of punishment that are nothing more than the expression of the will to power. In the context of a "history" of punishment, a particular historical instance of it is not a stable phenomenon that can be verified by documentary evidence; nor is it the result of purposeful human action. It is instead a sign of domination, "the reversal of a relationship of forces, the usurpation of power, the appropriation of a vocabulary turned against those who had once used it, a feeble domination that poisons itself as it grows lax, the entry of a masked 'other'" ("Nietzsche" 154).

The New Historicism that evolved in the 1980s, using Foucauldian techniques and concepts, was less a form of historiography than a "hermeneutics of culture." **Stephen Greenblatt**, Louis Montrose, and Catherine Gallagher were early practitioners and their work points toward a historical critique of representation, one that takes into consideration the context of literary works as fundamental to their interpretation. Greenblatt's *Renaissance Self-Fashioning* (1980) provided a template for the New Historicist method. He argues that the mode of identity formation in Shakespeare's time was intimately bound up with the cultural texts of the era and that opportunities for "self-fashioning" were constrained or delimited (e.g., rules for the courtier), but also open to the kind of semiotic play that poststructuralism had identified with the very power of language and that made possible a deeper historical understanding of race, class, ethnicity, religion, and sexuality. Greenblatt is interested in identifying cultural "control mechanisms" (here, he draws on Geertz) in Renaissance texts, "the cultural system of meanings that creates specific individuals by governing the passage from abstract potential to concrete historical embodiment" (*Self-Fashioning* 3–4). His "poetics of culture" – as much a form of anthropological criticism as of historiography – performs the genealogical task of throwing into relief the multiple social contexts in which the self (the historical subject, the reader, the author) undergoes a transformation. New Historicist analysis allows us to experience texts in an entirely new way, for when a text "reaches us powerfully, we feel at once pulled out of our own world and plunged back with redoubled force into it" (Gallagher and Greenblatt 17).

Understood in this way, the New Historicism is a form of literary analysis specifically designed to interpret the dense, web-like disposition of languages, texts, and other sign systems that determine historical identities and situations. It is hermeneutical to the extent that interpreting the "network of material practices" (Veeser xi) helps us understand the material social world out of which the text emerged. Scholars of the Renaissance and medieval, who produced many of the key New Historicist texts, tend to focus on identity, gender, and sexuality, for these were the most visible points at which power manifested itself as a form of social and cultural transformation. A good example is Jonathan Goldberg's *Sodometries*, which draws on Foucault's *History of Sexuality* at the same time that it puts pressure on Foucault's "epochal pronouncement" that "the sodomite had been a temporary aberration; the homosexual was now a species" (Goldberg 18; Foucault, *History* 43). Goldberg seeks in his study to clarify the "utterly confused category" of the sodomite. His method is exemplary of the New Historicist style, one that "occasionally glances" at historical questions, but with the focus less on "the legal codes or the law cases that will deliver records about sodomites, and more on the question of literary representation" (20). He explicitly aligns his work with the "promise of New Historicism and feminism – the promise, let us say, of the transformation of literary studies into a branch of cultural studies" (24). His ambitions coincide with Greenblatt's in that both aspire toward a renovated field of cultural study in which historical questions and methodologies are part of an ensemble of interpretive techniques and tactics.

Catherine Gallagher states explicitly a point that is implicit in so much New Historicist critique. She argues that there can be no "*single*, unequivocal political meaning" for New Historicist practice and that it is wrongheaded to reduce it to a politics or simple "relation of power." On the contrary, a principal insight of the field is "that no cultural or critical practice is simply a politics in disguise, that such practices are seldom *intrinsically* either liberatory or oppressive, that they seldom contain their politics as an essence but rather occupy particular historical situations from which they enter into various exchanges, or negotiations, with practices designated 'political'" (37). A good example of this phenomenon is Greenblatt's reading of Shakespeare's *Othello*, which he regards as "the supreme expression of the cultural mode" of improvisation (*Renaissance* 232). Self-fashioning in this context involves the displacement and absorption of symbolic structures found in the culture at large and is made possible by "the subversive perception of another's truth as ideological construct" (228). Identity in the Renaissance, according to Greenblatt, is not a matter of achieving or sustaining autonomy but of negotiating among social and cultural discourses whose DETERMINATIONS impose multiple and varied constraints. Shakespeare's play exists within a socio-historical matrix in which such discourses, emanating from institutions like the church and the state, help to determine the coordinates of the text's meaning. Greenblatt points to Christopher Marlowe, whose achievement can best be understood by looking not "at the playwright's literary sources, not even at the relentless power-hunger of Tudor absolutism, but at the acquisitive energies of English merchants, entrepreneurs, and adventurers, promoters alike of trading companies and theatrical companies" (194). For the New Historicist critic of the Renaissance, the important thing is to map the contours of the discourse environment in which literature was produced and consumed. For example, while the Church of England rejected the Roman Catholic concept of Purgatory forty years before *Hamlet* was written, Shakespeare's audience would have been able to grasp allusions to it. "There were many people who clung to the old beliefs," writes Greenblatt, "despite the official position, and Elizabethan audiences were in any case perfectly capable of imaginatively entering into alien belief systems" (Greenblatt, *Hamlet* 235).

Given this Nietzschean–Foucauldian framework, the task of the New Historicist is clear: it is to "map" the various connections and relations between literary texts and the social and cultural contexts. The result of these discursive negotiations and exchanges is the construction of what Tony Bennett calls a *reading formation*, specific determinations that "mediate the relations between text and context" (qtd. in Montrose 398). In a reading formation, context does not lie outside of discourses but is established by them and their interrelations. This textualist approach to historical context and textuality is characterized, as Louis Montrose puts it, by "a reciprocal concern with the historicity of texts and the textuality of histories." All texts and all modes of reading must be understood as historically embedded; but at the same time, "we can have no access to a full and authentic past, to a material existence that is unmediated by the textual traces of the society in question" (410). The emphasis on textuality has led some critics to claim that if history is a textual phenomenon there can be no historical "truth." **Fredric Jameson** describes New Historicism as a form of nominalism (a belief that ideas represented in language have no basis in reality). While he agrees that textualization is an inevitable outcome of the historical discipline, he insists that "history is not a text, not a narrative, master or otherwise, but that, as an absent cause, it is inaccessible to us except in textual form, and that our approach to it … necessarily passes through its prior textualization, its narrativization in the political unconscious" (35). Jameson's caution is echoed by Stanley Fish, who describes well the central problem, which is "reconciling the assertion of 'wall to wall' textuality – the denial that the writing of history could find its foundation in a substratum of unmediated fact – with the desire to say something specific and normative" (303). Fish is calling for a pragmatic mode of speaking truly (a mode governed by norms) that requires more than a guarantee offered by interpretation. New Historicism understood as a cultural poetics sees no stable ground for its work and in fact argues against the necessity for *any* guarantee. At its best, New Historicism operates on the presupposition of multiple truths about the past and accepts no single method or mode of truth as normative. The New Historicism does precisely more and less with historiography, invoking certain norms to solidify an argument, skirting some in the interests of a cultural poetics that seeks the truth of the past in the efficacy of the critic's engagement with the texts that communicate it.

Hayden White, a theorist of history and historiography, explicitly refutes the charge that textualism itself is ahistorical and argues that, at some level, all history is textual (see *Metahistory*). The critical issue is whether or not one can get beyond the textual level of analysis (of primary documents and historical accounts) to say something meaningful about the concrete social world. If the past can be known only through the negotiation of competing interpretations of the archival evidence and through the critical awareness of the historian's own role in the selection and representation of it, then an exploration of the archive is a prerequisite to understanding fully the relations of power in any given epoch and to subverting prevailing historical explanations. Gallagher resolves the dilemma by constructing a hybrid methodology; thus Foucault and Marx are brought into collaboration on projects that deal with local expressions of social and productive power. This combination in her work produces a critical discourse suited to a localized and highly mobile "micro-politics of daily life" (43). Gallagher's approach shares much with the British tradition of Marxist historiography that includes Christopher Caudwell, Raymond Williams, E. P. Thompson, and Eric Hobsbawm and with cultural studies theorists like Stuart Hall and Dick Hebdige, whose work focuses precisely on the "micro-politics" of marginalized groups and subcultures. Walter Benn Michaels, in *The Gold Standard and the Logic of Naturalism* (1987), did much the same thing in American studies by turning our attention to the relation between specific economic phenomena and literary naturalism.

Precisely because they emphasize textualism and interpretation over empirical methods, New Historicists are open to the charge that they play fast and loose with disciplinary protocols and standards of historiography, especially about sources and how they are used. As Morris Dickstein has remarked, historical criticism too often relies "on interesting but remote social anecdotes that could point up an ingenious parallel to a literary work without convincing the reader that it was truly relevant or illuminating." More important, "by avoiding the chronological approach of earlier historicists, which sought out the genesis of historical events and movements, it ran the risk of looking arbitrary or merely clever" (251). Dominick LaCapra has made the important point that New Historicism has a weak theoretical foundation, which means that its reliance on Foucault's notion of power/knowledge "threatens to become a universal solvent in explanation and interpretation" (*Soundings* 191). LaCapra views context less as a context for literature than as a context for the historian: "to historicize means to contextualize. Certainly, historical understanding requires contextualization even if the latter is problematized in certain ways and seen as a necessary rather than sufficient condition of a self-critical historiography that acknowledges the importance of self-understanding in the attempt to make one's assumptions explicit and to work critically through a relation to the past." LaCapra's view "is that one must combine the roles of historian and critical theorist or at least see them as intensely interactive and, in the best of circumstances, mutually supportive" (*Representing* 69–70). At its best, New Historicism does precisely what LaCapra suggests – it combines a historical viewpoint with critical interpretation. And while it did not last as a movement, the historical perspective it developed has had a powerful influence in fields like cultural studies, postcolonial studies, and feminism.

Works Cited

Benjamin, Walter. *Selected Writings*. Ed. Marcus Bullock and Michael W. Jennings. Vol. 4. Cambridge, MA; Belknap-Harvard University Press, 1996. 389–411.

Dickstein, Morris. "The Limits of Historicism: Literary Theory and Historical Understanding." In *The Mirror in the Roadway: Literature and the Real World*. Princeton: Princeton University Press, 2005. 248–58.

Fish, Stanley. "Commentary: The Young and the Restless." In *The New Historicism*. Ed. H. Aram Veeser. New York: Routledge, 1989. 303–16.

Foucault, Michel. *Discipline and Punish: The Birth of the Prison*. Trans. Alan Sheridan. New York: Vintage, 1979.

Foucault, Michel. *The History of Sexuality*. Vol. 1. Trans. Robert Hurley. New York: Pantheon, 1978.

Foucault, Michel. "Nietzsche, Genealogy, History." In *Language, Counter-Memory, Practice: Selected Essays and Interviews*. Ed. Donald F. Bouchard. Trans. Donald F. Bouchard and Sherry Simon. Ithaca: Cornell University Press, 1977. 139–64.

Gallagher, Catherine. "Marxism and New Historicism." In *The New Historicism*. Ed. H. Aram Veeser. New York: Routledge, 1989. 37–48.

Gallagher, Catherine and Stephen Greenblatt. *Practicing New Historicism*. Chicago: University of Chicago Press, 2000.

Geertz, Clifford. *The Interpretation of Cultures*. New York: Basic Books, 1973.

Goldberg, Jonathan. *Sodometries: Renaissance Texts, Modern Sexualities*. Stanford: Stanford University Press, 1992.

Greenblatt, Stephen. *Hamlet in Purgatory*. Princeton: Princeton University Press, 2001.

Greenblatt, Stephen. *Renaissance Self-Fashioning: From More to Shakespeare*. Chicago: University of Chicago Press, 1980.

Jameson, Fredric. *The Political Unconscious: Narrative as a Socially Symbolic Act*. Ithaca: Cornell University Press, 1981.

LaCapra, Dominick. *Representing the Holocaust: History, Theory, Trauma*. Ithaca: Cornell University Press, 1994.

LaCapra, Dominick. *Soundings in Critical Theory*. Ithaca: Cornell University Press, 1989.

Montrose, Louis. "New Historicism." In *Redrawing the Boundaries: The Transformation of English and American Literary Studies*. Ed. Stephen Greenblatt and Giles Gunn. New York: MLA, 1992. 392–418.

Nietzsche, Friedrich. *On the Genealogy of Morals*. Ed. Keith Ansell-Pearson. Trans. Carol Diethe. Cambridge: Cambridge University Press, 1994.

Nietzsche, Friedrich. "On the Uses and Disadvantages of History for Life." In *Untimely Meditations*. Ed. Daniel Breazeale. Trans. R. J. Hollingdale. Cambridge: Cambridge University Press, 1997. 57–123.

Veeser, H. Aram, ed. *The New Historicism*. New York: Routledge, 1989.

White, Hayden. *Metahistory: The Historical Imagination in Nineteenth-Century Europe*. Baltimore and London: Johns Hopkins University Press, 1973.

Postmodernism

The term *postmodernism* designates both an epoch following modernism and a discourse about modernity. The former is a more or less simple historical explanation (i.e., the postmodern comes *after* the modern), and it is useful for canon formation and other pedagogical tasks; but it can also provide a space, of reflection and theorizing, for calling into question the dominance of modernism, particularly in aesthetics and social theory. "Postmodernism can be seen," writes Anthony Appiah, "as a reauthorization of the proliferation of distinctions that reflects the underlying dynamic of cultural modernity, the need to clear oneself a space. Modernism saw the economization of the world as the triumph of reason; postmodernism rejects that claim, allowing in the realm of theory the same proliferation of distinctions that modernity had begun" (346). As a discourse about modernity, which includes but is not reducible to a critique of cultural modernism and its aesthetic program, postmodernism consolidates a particular ensemble of theoretical tendencies, some of which are shared by post-Marxism (e.g., toward non-dialectical models of contradiction and reconciliation, a semiotics of the commodity, and an anti-Platonic embrace of resemblance). Postmodernism also shares some tendencies with poststructuralism (e.g., toward a textualist understanding of language, the elaboration of the category of *difference*, deconstruction as a method).

Part of the difficulty in historicizing the postmodern lies in the fact that it was theorized well before the historical conditions that made it self-evident were in place. And this advance notice, which we can see clearly enough now, is the signature gesture of postmodernism, one that concedes belatedness at the very start. Samuel Beckett, one of the first postmodernist novelists, dramatizes this conundrum. "What have I omitted?" asks Malone, in *Malone Dies* (1951):

> Little things, nothings. They will come back to me later, make me see more clearly what has happened and say, Ah if I had only known then, now it is too late. Yes, little by little I shall see [a stranger] as he just has been, or as he should have been for me to be able to say, yet again, Too late, too late. There's feeling for you. (272–3)

The skepticism of Beckett's protagonists is grounded in the loss of what Winnie in *Happy Days* calls "the old style," which covers every ideal that culture has offered as a promissory note toward a better future. This disenchantment, this belatedness, finds its fullest expression in a postmodern aesthetics that repudiates dominant modernist techniques (e.g., expressive form, mythic structures, stream of consciousness) or redistributes them across different generic fields or in new combinations. The point is no longer that art stage its repudiation of aesthetics; it must vacate entirely the framework in which aesthetics produces its truth, including modernist *anti*-aesthetics. Thus, the postmodernist aestheticization of the *not*-aesthetic moves away from the "old style" of art toward art forms that seem to disappear into their materials and environment. On these terms, we can account for the preponderance of spatial concepts, techniques, and materials; of mass exhibitions (e.g., the Venice Biennale), installations and "wrappings"; and of rogue billboards, murals, and other forms of public art.

Postmodernist thought, no matter where it is found, is characterized by a principled skepticism about language, truth, causality, history, and SUBJECTIVITY. It rejects the modes of identification association with traditional dialects in favor of non-identity and non-totalizing strategies of dispersion in which identity becomes an ever-changing performativity. It rejects the concept of authenticity and the possibility of origins, regarding both as little more than retroactive propositions meant to legitimize or ground present social and political practice. Instead, postmodern thinkers explore the implications of repetition, deferral, and self-reference that constitute the EPISTEME of the postmodern. Across the academic and cultural spectrum, the postmodern world is indeterminate and contingent; it lacks stable foundations for truth, law, ethics, language, consciousness, even perception. Over against the UNIVERSALS and strategies of containment offered by philosophy and social theory, postmodernism embraces the unpredictable and ever-changing reality of particulars. Non-identity (Adorno), paralogy (Lyotard), heterology (De Certeau), the phantasm (Deleuze) – each designates a form of non-being, of negated being, and each militates against idealist visions of social unity. Though many postmodernists adopt poststructuralist theories of language, semiotics, and discourse, their aim is not the analysis of a structure but the practice of a discourse, one that is committed to going beyond the limits of metaphysical philosophy, beyond representation and mimesis, and beyond the possibility of a *gestalt* or "total situation" (e.g., a unity of being or culture, as in Yeats, or a "moment of being," as in Woolf).

These innovative features of postmodernism are, paradoxically, not new at all, for we can find most of them in Friedrich Nietzsche's theory of language, his concept "will to power," and his understanding of the individual as profoundly aesthetic and creative. "We have a different faith," Nietzsche writes in *Beyond Good and Evil*. We look "toward spirits strong and original enough to provide the stimuli for opposite valuations and to revalue and invert 'external values'" (117). For him, such spirits are artists who practice the "good deception" of using metaphors to "smash" existing frameworks or throw them into confusion. We fall into the traps of idealism and tradition when we forget that we are *"artistically creating* subjects," when we begin to believe that truth can be uncontaminated by any trace of human construction ("Truth and Lies" 90, 86). Throughout his work, Nietzsche challenges the transcendent origin and unchanging nature (the "truth value") of moral concepts and beliefs. Opposed to the *Truth*, transcendent or essential, lie *truths* on the very surface of things. "Oh, those Greeks!" he exclaims:

> They knew how to *live*. What is required for that is to stop courageously at the surface, the fold, the skin, to adore appearance, to believe in forms, tones, words, in the whole Olympus of appearance! Those Greeks were superficial – *out of profundity*! … Are we not, precisely in this respect, Greeks? Adorers of forms, of tones, of words? And therefore – *artists*? (*Gay Science* 38)

Nietzsche's paean to appearances celebrates the inessential, that which is overlooked as mere "given" nature or accidents of perception. It does not invert the priority of substance over appearance, but rather, and more radically, it plumbs the depths of appearance itself, explores *its* peculiar substance. Appearance is like the image as Jean-Luc Nancy describes it, whose "ontological content is sur-face, ex-position, ex-pression. The surface … is not relative to a spectator facing it: it is the site of a concentration in co-incidence" (*Ground* 9). For Nietzsche as for postmodernists in the twenty-first century, the surface of things is their "deep" truth.

The Nietzschean revaluation of the relation between appearance and substance strikes at the core of Western thought – its theories of being, knowing, acting, doing, making – and deconstructs a certain way of being human, one that is rooted in classical Greece by way of the Renaissance recovery of it and that flourished in the Enlightenment, particularly in the idealist philosophy of Immanuel Kant, Friedrich Schiller, and G. W. F. Hegel. In this sense, the prefix *post-* in postmodernism signifies an *epistemological shift* in how we see and know the world, a shift that began to register at the end of the nineteenth century. It implies the end of modernity and the beginning of something new. "In direct opposition to modern views," Steven Best and Douglas Kellner write, "postmodernists valorize incommensurability, difference, and fragmentation as the antidotes to repressive modern modes of theory and rationality" (38). Andreas Huyssen sees this valorization on display at the 1982 Documenta 7 exhibition of contemporary art in Kassel, Germany. The exhibition is a "total confusion of codes," both "anti-modern" and "anti-avantgarde," but also "anti-postmodern in that it abandons any reflection of the problems which the exhaustion of high modernism originally brought about." Documenta 7 is the "perfect aesthetic simulacrum … "a postmodern restoration of a domesticated modernism" (180–1). Huyssen concedes that postmodern art "in its better moments" addressed the disenchantment of modernism, but in the end, it appears to have fallen under its sway.

At stake in this epistemic shift is the subject/object (same/other) duality, which has grounded thought and science, ethics and art for millennia, particularly in the form of dialectical models of knowledge in which SELF-IDENTITY is the sign of a fullness of presence and being. Postmodernism privileges negativity and NEGATION on principle: on the one hand, the subject is no longer in a position of dialectical dominance over the object/*other*; on the other hand, the subject makes her own appeal (for being, for connection, for appropriation) from the position of non-identity. The tendency to define postmodernism by negation, to make statements about what postmodernism is *not* or to describe the postmodern as lack and the *un*presentable, invariably suggest an investment in negative dialectics. This tendency can be discerned as early as the late 1940s and 1950s with Surrealism and Dadaism, Beckett and the theatre of the absurd, and thinkers like Georges Bataille, Maurice Blanchot, and Gaston Bachelard, who were exploring the limits of representation and the knowable in an attempt to break the stranglehold of dualism, the "rigid geometries" (Bachelard) that keep us from knowing "limit events" (Bataille) such as the sacred, the erotic, and death – the kinds of experiences that for **Jacques Lacan** give us access to the painful excitements of JOUISSANCE. This line of development continued through the 1960s, with the *nouveau roman* in France and the postmodernist novels of Thomas Pynchon and Don Delillo, the Pop Art of Andy Warhol, and conceptual and performance art. In architecture, where the postmodern movement was prominent, a negative critique of the dominant modernist trend of Le Corbusier and Ludwig Meis van der Rohe led to a pastiche method that "quoted" modernism in a deconstruction of its formal principles as well as its use of space, materials, and perspective. Frank Gehry's whimsically sublime Symphony Hall in Los Angeles, for example, evacuates space and redefines form and function in a way that challenges the palette of aesthetic modernism. Surprising new combinations of materials and use of space have revolutionized the way artists create and exhibit their work, and pastiche styles dominate in popular entertainment (music, film, television, video games). Even simple objects of "mechanical art," which for Kant make "a possible object actual, adequately to our *cognition* of that object," can cross over and become a "way of cognizing," which is the mode of presentation in fine art (305). Or, conversely, the patently non-artistic (the found object, the empty factory, human waste) becomes art by virtue of framing, exhibition, and installation and the viewer's attitude toward it. Postmodernist relational aesthetics remains within this negative dialectics of non-art and art, even when, at its most extreme (i.e., most Nietzschean), it announces that there is no difference between the two terms.

Postmodernism repudiates the philosophical and cultural legacy of the Enlightenment, especially the forms of narrative legitimation that gave shape and unity to social, political, religious, and cultural life. Critical theorists like Jürgen Habermas address the crisis of legitimation from the standpoint of a renovated rationality and a theory of communicative action designed to facilitate forms of pluralism and political consensus. Postmodernists remain skeptical of such "returns to reason" and resist what they perceive to be its effects: the instrumentalization of rationality and ideological inscription of the subject, HEGEMONIC appropriation of divergent ideas and opinions, and the rise of commodity markets and a fully mediatized consumer culture. Behind this skepticism is the rejection of "the modern equation of reason and freedom" (Best and Kellner 38). As a result, and in order to preserve a space for genuine freedom and thus for genuine subjectivity, the question of legitimacy must be raised and answered in the context of multiple narratives of authority that avoid hegemony and the ideological interpellation of the subject and offer alternative modes of social belonging. Lyotard's *Postmodern Condition* (1979) diagnoses the problem of legitimation and expresses a complete disenchantment with *les grands récits*, the MASTER NARRATIVES of progress, education, and emancipation that, in the twentieth century, had proven to be bankrupt. "The contemporary decline of narratives of legitimation," Lyotard writes, "is tied to the abandonment of the belief" that science or anything else can provide "metaprescriptions" to unify all language games (i.e., the forms in which linguistic statements constitute specific areas of knowledge) (64, 66). He identifies two principal forms of legitimation: *narratives of emancipation*, which are driven by Enlightenment values of freedom and individuality (*Bildung*) and exemplified by the narrative dynamics of the French Revolution; and *narratives of speculation*, which are constructed along the lines of "customary knowledge" and exemplified by the Hegelian narrative of the world spirit coming into being. In the postmodern era, such modes of legitimation are met with incredulity, for they no longer serve the purpose of making sense of the world. According to Joseph Riddel, Lyotard rejects "the dialectical model of theory, and therefore the argument that theory must replace rather than displace, master and organize rather than criticize, and thus reorganize the authority of knowledge rather than participate in a general economy of production" (102).

Of special importance for Lyotard is the way knowledge becomes innovation within a "command system bent on efficiency" (*Postmodern Condition* 60–1), as when crisis in the productive forces leads to reform and reorganization, all within the scope of existing "customary" knowledge. Innovation in modernity is less about human creativity in production than about optimization of systems. We might therefore speak of a *renovating* spirit that takes reformation and reorganization *outside* the boundaries of customary knowledge. Lyotard believes that alternatives lie in the critical narratives of local experience (*le petit récit*), in paralogical forms of knowledge (e.g., informatics, fractal mathematics, chaos theory, game theory) that move beyond Enlightenment paradigms. This turn to paralogy and a "pagan" ideal is governed by a desire to present what cannot be presented, to bring non-being into being. These "unpresentable" features of social and aesthetic life can only be recovered through a "pragmatics of knowledge" (60–1) that remains open-ended, non-hierarchical, and non-dialectical. Such "open systems" could provide legitimacy without narrative hegemony and be more efficient and just. As Honi Fern Haber notes, language games are "endemic to the pagan ideal because they fight against the imposition of terror in all its forms by encouraging alternative ideas and modes of expression" (145).

Paralogy signals an epistemic rupture that separates the postmodern from the modern; but, for Lyotard, the rupture was *always already* in place: "The postmodern world would be that which, in the modern, puts forward the unpresentable in presentation itself, that which denies itself the solace of good forms" (*Postmodern* 81). In the modernist epoch, the attempt to "put forward the unpresentable" met with two kinds of success: on the one hand, W. B. Yeats, James Joyce, and T. S. Eliot moved beyond orthodox Western modes of representation (i.e., presenting what is presentable) by turning to mystical, heretical, and unorthodox forms of idealism (e.g., those espoused by Neo-Platonism, Giambattista Vico, William Blake, St. John of the Cross); on the other hand, Joyce, Virginia Woolf, Ezra Pound, Marcel Duchamps, Jean Artaud, Gertrud Stein, Wallace Stevens, H.D., and many others avoided this unorthodox reaffirmation of the ideal in favor of an acknowledgment of the "relational" or "contingent" nature of all things, most of all language, in the spirit of Stéphane Mallarmé, arch protopostmodernist:

> O Spirit of litigation, know,
> When we keep silent in this season,
> The stem of multiple lilies grew
> Too large to be contained by reason. (47)

Postmodernism, by privileging the unpresentable (i.e., the non-identical), resists the dialectic closure that raises mind over matter by annihilating sensation ("multiple lilies") in the production of abstract concepts. If modernism redefines closure by fighting within and against the "good forms" of modernity, postmodernism forecloses this option in the space of the negative and non-identity and thereby resists the reinscription of the duality that has frustrated philosophy for so long and that haunts modernism in the form of mysticism. Thus Michel de Certeau – whose theory of "heterologies" is meant to skirt the dialectical process required by identity theory – acknowledges the radical *other* but goes further and remains in the space of negation *just before* closure annihilates this necessary otherness. This tactical emancipation, which cannot be gauged in classical dialectical terms, is the liberating dimension of postmodernity, a dimension in which the subject is no longer at odds with the world and is able to achieve happiness in it without a doomed recourse to mythology or nostalgic fantasy. While postmodernists embrace non-identity, they do not find in it an *authentic* position. Indeed, for them, authenticity is a chimera, produced by the aesthetic regime and reinforced in the modernist rejection of aesthetics in favor of a more authentic *anti*-aesthetics. In the precession of simulations, in the non-being of difference, only the inauthentic and untrue can acquire the status of a "truth" and then only about its own *in*authentic status, its *un*truth. The simulation itself, the resemblance, the *act* of resemblance becomes the ground for any claim to truth.

The postmodernist stance toward truth would seem to confirm the claim, made by Lyotard and others, that there has been an epochal rupture, one that justifies our leaving behind the project of modernity, in which truth claims were adjudged according to universal principles. Habermas vigorously disagreed, in a widely influential essay, that admonished the postmodernists for abandoning one of the principal goals of the Enlightenment: the reintegration of economic, political, and cultural spheres based on "communicative action" and consensus, on the essentially humanist notion of an organic and meaningful social TOTALITY. He famously wrote that the "project of modernity has not yet been fulfilled" (12). Lyotard's postmodernism is, in some ways, a direct answer to Habermas's belief in the progressive potential that lies in a reintegration of social and cultural spheres, for he calls into question *what had before been self-evident* (i.e., Habermas's modernity). Hence Lyotard's interest in the *différend*, the condition of incommensurability that characterizes certain kinds of disputes "that cannot be equitably resolved for lack of a rule of judgment applicable to both arguments" (*Differend* xi). The *différend* designates "the unstable state and instant of language wherein something which must be able to be put into phrases cannot yet be." It is "born from a wrong and is signaled by a silence" (13, 58). The *différend* functions in legal and political discourse much as the sublime does in aesthetics – as the space of an interminable and vertiginous TEXTUALITY – and is characterized by deconstructionist tactics, such as deferral or displacement of meaning, undecidability, sophism, falsehood, and so on. While we may feel "the despair of never being able to present something within reality on the scale of the Idea," we enjoy the compensation of an "overrid[ing] joy of being nonetheless called upon to do so. We are more depressed by the abyss that separates heterogeneous genres of discourse than excited by the indication of a possible passage from one to the other" (179).

By installing the sublime within the very difference of language, postmodernist knowledge seeks to escape the burden of a philosophical tradition that polices the borderline between reason and the realm of sensibility that is often figured as the seat of unreason and the irrational. This is why postmodern philosophy and aesthetics redefine negation as a kind of internal otherness or HETERONOMY, as the space of the *non*-modern and the *non*-artistic. Lyotard's critique of Kantian aesthetics and Edmund Burke's theory of the sublime leads him to a recovery of what is implicit in the aesthetic regime. Drawing on Edmund Burke and Kant, he developed a conception of the *postmodern sublime* that designates an excess (or privation) of representation in the form of a gap between reality and its presentation, between "presentation" and the "unpresentable," that harbors the terrifying kernel of enlightenment. "There is something so over-ruling in whatever inspires us with awe," writes Burke, "in all things which belongs ever so remotely to terror, that nothing else can stand in their presence. There lie the qualities of beauty either dead or unoperative; or at most exerted to mollify the rigour and sternness of the terror, which is the natural concomitant of greatness" (304) (on Burke, see chapter one, "The Rise of Literary Theory" 13). Unlike the Romantic sublime, which was typically located in nature, the postmodern sublime has no object, there is no reference point in nature that can trigger a sublime reaction, in part because it is a response to the experience of privation, and to the despair of ever finding language adequate to that experience.

The postmodern sublime is caught up in the currents of nostalgia for something that can never be repossessed or re-presented; but it unveils the reality that this "something" has *never been* possessed or presented, has always been a matter of deferral and displacement. "A sorrow felt before the inconsistency of every object, [the sublime] is also the exultation of thought passing beyond the bounds of what may be presented. The 'presence' of the absolute is the utter contrary of presentation" (Lyotard, *Postmodern Fables* 29). Following Burke, who held that "all general privations are great because they are terrible" (125), Lyotard remarks that there is no privation more terrible than the privation of the future: "What is terrifying is that the *It happens that* will not happen, that it will stop happening" (*Inhuman* 99).

In line with this radical sublimity is the pervasive use of irony, parody, and other techniques for exploiting the semiotic excesses of language. This is particularly evident in postmodernist literature, especially the novel, which is characterized by irony and belatedness, by precocious renovation of key modernist techniques (e.g., disjunctive narratives, collage and pastiche forms, multiple and unreliable narrators), and by a willingness to integrate theoretical ideas in literary forms. In this regard, postmodernism shares with poststructuralism a desire to break free of limiting generic and linguistic structures and a tendency toward INTERTEXTUALITY and METAFICTIONAL forms. Ihab Hassan's *Dismemberment of Orpheus* (1971), one of the first major studies of postmodernist literature, argues that postmodernism rejects the commitment to realism behind modernist experimentation in favor of a literature of ludic self-reference. If there is no intrinsic relation between language and the "real" world, then language becomes the only thing that literary works can effectively "re-present." Linda Hutcheon writes, in a similar vein, of "narcissistic narrative," a self-conscious attitude toward literary structure and writing that often serves as the central theme of the work itself. According to Hutcheon, metafictional forms force readers to look at language and texts in new ways: "the narcissistic novel as incitement to revolutionary activity would be the ultimate defense of self-conscious fiction against claims of self-preening introversion" (155). However, from the materialist perspective of someone like **Fredric Jameson**, the self-referentiality and lack of affect that characterize the "narcissistic novel" would appear far from revolutionary, would in fact appear to have relinquished the goal of using language and literature in socially progressive ways.

For both Jameson and Hutcheon, as for many other theorists, intertextual citation is a critical component of a postmodernist theory of discourse. *Citation* conventionally signifies a relation of authority within a discourse, one in which certain statements serve a regulatory or evidentiary function: one *cites an authority* in order to advance an argument. Postmodern citation, by contrast, is a strategy of repetition and appropriation; texts cite each other not with the intent of invoking an authority or showing indebtedness but with the desire to create new expressive relations, new opportunities for enunciation and articulation, new models of cultural production and social action. Jameson describes a related postmodernist practice, *pastiche*:

> Pastiche is, like parody, the imitation of a peculiar or unique, idiosyncratic style, the wearing of a linguistic mask, speech in a dead language. But it is a neutral practice of

such mimicry, without any of parody's ulterior motives, amputated of the satiric impulse, devoid of laughter and of any conviction that alongside the abnormal tongue you have momentarily borrowed, some healthy linguistic normality still exists. Pastiche is thus blank parody, a statue with blind eyeballs. (*Postmodernism* 17)

Pastiche is parody without a referent; like other forms of intertextuality, it sustains a linguistic universe in which reference to the external world is neither necessary nor desirable. This renovated conception of parody is similar to the poststructuralist form theorized by **Julia Kristeva**, for whom the "pseudo-transgressive" character of traditional parody is no longer viable. Following **M. M. Bakhtin**, she prefers the parodic energies of the carnivalesque, in which the dualist structure of conventional parody is rejected for a form of parodic discourse that does not rely on an "incestuous" binarism that is not a law anticipating its own transgression, but "transgression giving itself a law" (71).

Jameson sees in such strategies a fundamental "effacement" of "aesthetic Modernism," that is, "of the older (essentially high-modernist) frontier between high culture and so-called mass or commercial culture, and the emergence of new kinds of texts infused with the forms, categories, and contents of that very culture industry so passionately denounced" by critics of modernity, particularly Adorno (*Postmodernism* 2). This rejection of aesthetic modernism does not, however, constitute a total break with the aesthetic regime. **Jacques Rancière**, in *Aesthetics and its Discontents* (2004), makes the case that postmodernism fails in the same way as modernism to resist an aesthetic regime that had decoupled aesthetics, as a mode of thought, from art as such. Modernism had fought against the aesthetic regime's foundational rupturing of the "representative regime," in which *poeisis* and *aisthesis* (making and sensing) were joined by *mimesis* (imitation). In the aesthetic regime, the opposition between *poeisis* and *aisthesis* situated art and sensuous materiality as dialectically opposed (rather than mutually operational within a system of representation governed by *mimesis*) within a new field of aesthetics. In other words, the rupture that inaugurated the aesthetic regime situated it within an idealist and dualistic framework. Modernism fought against this framework, but its anti-mimetic stance, which tends to reinscribe the very terms of the problem in dialectical and oppositional ways, made it impossible to heal the original rift that gave aesthetics the power to identify art *as such* (on the aesthetic regime, see Post-Marxist Theory 114–15). Postmodernist aesthetics, eager to leave behind the tarnished achievements of modernist idealism, counters aesthetic modernism with a "relational aesthetics" that removes the artwork and the work of art (creation and exhibition) from a specifically *anti*-aesthetic context (that of, say, a Duchamps installation or a Dada performance). The postmodern artist and the curator conspire to alter entire environments, to challenge the distinction between art and its materials and the spaces in which it is made and exhibited. At the cutting edge of this relational aesthetics is the non-aesthetic realm of primal materials, open space and uncontrollable variables that create new modes of aesthetic experience – new "distributions of the sensible," new ways of enjoying and even thinking of the sensible. In this way, postmodernism attempts to reintroduce the sensible through a radical mimesis that collapses the distinction between the sensible and thought, between the world and the artwork, in short, between art and *not*-art. When art and the world become indistinguishable we have the theatre of the absurd and Situationism, we have conceptual art and installations. And when mimesis is taken to the limit, we have the striking resemblances produced by the photographer Cindy Sherman or the sculptor Richard Serra. In the former, resemblance is carefully orchestrated and thus utterly unlike what it purports to represent (there is really nothing to represent); in the latter, it is located at the level of material (the artwork resembles what constitutes it: raw wood or iron, found objects, an open plaza). However, and this is Rancière's main point, relational aesthetics can all-too-easily replicate the modernist paradigm when the artwork (e.g., a Damien Hirst installation) becomes part of a permanent exhibit and when the system of instruction and of distribution (in galleries, museums, public spaces, private ownership) sustains a thriving art market.

This ambivalent break with modernist aesthetics is symptomatic of a larger ambivalence with respect to modernity. Jameson, for example, sees the postmodern as coeval with "late capitalism," so that the temporal linkage is not to modernity as such, but to its specifically capitalist manifestation (if that is not speaking tautologically). For him, postmodernism is a *reaction* to modernism that marks "the emergence of a new type of social life and a new economic order – what is often euphemistically called modernization, postindustrial or consumer society, the society of the media or the spectacle, or multinational capitalism" ("Postmodernism" 15). In such a context, nostalgia, pastiche and other "empty" representations without origin dominate consciousness and, inevitably, the unconscious; and where subjectivity is dispersed, identity opens up into non-identity, and being is subjected to a terrifying proximity to non-being. Disenchanted with material existence, living in a world of simulated reality, the postmodern subject experiences a "waning of affect," in which psychological and cultural depth is replaced by SIMULACRA. Cultural products still produce "feelings" (which Deleuze and Guattari and Lyotard call "intensities") but they are "free-floating and impersonal," no longer anchored to a stable, AUTONOMOUS subjectivity (*Postmodernism* 15–16). (On aesthetics, see chapter one, "The Rise of Literary Theory" 12–24, Marxist Theory, 89–90 and Post-Marxist Theory 114–17.)

The questions Jameson raises about the consumer society of postmodernity resonates in the work of **Jean Baudrillard**, whose early commitment to Marxism ultimately led to one of the most influential theories of postmodern societies. He is primarily concerned with the impact of the materiality of the sign and the image, particularly in new media environments. In *The Mirror of Production* (1973), he critiques the Marxist conception of production and argues that radical politics must move beyond the conception of the worker as a "production machine," for social systems are no longer driven by political economy but by signifying economies. The recognition of the importance of "sign value" led Baudrillard into the study of semiotics, simulations, and mediation as elements of a new postmodern system of symbolic exchange. Though some commentators read Baudrillard's work as "apocalyptic trumpeting" (Best and Kellner 44), it is more fruitful to see it as a gloss on Nietzsche's celebration of appearances and forms and therefore a reminder that the unassuming surface of things requires our serious study and consideration.

Baudrillard's chief contribution to postmodern theory is the idea of SIMULATION, which he regards as a precession of orders of simulacra, in which the image (1) reflects a "profound reality"; (2) "masks and denatures a profound reality"; (3) "masks the *absence* of a profound reality"; (4) "has no relation to any reality whatsoever: it is its own pure simulacrum." Postmodernism coincides with the turn from the second to the third orders. "In the first case, the image is a *good* appearance – representation is of the sacramental order. In the second, it is an evil appearance – it is of the order of maleficence. In the third, it plays at being an appearance – it is of the order of sorcery. In the fourth, it is no longer of the order of appearances, but of simulation" (*Simulacra* 6). The theory of simulation suggests that the postmodern world is one in which the real has been replaced by simulations of reality. "It is no longer a question of imitation, nor of reduplication, nor even of parody. It is rather a question of substituting signs of the real for the real itself." Whereas dissimulation involves "feign[ing] not to have what one has," simulation involves "feign[ing] to have what one hasn't" (*Simulations* 4–5). In the "hyperreal" space of simulation, there is no truth, causality, temporality, law – even nature and the human body are irrelevant in a world in which "signs of the real" replace the real and "God, Man, Progress, and History itself die to profit the code" (111). The hyperrealism of postmodernity takes mimesis to the limits of what resemblance can achieve until representation itself is left behind in the production of a pure, unanchored image.

Baudrillard draws a line of analogy and affiliation between Descartes' "Evil Demon," which is the principle that throws our knowledge of the world into doubt by actively manipulating our perception, and the way images work in highly mediated societies. The language of contagion that Baudrillard uses throws into vivid relief the forsaken purity of the REAL: "the image is interesting not only in its role as reflection, mirror, representation of, or counterpart to, the real, but also when it begins to contaminate reality and to model it, when it only conforms to reality the better to distort it, or better still: when it appropriates reality for its own ends, when it anticipates it to the point that the real no long has time to be produced as such" (*Evil Demon* 16). For Baudrillard, the postmodern media image is catastrophic; it induces and signals in the same moment "a radical, qualitative change in an entire system" (19). This is especially the case in television, the medium *par excellence* for deferring the real: "The cold light of television is inoffensive to the imagination (even that of children) since it no longer carries any imaginary, for the simple reason that *it is no longer an image*." Unlike cinema, which is "still an image" and belongs to the realm of the double and the mirror, television is a "terminal located in your head and *you* are the screen." It is a "magnetic tape … not an image" (19, 25).

Baudrillard's very insistence on the predominance of simulations has prompted some critics to wonder if he harbors a nostalgia for the real, for that which is authentic, grounded and present, stable and substantial, immutable and unmovable. This objection, of course, raises the question whether one can be nostalgic for what has never transpired. Jean-Luc Nancy's postmodernist approach to the image follows a different path, one that emphasizes the idea of the image as both a passage (a temporalized event) and a withdrawal, a refusal to disclose itself *as* image (i.e., as the "thingness" of the image). Unlike Baudrillard, Nancy can still speak of the *grounded* image: "The image is separated in two ways simultaneously. It is detached from a ground [*fond*] and it is cut out within a ground. It is pulled away and clipped or cut out. The pulling away raises it and brings it forward: makes it a 'fore,' a separate frontal surface, whereas the ground itself had no face or surface" (7). Whereas Baudrillard sees only the "marvellous indistinguishability" of simulations (*Evil Demon* 20), Nancy discerns a negative movement between image and ground, in which neither image nor ground can establish itself. The image is visible "because it does not belong to the domain of objects, their perception and their use, but to that of forces, their affections and transmissions." It is because of these latter, and because the image is always in some ways its own ground, that Nancy can say that "the image is always material" (12). In this doubling of the ground we find the suspended temporality of the image: "It is at once the profound depth of a possible shipwreck and the surface of the luminous sky. The image floats, in sum, at the whim of the swells, mirroring the sun, poised over the abyss" (13).

The questions raised by Nancy and Baudrillard resonate in the work of **Gilles Deleuze and Félix Guattari**, whose critique of capitalism rests on a similar refusal of traditional modes of constituting the real. For them, material and symbolic production can no longer be differentiated, which means that traditional modes of knowledge fail to grasp the complexities of advanced capitalist societies. In their two-volume study *Capitalism and Schizophrenia* (*Anti-Oedipus* and *A Thousand Plateaus*), they argue that capitalism and psychoanalysis have created forms of domination that are all-encompassing and that desire itself has been converted into the automatic satisfaction of simulated needs. The "major enemy" is totalitarianism. As **Michel Foucault** puts it in his preface to *Anti-Oedipus*, "the strategic adversary is fascism … And not only historical fascism, the fascism of Hitler and Mussolini – which was able to mobilize and use the desire of the masses so effectively – but also the fascism in us all, in our heads and in our everyday behavior" (xiii). For this reason, they reject Freud's theory of desire, particularly its determination in the Oedipus complex, in which it arises only to be repressed; nor do they agree with Lacan's emphasis on lack as the primary motivation of desire. Against the dyadic or binary structure of Freudian and Lacanian subjectivity, Deleuze and Guattari advance the notion of *schizophrenia*, which more aptly describes the heterogeneous and discontinuous experience of postmodernity. Thus instead of "cathexis" and "sublimation" (terms used in psychoanalysis for the way desire is expressed) and circulation (a term used to account for money and commodities in a capitalist market), Deleuze and Guattari speak of flows and intensities, of *desiring machines* that remap social and personal spaces.

The specific of this "libidinal economy" is determined by processes of DETERRITORIALIZATION and RETERRITORIALIZATION that traverse the social body, inscribing and reinscribing psychological, geographical, political, or social boundaries. Territorialized space is not governed by a "schizo" logic but rather by the logic of the Law, the Lacanian Symbolic. Deterritorialization refers to the process of breaking down these boundaries and mapping "demographic flows" of intensities that emanate from different points of the social matrix, while reterritorialization occurs once new boundaries are inscribed on this matrix-in-process. All of this plays out on a social landscape that resembles a "rhizome," which Deleuze and Guattari describe as "a subterranean stem" that is "absolutely different from roots and radicles. Bulbs and tubers are rhizomes. Plants with roots or radicles may be rhizomorphic in other respects altogether … Burrows are too, in all their functions of shelter, supply, movement, evasion, and breakout" (*Thousand Plateaus* 6–7).

Following Antonin Artaud and Spinoza, Deleuze and Guattari develop a theory of social space as a "body without organs" (BwO), the "full egg" free of any territorializing demand. A body without organs designates a node through which intensities or flows of forces pass and create interconnections, openings, passages, assemblages: "the BwO is not a scene, a place, or even a support upon which something comes to pass. It has nothing to do with phantasy, there is nothing to interpret" (*Thousand Plateaus* 153). Desire is the operation of the body without organs. Even when that body is threatened with annihilation, "it is still desire. Desire stretches that far: desiring one's own annihilation, or desiring the power to annihilate. Money, army, police, and state desire, fascist desire, even fascism is desire. There is desire whenever there is the constitution of a BwO under one relation or another" (*Thousand Plateaus* 165).

Of crucial importance for Deleuze and Guattari is the idea of the ASSEMBLAGE, a machinic unity that does not function in a context of stability/instability and produces difference in an enigmatic and unpredictable dispersion or flow. Like the concept *bricolage*, a random or "ready to hand" construction or analysis, the assemblage designates non-structured aggregates as well as flexible, multi-directional *valences* through which power (money, commands, information, verdicts, knowledge) flows. The assemblage is a radically *uncentered* formation that nevertheless "hangs together," largely by virtue of the integrity of elements within it, whose associations and CONSTELLATED meanings constitute a totality without totalization, a unity subject at any time to a disunifying event. The assemblage and the machinic desire that activates it depend on a concept of difference driven less by Saussurean formalism than by Nietzschean will to power. Unlike poststructuralist difference, which relies on the binarity of language for its constitution of the trace or DIFFÉRANCE that solicits meaning, Deleuzean difference disables the difference between terms. Or to put it another way, difference itself becomes differentiated. As Deleuze theorizes it, difference is not the "being of the negative," but the very posing of the question, the PROBLEMATIC of being understood as a form of differential repetition – not the "mere" repetition of copies generated by an original, but the iteration of images, models, or "bodies." As opposed to the representation of an original (an original "being") we find not simulations but an endless array of originals, each primed to signify in the same way. And what is signified is not a concept or object in the world, not a "being" but the *non*-being of the image or model or body itself. Deleuze's Nietzschean affirmation of "(non)-being" produces a form of repetition in which affirmation "finds the principle of its genesis" (*Difference* 64; see 49–51) and is governed by a principle of "qualitative multiplicity," a term he borrows from Henri Bergson. This form of multiplicity is "pure duration," "an internal multiplicity of succession, of fusion, of organization, of heterogeneity, of qualitative discrimination, or of *difference in kind*" (as opposed to the *difference in degree* characteristic of "quantitative multiplicity") (Deleuze, *Bergsonism* 38). "Our claim is not only that difference in itself is not 'already' contradiction, but that it cannot be reduced or traced to contradiction, since the latter is not more but less profound than difference" (51). In contradistinction to "infinite representation" (which is no better than the finite variety), Deleuze posits difference as Nietzschean affirmation: "difference is primary: it affirms difference and distance. Difference is light, aerial and affirmative. To affirm is not to bear but, on the contrary, to discharge and to lighten. It is no longer the negative which produces a phantom of affirmation like an ersatz, but rather a No which results from affirmation" (*Difference* 54). Deleuze argues that "(non)-being is Difference," but in the sense of *differentiation*, which marks the silence between terms, the gap that calls difference into being, the "non-space" of being. Differentiation opens up more of the difference in *différance*; it is the "differential element in which affirmation, as multiple affirmation, finds the principle of its genesis. As for negation, this is only the shadow of the highest principle, the shadow of the difference alongside the affirmation produced" (64). This is affirmation without the annihilation of dialectical closure that, as Timothy Wilson argues, takes Nietzsche's philosophy "to its logical extreme: where existence manifests itself as a mere simulacrum or phantasm" (158).

Unlike Baudrillard, for whom the simulacrum is a kind of pure immaterial sign, Deleuze seeks to theorize a new conception of materiality which Pheng Cheah has identified as the "power of nonorganic life," which does not presuppose an "originary difference" dependent on otherness but instead posits a "plane of immanence that generates actuality" (83–4). Deleuze's materialism is akin to theories of vitalism and multiple singularities, such as Nietzsche's "will to power," Foucault's "power/knowledge," and Negri's *potentia*. In all of them, we find a potentiality within human limits to change (or redistribute) the sensible world around us and to do so from the standpoint of what is *not* sensible, namely, philosophy and theory. In this scenario, we do not find a neutralizing or dehumanizing abstraction of thought from the world, but rather the abolition of the opposition between thought and the sensible. The Lyotardian sublime is a step in this direction, insofar as it claims that within what is present to us we find the horror of what is unpresented – a horror that becomes the norm in Alain Badiou's theory of the "event," which escapes being labeled postmodern by virtue of its explicit commitment to Platonism. (On Badiou, see Posthumanism 274–6.) For the postmodernist, everything needs to be reconsidered outside of the constraining presuppositions of ideology and idealism. "Rethink body, subjectivity, and social change," writes Brian Massumi, "in terms of movement, affect, force, and violence – before code, text, and signification. These latter reiterate arrest (the Law: where bodies cease, only to mean, and where meaning carries a sentence)" (66). Like theorists of performance and posthumanism, postmodernists share a concern with the phenomenologist Maurice Merleau-Ponty, who held that dualism and binary thinking have kept separate the two dimensions of our being, the sensible and the sensing, that are primordially joined as "Flesh," "an 'element' of Being" (139).

Postmodern materialism is a radical return to what is vital in our world experience, a foundational act that makes possible the idea of a situated subject free of constraints, except for those imposed upon the act of *being in a situation* (or of *not* being in a situation). It is relational, with the emphasis on the *fact* of relation within a given social situation, free of domination. In some cases, as in the poststructuralist feminism of **Hélène Cixous** and Julia Kristeva, the orientation to difference and materiality is decidedly postmodern and their work posits both structure and subject as mobile and permeable and repudiates patriarchal authority. Indeed, their work is at the forefront of postmodernist feminist ethics. As Marilyn Edelstein notes, with respect to Kristeva, deconstruction "of the seeming binary opposition between ethics and politics is a postmodernist but also a feminist move, in keeping with other feminist critiques of traditional oppositions between public and private, or between the personal and the political" (206). Kristeva's attitude toward ethical practice, her emphasis on the maternal and on "acknowledging and respecting one's own and others' ALTERITY," aligns feminist ethics with postmodern ontologies.

Another way of explaining the emphasis on matter and the sensible is to look at what feminism is doing with a postmodernist reframing (rather than rejection) of the subject. Postmodernists by and large reject the idea of the unified SUBJECT with its indivisible and sovereign core of being and seek instead to map the dispersion and regulation of behaviors and affects, to improvise new models for understanding how subjectivity should comport itself in a social world saturated with commodities, images, and other forms of simulated substance. Feminists, particularly those involved in the analysis of social and legal issues, have found the deconstruction of the subject to be problematic. While theorists like Mary Joe Frug, in *Postmodern Legal Feminism* (1992), challenge masculinist assumptions underwriting the subject of legal discourse, the category of the subject itself is rehabilitated. Jennifer Wicke believes that theorists like Lyotard and Baudrillard, who celebrate "the liberating potential of local, interlocking language games, which replace the overall structures," leave little room for reflection on "collective identities" and the "historical terrain of struggle" (17–18). Greater awareness is needed of the distinction between *identity politics*, which is tethered to traditional notions of the autonomous legal subject, and *relational politics*, which denotes "a multiple political dynamic that can see itself at work in the world in the back and forth of actual political engagement" (33). **Donna Haraway** takes the critique of the gendered subject beyond ethics and law and challenges the foundations of science and the limits of nature. Her aim, in *Simians, Cyborgs, and Women* (1991), is to deconstruct binomial models of human experience – mind/body, subject/object, nature/artifice, art/science, body/machine – and to posit an alternative model, the cyborg, which links biological nature structurally to the "interface" opportunities made possible by computer-generated and mediated environments. Especially for women, the cyborg model is better adapted to a relational politics and can help bridge the gap between postmodernism and a feminist theory that still presupposes, for political purposes, the existence and necessity of an autonomous subject (on Haraway, see Posthumanism 269–70, 305–6).

The twenty-first-century critique of postmodernism, in the work of thinkers like **Bruno Latour**, Badiou, and Rancière, reminds us that postmodernity is less a break with modernity (and postmodernism a break with modernism) than a convoluted detour, through irony and misrecognition, that returns us to the very heart of the modern. This return is seen most clearly in aesthetics, where it models the return of thought to certain fundamentals (Plato, Spinoza, Kant, Hegel, Heidegger) throughout the theoretical spectrum in postmodernity. Some contemporary critics claim that this apparent break is not a break at all but a kind of awakening to a long-repressed potentiality. "There is no postmodernist rupture," Rancière announces (*Aesthetics* 42), and he takes postmodernist philosophers like Lyotard to task for not sufficiently repudiating modernist themes, particularly in aesthetics. In a similar vein, Latour has noted that "postmodernism is a symptom, not a fresh solution" (46), a conclusion that Beckett had reached in *Endgame* (1957): "Use your head, can't you, use your head, you're on earth, there's no cure for that!" (53). By envisioning a world that can no longer be comprehended by dialectics and totalities, postmodernism offers a vision of the world free of domination and totalization by grand narratives and ideology and free too of the dualisms that foster the arrested development of subjects, communities, and the very thought that unites them. In this regard, postmodernists occupy common ground with post-Marxist and neo-Hegelian theorists like **Judith Butler**, Rancière, Laclau, Negri, and Žižek. And this common ground, far from being shaken by it, is in fact set into place and guaranteed by the dissensus of the general social field in which both the postmodernist and post-Marxist theorize. For while the two camps may diverge on the politics of representation or the question of theory's relation to social practice, they come together in the general repudiation of the One and the All.

Note
Many of the authors and themes in this section are discussed under the heading Posthumanism.

Works Cited

Appiah, Kwame Anthony. "Is the Post- in Postmodernism the Post- in Postcolonial?" *Critical Inquiry* 17.2 (1991): 336–57.

Baudrillard, Jean. *The Evil Demon of Images*. Trans. Paul Patton and Paul Foss. Sydney: Power Institute of Fine Arts, 1988.

Baudrillard, Jean. *Simulacra and Simulation*. 1981. Trans. Sheila Faria Glaser. Ann Arbor: University of Michigan Press, 1994.

Baudrillard, Jean. *Simulations*. Trans. Paul Foss, Paul Patton, and Philip Beitchman. New York: Semiotext(e), 1983.

Beckett, Samuel. *Endgame*. New York: Grove, 1958.

Beckett, Samuel. *Three Novels: Molloy, Malone Dies, The Unnamable*. New York: Grove, 1965.

Best, Steven and Douglas Kellner. *Postmodern Theory: Critical Interrogations*. Basingstoke: Macmillan, 1991.

Burke, Edmund. *A Philosophical Enquiry into the Origin of Our Ideas of the Sublime and Beautiful*. London: J. Dodsley, 1767.

Cheah, Pheng. "Non-Dialectical Materialism." In *New Materialism: Ontology, Agency, and Politics*. Ed. Diana Coole and Samantha Frost. Durham, NC: Duke University Press, 2010. 70–91.

Deleuze, Gilles. *Bergsonism*. Trans. Hugh Tomlinson and Barbara Habberiam. New York: Zone Books, 1988.

Deleuze, Gilles. *Difference and Repetition*. Trans. Paul Patton. London: Athlone Press, 1994.

Deleuze, Gilles and Félix Guattari. *Anti-Oedipus: Capitalism and Schizophrenia.*. 1977. Trans. Robert Hurley, Mark Seem, and Helen R. Lane Minneapolis: University of Minnesota Press, 1983.

Deleuze, Gilles and Félix Guattari. *A Thousand Plateaus: Capitalism and Schizophrenia*. Trans. Brian Massumi. London: Athlone, 1988.

Edelstein, Marilyn. "Toward a Feminist Postmodern *Poléthique*: Kristeva on Ethics and Politics." In *Ethics, Politics and Difference in Julia Kristeva's Writing*. Ed. Kelly Oliver. New York: Routledge, 1993. 196–214.

Haber, Honi Fern. *Beyond Postmodern Politics: Lyotard, Rorty, Foucault*. New York: Routledge, 1994.

Habermas, Jürgen. "Modernity versus Postmodernity." *New German Critique* 22 (Spring 1981): 3–22.

Hutcheon, Linda. *Narcissistic Narrative: The Metafictional Paradox*. Waterloo, OT: Wilfred Laurier University Press, 1980.

Huyssen, Andreas. *After the Great Divide: Modernism, Mass Culture, Postmodernism*. Bloomington: Indiana University Press, 1986.

Jameson, Fredric. "Postmodernism and Consumer Culture." In *Postmodernism and Its Discontents: Theories, Practices*. Ed. Ann Kaplan. London: Verso, 1988. 13–29.

Jameson, Fredric. *Postmodernism, or, The Cultural Logic of Late Capitalism*. Durham, NC: Duke University Press, 1991.

Kant, Immanuel. *Critique of Judgment*. 1790. Trans. Werner S. Pluhar. Indianapolis: Hackett, 1987.

Kristeva, Julia. *Desire in Language: A Semiotic Approach to Literature and Art*. Ed. Leon S. Roudiez. Trans. Thomas Gora, Alice Jardine, and Leon S. Roudiez. New York: Columbia University Press, 1980.

Latour, Bruno. *We Have Never Been Modern*. 1991. Trans. Catherine Porter. Cambridge, MA: Harvard University Press, 1993.

Lyotard, Jean-François. *The Differend: Phrases in Dispute*. 1983. Trans. Georges Van Den Abbeele. Minneapolis: University of Minnesota Press, 1988.

Lyotard, Jean-François. *The Inhuman: Reflections on Time*. Trans. Geoffrey Bennington and Rachel Bow. Cambridge: Polity, 1991.

Lyotard, Jean-François. *The Postmodern Condition: A Report on Knowledge*. Trans. Geoff Bennington and Brian Massumi. Minneapolis: University of Minnesota Press, 1984.

Lyotard, Jean-François. *Postmodern Fables*. Trans. Georges Van Den Abbeele. Minneapolis: University of Minnesota Press, 1997.

Mallarmé, Stéphane. *Collected Poems*. Ed. and Trans. Henry Weinfield. Los Angeles: University of California Press, 1994.

Massumi, Brian. *Parables for the Virtual: Movement, Affect, Sensation*. Durham, NC and London: Duke University Press, 2002.

Merleau-Ponty, Maurice. "The Intertwining – The Chiasm." In *The Visible and the Invisible*. Ed. Claude Lefort. Trans. Alphonso Lingis. Evanston: Northwestern University Press, 1968. 130–55.

Nancy, Jean-Luc. *The Ground of the Image*. Trans. Jeff Fort. New York: Fordham University Press, 2005.

Nietzsche, Friedrich. *Beyond Good and Evil*. Trans. Walter Kaufmann. New York: Vintage, 1966.

Nietzsche, Friedrich. *The Gay Science*. Trans. Walter Kaufmann. New York: Vintage-Random, 1974.

Nietzsche, Friedrich. "On Truth and Lies in a Nonmoral Sense." In *Philosophy and Truth: Selections from Nietzsche's Notebooks of the Early 1870s*. Ed. and trans. Daniel Breazeale. Atlantic Highlands, NJ: Humanities Press, 1979. 79–97.

Rancière, Jacques. *Aesthetics and Its Discontents*. Trans. Steven Corcoran. Cambridge: Polity, 2009.

Riddel, Joseph. "Coup de Man, or The Uses and Abuses of Semiotics." *Cultural Critique* 4 (Fall 1986): 81–109.

Wicke, Jennifer. "Postmodern Identities and the Politics of the (Legal) Subject." In *Feminism and Postmodernism*. Ed. Margaret Ferguson and Jennifer Wicke. Durham, NC: Duke University Press, 1994. 10–33.

Wilson, Timothy. "Foucault, Genealogy, History." *Philosophy Today* 39.2 (Summer 1995): 157–70.

3   Language/Systems/Texts/Readers

Phenomenology and Hermeneutics

The main concern of phenomenology is consciousness and its chief problem is to determine the relation between consciousness and its object. As Robert Holub puts it, "Consciousness is always consciousness *of* something; it has a direction towards or a goal in the object" (291). To some extent, the chief problem of phenomenology is the problem of philosophy as such: to understand the relation between thought and the world we think about. From Plato to Hegel to Marx, this has largely been considered in terms of dialectical or categorical logic, both of which presuppose non-negotiable dualities: form/matter, spirit/body, thought/sensation, history/eternity, finite/infinite, heaven/earth, and so on. Phenomenology investigates a similar dualism, consciousness/object, and is caught up in a unique dilemma, for as a study of consciousness, phenomenology is an instance of philosophy taking itself as an object. This trend in philosophy first emerges in Hegel's *Phenomenology of Spirit*, which is an attempt to understand Reason in terms of an absolute or universal consciousness coming into knowledge of itself. Edmund Husserl, the founder of phenomenology as we think of it today, tackled the problem of consciousness from a different angle. He focused on the problem of the object *for* consciousness, which entailed the isolation and bracketing of the object, a process which Husserl called the *epoché*. Bracketing is meant to limit philosophical investigation to the intentional act of the subject, free of all externality, including that of the object or the object world in which the act takes place. It is also a guarantee that analysis will yield an exact record of experience. This raises the question of the reliability of perception, which phenomenology would answer by saying that bracketing is a function of understanding and subject to the same limits as philosophy as a whole. (Maurice Merleau-Ponty will later raise the question of perception and its relation to being.) If it were not for the initial supposition that consciousness is *for* something, then phenomenology would be left only with the pure act of intention without an object.

For Husserl, consciousness is *of the world*, which entails a universal standpoint for grasping, in an essential way, the "multiplicities of consciousness":

> If it is the case that whatever is experienced, whatever is thought, and whatever is seen as the truth are given and are possible only within [the corresponding acts of] experiencing, thinking, and insight, then the concrete and complete exploration of the world that exists and has scientific and evidential validity for us requires also the universal phenomenological exploration of the multiplicities of consciousness in whose synthetic changes the world subjectively takes shape as valid for us and perhaps as given with insight. The task extends to the whole of life – including aesthetic life, valuing life of whatever type, and practical life – through which the concrete life-world with its changing content likewise continuously takes shape for us as a value-world and a practical world. ("Phenomenology" 85–6)

Husserl was specifically interested in the "essential structures" of intentional consciousness that "allow the objects naively taken for granted in the 'natural attitude' [i.e., in the "whole of life"] … to 'constitute themselves' in consciousness" (Beyer). His *Ideas* (1913) describes how the object is constituted for analysis, how to talk about materiality and its properties (e.g., extension, substance), and how to reveal the object's essence through a phenomenological analysis of its "given" nature. This "intuition of essences" is the goal of his practice. "The knowledge of essence is 'vision' of its object," writes Emmanuel Levinas, "which is not only *signified* or *sighted* … but *given* 'clearly and distinctly' with evidence." Even with the object "'originally given,' … it *is in the very nature* of essence to require examples in order to be grasped" (*Unforeseen* 28; Levinas quotes from Husserl's *Logical Investigations*). As in Kant, the object remains in its own domain, and we are left with what is "given" to consciousness. The category of knowledge achieved through the intuition of essence yields a conception of "pure consciousness," "*a self-contained complex of being* … into which nothing can penetrate and out of which nothing can slip, to which nothing is spatiotemporally external." The spatiotemporal world, on the other hand, "which includes human being and the human Ego as subordinate single realities is, *according to its sense, a merely intentional being*, thus one has the merely secondary sense of a being *for* a consciousness" (*Ideas* 1: 112).

The emphasis on the essence of the object, not on the thing as inert matter, means that "what is objective *becomes a theoretical object*, an object, that is, of an *actively performed positing of being* in which the Ego lives and grasps what is objective, seizes and posits it as a being." Temporality resides in this process as the "essence of thingly being" (*Ideas* 2: 13, 35). Husserl's phenomenology is transcendental in the sense that it posits a ground in the idea, which is born of an intention (a positing of judgment) and makes possible knowledge of essence. "Husserl's primary concern," writes Elisabeth Ströker, "is that what is essential to an act be considered not just in terms of the act-quality, but rather in terms of the unity of quality and matter: this unity is to be understood as the 'intentional essence' of the act." The intentionality of consciousness is a relation to a *given* state of affairs and Husserl's "genuine discovery" was of "*the modes of givenness* of the object," a discovery which clarifies our sense that knowledge "depends not merely upon the intentional relation between an act of consciousness and an object, but also, and indeed essentially, upon the manifold modes of objective givenness and the modes of consciousness that belong to them" (28). Horizons of possibility are defined by the orientation of consciousness (in space and in time) toward the object that is "co-given" with it; it is the space of the "intentional essence" and thus of the temporality of intentionality, which folds past and future into the moment of consciousness (on intentionality, see Crowell).

Husserl's successors, particularly his student, Martin Heidegger, sought to overcome the idealism of transcendental phenomenology. Heidegger claimed that Husserl's ONTOLOGY reproduced consciousness as an ideal (as a *primary* being) and reaffirmed the utter externality of the object. He avoids this latent idealism by shifting his attention from consciousness *as* being to the essence of being, which is always understood as "worldly," as being-in-the-world. Heidegger's phenomenology is concerned with a specifically *human* being (Da-sein) and with "the interpretation of the fundamental structures of Da-sein with regard to its usual and average way of being." Da-sein is historical in the sense that it is "entangled in the world in which it is." Heidegger declares in *Being and Time* that the "destructuring of the history of ontology essentially belongs to the formulation of the question of being and is possible solely within such a formulation" (18, 20). The bracketing which allowed Husserl to avoid the question of the object in relation to the world around it (that is, the object unavailable *for* consciousness) proved insufficient for Heidegger, who required a hermeneutic method that would enable the questioning of being, that would peel back layers of prior knowledge about objects to arrive not at the object itself but at its "unconcealment" in the space of its being, which is made possible by our already *being there*. In Heidegger's investigation of the temporality of being, we find the first concerted attempt to write a theory of the totality of multiples. What is at stake is grasping the "structural whole of the everydayness of Da-sein in its totality," which entails delineating "the being of Da-sein" as a unity which "ontologically supports the structural whole as such, becomes accessible by completely looking *through* this whole *at a* primordially unified phenomenon which already lies in the whole in such a way that it is the ontological basis for every structural moment in its structural possibility" (170).

For Heidegger, phenomenology does not simply boil down to the maxim "To the things themselves" (*Being* 30). Rather, it is the "science of the being of beings," that is to say, ontology, but it is also something more. "Both terms characterize philosophy itself, its object and procedure. Philosophy is universal phenomenological ontology, taking its departure from the hermeneutic of Da-sein, which, as an analysis of *existence*, has fastened the end of the guideline of all philosophical inquiry at the point from which it *arises* and to which it *returns*" (34). This kind of inquiry entails "a development and appropriation of an understanding," a totality of presuppositions which Heidegger calls "the hermeneutical situation." This situation guarantees the "primordiality that fundamental ontology requires" (that is, its *ground*) and permits us to proceed to "the question of the primordial unity of [the] structural totality" (214). In the "unity of the structure of care," temporality ceases to be measurable by chronology or sequence: "Primordially constituted by care, Da-sein is always already ahead of itself." Time is an "ecstatic unity of the actual," a saturation of being in temporality, which enables the paradoxical disclosure that is also an unconcealment, the ambiguous dialectics of being *in time*. This is not a mere "'succession' of the ecstasies" but something like a tensed and spiraled temporality in which "the future is *not later* than the having-been, and the having-been is *not earlier* than the present. Temporality temporalizes itself as a future that makes present, in the process of having-been" (315, 321).

In "The Origin of the Work of Art," a late and masterful essay that draws on every element of his philosophy, Heidegger argues that art permits the revelation of *aletheia*, or truth, in the form of a double gesture of withdrawal and unconcealment, of presence and absence: "Art is truth setting itself to work" (39). He points to the temple, or *temple-work*, which "opens up a world and at the same time sets this world back again on earth" (42): the temple is a "setting up" that is both a "setting forth," a jutting of earth into world, and a concealment, a settling back into earth. The "work as work sets up a world," because "the work-being of the work itself has the character of a setting forth" (43–5). It is not "a merely imagined framework" but a shining forth and that which grounds this shining: "*the world worlds*" (44). We come back to truth, to "what corresponds to the actual, and the actual is what is in truth. The circle closes again" (50). We are not talking about truth as correspondence, a viewpoint that regards truth as a matter of reference to the full presence of a fact or being in the world. For Heidegger, truth is more complicated. The very nature of truth is "the unconcealment of beings," which is "never a merely existent state, but a happening. Unconcealment (truth) is neither an attribute of matter in the sense of beings, nor one of propositions" (52, 54). This is why we cannot escape the fact that the *actuality* of truth is essentially *untruth* and also why misrecognition lies at the foundation of and is necessary for true recognition. The truth of the work of art (particularly the work of poetry) is possible because beauty is "one way in which truth essentially occurs as unconcealment" (56) Art is exemplary in part because in being the truth of an artwork it is a truth of work as such; it is the "work-being of the work," the realm of Da-sein in the world: "the work moves the earth itself into the open region of a world and keeps it there" (46). (On Heidegger, see Posthumanism 268–9, 274–5, 283–8.)

The French tradition of phenomenology continues the Heideggerian project, particularly the emphasis on what Heidegger called "the Others," who are implicit in the idea of Being. "They are rather those from whom, for the most part, one does *not* distinguish oneself – those among whom one is too" (*Being* 154). For Emmanuel Levinas, as for Jean-Paul Sartre, the position of the OTHER takes on a new urgency. The Hegelian *other* serves to confirm the identity of the concept (for understanding) in a dialectical process, in which the sign of otherness (ALTERITY) is cancelled in the coming into being of the concept. If there is a "remainder" in this process, it is indeterminable and therefore unthinkable, a non-being. Philosophy's task, according to Levinas, is to nurture the *other*, which is the true ground of being. "Is not identity itself a failure?" Levinas asks. "The reunion of self and self [absolute SELF-IDENTITY] is a flop. Interiority is not rigorously interior. *I is an other*" (*Humanism* 60). The "strangeness" of being arises precisely in this faulty process of identity in which the individual is "stitched of responsibilities" to the *other*. Through these responsibilities, "he lacerates essence." Being is not "posed in itself and for itself like a free identity" but is a matter of "the subjectivity of the subject, his non-indifference to others in limitless responsibility" (67). Like Sartre, Levinas links human essence to the *commitment* made to others in an existential context. But this fact of the *other* opens up the whole ontology of being in a new way, for it suggests the unceasing presence of a shadow in the form of a *resemblance*.

In art, the image exemplifies the operation of resemblance, "not as the result of a comparison between an image and the original, but as the very movement that engenders the image" (Levinas, "Reality" 6). Here too Levinas echoes Sartre, who rejects the *referential relation* between word and thing signified (which is what we might expect in the realistic language of prose, from journalism to the novel) and who argues that in art we see "a double reciprocal relation of magical resemblance and meaning" (Sartre 31). Reality discloses its truth, Levinas avers, only because it is also its "double, its shadow, its image." He uses the term *allegory* to designate this doubling up that is at the same time a distance; thus the image is an "allegory of being" ("Reality" 6). The double, or shadow, is the "incessant murmuring of [a] distancing ... like a night manifesting itself in the night." In art, as in ethics, the "errancy of being" leads us to a realm that is "more external than truth" and to a mode of authenticity "that is not truth" (*Proper* 132, 134–5). This amounts to short-circuiting of the dialectical interplay of being and non-being, of truth and non-truth, by founding being and truth outside of themselves in a space of radical difference, of their negation and *non*-being. Since this space is precisely that of the *other*, one's being is founded in alterity, which is a way of saying that one's being is "in the world" with other beings. "Experience, like language," Levinas writes, "no longer seems to be made of isolated elements lodged somehow in a Euclidean space where they could expose themselves, each for itself, directly visible, signifying from themselves. They signify from the 'world' and from the position of the one who is looking" (*Humanism* 12). Levinas here invokes some of the dominant themes of phenomenology at mid-century: the problem of space (inside/outside), of perception (visibility/invisibility), and of the gaze (looking/being looked at). In each of these cases, the dialectical or binary relation is discombobulated in a way that produces radical doubt about the underlying distinctions. This presence that insists on its own absence clearly draws on the Heideggerian notion of a disclosure that is also a withdrawal. But Levinas describes it in terms of a doubling that is marked by a shadow of what is not present, a shadow that subtends and gives outline to what *is* present. "The idea of shadow or reflection to which we have appealed – of an essential doubling of reality by its image, of an ambiguity 'on the hither side' – extends to the light itself, to thought, to the inner life. The whole of reality bears on its face its own allegory, outside of its revelation and its truth" ("Reality" 7).

The problem with art is that it locks up this resemblance in an image, a frozen moment of time, excluding it from engagement with others (other things) in the world. If an image is an idol, this means that "every image is in the last analysis plastic and that every artwork is in the end a statue – a stoppage of time, or rather its delay behind itself.... The statue realizes the paradox of an instant that endures without a future" ("Reality" 8–9). The temporality of being in art is the "eternal duration of the interval – the *meanwhile*" and it leads to art's disengagement from the world. The critic's task is to integrate "the inhuman work of the artist into the human world" (11–12). Unfortunately, as Sartre notes at about the same time (1949), critics are not always up to the task, for they have taken "quiet little jobs as cemetery watchmen" and are concerned only with dead things: "It is a whole disembodied world which surrounds him, where human feelings, because they are no longer affecting, have passed on to the status of exemplary feelings and, in short, of *values*" (41–2). The critic intent on *meaning* fails to grasp the *message* communicated in art, in "'true,' 'pure' literature, a subjective thing which reveals itself under the aspect of the objective, a discourse so curiously contrived that it is equivalent to silence, a thought which debates itself, a reason which is only the mask of madness, an Eternal which lets it be understood that it is only a moment of history" (45).

Mikel Dufrenne approaches this aspect of art – the curious "subjective thing" that reveals itself as objective – in terms of the "expressed world" it creates. This world is, in a sense, waiting for the work of art to bring it into being, for it "is not yet structured in accordance with space and time but is rather the potentiality of space and time – as it is of objects as well." The aesthetic object thus expresses "a preobjective space and time *as* this world" (182–3). Merleau-Ponty proceeds on just such a presupposition of a "preobjective space" prior to perception. In

Phenomenology of Perception (1945), he argues that perception is not available to objective thought, which is "unaware of the subject of perception. This is because it presents itself with the world ready made, as the setting of every possible event, and treats perception as one of these events" (140). The subject of perception is both inside and outside of sensation. "Sensation is intentional," Merleau-Ponty writes, "because I find that in the sensible a certain rhythm of experience is put forward." He makes clear that the "sensor and the sensible do not stand in relation to each other as two mutually external terms, and [that] sensation is not an invasion of the sensor by the sensible" (148). The "gaze" subtends and "pairs off" the sensations we receive, and there is no intrinsic reason to privilege the sensor or the sensible. "The unity of the sense, which was regarded as an *a priori* truth, is no longer anything but the formal expression of a fundamental contingency: the fact that we are in the world" (256).

In the later work, Merleau-Ponty sharpens his sense of this unity by abolishing any residual duality. Thus, his critique of René Descartes, in "Eye and Mind," is in part an attempt to accomplish what Gaston Bachelard said was needed: to move beyond geometrical opposition (e.g., subject/object) and the idea of perspectival distance, which only recognizes degrees of material space between objects in a field. Descartes locates the being of man on the "inside" (i.e., the side of the subject), while consigning the outside to the realm of resemblances and inessential matter; but no "mental image" can stand "like a breakthrough to the heart of Being" ("Eye," 132). Descartes' revolutionary act was to liberate space from two-dimensional being and thus to open experience to "the absolute positivity of Being": "space without hiding places which in each of its points is only what it is, neither more nor less." However, by liberating space, Descartes manages also, wrongly, to "erect it into a positive being, beyond all points of view, all latency and depth, devoid of any real thickness" (134–5). This raises the problem of vision – a sensation that must be brought under the aegis of thought – which Descartes resolved by making the body a unique space, "the place of the body the soul calls 'mine' ... and the matrix of every other existing space." Vision therefore doubles: it is "the vision upon which I reflect" and "the vision that actually occurs ... collapsed into a body" which cannot be thought, but only exercised. However, banishing vision to the unthinking body does not really resolve the problem, for the "enigma of vision is not done away with; it is shifted from the 'thought of seeing' to vision in act" (136). Merleau-Ponty's theory of "the flesh" eliminates the barriers, erected by Cartesian dualistic thinking, between the body and the space it occupies, between the soul or thought that "sees" and the sensations of sight that involve the body in space. Subject and object dissolve in the unfolding of being in "the flesh" where inside and outside coincide and in which what is visible enjoys Being (as such). On this view, depth is a kind of reversibility of dimensions, "of a global 'locality' in which everything is in the same place at the same time" (140). "The flesh," understood as a preobjective space, incessantly intervenes before experience becomes that of discrete subjects and objects. "The flesh is not matter, is not mind, is not substance. To designate it, we should need the old term 'element,' ... a sort of incarnate principle that brings a style of being wherever there is a fragment of being. The flesh is in this sense an 'element' of Being" ("The Intertwining" 139).

Bachelard and Georges Bataille both attack the basic question here – the status of the outside with respect to a privileged inside – by developing an anti-dialectical method that stridently resists the distinction between inside/outside. To retain this distinction is to limit philosophical investigation to a "language of agglutination" (Bachelard 174). Like his contemporaries, Bachelard is interested in "being," but not in a way that can be "settled" through dualistic thinking. For him, "the being of man is an unsettled being which all expression unsettles" (175). The unsettlement of being and the convolution of inside/outside are obvious in the poetic image, which allegorizes the internalization of the dangers (of alterity, of materiality) posed by the outside: "a becoming of being that is an awareness of the *being's inner disturbance*" (178). Bataille reached a similar limit in his writing, which put fresh and aggressive pressure on the dualism that continued to vex philosophical discourse. His focus on the abyss, sacrifice, and sexual transgression was meant to draw philosophy toward the questions that it could not ask, questions that, once asked, would undermine philosophy's foundation by unveiling the constitutive alterity of what is meant to be identical to it. The sacred time of transgression, of eroticism and sacrifice, is separated from the world of work, which requires efficiency and freedom from distractions. Philosophy is a kind of work that has been distracted from providing a true "sum of the possibles" – including the taboo and unthinkable. Its warrant has been instead to consider only "certain well-defined experiences aimed at knowledge" (Bataille 258).

Such a position would be foreign to the hermeneutist who considers all of human thought and experience to come under its "all-encompassing" universality (Gadamer, *Philosophical* 103). Modern hermeneutics begins with Friedrich Schleiermacher, the early nineteenth-century philosopher who established hermeneutics as "the art of understanding particularly the written discourse of another person correctly." Criticism, which establishes "the authenticity of texts and parts of texts from adequate evidence and data," thus presupposes hermeneutic understanding. But because hermeneutical "explication" can establish the meaning of a text only after the "authenticity of the text or part of the text can be presupposed, then the practice of hermeneutics presupposes criticism" (Schleiermacher 3–4). This "hermeneutical circle" constitutes "an opposition between the unity of the whole and the individual parts of the work, so that the task could be set in a twofold manner, namely to understand the unity of the whole via the individual parts and the value of the individual parts via the unity of the whole" (109). Schleiermacher believed that the logical contradiction of such a circle can be overcome by an intuitive leap into an understanding of the part and whole in conjunction (see Palmer 87f), a leap that Heidegger regarded as intrinsic to the questioning of being: "The 'circle' in understanding belongs to the structure of meaning, and this phenomenon is rooted in the existential constitution of Da-sein, in interpretive understanding" (*Being* 143). The philosopher moves back and forth from part to whole, from whole to historical tradition. Thus, as Heidegger illustrates, the truth of art is brought forth in the work, but the work is established in the truth that is this bringing-forth. It is the "strength of thought": "We are compelled to follow the circle.... Not only is the main step from work to art a circle like a step from art to work, but every separate step that we attempt circles in this circle" ("Origin" 18).

The interrelationship of hermeneutics and criticism constitutes a circle of mutually reinforcing power, one that ensures the validity of the enterprise. This hermeneutical practice is rooted in early Christian attempts to battle heresy and other threats through appeal to the authority of tradition; but the outlines of a science of hermeneutics were not visible until after the Reformation made the Bible available in the vulgate and opened up the possibility of new and even private ways of bridging the gap between the reader and ancient authorities. As Wilhelm Dilthey puts it, "the rise of Protestantism began to set exegesis free" (*Hermeneutics* 34). In this sense, hermeneutics was a special project of interpretation designed to understand the true intent of past authors by bridging the gap created by time, culture, and geography. Michael Forster shows that the emphasis on both language and psychology in hermeneutics can be traced to German idealism generally but specifically to Friedrich Schlegel and Johann Gottfried Herder (*German* ch. 2); he also shows that Schleiermacher's own contributions to this theory of interpretation stress the historically conditioned differences among writers and the holistic relation of the word with its textual and other contexts (see "Schleiermacher"). For example, in order to understand the true intent of epistles written by the Apostles under different circumstances and for different purposes, it is necessary for the interpreter to know as much as possible about those circumstances. "The certainty in the achievement of the hermeneutic task," writes Schleiermacher, "depends on the degree of knowledge which we have of the circumstances themselves" (148). As Richard Palmer puts it, hermeneutical understanding "as an art is the reexperience of the mental processes of the text's author." It is a scientific mode of grasping both the linguistic structure of the text's language and the "mental life" of the author. In short, hermeneutics is meant to "guide the process of extracting meaning from a text" (86, 91).

For Dilthey, the task of hermeneutics is to arrive at an objective understanding of the past. Schleiermacher believed that the "vocabulary and the history of the era of an author" were bound up in the hermeneutical circle presented to the critic for understanding (24). Dilthey made possible a clear distinction between the specific understanding proper to human sciences and the mode of explanation proper to the natural sciences. His aim was to see that the former ran along lines as rigorous and stable as the latter. If the problem for the classic tradition was to grasp the holism of the interpretive experience, for Dilthey it is to traverse the gap between understanding and analysis. "The art of understanding of intellectual life and history," therefore, centers "on the interpretation of written records of human existence." The limits of "general knowledge" in the human sciences depend on the alignment of understanding with "the analysis of inner experience." Language is what captures this human inwardness, and Dilthey believed that humanist understanding has developed in the same "orderly" fashion as does "the questioning of nature by experiment" (*Selected* 249). Following Schleiermacher, Dilthey argues that the principles of valid interpretation "can be deduced from the nature of understanding," which leads to the conclusion that "all individual differences are, in the last resort, conditioned not by qualitative differences between people but by differences of degree in their mental processes." The vital connection between two mental states is possible experimentally if the interpreter engages "some mental processes" more strenuously than others; in this way, he can "reproduce an alien life in himself" (258). By creating "empathy with the mental life of others," Dilthey held that one could achieve "the objective apprehension of the unique" which can provide a form of "general validity." The key question for him is whether we can reliably "reconstruct" and know objectively "the distinct individuality of another." Explanation, on the order of the logical and empirical sciences, cannot produce this kind of knowledge; only understanding through interpretation or exegesis can arrive at the "systematic understanding of recorded expressions" (247–8).

Historical hermeneutics, then, does not borrow a scientific status it has not earned but rather provides its own form of legitimation through a method of interpretation adequate to its task (i.e., reading particular texts written in a particular past) but also universal in the sense that it makes available to any interpreter the same horizon of understanding ("historicality"). The specific dimensions of this horizon change with each act of interpretation, but the act itself is made possible by the horizon that is *re*-formed from the state of universal potentiality in the act of reading.

Hans-Georg Gadamer and Paul Ricoeur take up the two main strands of thought on hermeneutics (Heidegger's and Dilthey's) and draw out the element of *self-understanding*, which the hermeneutist achieves through building bridges between different lived experiences in language. The aim is to discover an objective ground in an act of reading that effectively returns interpretation to a stable reference. Gadamer, a student of Heidegger's writing at mid-century, was the leading theorist of this new hermeneutical tradition. For him, the text did not lie on the far side of a temporal gap but was capable of being understood within the "horizon" of a present moment, in which interpretation is grounded in the "historicality" of the interpreter. In this, he follows Heidegger in positing the notion of a horizon that is projected even before our experience comes into shape within it. Commenting on Heidegger's critique of "modern subjectivism" and the new temporalities it enables, Gadamer writes that "[i]nterpreting being from the horizon of time does not mean, as it is constantly misunderstood to mean, that Dasein is radically temporal, so that it can no longer be considered as everlasting or eternal but is understandable only in relation to its own time and future." This misreading tends to strengthen the hold of subjectivism by making it existential, while the pertinent question for philosophy is the subjectivism itself. "The philosophical question asks, what is the being of self-understanding? With this question [subjectivism] fundamentally transcends the horizon of this self-understanding." Understood in this way, subjectivism opens itself up to a "hitherto concealed experience that transcends thinking from the position of subjectivity, an experience that Heidegger calls *being*" (*Truth* 86).

Hermeneutics does not merely comprehend context, nor does it merely record the complex and interrelated subjective experiences and intentions that constitute the past as represented in the text; its proper field of understanding is the "great matrix of the meaning of history" as presented to us *in its being* in language. The proposition "that being that can be understood is language" (*Truth* 103) supports the "all-encompassing" universality of the hermeneutical perspective. Dilthey had argued for the "general validity" of the unique apprehension derived from a "systematic understanding" of a text; Gadamer develops this insight, via Heidegger, in the direction of a method that avoids naïve historicism ("reconstructing what the author really had in mind"). Such a method refuses to reconstruct the "question to which a given text is an answer," preferring to attend to "the question that the text puts to us," which takes the form of "our being perplexed by the traditionary world, so that understanding it must already include the task of the historical self-mediation between the present and tradition" (*Truth* 366).

Tradition belongs to human Da-sein because the "fundamental constitution" of Da-sein's historicity is "to mediate itself to itself understandingly." Aesthetics, too, "belongs to the matrix of things we have to understand" and its aim is that of hermeneutics generally, "avoiding misunderstanding" (Gadamer, *Philosophical* 96, 98). The experience of art is "an encounter with the authentic," "a familiarity that includes surprise." Art captures experience as such (in "a real sense") and thus has "the task of integrating it into the whole of one's own orientation to a world and one's own self-understanding" (101–2). This is not a metaphysical position, however; for if the assertion "that being that can be understood is language" supports the idea of universality, it does so by describing "from the medium of understanding, the unrestricted scope possessed by the hermeneutical perspective" (103). As Gadamer notes, following Heidegger, this universal aspect is fulfilled only by art, which possesses the "symbolic character" that belongs to all beings; unlike the historical text, which makes the past available for the hermeneutical enterprise in the present moment of exegesis, the work of art is the "absolute present for each particular present, and at the same time holds its word in readiness for every future" (104).

Ricoeur agrees with this idea of readiness and locates within the attitude of receptivity and openness the material ground for interpretation *outside* the text. Ricoeur is in part responding to poststructuralists like **Jacques Derrida** who promote the idea of the "absolute text," which Ricoeur rejects because it cuts the text off from any ground in lived experience. In a hermeneutic framework, the text is capable of providing just such a ground in the referential function of language, which involves the reader in the "task of reading, *qua* interpretation, [which is] precisely to fulfill the reference" (148). This is why Ricoeur begins with the question, "what is a text?" To begin with, the text is more than a written form of speech, for it records what *could have been said*; indeed, it is "written precisely because it is not said" (147). "Fixation in writing" occurs where "speech could have emerged"; it describes directly the meaning of the text, in which writing splits discourse and creates "a double eclipse of the reader and the writer. It thereby replaces the relation of dialogue, which directly connects the voice of one to the hearing of the other." This "intention-to-say," which writing transcribes, is not the same as the "graphic inscription of the signs of speech." It is the "emancipation of writing" and the "birth of the text" (147). But this emancipation precipitates an "upheaval" in the relation between the *referential function* of language and the external world. Reference is not annulled or suppressed, as it is in the "the absolute text," but held in a state of suspension, which "leaves the text, as it were, 'in the air,' outside or without a world." Texts then are free to interact with each other. "This relation of text to text, within the effacement of the world … engenders the quasi-world of texts or *literature*" (148).

Roland Barthes, one of the architects of the absolute text, has similarly noted the birth of the text in the reader, though in his view, the suspense of reference is precisely the point. Ricoeur's radical departure from poststructuralism lies in his insistence that reference truly grounds the experience of reading and provides a foundation for knowledge and its legitimation. He makes his case by returning to Dilthey's two "fundamental attitudes" toward the text, *explanation* (natural sciences) and *interpretation* (human sciences): explanation enables the identification of objects in the natural sciences, while interpretation provides the "degree of objectification" for understanding in the human sciences, based on the "fixing" and preserving power that "writing confers upon signs" (150–1). Whereas Dilthey believed hermeneutics must extricate itself from the material and affective dimension of self-understanding, if it is to achieve the validity proffered by explanation, Ricoeur, like Gadamer, requires this dimension. Therefore, a ground for objectivity and universality had to be found in the one domain that exists for explanation *within* the human sciences. Structuralist linguistics provides just such a ground, which is established at the level of interpretation and self-understanding. For in hermeneutical interpretation, the reader does not act *on* the text but achieves self-understanding, in an objective sense, through a "process of interpretation that would be the act *of* the text" (162).

By the 1960s and 1970s, a new generation of European intellectuals were transforming phenomenology by combining it with new theoretical models from structuralism, psychoanalysis, and Marxism. One could say that with phenomenology and hermeneutics, philosophy is poised at the outer limits of idealism, the point at which it shatters into innumerable particularities that bear the imprint of being in its full PRESENCE. The next three sections explore the implications of this philosophy at the limits. For in reader-response theory, deconstruction, and poststructuralism we find new ways of thinking about language and aesthetics that are profoundly destructive of dualisms and the "rigid geometries" of dialectics.

Works Cited

Bachelard, Gaston. *The Poetics of Space*. Trans. Maria Jolas. Boston: Beacon Press, 1994.

Bataille, Georges. *Eroticism, Death and Sensuality*. Trans. Mary Dalwood. San Francisco: City Lights Books, 1986.

Beyer, Christian. "Edmund Husserl." *Stanford Encyclopedia of Philosophy* (Winter 2011). Ed. Edward Zalta. http://plato.stanford.edu/archives/win2011/entries/husserl/ (accessed November 2012).

Crowell, Steven. "Husserlian Phenomenology." In *A Companion to Phenomenology and Existentialism*. Ed. Hubert L. Dreyfus and Mark A. Wrathall. Oxford: Wiley-Blackwell, 2006. 9–30.

Dilthey, Wilhelm. *Hermeneutics and the Study of History*. Vol. 4 of *Selected Works*. Ed. Rudolf A. Makkreel and Frithjof Rodi. Princeton: Princeton University Press, 1996.

Dilthey, Wilhelm. *Selected Writings*. Ed. and trans. H. P. Rickman. Cambridge: Cambridge University Press, 1976.

Dufrenne, Mikel. *The Phenomenology of Aesthetic Experience*. Trans. E. S. Casey et al. Evanston: Northwestern University Press, 1966.

Forster, Michael N. *German Philosophy of Language: From Schlegel to Hegel and Beyond*. Oxford: Oxford University Press, 2011.

Gadamer, Hans Georg. *Philosophical Hermeneutics*. Trans. and ed. David E. Linge. Berkeley: University of California Press, 1976.

Gadamer, Hans Georg. *Truth and Method*. 2nd rev. ed. Rev. trans. Joel Weinsheimer and Donald G. Marshall. London and New York: Continuum, 2004.

Heidegger, Martin. *Being and Time*. Trans. Joan Stambaugh. Albany: SUNY Press, 1996.

Heidegger, Martin. "The Origin of the Work of Art." In *Poetry, Language, Thought*. Trans. Albert Hofstadter. New York: Harper and Row, 1971. 17–87.

Holub, Robert. "Phenomenology." In *The Cambridge History of Literary Criticism*. Vol. 8: *From Formalism to Poststructuralism*. Ed. Raman Selden. Cambridge and New York: Cambridge University Press, 1995. 289–318.

Husserl, Edmund. *Ideas Pertaining to a Pure Phenomenology and to a Phenomenological Philosophy*. 3 vols. Dordrecht, Netherlands: Kluwer Academic Publishers, 1982.

Husserl, Edmund. "Phenomenology." In *Psychological and Transcendental Phenomenology and the Confrontation with Heidegger (1927–1931)*. Ed. and trans. Thomas Sheehan and Richard E. Palmer. Dordrecht, Netherlands: Kluwer Academic Publishers, 1997. 80–198.

Levinas, Emmanuel. *Humanism of the Other*. Trans. Nidra Poller. Urbana: University of Illinois Press, 2003.

Levinas, Emmanuel. *Proper Names*. Trans. Michael B. Smith. London: Athlone Press, 1996.

Levinas, Emmanuel. "Reality and Its Shadow." *Collected Philosophical Papers*. Trans. Alphonos Lingis: Dordrecht, Netherlands: M. Nijhoff, 1987. 1–14.

Levinas, Emmanuel. *Unforeseen History*. Trans. Nidra Poller. Urbana and Chicago: University of Illinois Press, 2004.

Merleau-Ponty, Maurice. "Eye and Mind." In *The Merleau-Ponty Aesthetics Reader: Philosophy and Painting*. Ed. Galen A. Johnson. Trans. and ed. Michael B. Smith. Evanston, IL: Northwestern University Press, 1993. 121–50.

Merleau-Ponty, Maurice. "The Intertwining – The Chiasm." In *The Visible and the Invisible*. Ed. Claude Lefort. Trans. Alphonso Lingis. Evanston, IL: Northwestern University Press, 1968. 130–55.

Merleau-Ponty, Maurice. *Phenomenology of Perception*. Trans. Colin Smith. New York: Humanities Press, 1962.

Palmer, Richard, E. *Hermeneutics: Interpretation Theory in Schleiermacher, Dilthey, Heidegger and Gadamer*. Evanston, IL: Northwestern University Press, 1969.

Ricoeur, Paul. "What is a Text? Explanation and Understanding." In *Hermeneutics and Human Sciences: Essays on Language, Action and Interpretation*. Ed. and trans. John B. Thompson. Cambridge: Cambridge University Press, 1981. 145–64.

Sartre, Jean-Paul. "What Is Literature?" Trans. Bernard Frechtman. In *"What Is Literature?" and Other Essays*. Cambridge, MA: Harvard University Press, 1988. 21–245.

Schleiermacher, Friedrich. *Hermeneutics and Criticism and Other Writings*. Ed. and trans. Andrew Bowie. Cambridge: Cambridge University Press, 1998.

Ströker, Elisabeth. *Husserl's Transcendental Phenomenology*. Trans. Lee Hardy. Stanford: Stanford University Press, 1993.

Reader-Response Theory

If the hermeneutical tradition is concerned with self-understanding through interpretation, reader-response theory explores the specific mechanisms whereby this self-understanding is achieved through the act of reading. The importance of the reader in literary theory has long been acknowledged, but the reader's role has historically been subordinated to an understanding of the text's *content*. Twentieth-century formalist theories, including New Criticism, confirmed that the reader's experience is guided by formal cues inherent in the text, while rhetoricians, like the Chicago School Neo-Aristotelians, rely on predictable reactions on the part of readers when presented with specific kinds of rhetorical situations (e.g., an unreliable narrator). These approaches share in common a sense that reading is a part of a larger formal process that, far from being passive, is a skilled capacity for discovering the text's internal dynamics and structural unities. However, there were some figures in that movement who did significant work with reader response. For example, I. A. Richard's experiments in reading in his *Practical Criticism* (1929) took an "affective" approach that measured emotional responses and attitudes. We might also regard William Empson's work on ambiguity in poetry as implicitly a theory of reading that anticipates in some respects **Paul de Man**'s rhetorical deconstruction; but Empson's attention to formal structures leaves him little room to explore the reader's role in interpreting ambiguity, other than his own role as a kind of "master reader."

Formalist and structuralist theories of narrative attempt to account for the reader in terms of an overall textual *gestalt*. Important for such approaches is not the reader's emotional or intellectual disposition but rather her competence with respect to the codes employed in a given narrative. Vladimir Propp's theory of the folktale is exemplary in this regard, for in his view folklore is structured in such a way as to solicit certain reactions in the reader according to the arrangement of formal and thematic elements. The reader is, in a sense, a function of the text, a formal necessity quite separate from the equally necessary existence of "real" readers. Gerald Prince, in discussing the role of the "narratee," makes this point explicitly: "The reader of fiction, be it in prose or in verse, should not be mistaken for the narratee. The one is real, the other fictive. If it should occur that the reader bears an astonishing resemblance to the narratee, this is an exception and not the rule" (9). Umberto Eco's SEMIOTIC theory of reading similarly locates a "fictional" reader in the text, but his poststructuralist orientation overcomes to some degree the limits of formalist models of the reading process. Eco remains committed to a semiotic structure of sender and addressee but defines the two positions in terms of their "actantial roles" in the sentence (i.e., their roles in the narrative grammar), "not as *sujet de l'énonciation*, but as *sujet de l'énoncé*" (10). Reading takes place within "a given *field of relations*" that constitutes an *open text* in which these relations are governed by an "organizing rule." The reader's freedom inheres in the task of completing the text: "[T]he author offers the interpreter, the performer, the addressee a work *to be completed*." And while the author cannot know how the work will be completed, it "will still be his own. It will not be a different work" (62). Unlike a *closed text*, which may invite a variety of "aberrant" readings but only insofar as they are read independently of each other, the open text exhibits a plurality of potential interpretations made possible within a "semantico-pragmatic process" in which the Model Reader makes decisions that are in fact a "component of [the text's] structural strategy" (9). **Roland Barthes**' provocative and influential essay, "The Death of the Author," draws the inevitable conclusion from such textualist theories of reading: "[T]he reader is the space on which all the quotations that make up a writing are inscribed without any of them being lost; a text's unity lies not in its origin but in its destination.... [T]he birth of the reader must be at the cost of the death of the Author" (148).

Eco's point about the role of the reader completing the text is central to contemporary reader-response theory, which is concerned principally with the way readers frame interpretations. Early work in reader-response theory – by Georges Poulet, Roman Ingarden, and **Wolfgang Iser** – was grounded in phenomenological hermeneutics. Poulet, of the Geneva school of literary critics, developed a phenomenology of reading in which the text defines the "horizon" of the author's consciousness and the reader's relation to it. He argues that the act of reading is a process of opening oneself up to an "alien" consciousness. In the act of reading, "I am aware of a rational being, of a consciousness; the consciousness of another, no different from the one I automatically assume in every human being I encounter, except in this case the consciousness is open to me, welcomes me, lets me look deep inside itself" (54). Reading breaks down the barrier between subject and object in part by transforming the text-as-object into another subject, one that occupies the reader's consciousness, existing simultaneously within it. "You are inside [the text]; it is inside you; there is no longer either outside or inside" (54). It is not the author's consciousness that occupies the reader's mind as subject, though such things as biographical and bibliographical information are certainly important to the reader. What penetrates the reader's mind and exists within it as an "alien subject," what effectively "loans" the reader's SUBJECTIVITY to the text, is the consciousness of the text itself: "the subject which presides over the work can exist only in the work" (58). The "I" spoken in the reader's mind is the "I" of the work. Poulet's phenomenological approach was influential among critics in the 1960s and 1970s who were combating the formalism of the New Criticism, particularly the US deconstructionist **J. Hillis Miller**. Ultimately, however, as Iser has noted, Poulet's "substantialist conception of the consciousness that constitutes itself in the literary work" (*Implied Reader* 293) was ill-suited to the formation of pragmatic conceptions of the relationship between reader and work.

Reader-response theory in Europe since the 1970s has remained indebted to hermeneutics, even as it absorbs the lessons of structuralist linguistics and deconstruction. The most significant and influential advances have come from Ingarden and the Konstanz school theorists Iser and Hans Robert Jauss. For them, reading is fundamentally a process in which the reader activates or completes a text. Ingarden's phenomenological study of literary art presents a theory of "concretization" or "realization," the dynamic process by which the reader participates in the creation of a text's potential meanings. He found "absurd" the idea that "the literary work is nothing but a manifold of experiences felt by the reader during the reading" (*Literary* 15). Nor did he think that "the attributes, experiences, or psychic states of the reader" belong in the "structure of the work." While the reader may enjoy "pleasurable experiences" in the reading process, these experiences are not technically part of the text itself (23–4). Of signal importance is the "cognition of the literary work," which entails the "intentional reconstruction and then the cognition of the objectivities portrayed in the work." The act of reading is not "a mere experience or reception of something" or simply the act of "thinking the meaning of sentences" (*Cognition* 37). The difference between this passive form of reading and an active one lies in the orientation of the reader toward "signitive acts," which the active reader performs; the passive reader, on the other hand, "only experiences or feels that they are being performed" (38–9). The active reader not only understands "sentence meanings but also apprehends their objects and has a sort of intercourse with them." Only an active reading can enable the discovery of the text "in its peculiar, characteristic structure and in its full detail" (39, 41).

Iser develops further Ingarden's claim that "the reader to some extent proves to be the cocreator of the literary work of art" (*Cognition* 41). In fact, he argues that "the convergence of the text and the reader brings the literary work into existence" (*Implied Reader* 275). Iser postulates the existence of *expectations* (what the phenomenologist Edmund Husserl called *pre-intentions*) whose unfulfillment constitutes the structure of the literary text. Unlike a didactic text (for example, a cookbook or a chemistry textbook), the literary text is filled with gaps and blockages, "unexpected twists and turns, and frustration of expectations" (279). For this reason, it is constitutively indeterminate and inexhaustible, which explains why the same text can accommodate a variety of different interpretations. The literary text is far more than what is written in it; and this "far more" comes into existence precisely as part of a creative process whereby the reader's own faculties are brought into play. The reader's desire for consistency comes up against the text's recalcitrance, its tendency to allow "alien associations" to interrupt the smooth, consistent flow of reading. However, while the illusion of consistency is continually being shattered, the need for consistency persists, in large measure, Iser argues, because it is tied up with our desire to interpret the world: "The need to decipher gives us the chance to formulate our own deciphering capacity – i.e., we bring to the fore an element of our being of which we are not directly conscious" (294). In this way, the "'reality' of the reading experience illuminates basic patterns of real experience"; it confers upon the text what Iser calls a "dynamic lifelikeness" that "enables us to absorb an unfamiliar experience into our personal world" (281, 288). Grasping the "staging" of action in literature is, for Iser, central to this process of illuminating the reader's experience, for staging "makes conceivable the extraordinary plasticity of human beings" (*Fictive* 297).

The reader, Iser insists, discovers as much about the whole affective dimension of human experience as about herself or the text she reads. And by virtue of this discovery, she is equipped to comprehend her own being as a concrete historical subject. Hans Robert Jauss' work on reception theory focuses on this aspect of the reading process. For Jauss, *Rezeptionsästhetik* (aesthetics of reception) is both an approach to literary history and a critical means of determining the specific "horizons of expectation" that historical readers confront. It is, in essence, a reverse hermeneutics that attempts to recover, through analysis, the situation of past readers in the past. "The historical life of a literary work," Jauss writes, "is unthinkable without the active participation of its audience." Reception theory aims to enable the reader to experience the historical continuity of the literary work, a continuity in which "change occurs from simple reception to critical understanding" (8). *Rezeptionsästhetik* mediates between the "passive reception" of a "norm-setting" reading protocol and the "active understanding" bound up in establishing new modes of literary production. Literary history from this perspective enables both an understanding of past readers and the development of new modes of reading and writing.

Advances in US reader-response theory tend toward rhetorical and pragmatic modes of engagement with the text and literary history. Paul de Man, who champions a rhetorical approach, has criticized the Konstanz school for its commitment to "grammatical models or … traditional hermeneutical models," which for him means that it cannot "allow for the problematization of the phenomenalism of reading and therefore remain[s] uncritically confined within a theory of literature rooted in aesthetics" (18). De Man's own rhetorical theory of reading holds that the reader is constantly being misled or tempted into misrecognizing what the "figures" in the text signify. It presupposes that there can be no identity between the text and the world, and the reader and the text, for if there could be such an identity, then all readers would have the exact same experience. Since this is patently *not* the case, US poststructuralists like De Man and J. Hillis Miller have attempted to explain the difference in readings and in how we read. (On De Man and Miller, see Deconstruction 162–6.) The pragmatist **Stanley Fish** is interested in quite the opposite phenomenon: despite differences in class, gender, ethnicity, and so on, he argues, we still manage to read texts in *similar* ways. Like Iser, Fish believes that the reader is instrumental in the construction of meaningful texts. The only way to maneuver within a "scene of reading" riddled by contradictions, ellipses, gaps, and other inconsistencies is to learn the interpretive protocols of a given community of readers. In *Surprised by Sin* (1967), he argues that John Milton, in *Paradise Lost*, creates a form of empathy between the reader and Satan that leads the reader to experience the fall of Adam and Eve in an unorthodox way. The reader is thus in a position to grasp the powerful moral and religious lessons that Milton's depiction of the "fortunate fall" has to offer. In later essays, collected in *Is There a Text in This Class?* (1980), Fish explores the dangers of succumbing to the "affective fallacy," which substitutes subjective response for meaning, and advocates a form of "affective stylistics," which holds that our affective response to the text is not the text's *meaning* but part of a strategy for constituting the text *as a text*. The reader's experience (what the text actually *does*) is coextensive with the text *as such*. For Fish, "a stylistic fact is a fact of response" (*Is There* 65), which means there can be no point in separating poetic from non-poetic styles. In his theory of affective stylistics, he underscores the anti-formalist orientation of reader-response theory and argues, against critics like I. A. Richards and Michael Riffaterre, that the distinction between poetic and non-poetic language, and the consequent privileging of the former, limits the interpretive potential of language and texts.

Affective approaches to reading acknowledge the emotional investments made by readers in the text. According to Steven Katz, affective experience cannot be totally described or felt with the same immediacy as the original experience, nor can it be determined empirically as an object of knowledge. It thus exhibits a state of indeterminacy that would bring a theory of reading to the limits of what can be theoretically known (61ff). As Brian Massumi puts it, "emotion and affect … follow different logics" (27), and it is these logics that can be fruitfully conjoined with theories of how we read and, ultimately, with an ethics of reading that is based not on reading the ethical dimension of a given text, but on the ethical practice that reading puts into play and constitutes and that is only partly involved in explicit communication. Fish offers a powerful hedge against the subjectivism into which an affective approach might fall with his argument that the "informed" reader's response is not arbitrary or random, that there are "'regularizing' constraints on response." These constraints are produced by "the system of rules all speakers share" and by various forms of linguistic and semantic competence honed within "interpretative communities" (*Is There* 44–5). Like Iser, he argues that the meaning derived from literary texts is the product of a "joint responsibility." Meaning is thus "redefined as an event rather than an entity": "[T]he reader's response is not *to* the meaning; it *is* the meaning" (3). The "informed reader" learns the appropriate reading responses by being a member of a community "made up of those who share interpretive strategies" that "exist prior to the act of reading and therefore determine the shape of what is read rather than, as is usually assumed, the other way around" (171). Disagreements hinge not on a UNIVERSAL notion of the truth about texts or their meanings but rather on the conditioned and relative truth of each community. Thus, there can be both agreement among readers of the same community and principled disagreement between communities. Literary texts are always interpreted within the context of protocols and norms. There can be no such thing as a subjective reading (in the radical sense of a reading that emerges from a single person's own experience with what Eco calls a "closed text"), nor can a reading exist based solely on the "given" structures of language or text. The meanings generated by interpretive communities "are *both* subjective and objective: they are subjective because they inhere in a particular point of view and are therefore not universal; and they are objective because the point of view that delivers them is public and conventional rather than individual and unique" (335–6).

In response to Ralph Rader, who described Fish's approach as an extension of New Critical formalism, Fish defended the affective stylistics of reader response: "My unit of analysis is interpretive or perceptual, and rather than proceeding directly from formal units of language, it determines what those units are." The unit of analysis "is formed (or forms itself) at the moment when the reader hazards interpretive closure," that is, when she enters into a relationship with a proposition offered by the text (e.g., belief or approval of a given act or statement) ("Facts" 888–9). Herein lies what we might call an "ethics of reading," which emerges out of affective engagements bounded by interpretive communities. For many theorists, the ethical relation to the text is grounded on a version of Emmanuel Levinas' theory of the *other* in which the *other* already summons us, wordlessly and in advance. "There is a claim laid on the same by the other in the core of myself," writes Levinas, "the extreme tension of the command exercised by the other in me over me, a traumatic hold of the other on the same" (141). In terms of an ethics of reading, this conception of the *other* leads to an openness before the text. Thus, according to Leisbeth Altes, following Levinas, "reading should be envisaged not as the appropriation of the work, but as a double 'undoing': as a reader, one must agree to lose oneself in the submission to the call of the text as Other, and to lose the work as a graspable, coherent whole" (144). J. Hillis Miller's understanding of the ethics of reading, grounded in poststructuralist theories of language, moves in this direction. For him, ethics is a question that covers the whole domain of language and *is prior to* action precisely because it is embedded in language. And because reading is made possible by language and because human beings are confronted constantly with the task of reading, it follows that our ethical sense is a function of language and reading. "[E]ach reading is, strictly speaking, ethical, in the sense that it *has* to take place, by an implacable necessity, as the response to a categorical demand, and in the sense that the reader *must* take responsibility for it and for its consequences in the personal, social, and political worlds" (59). The problem with this approach, as Vincent Leitch has observed, is that it ignores precisely the social, political, and cultural contexts that structure our ways of reading. Leitch points out that, for Miller, reading makes social acts possible, that "social and political moments" are "all secondary, belated, SUPPLEMENTARY: first there is language and its law; then there is misreading and its ethical consequences. Evidently, after these come social, psychological, and political matters. Surely, Miller does not believe all this" (50). Well, assuming that he does, it should come as no surprise, especially in view of Fish's theory of interpretive communities. Miller belongs to a specific reading community for which the ethics of reading takes on a certain dimension, while Leitch belongs to another, quite different community, closer to the ethical pluralists associated with the Chicago school. That they can have a principled disagreement over the way reading and ethics intersect is the desirable outcome of a network of reading communities in which different points of view coexist in peaceful disagreement.

Note

On Propp, see Formalism and Structuralism; on Empson and Richards, see New Criticism; on the implied reader and ethics, see Chicago School Neo-Aristotelian Theory and Theory of the Novel; on affect theory, see Trauma Studies.

Works Cited

Altes, Liesbeth Korthals. "Ethical Turn." In *Routledge Encyclopedia of Narrative Theory*. Ed. David Herman, Manfred Jahn, and Marie-Laure Ryan. London and New York: Routledge, 2005. 141–6.

Barthes, Roland. "The Death of the Author." In *Image-Music-Text*. Trans. Stephen Heath. New York: Hill and Wang, 1977. 142–8.

De Man, Paul. *The Resistance to Theory*. Minneapolis: University of Minnesota Press, 1986.

Eco, Umberto. *The Role of the Reader: Explorations in the Semiotics of Texts*. Bloomington: Indiana University Press, 1984.

Fish, Stanley. "Facts and Fictions: A Reply to Ralph Rader." *Critical Inquiry* 1.4 (June 1974): 883–91.

Fish, Stanley. *Is There a Text in This Class? The Authority of Interpretive Communities*. Cambridge, MA: Harvard University Press, 1980.

Ingarden, Roman. *The Cognition of the Literary Work of Art*. Trans. Ruth Ann Crowley and Kenneth R. Olson. Evanston, IL: Northwestern University Press, 1973.

Ingarden, Roman. *The Literary Work of Art: An Investigation on the Borderlines of Ontology, Logic and Theory of Literature*. Trans. George G. Grabowicz. Evanston, IL: Northwestern University Press, 1973.

Iser, Wolfgang. *The Fictive and the Imaginary: Charting Literary Anthropology*. Baltimore and London: Johns Hopkins University Press, 1993.

Iser, Wolfgang. *The Implied Reader: Patterns of Communication in Prose Fiction from Bunyan to Beckett*. Baltimore: Johns Hopkins University Press, 1974.

Jauss, Hans Robert. "Literary History as a Challenge to Literary Theory." *New Literary History* 2.1 (Autumn 1970): 7–37.

Katz, Steven B. *The Epistemic Music of Rhetoric: Toward the Temporal Dimension of Affect in Reader Response and Writing*. Carbondale: Southern Illinois University Press, 1996.

Leitch, Vincent B. "Taboo and Critique: Literary Criticism and Ethics." *ADE Bulletin* 90 (Fall 1988): 46–52.

Levinas, Emmanuel. *Otherwise than Being*. Dordrecht: Kluwer Academic Publishers, 1991.

Massumi, Brian. *Parables for the Virtual: Movement, Affect, Sensation*. Durham, NC and London: Duke University Press, 2002.

Miller, J. Hillis. *The Ethics of Reading: Kant, de Man, Eliot, Trollope, James and Benjamin*. New York: Columbia University Press, 1987.

Poulet, Georges. "Phenomenology of Reading." *New Literary History* 1.1 (1969): 53–68.

Prince, Gerald. "Introduction to the Study of the Narratee." In *Reader-Response Criticism: From Formalism to Post-Structuralism*. Ed. Jane Tompkins. Baltimore: Johns Hopkins University Press, 1980. 7–25.

Deconstruction

Deconstruction refers to a set of practices, common throughout the poststructuralist and postmodern fields, whose chief task is to seek out the contradiction, gap, errancy, PLAY, or APORIA that defines and undermines the "structuration of structure," the TRANSCENDENTAL SIGNIFIED that stands behind and authorizes the very possibility of stable and centered structures. The approach developed by **Jacques Derrida** and other French poststructuralists emerged out of a tradition of philosophical thought strongly influenced by phenomenology and hermeneutics, particularly the work of Edmund Husserl, Martin Heidegger, and Emmanuel Levinas. Of special interest to Derrida was Heidegger's critique of Edmund Husserl's phenomenology, particularly the idealist notion of the "transcendental temporality of consciousness," and shifted attention to the essence of *being*, which is always understood as "worldly," as Being-in-the-world or *human* being (Da-sein). Derrida adopted Heidegger's method of critical "destructuring" – the stripping away of presuppositions around a concept or idea – that draws out the contradictions, fatally necessary, of idealist philosophy and structuralism. He used the same method to expose the lingering influence of metaphysical idealism, still legible in Heidegger's *being*, which "dwells" in the world and serves as a transcendental foundation for philosophy, an indivisible point of origin and history. "The privilege granted to consciousness signifies the privilege granted to the present; and even if one describes the transcendental temporality of consciousness, and at the depth at which Husserl does so, one grants to the 'living present' the power of synthesizing traces, and of incessantly reassembling them. This privilege is the ether of metaphysics, the element of our thought that is caught in the language of metaphysics" (*Margins* 16).

Derrida identifies here the chief obstacle for philosophy: the concept of PRESENCE, which in metaphysical ontologies is the sign of a "grounded" being, one that is neither a memory, an anticipation, or a resemblance; typically this grounded being is transcendental (as in Kant) or, as in Hegel and Marx, it is determined in a dialectical integration of the sensible in the transcendent spirit that culminates in an ideal form of itself, which is temporalized as "ultimate" (*telos*). For Derrida, this guarantee of presence is contradicted by the very language of the philosophy that issues it. Indeed, language models the very absence that defines any presence, the space or interval that gives meaning to whatever is expressed. Like so many French intellectuals at mid-century, Derrida follows Friedrich Nietzsche, via Heidegger, in his deconstruction of the metaphysics of presence (and of the TRANSCENDENTAL SIGNIFIER and SIGNIFIED). Deconstruction rejects "onto-theology," a world view in which meaning and value are invested in the transcendent ESSENCE (*onto*, being) of an unchanging principle or divinity (*theo*, God). Nor does it accept PHALLOGOCENTRISM, a world view in which social and cultural power are invested in a symbol of pure abstract presence (*phallus*) and articulated in the unchanging concepts of reason (*logos*). Out of his critique came the central idea of poststructuralist thought: that language does not refer in some stable and predictable way to the world outside of it but rather designates relationships of DIFFERENCE within signifying systems. It is, of course, an abiding irony that this idea is also central to structuralism itself, as Ferdinand de Saussure defined it.

Deconstruction takes seriously the difference between the SIGNIFIER and the SIGNIFIED, seeing in it the potentially destabilizing force of the signifier's non-identity with its concept. This is why the signifier is just as important as the signified, the word just as important as the world it purports to designate. It follows that speech is *not* more present to us for being spoken. This would be to misunderstand the role of the signifier. For Derrida, speech *enters into writing* even as it is heard, being grasped as language, as part of a signifying system and CONSTELLATION of meanings. *Speech* is not more authentic or present than *writing*; to think otherwise is to assume that speech *as presence* is either prior to writing (e.g., preobjective) or constituted as what is missing from writing. In *Of Grammatology* (1967), Derrida argues that the priority of speech over writing has obscured the problem of language and its relation to presence. On this view, deconstruction is both a critique of "phonocentrism" and an elaboration of a "general science of writing" (27). In this special sense, *writing* refers to the movement of and difference within language: "the signifier of the signifier" (7). Derrida called this capacity of language DIFFÉRANCE (the French term combines two meanings, "differing" and "deferring"), the condition in which signifiers endlessly refer to each other, as in the "discreet graphic intervention" of spelling "difference with an 'a'": "this graphic difference (*a* instead of *e*), this marked difference between two apparently vocal notations, between two vowels, remains purely graphic: it is read, or it is written, but it cannot be heard" (*Margins* 3). This play or "spacing" of difference is "permitted by the lack or absence of a center or origin" – it is "the movement of *supplementarity*" (*Writing* 289). For Derrida, SUPPLEMENTATION means more than simply adding something, "a plenitude enriching another plenitude, the *fullest measure* of presence." It means also, and perhaps primarily, a substitution, something that "insinuates itself *in-the-place-of*." The supplemental difference within language oscillates between nostalgia for lost unities and a joyful embrace of their loss. "If it represents and makes an image, it is by the anterior default of a presence" (*Of Grammatology* 167, 144–5).

Deconstruction calls our attention to the failure of philosophy to achieve or describe presence, and in the process of this negative critique it sustains the hermeneutical project, for the deconstructionist critic seeks primarily to hear what the text is saying, what Hans-Georg Gadamer calls the "intention-to-say," which, in the poststructuralist context, is to understand our own "ungrounded" understanding. Like hermeneutics, deconstruction does not sanction claims that only language exists or that the material world is a conjuring trick, an illusion of words. As Rodolphe

Gasché points out, deconstruction "is never the effect of a subjective act of desire or will or wishing. What provokes a deconstruction is rather of an 'objective' nature. It is a 'must,' so to speak." Though we can speak of a deconstructionist method, it "cannot be mistaken for anything resembling scientific procedural rules, in spite of its departure from a certain point outside philosophy." Cut free of the methodological limitations of philosophy and science, deconstruction "is also the deconstruction of the concept of method" (123). Thus, Derrida's famous remark, "*il n'y a pas de hors-texte*" (there is nothing outside of the text) (*Of Grammatology* 158), is not a repudiation of the material world but a testament to the text's radical ONTOLOGY, its material otherness and "being-as-text," and to its critical distance from a merely MIMETIC mode of reference. Deconstruction takes place within the horizon of the text, at the moments of rupture (or the space of contradiction or conflict, often called aporia) in which the text throws itself into doubt. These moments of instability provide the starting point for a critique of the philosophical, scientific, moral, ethical, and critical assumptions underlying a given text. The problem, however, is not with mimetic language but with language *as such*. The presumption of an adequate language – one that could faithfully represent the true being of things in the world – is precisely what deconstruction seeks to criticize. The purportedly stable and unified text can be shown to be internally inconsistent and this inconsistency is one of its foundational components. By its own terms, deconstruction must conclude that Western thought has *always already* been defined by PARADOX, inconsistency, contradiction, aporia, errancy, and incommensurability.

The very condition of "deconstructability" is the condition of possibility of the text itself, the sign of its intractable relation to what it purports to represent. Therefore, to *de*-construct is not to destroy; it is rather to unveil the seemingly hidden workings of language that constitute the very basis of linguistic and textual meaning. In the "Plato's Pharmacy" section of Derrida's *Disseminations*, for example, we learn that the term *pharmakon* means both remedy and poison. **J. Hillis Miller** makes a similar point about deconstruction by way of the reversibility of the parasite/host relation. Like Gaston Bachelard and Maurice Merleau-Ponty, Derrida was interested in the borderline between inside/outside and used deconstruction to interrogate it in aesthetics, philosophy, ethics, and politics. In a discussion of *parergon*, for example, which means ornamentation or, generally, a supplement (e.g., inessential elements like the frame of a picture), Derrida shows that the ornament is constitutive of the thing ornamented. Thus the frame both presents and includes the picture, but also signifies, by its boundary function, all that is *outside* the artwork. The inessential ornament, the frame, turns out to be decisive, even essential to the artwork's being. "The *parergon* stands out both from the *ergon* (the work) and from the milieu, it stands out first of all like a figure on a ground" (*Truth* 61). So too does the work, but the *parergon* has the additional property of merging with the work itself. "There is always a form on a ground," Derrida writes, "but the *parergon* is a form which has as its traditional determination not that it stands out but that it disappears, buries itself, effaces itself" (61). Deconstruction sustains the Heideggerian gesture of unconcealment and withdrawal as part of a critique that seeks to understand the ontology of artworks, their modes of being, which "neither reframe nor dream of the pure and simple absence of the frame" (73).

Throughout his career, Derrida elaborated on the technique of deconstruction, developing new figures by which to illustrate it, including the concept *hymen*, which can signify both a barrier (between men and women) and a fusion (marriage), and the *gift*, which signifies a relation to the presence of the OTHER that grounds all philosophy but also all deconstructionist critiques of philosophy. As Derrida points out, the ethical obligation of the gift in the West first arose when, at God's bidding, Abraham offered up Isaac as a sacrifice. Derrida's "ethics of the possible" (to use Richard Kearney's phrase) offers a compelling alternative both to traditional Kantian ethical imperatives and to nihilistic relativism. As a trope for the concept *presence* and its exchange within a system of signs, the gift provides a focal point for meditations on history, epistemology, biography, and autobiography. The ghostly doubleness of presence haunts Derrida's later works in the form of the *specter*, the uncanny presence of what can never be present, "a *frequency* of a certain visibility. But the visibility of the invisible." It is also "what one imagines, what one thinks one sees and which one projects" (*Specters* 100–1). In *Specters of Marx*, Derrida aligns deconstruction with Marxism's "interminable self-critique" (89), which renovates DIALECTICS and reconceives TOTALITY and UNIVERSALITY in terms of either singularized ensembles and multiples or dynamic and fluid states. Indeed, "deconstruction would have been impossible and unthinkable in a pre-Marxist space." He associates the "radicalization" of deconstruction with "*the tradition* of a certain Marxism, in a certain *spirit of Marxism*" (92). To keep faith with this spirit is to engage in "the deconstruction of Marxist ontology," both at the level of theory and in the practice of resistance. Deconstruction is, finally, not "a methodical or theoretical procedure" but a mode of experience, the possibility of experiencing the impossible, which is "never a stranger to the event, that is, very simply, to the coming of that which happens" (89). Thus the "specter of Marx" (of deconstruction) holds open the possibility of an impossible future in which the *revenant* marks "the promised return of the specter of living being" (99).

The *event* in deconstruction, like the event in postmodernist and posthumanist theorizing, is a situation in which difference, supplementation, multiplicity, absence, and temporal "disadjustment" give rise to a "questioning stance" but also to "a certain emancipatory and messianic affirmation" (*Specters* 54). Like Walter Benjamin, for whom messianism is an attitude toward the future of the past, Derrida affirms "the idea of emancipatory promise or the promise of a better future, a future to come that is promised in the here and now" (Joseph 250). Derrida's late concern with an ethics of futurity echoes what **Michel Foucault** calls "the care of the self": "to learn to live, to learn it *from oneself and by oneself*, all alone, to teach oneself to live ('I would like to learn to live finally'), is that not impossible for a living being … And yet nothing is more necessary than this wisdom. It is ethics itself: to learn to live – alone, from oneself, by oneself. Life does not know how to live otherwise" (*Specters* xviii).

Derridean deconstruction had a profound impact on US and UK readers, in part as a reaction New Criticism, Chicago School neo-Aristotelian rhetorical theory, and archetypal structuralism of the sort practiced by M. H. Abrams and Northrop Frye. US theorists – principally Miller, **Paul de Man**, and Geoffrey Hartman (the so-called Yale School), Joseph Riddell, Barbara Johnson, Rodolphe Gasché, and Josué Harari – shared much the same intellectual background as their continental peers. Miller's work on Dickens and other Victorian novelists is a good example of this, for he developed a deconstructionist style of interpretation that grew out of his interest in Georges Poulet's notion of "interior distance" and the horizon of narrative that enables the consciousness of the text to unfold. For Miller, language creates the world of the text, a point of view that undermines the naïve sense, to some degree a product of phenomenology itself, that language can capture the immediacy of one's experience of the world; the reader thus inhabits the consciousness produced by the author in narrative, a consciousness that constitutes the world of the text. In 1977, he published "The Critic as Host," an eloquent defense of deconstruction against the charge, made by Abrams, that deconstruction was "parasitic" upon normative or authoritative interpretations of literature. Miller deconstructed the opposition *host/parasite* in part by showing that the word "parasite" shares the same etymological root as the word "host." "On the one hand, the 'obvious or univocal reading' always contains the 'deconstructive reading' as a parasite encrypted within itself, as part of itself, and, on the other hand, the 'deconstructive' reading can by no means free itself from the metaphysical, logocentric reading which it means to contest" ("Critic" 444–5). This inner encryption, a condition for a specifically narrative meaning, is based on a differential repetition of the sign or image on a textual horizon. In "Ariadne's Thread" (1976), Miller used the metaphor of the labyrinth to describe non-linear, non-chronological narrative forms. He draws from Nietzsche and **Gilles Deleuze** to put forward a theory of "differential repetition" that attempts to account for the way that literary narratives work. Differential repetition lacks a ground or fixed origin against which to compare succeeding copies. Rather than produce copies, which is what we find in conventional, mimetic, or "unifying" repetition, differential repetition produces an incessant multiplication of originals, "ungrounded doublings which arise from differential interrelations among elements which are all on the same plane. This lack of ground in some paradigm or archetype means that there is something ghostly about the effects of this … kind of repetition" (*Fiction* 6). (On Deleuze and difference, see Postmodernism 137–8.) Reading, on this view, is not a matter of tracing language to its referents outside the text (either in the author's consciousness or in the external world) but of following the labyrinthine trajectory of signifiers as they produce significations in a theoretically endless process of repetition. Instead of the exact repetition of a signifier in harmony with its signified, we find the "infinite semiosis" of signifiers linked in chains of signification.

Paul de Man arrived at a similar conclusion about the nature and productive quality of language, but from a different starting point. Like Miller, he debated the question of theory with his contemporaries, and his early work on the New Criticism and literary history established a style of critique that owed as much to classical rhetoric as to the continental tradition of philosophy. In *Blindness and Insight* he argues that becoming aware of the "complexities of reading" is the necessary first step toward "theorizing about literary language" (viii). These complexities are the function of the critic's "blindness" with respect to a gap between practice and the theoretical precepts guiding it. Literary critics are thus "curiously doomed to say something quite different from what they meant to say" (105–6). And while critics may remain unaware of the discrepancy that informs their work, "they seem to thrive on it and owe their best insights to the assumptions these insights disprove" (ix).

De Man illustrates his thesis in a detailed analysis of Derrida's reading of Jean-Jacques Rousseau (in *Of Grammatology*), arguing that it is actually a *mis*reading. Derrida believes that Rousseau's theory of language is a reflection of his desire to link language to the world of objects in a direct and unmediated fashion – a reflection, in short, of his desire for presence. De Man, however, argues that Rousseau is always aware of the fundamentally *rhetorical* nature of language, that he in fact uses language not to make mimetic statements about the world but rather to make rhetorical statements that refer only to themselves, to their own figural nature. Rousseau's text thus "prefigures its own misunderstanding as the correlative of its rhetorical nature" (136). When Derrida deconstructs Rousseau, claiming that his theory of language and representation is committed to the "metaphysics of presence," he misses the point. For De Man, Rousseau "said what he meant to say" (135). Part of the problem is that Derrida refuses to read Rousseau as literature and thus fails to see the figural or rhetorical nature of his language. Derrida's reading of a "pseudo-Rousseau" is nevertheless instructive, for he seems to be aware of his own *mis*reading, which is "too interesting not to be deliberate" (140).

The importance of the rhetorical dimensions of language is explored in De Man's most famous essay, "The Rhetoric of Temporality," which focuses on two of the most common rhetorical tropes, symbol and allegory. De Man is chiefly concerned with the privilege historically granted to the symbol. The Romantic notion that the symbol exists in a kind of synthesis or union with what it designates is called into question, as is the denigration of allegory as a disjunctive figure, lacking any intimate association with what it signifies. De Man argues that the disjunctive quality of allegory is owing to its *temporal* nature: "in the world of allegory, time is the originary constitutive category" (*Blindness* 207). Allegory, like irony, always points to another sign that precedes it; it is always an instance of differential repetition in which the sign can never coincide, as the symbol is purported to do, completely and without remainder, with its object. It is, in a word, a *narrative* form of signification. This narrative temporality is precisely the *différance* that Derrida believes to be the function of language: deferral, spacing, the trace, play, specter, survival – all of these terms indicate the interminable and vertiginous temporality of the world of signs. For De Man, it is rarely possible to decide, when reading a literary text, whether we are reading, or should be reading, in a rhetorical or literal fashion. This critical "undecidability" is a property of both literary and critical language.

For De Man rhetoric is more suited to engaging the undecidable text than semiology, which is "derived from grammatical patterns." His "rhetorically conscious reading" of W. B. Yeats' "Among School Children" – with its enigmatic closing question, "How can we tell the dancer from the dance?" – allegorizes the fundamental undecidability of interpretation, for it suggests "that two entirely coherent but entirely incompatible readings can be made to hinge on one line, whose grammatical structure is devoid of ambiguity, but whose rhetorical mode turns the mood as well as the mode of the entire poem upside down" (*Allegories* 15–16, 12). De Man's critical practice maps the "figural pattern of contradiction" as a double deconstruction in which "the first undoing of the 'natural' metaphor" leads to the reinstatement of the metaphor's "figural status," thus "making it into the figural deconstruction of the prior deconstruction of the figure" (252–3). This double move is the "figural state of suspended meaning" (151) that evolves out of the tendency in rhetoric to dissemble. Indeed, the "resistance to theory" is precisely, for De Man, a resistance to this suspended and dissembling character of rhetoric *as such*. In short, theory resists *literariness*, a "rhetorical function" that is "a mere *effect* which language can perfectly well achieve, but which bears no substantial relationship, by analogy or by ontologically grounded imitation, to anything beyond that particular effect" (*Resistance* 10). This lack of "referential restraint" threatens logic and grammar (the other three elements of the classical *trivium*) with a destabilizing influence on a shared language. The uncertain relationship between grammar and rhetoric is apparent in the "uncertain status of figures of speech or tropes, a component of language that straddles the disputed borderlines between the two areas.... Tropes, unlike grammar, pertain primordially to language" (13–15). In a classic deconstructionist move, De Man invokes the paradox of a misreading that is at the same time irrefutable. Rhetorical readings are irrefutable because they are totalizable within the system of language (and its systemic failure): "they are indeed universals, consistently defective models of language's impossibility to be a model language.... They are theory and not theory at the same time.... Nothing can overcome the resistance to theory since theory *is* itself this resistance" (19).

As David Lloyd remarks, in a discussion of the violence that accompanies the founding of institutions, "deconstruction does not escape, or evade, the problematics of foundation, of its own establishment as a procedure or a style. If the specter of deconstruction already speaks from the cellarage of our state, is it possible not to follow its voice?" (346). Even as it founds a discourse, deconstruction resists the status of an authoritative origin. From another perspective, it can be regarded as another stage in the development of philosophical hermeneutics that intersects with phenomenology (especially Levinas and Heidegger) to become part of the general discourse of poststructuralism, indeed of theory as such. As **Elizabeth Grosz** points out, some feminist theorists see a danger in deconstruction, insofar as it is an "attempt to be all-pervasive, to occupy all specific positions – to speak as woman, as man, as decentered, as centered – opportunistically seeking any position momentarily or strategically while remaining committed to none" (81). But this is a danger that deconstruction would seem to deconstruct in advance, a danger that Derrida confronted throughout his career, and nowhere more vigilantly than in the late works, whose major themes – the gift, mourning, debt, hospitality, the specter – skirt the limits of the all-pervasive, and register our desire for something less, a commitment that has to say *no* even as it says *yes*, in order to remain open to the *other*.

Note
On Saussure, see Structuralism and Formalism; on Derrida, see Posthumanism and Poststructuralism.

Works Cited

De Man, Paul. *Allegories of Reading: Figural Language in Rousseau, Nietzsche, Rilke, and Proust*. New Haven: Yale University Press, 1979.
De Man, Paul. *Blindness and Insight: Essays in the Rhetoric of Contemporary Criticism*. New York: Oxford University Press, 1971.

De Man, Paul. *The Resistance to Theory*. Minneapolis: University of Minnesota Press, 1986.

Derrida, Jacques. *Margins of Philosophy*. Trans. Alan Bass. Chicago: University of Chicago Press, 1982.

Derrida, Jacques. *Of Grammatology*. Trans. Gayatri Chakravorty Spivak. Baltimore: Johns Hopkins University Press, 1976.

Derrida, Jacques. *Specters of Marx: The State of the Debt, the Work of Mourning and the New International*. Trans. Peggy Kamuf. New York: Routledge, 1994.

Derrida, Jacques. *The Truth In Painting*. Trans. Geoff Bennington and Ian McLeod. Chicago: University of Chicago Press, 1987.

Derrida, Jacques. *Writing and Difference*. Trans. Alan Bass. Chicago: University of Chicago Press, 1978.

Gasché, Rodolphe. *The Tain of the Mirror: Derrida and the Philosophy of Reflection*. Cambridge, MA: Harvard University Press, 1986.

Grosz, Elizabeth. "Ontology and Equivocation: Derrida's Politics of Sexual Difference." In *Feminist Interpretations of Jacques Derrida*. Ed. Nancy J. Holland. University Park, PA: Pennsylvania State University Press, 1997. 73–101.

Joseph, Jonathan. "Learning to Live (with Derrida)." In *Realism Discourse and Deconstruction*. Ed. Jonathan Joseph and John Michael Roberts. London and New York: Routledge, 2004. 246–61.

Lloyd, David, "Rage against the Divine." *South Atlantic Quarterly* 106.2 (Spring 2007): 345–72.

Miller, J. Hillis. "The Critic as Host." *Critical Inquiry* (Spring 1977) 3.3: 439–47.

Miller, J. Hillis. *Fiction and Repetition: Seven English Novels*. Cambridge, MA: Harvard University Press, 1982.

Poststructuralism

Poststructuralism designates a number of distinct theoretical principles and practices with a common aim: a critique of structuralism, the idea that human societies and their traditions can be understood according to universal and unchanging structures that are replicated in texts, artworks, rituals, and other modes of expression. The emergence of poststructuralism coincides with a high point of structuralist theorizing in the 1950s and 1960s, particularly in the work of the anthropologist Claude Lévi-Strauss and the semiotician and culture critic **Roland Barthes**. These thinkers, and the poststructuralists who followed, were drawn to the structural linguistics of Ferdinand de Saussure, whose lectures in the first decade of the twentieth century provided the foundation for formalism and structuralism. The SIGN, according to Saussure, consists of a SIGNIFIER (word or sound pattern) and a SIGNIFIED (concept). Its importance lies not in referencing an aspect of the material world but rather in functioning as part of a system. Saussurean linguistics thus refutes the referential theory of language and argues instead that phonemic DIFFERENCE (e.g., *b*at v. *c*at), which parallels but is not reducible to conceptual difference, is the primary operative feature of language. The significance of the sign is thus entirely arbitrary. While structuralism built on this insight a theory of how social and cultural forms (e.g., mythology, kinship, religious rituals) conform to structural patterns and transcend local and national boundaries, poststructuralism focuses on the notion of language as a system of differences, that is, the notion that meaning is derived not from *reference* (a sign designating an object in the world) but from internal *self-reference* (a sign designating a relation to other signs).

An important moment in *the poststructuralist turn* occurred in 1966, when Johns Hopkins University hosted a conference, "The Languages of Criticism and the Sciences of Man," which featured some of the most important thinkers in structuralism at the time, many of whom – preeminently Barthes and **Jacques Derrida** – had already made the transition to *post*structuralism. "Structure, Sign and Play in the Discourse of the Human Sciences," Derrida's inaugural essay in English delivered at the conference, sums up some of the chief ideas and themes of poststructuralism, including rupture, PLAY, SUPPLEMENTATION, *archē* (origin), PRESENCE, and *DIFFÉRANCE*. These ideas were used to explain a theory of language and interpretation in which difference, of the sort that Saussure theorized, determined meaning precisely by deferring it along a chain of signifiers. There could be no grounding concept, or original referent that could call a halt to the signification process. Understood in this way, language was *supplemental* to what it designated in a double sense: signifiers were both an addition to and a displacement of the referent or signified. Language so understood could not support the "concept of centered structure" (*Writing* 279). Derrida's essay takes Lévi-Strauss's structuralist anthropology to task for its naïve faith in centered structures. For Derrida, the center is always otherwise than *in the center of things*; it is, he argues, a HETERONOMOUS force (e.g., an external law or idea) whose absence from the structure calls structure *as such* into question. "The function of this center was not only to orient, balance, and organize the structure – one cannot in fact conceive of an unorganized structure – but above all to make sure that the organizing principle of the structure [i.e., *structuration*] would limit what we might call the *play* of the structure" (278–9). Derrida critiques Lévi-Strauss's structuralist method, which seeks, through the sign, to move outside the structural opposition between nature and culture, the sensible and the intelligible. "But the concept of the sign is determined by this opposition," Derrida argues, and with this insight, he is able to deconstruct Lévi-Strauss's structuralism because of its reliance on what it would seem to disavow, for it "will always remain faithful to this double intention: to preserve as an instrument that whose truth-value he criticizes" (255). Derrida invites us "to seek new concepts and new models, an *economy* escaping this system of metaphysical oppositions. This economy would not be an energetics of pure, shapeless force" (20). (On Derrida, see Deconstruction 160–5.)

Poststructuralism questions the ability of language to designate a center, to guarantee a stable and stabilizing authority, to provide an absolute criterion for assessing the truth, to construct a discourse in science or politics that could presuppose universal validity. Precisely by focusing its critical energies upon structured systems, poststructuralism commits itself to discovering alternatives through an *immanent critique* that maintains an indeterminate but essential relation with structure as such, which is why linguistics and semiotics play such an important role. Paul Ricoeur, in his analysis of structuralist linguistics, suggests that future inquiries will "escape the structuralist model" and "proclaim a new understanding of operations and processes; this new understanding will be situated beyond the antinomy between structure and event, between system and act, to which our structuralist investigation will have led us" (80). This goal, perhaps the general goal of poststructuralism, is always in the tense of the *future anterior*.

It is arguable that in poststructuralism, the epoch of Hegel and DIALECTICS was still very much felt as a contemporary moment, in part because of Alexandre Kojève's reading of the *Phenomenology of Spirit*, which emphasizes the role of desire and negation in the dialectical struggle for recognition. The chief concepts of poststructuralism – difference, POWER/KNOWLEDGE, the discourse of the OTHER, NEGATIVE DIALECTICS, the body and the subject, identity as PERFORMANCE, and dispersion of effects – derive their power precisely from a deconstructionist critique that recognizes both negation and desire *in their own right* and not as elements that must be SUBLATED (subsumed and assimilated) or sublimated. The same can be said for the way structuralism is overturned in a gesture that proliferates difference within a self-deconstructing structure. As Saussure demonstrated, the power of difference was first discovered in the controlled environment presented by the structure, with what was presumed to be its internal and stable center, the logic that regulated the play of difference and held the structure together. One of the most innovative poststructuralists, Roland Barthes, began his career trying to establish the workings of this logic in SEMIOTIC systems and in literary and cinematic narrative (on his structuralism, see Formalism and Structuralism 57–8). His essays in the late 1960s mark a decisive transition point at which the idea of a regulated and centered structure is displaced by the idea of an unregulated, decentered *process of reading*. In this process, there can be no final authority, certainly not the author who *originates* the work. In "The Death of the Author" (1968), Barthes argued that authorship is a linguistic function, "never more than the instance writing, just as *I* is never more than the instance saying *I*." The author is a SUBJECT POSITION in a text or discourse, not a psychological being who serves as locus and origin of meaning. In the place of the author, Barthes introduces the "modern scriptor," a force "in no way equipped with a being preceding or exceeding the writing." The scriptor is a "subject with the book as predicate," "born simultaneously with the text." So too is the reader, but "at the cost of the death of the Author" (*Image* 145, 148). **Michel Foucault** mounts a similar argument in "What is an Author?" (1969). For him the author's "proper name" is not "a function of the man's civil status, nor is it fictional; it is situated in the breach, among the discontinuities, which gives rise to new groups of discourse and their singular mode of existence" (*Language* 123). The function of an author, therefore, is "to characterize the existence, circulation, and operation of certain discourses within a society" (125). This function also delimits and sets the rules for selection of texts for circulation within DISCOURSE FORMATIONS. (On this essay, see Posthumanism 272.)

These pronouncements, which came in the space of a year, constituted a space-clearing gesture that freed theory of the burden of a subjectivist conception of how texts and discourses function in society. Barthes largely follows Derrida in recognizing that language is fundamentally "dilatory," a play of differences, deferrals, and displacements of meaning within semiotic and linguistic systems, which might include an author's œuvre (the aegis of the "proper name"), a doctrine's CANON, a discipline's discourse formation, a nation's cultural and literary traditions, legislative and judicial proceedings, and so on. The "scriptor" moves within these systems against the grain of their announced logic and opens up what is non-identical to it. In this sense, poststructuralism calls on negative dialectics, in which non-identity trumps the myth of an origin identical to the text: "[W]riting is the destruction of every voice, of every point of origin. Writing is that neutral, composite, oblique space where our subject slips away, the negative where all identity is lost, starting with the very identity of the body writing" (*Image* 142). Unlike the AUTONOMOUS *work*, which fixes signification and reference, the TEXT takes its shape and meaning from a fluid and multifarious network of signs. In *The Pleasure of the Text* (1973), Barthes describes the difference between *writerly* and *readerly* texts in terms of their openness to linguistic difference. The readerly text is a stable "work," a "classical text" that satisfies and edifies, one that gives pleasure by conforming to readers' expectations; it is "a *comfortable* practice of reading" (*Pleasure* 14; see also his *S/Z*). The writerly text, on the other hand, is a text of bliss that challenges or overturns expectations, that induces JOUISSANCE and leaves the contented reader behind. But even this dualism troubles Barthes, who makes a point of abandoning it (parenthetically):

> ("*Pleasure/Bliss*: terminologically, there is always a vacillation – I stumble, I err. In any case, there will always be a margin of indecision; the distinction will not be the source of absolute classifications, the paradigm will falter, the meaning will be precarious, revocable, reversible, the discourse incomplete.) (*Pleasure* 4)

Barthes' "vacillation" is a deconstructionist maneuver that concedes an important point: every interpretation is subject to the same principle of linguistic difference that is under investigation. But this methodological crisis is also a pedagogical opportunity, for it reinforces the primary drive toward overturning dualisms that constrains our "blissful" engagement with the open text.

Barthes' poststructuralist semiology has much in common with the work of **Julia Kristeva**. A practicing psychoanalyst herself, Kristeva "grafted" psychoanalytic theory onto semiology to produce a new form of "semanalysis," an "*analytical discourse* on signifying systems" (*Desire* 125). For Kristeva, as for Barthes, a *desire for language* is manifested *in* language as a material effect of difference and displacement. Like other French feminist philosophers, Kristeva focuses attention on how language and discourse penetrate and inhabit the body, sometimes leaving signs and significations on the flesh, and on how the body permeates language making it vital but also incomplete and non-abstract. She borrows and revises Freud's concept *libido* (the *quantum* of the sex drive) to signify a "prediscursive libidinal economy" that can serve as the "locus of cultural subversion" (Oliver 165). The structure, trajectory, and outcome of libidinal drives provide models for new forms of SEMIOTIC activity. Kristeva was influenced by **M. M. Bakhtin**'s theory of DIALOGISM and the CARNIVALESQUE in Rabelais and Dostoyevsky. Literary texts, according to Bakhtin, were dialogized and stratified by a variety of languages and idioms, which meant that language had a material social existence as a signifying system, implicated at every level with the material existence of culture. This dialogized HETEROGLOSSIA regards "language as a correlation of texts, as a reading-writing that falls in with non-Aristotelian syntagmatic, correlational, 'carnivalesque' logic" (*Desire* 88–9). Like Bakhtin, Kristeva emphasizes the polyphonic nature of literature and its constitutive AMBIVALENCE, its oscillation between monological and dialogical narrative structures. "Bakhtinian dialogism identifies writing as both subjectivity and communication, or better, as INTERTEXTUALITY" (*Desire* 68). For Kristeva, intertextuality is the capacity in discourse that enables language to map "historical and social coordinates" at "different structural levels of each text" or "semiotic practice" (*Desire* 36). It enables a form of parody that differs from traditional forms in that it does not pay homage to or satirize an antecedent text but rather signals a purely systemic relation to what came before, a form of repetition that amounts to what **Fredric Jameson** calls "blank parody." It is this very lack of a ground in an antecedent text that worries some critics of poststructuralism. "The problem for *any* intertextual reading," writes Toril Moi, "is to counter the charge of arbitrariness. Paradoxically, it is precisely because there is, in principle, no limit to the number of possible intertexts to any given text, that it becomes necessary explicitly to justify one's choice of any *particular* intertext" (1043). But I think Kristeva is less interested in justifying a "*particular* intertext" than in developing a methodology for reading the condition of intertextuality *as such*.

If intertextuality privileges the relations between texts in discourse systems, the role of the subject (of discourse, of speech, of writing) emerges as a central PROBLEMATIC in poststructuralist theory. Like other theorists, Kristeva tackles this problematic by referring to the "speaking subject," a position that accounts for modes of AGENCY and articulation not covered by the autonomous subject of idealist philosophy. Structural linguistics falls short, she argues, by refusing to recognize this subject position: "[I]n order to move from sign to sentence the place of the subject had to be acknowledged and no longer kept vacant" (*Desire* 127–8). Kristeva's model of the subject is in some ways indebted to Lacan's critique of the "unity of the subject" (*Écrits* 281) that had become doctrine in ego-psychology by the 1950s. For Lacan and Kristeva, the subject is by its very nature disunified but in a way that also signals a primordial, prelinguistic space that ejects and defies it; *abjection* is the term Kristeva uses for this intrinsic self-disavowal that roots the subject in desire for what it lacks. As subjects, we are *speaking* subjects because language shapes our conscious memories, reflections, anticipations but also our unconscious (e.g., dreams) and our aesthetic experiences. The Lacanian subject must accept "the signifier as the determinant of the signified," "through an enunciation that makes a human being tremble due to the vacillation that comes back to him from his own statement" (288–9). This trembling marks "the moment of a fading or eclipse of the subject – which is closely tied to the *Spaltung* or splitting he undergoes due to his subordination to the signifier – to the condition of an object" (301). Language does not so much dominate the subject as constitute every aspect of her existence.

Lacan follows Freud in grounding his theory of the subject in neurosis, specifically in the structure of the symptom. The symptom "speaks in the Other, I say, designating by 'Other' the very locus evoked by recourse to speech in any relation in which such recourse plays a part. If it speaks in the Other, whether or not the subject hears it with his ear, it is because it is there that the subject finds his signifying place in a way that is logically prior to any awakening of the signified" (275). This "locus" is the SYMBOLIC, which is the space of Lacan's big Other – the "treasure of the Symbolic," in Alain Badiou's felicitous phrase (7). The big Other ought not to be confused with *l'objet petit a*, the *other* that mediates our experience of the unconscious through the withholding of the object of desire. This withholding is, in an important sense, bound to the slippage and difference native to language. As Lacan famously claimed, "It is the whole structure of language that psychoanalytic experience discovers in the unconscious" (138). For Kristeva and other poststructuralist feminists, preeminently **Luce Irigaray**, the unconscious and the IMAGINARY realm that it opens up, which for Freud and Lacan are situated within the primal scene of Oedipal trauma, become associated with pre-Oedipal and pre-Symbolic experiences. These experiences signal "a *heterogeneousness* to meaning and signification" that "operates through, despite, and in excess of [meaning] and produces in poetic language 'musical' but also nonsense effects that destroy not only accepted beliefs and signification, but, in radical experiments, syntax itself" (Kristeva, *Desire* 133). In a manner similar to Lacan's *jouissance*, which arises in proximity to unconscious processes, Kristeva's *khora* designates an ecstatic experience of the Imaginary grounded on the "oceanic" bond of mother and child. In both cases, a structured system (i.e., the ego) is disrupted by an excess of signs, a boundless state or "semiotic disposition" rooted in the maternal body. It is a space and temporality prior to the Symbolic and the patriarchal system of gender differentiation, a new ground for psychoanalysis and feminist ethics. For poststructuralist feminists, the body is the ultimate structure: systematized at multiple levels, intricately cross-referenced, coded but capable of a wide range of random de- and recodings, fluid but contained. Understood in this radical sense, the body itself is simultaneously *énoncé* and *énonciation*, message and site of inscription.

As we have seen, the arbitrariness of the sign is rooted in the unrelenting conventionality of signifying systems and thereby undermines their structural integrity. But this does not mean that such systems lack coherence, consistency, and authority. Foucault's work is dedicated to demonstrating precisely this point, that signifying systems – or *discourse formations*, to use his terminology – can be understood according to their unique conditions of possibility. His methodologies, particularly GENEALOGY and ARCHAEOLOGY, transformed how we think and write about discourse formations, whether they be histories, the canons of a discipline, the statements clustered around a particular theme or problem. The discourse formation is an anti-historicist mode of analysis, interested not in chronology, causality, precedent, and continuity but rather in the emergence of institutional POWER/KNOWLEDGE and the discontinuities and ruptures that mark its temporal passage in the social body and the body of the subject. In *The Archaeology of Knowledge* (1969), Foucault offers a detailed account of the archaeological method and the principles governing discourse formations, which he describes as a "*system of dispersion*," a series of statements (e.g., on medicine or madness) that creates "an order in their successive appearance, correlations in their simultaneity, assignable positions in common space, a reciprocal functioning, linked and hierarchized transformations" (37). There is no attempt in the discourse formation to return to an origin or a time of plentitude (a "golden age"). Rather, it constitutes its own past in the distribution of the "field of antecedent elements" in which every statement in the formation is situated. This "enunciative past," this "acquired truth," is a form or *recurrence* that is not a return, but rather a refiguring and redistribution of discursive material. The historicity of formations is therefore purely discursive or textual; what we often think of as a "unity through time" is really the effect of a "temporality of accumulation," which Foucault calls a *historical a priori*, the limits governing a discursive formation, limits formed by "rules of enunciation" (129). The historical *a priori* designates the concrete, material conditions for discursive statements and for the rules governing formations and it guides archaeological analysis. It is important to emphasize that the term *archaeology* "does not imply the search for a beginning; it does not relate analysis to the geological excavation. It designates the general theme of a description that questions the already-said at the level of its existence: of the enunciative function that operates within it, of the discursive formation, and the general archive system to which it belongs. Archaeology describes discourses as practices specified in the element of the archive" (131). The discursive formation "deals with statements in the density of the accumulation in which they are caught up and which nevertheless they never cease to modify, to disturb, to overthrow, and sometimes to destroy" (124–5). Archaeological analysis uncovers a "series full of gaps, intertwined with one another, interplays of differences, distances, substitutions, transformations" (37).

Archaeology has a descriptive vocation and is concerned with how one negotiates discourses in formations, archives, and other aggregations. Genealogy, a concept Foucault borrowed from Nietzsche, works within the space cleared by this archaeological description and emphasizes the fundamental role of interpretation in the emergence of law and morality. Some critics believe the concept of *genealogy* to be a later refinement of archaeology; others believe that archaeology focuses on the SYNCHRONIC level of the discourse (contiguity of statements and ideas), while genealogy focuses on the DIACHRONIC level (historical development and other temporalities). Steven Best and Douglas Kellner regard both as modes of historiography. Archaeology focuses on "local discursivities," genealogy on "the material context of subject construction" and its aim is "to draw out the political consequences of 'subjectification,' and to help form resistances to subjectifying practices" (45–7). Foucault himself described genealogy as "the union of erudite knowledge and local memories which allows us to establish a historical knowledge of struggles and to make use of this knowledge tactically today." Genealogies are "anti-sciences," not because "they vindicate a lyrical right to ignorance or non-knowledge," but rather because they rise up against knowledges that centralize power and are "linked to the institution and functioning of an organised scientific discourse within a society such as ours" (*Power/ Knowledge* 83–4). Thus Foucault's *Discipline and Punish* seeks to understand punishment *not* through an *a priori* or transcendent concept or legitimizing grand narrative, but rather through the analytical activity of tracing the emergence of specific instances of punishment and formulating an interpretation of the function of those instances. For example, by tracing the shift (at the end of the seventeenth century) from a "criminality of blood" (i.e., "the attack of bodies") to a "criminality of fraud" (i.e., "direct seizure of goods") – from "mass criminality" to "marginal criminality" – Foucault is able to uncover the adjustments to the "mechanisms of power" that follow up on this shift. These adjustments did not lead to a "new respect for the humanity of the condemned," for torture and execution were still common; what we see instead is "a tendency towards a more finely tuned justice, towards a closer penal mapping of the social body" (*Discipline* 76–8). Within such shifts, the genealogist looks for "the hazardous play of dominations," "the emergence of different interpretations" (*Language* 148, 152); he identifies the ruptures in the flow of events, "the accidents, the minute deviations – or conversely, the complete reversals – the errors and the false appraisals, and the faulty calculations that gave birth to those things that continue to exist and have value for us" (146). In his late essays, Foucault elaborated on the way that power effects the constitution of social subjects. Perhaps his most influential genealogical work was *The History of Sexuality*, in which he considers the emergence of a discourse of sexuality, which he calls a "slow surfacing of confidential statements" (61, 63) produced and regulated by particular matrices of power.

The *History of Sexuality* and other later works offer not only a genealogy of the discourse of sexuality but a new conception of the subject and a theory of its care. The term *care* resonates within a theoretical tradition that goes back to Heidegger, for whom care is synonymous with Da-sein (human being). For Foucault, the care of the self involves attention both to the body and to the way power determines it. Foucault's reassessment of the possible relations to power enjoyed by the subject led him to rethink the Nietzschean creative power of the subject *with* and *in* power. There is a continuity here that is not dialectical, nor is it organic or mechanistic; it is a continuity that attests to a lack of distinction between the subject and power, between subject and the object, between actor and event, between spectator and spectacle. It is the logic of dispersion. Under conditions of domination, the subject is a *subject of* a hegemonic discourse that restricts the dispersion of identity (and much else) and requires the consent, in some tacit way, of the subject herself. To rethink the relation between power and the subject of power, Foucault needed to rethink power in terms of the body and sexuality, in terms of *biopower*, the materiality of power as *subject to* historical development. Foucault sees a decisive shift in the eighteenth century, when the idea of power understood as emanating from the state "as *institutions* of power" that ensured "the maintenance of production relations" evolved into the idea of power as a form of bureaucratic surveillance (e.g., regulatory controls, "a bio-politics of the population"). In the nineteenth century, the era of Darwin, Marx, and the polymath Francis Galton (Darwin's cousin), "the rudiments of anatomo- and bio-politics" took form as *techniques* of power, forces that guaranteed "relations of domination and effects of hegemony." With the techniques of biopower came "the entry of life into history, that is, the entry of phenomena peculiar to the life of the human species into the order of knowledge and power" (139, 141–2).

While Foucault reveals vividly the subjection of the subject in modernity, his late essays on governmentality reveal a more complex vision of the subject and her own will to power. "At the very heart of the power relationship," he claims, "and constantly provoking it, are the recalcitrance of the will and the intransigence of freedom. Rather than speaking of an essential freedom, it would be better to speak of an 'agonism' – of a relationship which is at the same time reciprocal incitation and struggle; less of a face-to-face confrontation which paralyzes both sides than a permanent provocation" ("Subject" 221–2). To be a subject *of* power is not necessarily to be subjected *by* it, but rather to use it as the agonistic space of the dispersal and disarrangement of forces within the strategic confines of a formation (political, economic, institutional, pedagogical): this concatenation of the subject and the discourse of power produces material effects, one of which is to delimit the subject's intelligibility and thus her authority and influence.

Because there is no way to TOTALIZE power/knowledge, we can speak only of its absolute contingency. Foucault, like Nietzsche before him, goes to considerable lengths to debunk in advance the criticism that he practices a form "negative theology" that reinscribes the very absolute authority he seeks to disavow through appeal to an undifferentiated power that is absolutely immeasurable. Timothy Wilson, for example, argues that Foucault and Nietzsche are "anti-Platonists" who end up "rewrit[ing] Plato based on an inversion of his metaphysics – an inversion that remains metaphysical" (158–9). The critical consensus, however, is that Foucault's concept of power/knowledge offers a credible and effective alternative to metaphysical universalisms and a revolutionary way of thinking about ensembles or "multiples" as events within a horizon that can be mapped by the archaeologist and historicized by the genealogist without at the same time being totalized or exhausting all possible events. **Gilles Deleuze** and Alain Badiou are his successors in this task of reassigning the function and value of the multiple and the one, but they too have been charged with being inverted Platonists.

Slavoj Žižek has faulted poststructuralist theories of identity in a similar way for failing to offer a decisive critique of existing social conditions: "The predominant form of ideology today is precisely that of multiple identities, non-identity and cynical distance. This includes even sexual identities … these Foucauldian practices of inventing new strategies, new identities, are ways of playing the late capitalist game of subjectivity" (40). This is perhaps an unsurprising outcome of a theoretical formation rooted in philosophical modernity, an outcome that Žižek reads as belated, as yet another twist in the production of the subject that modern capital and modern philosophy have encouraged since the time of Kant. For Žižek, Foucault's solutions are somehow variants of existing forms of subjectivity. Of course the Foucauldians could reply that Žižek's position presupposes a space in which a different game can be played and a subjectivity that is something other than a game. The transition in Foucault's thinking about power – seeing it first as an all-pervasive mode of social oppression and surveillance, then coming to see that the subject is capable of agency and resistance that amount to more than token efforts – complicates the question in a way that Žižek does not allow himself to appreciate. The mode of identity formation that Foucault and others describe is a form of social construction – that is, identity is determined by social forces, media, discourses, and so on – that is not entirely determined by capitalist modes of self-formation. In any case, it is entirely consistent for poststructuralism to remain within the structures of the "capitalist game of subjectivity" and therein find innovative and subversive ways to play these games. Take, for example, the tactical maneuvers within strategic systems that Michel de Certeau theorizes in *The Practice of Everyday Life* (1980). Even though subjects exist within the "constraining order of the place or of the language," they can nevertheless find *ways of using* the system and its products, thereby enabling "a degree of *plurality* and creativity" (30). A striking example of this tactical mode of internal disruption (which De Certeau calls *la perruque*) is the practice of *street parkour*, or *free running*, which uses the existing structures of the urban environment as an opportunity for tactical play and mobility. At the limits of the poststructuralist domain is the uneasy coexistence of dispersion and constraint. It is difficult at this limit to discern a separate *place* for the "proper," for the strategic, but it is quite easy to see how tactics can break free of traditional "stable local units." The RETERRITORIALIZATION of strategic institutions creates new grounds for negative dynamics, for contorted structures and diversified and multiplied dialectics. "One would thus have a proliferation of aleatory and indeterminable manipulations within an immense framework of socioeconomic constraints and securities" (40). De Certeau's theory of practice is in part a response to **Pierre Bourdieu**'s theory of the HABITUS, a socialized subjectivity that has an almost infinite range of possibilities within a bounded framework. But De Certeau takes aim less at the systematic or bounded nature of the habitus than at the socialized nature of a closed system in which one is perpetually constrained by social habits, distinctions, and status. Negative innovations within such structures are initiated through tactics, through resignified norms, through reconfigured technologies, and through ironic modes of compliance with strategic regulations and goals. This is poststructuralism as sabotage, the ultimate breaching of the limits of structure from within as a form of immanent critique. (On Bourdieu, see Cultural Studies 222–3.)

If poststructuralism is grounded in linguistics, structuralism, semiology, discourse analysis, hermeneutics, then the contemporary philosopher **Giorgio Agamben** falls within its ambit, though to characterize him as a poststructuralist understates the range of his interests (which includes classical and medieval philosophy). Agamben's interest in language places him close to Derrida in scholarly style and temperament. "Following Wittgenstein's suggestion," he writes, "according to which philosophical problems become clearer if they are formulated as questions concerning the meaning of words, I could state the subject of my work as an attempt to understand the meaning of the verb 'can' [*potere*]. What do I mean when I say: 'I can, I cannot'?" (*Potentialities* 177). Agamben argues that existence is potentiality (in this he follows **Antonio Negri**), and thus puts into play the question of being and the limits of being within dualistic structural frameworks – inside/outside, subject/object, matter/spirit – that are the chief targets of phenomenologists and poststructuralists alike. With Agamben, the question of being becomes the question of "the being-given of the word" (*Language* 68). This question is posed in a genealogical examination of medieval "logico-grammatical" systems of thought that did not quite take the decisive step, taken by modern linguists like Émile Benveniste, toward the idea of language as an instance of being. Benveniste had proven that pronouns served a *deictic* function (i.e., they indicated a relation): "Indication is the category within which language refers to its own taking place." Agamben seizes on "this return to the instance of discourse," the space of being that the word "gives," the "event of language" (25). In a deft *ricorso*, he revives (and inverts) a seminal poststructuralist problematic – the privilege of *speech* as opposed to *writing*, of *voice* as opposed to *text* – initiated by Derrida's *Of Grammatology* (1967). Though, like many poststructuralists, his orientation is broadly Hegelian and Heideggerian, Agamben often reads the problems that preoccupy them through the lens of Christian texts and has rehabilitated a sacred theory of voice in a contemporary philosophical setting. In a meditation that opens with a query about Da-sein, "Being-the-there," Agamben begins with the "question of the horizon of negativity": the space in and for the speaking subject whose voice is the negative instance in the event of a language. For Hegel and Heidegger both, "negativity enters into man because man has to be this taking place, he wants to seize the event of language"; but Agamben wants to know how the event of language causes us to be *thrown into* negativity. He also wants to know what it means "to *indicate* the instance of discourse" (*Language* 31), particularly how the pronoun "I" becomes such an instance. In one sense, it is legible as a sign, the written "I," which is indicated lexically and grammatically. But in another sense, it must be "existential" and "contemporary" (criteria borrowed from Benveniste) and can only be satisfied in the form of voice. "*The utterance and the instance of the discourse are only identifiable as such through the voice that speaks them,* and only by attributing a voice to them can something like a taking place of discourse be demonstrated" (32). Agamben's project, like so many in the late twentieth century, is a return to the idealist philosophical tradition – not in order to attack it for being idealist, but to explore the vicissitudes of negativity, which is the founding non-being of all discourse of being. "If our analysis is correct," Agamben confidently writes, "we ought to be able to find in both Hegel and Heidegger a notion of the Voice as the originary negative articulation" (37).

It is the productive quality of the event that counts, the potential for new events and combinations of events. "To traverse being does not mean to dominate it," writes Antonio Negri. "It means taking it for what it is: destructuring it and displaying it as the figure of the collective voice and its continual dislocation in accordance with the rhythm of the voice. In this way, Agamben also ends up the most determined representative of the second generation of poststructuralism." Agamben's project, far from being a "'weak' postmodernism," is in fact a "strong" poststructuralism whose warrant is to "dissolve the ambiguity of the phenomenological reference" that haunts poststructuralist thought and to "a new problematic and constructive tableau: that of deconstruction, desire, and politics" (116). This strikes me as a good way to describe both the ambitions and the limits of poststructuralism and of so much theoretical work that follows, particularly in various domains of posthumanism.

Note

For more on Foucault and Nietzsche, see New Historicism; on Foucault and the history of science, see Posthumanism; on Saussure, Bakhtin, and Barthes, see Formalism and Structuralism; on Kristeva, see Feminism; on Lacan, see Psychoanalysis; on Deleuze and Guattari, see Post-Marxist Theory and Psychoanalysis; on Bourdieu, see Cultural Studies; on Agamben, see Posthumanism.

Works Cited

Agamben, Giorgio. *Language and Death: The Place of Negativity*. Trans. Karen E. Pinkus. Minneapolis: University of Minnesota Press, 1991.

Agamben, Giorgio. *Potentialities: Collected Essays in Philosophy*. Ed. and trans. Daniel Heller-Roazen. Stanford: Stanford University Press, 1999.

Badiou, Alain. *Handbook of Inaesthetics*. Trans. Alberto Toscano. Stanford: Stanford University Press, 2005.

Barthes, Roland. *Image-Music-Text*. Trans. Stephen Heath. New York: Hill and Wang, 1977.

Barthes, Roland. *The Pleasure of the Text*. Trans. Richard Miller. New York: Hill and Wang, 1975.

Barthes, Roland. *S/Z*. Trans. Richard Miller. New York: Hill and Wang, 1974.

Best, Steven and Douglas Kellner. *Postmodern Theory: Critical Interrogations*. Basingstoke: Macmillan, 1991.

De Certeau, Michel. *The Practice of Everyday Life*. Trans. Steven Rendall. Berkeley: University of California Press, 1984.

Derrida, Jacques. *Writing and Difference*. Trans. Alan Bass. Chicago: University of Chicago Press, 1978.

Foucault, Michel. *The Archaeology of Knowledge and the Discourse on Language*. Trans. A. M. Sheridan Smith. New York: Pantheon Books, 1972.

Foucault, Michel. *Discipline and Punish: The Birth of the Prison*. Trans. Alan Sheridan. New York: Vintage Books, 1979.

Foucault, Michel. *The History of Sexuality*. Vol. 1. Trans. Robert Hurley. New York: Pantheon Books, 1978.

Foucault, Michel. *Language, Counter-Memory, Practice: Selected Essays and Interviews*. Ed. Donald F. Bouchard. Trans. Donald F. Bouchard and Sherry Simon. Ithaca: Cornell University Press, 1977.

Foucault, Michel. *Power/Knowledge: Selected Interviews and Other Writings, 1972–77*. Ed. Colin Gordon. Trans. Colin Gorden et al. New York: Pantheon Books, 1980.

Foucault, Michel. "The Subject and Power." In *Michel Foucault: Beyond Structuralism and Hermeneutics*. Ed. Herbert L. Dreyfus and Paul Rabinow. Chicago: University of Chicago Press, 1984. 208–26.

Kristeva, Julia. *Desire in Language: A Semiotic Approach to Literature and Art*. Ed. Leon S. Roudiez. Trans. Thomas Gora, Alice Jardine, and Leon S. Roudiez. New York: Columbia University Press, 1980.

Lacan, Jacques. *Écrits: A Selection*. Trans. Bruce Fink. New York: Norton, 2002.

Moi, Toril. "Appropriating Bourdieu: Feminist Theory and Pierre Bourdieu's Sociology of Culture." *New Literary History* 22.4 (Autumn 1991): 1017–49.

Negri, Antonio. "The Discreet Taste of the Dialectic." In *Giorgio Agamben: Sovereignty and Life*. Ed. Matthew Calarco and Steven DeCaroli. Stanford: Stanford University Press, 2007. 116–25.

Oliver, Kelly, ed. *Ethics, Politics and Difference in Julia Kristeva's Writing*. New York: Routledge, 1993.

Ricoeur, Paul. *The Conflict of Interpretations: Essays in Hermeneutics*. Ed. Don Ihde. Evanston, IL: Northwestern University Press, 1974.

Wilson, Timothy. "Foucault, Genealogy, History." *Philosophy Today* 39.2 (Summer 1995): 157–70.

Žižek, Slavoj. "Postscript." Interview. In *A Critical Sense: Interviews with Intellectuals*. Ed. Peter Osborne. London: Routledge, 1996. 36–44.

4   Mind/Body/Gender/Identity

Psychoanalysis

Psychoanalysis offers a systematic theory of the mind and human psychic development. As early as the 1890s, Sigmund Freud had established the fundamental importance of dreams, which offer a glimpse of the nature of neurotic symptoms and their origin in the unconscious. His early collaboration with Josef Breuer in the study of hysteria was the starting point for a theory of *neurotic symptoms*, which he believed were derivatives of memories that had been repressed and existed only in the unconscious. *Neuroses* are psychological disorders in which the self is in conflict with the world; they include hysteria, obsessive and compulsive disorders, depression, phobias, and so on; they are the focus of psychoanalysis and can be treated. *Psychoses*, like schizophrenia and manic depression, are more serious disorders, often with an organic basis, that involve a breakdown of some kind in the balance between conscious self and unconsciousness: they are typically not treatable by psychoanalysis. Neuroses, therefore, lie at the foundation of Freudian psychoanalytic theory. The early case histories – for example, "Dora: A Case of Hysteria" and "History of an Infantile Neurosis (Wolf Man)" – show the development of Freud's thinking about unconscious processes and the way in which dreams provide insight into the etiology, or cause, of neurotic symptoms. These case histories, particularly "History of an Infantile Neurosis," illustrate a method of dream interpretation that seeks to reveal the repressed trauma underlying neurotic symptoms. And while this method has been criticized (famously by Gilles Deleuze and Félix Guattari, in *Anti-Oedipus*) for being reductive, it remains a vital component of psychoanalysis and other forms of psychotherapy.

Like the symptom, the dream is an indirect or coded message, the interpretation of which holds the key to the meaning of the symptom. Dream interpretation is a complex process involving considerable skill on the part of the analyst; but Freud was confident that proper training would ensure reliable, scientific results. Dreams have two kinds of content, *manifest* and *latent*. The manifest level is the dream itself, the object of interpretation; the latent level is the actual thought that cannot be known or expressed consciously because it has been repressed or "censored" by the super-ego that normally screens perceptions for consciousness and holds back whatever could result in a trauma to the ego. The material prohibited by the censor may include violations of culturally specific taboos (e.g., anti-normative behaviors) as well as those of a more universal character (e.g., the prohibition against incest). Freud believed that the unconscious was the location of wishes of various kinds (from the simplest to the most profound) that could not be consciously fulfilled; however, enough of this primal material makes its way to consciousness in dreams and finds a kind of symbolic fulfillment. "[A] dream is not an intention represented as having been carried out, but a wish represented as having been fulfilled" (*SE* 7: 85). The distortions that convert wishes into often bizarre and obscure dreams Freud called the *dream-work*, a process in which unconscious material is allowed a disguised or coded expression during sleep, when the dream-censor relaxes its vigilance. This dream-work entails the primary mechanisms of *displacement* and *condensation* by which unconscious material is formed into the manifest content of the dream. In other words, the dream-work performs what many (including Freud) recognize as a literary activity in which metaphor, metonymy, and other figures represent in a disguised form the secret wish that lies hidden in the unconscious. In order to comprehend the manifest content of the dream, the analyst must lead the analysand to the latent level of unconscious, repressed meaning.

Dreams are important because they hold the key to neurotic symptoms that usually originate in an individual's earliest experiences of instinctual satisfaction and repression. For this reason, childhood sexual experiences are fundamentally important. Freud's *Three Essays on Sexuality* argues that these experiences are structured diphasically, which means that sexual development is interrupted by a latency period that effectively separates it into two distinct phases, pre-genital (oral and anal states) and genital, each incorporating multiple stages and, quite often, regression to prior stages. Children are *polymorphously perverse* and can therefore respond along a number of erotic pathways (or "sexual aims") to a number of "sexual objects" (including the child herself). For Freud, "normal" development entailed the integration of the component "perversions" (scopophilia and exhibitionism, auto-eroticism, sadism and masochism) into a healthy, heterosexual instinct. He was well aware that "normal" sexuality and sexual identity were not often achieved, that an individual could fixate at one or another of the early stages; but he strongly believed that the heterosexual norm was best suited to fulfill the destiny of the human species, to fend off death and produce more life. The *pleasure principle*, which is the pure and unfettered energy of the sexual instinct, motivates childhood sexuality. In normal development, particularly during the genital phase and the "dissolution" of the Oedipus complex, the narcissistic pursuit of pleasure "comes under the sway of the reproductive function" and the instincts are "organized" more firmly "towards a sexual aim attached to some extraneous sexual object" (*SE* 7: 197). This form of *primary narcissism*, which refers to the auto-erotic tendencies of infants, is to be distinguished from *secondary narcissism*, the unhealthy fixation of the ego on itself at later stages of sexual development. The *reality principle* keeps individuals from succumbing to the whim of their sexual instincts and forces them either to sublimate some of their libido in non-sexual or non-violent activities (art, religion, philosophy) or to repress the desire for such activities through *reaction-formation* (moral reactions like disgust and shame), the mental forces that come into play to oppose or block perverse impulses. Under the influence of the reality principle, the child learns to direct sexual libido away from the ego (in order to avoid the danger of secondary narcissism) and onto a suitable sexual object.

For Freud, the central event in early development is the *Oedipus complex*, working through which allows the individual to overcome "incestuous phantasies" and permits "one of the most painful, psychical achievements of the pubertal period ... detachment from parental authority" (*SE* 7: 227). The Oedipus complex springs from Freud's reading of Sophocles' *Oedipus Rex*, the tragic story of a man who unknowingly kills his own father and marries his mother and who, upon learning all of this, puts out his eyes. Freud derived from his reading of Sophocles an understanding of desire that is essentially triangular: the young male child desires his mother, but feels thwarted by his father with whom he must ultimately identify, but only at the cost of giving up his mother. The prohibition against the mother throws up defenses against the father, who is perceived as a threat to the boy's bond with his mother, a threat that for Freud was akin to a fear of being castrated, which is made all the more real when the young boy happens to see a young girl undressing or his own mother in bed with his father and realizes that women have already suffered this fate. A "normal" dissolution of the Oedipus complex would involve the child repudiating his mother, with whom he was closely identified and to whom he was most attracted, identifying with his father, and finding another love-object. For young girls, this process is doubly traumatic, for girls must not only turn away from their initial love objects, they must also shift their desire from female to male objects.

Additionally, the threat of castration appears to the girl as a past event, her own body standing as evidence of its terrible effects; and while the boy is free to find a female substitute for his mother, the girl is absolutely prohibited from finding another female object of desire and so is separated from the very person with whom she would "normally" identify. These events lead girls to experience a loss or lack which they attempt to alleviate by having a baby, a phallic gift from the father. The Oedipal process for girls (sometimes called the *Electra complex*) thus issues a double imperative: preserve life through heterosexual object choices and repudiate the most natural bond of attachment (the mother), which necessarily entails an identification with the father. For boys and girls, the Oedipus complex installs repression as a means by which to manage prohibited desires; it involves "the transformation into affects, and especially into anxiety, of the mental energy belonging to the instincts" (*SE* 14: 153). The onset of repression is simultaneously the destruction of the Oedipus complex. Subsequent repressions are made under the aegis of the super-ego that emerges as a result of a successful Oedipal experience. The super-ego is thus "the heir of the Oedipus complex" (*SE* 19: 36).

The importance of "metapsychological" ideas like the Oedipus complex is hard to underestimate. It guarantees the structural integrity of the nuclear family and, in a broader cultural context, could be regarded as the foundation of civilization, but it also motivates "the young phantasy-builder" (*SE* 9: 240) who wishes to replace his family with one of a higher rank or rescue his mother from an abusive father. Despite the importance of the Oedipus complex, the chief and enduring elements of Freud's thought – the unconscious, the instincts, neurotic symptoms and defenses, dream interpretations – are grounded in psychoanalytic therapy, the object of which is to bring to light the origins of neurotic symptoms that Freud believed lay in the traumas of sexual development. Of crucial importance in therapeutic contexts is *transference*, in which desire for a repressed object is transferred to the analyst himself, who is then in a position to bring to consciousness, through dream interpretation and free association, the latent wish or desire that is at the root of the original neurosis. As Freud put it in the famous case history of Dora, transferences are "new editions or facsimiles of the impulses and phantasies which are aroused and made conscious during the progress of the analysis; but they have this peculiarity, which is characteristic for their species, that they replace some earlier person by the person of the physician" (*SE* 7: 116). This potentially problematic interaction between analyst and analysand is, in a sense, the goal of the analytical process itself, for a desire that has been brought to consciousness no longer manifests as a neurotic symptom.

As he developed the theory of the ego, especially in such controversial later works as *Beyond the Pleasure Principle* (1920) and *The Ego and the Id* (1923), Freud formulated a "structural" theory of the mind, one in which the *ego*, the *super-ego*, and the *id* signify certain kinds of relationships between conscious and unconscious elements of the psyche. The *ego* is that part of the mind that confronts the world, the *id* that portion of the ego that remains unconscious and is the seat of the drives or instincts; the super-ego protects the conscious ego from the id and from hostile external simulations. The human psyche is, by its very nature internally split, both threatened and nourished by instinctual drives. Because instincts constitute the limit of what can be studied scientifically, the aim of psychoanalysis is restricted to "demonstrating the connection along the path of instinctual activity between a person's external experiences and his reactions" (*SE* 11: 136). Freud had started by positing two primary instincts: *sexual*, linked to fantasy, wish fulfillment, and the pleasure principle; and *ego*, linked to consciousness and the reality principle. In *Beyond the Pleasure Principle*, he revised this theory by fusing the ego and sexual instincts into a single drive toward self-preservation (*Eros*) and posited the death instinct (*Thanatos*), which is dedicated to the quest of short-circuiting the sexual instinct and ending life. "[A]n instinct," Freud writes, "is an urge inherent in organic life to restore an earlier state of things which the living entity has been obliged to abandon under the pressure of external disturbing forces; that is, it is a kind of organic elasticity, or, to put it another way, the expression of the inertia inherent in organic life." The death instinct seeks to return to an original *inorganic* state: "the aim of all life is death" (*SE* 18: 36, 38). Paradoxically, the pleasure principle, because it seeks the repetition of desires and wishes that could bring harm to the individual, appears to be in the service of the death instinct.

Freud's reflections on culture have been controversial, in part because they attempt to derive concepts like the Oedipus complex from what appear to us now to be inadequate anthropological and historical materials. For example, in *Totem and Taboo* (1913), Freud suggests that "[t]he beginnings of religion, morals, society and art converge in the Oedipus complex" (*SE* 13: 156). He speculates that there existed a primal moment in humankind's early development when the brothers in the "primal horde" murder the father in order to gain freedom and women. A totem system emerges, one that reduplicates the crime but also puts in place prohibitions against the crime itself as well as the possession of women that made it necessary. From the primal horde emerged the "fraternal clan," and from this clan there ultimately emerged complex PATRIARCHAL social structures, religion, and morality. In *Civilization and Its Discontents*, he argues that modern humanity is caught between a civil and a savage condition:

> What makes itself felt in a human community as a desire for freedom may be their revolt against some existing injustice, and so may prove favourable to a further development of civilization; it may remain compatible with civilization. But it may also spring from the remains of their original personality, which is still untamed by civilization and may thus become the basis in them of hostility to civilization.... A good part of the struggles of mankind centre round the single task of finding an expedient accommodation – one, that is that will bring happiness – between this claim of the individual and the cultural claims of the group. (*SE* 21: 95–6)

Civilization becomes a kind of negative compensation for the repression of desires that led to the destruction of the father in the first place. Religion, specifically the worship of the fallen father as a god, sublimates primal desire and symbolically reenacts its tabooed fulfillment in the form of religious ritual.

Almost as soon as it became a legitimate field of study within the medical establishment (that is, around the time of World War I), psychoanalysis experienced schisms and factional movements that reduced Freud's centralizing authority and made psychoanalysis more varied, more popular, and more accessible. C. G. Jung's break with Freud in 1913 was due mainly to their divergent views on sexuality and the unconscious; because it occurred early in the development of psychoanalysis, Jung's own subsequent work in "analytical psychology" is not usually regarded as revisionist Freudianism. The more serious threat to Freud's theoretical hegemony came from ego psychologists, like his daughter Anna Freud, and object-relations theorists like D. W. Winnicott, Otto Rank, and Melanie Klein. Ego psychologists tend to focus on the dynamic qualities of the ego, rather than on the id and the unconscious, while object-relations theorists reject the priority of the Oedipus complex and emphasize instead the mother–child relationship.

Object-relations theory has been particularly influential (see Greenberg and Mitchell), in part due to Klein and Anna Freud's analysis of infantile experiences. Both accepted the Oedipal complex but located its time of emergence at a much earlier phase of childhood and shifted attention away from the complex itself to the period before it (the "pre-Oedipal phase") and the relations between the infant and her world, particularly her IDEALIZATIONS of the mother's body. Klein was especially interested in the complexities of the child's inner world and how objects from the outer world, particularly the mother, could be transformed into a part or whole object invested with intense feelings in the child's psyche. Winnicott also focused on early childhood development and introduced into psychotherapy concepts like "transitional objects" and "good-enough mothering." The transitional object, an "other-than-me object," is woven into a "personal pattern" and determines an "intermediate area of experience … between the oral eroticism and true object relationship, between primary creative activity and projection of what has already been introjected" (230–1). This object is typically something in which the infant is emotionally invested, such as a blanket or a teddy bear, that enables her to slowly relinquish her dependence on the mother's body, which, in early development, is indistinguishable from the child's. These transitional objects, which are neither purely subjective nor purely external, are actively chosen for comfort and security. They are the infant's first "not-me possession," which enables an awareness of the spatial distinction between herself and her external environment. Winnicott's "good-enough mother" creates a protective "holding environment" of shared emotions and mutual understanding in which the infant's autonomous identity can eventually emerge. Without such mothering the child's "true self" will be inhibited and a "false self" will develop that can interfere with the formation of adult relationships. While the emphasis on mothering in psychoanalysis was welcomed by many, Winnicott was criticized by some who found his theory put all the pressure of parenting back on the mother, who could now be blamed for her child's failures.

While object-relations theorists emphasized the mother–child relationship, ego psychologists, including R. D. Laing and Heinz Kohut, sought to reestablish the whole ego through a purging or healing of the divided self. It was this latter development in psychoanalysis – with its emphasis on the "sociological poem of the 'autonomous ego'" – that drove **Jacques Lacan** to "return to Freud" (*Écrits* 162). Lacan's revision of Freud, influenced by Saussurean linguistics and Lévi-Strauss's structuralist anthropology, together with his own clinical experience, enabled him to claim, in 1957, that it is "the whole structure of language that psychoanalytic experience discovers in the unconscious." Therefore, the idea that the unconscious "is merely the seat of the instincts will have to be rethought" (138). Note that Lacan does not say the unconscious is structured *like* a language but that the structure of language is found *in* the unconscious. As such, the unconscious constitutes what Lacan calls the "big Other," which speaks to us, provided we are willing to listen, from within the Symbolic realm of language. "The unconscious is neither the primordial nor the instinctual and what it knows of the elemental is no more than the elements of the signifier" (161).

This revolutionary rethinking of the SUBJECT and his relation to the unconscious began with Lacan's theory of the "mirror stage" of childhood development. He argued that children (typically in their second year) think they see themselves as an entire being, fully present before themselves (as in a mirror), disconnected from the oceanic unity of the maternal body. However, the image obscures the figure of the mother-as-prop (or prosthesis), so that the image becomes a fantasy of the self. The mirror stage is a *mise-en-scène* of misrecognition (*méconnaissance*) that inaugurates the IMAGINARY order, a narcissistic realm of fantasy and imagination. For Lacan, the original fused state of the child and mother fostered a quasi-narcissistic state of pleasurable plenitude, a unity of self and other. This fusion is ruptured by the "No" of the father, at which point the child gives up the mother and enters the Symbolic realm, by acquiring an ability to symbolize. Symbolization means that a sign takes the place of the thing. To symbolize therefore is to give up the object. If the longing for re-fusion with the mother defines the Imaginary dimension of the psyche, the entry into the Symbolic order through the "Name-of-the-Father" installs the mother in the realm of the REAL – a domain of primal needs and the unattainable materiality of experience – where she becomes resistant to symbolization. Lacan believed that all children undergo a "mirror stage" in which the subject is formed out of narcissistic fantasies. The ego is therefore a realm of delusion, for the "truth" of the human psyche resides in the unconscious. "The Other is the locus in which is situated the chain of the signifier that governs whatever may be made present of the subject – it is a field of that living being in which the subject has to appear" (*Four* 203). Misrecognition forms the ego at the same moment that it thwarts desire: it constitutes the "vital dehiscence constitutive of man," which Lacan also calls "negative libido" (*Écrits* 22–3).

The ascension to the Symbolic entails a transition from *demand*, associated with the Imaginary, to *desire* or *lack*, which can never be fulfilled. In a sense, lack defines the relationship to the Real, which is the space of an impossible plenitude. Or, as Ernesto Laclau puts it, "the Real becomes a name for the very failure of the Symbolic in achieving its own fullness. The Real would be, in that sense, a retroactive effect of the failure of the Symbolic" (68). The Real is not a "thing-in-itself" in the Kantian sense, but a domain of experience; its inaccessibility has nothing to do with its ideal nature but rather with the opposite: it is the realm of the *un*ideal, the raw materiality of things before they have gotten a name or a purpose. Lacan, in the seminar on Freudian technique, describes the Real as that which "resists symbolization absolutely. In the end, doesn't the feeling of the real reach its high point in the pressing manifestation of an unreal, hallucinatory reality?" (*Seminar* 66). But, **Slavoj Žižek** notes, Lacan's attempt to define the Real slips into the Symbolic register. "Drawing a clear line between the real and the symbolic is a symbolic operation *par* *excellence....* [W]hat Lacan calls 'the real' is nothing beyond the symbolic, it's merely *the inherent inconsistency of the symbolic order itself*" ("Postscript" 41).

The Real is unavailable to us, but we do receive messages from it via the unconscious (the big Other) and these messages (literally *letters*) enjoy the same status as the "purloined letter" in Edgar Allan Poe's eponymous story: manifest rather than latent, always in plain sight. The constitution of the subject in language takes place along a path of signification: "only signifier-to-signifier correlations provide the standard for any and every search for signification" (*Écrits* 145). Because only the signifier, the letter, is available to us, the signified effectively disappears *beneath* the signifier (hence Lacan's algorithm, S/s, in which the signified rests beneath the Signifier). This "signifying structure," which Lacan also finds in the symptom, signals "the omnipresence for human beings of the symbolic function stamped on the flesh" (*Écrits* 119), that is to say, the PHALLUS. For Freud, the phallus is significant primarily for the role it plays in the Oedipus and castration complexes. Lacan recognizes this important role, but goes further by equating the phallus with the concept of the TRANSCENDENTAL SIGNIFIER of authority, rationality (*logos*), and power. Hence, "[t]he phallus is the privileged signifier of this mark in which the role of Logos is wedded to the advent of desire" (277). Neither a fantasy, nor an object, nor an organ, "it is the signifier that is destined to designate meaning effects as a whole, insofar as the signifier conditions them by its presence as signifier" (275). This conditioning is in part accomplished through a double move: the "incessant sliding of the signified under the signifier" and the entrance of the signifier into the signified, "namely, in a form which, not being immaterial, raises the question of its place in reality" (152, 142). The only thing that can stop this movement is the POINT DE CAPITON (quilting point, anchoring point), which serves as the site of the gaze and the "schema for taking into account the dominance of the letter in the dramatic transformation that dialogue can effect in the subject" (152). It captures and mediates desire in the Other – a circular articulation, "from the subject called to the Other, to the subject of that which he has himself seen appear in the field of the Other" (*Four* 207). In **Judith Butler**'s formulation, it refers to the situation in which "an arbitrary sign not only appears essential to what it signifies, but actively organizes the thing under the sign itself" (26). The shark in *Jaws* is an instance of this organization, for it serves as a nodal point for free-floating fear and anxiety (see Žižek, *Looking Awry* 133–4).

Of crucial importance for Lacan is the subject's relation to the signifier, which occurs "through an enunciation that makes a human being tremble due to the vacillation that comes back to him from his own statement" (*Écrits* 289). This is also the moment of the "*Spaltung* or splitting" that the subject endures "due to his subordination to the signifier – to the condition of an object" (301). Alain Badiou has written that Lacan is "our Hegel," in that "he presents the (idealist) dialectic of our time" (132) precisely in the account of this splitting and in providing the Hegelian "dialectical torsion" with a new paradigm of the subjective as disjunctive. The "vanishing term" of the subject, the traversal of the subject through the "fantasmatic image" and lack, "is governed by the ignorance of loss that constitutes it. It follows that there is no truth which is not mutilated, and no subject which is not subjected" (Badiou 137–8). This loss is marked by the crucial function of the signifier, in the field of the Other within the Symbolic, which allows subjectivity to "manifest" itself to itself. Language is *for the subject* in the sense that it is suited to subjectivity and that it precedes it. Lacan argues that the "I" (*je*) speaks only in order to secure an answer that validates, in the Symbolic order, what the self (*moi*, me) imagines itself as being; it seeks to elicit messages from the Other (through, for example, woman-as-other [*objet petit a*]) that the "paranoid" *moi* (the Imaginary conception of the self) needs to hear in order to believe in his existence. "The Other is, therefore, the locus in which is constituted the I who speaks along with he who hears, what is said by the one being already the reply, the other deciding, in hearing [*entendre*] it, whether the one has spoken or not" (Lacan, *Écrits* 132–3).

In the Other too we find the crucial possibility of FORECLOSURE of the Symbolic and the paternal metaphor (e.g., phallus, Name-of-the-Father). For Jöel Dor, *foreclosure* "seems to be the very mechanism that can cause primal repression to fail," and this insight is Lacan's "most explicit contribution to Freudian thought." For if "the Name-of-the-Father is foreclosed in the place of the Other, the paternal metaphor fails" and psychosis ensues (122, 124). Lacan derives his concept of foreclosure from Freud's use of the term *Verwerfung* (rejection, dismissal), which refers to the psychotic's break with reality. Lacan defines it at one point in reference to the emergence of "the Thing" (i.e., the "thing as such") and its repudiation or foreclosure within scientific discourse, for "what is foreclosed in the symbolic reappears in the real," which is why, Lacan concludes, "at the end of physics, it is something as enigmatic as the Thing that is glimpsed" (*Ethics* 131). Foreclosure is a "type of alienation of the authentic subject in favor of a privileged stand-in designated, for the occasion, as the *knowing subject* or the *subject of knowledge*" (Dor 167). Thus foreclosure is either a state of being *outside* the Symbolic (i.e., an experience of JOUISSANCE) or the complete disavowal of the self in the space of the Symbolic. The concept of *jouissance* is important for Lacanian theory, for it enables the illusion, in the space of the Imaginary, of stepping outside of the Symbolic; another way of putting this is to say that *jouissance* is merely an instance of the Imaginary misrecognizing the Symbolic for the Real. Some theorists believe that *jouissance* is a form of foreclosure that places it outside the unconscious and thus free of the phallic power. In Colette Soler's reading, feminine *jouissance* is not *in* the Other but is rather "the signifier of the *jouissance* of the Other, insofar as that *jouissance* is foreclosed from the Other of the signifier" (107). She notes further that women can be situated "quite easily in relation to these terms," which means that foreclosure becomes linked not only with *jouissance* but also with female sexuality in a way that decouples it from a phallic economy. One could say that Lacan's discourse does not so much reinscribe PHALLOGOCENTRISM as circumscribe it for interrogation, enclose it in order to allow for its *foreclosure* (see Lacan, *Four* 217f). (On the question of female sexuality and foreclosure, see Gender Studies 203–4.)

Like Freud, Lacan regarded woman (and female sexuality) as enigmatic, in part because woman sustains the power of the phallus, and in part because she creates a possibility of divine *jouissance*: Woman "grounds itself in not-wholly situating itself in the phallic function." Lacan believed that Woman (with a capital W) did not exist, for she is the "not-whole," the non-universal (*Encore* 72–3). Therefore "Woman can only be written with a bar through it" (thus ~~Woman~~). (In French, this cancellation of the universal category or essence of woman would be marked in the article:

thus, ~~la~~ *femme*.) As a cancelled universal, as a "not-whole" non-essence, woman functions *in the phallic system* not as a full subject but as an instrument for the subjectivity of men, a partial "thing" that enables the construction of a whole essence (i.e., "man"), the *other* through which man constitutes himself *in* the big Other (the unconscious). Woman is thus a symptom, a screen for the projection of lack, but also a space of desire fulfilled, the space of the Other/*other* in which man finds his identity and being.

> What constitutes the symptom – that something which dallies with the unconscious – is that one believes in it.... [I]n the life of a man, a woman is something he believes in. He believes there is one, or at times two or three, but the interesting thing is that, unable to believe only in one, he believes in a species, rather like sylphs or water-sprites. (*Feminine* 168)

This relation of the subject to the Other and the Woman is especially marked in film, where the gaze situates the viewer at the *point de capiton* of the Other. Kaja Silverman is especially interested in how the camera functions in the field of the gaze. "I understood," Silverman writes, "that in order for the gaze to be perceived in this way, the male eye had necessarily to be aligned with the camera. I also saw that the endless subordination of woman-as-spectacle was necessary to the establishment of this alignment" (136). Laura Mulvey illustrates this practice by which a critique of Lacan's discourse makes possible a new theory of desire and the gaze. Her work on visual pleasures in film draws on Freudian and Lacanian theories of the gaze (both the gaze of the Other and that of the voyeur or scopophile, who "loves to look") in order to critique the "determining male gaze" that constitutes "[t]he presence of woman" as "an indispensable element of spectacle in normal narrative film" (27). As the signifier of maleness (the "male other"), woman stands unnoticed *as a woman*. She is, as **Luce Irigaray** has pointed out, a screen for man's desire, a "bearer of meaning, not maker of meaning" (15).

Of crucial importance for Lacanian and post-Lacanian feminists, including Irigaray, **Julia Kristeva**, Juliet Mitchel, and Jane Gallop, was a reconsideration of the Oedipus complex and the role of the mother in pre-genital phases of development and object relations. Though Kristeva was influenced to some degree by Lacan's seminars of the 1970s, her own approach as an analyst was defined by a feminist resistance to some of his key formulations. Kristeva posits a condition of *abjection*, of being refused, ejected, rejected, and disavowed as the "not I": "a vortex of summons and repulsion places the one haunted by it literally beside himself" (*Powers* 1). The temporality of abjection moves between "oblivion and thunder" as a form of "veiled infinity and the moment when revelation bursts forth" (9). She suggests that abjection is a form of primal repression, for having been effected "prior to the springing forth of the ego, of its objects and representations" (11). Something outside the unconscious makes it possible, which is to say that the foreclosure of the subject signals a "narcissistic crisis," by which the self is depleted, subtracted, abjected. This foreclosure abjects the self into "a world in which the Other has collapsed," a world in which the "border between inside and outside" collapses as well, so that abjection "takes the place of the other" and ushers the abject "into the site of the Other" (18, 53–4). The condition of abjection makes legible "the fragile limits of the speaking being," the "bottomless primacy" (18) that she called *khora*, analogous in many ways to the pre-Oedipal state of indifferentiation.

The general tendency away from the Oedipus complex, especially in Kristeva, signals a repudiation of patriarchy and phallogocentric thought and a privileging of the maternal body. In "Stabat Mater," Kristeva asks if it is possible "to say of a *woman* what she *is* (without running the risk of abolishing her difference)," and if so, "would it perhaps be different concerning the *mother*, since that is the only function of the 'other sex' to which we can definitely attribute existence?" (*Tales* 234). The problem with this argument is that it blurs the distinction between real experience and fantasy formations based on it; even for feminists this confusion leads to the rejection of motherhood as a model for feminine identity. The point, however, is not that motherhood is privileged, but that it is the indelible marker of a space outside phallic economies. Irigaray, a philosopher as well as a psychoanalyst, takes just this view in her critique of the Western philosophic tradition. She finds that women are associated consistently with the material world and thereby serve as the basis for philosophic speculation that is always defined in terms of a male identity that transcends maternal matter. Irigaray points to one reason why women and women's bodies are "excluded by the nature of things," as Lacan claimed. If they are associated with the material ground of existence, the non-essential ESSENCE that grounds male subjectivity, they cannot reflect (for) themselves. This would make woman a mere "speculum" or mirror for the production of male subjectivity. Irigaray asks, "Is [woman] the indispensable condition whereby the living entity retains and maintains and perfects himself in his self-likeness?" (*Speculum* 165). (On Irigaray, see Feminism 191–4.)

Gilles Deleuze and Félix Guattari have mounted a similar attack against the centrality of the Oedipus complex. In *Anti-Oedipus* Deleuze and Guattari argue that the "Oedipal triangle ["father-mother-me"] is the personal and private territoriality that corresponds to all of capitalism's efforts at social RETERRITORI-ALIZATION. Oedipus was always the displaced limit for every SOCIAL FORMATION, since it is the displaced represented of desire" (*Anti-Oedipus* 266). In other words, the mechanisms of repression and conscience that are unleashed by the Oedipus complex are perfectly suited to those of capitalism: both destroy traditional structures and both create new pathways and economies of desire. The emphasis on desire and lack in psychoanalysis distracts us from the true nature of desire, which is not to be located in the feelings or experiences of the "oedipalized subject" but rather in a circulating flow of "intensities." Human desire is only one kind of "desiring machine" that springs up spontaneously and without centralization, all over the social body. "If desire produces, its product is real. If desire is productive, it can be productive only in the real world and can produce only reality ... Desire and its object are one and the same thing: the machine, as a machine of a machine. Desire is a machine, and the object of desire is another machine connected to it" (26). The schizophrenic is especially sensitive to this conception of desire, and for this reason Deleuze and Guattari use the "schizo" rather than the neurotic as the basis for their critique of psychoanalysis and its complicity with capitalism.

Psychoanalysis continues to be an important method for treating mental illness in the Anglophone world, and it continues to generate new theoretical work regarding such conditions as narcissism, borderline personalities, and such pathologies as incest. Freudian and Lacanian schools of psychoanalysis continue to thrive in the academy in part because the leading discoveries of the field – the unconscious, the interpretation of dreams, the drives and the pleasure/reality principles, the structure of neurotic symptoms, the phallus, the feminine as radically unknown – have undergone extensive renovation by a wide range of contemporary theorists. Lacan's turn in the 1970s to James Joyce, whom he claimed was the inspiration for a new theory of the symptom (or *sinthome*), has revitalized literary studies. Lacan's ideas have been fruitfully applied in post-Marxist analyses of ideology and hegemony, especially in the work of **Louis Althusser** and Ernesto Laclau. Perhaps the most influential partisan of Lacanian ideas is **Slavoj Žižek**, who has done more than anyone else to cement Lacan's preeminence in the cultural field (the reader is encouraged to log on to *Lacanian Ink* at www.lacan.com). Žižek has famously applied Lacanian theory to everything from Kant to Hitchcock and has developed a unique perspective on European nationalism indebted to Lacan's theory of lack and the relation of lack to the Symbolic order. If Lacan truly is "our Hegel," as Badiou claims, then we are faced with the ironic possibility that Lacan will become himself the Name-of-the-Father that his thinking in some ways warns us against.

Note
For more on Lacan, see Poststructuralism; on Deleuze and Guattari, see Postmodernism; on Butler, Žižek, and Laclau, see Critical Theory and Post-Marxist Theory.

Works Cited

Badiou, Alain. *Theory of the Subject*. Trans. Bruno Bosteels. London and New York: Continuum, 2009.

Butler, Judith. "Restaging the Universal: Hegemony and the Limits of Formalism." In Judith Butler, Ernesto Laclau, and Slavoj Žižek. *Contingency, Hegemony, Universality: Contemporary Dialogues on the Left*. London and New York: Verso, 2000. 11–43.

Deleuze, Gilles and Félix Guattari. *Anti-Oedipus: Capitalism and Schizophrenia*. Trans. Robert Hurley, Mark Seem, and Helen R. Lane. Minneapolis: University of Minnesota Press, 1983.

Dor, Joël. *Introduction to the Reading of Lacan: The Unconscious Structured Like a Language*. New York: Other Press, 1998.

Freud, Sigmund. *Standard Edition of the Complete Psychological Works of Sigmund Freud*. Ed. James Strachey. 24 vols. London: Hogarth Press, 1953–74. (*SE*)

Greenberg, Jay R. and Stephen A. Mitchell. *Object Relations in Psychoanalytic Theory*. Cambridge, MA: Harvard University Press, 1983.

Irigaray, Luce. *Speculum of the Other Woman*. Trans. Gilliam C. Gill. Ithaca: Cornell University Press, 1985.

Klein, Melanie. *Contributions to Psycho-analysis, 1921–1945*. London: Hogarth Press, 1948.

Kristeva, Julia. *Powers of Horror: An Essay on Abjection*. Trans. Leon S. Roudiez. New York: Columbia University Press, 1982.

Kristeva, Julia. *Tales of Love*. Trans. Leon S. Roudiez. New York: Columbia University Press, 1987.

Lacan, Jacques. *Écrits: A Selection*. Trans. Bruce Fink. New York: Norton, 2002.

Lacan, Jacques. *The Ethics of Psychoanalysis, 1959–1960. The Seminar of Jacques Lacan, Book VII*. Ed. Jacques-Alain Miller. Trans. Dennis Porter. New York: Norton, 1992.

Lacan, Jacques. *Feminine Sexuality*, by Jacques Lacan and the École Freudienne. Ed. Juliet Mitchell and Jacqueline Rose. Trans. Jacqueline Rose. New York: Norton, 1982.

Lacan, Jacques. *On Feminine Sexuality: The Limits of Love and Knowledge, 1972–1973. The Seminar of Jacques Lacan, Book XX*. Trans. Bruce Fink. New York: Norton, 1998.

Lacan, Jacques. *The Four Fundamental Concepts of Psychoanalysis. The Seminar of Jacques Lacan, Book XI*. Ed. Jacques-Alain Miller. Trans. Alan Sheridan. New York: Norton, 1981. French edition 1973; first US edition 1978.

Lacan, Jacques. *The Seminar of Jacques Lacan*. Ed. Jacques-Alain Miller. Vol. 1. Trans. John Forrester. Cambridge: Cambridge University Press, 1988.

Laclau, Ernesto. "Identity and Hegemony: The Role of Universality in the Constitution of Political Logics." In Judith Butler, Ernesto Laclau, and Slavoj Žižek. *Contingency, Hegemony, Universality: Contemporary Dialogues on the Left*. London and New York: Verso, 2000. 44–89.

Mulvey, Laura. "Visual Pleasure and Narrative Cinema." *Screen* 16.3 (Autumn 1975): 6–18.

Silverman, Kaja. *Threshold of the Visible World*. New York: Routledge, 1996.

Soler, Colette. "What Does the Unconscious Know about Women?" In *Reading Seminar XX: Lacan's Major Work on Love, Knowledge, and Feminine Sexuality*. Ed. Suzanne Barnard and Bruce Fink. Albany: SUNY Press, 2002. 99–108.

Winnicott, D. W. *Collected Papers: Through Paediatrics to Psycho-Analysis*. New York: Brunner-Routledge, 1992.

Žižek, Slavoj. *Looking Awry: An Introduction to Jacques Lacan through Popular Culture*. Cambridge, MA: MIT Press, 1991.

Žižek, Slavoj. "Postscript." Interview. In *A Critical Sense: Interviews with Intellectuals*. Ed. Peter Osborne. London: Routledge, 1996. 36–44.

Feminist Theory

In some ways feminism is the discourse that Freudian psychoanalysis failed to produce: an account of female sexuality, of gender difference, and of the gendered knowledge on which modern science, philosophy, arts, and politics depend. As such, feminist theory is both an exploration of the gendered subject and a political theory of equality and emancipation. Modern feminism began with Mary Wollstonecraft's *A Vindication of the Rights of Woman* (1792), a work that criticizes stereotypes of women as emotional and instinctive and argues that women should aspire to the same rationality prized by men. A product of the Enlightenment, Wollstonecraft believed that women should enjoy social, legal, and intellectual equality with men and drew for support from the work of progressive social philosophers. Liberal intellectuals like John Stuart Mill and his wife, Harriet Taylor, developed this argument, infusing it with the principles of individualism that Mill had developed out of the utilitarian philosophy of Jeremy Bentham. In 1866, Mill introduced a bill in parliament that called for an extension of the franchise to women and, in 1869, published *The Subjection of Women*. In that essay he argued that women ought to enjoy equality in the social sphere, especially in marriage, and condemned "forced repression" and "unnatural stimulation" (276): "All women are brought up from the very earliest years in the belief that their ideal of character is the very opposite to that of men; not self-will, and government by self-control, but submission, and yielding to the control of others" (271). Mill's views, influenced strongly by Taylor, marked a significant advance for women and contributed to the rise of the New Woman movement at the end of the nineteenth-century and the early twentieth-century suffragette movement, both of which were committed to social equality and individual freedom.

The first phase or "wave" of modern feminism, then, was concerned primarily with the issue of suffrage (the right to vote). The dominant figures at mid-nineteenth century in the United States were Elizabeth Cady Stanton and Susan B. Anthony, whose political roots were in anti-slavery activism and, to a lesser degree, temperance movements. Stanton composed the "Declaration of Sentiments" for the Seneca Falls women's rights convention in 1848, a watershed moment in US feminism. Modeled on the US Constitution, the Declaration asserts "that all men and women are created equal," and indicts a PATRIARCHAL culture for repressing the rights of women: "The history of mankind is a history of repeated injuries and usurpations on the part of man toward woman, having in direct object the establishment of an absolute tyranny over her" (*Internet Modern History Sourcebook*). Together with Matilda Joslyn Gage, Stanton wrote the "Declaration of Rights of the Women of the United States" for the Centennial celebration in Washington in 1876. Anthony and Stanton later founded the National Woman Suffrage Association, which in 1890 merged with the more conservative American Woman Suffrage Association. These organizations were instrumental in securing suffrage for women – in 1920, with the Susan B. Anthony Amendment – and served as the foundation for modern feminism.

Not all early feminist movements involved political activism, however. Literary modernism produced foundational feminist writers, including preeminently Virginia Woolf, H.D. (Hilda Doolittle), Mina Loy, and Djuna Barnes. While they supported political movements for the emancipation of women, they also dramatized the potentially damaging effects of the rationalism that Wollstonecraft and Mill proffered as the birthright of both men *and* women. They are united in their willingness to criticize representations of women by male authors and propose a new model of female IDENTITY and AGENCY. Woolf's *Room of One's Own* (1929), for example, insists that women be allowed the economic and social freedom to follow their aspirations and to forego the traditional role of serving as an enlarging mirror for male identity. "How is he to go on giving judgement, civilising natives, making laws, writing books, dressing up and speechifying at banquets," she asks, "unless he can see himself at breakfast and at dinner at least twice the size he really is?" (60). Woolf's insight into the relationship between men and women, in which women serve as the non-essential reflective surface on which men constitute their subjectivity, looks forward to the poststructuralist feminism of **Luce Irigaray** and **Hélène Cixous**.

A second wave of feminism, cresting in the 1960s, was two-pronged: it focused on civil rights, specifically social and economic equality, and it explored the philosophical dimension of gender difference. Both of these tendencies are rooted in Simone de Beauvoir's *The Second Sex* (1949), which noted not only the subordination of women to men at every level of social life but also the fact that "one is not born, but rather one becomes, woman" (283). This insight, and the SOCIAL CONSTRUCTIONIST thesis it entails, was further developed by US feminists in the 1960s, preeminently in the work of Germaine Greer and Betty Friedan. In *The Feminine Mystique*, for example, Friedan follows Beauvoir in arguing that there is no "natural" distinction between the sexes and that the assumption of such a distinction has led to a pervasive sense of dissatisfaction:

> I have heard so many women try to deny this dissatisfied voice within themselves because it does not fit the pretty picture of femininity the experts have given them. I think, in fact, that this is the first clue to the mystery; the problem cannot be understood in the generally accepted terms by which scientists have studied women, doctors have treated them, counselors have advised them, and writers have written about them. (27)

For Kate Millett, the problem was fundamentally political. Also like Beauvoir, she argued against the concept of "biologism," the idea that gender difference is "natural." More explicitly than others, Millett takes aim at the "power-structured relationships" of domination characteristic of patriarchy, relationships that condition gender and cause the oppression of women (23). She dismisses the arguments of contemporary science, religion, philosophy, and law that insist upon patriarchy as the original and therefore most natural form of social organization, calling them the "evanescent delights afforded by the game of origins" (28). Anticipating the work of radical feminists of the 1980s and 1990s, Millett criticizes "cultural programming," especially the infantilization of women perpetuated by social surveillance and the violence directed against them, a "patriarchal force" that is "particularly sexual in character and realised most completely in the act of rape" (42–4).

The 1970s saw the emergence of feminist literary history, a project of discovery and CANON formation that has altered significantly our sense of what literature has been and the role it plays in society. **Elaine Showalter**'s *A Literature of Their Own* (1976) examines the novels of the Brontë sisters, George Eliot, and writers in the suffragette movement and compares them to the sensationalist "feminine novel" of the day that did little to combat sexist stereotypes. **Sandra Gilbert and Susan Gubar**, too, fought against the tendencies of conventional fiction and the patriarchal culture that nurtured it. Their landmark work, *Madwoman in the Attic* (1979), draws on phenomenology and Harold Bloom's theories of influence to describe new relationships between women writers and their audiences and between these writers and their male predecessors. In part by deconstructing or re-visioning male discourses and images of women, in part by exploring the unexplored terrain that sustained women's writing, Gilbert and Gubar uncover "the crucial ways in which women's art has been radically qualified by their femaleness" (82).

These projects constitute significant advances, though Toril Moi believes they did not go far enough. In her widely read *Sexual/Textual Politics* (2002), Moi takes "humanist feminism" to task for its rejection of theory and its adoption of New Critical aesthetics. "What 'knowledge,'" Moi asks, "is ever uninformed by theoretical assumptions?" (76). Moi believes an alternative can be found in the French tradition of feminists – principally Irigaray, Hélène Cixous, Catherine Clément, and **Julia Kristeva** – who also take Beauvoir as the starting point. As Alice Jardine and other feminists have pointed out, poststructuralist thought, especially that of **Jacques Derrida** and **Michel Foucault**, offers especially fruitful points of collaboration for these feminists, while **Jacques Lacan**'s work has been attacked and (often at the same time) used tactically. Though very different in terms of method and style, these writers all interrogate the foundational principles of a patriarchal culture that developed the concept of "rights" as part of a stable, AUTONOMOUS subjectivity. The Centre d'Études Féminines at the University of Paris VIII (Vincennes), founded by Cixous in 1974, provided an institutional structure for this ongoing critique and for the development of new feminist standpoints. One example of the latter is Jardine's theory of "gynesis" (i.e., "putting into discourse of 'woman'"), which frees women from patriarchal domination and HETERONORMATIVITY, "paternal fictions" that guarantee "the right to govern, the succession of kings," and other political prerogatives. Gynesis, like Showalter's "gynocriticism," liberates the "non-knowledge" of Enlightenment thought that "eluded" and "engulfed" men. "This other-than-themselves is almost always a 'space' of some kind (over which the narrative has lost control), and this space has been coded as feminine, as woman" (24–5).

One of the principal concerns of this cohort of French theorists is a specifically feminist critique of philosophy, psychoanalysis, and literature. Irigaray's critique of Freud exemplifies this approach. Defying rhetorical, syntactical, and thematic conventions, Irigaray's theoretical writings offer a penetrating critique of those conventions as well as alternatives to them. Borrowing from Derrida and Lacan, Irigaray calls into question the Freudian discourse on femininity, particularly the role played by the Oedipus and castration complexes and Freud's seeming cluelessness with respect to the experience of girls. Her chief point is that women are trapped in a masculine world of representation, forced to be the reproductive medium or essence in which men find their ESSENTIAL being, but are themselves debarred from actually possessing essence. "The girl," she writes, "has no right to play in any manner whatever with any representation of her beginning, no specific mimicry of origin is available to her: she must inscribe herself in the masculine, phallic way of relating to origin, that involves repetition, representation, reproduction. And this is meant to be 'the most powerful feminine wish'" (*Speculum* 78). Cixous and Catherine Clément, in *The Newly Born Woman* (1975), echo Irigaray's critique in their investigation of the Freudian seduction scene, in which the daughter seduces the father, the "pivotal" point at which the SYMBOLIC order enters into the young girl's life. For Freud, the daughter, though pivotal, is relegated to the margins, sexually and socially, and takes the blame for "fantasiz[ing] a reality that, it seems, is to remain undecipherable" (47). She is thus an unreadable, non-essential ground for masculine sexual identity. In this sense, the girl's body, her desire and availability, become for the type of symbolic exchange between men that Gayle Rubin analyzes in "The Traffic in Women" (1975). Irigaray's theory of the "speculum" tries to account for this "non-essentiality" and ritual exchange by showing how speculation (both visual and philosophical) constitutes gender identity: "The masculine can partly look at itself, speculate about itself, represent itself and describe itself for what it is, whilst the feminine can try to speak to itself through a new language, but cannot describe itself from outside or in formal terms, except by identifying itself with the masculine, thus by losing herself" ("Women's Exile" 65). (On Irigaray, see Psychoanalysis 187–8.)

Alternative modes of writing that reject the styles of masculine discourse are offered by a number of French feminists. This work has sometimes been called ÉCRITURE FÉMININE (variously translated as "feminine writing" and "writing the body"), and in some forms it takes an ESSENTIALIST position. Irigaray's reflections on language and the body exemplify this approach:

> If we don't invent a language, if we don't find our body's language, it will have too few gestures to accompany our story. We shall tire of the same ones, and leave our desires unexpressed, unrealized.... Never settle. Let's leave definitiveness to the undecided; we don't need it. Our body, right here, right now, gives us a very different certainty. Truth is necessary for those who are so distanced from their body and have forgotten it. (*This Sex* 214)

Diana Fuss has described this style and approach as a "strategic deployment of essence" (62), according to which a woman's body determines not only her identity but also a mode of writing and thinking fundamentally different from and in revolt against masculine modes. Irigaray calls it "hysteria scenario, that privileged dramatization of feminine sexuality" (*Speculum* 60). This practice is strongly associated with Cixous' literary and theoretical work, especially her influential essay "The Laugh of the Medusa." "It is impossible to define a feminine practice of writing," Cixous claims, but she goes on to insist that such a practice "will always surpass the discourse that regulates the phallocentric system" in part because it lies outside the arena of "philosophico-theoretical domination" (46). The space marked out by this new practice is a woman's body, where her own desires, banned from patriarchal discourse, can find expression. It is also a space defined by the blanks and gaps in that discourse where a woman's voice can find, in Irigaray's phrase, its "silent plasticity" (*Speculum* 142). The Lacanian concept of JOUISSANCE is often used to define this inexplicable site of "female writing," where women's experience can be freed from the unforgiving dialectic of Oedipus and the HEGEMONY of the Symbolic in order to embrace the IMAGINARY realm of mystical and pre-Oedipal experiences, the "oceanic" unity with the body of the mother. These experiences are linked, in Kristeva's "semanalysis," to the "semiotic *khora*," the pre-Oedipal dissolution of boundaries. Thus the maternal body becomes the foundation both for a resistance to patriarchal discourse and for a feminist ethical practice ("herethics") that does not derive from it. Like other French feminists of her generation, Kristeva struggled to lift prohibitions on the maternal body imposed by the Oedipal and castration complexes. In the Preface to *Desire in Language* (1980), she confesses that "[i]t was perhaps also necessary to be a *woman* to attempt to take up that exorbitant wager of carrying the rational project to the outer borders of the signifying venture of men" (x). (On Kristeva, see Psychoanalysis 187–8.)

Judith Butler's philosophy of gender difference moves in a different direction, away from any hint of essence (even a strategic form of it) toward theories of SOCIAL CONSTRUCTION and PERFORMANCE that emphasize the subversive and empowering dimension of gender identity. The fundamental question that leads to such radical redefinitions has to do with how social construction and performance have been used in oppressive ways. "To what extent," Butler asks, "do *regulatory practices* of gender formation and division constitute identity, the internal coherence of the subject, indeed, the self-identical status of the person?" (*Gender Trouble* 16). (On Butler, see Gender Studies 202–4.) Butler's concern for the hegemonic power of universality and its impact on the subject is part of a more general concern that Western feminism remains bound to the Enlightenment tradition of knowledge it disavows and the heteronormativity at the core of Western cultural values. Lesbian feminism has been particularly valuable for its critique of sexism, homophobia, and the "compulsory heterosexuality" at the heart of patriarchal cultures. Adrienne Rich and Jeffner Allen have advocated new forms of community based on lesbian desire, which they believe is an unacknowledged and powerful force for social change. In a similar way, Monique Wittig emphasizes the "lesbian body" and lesbian consciousness as a precondition for a more inclusive and politically effective feminism. (On lesbian feminism, see Gender Studies 206–8.)

As we have seen, many Western feminists share an interest in exposing patriarchal forms of power as the cause of the unequal and subordinate status of women in Western societies. However, they tend to speak from the standpoint of white, middle-class privilege – even as they criticize that very privilege in the form of suburban complacency. And while feminist critique is aimed at patriarchal authority, the standpoint of that critique tended to be Eurocentric and at times complicit with imperialist ideas about the social role of women. It is just this standpoint – and the abstract notion of "third-world woman" – that feminists of color reject. **bell hooks**, for example, insists that the fight against racism is the fundamental conflict, the one that all feminists must fight who desire an end to sexism. hooks, in her landmark work *Feminist Theory: From Margin to Center* (1984), responds to what she sees as a dominant trend in US feminism toward seeking "social equality with men" (19) and advocates a more general critique of male domination and a transformation of social relationships, especially marriage and childrearing. Most important, she decries the lack of attention to race and sexism. "Racism is fundamentally a feminist issue," she argues, "because it is so interconnected with sexist oppression" (53–4). Along with **Gayatri Chakravorty Spivak** and other postcolonial feminists, hooks insists that race and class cannot be ignored or downplayed in the formulation of a feminist politics. Spivak recognizes the "important advantages won by US mainstream feminism," primarily in the treatment of female subjectivity and its representation, but prefers to think in historical terms. She hopes at least to "incite a degree of rage against the imperialist narrativization of history" that produces "so abject a script" for the artist. Her aim, then, is to "situate feminist individualism in its historical determination" (244). Postcolonial feminism, like African American and Chicana feminism, must contend with a form of double consciousness and double discrimination that links sexual and gender inequality with racial and/or ethnic identity. Postcolonial nationalism and neocolonial relations complicate these duplicities. In the postcolonial era, economic inequality and retrograde gender roles continue to put women at a disadvantage, when it does not silence them altogether. One of the common threads among the thinkers in this fourth wave is the critique of sexist oppression, particularly violence against women, whether in the form of domestic abuse or ritualized social practices like genital mutilation, which is the physical manifestation of this oppression on women's bodies. Feminists of color have in common a desire to overcome a twofold domination, for they are oppressed because of their gender and because of their race/ethnicity. (On these issues in feminism, see Ethnic and Indigenous Studies 234 and Postcolonial Studies 250–1.)

This trend in feminism is allied to a renovated materialist approach to identity and gender. **Elizabeth Grosz,** for example, argues that we need to rethink how we speak of such concepts as freedom, autonomy, and subjectivity, which have, "over the last century," been largely considered "through the discourses of political philosophy and the debates between liberalism, HISTORICAL MATERIALISM, and postmodernism regarding the sovereignty and rights of subjects and social groups." Recourse to ONTOLOGY and metaphysics, for Grosz, represents a way of progressing beyond the "paradigm of recognition," but only if we regard the ontological and metaphysical from the point of view of what she calls "the philosophy of life," found in pre-Socratic philosophy and the work of philosophers like Nietzsche and Henri Bergson. Grosz is drawn to Bergson because of his belief that freedom can be found only in actions, not in the subject as an essence or property. Of course this freedom is made possible by the ability "to harness and utilize matter for one's own purposes and interests" (140, 147–8). In a renewed conception of "the materiality that life and the nonliving share" (142), feminists can arm themselves against abstractions that tend to obscure the material conditions of women's lives. Grosz is aware that an emphasis on materiality "tends to determination," and that it can lead to the very form of instrumental rationality that pigeonholes individuals according to gender, sexual orientation, race, and other identity markers. But she insists that a critical reappropriation of materiality can serve as the space in which "free acts are generated through the encounter of life with matter and the capacity of each to yield to the other its forms and forces, both its inertia and dynamism" (150). This turn to materiality raises old questions in new ways, especially about ontology, ethics, politics, and about the relation of the Real and "nonhuman agency" science (Alaimo and Hekman 7; see also Hekman).

To open feminism to materiality and a materialist method is to foreclose the patriarchal construction of essence – or rather the subordination and devaluation of *non*-essence – and the gender and sexual identities that it authorizes. Judith Butler has remarked, echoing Fuss, that it is "no longer useful to come up with an essentialist description of what women are, if 'essentialism' means a category that adequately describes the range of women's experience and that attempts to unify that experience in some way. There have been some innovative efforts to try to rethink what essentialism is if it is no longer making the claim to be descriptive. Strategic essentialism was one way to do that" (Butler, "Changing" 742). We could read the new materialist studies as just such a strategic essentialism, insofar as it presupposes (as Jane Bennett does) a "vital matter" that allows for new forms of intersubjectivity and political action. The future of feminism, and its principal intellectual value, lies in its continued ability to critique its own assumptions and, by doing so, to open up the discourse to the new problems created by the globalization of economies, cultures, and discourse. It must be said that by the turn of the twenty-first century, and despite backlashes in the academy and the popular media, feminism has become a recognized and powerful standpoint in nearly every branch of the academy.

Note

On feminism and feminists discussed here, see the following entries: African American Studies, Ethnic and Indigenous Studies, Gender Studies, Postcolonial Studies, Posthumanism, Poststructuralism, Postmodernism, and Psychoanalysis.

Works Cited

Alaimo, Stacy and Susan Hekman. "Introduction: Emerging Models of Materiality in Feminist Theory." In *Material Feminisms*. Ed. Stacy Alaimo and Susan Hekman. Bloomington: Indiana University Press, 2008. 1–19.

Beauvoir, Simone de. *The Second Sex*. 1949. Trans. Constance Borde and Sheila Malovany-Chevalier. New York: Vintage, 2011.

Bennett, Jane. *Vibrant Matter: A Political Ecology of Things*. Durham, NC: Duke University Press, 2010.

Butler, Judith. "Changing the Subject: Judith Butler's Politics of Radical Resignification." Interview with Gary A. Olson and Lynn Worsham. *Journal of Advanced Composition* 20.4 (2005): 727–65.

Butler, Judith. *Gender Trouble: Feminism and the Subversion of Identity*. New York: Routledge, 1990.

Cixous, Hélène. "The Laugh of the Medusa." *Signs* 1.4 (Summer 1976): 875–93.

Cixous, Hélène and Catherine Clément. *The Newly Born Woman*. Trans. Betsy Wing. Minneapolis: University of Minnesota Press, 1986.

Friedan, Betty. *The Feminine Mystique*. New York: Norton, 1963.

Fuss, Diana J. "'Essentially Speaking': Luce Irigaray's Language of Essence." *Hypatia* 3.3 (Winter 1989): 62–80.

Gilbert, Sandra and Susan Gubar. *Madwoman in the Attic: The Woman Writer and the Nineteenth-Century Literary Imagination*. 1979. 2nd ed. New Haven and London: Yale University Press, 2000.

Greer, Germaine. *The Female Eunuch*. London: MacGibbon and Kee, 1970.

Grosz, Elizabeth. "Feminism, Materialism, and Freedom." In *New Materialism: Ontology, Agency, and Politics*. Ed. Diana Coole and Samantha Frost. Durham, NC: Duke University Press, 2010. 139–57.

Hekman, Susan. "Constructing the Ballast: An Ontology for Feminism." In *Material Feminisms*. Ed. Stacy Alaimo and Susan Hekman. Bloomington: Indiana University Press, 2008. 85–119.

hooks, bell. *Feminist Theory: From Margin to Center*. Cambridge, MA: South End Press, 2002.

Internet Modern History Sourcebook. "The Declaration of Sentiments, Seneca Falls Conference, 1848." http://www.fordham.edu/halsall/mod/ Senecafalls.asp, accessed November 2012.

Irigaray, Luce. *Speculum of the Other Woman*. Trans. Gilliam C. Gill. Ithaca: Cornell University Press, 1985.

Irigaray, Luce. *This Sex Which Is Not One*. Trans. Catherine Porter. Ithaca: Cornell University Press, 1985.

Irigaray, Luce. "Women's Exile." *Ideology and Consciousness* 1 (May 1977): 62–76.

Jardine, Alice. *Gynesis: Configurations of Women and Modernity*. Ithaca: Cornell University Press, 1985.

Kristeva, Julia. *Desire in Language: A Semiotic Approach to Literature and Art*. Ed. Leon S. Roudiez. Trans. Thomas Gora, Alice Jardine, and Leon S. Roudiez. New York: Columbia University Press, 1980.

Mill, John Stuart. "The Subjection of Women." In *Essays on Equality, Law, and Education*. Vol. 21 of *The Collected Works of John Stuart Mill*. Ed. John M. Robson. Toronto: Toronto University Press, 1984. 259–340.

Millett, Kate. *Sexual Politics*. Garden City, NY: Doubleday, 1970.

Moi, Toril. *Sexual/Textual Politics: Feminist Literary Theory*. 2nd ed. London and New York: Routledge, 1985, 2002.

Spivak, Gayatri Chakravorty. "Three Women's Texts and a Critique of Imperialism." *Critical Inquiry* 12 (1985): 243–61.

Woolf, Virginia. *A Room of One's Own*. London: Hogarth Press, 1929.

Gender Studies

Gender studies encompasses a number of discrete fields of study that share common concerns and themes, including gender roles and identity; sex, sexuality, and sexual identity; and the body and its social, cultural, and political significance. As some critics have noted, the study of gender and sexuality is a late phase of feminism, which is not to say that feminism assimilates or legitimates gender and sexuality, but rather that feminism was the first theoretical standpoint to make gender and sexuality not only the keynotes of a theoretical platform but also the ground for a practical politics of the body. One of the things that distinguishes gender studies as a separate field is its focus on IDEOLOGY and the social construction of identity, the study of which entails the deconstruction of cherished assumptions about gender roles and gender identity, particularly the idea that gender is identical to sex and that both are biologically determined categories. This is a thoroughly interdisciplinary task in large measure because gender is a significant category in nearly every discipline, especially in the human and social sciences, where the gender analysis and critique have become vital components of literary studies, film and media studies, religious studies, history, political science, sociology, and so on. Indeed, in recent years (e.g., in the work of Anne Fausto-Sterling), we have seen to what extent it conditions certain aspects of the natural sciences (e.g., methodologies, objects of study, funding, academic hiring). **Michel Foucault** exercises considerable influence in gender studies, in large measure by providing theoretical models for an understanding of gender outside the categories established by modern science and philosophy. This "outside," however, is really an "inside," a standpoint for immanent critique *within* the very PATRIARCHAL culture that characterizes modernity.

Gender studies is by and large driven by theories of SOCIAL CONSTRUCTION that draw on a number of disciplines, including sociology, social history, feminism, Marxism, and anthropology. Social constructionism is primarily concerned with a "general critique of biological determinism, in particular of received knowledge about the biology of sex differences." Social constructionism holds that "the relationship between sexual acts and sexual meanings is not fixed" and that "it is projected from the observer's time and place at great peril." Even sexual desire "is itself constructed by culture and history from the energies and capacities of the body" (Vance 38, 42–3).

This social constructionist perspective, strongly influenced by Foucault's theories of sexuality, is predicated on the idea that subjectivity and identity are not natural categories or essential features of human existence, but rather the material effects of the discourses and images that surround us. Nowhere is this more evident than in the social inscription of women's bodies. Historically, writes **Elizabeth Grosz**, "women's corporeal specificity [has been] used to explain and justify the different (read: unequal) social positions and cognitive abilities of the two sexes" (*Volatile* 14). Though social constructionists sometimes promote "a biologically determined, fixed, and ahistorical notion of the body" and thereby retain "the mind/body dualism," Grosz believes that they are by and large open to seeing the body and sexuality as biologically outside the framework of a hegemonic science, for "it is not biology per se but the ways in which the social system organizes and gives meaning to biology that is oppressive to women" (16–17). For this reason "we need to look outside the traditions of thought that have considered subjectivity as the realm of agency and freedom only through the attainment of reason, rights, and recognition: that is, only through the operation of forces – social, cultural, or identificatory – outside the subject" ("Feminism" 140). In a similar vein, concentrating on how the body bears emotion, Susan Bordo's *Unbearable Weight: Feminism, Western Culture, and the Body* explores the discourse of the body but from the perspective of the "disordered" body (e.g., the "slender body" of anorexia nervosa), which offers the alternative of another order. In calling for "an effective discourse about the female body," Bordo hopes to find a discourse "adequate to an analysis ... of modern social control." Such a task would require rejecting the notion that gender is a function of norms and normative behaviors and identities. "We must think instead," Bordo writes, "of the network of practices, institutions, and technologies that sustain positions of dominance and subordination in a particular domain" (167). By doing so, we can avoid the temptation to which Grosz refers of unthinkingly reinscribing mind/body dualisms.

At the foundation of most theories of gender and sexuality is a thoroughgoing critique of the SUBJECT and SUBJECTIVITY. As a social and political category, the subject cuts across all disciplinary and theoretical boundaries. Being a subject can mean many things – a citizen of a particular community, an AUTONOMOUS being in possession of a sense of personal wholeness and unity, the subject of an oppressive ruler or of a discourse. In all of these senses, what is invoked is the *philosophical concept* of the sovereign, SELF-IDENTICAL subject. This notion of the modern subject has its origin in the Enlightenment, particularly in the philosophy of John Locke, who regarded personal identity as stable, coherent, and continuous. Subjectivity, the consciousness of one's historical and social agency, was the prerogative of the Western individual who defined himself in opposition to the OTHER, to that which was not a subject and did not possess subjectivity. The classic philosophical expression of this relationship of the subject to what it is not is Hegel's dialectic of the master and slave. In this context, the autonomy of the subject is precarious, for not only does the subject absolutely require the *other*, but the *other* is, by virtue of the dialectical process, *misrecognized* (see Fraser 113–18; Oliver 11–12). Gender studies is concerned not only with finding non-dominative modes of identity formation but also with understanding the non-identity of the *other* outside of the dialectical process that eliminates otherness in the establishment of self-identity.

Closely linked to the concept of the subject is the concept of IDENTITY, which could be said to refer to the process by which a subject becomes a particular *kind* of subject. Rather than a fixed quality or ESSENCE, identity is understood by theorists of gender and sexuality as an ongoing process of construction, performance, appropriation, or mimicry. The crucial questions raised by theories of gender and sexual identity have to do with agency and determination: Who or what determines the construction of gender and sexuality? How is social agency acquired and maintained by these constructions? Is one constructed solely by social ideologies and institutions? Or do individuals have the freedom to act reflexively, to engage in what Anthony Giddens calls "projects of the self"? Foucault's work provides a range of answers that move between two conditions of the subject: on the one hand, the subject is utterly determined by power and its discourses; on the other hand, the subject of this POWER/KNOWLEDGE has some agency in determining how to be determined. There is also, in the late Foucault, a greater value accorded to contingency and a greater willingness to see power as a permeable and pervasive *biopower* in which contingency can be productive in terms of a logic of dispersion. The insights in this late work on the subject, gender, and sexual identity were decisive in the formation of a theory of gender that builds on the critique of gender inaugurated by feminism and that develops in a number of directions, including masculinity studies, queer theory, and lesbian studies.

Sexuality and the identities that it helps create have played a fundamental role in developing modern modes of social organization and regulation. The idea that sexuality had long been repressed and that only in the post-Freudian era did sex become an open topic of discourse is overturned in Foucault's *History of Sexuality* (1976). If sexuality comes to our notice by way of discourse – Foucault focuses on medicine, psychiatry, education, and other fields associated with reproduction, hygiene, and the classification of sexual difference – then it is to these discourses that the GENEALOGIST must turn to find the matter for his history. Within the discourse of sexuality we see how the "function of reproduction" came to dominate sexual life; all that could not be recognized as part of this function was repressed. Not only was this repression a "sentence to disappear, but also an injunction to silence" (*Sexuality* 4). According to Foucault, "sexual heterogeneities" were, at first, governed by three codes: canonical law, Christian pastoral, and civil law. Prohibitions on sex were "essentially of a juridical nature" for both the church and civil law; perversions were separated out from transgressions within the heterosexual norm. The result was two different kinds of infractions: violations of the law and perversions of practice, the latter subject to the proliferation of medicalized discourses that, while removing "perverts" from the rule of law, subjected them to surveillance and invasive adjustment and manipulation (37–40). The regime by which sexual identity was locked into step with a binomial gender identity consisted of four operations that were not simple prohibitions: (1) control and regimentation; (2) incorporation of perversions and "new specification of individuals" (i.e., homosexual acts displaced by the homosexual persona) (42); (3) proximity and contact, which creates a "double impetus": pleasure and power in "perpetual spirals" (45); (4) devices of sexual saturation. Far from being proscribed or repressed in the nineteenth century, sexuality became a discourse formation the main task of which was to identify and regulate all forms of sexual behavior. "Instead of a massive censorship," Foucault claimed, "what was involved was a regulated and polymorphous incitement to discourse" (34). Religious confession, psychoanalysis, sexology, literature – all were instrumental in this incitement, which simultaneously made sexuality a public matter and a target of social administration. "Under the authority of a language that had been carefully expurgated so that it was no longer directly named, sex was taken charge of, tracked down as it were, by a discourse that aimed to allow it no obscurity, no respite" (20).

The discourse on sexuality is a specific manifestation of "juridico-discursive" POWER, "a rule of law" that reaches into every corner of human experience (82–3). In this regulatory form, "power is tolerable only on condition that it mask a substantial part of itself" (86). By suppressing certain sexual identities, "intolerable" forms of sexual power can be repudiated or rendered invisible in discourse. This of course means that certain forms of freedom are denied as well, for the discourse on sexuality creates systems of social inequality, in which proscribed sexual identities and practices lead to the withdrawal of social recognition and thus of resources. By the nineteenth century, "four great strategic unities" had emerged and formed "specific mechanisms of knowledge and power centering on sex": hysterization of women's bodies, pedagogization of children's sex, socialization of procreative behavior, and psychiatrization of perverse pleasure (103–5). These techniques of power, which Foucault calls the "deployment of sexuality," both overtake and are entwined with an older technique of power rooted in sexual affiliation through "blood" (the "deployment of alliance ... a reality with a symbolic function") (147–8). In the modern deployment of sexuality, biopower emerges as the distribution of power within institutions and practices that regulate, punish, protect, and reproduce the body. With biopower came new technologies for managing life (and thus staving off death), new disciplines for the body, and new modes of regulating populations. With these new "political techniques," we discern "the entry of life into history, that is, the entry of phenomena peculiar to the life of the human species into the order of knowledge and power" (141–2; see Lee 101f).

In the late essays on governmentality and power, Foucault recognized that the individual possessed a freedom from power that was in fact native to it, which is "exercised only over free subjects ... and only insofar as they are free. By this we mean individual or collective subjects who are faced with a field of possibilities in which several ways of behaving, several reactions and diverse comportments may be realized" ("Subject" 221). This "field of possibilities" has been mapped by gender theorists from a number of perspectives that make much the same point about the constructedness of gender within social systems. Gayle Rubin, for example, describes the "sex/gender system" by means of which PATRIARCHAL power maintains its control over women and those who fail to abide by heterosexual norms. It may in fact be the original, even foundational contradiction in human societies, "the set of arrangements by which a society transforms biological sexuality into products of human activity, and in which these transformed sexual needs are satisfied" (159). As Fausto-Sterling has shown, the biological body is more multiple and less disciplined than the sex/gender system can tolerate. "[I]f the state and legal system has an interest in maintaining only two sexes, our collective biological bodies do not" (31). The power of discourse to counter what our bodies tell us testifies to the kinds of gender determinations that create the conditions for the subordination of women in patriarchal societies. Recent work in masculinity studies by Tim Carrigan, Bob Connell, and John Lee has shown that the "social organization" of masculinity is produced in historically determined, collective practices (Carrigan et al. 65). In patriarchal societies, Connell argues, such practices include systematic dominance over women that reinforces or alters the balance of power among men. Violence is constitutive of masculinity *as such*, particularly violence as a function of the state. But it is only one among an ensemble of behaviors coded masculine, one that Connell regards as a key feature of *hegemonic masculinity*, a dominant position (the others being subordinate, complicit, and marginalized) but one that is "always contestable" (76–7). Because most men benefit from the ideal of hegemonic masculinity, they are therefore complicit in the sex/gender system that distributes power unevenly between men and women. The measure of the crisis of masculinity can be taken in Judith/Jack Halberstam's work, which rehabilitates masculinity for lesbian identity and calls into question the distribution of gender identities across male and female bodies. Female masculinity is not an imitation of the male form, but an opening onto the way "masculinity is constructed as masculinity." The idea that masculinity is the essence of man is deconstructed in Halberstam's radical appropriation of the masculine for a female body. She opposes "heroic masculinity," which "has been produced by and across male and female bodies" and depends "absolutely on the subordination of alternative masculinities." Male masculinity serves in her project as "a hermeneutic, and as a counterexample to the kinds of masculinity that seem most informative about gender relations and most generative of social change" (1–3). That is to say, alternative masculinities, in their very performance, strike a fatal blow to the idea that gender identity is a "natural fact."

The subordination of women that makes hegemonic masculinity possible is a gendered form of subordination that is at the heart of the subject as such, at least according to **Judith Butler**. In her rereading of Hegel's master/slave dialectic (in *Phenomenology of Spirit*), she argues that the emergence of the slave into self-consciousness is precisely the starting point of subjection, for "the subject emerges as an unhappy consciousness through the reflexive application of … ethical laws" (*Psychic* 32). In the wake of Freudian and Nietzschean critiques of the subject, Butler sees a heightening of the self-enslavement that is attendant upon self-consciousness, which she calls "self-beratement" (following Freud's theory of the super-ego; see 22–3) and which can lead in some cases, as in states of loss, to a FORECLOSURE in which the subject is threatened with dissolution at the very moment of its emergence (23). The "rift" in subjectivity that defines the "unhappy consciousness" can be overcome only "by finding a body which embodies the purity of its unchangeable part," but this leads to IDEALISM, in which the very body that offered salvation is dismissed as inessential. This logic is to be found in Nietzsche (where the body that acts disappears into a trope, a "shadow of a body … in spectral and linguistic form") and in Foucault (where the body is "a destruction on the occasion of which a subject is formed") (68, 92). Butler concedes that, despite this tendency to lose track of the body, Nietzsche and Foucault have been instrumental in forming a perspective from which to perform a "critical analysis of subjection." Such a critique would look at how "regulatory power maintains subjects in subordination" and would also recognize the subject produced by such power is "nevertheless haunted by an unassimilable remainder, a melancholia that marks the limits of subjectivation." The prohibition of homosexuality is one of the losses the subject mourns (29).

It is precisely the unhappy consciousness attendant upon subjectivity that subversive forms of gender PERFORMANCE meant to overcome, and they do so in large measure because they allow us to regain consciousness of the body and to throw off the constraints of a reflexive idealism and the abstraction of subjectivity that goes with it. Understood in performative terms, gender is "*a corporeal style*, an 'act,' as it were, which is both intentional and performative, where 'performative' suggests a dramatic and contingent construction of meaning": "strategies of survival within compulsory systems" (*Gender Trouble* 177–8). As an alternative to regulatory practices and strategies of naturalization and containment of identity, Butler developed a model of *performativity*, which she distinguished from a normative model of *performance*:

> [performance] presumes a subject, but [performativity] contests the very notion of the subject.… What I'm trying to do is think about performativity as *that aspect of discourse that has the capacity to produce what it names*. Then I take a further step, through the Derridean rewriting of [J. L.] Austin, and suggest that this production actually always happens through a certain kind of repetition and recitation. So if you want the ontology of this, I guess performativity is the vehicle through which ontological effects are established. Performativity is the discursive mode by which ontological effects are installed. ("Gender" 111–12)

According to Butler, gender and sexual identity has always been a matter of performance, understood as "a sedimentation of gender norms [that] produces the peculiar phenomenon of a 'natural sex' or a 'real woman' or any number of prevalent and compelling social fictions." What is often read as the "cause" of gender (i.e., the sedimentation of norms) is actually an effect of social inscription on the body. The authority of normative gender performance presupposes "stable identity or locus of agency" (*Gender Trouble* 178–9). Performativity challenges the very notion of such a subject and thus of gender and sexual difference. The "ontological effects" to which Butler refers are all that we can see or know of "true" gender or sexual identity, a situation dramatized most clearly in drag and other forms of transvestism. Performativity is the provisional result of a process of construction *and* the material sign of an authentic self. For while the drag queen prides himself on getting every detail right and being true to a particular vision of femininity, his performance is a critique of the very category of woman he strives to imitate faithfully. Gender understood as a performative process has a social temporality, one that serves as its ground, foundation, and "inner core," a "gendered corporealization of time" (179).

If we look at the question from a Lacanian perspective, we can regard this kind of performativity as a form of foreclosure, a refusal to be the *subject of* the Symbolic order. However, Butler sees foreclosure as something more sustaining and sustainable than the "foundational" sense it has for Lacanians: "[I] don't think that the foreclosures that produce the subject are fixed in time in the way that most Lacanians do. They really understand foreclosure as a kind of founding moment. My sense is that it is always the case that the subject is produced through certain kinds of foreclosure" ("Changing" 738; see Oliver 61–75). Thus foreclosure is a kind of enduring schism or rupture, a cohesive identity founded on the incessant refusal to be subordinated to a regulatory regime of gender.

This form of foreclosure radically challenges our assumptions about the relation between gender and social power. As Susan Hekman points out, gender studies has contributed significantly to the development of identity politics, which focuses on the political agency of identities formed in social constructionist terms: if one performs one's gender in social and institutional contexts, then one's gender identity is politicized in a way that is determined by these contexts. But the chief problem with identity politics is that it appears to place a barrier between individual freedom and collective action. "The most obvious criticism of identity politics," Hekman writes, is that "it celebrates personal identity over the identity of the universal citizen" (92). Butler and other theorists have attempted to rehabilitate a form of foundationalism that might serve to remedy this criticism, but Hekman regards this return, however critical, to the foundations of identitarian thought will reestablish a claim on gender "that entails the fixing of identity" (93). This criticism goes against the grain of what Butler appears to say about the body and its relation to identity and identity politics, which is that theory in gender studies seeks not to fix identity but rather to grasp the very foreclosure of stable identity, the provisional foundation of non-identity that *is always the case.*

Gay and Lesbian Studies

The critical standpoint defined by the Foucauldian strand of thought about gender made possible new ways of thinking about issues in gay and lesbian studies, which is rooted in political activism and the equal rights struggle. There has been a more or less "closeted" discourse about gay identity from at least the time of Oscar Wilde, when homosexuality was considered aberrant behavior (thus the figure of the "sodomite"). The early sexologists (Krafft-Ebbing) with their theories of *inversion* and ultimately Freud with his idea of primal bisexuality (and the unsurprising existence of homosexuality as a *perversion*) created a psycho-medical regime of identification that kept homosexuality either criminalized, pathologized, or both until the last decades of the twentieth century (in the West, for the most part). By the 1970s, gay/lesbian activist movements were well in place (e.g., the Lavender Menace, Act Up). This long tradition of resistance to gender and sexual discrimination emboldened a generation of scholars who, by the 1980s, began writing theoretically about gay and lesbian experience, using the techniques and concepts already available in feminism, psychoanalysis and psychology, sociology, anthropology, literary studies, and philosophy. The 1980s saw the rise of gay and lesbian studies programs in universities, particularly in the United States. At this time gay studies was strongly oriented toward male sexuality. "The gay movement," write Carrigan, Connell, and Lee, "has been centrally concerned with masculinity as part of its critique of the political structure of sexuality. In this, it should be noted, the contemporary movement represents a distinct break with previous forms of homosexual activism" (93).

Eve Kosofsky Sedgwick, working within this new framework, pioneered a way of talking about sexual and gender difference that challenged the HETERONORMATIVITY of the mainstream culture but also prevailing ideas about homoeroticism and homosexual relations. Her work was critical to development of *queer theory*, primarily by introducing new theoretical approaches to sexuality and gay experience (the Q series at Duke University Press began with Sedgwick's *Tendencies* in 1993). Her landmark study *Between Men* (1985) explored the complexities of same-sex relations, particularly the way that heterosexual norms both repudiate and disavow homoeroticism and homosexual relations. This curious duplicity results in a complex and partially repressed continuum that articulates the parameters of HOMOSOCIALITY, which designates a set of social behaviors grounded in an "epistemology of the closet" (i.e., what is true or what really exists is what you cannot see but is nevertheless there) and a conception of desire as mediated by another (either another person, a woman, or an ideal). In a heteronormative context, homosociality affords men a privileged access to social power that simultaneously requires women and excludes them. Her emphasis on "male friendship, mentorship, entitlement, rivalry" (1) within the context of a sex/gender system provides a new way to define masculinity and the subordination of women. The term homosocial comes from the social sciences where it is used to define forms of same-sex bonding, and Sedgwick argues for the focus on masculinity by saying that the "diacritical opposition between the 'homosocial' and the 'homosexual' seems to be much less thorough and dichotomous for women, in our society, than for men" (2; see also 4–5). Sedgwick suggests that due to the structure of patriarchal societies, male homosociality tends to enforce heterosexuality as a norm and to encourage (and even incite) homophobia, though theoretically, the homosocial continuum would allow for the encouragement and even incitement of homoeroticism (as it did in classical Greece).

For this and other reasons, homosocial relations and networks are constantly policed for expressions of homoerotic desire and homosexual (i.e., genitalized) relations. Sedgwick suggests, however, by linking the word "desire" to "homosocial," that there is an "unbroken continuum" between the homosexual and the homosocial, a continuum that is typically repressed, and between homoerotic desire and the pathologized form of disavowal that Sedgwick calls *homosexual panic*, a violent reaction against any manifestation of homoeroticism or homosexual behavior that might threaten homosocial bonds. Drawing on René Girard's theory of "triangular desire" and on Gayle Rubin's work on sex/gender systems, Sedgwick argued that homosocial desire between men is expressed in a triangular structure with a woman (or a discourse of "woman") standing as a putative object of at least one of them: "the ultimate function of women is to be conduits of homosocial desire" (99). Social regulation and control tend to "convert homophobia into an all-pervasive anxiety" (88) and serve as an institutionalized check on repressed homosexual desire; but they also allow for "changes in men's experience of living within the shifting terms of compulsory heterosexuality" (134). Her chapter on Henry James in *Epistemology of the Closet* (1990) illustrates the divide between homosocial networking, which confirms the heterosexual status quo, and homosexual panic, which reacts violently against any manifestation of eroticism or sexual behavior that might emerge out of such networks.

Carrigan, Connell, and Lee point out that the "making of modern homosexuality is plainly connected to the development of industrial capitalism, but equally clearly has its own dynamic" (Carrigan et al. 89). This dynamic is determined in complex and varying ways by sex and sexuality, which are revalued and embraced as central to identity, particularly in "queer culture," which became increasingly visible in academic and activist discourse. As Michael Warner argues, queer culture is more accepting and open about sex and also more willing to deploy the stigma associated with homosexuality in the general culture as a tactical opportunity "to test the limits of shame."

> For all the variability of queer culture – and all its limitations – it is possible to find, running through its development over the past century, and especially in its least organized and least "respectable" circles, an ethical vision much more at home with sex and the indignities associated with sex. Nowhere, after all, are people more aware of the absurdity and tenacity and shame than in queer culture. (33–4)

The ambivalence of queer identity is powerfully dramatized in the study of black queerness, which has, since the time of the Harlem Renaissance, been the hushed shadow form of W. E. B. Du Bois' "double consciousness" that runs the gamut from denial to "living the down low" to openly embracing a gay identity. Each option entails the acceptance of ambivalence, the "caught-betweenness" of being queer and black. Referring to Harlem Renaissance writers and artists Bruce Nugent and Langston Hughes, David Gerstner remarks that they "enacted their otherness while cognizant of the cultural inscribed repetitions that informed and contained ('straightened') their queer black lives every day" (28). Sara Ahmed's "queer phenomenology" reads this *dis*orienting experience in terms of the "queer moment, in which objects appear slantwise and the vertical and horizontal axes appear 'out of line.'" Her phenomenological approach broadens the notion of queer at the same time that it provides a theory of the orientation of bodies in normative social spaces, where the "straight body appears 'in line'" (66).

Given heterosexual norms in the general culture and a male emphasis in the early days of the gay movement, female homosexuality was doubly problematic in much the same way that black feminism was, for being queer and female created a split or "double consciousness." Lesbian studies therefore evolved with slightly different theoretical foundations and thematic interests. For example, Monique Wittig's *The Lesbian Body* attacks the tradition of anatomy based on the orderly and ordered male body and offers instead the lesbian body as a model of the desiring subject. Like other feminists who challenge the authority of PATRIARCHAL discourse, Wittig openly confronts the problem of the SUBJECT POSITION she occupies as a theorist and writer by disrupting the texture of her writing and thereby repeating, at the level of her discourse, the disorderly nature of the lesbian body itself. She espouses a form of "materialist lesbianism," but also believes that "dialectics has let us down. Therefore the comprehension of what 'materialism' and materiality are belong to us" (*Straight* xiv). It is the materialism of "an escapee, a fugitive, a slave, a lesbian," one that calls for "the destruction of the class of women within which men appropriate women," which can be accomplished "only by the destruction of heterosexuality as a social system" based on oppressive gender difference (xii, 20).

Lesbian materialism focuses on structural inequalities that originate in masculinist philosophical traditions and that are perpetuated by each new generation educated in those traditions. The "man-hating" trope that is often used by lesbian separatists targets this structural inequality rather than individual men. Jeffner Allen has written about a condition of man-hating that is really a form of protest against the structural dominance of patriarchy and masculinism in both social institutions and everyday life. "Man-hating may be considered an antagonistic division between object (woman) and subject (man)." But it is not "the 'battle of the sexes.' It is not an incessant cycle of men vs. women, women vs. men. Nor is man-hating a 'heroic hatred.' Heroic hatred is insatiable; upon vanquishing its enemy, heroic hatred goes off to seek another. Man-hating places in question all heroic ability, all antagonistic activity that exists solely for its own sake." Allen's critique echoes that of feminists like **Luce Irigaray**, who believes that women have been robbed of essence and even material substance. "My man-hating," Allen writes, "is grief for myself and other women at the loss of our bodies and memories, time and history" (21–3). Patriarchal "terrorization" and the oppressive estate of motherhood (in which a woman's body "is used as a resource to reproduce men and the world of men" [61]) prevent the "aqueous" freedom of female friendships in which women can establish what is most dangerous to a patriarchal ideology bent on subordinating women: "an ethics of care and a metaphysics of touch. Apart from the ties that bind men, *a fundamental ontological rupture is effected by women*" (90). This ontological rupture defines female sexuality and the female body as the space of a feminist phenomenology, in which touch and care have a role in demarcating the being of women outside the dimorphic division of sexual labor native to patriarchy and phallocentric rationality.

Adrienne Rich, in her much-anthologized essay, "Compulsory Heterosexuality and the Lesbian Existence," attacks "heterocentricity" as a covert mode of socialization that seeks willfully to repress the "enormous potential counterforce" (39) of lesbian experience. Because heterosexuality is the compulsory cultural norm, the oppression of women – their sexual slavery – is more difficult to name. Rich revalues the so-called perversity of lesbian desire and posits a "lesbian continuum" free of invidious binary sexual typologies. Lesbian feminism is not concerned with hating men but rather with celebrating the life choices of women who love women. Heterosexuality is not, in and of itself, oppressive; but "the absence of choice remains the great unacknowledged reality" (67). Acknowledging this reality has motivated theorists like **Teresa de Lauretis**, who challenges psychoanalytical theories of sexuality. Her critique of Freud's *Three Essays on Sexuality* (1905) deconstructs the normative status of heterosexual desire, which strikes her as "the imposition of a historically determined social norm on a field of instinctual drives" (24) that even Freud's evidence would seem to suggest a more diverse and "perverse" field of orientations.

Whether or not lesbian sexuality leads a woman to take a separatist position, the chief object of critique is the normative and at times compulsory status of heterosexual identity and heterosexual relations. These struggles take place within a material environment and have a material effect. The array of arguments about the material conditions and orientation of the queer body may account for the current, more broadly conceived idea of gender and sexual identity, one that focuses on the common roots of the problems gay men *and* women face: structural inequalities based on a sex/gender system and a late capitalist culture industry that continues to enforce a heterosexual norm. The "queering" of academic discourse is only the first step toward a more general queer/lesbian turn in society at large, which has become (in the West at least) more knowledgeable about and accepting of sexual and gender differences outside the categories straight/gay, man/woman. The urgency of the problem outside the West (and in some areas within it) may require more than literary theory can muster if substantial change is to occur.

Note

For more on issues related to gender and sexuality, see Feminist Theory, Ethnic and Indigenous Studies, and Postcolonial Studies. On Lacan, see Psychoanalysis. On Foucault, see Posthumanism and Poststructuralism. On materialism, see Posthumanism.

Works Cited

Ahmed, Sara. *Queer Phenomenology: Orientations, Objects, Others*. Durham, NC: Duke University Press, 2006.

Allen, Jeffner. *Lesbian Philosophy: Explorations*. Palo Alto: Institute of Lesbian Studies, 1986.

Bordo, Susan. *Unbearable Weight: Feminism, Western Culture, and the Body*. 10th Anniversary Ed. Berkeley: University of California Press, 2003.

Butler, Judith. "Changing the Subject: Judith Butler's Politics of Radical Resignification." Interview with Gary A. Olson and Lynn Worsham. *Journal of Advanced Composition* 20.4 (2005): 727–65.

Butler, Judith. "Gender as Performance." Interview. In *A Critical Sense: Interviews with Intellectuals*. Ed. Peter Osborne. London: Routledge, 1996. 108–25.

Butler, Judith. *Gender Trouble: Feminism and the Subversion of Identity*. New York: Routledge, 1990.

Butler, Judith. *The Psychic Life of Power: Theories of Subjection*. Stanford: Stanford University Press, 1997.

Carrigan, T., Connell, R., and Lee, J. "Toward a New Sociology of Masculinity." In *The Making of Masculinities: The New Men's Studies*. Ed. Harry Brod. Boston: Allen and Unwin, 1987. 63–100.

Connell, R. W. *Masculinities*. 1995. 2nd ed. Cambridge: Polity Press, 2005.

De Lauretis, Teresa. *The Practice of Love: Lesbian Sexuality and Perverse Desire*. Bloomington: Indiana University Press, 1994.

Fausto-Sterling, Anne. *Sexing the Body: Gender Politics and the Construction of Sexuality*. New York: Basic Books, 2000.

Foucault, Michel. *The History of Sexuality*. Vol. 1. Trans. Robert Hurley. New York: Pantheon Books, 1978.

Foucault, Michel. "The Subject and Power." In *Michel Foucault: Beyond Structuralism and Hermeneutics*. Ed. Herbert L. Dreyfus and Paul Rabinow. Chicago: University of Chicago Press, 1984. 208–26.

Fraser, Nancy. "Rethinking Recognition." *New Left Review* 3 (2000): 107–20.

Gerstner, David A. *Queer Pollen: White Seduction, Black Male Homosexuality, and the Cinematic*. Urbana: University of Illinois Press, 2011.

Grosz, Elizabeth. "Feminism, Materialism, and Freedom." In *New Materialism: Ontology, Agency, and Politics*. Ed. Diana Coole and Samantha Frost. Durham, NC: Duke University Press, 2010. 139–57.

Grosz, Elizabeth. *Volatile Bodies: Toward a Corporeal Feminism*. Bloomington: Indiana University Press, 1994.

Halberstam, Judith. *Female Masculinity*. Durham, NC and London: Duke University Press, 1998.

Hekman, Susan. *Private Selves, Public Identities: Reconsidering Identity Politics*. University Park, PA: Penn State Press, 2004.

Lee, Theresa Man Ling. *Politics and Truth: Political Theory and the Postmodernist Challenge*. Albany: SUNY Press, 1997.

Oliver, Kelly. *Witnessing: Beyond Recognition*. Minneapolis: University of Minnesota Press, 2001.

Rich, Adrienne. "Compulsory Heterosexuality and the Lesbian Existence." In *Blood, Bread and Poetry: Selected Prose 1979–1985*. New York: Norton, 1986. 23–75.

Rubin, Gayle. "The Traffic in Women: Notes on the 'Political Economy' of Sex." In *Toward an Anthropology of Women*. Ed. Rayna R. Reitor. New York: Monthly Review Press, 1975. 157–210.

Sedgwick, Eve Kosofsky. *Between Men: English Literature and Male Homosocial Desire*. New York: Columbia University Press, 1985.

Sedgwick, Eve Kosofsky. *Epistemology of the Closet*. Berkeley: University of California Press, 1990.

Vance, Carole S. "Social Construction Theory and Sexuality." In *Constructing Masculinity*. Ed. Maurice Berger, Brian Wallis, and Simon Watson. New York and London: Routledge, 1995. 37–48.

Warner, Michael. *The Trouble with Normal: Sex, Politics, and the Ethics of Queer Life*. New York: Free Press, 1999.

Wittig, Monique. *The Straight Mind and Other Essays*. New York: Harvester Wheatsheaf, 1992.

Trauma Studies

Trauma studies arose initially to help us understand the impact of world-historical events like the Holocaust but has evolved to include a wide array of personal, social, and historical experiences. Common to the various approaches found today is the temporality of trauma, which moves from the traumatic event to recovery and then to various forms of representation. At each stage, from event to recovery, the acts of witnessing and giving testimony come into play. There are a number of theoretical approaches in trauma studies, but underlying them all, especially early on, is a psychoanalytic approach to psychic events and, in the case of domestic and sexual trauma, a feminist and gender studies critique. By the 1970s, two distinct strands of development were dialectically entwined, based on two different kinds of experience: intensely personal and world historical. On the one hand, a strand of research in psychology developed around the study of personal trauma, for example, incest, physical and mental abuse, domestic violence, post-traumatic stress disorders (PTSD), and so on; on the other hand, a strand of research emerged on the trauma of world-historical events, initially the Holocaust, or *Shoah* (האושה, "catastrophe"), but also including war, genocide, and other natural and human calamities. In trauma studies, the personal and the historical come together in a cleavage that is both the sign of an unhealable rift and of a suture that knits together the survivor-witness and the discourse of the traumatic event. This complex double relation testifies to the *unsayable* quality of trauma, which seems to have its real existence outside the framework of a discourse.

The inaugural work on trauma might well be *Studies on Hysteria* by Freud and Josef Breuer, published in 1895. The idea that behind hysterical symptoms lay childhood sexual trauma shocked and scandalized both the medical and lay communities. In Freud's later work, trauma became central to the theory of the unconscious and the Oedipus complex. Cathy Caruth shows that from the early studies on hysteria to late culture works like *Moses and Monotheism* (1937), "Freud seems to have been concerned … with the way in which trauma is not a simple or single experience of events but that events, in so far as they are traumatic, assume their force precisely in their temporal delay." The interplay of forgetting and remembrance in which what cannot be recalled is displaced by the account of that failure, is itself a repetition of the traumatic event. In the temporality of trauma, "experience is repeated after its forgetting," and an "inherent latency" produces a structure of belatedness, "since the traumatic event is not experienced as it occurs, it is fully evident only in connection with another place, and in another time" ("Trauma" 8–9). That other time and place unfolds in narrative, particularly memoirs, autobiographies, and other variants of "life-writing," *Bildungsromane*, and documentary forms. Laurie Vickroy voices a common view when she describes the trauma narrative as a space in which the personal element of public pain can be shared with others. Such narratives "position their readers in ethical dilemmas analogous to those of trauma survivors" (3) and in this way attempt to raise awareness about trauma by creating a reading experience that in some ways compensates for the inaccessibility of trauma (an event that occurred but that cannot be recalled) and creates healing forms of repetition. This is evident in PTSD, which, since the 1970s, has provided clinical evidence of the temporality of trauma, in which the remembered event has the immediacy of the present (see Horvitz 12).

Bearing witness to trauma is a form of cultural memory that has to do less with a primordial traumatic event than with the "discourse of trauma" initiated by it. The model for this discourse delay and repetition is the temporal dynamic of Oedipal trauma, which depends for its reverberating effect on unconscious memories and traces of desires that have not been satisfied and that return again and again, inscribing their repetition as a separate reality. For many trauma theorists, the utterly unique event of the twentieth century was the Holocaust and, in the attempt to understand the experience of this trauma, a new set of theoretical problems arose. As Dominick LaCapra instructs us, historical trauma like the Holocaust "is specific, and not everyone is subject to it or entitled to the subject position associated with it." The scholar's identification with the victim is not the point when attempting to make sense of such traumatic events or when gathering testimony about it. As opposed to "empathy and empathic unsettlement," the "secondary witness" experiences trauma "virtually" by putting oneself "in the other's position while recognizing the difference of that position and hence not taking the other's place" (*Writing* 78). LaCapra believes that we must combine the view of historian and critic and take a hermeneutical position that "acknowledges the importance of self-understanding in the attempt to make one's assumptions explicit and to work critically through a relation to the past" (*Representing* 69). This is altogether appropriate for a field of study in which witness representations must aspire toward a very high level of nuance and tolerance. LaCapra argues that a form of transference takes place between the historian and the past event, a process driven by the need to know the past. "[T]he Holocaust presents the historian with transference in the most traumatic and disconcerting form conceivable." While transference alone does not offer insight into the traumatic event, it does point to the existence of the event and creates opportunities for "more or less critical vigilance and a measure of responsible control" (72). Indeed, narratives developed through transference may themselves be traumatic.

The line separating ordinary experience from that of trauma, the experience of which is singular and untransferable, is traversed and sometimes crossed through representation, which attempts to capture not only the traumatic event but the temporality it puts into play. In the discourse of trauma, temporality varies between the ecstatic and epiphanic reenactment of the primordial event that occurs in a flash, and the complex temporality of remembrance that is part of healing. This experience of timelessness can erase the present and foreclose the future, overtaking one's world view. "Is the prevalence of the concern with trauma," asks Andreas Huyssen, "due to the fact that trauma as a psychic phenomenon is located on the threshold between remembering and forgetting, seeing and not seeing, transparency and occlusion, experience and its absence in traumatic repetition?" (16). He notes that memory can have the paradoxical effect of overcoming our ability to see past the very thing we wish to overcome. "Our culture's sense of time is being renegotiated. But time is not only the past. Some warn that we are suffering from a surfeit of memory. Perhaps it is time to remember the future" (28–9). Memory can also produce a layered temporality, within discourse, that entwines the event in real time with the narrative time of healing and testimony. But while testimony, oral sources, and other documents of the past can support and substantiate memory, they do not replace it. "Testimony is not history," notes Esther Faye, because in "the testimonial act" time collapses, as does the distinction between the past and the one remembering it. Traumatic memory can telescope decades into the space of days, so that understanding a traumatic event requires the effort through interpretation to grasp the traumatic event in an entirely different temporal framework. But lest we think that this is a form of relativism, Faye reminds us that "the work of remembering that takes place in testimony is more than an individual's way of interpreting and narrating a personal past from the vantage point of the present." This "more" has to do with preserving the *otherness* of the past but also with bringing "the historian's work closer to the psychoanalyst's…. [I]t is this other way that allows us to value memory as a source *of* history and not merely a source *for* history" (161).

The dialectics of memory and trauma, of repetition that congeals into a permanent image displacing reality, is dramatized in one of the most influential witness narratives, Claude Lanzmann's film *Shoah*. This documentary, which relies almost exclusively on the oral accounts of witnesses, survivors, and family, brings the unthinkable to consciousness. The recognition of what lies beyond thought – madness, evil, nothingness – is the opposite of denial. Vickroy writes that "Lanzmann's use of dialogism creates a narrative wherein many voices, emotions, and experiences intermingle to produce memory. Individual witnesses counteract collective denial and repression, traditional historical accounts, and perpetrator evasions" (20–1). That Lanzmann's *Shoah* was able to retain the unsayable event precisely by means of a documentary featuring little else but talk is a striking example of **Jean-François Lyotard**'s notion of the presentation of the "unpresentable." Lyotard notes that even the best films of the Holocaust, those "best qualified not to let us forget," tend to "represent what, in order not to be forgotten as that which is the forgotten itself, must remain unrepresentable." He points to *Shoah* as the exception,

> maybe the only one. Not only because it rejects representation in images and music but because it scarcely offers a testimony where the unpresentable of the Holocaust is not indicated, be it but for a moment by the alteration in the tone of a voice, a knotted throat, sobbing, tears, a witness fleeing off-camera, a disturbance in the tone of the narrative, an uncontrolled gesture. (26)

Lanzmann's film, as Lyotard describes, anticipates **Giorgio Agamben**'s call for a new ethical position with respect to traumatic events that fail to coincide with the language used to represent them. For him, the ethical problem of this "non-coincidence" lies not in the non-coincidence itself but in our attitude toward our own role as speaking subjects within the discourse about trauma. The "I" of such a discourse, which, Agamben argues, serves as a purely linguistic marker, must be simultaneously inhabited and abandoned so that testimony can resound: "in the absolute present of the event of discourse, subjectification and desubjectification coincide at every point and both the flesh and blood individual and the subject of emancipation are perfectly silent" (117). In this "perfect" silence, the unsayability of trauma is itself articulated.

Despite the unsayable status of historical trauma, Kalí Tal finds that the reclamation of memory in projects like *Shoah* enable witnesses to participate "in a communal, reconstitutive act" (228). But this act exacts a price. Speaking of Elie Wiesel, whom she calls a "professional Holocaust survivor," Tal notes that the "survivor-witness bears a terrible burden – a duty to both the living and the dead to testify, to tell the world of the horrors he has seen" (2). Such testimony ultimately fails to break down the barrier between traumatic experience and the language used to explain it. Caruth notes that "traumatic recollection" is a far from simple task, for it must try to capture the reality of what is in fact not real at all. Memory, before it has been shaped into a narrative or an interpretation of the past, is already a memory of something more primordial, the singular event whose actuality is lost in representations. Caruth points to a difference between memory and reenactment in which the latter is "absolutely accurate and precise" and the former "largely inaccessible to conscious recall and control." The dynamic here is a suspended dialectic: "The phenomenon of trauma … both urgently demands historical awareness and yet denies our usual modes of access to it. How is it possible … to gain access to traumatic history?" Conscious memory is unreliable and open to interpretation, as analysts readily concede; and while reenactment brings to the fore what cannot be recalled, it serves a powerful purpose in being itself an *original* event that can, unlike the primordial unsayable event, be said. Reenactment thus conveys "both *the truth of an event*, and *the truth of its incomprehensibility*" ("Recapturing" 151, 153; see also "Trauma" 6).

Like Caruth, Vickroy believes that the truth of traumatic events is prospective and can only be known (and then only partially) in the future, specifically in the future of the survivor or witness accounts. In this sense, they are forms of misrecognition, for structurally they are bound to be unrecognizable, and take the form of dissimulations that seek to transform themselves into reality. Indeed, most trauma narratives "acknowledge ambivalence and doubts about successful retelling" even as they provide "ways for traumatic experience to be re-created" (11). Toni Morrison's fiction illustrates one strategy – engaging the reader in a kind of intimate relation with character's consciousness (Vickroy) – while memorials like Jochen Gerz's installation *2,146 Stones: Monument against Racism* (1993) exemplify another. In the latter, as Nicholas Miller describes it, the "forgotten names of German Jewish cemeteries in use during the war" were inscribed on cobblestones clandestinely removed for the purpose from a square in Saarsbrücken, Germany, directly above an old underground Gestapo detention cell, and replaced with the inscriptions face down. The point of the installation is that history is forever being buried or, to use the etymological pun Miller favors, "en-graved" in the language that memorializes it. Gerz's counter-discourse of memory resists forms of public commemoration that can produce little more than "an ideal narrative to commemorate or memorialize a past that is in itself unrepresentable" (22, 26). The public memorial is a paved-over indication (as opposed to a representation), a flagstone in the primal scene of memory.

Trauma studies both responds to and collaborates with what Huyssen calls a "culture of memory," which, in the late twentieth century, was rapidly diversified as new technologies made possible myriad forms of oral history and testimony, the most famous of which is the ongoing archive at Yad Vashem, the Holocaust Museum in Israel. Public memorials for Holocaust victims and memorials for other atrocities (e.g., Ground Zero in New York) create a well-marked public zone of memorialization, where mourning is severed from loss and transformed into a renewed sense of community. **Frantz Fanon**, the French-trained psychiatrist from Martinique who practiced in Algeria during the war of independence in the 1950s, concluded that "colonial war is a new phenomenon even in the pathology it produces" (184). What Fanon witnessed has come to characterize late twentieth-century conflicts (e.g., in Vietnam, Cambodia, Yugoslavia, Biafra, Rwanda, Sierra Leone, Darfur, and on and on), which have created a new norm with regard to human suffering and atrocity. These world-historical traumas have also called forth new forms of commemoration and mourning and new forms of resolution, such as the Truth and Reconciliation Commissions that emerged in South Africa after the fall of the white government and apartheid, which produced countless personal narratives and put an official (that is to say, historical) imprimatur upon them.

Yet if trauma leads, as many psychologists attest, to dissociative personality disorders and the shattering of the self, "[h]ow can such a lost, indefinable state of existence be narratively represented? Can narrative, itself, by compelling victim-survivors to remember and to repeat stories suffused with terror, panic, and pain, serve a palliative role in the healing process?" (Horvitz 6). Though trauma remains inaccessible, resistant to "full theoretical analysis," it nevertheless facilitates survival through "the different modes of therapeutic, literary and pedagogical encounter," and it is through these modes of survival that "we are implicated in one another's traumas" (Caruth, "Trauma" 10; *Unclaimed* 24). The key word here is "encounter," for in the circumstances of traumatic memory and reenactment, memory is at bottom interpersonal, which means that we bring that element of interpersonal connection to history, but we also take from the traumatic memory an image of it that is neither a distortion of reality nor "the repression of what once was wished" ("Trauma" 4–5). This amounts to saying that it cannot be known, but it makes possible knowledge of the future.

This knowledge is, by and large, *for* the listener, who performs the "work of remembering" as the *other* within the discourse of trauma. Wendy Hui Kyong Chun believes that "a politics of listening [is] a necessary complement to a politics of speaking." She points out that feminism has taught us to create a voice, but not so much how to listen. "The question of how to listen and respond to these testimonials has been largely unaddressed, since the question of listening in general tends to be under-theorized and under-valued: more often than not, we assume we know how to listen" (145). Testimony, which stands or falls on the sensitivity and perspicacity of the listener, is thus a precarious and fragile mode of documentation the authenticity of which is entwined with what Shoshana Felman calls a "crisis of truth" (Felman and Laub 5ff). Felman and Dori Laub raise the principal question: "Why has testimony become at once so central and so omnipresent in our recent cultural accounts of ourselves?" (6). Drawing on the poet Paul Celan, for whom a poem "'takes its position at the edge,'" Felman argues that "[t]estimonial teaching fosters the capacity to witness something that may be surprising, cognitively dissonant. The surprise implies the crisis. Testimony cannot be authentic without that crisis, which has to break and to transvaluate categories and previous frames of reference" (52–3). This Nietzschean desire to shatter constraining categories in order to utter the truth about what is unsayable, even unthinkable, plays out, for Felman, in a pedagogical framework in which reflection on the crisis can lead to transvaluation. The suggestion, of course, is that all witnessing is a form of pedagogy.

Some trauma studies scholars take issue with the over-reliance on a psychoanalytic framework. Tal is especially critical of the psychoanalytic dialogue that introduces the analyst into the situation of the survivor's testimony. She distrusts this mediation, as she does the fuzzy distinction, made by Felman and Laub, between real and metaphorical "crossings" "'from the inside of the Holocaust to the outside world'" (Felman and Laub, qtd. in Tal 58). This faultline of authenticity, which suggests that only the inaccessible REAL counts as authentic, threatens to leave trauma studies with no recourse but to adopt a Platonic or Freudian attitude to the primal event of trauma. Both the philosopher and the analyst, the poet and the confessor, are trumped by the uncompromising dualism behind the plea for absolute authenticity. Horvitz does not mince words: "Second-hand or vicarious perception of trauma is not tantamount to experiencing it." By emphasizing the first-hand experience of trauma – and she speaks primarily of violence against women – she is able to "examine a particular facet of women's subjugation, which includes not just the sadism forced upon them, but also how powerlessness becomes eroticized, then entrenched within the victim's self-identity" (21). Where psychoanalytic feminism can be of use is in the analysis of what Horvitz calls "cultural and political trauma":

"an officially sanctioned, sadomasochistic system of oppression in which a targeted group, perceived by the dominant culture as an obstacle to the goals of the existing hegemony, are tortured, imprisoned, or killed" (11).

The questions raised by Horvitz indicate a deep discomfort with the possibility that a traumatic experience can be shared. Judith Herman sees the event of trauma as a limit beyond which exists a world that is gone forever. "Traumatic reactions occur when action is of no avail.... Traumatic events produce profound and lasting changes in physiological arousal, emotion, cognition, and memory" (34). They also produce something like a readable script of what goes on in the "realms of the unthinkable" (7), for the discourse of trauma tends to map event, symptom, and reaction in a gridlike arrangement suggestive of the suspended temporality of the unthinkable. Because traumatic events undermine all stable and conventional supports (because time is "out of joint," because one feels dissociated and isolated), recovery is itself traumatic. Healing, therefore, is a crucial feature in the discourse on trauma. Recovery, theorists agree, is not a return to normal but the establishment of a new normative mode of being. But since, as Herman insists, "[r]ecovery can take place only within the context of relationships" (133), it cannot amount to a complete severance of all social contacts associated with a prior "normal" life. This means that the interpersonal component of traumatic witnessing and testimony must be sustained through all stages of recovery and that the narrative and dialogic modes of witness and testifying are equally useful in recovering and taking account of one's recovery (a prominent theme in the contemporary memoir).

This raises the question of the status of the writer, who serves or has the potential to serve as a witness and healer. The same period that saw the rise of medical, psychological, and theoretical interest in trauma (from, say, the 1950s) saw as well the rise of a literature of witness, those who, like Paul Celan, have survived historical trauma (in his case, a labor camp in Romania during World War II), but also those who, like Carolyn Forché and Cynthia Hogue, fashion a poetics of public memory in which aesthetics returns to its roots in the sensible, in the affective and bodily. Poets of witness do not so much represent trauma as create its environment of dislocation in language. This ethical desire to witness is unique to the literature of trauma (and it is not without controversy), and in Celan, this desire is unfurled in a *dischronic* temporality: "Black milk of daybreak we drink it at nightfall," he writes in "Fugue of Death." "Your ashen hair Shulamith we are digging a grave in the sky it is / ample to lie there." The entwinement of the historical and personal in Celan's poem lays bare the wound of trauma. In contemporary poetry we are more likely to see a veiled, but no less powerful, entwinement of traumatic experiences, some direct, some experienced via metaphor. Hence the intense psychic anguish of Sylvia Plath, whose work sometimes invokes the historical trauma of the Holocaust in a jarringly inappropriate rhetoric that ramifies the personal quality of that anguish, as when she writes, "my skin / Bright as a Nazi lampshade" ("Lady Lazarus"). But we also find, in the late twentieth century, especially in Eastern Europe, Northern Ireland, Latin America, and the Middle East (particularly in Palestine), the figure of the witness as an ironic spectator, a position that allows understatement to overstate the case. Writing in the 1970s, when Poland was still part of the Soviet empire, Zbigniew

Herbert allegorized historical trauma in the figure of Mr. Cogito who laconically notes that "the proof of the existence of the monster / is its victims" ("The Monster of Mr. Cogito").

Trauma narratives are not representations of trauma but rather accounts of recovery, of dealing with the effects of a traumatic experience. As Vickroy notes, the "contemporary trauma genre" is typically a narrative of "working through" (10) that seeks to represent the disjunctive effects of trauma. This is particularly evident in narratives of the terrorist attacks in the United States on September 11, 2001. These narratives frequently employ allegory in a way that reverses its rhetorical charge: rather than Mr. Cogito's vague and mythic "monster" standing in for totalitarian authority, we have, in Jonathan Foer's *Extremely Loud and Incredibly Close*, a cataclysmic act of terrorism that, through a massive reduction, comes to stand, by way of its displacement into its own aftermath, for the recovery of a small circle of strangers. The novel focuses on nine-year-old Oskar Schell, whose father was killed in the World Trade Center, and uses allegory to substitute a sayable experience (personal loss) for the unsayable event (the attacks themselves). In a similar way, Patrick McGrath's novella "Ground Zero" depicts the immediate aftermath of the 9/11 attacks, and the narrative conceit – the protagonist, Danny Silver, is in and out of therapy and in a precarious relationship with a woman that spirals into indifference and neglect – conveys the temporal discombobulation, the unreality and confusion of the attacks. The traumatic event is refracted in hundreds of personal reflections and experiences out of which the therapist attempts to weave a narrative. The story is an allegory not only of trauma, but of the therapy that is meant to alleviate the survivor's suffering. And therefore Danny's rage is itself an allegory of the incoherent emotions that mobilized a stunned citizenry to congregate at ground zero. "As I began to walk back uptown I attempted to find a few sticks of thought with which to build a structure that might explain why those men had done what they had to us. To *us*. But I could not, and all at once I felt what was, for me, a most rare emotion, I felt *rage* – which I imagine drove those men to attack us as they did" (196).

McGrath's response to the 9/11 attacks reminds us that the unpresentable is always having its impact on us and that we compulsively repeat the event in the discourse of trauma for decades afterwards. At stake, as we have seen, are two kinds of experience: the original trauma, inaccessible to representation, and the traumatic space of memory and writing. Curiously, this discourse that enables our witnessing and that records our survival yields its share of artistic and intellectual pleasures. Patricia Yaeger reflects on the "academic consumerism" in which "circulating the suffering of others" supports the discourse on trauma, a "self-pleasing, self-consuming" field in which discourse and affect intertwine in their separate circulations: "a world of words where we can channel-surf from trauma to pleasure and back to trauma again with so little cost" (30, 46). The pleasure in consumption is perhaps unavoidable, and so too might be the guilt we feel about it; but at bottom, trauma studies is a hermeneutic enterprise that seeks to build self-understanding and intersubjective connection. "In a catastrophic age," writes Caruth, "trauma itself may provide the very link between two cultures: not as a simple understanding of the pasts of others but rather within the traumas of contemporary history, as our ability to listen through the departures we have all taken from ourselves" ("Trauma" 11). If trauma studies teaches us anything, it is the pleasures and costs of survival, which are both forms of departure that allow us (once again) to envision the future.

Works Cited

Agamben, Giorgio. *Remnants of Auschwitz: The Witness and the Archive*. Trans. Daniel Heller-Roazen. New York: Zone Books, 2000.

Caruth, Cathy. "Recapturing the Past: Introduction." In *Trauma: Explorations in Memory*. Baltimore and London: Johns Hopkins University Press, 1995. 151–7.

Caruth, Cathy. "Trauma and Experience: Introduction." In *Trauma: Explorations in Memory*. Baltimore and London: Johns Hopkins University Press, 1995. 3–12.

Caruth, Cathy. *Unclaimed Experience: Trauma, Narrative, and History*. Baltimore: Johns Hopkins University Press, 1996.

Celan, Paul. *Poems of Paul Celan*. Trans. Michael Hamburger. London: Anvil Press, 1995.

Chun, Wendy Hui Kyong. "Unbearable Witness: Towards a Politics of Listening." In *Extremities: Trauma, Testimony, and Community*. Ed. Nancy K. Miller and Jason Tougaw. Urbana: University of Illinois Press, 2002. 143–65.

Fanon, Frantz. *The Wretched of the Earth*. Trans. Constance Farrington. New York: Grove Weidenfeld, 1963.

Faye, Esther. "Impossible Memories and the History of Trauma." In *World Memory: Personal Trajectories in Global Time*. Ed. Jill Bennett and Rosanne Kennedy. New York: Palgrave Macmillan, 2003. 160–76.

Felman, Shoshana and Dori Laub. *Testimony: Crisis of Witnessing in Literature, Psychoanalysis, and History*. New York: Routledge, 1992.

Herman, Judith. *Trauma and Recovery*. New York: Basic Books, 1992.

Horvitz, Deborah. *Literary Trauma: Sadism, Memory and Sexual Violence in American Women's Fiction*. Albany: SUNY Press, 2000.

Huyssen, Andreas. "Trauma and Memory: A New Imaginary of Temporality." In *World Memory: Personal Trajectories in Global Time*. Ed. Jill Bennett and Rosanne Kennedy. New York: Palgrave Macmillan, 2003. 16–29.

LaCapra, Dominick. *Representing the Holocaust: History, Theory, Trauma*. Ithaca: Cornell University Press, 1994.

LaCapra, Dominick. *Writing History, Writing Trauma*. Baltimore: Johns Hopkins University Press, 2001.

Lyotard, Jean-François. *Heidegger and "the Jews."* Trans. Andreas Michel and Mark Roberts. Minneapolis: University of Minnesota Press, 1990.

McGrath, Patrick. "Ground Zero." In *Ghost Town: Tales of Manhattan Then and Now*. New York: Bloomsbury, 2005. 175–243.

Miller, Nicholas Andrew. *Modernism, Ireland and the Erotics of Memory*. Cambridge: Cambridge University Press, 2002.

Tal, Kalí. *Worlds of Hurt: Reading the Literatures of Trauma*. Cambridge: Cambridge University Press, 1996.

Vickroy, Laurie. *Trauma and Survival in Contemporary Fiction*. Charlottesville: University of Virginia Press, 2002.

Yaeger, Patricia. "Consuming Trauma; or, The Pleasures of Merely Circulating." In *Extremities: Trauma, Testimony, and Community*. Ed. Nancy K. Miller and Jason Tougaw. Urbana: University of Illinois Press, 2002. 25–51.

5   Culture/Ethnicities/Nations/Locations

Cultural Studies

Cultural studies encompasses an array of approaches to culture, from the traditional domain of the fine arts to the most ephemeral, mass-produced entertainments. As a concept, *culture* is relatively new, arising in its contemporary sense in the late eighteenth-century German milieu of Johann von Goethe and Friedrich Schiller, when the terms *culture* and *cultivation* began to be used in connection with the formation of the self (*Bildung*) and the anthropological perspective on human societies. By the 1870s, the English social critic Matthew Arnold and his contemporary E. B. Tylor had, in separate disciplines (social criticism and anthropology), put forward a similar vision of culture defined, in Tylor's terse formulation, as "a complex whole which includes knowledge, belief, art, morals, law, custom, and any other capabilities and habits acquired by man as a member of society" (1). (On Arnold, see chapter one, "The Rise of Literary Theory" 15–16.) By the early twentieth century, Western culture was being transformed by the technologies of mass production, near-universal literacy, widespread availability of museums and exhibits, and the emergence of new work in anthropology and sociology. As the Frankfurt School critical theorists demonstrated, beginning in the 1940s, every product of culture, from fine to popular, had become thoroughly commodified, appropriated by totalitarian ideology and transformed into *kitsch* and spectacle. The rise of mass culture coincided precisely with one of the most devastating crises in the history of capitalism: the irrational development of totalitarianism, which distorted markets, at home and abroad, and caused historical upheavals that threatened the stability of a global system of circulation and exchange. On this view, exemplified by the work of **Theodor Adorno**, the possibility of collective forms of culture is irredeemably lost.

In the 1950s, British cultural studies began to look more closely at collective forms of culture, a tendency best exemplified by the work of **Raymond Williams,** whose *Culture and Society: 1780–1950* (1958) and *The Long Revolution* (1961) mark a decisive point at which an Arnoldian idea of culture as a coherent and unified complex begins to lose ground to an idea of culture as a "general structure of feeling," a matrix of social relations that are "only ever apprehended directly" as lived experience (*Culture and Society* 72). Unlike Arnold, who regarded some elements of society (i.e., the working classes) as inimical to culture as he defined it, Williams understood culture in terms of the "relationships between elements in a whole way of life. The analysis of culture is the attempt to discover the nature of the organization which is the complex of these relationships" (*Long Revolution* 46). This "whole way of life" constitutes a "structure of feeling," which registers "the particular living result of all the elements in the general organization" (48). And while they often "correspond to the dominant social character," they also include the interaction and struggle of the different social classes (63). Williams' approach was revolutionary in that he sought to analyze culture by way of a TOTALIZING concept ("structure of feeling") that was constituted by the "distilled residue" of multiple, interconnecting, unpredictable, and contingent elements in the community.

This totality includes overlapping social and cultural IDEOLOGIES. Thus we find, coexisting with a *dominant* culture, "alternative and oppositional forms of social life and culture," the possibility of which depends on "historical variation in real circumstances" and on "very precise social and political forces." These alternative and oppositional forms can be either *residual* (i.e., a holdover from a previous SOCIAL FORMATION) or *emergent* (i.e., "new practices, new significances and experiences") (*Culture and Materialism* 40–1). This model of culture not only accounts for the complexities and contradictions of late capitalism, it also acknowledges the presence of revolutionary potentialities within the social totality. (On Williams, see Post-Marxist Theory 103–5.)

Following the Italian Marxist Antonio Gramsci, Williams reconceived the relationship between BASE and SUPERSTRUCTURE within culture at large, which he divides into "three general categories": (1) the "ideal, in which culture is a state or process of human perfection, in terms of certain absolute or universal values"; (2) "the 'documentary,' in which culture is the body of intellectual and imaginative work, in which, in a detailed way, human thought and experience are variously recorded"; and (3) the "social," in which culture is "a description of a particular way of life, which expresses certain meanings and values not only in art and learning but also in institutions and ordinary behaviour" (*Long Revolution* 41). Each of these categories offers something of value to the critic, for each registers the complex ARTICULATIONS of various social groups and the "micro-politics" that represent and animate them. Gramsci's theory of HEGEMONY enabled Williams to analyze dynamic and complex cultural formations, particularly the web-like connections that link subcultures and the various class formations within overlapping regional and national frameworks. His consciousness of social DETERMINATION as a complex function of IDEOLOGY (rather than economics) meant that he, like Gramsci, refused the narrow Marxist view of history as the deterministic and mechanical relation between the productive base of society and superstructural phenomena. Williams was able, according to **Stuart Hall**, to counter "vulgar materialism and an economic determinism" with "a radical interactionism: in effect, the interaction of all practices in and with one another, skirting the problem of determinacy" (60).

Richard Hoggart, a contemporary of Williams and, like him, a teacher of adult education, embarked on a similar project of revisionary cultural analysis in *The Uses of Literacy: Changing Patterns in English Mass Culture* (1957). For him, as for Williams, the emphasis on mass culture entailed the analysis of new modes of cultural production, especially the popular media (newspapers, magazines, television, film), as well as patterns of cultural consumption, including individual behaviors as well as the audiences of new mass entertainments. This new orientation to cultural studies achieved disciplinary legitimation in 1964 with the foundation of the Centre for Contemporary Cultural Studies at the University of Birmingham, which was pivotal in establishing the field initially in Britain (Turner 71–2). Hoggart became the first director of the Centre, and his emphasis on sociology and empirical research methods was designed to facilitate a rigorous, empirical study of cultural trends, practices, and institutions. (The parallel with the Frankfurt Institute for Social Research is striking; see 91–3.) Stuart Hall took over as director of the Centre in 1968, and sought to legitimize not only new methods for defining and studying culture but also whole new domains of cultural production. His analysis of television typifies a point of view that remained grounded in the cultural materialism of Williams but that also pointed in striking new directions. For example, in "Encoding, Decoding" (1980), Hall shows television "to have achieved a 'near-universality'" by virtue of appearing to be "naturally given." This apparent absence of cultural code only testifies to the mastery of the encoding, of the profound *naturalization* that produces "apparently 'natural' recognitions," which are of course *mis*recognitions, of a different order from the "misunderstandings" that threaten the effectiveness of mediated communication ("Encoding" 110–11). Tony Bennett, a key figure in the Centre, attributes the shift indexed by Hall's influence to "the Foucault effect": "Foucault's perspectives, in encouraging us to focus on the detailed routines and operating procedures of cultural institutions, allow us to see how cultural resources are always caught up in, and function as parts of, cultural technologies which, through the ordering and shaping of social relations which they effect, play an important role in organizing different fields of human conduct" (82).

Vital to this task was the emphasis on race, class, ethnicity, immigration, and DIASPORIC identities, which signaled a new direction in British cultural studies that intersected with the emerging discourses of postcolonial studies. Of special note is *Policing the Crisis: Mugging, the State and Law and Order* (1978), by Hall and his colleagues at the Centre, which responded to a 1973 case in Birmingham, UK, in which young people of mixed race were given prison sentences for an assault, sentences which many felt were extreme. This kind of critical analysis formed a crucial counter-balance to the conservative policies of Margaret Thatcher's government (1979–90), which polarized British society and created the conditions for both new class antagonisms and new counter-hegemonic social formations. Dick Hebdige's *Subculture: The Meaning of Style* (1979) explores some of these new formations in its study of ethnic and musical subcultures (Rastafarians, "hipsters, beats and teddy boys," glam and glitter rockers, and so on). Hebdige shows how style functions as the dominant signifier in local discourses that may have far-flung participants, known to each other only at a concert or other events that mobilize communities contingently and sporadically. Subcultures, with their patently "unnatural" effects, can be read as a mode of resistance to dominant culture. Hebdige and Iain Chambers, in *Migrancy, Culture, Identity* (1994), were able to expand on Williams' interest in marginalized social groups by rethinking the idea of marginalization: a subculture is not an excluded or ignored class with a distinct identity and sense of solidarity; it is a contingent, often nebulous formation, characterized by a specialized *activity*, such as playing darts, nightclubbing, or reading fashion magazines, rather than by class consciousness. The emphasis on subcultures and marginalized groups also highlights the fact that culture is not a homogeneous and evenly distributed matrix of forces and relations. With these developments, the *idea* of culture became the *problem* of culture.

By the 1980s, the Centre, and a number of people associated with the Open University in London – notably Bennett, Hall, Colin Mercer, and Janet Woollacott – had developed a mode of cultural analysis that avoided an older, humanistic, top-down model of culture (see Turner 68f). At the same time, as Hall notes, cultural studies was confronted with a dilemma: either embrace Claude Lévi-Strauss's structuralist anthropology and analyze culture as a coherent, predictable structure or remain loyal to the dominant "culturalist" tradition of Williams and Gramsci ("Cultural Studies" 62–4). While Hall rejects "any easy synthesis between them," it is clear that a combined approach is needed. "Something fundamental" comes out of a comparative critique of both schools, he avers, which means that cultural studies retains its materialist foundation but absorbs the techniques and methodologies of structuralists and, as time goes by, poststructuralists. "[T]he line in Cultural Studies which has attempted to *think forwards* from the best elements in the structuralist and culturalist enterprises, by way of some of the concepts elaborated in Gramsci's work, comes closest to meeting the requirements of the field of study" (72). In short, the cultural studies of the future would have to be a hybrid discourse.

That said, British cultural theorists were generally hostile to structuralism, largely because it ignored the social and cultural determinations that shaped institutions, beliefs, and social practices. For this reason, the culturalist trend was more popular, especially after the "Gramscian turn" had reoriented cultural studies toward the study of hegemony and "the PROBLEMATIC of relative autonomy and 'over-determination'" (Hall, "Cultural" 69). Melissa Gregg describes this new orientation in terms of conjuncture, an emphasis on "the particularities of the present" that serves as the corollary of the "affective voices" of scholars who "convey compassion for those that have not always been the focus of academic concern" (55). She sees Hall's work as representative of the conjunctural approach, a Derridean strategy by which Hall "makes arbitrary closure for politics what DIFFÉRANCE is for language: a necessary fiction summoned in the service of a further project of sense-making" (59). Drawing on Gramsci and Ernesto Laclau, Hall theorizes new social articulations and CONSTELLATIONS that build on existing social elements. "The so-called 'unity' of a discourse," he writes, "is really the articulation of different, distinct elements which can be rearticulated in different ways because they have no necessary 'belongingness'" ("On Postmodernism" 141). As Lawrence Grossberg points out, the rearticulation to which Hall refers entails also a "delinking or disarticulating" process that provides the elements for a new provisional social unity that avoids the "bad totality" of poststructuralist absolutism (the hegemony of *différance*, of power, of the Other) (55). Hall himself called this bad totality the "devious path into the absolute" and promoted as an alternative "the relative autonomy of practices, via their necessary heterogeneity and 'necessary non-correspondence'" ("Cultural" 68).

It is just this "devious path" that Catherine Belsey attempts to demystify alongside a critique of "culturalism," which she associates with SOCIAL CONSTRUCTION THEORY. Culturalism assumes that reality is always already mediated by culture and context; therefore, culture is all we *can* know. In her reading, poststructuralism can be differentiated from culturalism by its refusal to "incorporate what exists into what we know exists, leaving open the possibility of a terrain of unmapped ALTERITY which **Jacques Lacan** calls 'the real'" (4). The poststructuralist position, as Belsey outlines it, is evident in contemporary cinema, which does not make the "easy constructivist assumption that there is no difference between illusion and reality": rather, it calls that difference into question (7). Once culturalism has eliminated the barriers between an authentic ("real") and an inauthentic ("illusion") action or standpoint, resistance to ideology becomes futile. Following Lacan and **Slavoj Žižek**,

Belsey argues for a conception of the cultural in which there is something subtracted from it, not included within it, a "beyond" that produces a creative unease. For her, as for many cultural studies scholars in the United States and Europe, the critique of culture needs to draw on psychoanalysis and theories of the body and of social space, but it also needs to be open to the space beyond culture. Art provides this open space by "inscrib[ing] in culture itself the limits to which culture is subject" (93).

The French sociologist **Pierre Bourdieu**'s theory of the SOCIAL FIELD and the HABITUS that constructs SUBJECTIVITY within it exemplifies a culturalist approach that has proven extremely influential, in part because it envisions society as a dynamic network of relations and links that can be totalized only in the sense that the theorists can arrive at a taxonomy of practices within it.

> A field – even the scientific field – defines itself by (among other things) defining specific stakes and interests, which are irreducible to the stakes and interests specific to other fields (you can't make a philosopher compete for the prizes that interest a geographer) and which are not perceived by someone who has not been shaped to enter that field … In order for a field to function, there have to be stakes and people prepared to play the game, endowed with the *habitus* that implies knowledge and recognition of the immanent laws of the field, the stakes, and so on. (*Sociology* 72)

The *social field* is not an "arbitrary social construct" but a product of slow development into a "relatively autonomous" state, which functions "in accordance with rigorous mechanisms capable of imposing their necessity on the agents" within the field. Paradoxically, as Bourdieu points out, it is this very quality of autonomy that prevents "those who are in a position to command the mechanisms" from formulating "strategies aimed expressly at the domination of individuals" (*Logic* 131–2). Thus, social fields are "games 'in themselves' and not 'for themselves,' and one does not embark on the game by a conscious act, one is born into the game, with the game" (67).

Being "born into the game" is to be endowed with the *habitus*, which in one sense is the measure of "cultural" capital, "the degree of accumulated prestige, celebrity, consecration or honour" one achieves in the social field (*Field* 7). The *habitus* refers to the half-conscious, unspoken limits of a given field, the "acquired, socially constituted dispositions" formed by experience with the rules of a particular social practice. It is a "'creative,' active, inventive capacity" of an "active agent," not "a transcendental subject in the idealist tradition" (*In Other Words* 12–13). As a mobile structure of "durable, transposable dispositions," the *habitus* organizes "practices and representations" as a form of objective adaptation that requires neither conscious aims nor mastery of technique (*Logic* 53). The *habitus* engages dialectically with conditions in the field to produce "a distribution of symbolic capital, legitimate capital, whose objective truth is misrecognized" (*Distinction* 172). Yet these misrecognitions are "in no way illusory, since they can orient real practices" and, at the individual and collective level, make "a real contribution toward actual revaluation" of social dispositions and distinctions (143). Michel de Certeau, in *The Practice of Everyday Life*, has criticized Bourdieu's approach on the grounds that it forecloses opportunities for tactical subversion of strategic structures in the social field, subversions that can provide the glimpses of the "real" that for Belsey constitute the limits of culture.

A radical form of culturalism emerged in the United States beginning in the 1970s among anthropologists and ethnographers who challenged traditional modes of representing culture. The breakthrough in this context was Clifford Geertz's *Interpretation of Cultures* (1973), which takes issue with structuralist and functionalist anthropology by arguing that cultural forms and "local knowledge" are texts circulated and read among people, as in the Balinese cock-fight, which is "a story they tell themselves about themselves" (448). Geertz was committed to a form of "thick description" that grew out of the deep immersion methods of early anthropologists like Bronislaw Malinowski; but rather than insert these descriptions into the scientific narrative of the ethnographer, Geertz demonstrated how cultural knowledge was distributed across different levels of narrative understanding and transmission. Just as the view of culture changed, so too did the methods of representing it, as is evident in James Clifford and George Marcus's influential collection, *Writing Culture* (1986), which privileged what Clifford calls "poetic dimension of ethnography" (26). However, *Writing Culture* invited criticism on the grounds that it focused less on material cultural conditions than on the texts those conditions constitute by virtue of a standpoint that predisposes the ethnographer to regard such conditions *as texts*. This criticism was answered, partially at least, in Richard G. Fox's *Recapturing Anthropology: Working in the Present* (1991), which came out of a seminar at the same School of American Research in Santa Fe that generated *Writing Cultures*. We see in Fox's volume a greater attention to materialist and postcolonial approaches to cultural representation than is matched elsewhere in US cultural studies.

As Graeme Turner and Patrick Brantlinger have demonstrated, there are significant differences between British and US cultural studies in the late twentieth century. The British form tends to emphasize MULTICULTURALISM and the problems of immigration, exile, and DIASPORA, as well as the new class formations and conflicts that a multicultural society brings in its train. In the United States, especially in the 1980s and 1990s, the dominant tendency was toward the study of popular culture. These trends are often fluid and interdisciplinary, which means that collaboration and theoretical hybridity is the norm. And while this broad distinction may be generally accurate, there are many points of crossover and convergence. Iain Chambers and Angela McRobbie in Britain and Janice Radway in the United States share an interest in popular culture (especially film) and an analytical approach to questions of gender and sexual identity. McRobbie's *Feminism and Youth Culture: From "Jackie" to "Just Seventeen"* (1991), for example, explores subcultures from a feminist perspective, focusing on the unique experiences of young women, while Radway's *Reading the Romance* (1984) considers the importance of genre fiction in a critique of PATRIARCHAL culture. In another study, McRobbie focuses on fashion and expresses her ambition that "a sociological and cultural studies approach might be able to offer better insight into fashion as a cultural practice, fashion as something more than the possession of unique insight, vision, talent or even genius" (758). The intense interest in popular culture, especially alternative textual forms that involve individuals in sustained "fantasy" environments (e.g., film, rock and roll, the internet, video games), is part of a more general critique of cultural CANONS in literature, art, and music. Throughout the 1990s, as "discourse" became increasingly prominent in the analysis of cultural formations, the categories *culture* and *nature*, and the relation between them, were called into question. **Donna Haraway**'s "reinvention of nature" is a good example of this form of culture critique. Focusing on "the categories of reproduction and production," she outlines the "major positions on human history and human nature," all of which "argued strictly within the boundaries of modern physiology, genetics, and social theory" and "hinged on the concept of function and recognized the 'liberal' doctrine of the autonomy of nature and culture." These positions articulate "a picture of human universals, of human nature as the foundation for culture" (42). Her work on subject positions like the "cyborg" is an attempt to move beyond this limited view of the human. The importance of nature as a category that imbricates with and defines culture continues to define the limits of cultural studies, as is evidenced in Beth Fowkes Tobin's *Colonizing Nature* (2005), which examines the flora and fauna of tropical outposts of empire and how they contribute to our understanding of British culture in the eighteenth and nineteenth centuries.

The trend in cultural studies toward popular culture has led to an emphasis on *material culture*, on cultural objects and their production, consumption, collection, and preservation. Susan Pearce, for example, argues that the analysis of the way individuals collect objects has much to say about how material culture impacts broader issues such as gender and class, for collecting "is as much a social activity as it is a form of solitary pleasure" (132). As the following sections illustrate, the analysis of culture has become widespread in literary theory, which makes it difficult, in the twenty-first century, to speak of "cultural studies" as a discrete field of study. Moreover, the renewed interest in theories of materialism and in new approaches to phenomenology and ONTOLOGY has meant that the cultural field has opened up to include innumerable new objects of study (see, for example, Posthumanism 283–90). All of these developments support Margaret Morse's argument that the very notion of cultural space needs to be rethought. She suggests that much of culture takes place in *non-space*, which "is not mysterious or strange to us, but rather the very haunt for creatures of habit." It is the ground of communication understood "as a flow of values between and among two and three dimensions and between virtuality and actuality" (102). Culture becomes a network or web that sustains "the institutions of mobile privatization" (118), the *non-spaces* of the freeway, the shopping mall, and, not surprisingly, television. The "ontology of everyday distractions" unveils the micro-practices and technologies of culture in a way that eludes grand theoretical schemes to create a coherent, unified cultural field.

Note

On the "culture industry" see Critical Theory. On media and culture, see Postmodernism. On Foucault and De Certeau, see Poststructuralism. On the critique of the human and the idea of culture, see Posthumanism.

Works Cited

Belsey, Catherine. *Culture and the Real: Theorizing Cultural Criticism.* London: Routledge, 2005.
Bennett, Tony. *Culture: A Reformer's Science.* London and Thousand Oaks, CA: Sage, 1998.
Bourdieu, Pierre. *Distinction: A Social Critique of the Judgement of Taste.* Trans. Richard Nice. 1979. Rpt. Cambridge, MA: Harvard University Press, 2002.

Bourdieu, Pierre. *The Field of Production: Essays on Art and Literature*. Ed. Randal Johnson. New York: Columbia University Press, 1993.

Bourdieu, Pierre. *In Other Words: Essays Towards a Reflexive Sociology*. Trans. Matthew Adamson. Stanford: Stanford University Press, 1990.

Bourdieu, Pierre. *The Logic of Practice*. Trans. Richard Nice. Stanford: Stanford University Press, 1990.

Bourdieu, Pierre. *Sociology in Question*. Trans. Richard Nice. London: Sage, 1993.

Clifford, James. "Partial Truths." In *Writing Culture: The Poetics and Politics of Ethnography*. Ed. James Clifford and George E. Marcus. Berkeley: University of California Press, 1986. 1–26.

De Certeau, Michel. *The Practice of Everyday Life*. Trans. Steven Rendall. Berkeley: University of California Press, 1984.

Fox, Richard G., ed. *Recapturing Anthropology: Working in the Present*. Santa Fe: School of American Research Press, 1991.

Geertz, Clifford. *The Interpretation of Cultures*. New York: Basic Books, 1973.

Gregg, Melissa. *Cultural Studies' Affective Voices*. New York: Palgrave Macmillan, 2006.

Grossberg, Lawrence. *We Gotta Get Out of This Place: Popular Conservatism and Postmodern Culture*. New York and London: Routledge, 1992.

Hall, Stuart. "Cultural Studies: Two Paradigms." *Media, Culture and Society* 2 (1980): 57–72.

Hall, Stuart. "Encoding, Decoding." In *Culture, Media, Language*. Ed. Stuart Hall, D. Hobson, A. Lowe, and P. Willis. London: Routledge, for the Centre for Contemporary Cultural Studies, 2005. 107–16.

Hall, Stuart. "On Postmodernism and Articulation: An Interview with Stuart Hall." 1986. Ed. Lawrence Grossberg. In *Critical Dialogues in Cultural Studies*. Ed. David Morley and Kuan-Hsing Chen. London and New York: Routledge, 1996. 131–50.

Haraway, Donna. *Simians, Cyborgs, and Women: The Reinvention of Nature*. New York: Routledge, 1991.

McRobbie, Angela. "Fashion as a Culture Industry." In *Cultural Studies: An Anthology*. Ed. Michael Ryan. Oxford: Blackwell, 2008. 753–63.

Morse, Margaret. *Virtualities: Television, Media Art, and Cyberculture*. Bloomington: Indiana University Press, 1990.

Pearce, Susan. *Collecting in Contemporary Practice*. London: Sage; Walnut Creek, CA: AltaMira Press, 1998.

Turner, Graeme. *British Cultural Studies*. London and New York: Routledge, 1996.

Tylor, E. B. *Primitive Culture*. Vol. 1. New York: Harper, 1958.

Williams, Raymond. *Culture and Materialism*. London and New York: Verso, 2005.

Williams, Raymond. *Culture and Society: 1780–1950*. 1958. Rpt. New York: Columbia University Press, 1983.

Williams, Raymond. *The Long Revolution*. New York: Columbia University Press; London: Chatto and Windus, 1961.

African American Studies

Modern African American studies is rooted in the pioneering work of W. E. B. Du Bois and the Harlem Renaissance, which enabled the formation of an interdisciplinary framework in the late 1960s. By the 1980s, the field included theorists in philosophy, history, religious studies, political science, literary and cultural studies. Key figures such as **Henry Louis Gates** and Kwame Anthony Appiah have revealed the theoretical richness of African and African American literature and philosophy and shown how contemporary European theories of language, gender, TEXTUALITY, and the SUBJECT can be used to critique discourses of race and racial difference. African American studies is by no means alone in furthering these aims. Chicano/a studies has, at least since the 1960s, been building an impressive CANON of theoretical works, and native American and indigenous studies has more recently started to explore the links between native literary and cultural practices and mainstream Anglo-European theory. But the African American experience is unique in having founded the critical discourse on race, which has proven relevant across disciplines. The originary traumatic experience of slavery, the long tradition of racism in the United States, the linked hybrid identities forged through memory and storytelling – these are the foundations of the African American theoretical standpoint.

Speaking from an African American perspective, Du Bois in 1903 articulated succinctly the central issue of modernity: "The problem of the twentieth century is the problem of the color-line" (16). For him, race and the difference that it marks have a profound effect on the social development of individuals. For if race is a problem, so too is the individual whose race differs from that of the dominant group. "It is a peculiar sensation," Du Bois writes in *The Souls of Black Folk*, "this double consciousness, this sense of always looking at one's self through the eyes of others, of measuring one's soul by the tape of a world that looks on in amused contempt and pity. One ever feels his two-ness, – an American, a Negro; two souls, two thoughts, two unreconciled strivings; two warring ideals in one dark body, whose dogged strength alone keeps it from being torn asunder" (8–9). Quintessential expressions of this syndrome in literature include Richard Wright's *Native Son* and Ralph Ellison's *The Invisible Man*, novels that depict the alienating and destructive effects of double consciousness on young men growing up black in the United States. The sense of this double consciousness is all the more striking, in Ellison's novel, for being communicated through one side of it, in defiance of white America. After hearing Jack discourse on "political consciousness" in Harlem, the narrator claims his own awareness and thus authenticity. "'Have it your way, Brother,'" he tells him; "'only the political consciousness of Harlem is exactly a thing I know something about. That's one class they wouldn't let me skip. I'm describing a part of reality which I know'" (471).

The Harlem Renaissance, which flourished in the 1920s and 1930s, expanded on Du Bois' work by addressing the problem of double consciousness in intellectual and cultural life. Hazel Carby, for example, has pointed to conflicts between northern intellectuals (the "Talented Tenth") and the rural "black folk" they IDEALIZED and between middle-class intellectuals and an emergent radical working class. Harlem Renaissance critics, like Bruce Nugent and Alan Locke – "the great proponent of African American 'high culture'" (Gerstner 23) – did much to build the canon of African American literature. Nella Larsen and Zora Neale Hurston defied the stereotypes of black women at the same time that they questioned the responsibility to "uplift" the race. They also addressed the phenomenon of colorism, in which the double consciousness that pits African Americans against the dominant culture is itself redoubled within African American communities, where light-skinned individuals often find themselves tempted to choose between a "native" black culture and a "foreign" white one. Clare, Larsen's protagonist in *Passing* (1929), illustrates one option for light-skinned black people. For her, *passing* is not difficult: "If one's the type, all that's needed is a little nerve" (31). But "nerve," as Brian Carr points out, "is not a determinate set of descriptions about how Clare passes but is rather a decontextualized, unverifiable principle" (287). She presents her own passing as an attempt to get around social restrictions; plus, she "wanted things" (Larsen 24). Passing and consumption are linked for her, and so through passing she gets the things she desires, presumably the white husband she marries and the middle-class life they lead. For her friend Irene, "racial consciousness" comes in the form of anxiety about her own presentation *as black*: "She was caught between two allegiances, different, yet the same. Herself. Her race. The thing that bound and suffocated her" (93, 152).

Du Bois was tremendously influential in defining the terms of debate in contemporary discourse on race in African American studies. However, as Appiah has shown, he confused biological and socio-historical conceptions of race: "[W]hat Du Bois attempts, despite his own claims to the contrary, is not the transcendence of the nineteenth-century scientific conception of race ... but rather, as the dialectic requires, a revaluation of the Negro race in the face of the sciences of racial inferiority" (25). Appiah's critique testifies to the tenacity of a concept that has no biological basis. As Richard Lewontin and his colleagues have discovered, "the differences between major 'racial' categories, no matter how defined, turn out to be small. Human 'racial' differentiation is, indeed, only skin deep," which means biology cannot justify racial categorization (126–7). Contemporary African American studies by and large finds its justifications elsewhere, regarding race as an ideological category that, like the category of "sex," enables the surveillance of difference and maintains the mythology of ESSENTIALISM that continues to flourish around the idea of "race." This is nowhere more evident than in the multicultural West, where racism persists, despite our steady enlightenment about non-Western cultures gained through centuries of immigration and integration, social and legal policymaking, and the discourse produced by dissident intellectual positions. "[I]f 'race' is real," write Antonia Darder and Rodolfo D. Torres, "it is so only because it has been rendered meaningful by the actions and beliefs of the powerful, who retain the myth in order to protect their own political-economic interests" (5, 12). Resistance to racism and the "color consciousness" that drives it can shape itself freely to a limited degree, "even if we cannot escape the consciousness itself" (Appiah and Gutmann 168). Critical race theory, which developed out of African American studies (particularly the work of Du Bois), presupposes the ideological character of race and sees the idea of "color consciousness" as a structural problem. As legal theorists such as Derrick Bell and Alan Freeman have shown, social and legal inequalities stem from the normalization of perceptions of racial difference and of the status of inferiority that comes with these perceptions.

Despite the deeply problematic nature of the concept, the cultural interpretations of race and the very real material conditions that are the direct result of policies and legislation aimed at "racial" issues remain entrenched in the social and political imaginary. Indeed, race supplies the ballast and teleological thrust of several important revisionist histories of Africa and its relation to the rest of the world. One of the most influential of these projects was Martin Bernal's *Black Athena* (1987), which challenges our historical understanding of Europe, empire, and the role that Africa has played in shaping the modern world system. Bernal posits that Africa (specifically Egypt) lies at the center of Western civilization, rather than on its periphery. On this view, racial difference is the result of the "fabrication" of ancient Greek culture. Extensive geological, archaeological, and linguistic analysis led Bernal to argue that the origin of Greece lies in "Egyptian and Semitic cultural areas" and that "there seems to have been more or less continuous Near Eastern influence on the Aegean" in the period during which Greek culture emerged (2100–1100 BCE) (1, 18). His assertion that we must rethink "the fundamental bases of 'Western Civilization'" and "recognize the penetration of racism and 'continental chauvinism' into all our historiography" (1–2) has been hotly contested by classicists, archaeologists, historians, and other scholars. To some degree, *Black Athena* is part of a larger "Afrocentric" project, which flourished in the 1970s and 1980s, of "recentering" Africa in response to its "peripheralization" by Western cultures. Afrocentricity is not a separatist discourse; it does not argue for the exclusion of other traditions of thought, nor does it designate practices of cultural revival. According to Molefi K. Asante, "Afrocentricity liberates the African by establishing agency as the key concept for freedom" and "provides the shuttle between the intransigence of white privilege and the demands of African equality" (21, 41). However, as Appiah and Gutmann argue, because the Afrocentric position ties self-formation to the social requirements and ideals of a group, there is the ever-present "potential for conflict between individual freedom and the politics of identity" (99).

These dangers are by and large avoided in the African American literary theory developed by Gates and Houston Baker, who worked within Western theoretical and philosophical traditions. Gates builds on Houston Baker's early work, which argues that "Black America" possessed its "own standards of moral and aesthetic achievement" and distinguished itself from white America by virtue of its commitment to an oral tradition and a collectivist ethos. Additionally, "black American culture is partially differentiated from white American culture because one of its most salient characteristics is an index of repudiation," especially of Western cultural theory (6, 16). In *The Signifying Monkey* (1988), Gates pursues a more progressive and enabling mode of differentiation in his analysis of trickster figures found in African cultures (particularly among the Yoruba) and in the black vernacular of African America. For Gates, the Esu-Elegbara and the "signifying monkey" are bound up with the idea of Signification or Signifyin(g) (capital *S*) – which he distinguishes from the poststructuralist conception of signification (lower-case *s*) – in order to argue that in Signifyin(g) the SIGNIFIER itself becomes the SIGNIFIED in a self-consciously rhetorical performance of language. (On **Roland Barthes'** mythic signifier, see 57.) In essence, Gates doubles up on the signifier and (re)discovers double consciousness within language itself. Black vernacular performances like "the dozens" (a form of ritual insult), which can be traced to sources in Africa, exemplify this Signifyin(g) practice. As Gates demonstrates in his analysis of Esu-Elegbara, the PROBLEMATIC of language and of representation is itself the centerpiece and subject of the stories. "Esu is our metaphor for the uncertainties of explication, for the open-endedness of every literary text.... Esu is discourse upon a text; it is the process of interpretation that he rules." The related trope of the signifying monkey is "the great trope of Afro-American discourse, and the trope of tropes, his language of Signifyin(g), is his verbal sign in the Afro-American tradition" (21). Signifyin(g) is about naming and revising discourse, a process of revision and repetition that works within a black vernacular tradition but also within (and against) a dominant Euro-American one. It is a form of "double voiced" utterance (an idea Gates borrows from **M. M. Bakhtin**), a "speakerly" text in which parody, pastiche, and a general facility with language permit a negotiation between two discourse communities as well as the creation of a new oppositional discourse.

African feminism had begun developing just such a discourse in the 1970s, beginning with Barbara Smith's influential article, "Toward a Black Feminist Criticism" (1977). Smith claims that the "politics of feminism have a direct relationship to the state of Black women's literature. A viable, autonomous Black feminist movement in [the US] would open up the space needed for the exploration of Black women's lives and the creation of consciously Black woman-identified art" (7). The woman who most effectively answered this call was **bell hooks**, whose work from the mid-1980s was part of a third wave of feminism that emphasized the experiences of women of color. Like her contemporaries in postcolonial feminism, she called white Western feminists to task for failing to address the fundamental problems of race and racism: "Although ethnocentric white values have led feminist theorists to argue the priority of sexism over racism, they do so in the context of attempting to create an evolutionary notion of culture, which in no way corresponds to our lived experience." In fact racism is the very means by which white women "construct feminist theory and praxis in such a way that it is far removed from anything resembling radical struggle" (53–4). For Smith and hooks, race is the category that orients thinking about women's experience because it is the "color-line" that dominates individual experience and collective political action. Barbara Johnson's reading of Larsen's fiction shows how deeply that line cuts. "Racial pride and prejudice are not merely interpersonal phenomena, but institutionalized structures in history and culture" (53). As with Larsen and Ellison, Toni Morrison's fiction does much-needed theoretical work. J. Brooks Bouson shows how *Beloved* "examines the painful and secret legacy of slavery and focuses attention on the pernicious effects of internalized racist assumptions about black inferiority on the construction of African-American identities" (137). Morrison explores the "intergenerationally transmitted and internalized ... wounds cause[d] by racist oppression" (137) and employs "countershame" tactically to reveal the inner strength of women and the utter lack of nobility that lies behind the social forces arrayed against them.

Though it typically focus on local conditions, African American fiction testifies to the broader historical contexts that drive double consciousness and the racial double-bind, for historical trauma (like slavery and racism) bespeaks an utterly private and singular event that unfolds within a community and a cultural politics that must combat not only racism but the tendency within the community to marginalize radical responses to it. Paul Gilroy has put forward the idea that marginalized communities can invert the "ideas of racial particularity ... so that they provide sources of pride rather than shame and humiliation." Too often "minor, dissident traditions" are overlooked as "insufficiently respectable, noble, or pure," but these very traditions and "the stubborn social movements that were built upon their strengths and tactics" have proven vital to the "pursuit of freedom, democracy and justice" (12–13). What is needed is a "pragmatic planetary humanism" that can respond explicitly "to the sufferings that raciology has wrought" (18; see also 327ff).

A good example of this pragmatic humanism is David Gerstner's *Queer Pollen: White Seduction, Black Male Homosexuality, and the Cinematic* (2011), which attempts to find a cultural space of recognition for queer black people in film, though he is less concerned with the representation of gay black people than with fostering the queer dimension within the operation of the cinema, which "facilitates experiences that illuminate the tensions with which queer black identity is fraught" (16). In the twenty-first century, such projects remind us of the power and humanity of "dissident traditions" and "stubborn social movements" that refuse to be marginalized. Indeed, as Gerstner argues, the "efflorescent queer-aesthetic dynamic generated by a roundtable of intimately situated artists" (23) is not an aberration within African American literary history but a crucial constitutive part of its historical emergence. At the time Gerstner was writing, African American studies could easily contain the kind of radical interdisciplinary project that not long ago would have been unthinkable.

Works Cited

Appiah, Kwame Anthony. "The Uncompleted Argument: Du Bois and the Illusion of Race." In *"Race," Writing, and Difference*. Ed. Henry Louis Gates. Chicago: University of Chicago Press, 1986. 21–37.

Appiah, Kwame Anthony and Amy Gutmann. *Color Conscious: The Political Morality of Race*. Princeton: Princeton University Press, 1996.

Asante, Molefi K. *The Afrocentric Idea*. 1987. Rev. ed. Philadelphia: Temple University Press, 1998.

Baker, Houston. *Long Black Song: Essays in Black American Literature and Culture*. Charlottesville: University of Virginia Press, 1972.

Bernal, Martin. *Black Athena: The Afroasiatic Roots of Classical Civilization*. Vol. 1. London: Free Association Books, 1987.

Bouson, J. Brooks. *Quiet as It's Kept: Shame, Trauma, and Race in the Novels of Toni Morrison*. Albany: SUNY Press, 2000.

Carr, Brian. "Paranoid Interpretation, Desire's Nonobject, and Nella Larsen's *Passing*." *PMLA* 119.2 (March 2004): 282–95.

Darder, Antonia and Rodolfo D. Torres. *After Race: Racism after Multiculturalism*. New York: New York University Press, 2004.

Du Bois, W. E. B. *The Souls of Black Folk*. New York: Vintage Books/Library of America, 1990.

Ellison, Ralph. *Invisible Man*. New York: Vintage, 1995.

Gates, Henry Louis. *The Signifying Monkey: A Theory of Afro-American Literary Criticism*. New York: Oxford University Press, 1988.

Gerstner, David A. *Queer Pollen: White Seduction, Black Male Homosexuality, and the Cinematic*. Urbana: University of Illinois Press, 2011.

Gilroy, Paul. *Against Race: Imagining Political Culture Beyond the Color Line*. Cambridge, MA: Belknap Press of Harvard University Press, 2000.

hooks, bell. *Feminist Theory: From Margin to Center*. Cambridge, MA: South End Press, 2002.

Johnson, Barbara. *The Feminist Difference: Literature, Psychoanalysis, Race, and Gender*. Cambridge, MA and London: Harvard University Press, 1998.

Larsen, Nella. *Passing*. New York: Penguin, 2003.

Lewontin, Richard C., Steven Rose, and Leon J. Kamin. *Not in Our Genes: Biology, Ideology and Human Nature*. New York: Pantheon Books, 1984.

Smith, Barbara. "Toward a Black Feminist Criticism." In *Black Feminist Cultural Criticism*. Ed. Jacqueline Bobo. Oxford: Blackwell, 2001. 7–23.

Ethnic and Indigenous Studies

Ethnic and indigenous studies is a rubric that covers a number of literary and theoretical projects, including the ones featured here: native American and indigenous studies, Chicano/a studies, and Asian American studies. These are the main disciplinary formations to emerge, beginning in the 1980s, in universities, museums, libraries, archives, and other cultural institutions. My consideration of Chicano/a studies relies on a fairly discrete, not to say small, body of work (literary, artistic, theoretical, historical and so on), produced in the United States, primarily in the Southwest; however, the issues raised here are relevant to the study of Mexican, Central American and Caribbean people who have settled in the United States. The larger category, Latino/a studies (sometimes called Latin American studies or inter-American studies; see Sadowski-Smith 16–19), encompasses not only a much broader geographic range but also includes many more disciplines, including politics, international relations, trade, economics, and urban development. Chicano/a studies very well represents the broader interests of Latino/a studies not so much because it is a subset of the latter (as some scholars believe), but because it pursues the central themes and puts forward key strategies in a particularly striking and influential fashion. (It should be noted that the terms are often used interchangeably.) Like many Chicano/a traditions, those of native and indigenous peoples are tied to a sense of *ethnos*, of community and humanity rooted in particular locations through long periods of history. The experiences of Asian Americans (from the era of Chinese labor to that of political and economic refugees) present entirely different geographic coordinates for ethnicity (and thus of cultural authenticity), but confront some of the same problems of negotiating within a dominant culture.

There are certainly critical traditions in other ethnic literatures and cultures (e.g., Irish American, Jewish American), and, perhaps unsurprisingly, they share some of the same theoretical assumptions and use the same techniques as the writers featured in this section. Most scholars of ethnicity and MULTICULTURALISM are interested in DIFFERENCE, both in the obvious sense of ethnic difference and in the philosophical sense that **Jacques Derrida** gives it, for difference in the field of ethnic and indigenous studies is manifested in signifiers (e.g., skin color, hair, eye shape, dialect, clothing) that establish and mark off OTHERNESS. For example, US theories of indigeneity are akin to those found in Canada, Australia, and New Zealand, where the concept is part of the cultural and legal discourses. Lack of space forbids my attempting to draw out the salient features of these critical traditions, except to say that the parallelisms found in native, Chicano/a, and Asian American traditions will be easy to discern by virtue of the general principles discussed here. I might add that in many cases in the United States, immigration, which is spread out generationally and in diminished intensities, constitutes a kind of fluid stability, in which individuals are simultaneously mobile and rooted. *Ethnos*, in this context, is defined less by the idea of the nation (or the nation's historical temporality) than by transition between nations, by translation into the language of multiple nations, and by the individual's own self-motivated transit.

Chicano/a Studies

Ethnic and indigenous studies is grounded in the genealogy of dispossession, colonialism, and oppression. On these grounds, Chicano/a studies is particularly close in its concerns to what animates native and indigenous writers, for in both the concern for nationalism, cultural as well as political, is tied to the ideal of sovereignty over native land, and much theoretical and creative activity is directed toward reappropriating that sovereignty in political, aesthetic, and personal ways. In this context, then, Chicano/a studies fosters an indigenous national identity, one that is not defined by ethnic purity but rather by linguistic and cultural continuities that survive the experiences of disruption, disconnection, and deprivation. This strand of nationalism should be distinguished from what is common in the Anglo-European traditions (see, e.g., Ernest Gellner and Eric Hobsbawm), for here we find a holistic environmentalism that supports a spiritual humanism extending from the family to the clan, from the tribe to the nation. There is no dialectical TOTALITY (e.g., the Hegelian nation-state), but rather the transmission of an attitude that encompasses the people, the land, and the spirits that inhabit it. This attitude, or rather its transmissibility, takes on the social and discursive force of a national imaginary.

Like African American studies, Chicano/a studies grew largely out of political activism and began to cohere into a discipline by the mid-1980s. As Alurista points out, Chicano/a (or, as he prefers, *Xicano*) literature grew out of and affirmed "a nationalist fervor founded on the most ancient and precolonial cultural origins available" (22). To traverse the centuries between the time of the "modern Xicano writer" and these origins in pre-Columbian societies would require a hermeneutic method and a willingness to critique what is transmitted in the chain of tradition. Following Fanon's call to reaffirm the "precolonial springs of life" (Fanon 170), Alurista declares the need "for the redefinition of Xicano identity [which] was clearly at the fore of the search for the historical self" that predated colonial dispossession (23). This is precisely Fanon's theoretical task in *The Wretched of the Earth* – to reinsert the subject into history. In his reading of Xicano literature in the period 1965–75, Alurista identifies a historical dialectic that weaves cultural heritage into national consciousness, the Fanonian goal of a nation whose people are conscious of themselves *as a people*. Literature had a role to play in this dialectical passage, and not a passive one of merely "reflecting" the social world. "Xicano literary production in the poetic mode, like Xicano theatre, brought out its message to the people rather than wait for the people to pick up a manuscript and legitimize the birth of a new consciousness" (29). This gives the power of agency to the people who receive the message and respond spontaneously to its theoretical program. The fact that national consciousness as Alurista defines it can exist only as an idea does not diminish its capacity to bind people into a community and justify resistance against neocolonial oppression. However, Américo Paredes believes that the narrative of the Chicano/a struggle, which is typified by Alurista's essay, lacks historical perspective. "Mexican-American dependence on the Mexican government in the matter of civil rights in the United States has not been given due notice in the history of the present Chicano movement, which too often is seen as a sudden awakening of the Mexican minority in the United States to a consciousness of themselves and of their rights as human beings" (27). He sees the Chicano/a struggle as stretching back to the nineteenth-century battles between the United States and Spain, then between the United States and Mexico.

The focus on language, race, and ideology defines much of the work in Chicano/a studies and native American studies, particularly in the 1990s, when both fields began to develop a strong institutional presence. Unlike African American studies, however, slavery was not part of this focus. Instead, theorists turned to the special problems of foreign conquest and the question of native identity and native rights. As Ramón Saldívar has pointed out, however, the Mexican American experience is not unlike what African Americans and Native Americans have gone through, for their experiences are defined by the interrelationship of two cultures, a "minority" and a "dominant" (13f). This is why it is necessary for Chicano narratives to mediate "truth about a culturally determinate people in a historically determinate context" and to find their ground "in the concrete social interests of historical and contemporary events" (24). Not content with mirroring a problematic real world of social hardship and economic deprivation, "Chicano narratives seek systematically to uncover the underlying structures by which real men and women may either perpetuate or reformulate that reality" (5–6). Unlike Gates, who sees African American literary traditions as involved in a kind of MIMICRY based in linguistic difference, Saldívar sees a "dialectical relationship" between Mexican American culture and "both of its original contexts," Mexico and the United States (17).

In the analysis of identity in Chicano/a contexts, the dialectical production of the subject involves multiple terms and multiple points of synthesis. To be sure, this is the case in African American contexts, as Du Bois pointed out in his discussion of "the phenomena of race-contact" (120). What differs is the Chicano/a experience of geographic borderlands, spaces of difference that complicate binary structures of knowledge and monolingual conceptions of human communication. Recent research in the literature and culture of the borderland – a term coined by the historian Herbert Eugene Bolton to describe the combination of conflict and belonging that defines many border communities (see Sadowski-Smith 1–2) – reveals a concrete social context for political action and cultural production *and* a SUBJECT POSITION characterized by ethnic, linguistic, and sexual HYBRIDITY. It is in such contexts that we discover the conditions for what Manuel Rafael Mancillas calls "collaborative empowerment" and a "globalized grassroots consciousness ... manifested in transborder alliances, partnerships, and collaborations, which transform *rasquachi* bands of disenfranchised community artists and political activists from the lunatic fringe into major players in the struggle for survival and the production of power" (209, 213). The border is a space of pain and merger, of struggle and communication. As Gloria Anzaldúa writes in *Borderlands/La Frontera: The New Mestiza* (1987), "The US–Mexican border *es una herida abierta* where the Third World grates against the first and bleeds. And before a scab forms it hemorrhages again, the lifeblood of two worlds merging to form a third country – a border culture" (3). Anzaldúa, like so many other Chicano/a writers, opposes a MANICHAEAN "counterstance" that "locks one into a duel of oppressor and oppressed." It is not enough, she writes, "to stand on the opposite river bank, shouting questions, challenging patriarchal, white conventions" (78). Anzaldúa's focus on the conflicts between and within dominant, immigrant, and *mestizo* cultures implicitly takes Western feminism to task. "Life as feminists on the border," Sonia Saldívar-Hull explains, "means recognizing the urgency of dealing with the sexism and homophobia within our culture; our political reality demands that we confront institutionalized racism while we simultaneously struggle against economic exploitation" (34).

As Claudia Sadowski-Smith shows, twenty-first-century conditions of globalization have changed how we think about borders and focused our attention on the transnational spaces they constitute. Amid a "triadic regionalization of the world" (Europe, Asia, the US), free-trade pacts, and "border militarization," the coherence of border communities, which are not contingent on the nation-states whose limits constitute the borderland, suffers profound destabilization. In fact, Sadowski-Smith notes, integration between the United States and Mexico "is not primarily achieved in border locations," which are dominated by no-go zones controlled by drug cartels or free-trade industrial parks, known as *maquiladoras* (6–7). In this transnational framework, the border is not simply a fluid geographic space but a mode of temporal and spatial disjunction that avoids cultural disintegration through hybrid modes of self-identification. The authors she discusses cannot be considered "in terms of their regional or spatial affiliation because they have led lives that cross ethnic and national frontiers" and "engage in fascinating and complex strategies of self-identification that draw selectively on aspects of their own identities and experiences to articulate affinities with a particular group or sometimes with multiple communities" (13). The term "transborder," which has evolved in American studies to account for these "contact zones," can also be used to discuss the new issues arising in Europe in the wake of the abolition of internal borders, in the new nations of the former Soviet Union and Africa, where the newest nation (South Sudan) has arisen by drawing a new border. In this context, indigenous territories, for example the Navajo Nation and the Aboriginal *reserves*, institute an internal border insofar as they demarcate a line that can be crossed but cannot be moved or *removed*, a line that separates incommensurate societies. Mancillas describes this situation with a grimly comic analogy: "As a native of the Tijuana/San Isidro border region, I have become a master of transborder crossings, a *zopilote* [buzzard] who has wagged the tales of *la linea* [the border] and lived to tell you about it, perched unvacillating high on the fence" (203).

Native and Indigenous Studies

Continuities between Chicano/a studies and Native American studies are based on similar experiences of colonial power; both have had to undergo cultural and linguistic trauma that has destabilized and broken up communities but which also has provided the means to overcome colonial subjection and oppression. As Simon Ortiz writes, "the indigenous peoples of the Americas have taken the languages of the colonialists and used them for their own purposes. Some would argue that this means that Indian people have succumbed or become educated into a different linguistic system and have forgot or have been forced to forsake their native selves. This is simply not true." The truth, for Ortiz, lies in the oral tradition, which carries out resistance ("political, armed, spiritual"); and the continuance of the oral tradition "is evidence that the resistance is on-going," evidence, in short, of its "nationalistic character" (10). This oral tradition comes with a responsibility, for the Indian writer must "advocate for [the] people's self-government, sovereignty, and control of land and natural resources; and to look also at racism, political and economic oppression, sexism, supremacism, and the needless and wasteful exploitation of land and people" (12).

Ortiz insists that authenticity lies in the indigenous oral traditions, but at stake here is not so much the traditions themselves (which can be preserved inauthentically) as the means of securing their *transmission* through local knowledge, genealogies, stories, and anecdotes, in a social context that is free of the homogenizing and demythologizing discourse of a dominant culture. This is the underlying philosophy of the Red Power movement. According to Joane Nagel, urbanization after World War II produced the conditions for the "emergence of supratribal 'Indian' identity" and Red Power activism (118), which reached a peak with the occupation of Alcatraz Island by "Indians of All Tribes" in 1969 and the occupation of Wounded Knee in 1973 by the American Indian Movement (120ff). The Red Power movement, Nagel argues, "sparked American Indian ethnic renewal" and "galvanized native and non-native public attention." This resulted not only in a "surge in Indian self-identification" and a revival of native culture, but ultimately in a "reversal of federal Indian policy" (13).

Native and indigenous nationalism, therefore, is not an ideology of the state (it is patently anti-colonial) but rather continuity of traditions and stories that identify a people in relation to place conjoined with a struggle against an oppressive national power that disavows this continuity as a part of its own national consciousness. Ortiz's call for an authentic Indian nationalism has led to a greater awareness of the internal dynamics of native traditions and of how these traditions generate patterns of coherence and legibility that have not been noted by prevailing theoretical frameworks of the nation. Ironically, his concern for the oral tradition was answered with another call for authenticity, this one in the name of the modern "red power novel." According to Sean Kircummah Teuton, the "red power novel" deals with a form of decolonization "in which the interaction between the concepts of identity and experience drives a dynamic of political awakening and cultural recovery" (8). For Teuton, identity is not "a self-evident fact of birth." He follows M. Scott Momaday's "corrected vision of a tribal past, land, and self," which entails a knowledge of the national borders "where Indian–US colonial relations frequently present competing histories" (8). He thus issues a call to scholars "to respond to the political urgency in Native studies by historicizing their work, by 'hearing the callout' of subjugated Indians such as Native prisoners."

Sherene Razack has issued a similar call with respect to issues of racism and sexism in indigenous communities. "When the terrain is sexual violence," she avers, "racism and sexism intersect in particularly nasty ways to produce profound marginalization." Culture is for Razack "the framework used by white society to preempt both racism and sexism in a process [of] culturalization." The question is "how Aboriginal women [in Canada] and women of color might talk about the specificities of their cultural experiences" without losing those specific experiences within an idealizing or totalizing concept. This retention of specificity is essential if one is to see clearly the heterogeneous quality of categories like "Aboriginal women" and "women of color" (897). To acknowledge difference is often to acknowledge violence directed at otherness (race, sexuality, religion, ethnicity, disability, and so on), but too often political and intellectual discourse (both from the dominant culture and from native intellectuals) subsumes the particularities of native women's experiences of otherness under the general rubric of racial and ethnic difference.

Teuton's emphasis on decolonization and Razack's on Aboriginal women register the emergence in native and indigenous studies of theoretical models borrowed from postcolonial theory in order to describe social and cultural situations – e.g., the denial of social services, chronic unemployment, relocation of populations, and suppression of native traditions, languages, and cultural practices – in which domination takes on the characteristics of colonial oppression. For many theorists in Native American studies, the solution to these problems lies in a form of "cosmopolitan comparativism" committed to "cross-cultural translation" (Krupat ix–x). Building on the work of Gerald Vizenor, Vine Deloria, Jr., and others, Arnold Krupat outlines a Native American literary theory that goes beyond a nationalist perspective that frames the struggle for sovereignty within a context of "anticolonial nationalism." The most fruitful alternative to the imperial "world of nations and nationalisms" lies in a critical perspective grounded in "the animate and sentient earth" (11). Krupat's cosmopolitan perspective, which situates Native American literatures "in relation to other minority or subaltern literatures elsewhere in the late-colonial or postcolonial world" (19), echoes Kwame Appiah's notion of "cosmopolitan patriotism" (see *Ethics* 223ff), which can be defined as a condition of transportable rootedness. Krupat's Native American literary theory seeks to transcend the necessarily narrow limits of national and indigenous literatures in order to find a point of contact with other literatures elsewhere in the world. Its engagement with Western forms of theoretical reflection is more problematic, however, and has been criticized by Elvira Pulitano, whose quarrel with Krupat appears less a matter of his commitments to the West than of how he positions himself with respect to those commitments.

This critical repositioning can be accomplished by the European as well as the indigenous critic but it requires something like an ethnographic method, one that rejects a totalizing, Eurocentric perspective. Brill de Ramirez and Susan Berry describe this method as "intersubjective ethnography," which is "grounded within the people's tribal culture and values, and developed through meaningful interpersonal relations." This renovated form of ethnography permits the critic to convey "the promise of storytelling insights and wisdom and the fruits of conversively informed texts whose authenticity is evident and whose value will endure" (205). The dialogic and dynamic structure of this "conversive" text guarantees a form of authenticity that is less a property of the text itself than of the voices, including the critic-ethnographer, that constitute it. And as for the endurance of values, that is a function of readers who affirm them when they harmonize with their own experience. And this is why ethnic and indigenous literary traditions are at the center of these social and political issues (of identity, of community, of borders, of sovereignty), because in literature we can represent our ongoing and changing engagement with communal values.

The turn of the twenty-first century has witnessed a significant development in theoretical writings from within the native and indigenous communities, some strongly influenced by European ideas, some in resistance to them. The critique of Western philosophy, anthropology, and science was fundamental to the creation of indigenous forms of knowledge, which some theorists have called a *third space*. Vine Deloria, according to Kevin Bruyneel, was one of the first theorists to envision such a space. His vision "was that of tribes whose identity and expression of sovereignty transcend the boundaries of colonial time" and who are able "to secure and expand the location of indigenous people in postcolonial space, across the boundaries of colonial rule" (221). For Bruyneel, the idea of a *third space* offers an escape from the dualistic traps of colonial and racial discrimination and oppression, one that can also provide indigenous tools for navigating Native American literature and culture. The "third space of sovereignty" opens opportunities for resistance to "the American settler-state and nation"; it is a space in which "indigenous political actors speak against and across the boundaries of colonial rule by articulating and fighting for a third space: a space of sovereignty and/or citizenship that is inassimilable to the modern liberal democratic settler-state and nation" (217). Native American peoples were not often given the option of assimilating, since the US government preferred a policy of containment through treaties (often broken) and reservations. The third space, according to Bruyneel, is only "inassimilable" according to rigid dialectical or binary models of historical and interpersonal relations. He believes the third space concept can "positively reshape the language and therefore the terms of and possibilities for indigenous–settler–society relations" (217). The presupposition here, as in Chicano/a studies, is that such relations will take into account alternative histories that are grounded in memory and storytelling, ritual and mythology, and the contours of the land.

Asian American Studies

One of the most pressing issues in ethnic studies today (particularly in the United States) is immigration, and nowhere is this issue theorized with more urgency than in Asian American studies. This is in part due to a long and tempestuous history that began in the mid-nineteenth century with the arrival of Chinese laborers working on the railroads. Immigration continued through periods of quotas, restrictions, and outright bans by the time of World War II, only to increase again in the 1970s after the war in Vietnam. These experiences represent entirely different geographic coordinates for ethnicity (and thus of cultural authenticity) than what we find in Latino/a and native and indigenous experiences, although it should be said that Latino/a immigrant experience in the United States is fraught with some of the same difficulties and challenges that Asian Americans face. The differences are significant, however; first, Latino/a immigration might be considered "inter-American" migration, while Asian American immigration constitutes a cross-hemispheric movement. Second, the cultural imaginary concerning Asian ethnicity provokes feelings of uncertainty and fear about the "yellow peril" (Palumbo-Liu 35–48), along with a certain curiosity about "oriental" exoticism. Finally, Asian Americans are often confronted with the paradox of a set of prejudicial attitudes that derive from the very success of their assimilation into US culture.

The most compelling reason to focus on Asian American experience lies in the fact that it has come so strongly to stand as the *other* in the process of US national development. Since the mid-nineteenth century, according to Lisa Lowe, "the American *citizen* has been defined over against the Asian *immigrant*, legally, economically, and culturally" (4). In a classic Hegelian dialectical structure, the American becomes identified *as such* over against what she is not: Asian. Of course this dynamic was already in place with respect to the indigenous native peoples and to African slaves, but in both of these cases the *other* was simply *too much of an other*; thus the African slave, reduced to three-fifths of a human being, had no stake in the dialectics of identity, while native people were violently disavowed, slaughtered, or relegated to reservations where they too had no stake in this dialectical procedure (Latino/as have to some degree escaped this radically excessive othering). The fact that these unassimilated *others* would go on to do just what they were refused the right to do – contribute to the self-determination of the United States as a nation – is a classic example of the Freudian notion of the "return of the repressed." European immigrants were the privileged stock of pioneers and settlers whose social status was conferred precisely by their having been early arrivals; the Irish and Italians by the early twentieth century were beginning to achieve a similar kind of legitimacy within the mainstream. At precisely this time, Asian American difference came to stand for difference *as such* and, in the form of immigration and immigration policy, had a decisive impact on a vital period of US development after the Civil War. In other words, the Asian *as immigrant* was openly avowed as the *other* and allowed access to the dialectics of identity, albeit as the "negative term" that must be assimilated while retaining the brand of *having had* to assimilate. The distinction between American citizens and Asian immigrants cast the latter, in Lowe's view, "both as persons and populations to be integrated into the national political sphere and as the contradictory, confusing, unintelligible elements to be marginalized and returned to their alien origins" (4). The legislation limiting or banning immigration is a perverse corollary of this dialectical passage from alien to citizen.

As Lowe describes it, the "legal genealogy" of Asian immigration is a variety of racial formation, a "shifting construction of racial meanings formed in the dialectic between state categorization and social challenges to those categorizations, and the socio-historical process by which racial meanings are created, lived, and transformed" (21). Thus the hysterical affect associated with the "yellow peril" served the ends of a state whose primary concern was classifying, regulating, and containing "alien" populations. For the "discursive fixing of the Asian ... has historically been instantiated through the state's classification of racialized Asian immigrant identities." Because the Asian person presents to the "national consciousness ... a transgressive and corrupting 'foreignness,'" she continues to be "object of the law" (19). Classic definitions of individuality (e.g., *Bildung*) emphasize freedom and self-determination, but in the situation described by Lowe we find a form of radical *unfreedom* in which the Asian American serves a primarily negative function with respect to white America's sense of its own freedom.

The relation to the past and to a homeland that Lowe and others see as part of the immigrant experience is, in the Asian American context, complicated by "war, occupation, and displacement," which sever the past from *its* homeland and make of memory a process of "re-member[ing] the past in and through the fragmentation, loss, and dispersal that constitutes that past" (Lowe 29). Memory (and the whole arsenal of temporal figures that constitute the "backward glance") stands opposed to the historical imagination that triumphs over this loss, which is for the greater good of the nation-state. Connected to this temporality of memory is the larger temporality of transnational communication, return (to the old homeland and then back to the new), and generational change. The latter is particularly important because the immigrant experience is not the same as that of the children of immigrants or their grandchildren, who may have no inkling of the personal trauma caused by immigration. The nuances of ethnic identification are so important that Japanese has a series of words to denote stages of immigration: *Issei* (first generation, born in Japan), *Nisei* (second generation, at least one *Issei* parent), *Sansei* (born abroad, at least one *Nisei* parent), and *Yonsei* (born abroad, at least one *Sansei* parent). For Japanese immigrants and, in less systematic ways, for other immigrants, the experience of assimilation is a negotiation of multiple and conflicting traditions at finely calibrated distances, each stage of which offers a new temporality of generational difference in which the subject becomes, with each passing generation, more native to the United States. So it is always important to know what kind of ethnic mark is being made. The trauma of *passage*, both from a homeland to the United States and from first to subsequent generations of experience as an ethnic American (what is sometimes called a "hyphenated American"), is sustained by institutionalized racism that persists, long after an immigrant becomes a *citizen* and should no longer be cast as the alien *other*. In the Asian American case, more so than in other cases, this disjunction and contradiction, which emanates from the state like a fault line, is the effect of a dialectical procedure whereby the immigrant is *necessarily other and citizen*, simultaneously but asymmetrically, for the *other* identity is subsumed under and canceled by the *citizen* identity, a process that *reproduces* the *other* as citizen.

For Claudia Sadowski-Smith, the nation-state is not the best framework in which to grasp Asian American experience, especially when it has been persuasively indicated that identity is no longer fixed on it, or at least not in the same way as in the past. The sublimation of the self into the state, a process that is allegorized in the classic form of *Bildung*, can no longer account for the transgenerational shifts in the Asian American individual's attitude toward the United States or toward the homeland.

Sadowski-Smith sees "denationalization" as the outcome of the immigration experience that extends over generations, in which we see a turn away from identification with the nation toward an identification with new DIASPORIC subject positions (52f). Lowe notes the same shift and examines the "'cultural institutions' of subject formation," especially novels written in English, that help to keep identifications unitary and assimilationist (i.e., they narrate the subject's identification with the state) (see 161–2). The denationalization process suggests that in the immigrant experience a singular, monological conception of national identity (e.g., community-based) is an inadequate way to describe what is at bottom an experience of social and cultural hybridity. The contradiction between the cultural values of the *citizen* and the social and legal policies toward the *immigrant* creates the conditions for a literary resistance (what Fanon calls "fighting literature") that refuses to submit its imaginary procedures to the needs of dialectical closure. Precisely because of the "uneven material histories" of colonization and racism, Lowe contends, "the sites of minority or colonized literary production are at different distances from the canonical nationalist project of reconciling constituencies to idealized forms of community and subjectivity" (100). To escape the oppressive, stultifying effects of identification, which in the Asian American immigration experience entails a traumatic self-*othering*, one must convert "displacement, decolonization and disidentification" into counter-hegemonic tactics (for example, the novel in which "alternative 'histories'" can be written), for they are "crucial grounds for the emergence of Asian American critique" (104).

In recent years, David Palumbo-Liu has built on the dialectical critique offered by Lowe by focusing on the way Asian Americans persist in serving as the *other* to white America, but he has moved onto new ground when he explores the "tropology of the psychic," that rhetorical and imagistic archive that supplies the US imaginary when it comes to race and to immigrant identity. This tropology "posits in the Asian/American subject a particular set of mental and spiritual capabilities and weaknesses, dispositions, encumbrances, and values" (12). It also posits the subject as a *subject in transit*, "as a point of reference on the horizon that is part of *both* a 'minority' identity and a 'majority' identity. This constant transitivity evinces precisely the malleability and resistance of 'America' with regard to racial reformation" (5). Palumbo-Liu's description of how Asian America is conceived in the US imaginary involves a complex dialectic of ethnicity and location in which being and rhetoric, person and image coalesce:

> [W]hat has most deeply informed, and continues to inform, attitudes and actions toward Asians in America has been an image of Asia located not "in" Asia nor in the United States, but of shifting and often contradictory predications of "Asia" onto and into the US imaginary. These predications have been and continue to be caught up in a process of transition and transformation, drawing on images of a highly reified "traditional Asia," a vacillating often contradictory set of images of "American," and incipient forms of an Asian American ontology. (21)

Assimilation as a social practice, however, increases the stakes, for assimilating means altering the social and physical body. The "racialized body" marks the site both of production and consumption within a capitalist economy and of symbolic investments of the sort that constitute a racial discourse (see 81–2). Like so many other theorists, Palumbo-Liu is skeptical of the claim that we have overcome race or that race has become effaced in the gradual hybridization of humanity. This way of thinking ignores "the actual possibilities of socially sanctioned intermarriage" and of "a more enlightened, less racist America" (85). One of the reasons that race remains a persistent marker is that assimilation is always as much about the body as the mind, and the Asian body is a *resistant* body. "[I]f certain bodies *won't* change, or do so only recalcitrantly, then it is taken as an index to their resistance or inability to assimilate" (85). This is especially true, Palumbo-Liu argues, of the "distinctly racialized face" that explicitly images race but in way that forces our thought to what race has *displaced* (i.e., white America). In short, the Asian body, the Asian face, are symptoms of a contradiction vis-à-vis the racial *other*, "a vacillation between 'race-neutral' symmetry and the visibility of race produced by demographic 'asymmetry.'" This is graphically illustrated in computer-generated images of multicultural America, one of which was featured on the cover of *Time* magazine in 1993. These gimmicks are a symptom of a deeper problem, however. "The notion of following the illusory ideal form of otherness into an assimilated core of national identity, as transacted upon the facial contours and bodies of the Asian/American, finds similar articulation in the imaginative constructions of the Asian body in Asian American literary texts" (114–15). The transnational body takes its place in a politically charged environment that is defined by the "shock of misrecognition" that the other incites, for we encounter in her both the *immigrant* who comes from elsewhere and the *citizen* (or potential citizen) who is recognized by the state.

The richness and variety of ethnic and indigenous studies testifies to the struggle for self-determination both in the community and in the academy. The chief lessons that indigenous and immigrant artists and theorists teach us is that there are alternatives to the dialectical hegemony of the nation-state as well as to the "ethnic absolutism" and institutional isolation of the academy that is one of the pitfalls of ethnic studies (Sadowski-Smith 8–9). These alternatives can be seen throughout the US intellectual spectrum, particularly postcolonial studies and the emergent field of transnationalism, where the themes and issues discussed here take on quite different local, national, and international significance.

Note
See African American Studies. On historical trauma, see Trauma Studies. On the subject, see Critical Theory, Post-Marxist Theory, and Gender Studies. On environmental issues, see Posthumanism.

Works Cited

Alurista. "Cultural Nationalism and Xicano Literature During the Decade of 1965–1975." *MELUS* 8.2 (Summer 1981): 22–34.

Anzaldúa, Gloria. *Borderlands/La Frontera: The New Mestiza*. 1987. 2nd ed. San Francisco: Aunt Lute Books, 1999.

Appiah, Anthony. *The Ethics of Identity*. Princeton: Princeton University Press, 2005.

Bruyneel, Kevin. *The Third Space of Sovereignty: The Postcolonial Politics of U.S.–Indigenous Relations*. Minneapolis: University of Minnesota Press, 2007.

Du Bois, W. E. B. *The Souls of Black Folk*. New York: Vintage Books/Library of America, 1990.

Fanon, Frantz. *The Wretched of the Earth*. Trans. Constance Farrington. New York: Grove, 1963.

Krupat, Arnold. *Red Matters: Native American Studies*. Philadelphia: University of Pennsylvania Press, 2002.

Lowe, Lisa. *Immigrant Acts: On Asian American Cultural Politics*. Durham, NC: Duke University Press, 1996.

Mancillas, Manuel Rafael. "Transborder Collaboration: The Dynamics of Grassroots Globalization." In *Globalization on the Line: Culture, Capital, and Citizenship at US Borders*. Ed. Claudia Sadowski-Smith. New York: Palgrave, 2002. 201–20.

Nagel, Joane. *American Indian Ethnic Renewal: Red Power and the Resurgence of Identity and Culture*. New York: Oxford University Press, 1996.

Ortiz, Simon. "Towards a National Indian Literature: Cultural Authenticity in Nationalism." *MELUS* 8.2 (Summer 1981): 7–12.

Palumbo-Liu, David. *Asian/American: Historical Crossings of a Racial Frontier*. Stanford: Stanford University Press, 1999.

Paredes, Américo. *A Texas-Mexican Cancionero: Folksongs of the Lower Border*. 1976. Urbana: University of Illinois Press, 1995.

Ramirez, Brill de and Susan Berry. *Native American Life-History Narratives: Colonial and Postcolonial Navajo Ethnography*. Albuquerque: University of New Mexico Press, 2007.

Razack, Sherene. "What Is to Be Gained by Looking White People in the Eye? Culture, Race and Gender in Cases of Sexual Violence." *Signs* 19.4 (1994): 894–923.

Sadowski-Smith, Claudia. *Border Fictions: Globalization, Empire and Writing at the Boundaries of the United States*. Charlottesville: University of Virginia Press, 2008.

Saldívar, Ramón. *Chicano Narrative: The Dialectics of Difference*. Madison: University of Wisconsin Press, 1990.

Saldívar-Hull, Sonia. *Feminism on the Border: Chicana Gender Politics and Literature*. Berkeley: University of California Press, 2000.

Teuton, Sean Kircummah. *Red Land, Red Power: Grounding Knowledge in the American Indian Novel*. Durham, NC: Duke University Press, 2008.

Postcolonial Studies

Postcolonial studies is an interdisciplinary domain in which we can discern two very broad trends: on the one hand, we see a concentration on IMPERIALISM and COLONIALISM, while on the other hand, we see primarily accounts of postcolonial literature, culture, society, and politics. There is a historical progression at work here, with the foundational works in the field focusing on imperialism and colonial locations and later work, much of it emanating from new postcolonial states, laying stress on questions of nationalism, local literatures and languages, religion, and culture and social conditions. The prefix "*post-*" thus refers, in one sense, to a historical relation to and a period *after* colonialism. But there is also an entwinement of the two strands, since to speak of empire is to speak of socio-historical conditions that will provide the foundations, precarious as they may be, for postcolonial states, and to speak of such states is to speak always in terms of the imperialism and colonialism that had to have been overcome. Were we to press forward with this analysis we would find that the two strands are dialectically interdependent, which means that postcolonial studies is always, in some way, concerned with the idea of *colonialism*.

As many theorists have noted, the historical relation alone is insufficient to cover the meaning of the "*post-*" in postcolonial. Kwame Anthony Appiah has argued that the significance of the term *postcolonial* extends beyond the historical relation of colonialism to include other times, themes, and discourses. "All aspects of contemporary African cultural life," Appiah writes, "have been influenced, often powerfully, by the transition of African societies *through* colonialism, but they are not all in the relevant sense *post*colonial. For the *post-* in postcolonial, like the *post-* in postmodern, is the *post-* of the space-clearing gesture" (346). This gesture, with its echo of Heideggerian being emerging in a cleared space of withdrawal and unconcealment, is accomplished through the "construction and the marking of differences." Difference marks the simultaneous presence and absence of the African *other* in an institutional space that both invokes colonialism and celebrates the glories of a precolonial culture. Anne McClintock has noted that this curious dialectical erasure of difference is predicated on the retention, in the very term *postcolonial*, of "a single, binary opposition: colonial, postcolonial." More crucially, she argues, the "postcolonial scene occurs in an entranced suspension of history," delineated by a prefix (*post-*) that isolates the postcolonial from the "prestige of history proper." In this way, "the world's multitudinous cultures are marked, not positively by what distinguishes them but by a subordinate, retrospective relation to linear, European time" (10–11).

The point that Appian and McClintock drive home is that the "*post-*" is not so much a historical marker as an indication of a position *within* the colonial (or the modern) that is somehow inaccessible or unrealizable. Adapting **Jean-François Lyotard**'s description of the postmodern as "that which, in the modern, puts forward the unpresentable in presentation itself" (81), we might say that the postcolonial refers to the unpresentable condition of time (past and future) beyond colonialism that lies in wait within the "presentation" of the colonial. Thus, in a world of MANICHAEAN struggle and massive inequalities, the "unpresentable" aspects of race, indigenous knowledges, kinship and family structures, and linguistic difference disrupt the smooth surface of empire's self-presentation (i.e., its SELF-IDENTITY) through strategies of appropriation, MIMICRY, and HYBRIDITY. In this sense, the prefix (*post-*) retains its capacity as a historical marker but it also subverts that "marking" by suggesting an alternative temporality to the historical, namely, the temporality of the *ricorso* by which the colonial subtends the postcolonial and the postcolonial is already emergent in the colonial. The postcolonial presents itself – typically in uncanny and sublime forms – in the colonial epoch, especially during periods of DECOLONIZATION, when the contradictions of colonialism, exacerbated by anti-colonial resistance, make such presentations of the unpresentable legible.

As a strictly historical phenomenon, postcolonialism is a critical reflection on the history of conquest and colonization that spanned most of the habitable globe and that separated the world into imperial or METROPOLITAN centers and peripheral territories. European colonialism began with conquest and encounter, the confrontation of Europeans with the *other* (and of indigenous peoples with Europeans). Peter Hulme's *Colonial Encounters: Europe and the Native Caribbean, 1492–1797* (1986) was one of the first major studies to analyze the phenomenon of cultural contact from a postcolonial perspective. In order to recover the full discursive context of the "discovery" of America, Hulme explores the DISCOURSE FORMATION constituted by the letters, journals, ship log entries, and other documents associated with the voyages of Columbus, but he also includes the discourse of the Carib people, a discourse that was frequently misunderstood and, for that very reason, had a profound impact on European attitudes about "primitive" peoples. Early colonial efforts in the Americas, by England, Spain, Holland and Portugal, yielded great wealth, and by the late eighteenth century England emerged as the most powerful imperial nation, in part due to its ability to exploit "triangular trade," the movement from the slave markets in West Africa to the plantations in the United States and Caribbean and then to consumers (of cotton, molasses, rum, and other commodities) throughout the world. While the Caribbean was colonized on the plantation system using African and local indigenous slaves, the East India Company, which began trading in 1612 and ruled for 100 years from 1757, was a commercial venture; in 1858 the British Raj ruled until independence and partition in 1947. Imperial rule in Africa and the Arab lands was a late development. In the 1880s, Africa was formally divided up among the European powers, while the Arab lands were dominated by the British and French until after World War II.

As this brief sketch indicates, imperialism was a complex affair, one that mixed myriad state-sponsored and commercial enterprises in a way that is difficult to grasp as a TOTALITY. For John Darwin, imperialism "was not a structure of global hegemony, holding in thrall the non-Western world," save in a few particular times and places, but a world-system of almost unfathomable complexity:

> It embraced an extraordinary range of constitutional, diplomatic, political, commercial and cultural relationships. It contained colonies of rule (including the huge "sub-empire" of India), settlement colonies (mostly self-governing by the late nineteenth century), protectorates, condominia (like Gibraltar and Malta), "occupations" (like Egypt and Cyprus), treaty-ports and "concessions" (Shanghai was the most famous), "informal" colonies of commercial pre-eminence (like Argentina), "spheres of interference" … like Iran, Afghanistan and the Persian Gulf, and (not least) a rebellious province at home. (1)

By far the most important formations within this system were *crown*, *settler*, and *administrative* colonies. Crown colonies, such as those in America and Ireland, were governed directly by the English monarch through appointed governors. To some extent, Ireland presents us with an exceptional case, for the Anglo-Irish ruling class was often caught in the middle between a colonized Catholic population and the British colonizing power. Administrative colonies supervised exports (rubber, ivory, spices, and, until the early nineteenth century, slaves), participated in world markets, and guaranteed freedom of movement for religious missions and sociological and anthropological inquiry. Settler colonies were developed by the colonial powers to absorb "excess" populations from the home country. In some cases, as in Rhodesia and French Algeria, these new populations were working- and middle-class settlers seeking land and economic advancement that would otherwise be out of reach. In Australia and New Zealand, through the nineteenth century, the new populations were primarily impoverished Irish, Scottish, and English families and transported convicts, and their relations with the Aborigines were not unlike those between

Europeans and Native Americans. "Early relations between Aborigines and white settlers," Graham Huggan points out, "were characterized by the often extreme racial antagonism that is a staple of violent frontier societies, occasionally leavened by the type of moralizing Christian sentiment that permitted itself to express sympathy for the unfortunate natives without doubting for a moment that they belonged to an inferior, quite possibly a dying, race" (18).

Postcolonial studies, grasped as a critique of colonialism from the perspective of the colonized, began in the 1930s with the Négritude movement, which included French-speaking colonial writers and intellectuals from the Caribbean and French North Africa. Aimé Césaire, from Martinique, and Léopold Sédar Senghor, from Senegal, were among the key figures. Césaire states the case:

> I have a feeling that [Négritude] was somewhat of a collective creation.... It was really a resistance to the politics of assimilation.... We didn't know what Africa was. Europeans despised everything about Africa, and in France people spoke of a civilized world and a barbarian world. The barbarian world was Africa, and the civilized world was Europe. Therefore the best thing one could do with an African was to assimilate him: the ideal was to turn him into a Frenchman with black skin. (73)

The resistance to assimilation, which is clearly a resistance to racism, became one of the foundational principles of postcolonial studies. **Frantz Fanon**'s first major study, *Black Skin, White Masks* (1952), analyzes the ideal of "a Frenchman with black skin" and concludes that it is an *impossible* ideal because the black man can never achieve self-identity. When a black man "is among his own," he writes, "he will have no occasion, except in minor internal conflicts, to experience his being through others." The Hegelian dialectical relation to the other is "unattainable in a colonized and civilized society." ONTOLOGY, which we must admit at last has left "existence by the wayside," does not help us understand the black man. "For not only must the black man be black; he must be black in relation to the white man." The converse, Fanon notes, cannot be allowed. "The black man has no ontological resistance in the eyes of the white man." Even the black body is plunged into "an atmosphere of certain uncertainty." The frightening specter of the "Negro" is what the black man offers to the white world (111–13).

Fanon and Albert Memmi, the leading figures of the first generation of postcolonial theorists, introduced one of the most pressing questions to occupy postcolonial studies, that of the relation between colonizer and colonized. They wrote their most important works in the 1950s and early 1960s and were strongly influenced by the dialectical and materialist traditions of Hegel and Marx. Both were interested in understanding the social and personal costs of colonialism, specifically the devastating psychological damage perpetrated by the colonial system and the racism at its core. "Colonial racism," Memmi writes, "is built from three major ideological components: one, the gulf between the culture of the colonialist and the colonized; two, the exploitation of these differences for the benefit of the colonialist; three, the use of these supposed differences as standards of absolute fact" (71). Fanon's ideas about the nation, nationalism, and national consciousness have been especially influential. He rejected the Western conception of the nation as a "universal standpoint" that subsumes all particulars (i.e., individual human lives) in the fulfillment of its own abstract freedom. In this idealist view, rooted in Hegel, the nation is merely a stage in the development of the world spirit, a particular manifestation of the state coming into being.

> The nation to which is ascribed a moment of the Idea in the form of a natural principle is entrusted with giving complete effect to it in the advance of the self-developing self-consciousness of the world mind. This nation is dominant in world history during this one epoch, and it is only once that it can make its hour strike. In contrast with this its absolute right of being the vehicle of this present stage in the world mind's development, the minds of the other nations are without rights, and they, along with those whose hour has struck already, count no longer in world history. (217–18)

One way of reading this extraordinary passage is to see the legitimacy behind world-historical nations (i.e., those with imperial power and ambitions) as the transcendent Idea that "ascribes" a moment of itself to a favored nation as part of its overall plan of fulfillment. This same Idea oversees the inevitable fall of even the world-historical nation. Fanon, and other theorists of the colonial state, are confronted with a dilemma, for this transcendent standpoint (understood as a universal source of value and legitimation) is precisely what is required to inaugurate the *postcolonial* nation. The Hegelian dialectic needs to be itself confronted dialectically, which means that Fanon does not so much reject the universal standpoint as appropriate it for the people – in order "to make the nation in its totality a reality to every citizen" (*Wretched* 140).

In an era of decolonization and anti-colonial struggle, violence is the only way for the native to become "human" and to enter into history as something other than a mere slave: "at the very moment when they discover their humanity, they begin to sharpen their weapons to secure its victory" (Fanon, *Wretched* 8). In Fanon's revolutionary conception, violence is a means of attaining the goal of independence; it is thus a form of *continuance*, for the "people realize that life is an unending struggle" (51). "Fanonian 'continuance,'" **Homi Bhabha** writes, "is the temporality of the practice of action: its performativity or agency is constituted by its emphasis on the singularity of the 'local'; an iterative structuring of the historical event and political pedagogy[,] and an ethical sense constructed from truths that are partial, limited, unstable" ("Unsatisfied" 40). At the foundation of this political pedagogy is Fanon's call to change human beings by raising their standard of consciousness. Too often, though, this process is left incomplete and the colonizer is free to try to force concessions and to let loose "psychological windfalls," for the "colonized subject is … starved of anything that humanizes him, even if it is third rate" (*Wretched* 90). The struggle ends only with the formation of national consciousness. "The Nation is the precondition for culture," Fanon writes, and culture "is first and foremost the expression of the nation, its preferences, its taboos, and its models" (*Wretched* 77). This expression is not limited to the geographic boundaries of the nation. For Fanon "[n]ational consciousness, which is not nationalism, is alone capable of giving us an international dimension" (*Wretched* 179). This *nationalitarian* standpoint, according to Anouar Abdel-Malek, "has as its object, beyond the clearing of the national territory, the independence and sovereignty of the national state, uprooting in depth the positions of the ex-colonial power" (quoted in Lazarus 255).

Much of the ambivalence that critics note in Fanon's work, indeed in a good deal of postcolonial theory, can be attributed to the gap between the non-dialectical binomialism of colonial relations and the dialectical critique of those relations that issues from anti-colonial nationalism. Moreover, Fanon's dialectical procedure is complicated by its "constitutive Gramscian politicism and therefore its openness," as Ato Sekyi-Otu puts it. But more than being open, Fanon's dialectical critique appears to privilege non-identity (i.e., "the colonized subject in revolt") and to lead not to "the comedy of self-recognition and absolute knowledge" but rather to "the disclosure of yet more tangled manifestations of the problems of freedom and community." Sekyi-Otu frames the question in a way that places Fanon on the boundary between two theoretical positions: "Is it possible," he asks, "for a narrative to remain dialectical after renouncing its Hegelian antecedents, but without quite ending up with something like a Foucauldian genealogy resolutely abstentious of the discourse of the universal?" (29–30). The narrative referred to here is the "dialectical dramatic narrative" (5) of Fanon's texts, which exemplify a NEGATIVE DIALECTICS of colonialism written against the grain of a *positive* dialectics of empire.

If Fanon hews closer to Hegel in his negative dialectical critique, **Edward Said**, in *Orientalism* (1978), embraces Foucault's GENEALOGICAL method. Said is interested in the way in which the Orient had become conceptualized by Western scholars, historians, anthropologists, missionaries, literary writers, and artists. Over against the neoconservative, neo-imperialist thesis, advanced by Samuel Huntington and Bernard Lewis, that the East/West divide represented an irresolvable "clash of civilizations," Said maps the complex relations of POWER/KNOWLEDGE formed by philological and scholarly writing about the East. His goal is to "unlearn" "the inherent dominative mode" (28) of imperialism, the forms of "executive" knowledge that regulate and control "subject peoples." Orientalism circumscribes and delimits the East as an OTHER in relation to the West; it is thus a form of *Manichaeism*, which posits an absolute difference "between the familiar (Europe, the West, 'us') and the strange (the Orient, the East, 'them')" (43). Discourses about the East, like the massive Napoleonic *Description de l'Égypte*, bear no "natural" or MIMETIC relation to the geographic and social realities of Eastern nations. Said notes a distinction between *latent* Orientalism, what a traveler or a native might experience in a specific geographic space, and *manifest* Orientalism, the discourses produced by Western art and ideology. New knowledge gained by direct experience at the latent level (e.g., E. M. Forster traveling in India) flows into the manifest level in the form of a novel representing India, *Passage to India*. The parallel with Freudian dream-work suggests that Orientalist discourse represses a good deal more than it represents.

One thing it represses is the disparity between discourse and reality, particularly the gap between the stated goal of civilization and the actual goal of economic exploitation and strategic occupation. "To colonize meant at first the identification – indeed, the creation – of interests" (100). This is what the African philosopher V. Y. Mudimbe calls "epistemological ethnocentrism," which is "the belief that scientifically there is nothing to be learned from 'them' unless it is already 'ours' or comes from 'us'" (15). Said's argument confirms this, but also suggests that the internal (and perhaps constitutive) fracture of Orientalism consists in our discovering that what we think we know "scientifically" is really fantasy. Once this is sensed, well before it is known critically, disappointment, especially among artists, sets in; the Orient does not match up with Orientalism and the latter supersedes the former as an account of "reality." Moreover, Orientalist generalities were used in a widespread fashion that suggests scholars and writers were talking to each other rather than listening to natives of non-Western lands. The Orient is *watched* (by anthropological voyeurs) and its foreignness translated. Thus we find a rather complacent (i.e., uncritical) hermeneutical circle in which the Orient of the Orientalist is the Orient Orientalized. At a discursive level, the "scope of Orientalism exactly matched the scope of empire, and it was this absolute unanimity between the two that provoked the only crisis in the history of Western thought about and dealings with the Orient" (Said 104). The Foucauldian orientation of his thesis leads Said to treat key figures and ideas not as influences or causes on a line of succession but rather as developments, changes, ruptures within a more or less stable discourse formation that transmits dogma and received ideas from generation to generation and across disciplines, trickling down, finally, to "literary" and "popular" culture. In this way, Orientalism becomes a form of hegemony, a system of truths, almost "totally ethnocentric," that mixes "narrative description regularly ... with passages of rearticulated definition and judgment that disrupt the narrative" (204, 228).

Though widely read and well received, Said's *Orientalism* attracted criticism. Aijaz Ahmad, for example, took Said to task for his Nietzschean and Foucauldian anti-humanism, his unwillingness to critique the idea of "third world" authenticity, and his reluctance to include COUNTER-HEGEMONIC alternatives to Orientalist discourse. Mudimbe's analysis of the "invention of Africa" answers Ahmad's call for a perspective that emerges from the *inside* of colonialism. In the case of Africa, Mudimbe discerns "two very different discourse formations – the discovery of African art and the constitution of the object of African Studies, that is, the 'invention' of Africanism as a scientific discipline" (9). This discipline leads to a form of primitivism that casts the African native in the ethnographic "timeless present," subtracted from the historical totality rather than dialectically absorbed or negated within it. Mudimbe suggests as much when he notes that "the African is a negation of all human experience, or is at least an exemplary exception in terms of evolution" (71). One cannot help but read this remark ironically, for to be exempt from historical evolution is to be outside the currents of world history.

Homi Bhabha makes much the same point in his analysis of the negative dialectics of colonial MIMICRY, which signals both the polarization of dialectical relations and the opening up of an opportunity for the non-identity of the colonized to take on genuine historical agency. Mimicry is the outcome of an ambivalent colonial presence, "a disjunction produced within the act of enunciation as a specifically colonial articulation of those two disproportionate sites of colonial discourse and power: the colonial scene as the invention of historicity, mastery, mimesis or as the 'other scene' of *Entstellung*, displacement, fantasy, psychic defense, and an 'open' textuality" (*Location* 153). In such an open textuality, *negation* (the principal move in dialectics) is evaded in a tactical *negotiation* that multiplies the possibilities of discursive and performative resistance. "Colonial mimicry," Bhabha writes, "is the desire for a reformed, recognizable other, *as a subject of a difference that is almost the same but not quite.* Which is to say that the discourse of mimicry is constructed around *ambivalence"* (*Location* 86). Mimicry is terrifying for the colonizer, for it communicates the threat of the *other* mirroring back the colonizer's own exorbitant, decentered inhumanity – as we see happen in Conrad's *Heart of Darkness*, when Marlow recognizes the *other*'s humanity and thus sees himself in the *other*. For while the colonizer consigns the colonial subject to a space of otherness, dehumanizing and infantilizing her in the process, the colonizer's discriminatory gaze, returned in the form of a destabilizing mimicry, simultaneously undermines the colonial enterprise by revealing that it is constructed on the "blank spot" of a people and culture that must be violently disavowed. Mimicry, as "the sign of a double articulation," both regulates and "'appropriates' the Other as it visualizes power" and introduces indecorum, inappropriateness, and "recalcitrance" into the "strategic function" of the colonial state (*Location* 86). Mimicry poses such a danger to empire because it uncovers the lie of its civilizing mission and, as Ashis Nandy points out, leaves the colonizer "with the fear that the subjects might begin to see their rulers as morally and culturally inferior, and feed this information back to the rulers. Colonialism minus a civilizational mission is no colonialism at all. It handicaps the colonizer much more than it handicaps the colonized" (11).

Bhabha's *colonial mimicry* creates a new SUBJECT POSITION defined by HYBRIDITY. Myriad possibilities for hybrid identity formation spring from the very ethnic, racial, and religious differences that delimit and destabilize the "other scene" of colonial power. **Stuart Hall** has theorized one of these possibilities, DIASPORA, in terms of its ambivalent role in the formation of identity in the Caribbean. Cultural identity, he writes, is "as an enigma, as a problem, as an open question" (286):

> everybody [in the Caribbean] comes from somewhere else.... That is to say, their true cultures, the places they really come from, the traditions that really formed them, are somewhere else. The Caribbean is the first, the original and the purest diaspora.... [I]n the histories of the migration, forced or free, of peoples who now compose the populations of these societies, whose cultural traces are everywhere intermingled with one another, there is always the stamp of historical violence and rupture. (283–4)

African, European, Indian, Chinese, and indigenous peoples have been dispersed throughout a system of islands bound together primarily by colonial commerce, which had its roots in the slave trade. The ambivalent potential of hybrid identities raises the question of the colonial subject's agency, for it is unclear to what extent the subject is in control of his destiny within the colonial context, a problem that Aimé Césaire's *Une Tempête* (1969), a rewriting of Shakespeare's *The Tempest*, dramatically realizes. The question of agency is at the heart of **Gayatri Chakravorty Spivak's** "Can the Subaltern Speak?," which investigates the dynamics of a SUBALTERN subjectivity silenced by Western theory. She takes issue with "French intellectuals" who are "complicit in the persistent constitution of the Other as the Self's shadow," a complicity that aligns theory (particularly that of **Michel Foucault**) with the "EPISTEMIC violence" that orchestrated the "far-flung, and heterogeneous project to constitute the colonial subject as Other" ("Subaltern" 280–1). The theorist's task, she suggests, is perhaps "no more than to ask that the subtext of the palimpsestic narrative of imperialism be recognized as 'subjugated knowledge'" that is now

inadequate, "'insufficiently elaborated'" and "'beneath the required level of cognition or scientificity'" (281; Spivak quotes from Foucault's *Power/Knowledge*). Her
main point is that Western theory cannot ask the appropriate question, or lacks the
location from which to ask it. Poststructuralist such as Foucault and **Gilles Deleuze**,
for example, hide an "essentialist agenda" within a "post-representationalist vocabulary" (285). This theoretical perspective presumes the right to speak, the knowledge
of speaking, and the cultural position from which one might speak (the idea does not
arise that a non-Western woman might lack such a position). The critique of colonialism must clear a space for the pertinent question – "*can the subaltern speak?*" –
but, of course, such a space exists only *within* colonial discourse, as an "inaccessible
blankness circumscribed by an interpretable text," a "*text-inscribed* blankness"
("Subaltern" 293–4).

Spivak's analysis of power relations in colonial and postcolonial India reveals
dramatic and persistent gender inequalities. "Both as object of colonialist
historiography and as subject of insurgency, the ideological construction of gender
keeps the male dominant. If, in the context of colonial production, the subaltern has
no history and cannot speak, the subaltern as female is even more deeply in shadow"
(287). Her example of *sati* (widow sacrifice) illustrates the ways that imperialism
codified and redefined a native practice as a crime, transforming a realm of free
choice and power into one of juridical repression. Because the female subaltern
disappears into a violent shuttling between tradition and modernization, she cannot
speak. At best, she may possess what Anne McClintock, speaking of Fanon's
representation of Algerian women, calls a *designated agency* – "an agency by
invitation only" (365). This blindness to the question of female agency is paradoxically
a feature of Western feminism, which is bound by conceptual constraints that prevent
an accurate assessment of the material conditions of women's lives outside the West.
Chandra Talpade Mohanty makes the point that the "connection between women as
historical subjects and the representation of Woman produced by hegemonic
discourses is not a relation of direct identity or a relation of correspondence or
simple implication." Western feminists are in part responsible for perpetuating this
non-relation, because they "discursively colonize the material and historical
heterogeneities of the lives of women in the third world, thereby producing/
representing a composite, singular 'third-world woman' – an image that appears
arbitrarily constructed but nevertheless carries with it the authorizing signature of
Western humanist discourse" (19). Mohanty is especially critical of a methodological
universalism that "assumes an ahistorical, universal unity among women based on a
generalized notion of their subordination" (31). This kind of unity can only be
imagined if one accepts as real the abstract idea of the "'postcolonial Woman,'"
which Sara Suleri believes complicates the question of "the 'authenticity' of female
racial voices in the great game that claims to be the first narrative of what the
ethnically constructed woman is deemed to want" (758, 760). The problem with the
"radical subjectivity" promoted by Western feminism is that it "too frequently
translates into a low-grade romanticism that cannot recognize its discursive status as
pre- rather than *post-*": a kind of transcendentalism that "emanates from [a]
somewhat free-floating understanding of 'postcoloniality'" (761–2). What is required,
as postcolonial feminists have discovered, is a talent for negotiating transnational

and global institutions and systems, which is difficult in an epoch when the people benefiting the least from the new possibilities of globalization are, as Ania Loomba notes, "women from once-colonized countries or peoples" (230). An emphasis in postcolonial studies on local issues, politics, culture, and language has led to significant progress for postcolonial women, who have greater participation "in the full range of postcolonial politics … from the more established forms of political action to the new social movements." What Spivak called for appears to Loomba to be near to hand, the articulation of "both the specificity of women's issues and their profound inter-linkage with the community at large" (230–1).

As Partha Chatterjee points out, speaking of Indian nationalism, the "woman question" was not ignored in the interests of ideological concerns. On the contrary, "nationalism had in fact resolved 'the women's question' in complete accordance with its preferred goals" (154). Chatterjee sees these goals in terms of a dualistic cultural framework, the material and the spiritual. "The discourse of nationalism," he writes, "shows that the material/spiritual distinction was condensed into an analogous, but ideologically far more powerful, dichotomy: that between the outer [*bahir*, world] and the inner [*ghar*, home]" (155). This arrangement differs from traditional PATRIARCHY, primarily by virtue of "the colonial situation" that transforms these two spheres by failing to colonize one of them, the home, the "inner core of the national culture." The sphere of the world proper "was a place of oppression and daily humiliation … where the norms of the colonizer had perforce to be accepted," while home was the place "where the East was undominated, sovereign, master of its own fate" (156). This bifurcation of experience maps onto a binomial division of gender and sexual labor, with men involved in the world and women in the home. Though the historical conditions of each location will give to this gendered nationalism a specific character, it is not difficult to see something like a transnational pattern. As Loomba remarks, the "identification of women as national mothers stems from a wider association of nation with the family. The nation is cast as a home, its leaders and icons assume parental roles" (216). This model of family and the vocabulary it introduces into political discourse "translated easily to the colonial situation." The ambivalence of this rhetorical appropriation of gender rests in the way family and woman are both embraced as metaphors for sovereignty, nativity and spirituality but are also "cast as the antithesis of the nation" (217). The same can be said for the construction of masculinity in colonial contexts. As Revathi Krishnaswamy points out, masculinity is a "foundational notion of modernity" and the cornerstone "in the ideology of moral imperialism" that was modeled on an ideal that "combined a Greek aesthetics of the body with Roman militarism and medieval chivalry" (292). Opposed to this hegemony are the various forms of subordinated masculinity, typically associated with minorities within and foreigners outside of Europe. The effeminate colonized Indian man, like the colonized woman, threatens not only the edifice of colonial power but also the nationalist project. "Homosexual yet manly, heterosexual yet effeminate, Indian masculinity injects a fearful indeterminacy into the economy of colonial desire" (302).

Chatterjee and Krishnaswamy touch on an issue that constitutes the fault line between colonial power and anti-colonial resistance: the problematic status of the nation. Fanon's faith in national consciousness is difficult to uphold in the face of postcolonial crisis and transnational capitalism, in which the postcolonial state must find its place. If a "Third Space of enunciation ... destroys [the] mirror of representation in which cultural knowledge is customarily revealed as an integrated, open, expanding, code" (*Location* 37), then what are we to make of the fate of the postcolonial nation that is, in many ways, a mirror image of the imperial nation? Bhabha's own response is to posit a condition of "nation-time," a "disruptive temporality of enunciation [that] displaces the narrative of the Western nation" (142). The emergence of the "People," a national body, is a "complex rhetorical strategy of social reference" rather than a world-historical event as imagined by Hegel. This produces a "contested conceptual territory" and introduces a new temporality:

> [T]he nation's people must be thought in double-time; the people are the historical "objects" of a nationalist pedagogy, giving the discourse an authority that is based on the pre-given or constituted historical origin in the past; the people are also the "subjects" of a process of signification that must erase any prior or originary presence of the nation-people to demonstrate the prodigious, living principles of the people as contemporaneity: as the sign of the present through which national life is redeemed and iterated as a reproductive process. (145)

Bhabha's aim is to rethink the temporality of nationalism; to supplant the Manichaean structure of exploitation with new modes of interaction between the "continuist, accumulative temporality of the pedagogical, and the repetitive, recursive strategy of the performative" (145).

For Achille Mbembe, these temporal possibilities take the form of the *postcolony*, the spatio-temporal domain of a reterritorialized Africa, the aim of which is not "to denounce power as such," but to "rehabilitate" the idea of the *age*. Mbembe means by age "not a simple category of time but a number of relations and a configuration of events.... As an age, the postcolony encloses multiple *durées* made up of discontinuities, reversals, inertias, and swings that overlay one another, interpenetrate one another, and envelope one another: an *entanglement*." It is in the multiple temporalities of the postcolony that the African nation can establish itself and make possible "an autonomous African subject" (14). Benedict Anderson's theory of "imagined communities" similarly rethinks the temporality of the nation in terms of simultaneity and seriality, which in his view grounds national identity. Michael Hardt and **Antonio Negri** alert us to the dangers that arise when postcolonial nationalism of the sort Anderson describes reinscribes the very forms of "national sovereignty" that have driven the imperial world order (see Transnationalism 256–8). They hold that the great age of national sovereignty has passed, and that this passage has provoked a crisis in modern global capital. "Colonial sovereignty," they note, "is another insufficient attempt to resolve the crisis of modernity" – a crisis that they argue has been from the beginning bound up with "racial subordination and colonization" (114–15). Transnationalism is, in this new geopolitical context, an alternative to the imperial world view, with its conflicts and collusion among nations. So too are various "critical localisms" and "indigenous struggles" that erupt in response to global capital and the continued exploitation of the under- and undeveloped regions of the world. But such a response, warns Peter Hallward, "deliberately risks a dangerous coordination with transnational capital" (64). The condition of "glocalization" leads us beyond the limit of postcolonial studies. It is at this stage historically that we see arising new frameworks for understanding the postcolonial world, frameworks that include the entire assortment of national and post-national developments. Transnationalism, globalization, cosmopolitanism, world-systems theory – all of these approaches speak to a renovation in how we think about the postcolonial nation. For the "temporality of continuance" that Fanon recognized and promoted takes on new, more complex and interconnected significance under the heading *transnationalism*.

Works Cited

Appiah, Kwame Anthony. "Is the Post- in Postmodernism the Post- in Postcolonial?" *Critical Inquiry* 17.2 (1991): 336–57.

Bhabha, Homi. *The Location of Culture*. London and New York: Routledge, 1994.

Bhabha, Homi. "Unsatisfied: Notes on Vernacular Cosmopolitanism." In *Postcolonial Discourses: An Anthology*. Ed. Gregory Castle. Oxford: Blackwell, 2001. 38–52.

Chatterjee, Partha. "The Nationalist Resolution of the Women's Question." In *Postcolonial Discourses: An Anthology*. Ed. Gregory Castle. Oxford: Blackwell, 2001. 151–66.

Darwin, John. *The Empire Project: The Rise and Fall of the British World-System, 1830–1970.* Cambridge: Cambridge University Press, 2011.

Fanon, Frantz. *Black Skin, White Masks*. Trans. Charles Lam Markmann. New York: Grove Press, 1982.

Fanon, Frantz. *The Wretched of the Earth*. Trans. Constance Farrington. New York: Grove Weidenfeld, 1963.

Hall, Stuart. "Negotiating Caribbean Identities." In *Postcolonial Discourses: An Anthology*. Ed. Gregory Castle. Oxford: Blackwell, 2001. 280–92.

Hallward, Peter. *Absolutely Postcolonial: Writing Between the Singular and the Specific*. Manchester and New York: Manchester University Press, 2001.

Hardt, Michael and Antonio Negri. *Empire*. Cambridge, MA and London: Harvard University Press, 2000.

Hegel, G. W. F. *The Philosophy of Right*. Trans. T. M. Knox. Oxford: Oxford University Press, 1975.

Huggan, Graham. *Australian Literature: Postcolonialism, Racism, Transnationalism*. Oxford: Oxford University Press, 2007.

Krishnaswamy, Revathi. *Effeminism: The Economy of Colonial Desire*. Ann Arbor: University of Michigan Press, 1998.

Lazarus, Neil. *The Postcolonial Unconscious*. Cambridge: Cambridge University Press, 2011.

Loomba, Ania. *Colonialism/Postcolonialism*. 1998. 2nd ed. London: Routledge, 2002.

Lyotard, Jean-François. *Postmodern Fables*. Trans. Georges Van Den Abbeele. Minneapolis: University of Minnesota Press, 1997.

Mbembe, J.-Achille. *On the Postcolony*. Berkeley: University of California Press, 2001.

McClintock, Anne. *Imperial Leather: Race, Gender, and Sexuality in the Colonial Conquest*. New York: Routledge, 1995.

Memmi, Albert. *The Colonizer and the Colonized*. Trans. Howard Greenfeld. New York: Orion, 1965.

Mohanty, Chandra Talpade. *Feminism without Borders: Decolonizing Theory, Practicing Solidarity*. Durham, NC: Duke University Press, 2003.

Mudimbe, V. Y. *The Invention of Africa: Gnosis, Philosophy and the Order of Knowledge.* Bloomington: Indiana University Press, 1988.

Nandy, Ashis. *The Intimate Enemy: Loss and Recovery of Self under Colonialism.* Delhi and New York: Oxford University Press, 1988.

Said, Edward W. *Orientalism.* London: Penguin, 1985.

Sekyi-Otu, Ato. *Fanon's Dialectic of Experience.* Cambridge, MA: Harvard University Press, 1996.

Spivak, Gayatri Chakravorty. "Can the Subaltern Speak?" In *Marxism and the Interpretation of Culture.* Ed. Cary Nelson and Lawrence Grossberg. Urbana: University of Illinois Press, 1988. 271–313.

Suleri, Sara. "Woman Skin Deep: Feminism and the Postcolonial Condition." *Critical Inquiry* 18.4 (Summer 1992): 756–69.

Transnationalism

Transnationalism is a field of recent vintage that, taken broadly, encompasses nearly every academic discipline in the humanities and social sciences and takes in as well business, economics, finance, political science, international relations, and diplomacy. The general premise of transnationalism is that the nation-state and the IDEOLOGY of nationalism, particularly in their modern forms (i.e., from the 1780s), no longer adequately explain social, cultural, and geographic realities. The Hegelian model of the nation, in which the individual is dialectically identified with (by being subsumed conceptually under) the idea of the nation, sustained the great period of national development in the nineteenth and twentieth centuries. The nation, in Hegel's view, is a manifestation in the world of a phase or stage of the "world mind," a term that for Hegel signified the movement not only of the absolute Idea but also of history. The nation is not a permanent ideal existence (like the idea of the state), but rather an embodiment of a moment in its passage toward self-fulfillment. The individual reflects this, in being a particularity that embodies a moment of passage to self-consciousness. "Pursuant to the moment of particularity of the will, it has in addition a content consisting of determinate aims and, as exclusive individuality, it has this content at the same time as an external world directly confronting it" (*Right* 39). These aims are associated with individual desire (in its particularity) that confronts dialectically a world in which it will be fulfilled or inhibited. Hegel compares the individual to the nation in just this ability to achieve SELF-IDENTITY (or "personality") in the midst of (as the result of) a confrontation with particularity. "Individuals and nations have no personality until they have achieved this pure thought and knowledge of themselves" (*Right* 39).

This vision of the nation is ratified by numerous nation-building projects in Europe and the Americas, as well as in theoretical explanations of the particularities of the transition or passage of a people to a "National Spirit belonging to Universal History": "In order that a truly universal interest may arise, the Spirit of a People must advance to the adoption of some new purpose; but whence can this new purpose originate?" Hegel's answer is that this purpose comes from a higher conception of itself, "a transcending of its principle" which entails the emergence of a new principle and a "new order, a new National Spirit" (*History* 75). This idea of the nation-state as a spiritual individual (see *History* 73–6) is meant to underscore the fact that it is an "ethical idea or ethical spirit." The "supreme duty" of the individual is to be a "member of the state." And while the idea of the state may not be concerned with "the historical origin of the state in general" or with "the origin of any particular state" (*Right* 156), its actualization in the nation-building process brings the ideal into contact with the particularity that it dialectically negates and subsumes. Most theories of the nation and nationalism since the late nineteenth century try to describe the relation between individuals and the state (i.e., the Ideal that takes form as a nation) and thereby define the particular dynamics of nationalism.

In the West, the crisis of nationalism coincides with the breakdown of empire and the rise of new postcolonial nations. The latter brought to light the contradictions that beset the former precisely by virtue of its imperial ambitions, which were driven by capitalist expansion and the principle of self-identity in which the colonial *other* served as the SUBLATED negative term. "Nationalism is a theory of political legitimacy," writes Ernest Gellner, "which requires that ethnic boundaries should not cut across political ones, and, in particular, that ethnic boundaries within a given state – a contingency already formally excluded by the principle in its general formulation – should not separate the power-holders from the rest." Gellner notes that the "nationalist principle" can be asserted in universal ethical terms but that it is not always "so sweetly reasonable, nor so rationally symmetrical" as such universal terms aspire to be (1–2). Postcolonial nationalism and the phenomenon of transnational development underscore the failure of the "national Spirit" once the colonial *other* refuses dialectical closure and embraces non-identity in opposition to the West. Steadily through the last half of the twentieth century, anti-colonial struggles and radical politics in the West gave way to a new imperial order driven by a new form of sovereignty that was not beholden to that of the old imperial nation. The old global order, which sustained nationalism in inter-state antagonism and alliances, gave way to a new world-system, an empire of information, population, and cultural flows, complex and interconnected financial systems, and new forms of transnational capitalist production (see Wallerstein and Appadurai). In this context, as Sanjay Krishnan argues, the *global* "does not point to the world as such but at the conditions and effects attendant upon institutionally validated modes of making legible within a single frame the diverse terrains and peoples of the world" (41). A transnational critique entails a focus both on the nation as a residual SOCIAL FORMATION in the midst of a new global one and on alternative models for global relations of power, for example, regional affiliations and models of identity on the order of "Caribbeanness" (Edouard Glissant's *antillanité*) (see Hitchcock, *Imaginary States* 27–33).

The Marxist critique of globalization, which motivates a good deal of discourse on transnationalism, emerges out of history, political science, and economics. "The major paradigm of transnationalism," writes Peter Hitchcock, "has not been provided by culture, but by economics – how, then, can transnationalizing culture avoid, or indeed challenge, a form of economic worldliness that currently gives to global capital its hegemonic stature?" Hitchcock's concern is that the "arbiters of cultural transnationalism" may well be among those political and "worldly" figures (politicians and the wealthy, the "one percent") that influence transnational relations. Criticism and theory need therefore to take care that the idea of the transnational retain its potential for openness and innovation, that it not be appropriated by elites as a strategy of containment. Hitchcock sees the "transnational imperative" as a "resource of hope ... not something to be either feared or suppressed but rather something to be approached as a condition of possibility in the analysis of global difference" (*Imaginary* 4–5). On this view, transnationalism is a critical mode of postnationalism and is related conceptually to other fields of study (e.g., transborder studies, globalization, cosmopolitanism) that take borders and their crossing as a central PROBLEMATIC, and that query the institutions that seek to legitimize these borders and regulate or prevent those who wish to cross (or erase) them. The transnational subject sees borders not as constraints but as invitations to cross over, to explore the new spaces and temporalities that such crossings open up.

Transnationalism also names the contested relation of the postcolonial nation to the world-system as a whole and to the "sovereignty of the nation-state" in particular. It is a mode of critique that seeks to "de-naturalize" the concept of the nation. "[W]hat is a nation," Michael Hardt and **Antonio Negri** ask, "and how is it made, but also, what is a people and how is it made? Although 'the people' is posed as the originary basis of the nation, *the modern conception of the people is in fact a product of the nation-state*, and survives only within its specific ideological context" (102). The problem arises when the nation-state model no longer serves adequately to organize existing social relations. This dynamic, by which the nation is reinscribed in the postcolonial state is exemplified in Benedict Anderson's theory of the nation as an "imagined community," held together by communal cultural practices (e.g., newspapers, novels). Nationalism so understood creates new forms of disjunctive temporality in which simultaneous and serial cultural developments displace the "homogeneous, empty time" that **Walter Benjamin** associates with traditional progressive views of history. Anderson's imagined community is a form of "cosmopolitan-local" that is expressed in forms of serialization (e.g., newspapers are an "unbound" serial, the census "bound"), which he argues are basic "to the modern imagining of collectivity" (*Spectre* 40). "Transnational culture" and "transnational space" are the terrain of open or unbounded seriality, whose formal logic "pins time to the space and place of postcolonial narration" (Hitchcock, *Long Space* 42). New narratives of identity are required to articulate this "long space" of postcolonial narration. Anderson, for his part, follows Hegel in seeing "modern persons" as analogous to nations in terms of development. "Awareness of being embedded in secular, serial time, with all its implications of continuity, yet of 'forgetting' the experience of this continuity ... engenders the need for a narrative of 'identity'" (*Imagined* 205). Yet, as Hardt and Negri have argued, Anderson's theory of the imagined community is constrained by the very idea of the nation it seeks to transform, for "*the nation becomes the only way to imagine community*. Every imagination of a community becomes overcoded as a nation and hence our conception of community is severely impoverished" (107).

Richard Kearney has attempted to theorize a *postnationalism* that avoids this complicity with the Hegelian model of the nation-state. Speaking of Ireland, Kearney describes postnationalism as a rupture of certain kinds of relation, for example, the mirror relation of Britain and Ireland – the "Siamese Twins" of nationalism (10) – or the competitive relations that lead to devastating "total warfare." This does not require the absolute repudiation of the nation, however, for the transition "from traditional nationalism to a postnationalism" should preserve "what is valuable in the respective cultural memories of nationalism (Irish and British) while superseding them. Postnationalism is not Pol-Potism. It does not solicit a liquidation of the past but its reinterpretation or *Aufhebung* [sublation]" (47). Kearney's patently dialectical theory depends on a kind of transformation, not one that merely annihilates the national past as an aspirational ideal (as if that were possible), but rather one that amounts to a reinterpretation that is also a negation or suppression of the past (i.e., the process of *aufheben*) that allows it to reemerge, in the new interpretation, at a "higher" or more conscious level. The national past is thereby subordinated to the postnational present that subsequently raises it up as a standard, an icon, or a lesson (perhaps all three).

If Kearney's *post*nationalism seeks to remain within a dialectical tradition, a *trans*national perspective is part of a NEGATIVE DIALECTICAL critique (as in the work of David Lloyd and Pheng Cheah) by which a new model emerges that acknowledges and even champions the "negative" element without sublating it (which is the outcome of the Hegelian dialectical process). These theorists seek to open a negative space for a variety of subject positions – the *non-modern*, the "recalcitrant" *other* (unemployed, immigrants, minorities, and so on) – not in order to make them equivalent to the dominant social class but in order to show how non-identity functions within a larger social framework without suffering the trauma of dialectical cancellation. As Lloyd argues, "if the nationalisms with which we are in solidarity are to be emancipatory, rather than fixed in the repressive apparatuses of state formations, it is their conjunctural relation to other social movements [e.g., trade unions and women's rights groups] that needs to be emphasized and furthered, at both theoretical and practical levels" (36). For both Lloyd and Cheah, the nation remains a powerful *negative* presence in transnationalism. "[I]f nationalism as a mode of consciousness and the nation-state as an institution are both undesirable and outmoded," Cheah wonders, "it is not entirely clear what the alternatives are and whether these alternatives actually exist or are capable of being realized" ("Introduction" 21). Cheah's *Spectral Nationality* (2003) critiques the Hegelian concept of national *Bildung* that preserves the classical ideal of harmonious integration of self and national body, and attempts to theorize the non-identity of what has been excluded. In his view, the national body is haunted by recalcitrant elements that fail to constitute the nation (through sublation) and that take on a spectral form outside of it, "a defective form of mediation that does not return to and augment the nation's proper body," which brings into prominence the residual form of the nation even as the effective political form of it now longer seems tenable (*Spectral* 246).

From the transnational perspective, postcolonial nations (by far the majority of "postnations") enter into relations and form alliances across a vast, increasingly interconnected and technologically complex global environment, which tests the limits and resilience of the idea of the nation and of nationalism. **Frantz Fanon** had tried to retain the notion of "national consciousness" in an international dimension (see 179), which **Homi Bhabha** calls "a temporality of continuance" ("Unsatisfied" 40). According to Bhabha, Fanon "introduces a *temporal* dimension into the discourse of decolonization," which "suggests that the *future* of the decolonized world ... is imaginable, or achievable, only in the process of resisting the peremptory and polarizing choices that the superpowers impose on their 'client' states" ("Forward" xiv). The "temporality of continuance" is therefore a transnational development that produces the temporality of the "in-between": "The boundary that marks the nation's selfhood interrupts the self-generating time of national production and disrupts the signification of the people as homogeneous" (*Location* 148). The "disjunctive temporality of the nation" makes possible a break from repressive history, in part by allowing for the multiple temporalities *in time* and *in-between* times that make possible *performative* investments in national identity. A temporality of continuance links the transnational condition to the national one in the form of a residual framework in which disjunctive and PERFORMATIVE modes of identity-formation can emerge.

The critique of nationalism in the late twentieth and twenty-first centuries has led to a disenchantment with national consciousness. Hardt and Negri, for example, believe that postcolonial theorists like Bhabha too often fail to appreciate that colonial structures of power persist in the postcolonial world. "The only form of domination Bhabha recognizes," they assert, "is that of modern [i.e., national] sovereignty" (145). Truly to embrace disjunctive temporalities would mean to recognize the breakdown of national coherence and interrelation in a world governed by global flows of power, knowledge, money, signs, and people. New conceptions of history (e.g., world-systems theory) and new modes of recursive, serial, and simultaneous temporalities incorporate micro-dialectics as part of a larger project (e.g., Foucauldian GENEALOGY, post-Marxist critique). Theories of transnationalism must account for a new transient internationalism of migrants, refugees, exiles, émigrés, and stateless peoples like the Palestinians and the Kurds. Some theorists remain optimistic about the *nation* in the transnational condition; for example, Hitchcock, following **M. M. Bakhtin**, envisions a "responsible interdetermination" that grounds the "answerability to the nation" and the "*trans* in the *transnational*" (*Long Space* 92). But the rise of free-floating, stateless collectivities and networks of terrorist groups whose members are often marginalized or excluded by their own nations suggests an *irresponsibility* that refuses even to hear the questions raised by the people, often urgently and violently. This is the message of the "Arab spring," which began in December 2010 and went horribly wrong in the devastation of Syria during the uprising against the regime of Bashar al-Assad. These seismic events are teaching us that transnationality is by its very nature subject to contradictions and upheavals the destabilizing effects of which introduce transience and displacement as a quasi-permanent state. A state of emergency characterizes a residual national sovereignty.

Transnationalism thus produces a double-edged consequence: on the one hand, new models of mobility and transnational connectivity emerge out of the new population flows that are legible in a variety of ways (e.g., Foucauldian biopower, post-Marxism, world-systems theory); on the other hand, these same flows destabilize inter-state infrastructures that are not designed to handle them. Refugee crises, for example, have become an unpredictable but permanent feature of transnational relations, which, unlike the national struggles in the past over territory or regional influence, cannot be localized and contained in dialectical terms. These continuous, overlapping, and factionalizing conflicts (e.g., in Latin America, the Eurozone, the

Middle East) are part of the transnational condition, in the sense of the nation going beyond itself, going to its farther side (as Sudan goes across itself to become Sudan and South Sudan). They also remind us of the transitivity of contemporary immigration and migration, the easy travel that allows the traversal of continents. It is indicative of the transnational perspective that the behaviors and attitudes suggested by phrases like "globe-trotting" and "jet set" now describe the global norm for anyone who can afford an airline ticket.

Some theorists, like Arjun Appadurai, speak of a transnational DIASPORA that links people and communities across discrete regions (e.g., the Caribbean, Europe, North America, and so on) throughout the global grid in ways that stop short of a pure dispersion of elements, for the idea of the nation remains as a kind of spectre that haunts the postnational future. Diaspora is the result of a "disjunctive relationship between nation and state": "while nations (or more properly groups with ideas about nationhood) seek to capture or co-opt states and state power, states simultaneously seek to capture and monopolize ideas about nationhood" (39). Following postcolonial critics like Partha Chatterjee and Ashis Nandy, Appadurai argues that "this disjunctive relationship is deeply entangled" with the nation-state ideal:

> Ideas of nationhood appear to be steadily increasing in scale and regularly crossing existing state boundaries, sometimes, as with the Kurds, because previous identities stretched across vast national spaces or as with the Tamils in Sri Lanka, the dormant threads of a transnational diaspora have been activated to ignite the micropolitics of a nation-state. (40)

This "activation" is made possible by a globalization process that provides, according to Peter Mandaville and Terrence Lyons, "openings for new actors and issues to rise to prominence and for novel forms of political action to gain salience." Like theorists of cosmopolitanism, they believe that new political processes and massive changes in communications and mobility have transposed the model of diaspora to a transnational formation outside the framework of postcolonial migrations and immigrations. They speak of new "diasporas in politics, where accelerating and expanding patterns of human mobility have resulted in significant populations that identify with a particular community" in the absence of a mutual "homeland" (2–3). The same can be said of economic exchange, as Alex Callinicos points out, for globalization means a transformation in capital production and an intensification of the "cross-border integration of production and markets" (64). As in the study of immigrant cultures, the nation emerges as a space of *transit* and *traversal*; not a point of origin but a space across which one travels. It is transnational passage, not the national past, that counts.

The phenomenon of the transnational is both an erasure and an elaboration of the border: on the one hand, the European Union (EU), for example, creates a transnational entity that eliminates borders; on the other hand, the persistence of these borders is reinforced at times of global economic crisis (as in 2011–12, when Ireland, Italy, Greece, and Spain threatened the stability of the Eurozone). The same double stroke of erasure and reinforcement, over a much longer period of time, played out in Yugoslavia, in which borders were erased, only to reassert themselves in the period after Tito's fall (the irony here is that the borders that reasserted themselves as authentic were constructed largely as a result of diplomacy and foreign occupation). Indeed, as a state of permanent crisis, the transnational marks the passage of a new form of empire that Hardt and Negri call "imperial sovereignty." The world is a total zone of conflict:

> Antagonisms to exploitation are articulated across the global networks of production and determine crises on each and every node. Crisis is coextensive with the postmodern totality of capitalist production; it is proper to imperial control. In this respect, the decline and fall of Empire is defined not as a diachronic movement but as a synchronic reality. (385)

This shift from a DIACHRONIC to a SYNCHRONIC temporality (the latter is the experience of disjunctive and recursive timeframes, the former "homogeneous, empty time") marks the transnational and a new vision of empire as a *passage*, a tectonic transition from national to imperial sovereignty. In a sense, we could (or should) reread postcolonial theory as a mode of the transnational, of a global system in which the *idea* of the nation is no longer the polestar of theoretical reflection.

This condition of being *in transit* with respect to nations, communities, cities, and villages, of being territorialized by borders and boundaries, has informed policy on everything from immigration to agricultural production to economic planning to politics and business. In a paradox that continues in the twenty-first century, we find a global world of economic and cultural production subtended by fierce articulations, critical and reactionary, of local interests and national requirements. Multiple micropolitical interactions – coupled with global capital markets that reach into every remote village and corporations that have obscure and multiple "centers" of operations – bind national sovereignty to CONSTELLATIONS of power and knowledge that seek to maintain that sovereignty, however diseased and dysfunctional, for purely strategic reasons. Thus the crisis of the Eurozone was largely a breakdown at the *national* level, where economic failure threatened the strategic *transnational* goals of the European Union.

The globalized space of transnationalism is in part an effect of multiple technological innovations that have made the exchange of information (as a commodity) almost instantaneous, while the exchange of other sorts of commodities is transformed from the transfer of goods made under the aegis of the nation to the disarticulated production of parts and components that are rearticulated elsewhere in a secondary production level and are exchanged on a global market. Global capitalism produces a transnational marketplace, in which a multitude of stakeholders thrive. The massive technological breakthroughs in communications and commodity production and marketing have created a sense of "globality" both quantitatively and qualitatively different from what we have seen historically in other forms of global totality. It is a world with an economy so interconnected that a seemingly isolated crisis in one hemisphere can have devastating effects on the other. Partly these effects are the result of investment patterns among multinational corporations and sovereign funds that link global financial technologies to a web of national and corporate entities whose value on the market registers the social and political conditions at any given moment. The economic crisis of 2008, still going at the time I write this in 2012 – which some call the Great Recession – is "great" for the same reasons the Great Depression was "great": it crossed national boundaries. What makes the Great Recession so different is the extensive penetration of crisis conditions globally. Indeed, one might argue from a transnational perspective that this event has served both to extend the prerogatives of global capital and to reassert, in surprising and sometimes violent, retrogressive ways, the very borders that transnationalism foundationally calls into question.

This consciousness of borders and boundaries (or, as is often the case, their removal) creates unique social subjectivities, with investments in residual and still socially effective indigenous strata of knowledge, traditions, and practices. Spaces formed by transnational and transborder crossings do not respond to dialectical treatments that fail to factor in these investments as *positivities* on their own terms and that persist in trying to assimilate them through negation. In multicultural societies like the United Kingdom and the United States, this refusal to assimilate is *the transgression of the idea of the nation* (the particularized and contingent form of the ideal state), a transgression that is, paradoxically, a precondition for local communities and micro-political projects. In both cases, we see the rise of a multicultural state consisting of "multitudes" (to use Hardt and Negri's term), each formed by geographic movement, by settlement, by emigration and exile, by internal migration and internment, and each is the expression of a different historical emergence. The United States and the United Kingdom, as global entities, are thus multitudes of particular historical moments of emergence. The kinds of subjectivities created by immigration, conquest, and the slave trade are now residual with respect to our contemporary moment that urges upon us the consideration of new *transnational* subjectivities grounded in transience and travel, on sojourning and exile, and that bear the imprimatur(s) of the nation only as a kind of legal requirement, a marker (e.g., a passport) for a being in transit. (On immigration, see Ethnic and Indigenous Studies 237–41.)

If transnational relations are native to a globalized world, MULTICULTURALISM arises as the chief characteristic of global societies, in which people may live for generations but still carry with them the flavor (or burden) of exile, migrancy, sojourning, all of which have served as tropes for the condition of postcolonial and transnational subjectivity. Multiculturalism refers both to a state ideology (as in the UK and, in some respects, the US) regarding race, immigration, and related issues and to a transnational condition defined by patterns of immigration, travel, diplomacy, warfare, and population displacements that spring from the near-total globalization of capitalism. NEOCOLONIALISM (the persistence of colonial relations in postcolonial contexts) has played a powerful role in the multicultural character of European nations (e.g., England, Germany, France), particularly after the Maastricht treaty and the formation of the European Union in 1992, which facilitated inter-European migration.

Multiculturalism and transnational population flows have created the conditions of a new kind of cosmopolitanism that modifies significantly the conventional model. "The international sphere," writes Nels Pearson, "can no longer be imagined as an undifferentiated, homogeneous space of common humanity, as in Enlightenment ideals of cosmopolitanism" (644). In fact, what we find increasingly since at least

1990, with the decisive end to the politics of the Cold War, is a new framework for cosmopolitanism. The idea of universal humanity, as theorized by German idealist philosophy in the late eighteenth century, presupposes an ideal of the cosmopolitan, a citizen of the world (Gr. *kosmopolites*). For Immanuel Kant, the "law-governed organization of society" requires the universal administration of justice (i.e., *recht*, right, law); but this *civil* goal is dependent on "the problem of a law-governed external relation between states" (6, 9). Kant posits a "civil commonwealth" in which the historical "law of equilibrium" yields a new mode of social being. "A cosmopolitan condition of public security is thus introduced, which is not completely free of *danger*, so that humankind's powers do not fall into slumber, but also not without a principle of the *equality* of their mutual *actions and reactions*, so that they do not destroy one another" (11–12). This UNIVERSAL notion of cosmopolitanism, which sustained the long development of national sovereignty and imperialism, is no longer effective in organizing the multitudinous particularities that characterize a transnational world-system. Bruce Robbins sums up the importance of new cosmopolitanisms in a globalized world. "[M]any voices now insist ... that the term should be extended to transnational experiences that are particular rather than universal and that are unprivileged – often coerced" ("Introduction" 1). This statement anchors *Cosmopolitics*, a volume Robbins co-edited (with Pheng Cheah), whose contributors, according to Cheah, are interested in exploring "the feasibility of cosmopolitanism as an alternative to nationalism in our contemporary era" ("Introduction" 21). Robbins' reflections ten years later confirm what the "many voices" were telling him: "Cosmopolitanism posits the option that fidelity to a particular place and tradition can be understood, like Aymara-speaking Bolivian rappers, as simultaneously and successfully participating in the global, the modern, and the innovative" ("Cosmopolitanism" 49). The spatial displacements and temporal disjunctions at play in these cosmopolitan variations resemble the simultaneity and seriality in Benedict Anderson's conception of the imagined community.

This is not unlike Homi Bhabha's *vernacular cosmopolitanism*. Partly in response to the universalism promoted in Martha Nussbaum's "Patriotism and Cosmopolitanism," which appeared in the *Boston Review* in 1994, Bhabha argues for a form of negotiation, a vernacular cosmopolitanism, in which "concepts of community come from a precarious sense of survival: on the liminal borders of the homogenizing discourses of nationality; in contention with the domineering narratives of civil society; effecting salutary acts of cultural translation between here and there, private and public, past and present" ("Unsatisfied" 43). This kind of cosmopolitan negotiation is a fact of life in a transnational space, and the "temporality of continuance," once anchored in a residual idea of the nation, must now acknowledge "both the emergence and erasure of the consciousness of nationness in the anticolonial struggle." The "cosmopolitical" is a "praxis of contingent articulation" that marks the discrepant and conflicting relations between "the moment of abstract systemic causality that produces a singular mode of difference – race, gender, class at the (pedagogical) level – and the performative articulation of the social as an *ensemble or problematic of differentiation*" (47). The effect on national identity is to multiply and diversify subjectivity, to produce, as John Tomlinson puts it, "a portfolio ... of identities, each with implications for our material and psychological well-being, each, thus, with a 'politics.'" This modern sense of identity is the result of multiple strands of local, national, and global development; this identity, Tomlinson writes, arose where there was none before, though before "there were perhaps more particular, more inchoate, less publicly represented and symbolized, less socially policed belongings" (161). The recalcitrant subject of the (trans)national narrative is the new cosmopolitan subject.

In an era of globalization, nation-states are increasingly involved in multiple and overlapping alliances and regional partnerships (e.g., the South Asian Association for Regional Cooperation and the Association of Southeast Asian Nations, the Union of South American Nations, the African Union, the League of Arab States). These involvements make for shifting, multiple, and easily destabilized centers of dominance and require a renovative historical framework in which to analyze their development. Immanuel Wallerstein attempts to provide one with his "world-systems" approach. He begins by positing a "unit of analysis" larger than the nation-state, one that could account for new globalized divisions of labor. His work is indebted both to Fernand Braudel, whose theory of *longue durée* provided him with the epochal framework for studying global history, and to Marx, whose theory of capital and labor helped him to explain the kind of systematic linkages (or "articulations") found within an historically bounded (i.e., epochal) world-system. Wallerstein avoids a particular way of talking about national development that "presume[s] that all states followed parallel independent paths to something called 'development.'" He believes that historical analysis should not be performed "country by country," that local developments need to be examined in larger historical terms (e.g., the epoch that extends from the sixteenth to the twenty-first centuries) that capture the mechanisms of a "world system – (the word *world* not being synonymous with *global*) – a world, not *the* world, as Fernand Braudel would phrase it" (*Modern* xviii). For Wallerstein and others of his school, the old order of national empires has been displaced by shifts in labor, transformations in the means and relations of production, and new networks of trade and consumption. Where Wallerstein parts company with Marxism, and with idealist historiography, is in the necessity of universal norms for development. What is striking about the relations of power in the world-system, he notes, is that they appear to accommodate two kinds of norms: a positive norm of universalism ("the priority to general rules applying equally to all persons") and a negative norm of anti-universalism ("the active institutional discrimination against all persons in a given status-group or identity" that constitutes a "negative norm") (*World* 38–9). This "antinomic duo" is fundamental to the division of labor within the core–periphery model of imperialism (41).

Like other post-Marxist historians, Wallerstein is interested in moving beyond the monadic view that would take the individual actor as the main focus of revolutionary social change. For world-systems analysis, actors, "just like the long list of structures that one can enumerate, are the products of a process" (*World* 21). And this process distributes power in new ways, in part because it has reached a degree of technological interconnection and interdependence that both insures efficiency by coordinating micro-economics into larger global structures and multiplies the opportunities for crisis. As Hardt and Negri point out, the new order of global capital exists in a state of permanent crisis, in part because in a global economy, fully integrated and online, the potential for crisis rises exponentially for every new DETERRITORIALIZATION of the labor market (e.g., deindustrialization, outsourcing, for-profit education, call centers). Tomlinson's "phenomenology of globalization" refocuses critical analysis "at the level, not just of macro-social phenomenon, but of everyday 'lived experience,' reaching down ultimately into transformations in the very constitution of that experience, particularly in respect of telemediatization" (164). The process of "telemediatization" – by which our experience with global reality is mediated by telecommunications – is native to the transnational cosmopolitical situation, in terms both of "the reach of global connectivity into everyday experiences, and the 'accessing of the world' by locally situated individuals" (156).

The transnational carries within it the concept of the national both as a model and as a space of resistance (of non-identity, of recalcitrance). In a post–Cold War era, in a world-system that is no longer controlled by a dialectical struggle between "super-nations" (e.g., US, USSR), a residue of national sovereignty is discernible in contemporary concerns about "emerging national powers" (e.g., Brazil, India, China). From a world-systems perspective, a transnationalist critique would have to accommodate this residual national sovereignty. Some recent critics, like David Palumbo-Liu, have followed Wallerstein in using a world-systems approach to fashion a "revised notion of rationality" that could counter the instrumental rationality of imperialism. Palumbo-Liu draws on Fanon's work to argue that, "in making the move to the world scale [i.e., of a world-systems approach to history and social science], we cannot ignore the particularities of race, nation, and location." Like other theorists, preeminently Bhabha, Palumbo-Liu insists on the centrality of a "counter-knowledge," "a mode of rationality deeply informed by race and history that came precisely from 'the other side' of what was presumed to be rational" and that could further a "revolutionary politics" (203–4). While Palumbo-Liu is right to pursue new modes of rationality, we should not lose faith in that which contests rationality as such, namely, the "recalcitrant" subject of counter-knowledge, the *non-modern* subject of a new transnational, globalized world, whose *non-identity* is a positivity in its own right. The transnational condition, if it is to guarantee a future of open possibilities, needs to embrace this positivity and its passage into new modes of community and connection.

Works Cited

Anderson, Benedict. *Imagined Communities: Reflections on the Origin and Spread of Nationalism*. Rev. ed. London and New York: Verso, 1991.

Anderson, Benedict. *The Spectre of Comparisons: Nationalism, Southeast Asia and the World*. London and New York: Verso, 1998.

Appadurai, Arjun. *Modernity at Large: Cultural Dimensions of Globalization*. Minneapolis: University of Minnesota Press, 1996.

Bhabha, Homi. "Forward: Framing Fanon." In *Wretched of the Earth*. By Frantz Fanon. Trans. Richard Philcox. New York: Grove Press, 2004. vii–xlii.

Bhabha, Homi. *The Location of Culture*. London and New York: Routledge, 1994.

Bhabha, Homi. "Unsatisfied: Notes on Vernacular Cosmopolitanism." In *Postcolonial Discourses: An Anthology*. Ed. Gregory Castle. Oxford: Blackwell, 2001. 38–52.

Callinicos, Alex. "Globalization, Imperialism and Capitalism." In *Globalization Theory: Approaches and Controversies*. Ed. David Held and Anthony G. McGrew. Cambridge: Polity, 2007. 62–78.

Cheah, Pheng. "Introduction Part 2: The Cosmopolitical – Today." In *Cosmopolitics: Thinking and Feeling Beyond the Nation*. Ed. Pheng Cheah and Bruce Robbins. Minneapolis: University of Minnesota Press, 1998. 20–43.

Cheah, Pheng. *Spectral Nationality: Passages of Freedom from Kant to Postcolonial Literatures of Liberation*. New York: Columbia University Press, 2003.

Fanon, Frantz. *Wretched of the Earth*. Trans. Richard Philcox. New York: Grove Press, 2004.

Gellner, Ernest. *Nations and Nationalism*. 1983. 2nd ed. Oxford: Blackwell, 2006.

Hardt, Michael and Antonio Negri. *Empire*. Cambridge, MA and London: Harvard University Press, 2000.

Hegel, G. W. F. *Lectures on the Philosophy of World History: Introduction*. Trans. H. B. Nisbet. Cambridge: Cambridge University Press, 1975.

Hegel, G. W. F. *The Philosophy of Right*. Trans. T. M. Knox. Oxford: Oxford University Press, 1967.

Hitchcock, Peter. *Imaginary States: Studies in Cultural Transnationalism*. Urbana: University of Illinois Press, 2003.

Hitchcock, Peter. *The Long Space: Transnationalism and Postcolonial Form*. Stanford: Stanford University Press, 2010.

Kant, Immanuel. "Idea for a Universal History from a Cosmopolitan Perspective." In *Toward Perpetual Peace and Other Writings on Politics, Peace and History*. Ed. Pauline Kleingeld. Trans. David L. Colclasure. New Haven and London: Yale University Press, 2006. 3–16.

Kearney, Richard. *Postnationalist Ireland: Politics, Literature, Philosophy*. London and New York: Routledge, 1997.

Krishnan, Sanjay. "Reading Globalization from the Margin: The Case of Abdullah Munshi." *Representations* 99 (Summer 2007): 40–73.

Lloyd, David. *Ireland after History*. Notre Dame: University of Notre Dame Press, 1999.

Mandaville, Peter and Terrence Lyons. "Introduction: Politics from Afar: Transnational Diasporas and Networks." In *Politics from Afar: Transnational Diasporas and Networks*. Ed. Peter Mandaville and Terrence Lyons. New York: Columbia University Press, 2012. 1–24.

Palumbo-Liu, David. "Rationality and World-Systems Analysis: Fanon and the Impact of the Ethico-Historical." In *Immanuel Wallerstein and the Problem of the World: System, Scale, Culture*. Ed. David Palumbo-Liu, Bruce Robbins, and Nirvana Tanoukhi. *Immanuel Wallerstein and the Problem of the World*. Durham, NC: Duke University Press, 2011. 202–22.

Pearson, Nels C. "'May I Trespass On Your Valuable Space?': *Ulysses* on the Coast." *Modern Fiction Studies* 57.4 (Winter 2011): 627–49.

Robbins, Bruce. "Cosmopolitanism: New and Newer." *Boundary* 2 34.3 (2007): 47–60.

Robbins, Bruce. "Introduction Part I: Actually Existing Cosmopolitanism." In *Cosmopolitics: Thinking and Feeling Beyond the Nation*. Ed. Pheng Cheah and Bruce Robbins. Minneapolis: University of Minnesota Press, 1998. 1–19.

Tomlinson, John. "Globalization and Cultural Analysis." In *Globalization Theory: Approaches and Controversies*. Ed. David Held and Anthony McGrew. Cambridge: Polity, 2007. 148–68.

Wallerstein, Immanuel. *The Modern World-System*. Vol. 1. 1974. Berkeley: University of California, 2011.

Wallerstein, Immanuel. *World Systems Analysis: An Introduction*. Durham, NC: Duke University Press, 2004.

6   People/Places/Bodies/Things

Posthumanism

Posthumanism began to emerge in the last decades of the twentieth century, and has since served as a general rubric for a host of theoretical investigations into the nature of humanity and of being human. The prefix *post-* in this instance, as in so many others, has multiple connotations, for while it signals a historical relation and position, it paradoxically marks what is quite the opposite of "post" in the historical/chronological sense, so that the prefix indicates something that has been repressed or neglected, occluded or disavowed, but can only now be describe or analyzed. (On the question of the prefix *post-*, see Postcolonial Studies 242–3.) In the present case, the term *posthuman* could designate (a) an epoch in which humanity undergoes a fundamental change in being (in every sense: social, cultural, physical, psychological and intellectual, and so on); (b) an immanent critique of humanity, humanism, the human being; (c) a rediscovery of the *non-human*. In each of these cases, theory undermines the myth of a stable, inviolate, and autonomous "human nature." If we take the historical view, we could define a posthuman era that effectively began in the fifteenth century with the Italian Renaissance, a cultural epoch that consolidated and modernized a *classical* vision of humanity whose meaning is decoupled from that sanctioned by traditional religious authorities. This era inaugurated a long tradition of philosophical inquiry that peaked with Kant, Hegel, and the German idealists, for whom human beings, though subject to HETERONOMOUS forces, were nevertheless autonomous because they possessed the power of reason. The essence of humanity became stable and inviolate, sovereign in the sense that its autonomy was more than simply species-based. The human being is *a better class of being*, the favorite of God ("crown of creation"). By the eighteenth century, Enlightenment philosophers and natural scientists regarded the human being not only as a better class of being but a *perfectible* one. William Godwin, writing in 1793, sums up this ideal:

> The voluntary actions of men are in all instances conformable to the deductions of their understanding, [and] are of the highest importance. Hence we may infer what are the hopes and prospects of human improvement ... Sound reasoning and truth, when adequately communicated, must always be victorious over error: Sound reasoning and truth are capable of being so communicated: Truth is omnipotent: The vices and moral weakness of man are not invincible: Man is perfectible, or in other words susceptible of perpetual improvement. (86–7)

The Enlightenment conception of humanity to which Godwin's idea of perfectibility coincides is the chief object of the posthumanist critique.

   At the peak of the Enlightenment era, the mid-nineteenth century, we begin to see this conception generate an immanent, dialectical critique, first with Marx, who redefined humanity in terms of a common "species-being" according to which each individual should treat himself as the actual, living species; because he treats himself as a *universal* and therefore a free being" (Marx and Engels 75). Marx's Hegelian formulation is based on a dialectical relation not between humanity and the "world mind," but rather between the worker and the capitalist. Marx might be said to be the first to understand humanity in purely social terms. Darwin's influence is crucial for much the same reason as Marx's: it dethroned the idealized human being. The notion that humanity evolved through fortuitous adaptations to the environment – adaptations that were then passed down to succeeding generations, thus improving the odds of their survival – from less evolved forms of itself, overturned the Christian and, to some extent, the Enlightenment conceptions of humanity. Despite attempts to splice evolution onto Providential design (by arguing, in effect, that God created evolution), the idea that humanity was *not* divinely created and favored had the dual effect of driving people *out of* the churches into a secular sphere in which "humanism" (variously understood) filled the gap of a "dead god" (Nietzsche) and of driving people *into* the churches in fear of such a world and ready to embrace religion all the more after science announced the "death of divine man" (Plato). By the end of the nineteenth century, however, with the influence of Darwin and Marx still hotly contested, with partisans and detractors filling the pages of reviews, journals, monographs, and lectures, a decisive blow was delivered by the very philosophical tradition that had ennobled humanity in the first place. Friedrich Nietzsche's philosophical attack on metaphysics is often reduced to the notion that "God is dead," but perhaps the more important claim that he makes is that *man is dead*, for the Nietzschean concept of the *Übermensch* ("overman") is the name for a humanity that has overcome itself. The human standpoint was unquestioned until Nietzsche put forward the proposition that human *being* is neither a natural estate nor a transcendent one, that humanism and all that is noble about humanity is not a fact of nature but the result of an interpretation. From the start, he saw the human being as fundamentally artistic, a creative liar who shattered truths that had become, in a devious irony of reason, *untrue*, had ceased to correspond to reality. But this "artistically creative subject," the paragon of which is Zarathustra, has been sickened by religion and culture and so has lost vitality and relevance. "A thousand goals have there been so far," writes Nietzsche, "for there have been a thousand peoples. Only the shackles for the thousand necks are still lacking: there is lacking one goal. Humanity still has no goal … But say to me now, my brothers: if humanity still lacks a goal, does it not also still lack – itself?" (*Zarathustra* 52). Zarathustra retreats from the flatlanders to his mountain aerie, where "this secret did Life herself tell me. 'Behold,' she said, '*I am that which must always overcome itself* … That I must be struggle and Becoming and purpose and conflict of purposes: ah, whoever guesses my will also guesses along what *crooked* ways it has to walk!" (99–100). In the *Gay Science* this struggle of artistic self-overcoming takes place under the cloud of a new necessity, for "God is dead. God remains dead. And we have killed him" (181). This god-slaying species, a far cry from the human being celebrated by Renaissance and Enlightenment thinkers, traces the lineaments of a new posthuman being. (On Nietzsche, Marx, Freud, and Darwin, see chapter one, "The Rise of Literary Theory" 16–18.)

By the time Sigmund Freud was establishing the science of psychoanalysis, the idea of the human had become *the problem of the human*. From Freud's early work on hysteria, dreams, and the unconscious, to his late works on the pleasure principle, the ego, and cultural psychology such as *Future of an Illusion* and *Civilization and*

Its Discontents, we cannot escape the reality of the human being as psychically split, a prey to instincts and obsessions, bound up with repressed memories and traumas, tantalized by dreams that are really secret messages from a repressed past and tempted to regress along developmental lines in order to gain a purchase on the forever-allusive object of desire. Humanity is a fragile species that suffers under the very culture that protects it from the ravages of nature, for its "seriously threatened self-regard requires solace; the terrors of the world and of life must be eliminated. And human curiosity – albeit driven by the strongest practical interest – wants an answer too" (*Future* 82). But as Freud well knew, humanity must repudiate, at least in part, this very solace.

> What makes itself felt in a human community as a desire for freedom may be their revolt against some existing injustice, and so may prove favourable to a further development of civilization; it may remain compatible with civilization. But it may also spring from the remains of their original personality, which is still untamed by civilization and may thus become the basis in them of hostility to civilization. The urge for freedom, therefore, is directed against particular forms and demands of civilization or against civilization altogether. (*Civilization* 49–50)

The precarious psychological equilibrium that the individual must maintain with the community is, for Freud, the lynchpin of "human nature"; his ideas of normative behavior, sexual and otherwise, arise precisely in order to calibrate this psychic balance.

At about the same time that Freud was developing his theories of the human psyche, and implicitly equating human being with psychic life, phenomenology, starting with Edmund Husserl, was exploring the condition of humanity not as psychic or psychological but as phenomenal: to be human was *to be* human. Heidegger's concept of Da-sein – the human being's self-consciousness of being and of being-in-the-world – transformed our way of thinking about human experience. From Heidegger to Maurice Merleau-Ponty and then on to poststructuralists like **Michel Foucault**, the question of humanity, of humanness and human being, could no longer be coupled to metaphysics or theology, nor to psychology or sociology. The answer lay in new theories of ONTOLOGY and epistemology (i.e., of being and knowing). In his *Letter on Humanism* (1947), Heidegger explores the concept of *humanitas*, which "really does remain the concern" of thinking about the human. "For this humanism: meditating and caring, that man be human and not inhumane, 'inhuman,' that is, outside his essence. But in what does the humanity of man consist? It lies in his essence" (224). Metaphysics, however, succeeds in evading the question of "Being" and its relation to "the essence of man" (226). What constitutes humanity, what makes up a singularly *human* being, is dwelling within the cleared space of being (a dwelling which is also the possession of language). "Such standing in the clearing of Being I call the ek-sistence of man. This way of Being is proper only to man." Thus Heidegger is able to say that the "human body is something essentially other than an animal organism" (228). This claim results in a paradox that defines the field of posthumanism, for on the one hand, Heidegger returns to humanity the absolute difference it had surrendered to science in the nineteenth century; on the other hand, he acknowledges and embraces a multitude of other beings, albeit under the aegis of Da-sein. The being of things may be forever withheld from us, but the opportunity for things to enjoy being is nevertheless created by the Being of Da-sein, for in Heidegger's ontology, being is a dance of veils, of unconcealment and withdrawal, orchestrated by *human* being. Not only does human being constitute an absolute difference from other beings, it stands for (and in) the very principle of difference (of different beings), which language is preeminently suited to convey. Our *human* being is not so much meditated by language as conditioned by it; language is "at once the house of Being and the home of human beings" (262). (On Heidegger, see Phenomenology and Hermeneutics 143–5.)

Contemporary posthumanism arises at the (re)convergence of all these pathways fanning outwards from the classical conceptions of humanity and humanism. Of particular importance for thinkers like Foucault and **Bruno Latour** is the convergence of Nietzschean thought, phenomenology, post-Marxism, and the history of science, particularly as the latter was being reconceived in France in the 1960s. As Latour has noted, our inability to overcome our humanism means that we have failed to be properly modern (let alone *post*modern). "Postmodernism is a symptom," he avers, "not a fresh solution" (*We Have Never* 46). Because it refers to what in modernity is pathological, disjunctive, excessive, deformed, or distorted, postmodernism cannot move forward. Indeed, for Latour, the chief problem is that postmodernism misrecognizes its own mission.

> Modernity has never begun. There has never been a modern world ... I am not saying that we are entering a new era; on the contrary we no longer have to continue the headlong flight of the post-post-postmodernists; we are no longer obliged to cling to the avant-garde of the avant-garde ... No, instead we discover that we have never begun to enter the modern era. Hence the hint of the ludicrous that always accompanies postmodern thinkers; they claim to come after a time that has not even started! (47)

Posthumanism needs to come first, Latour argues, it needs to *arrive at the modern* in order to transcend it. This is a variation of Jürgen Habermas's claim that modernity is an unfinished project, one that Latour and other posthumanists believe is possible in renovated forms of reason and rationality, forms that are non-instrumental, non-hierarchical, and inclusive of the *non*-human.

Renovations in the history of science typically lead us away from cherished assumptions that turn out to be erroneous or to lack explanatory power. Simple distinctions, like those between nature and culture, and between science and culture, are deconstructed in posthumanist critique, which shows scientific facts about nature to be as constructed as our "notions" about culture. Latour's work challenges the objectivity of science, but his conclusion is not so much that human being (as well as the concept of the human) is in grave jeopardy but that the *non-human* has been handicapped by philosophical and scientific traditions that posit the human as the transcendent ground of all other things. "You know," **Jean-François Lyotard** reminds us, "technology wasn't invented by us humans. Rather the other way around" (132). Despite Latour's dismissal of postmodernism, we can see in postmodernist thought alternatives to the "all-too-human" model of being in the world. **Donna Haraway**'s concept of the *cyborg* – digitally engaged and virtually embodied – and **Katherine**

Hayles' work on "virtual bodies" are both attempts to expand the very body as well as the definition of the human. Like Michel Foucault and other poststructuralists, Haraway and Hayles are interested in the Nietzschean project of "overcoming" the Enlightenment and all of its intellectual categories, including the idealized vision of the human (iconically rendered in Da Vinci's "Vitruvian Man"). In very different ways, they are concerned with deconstructing ESSENTIALIST and UNIVERSALIST claims that human beings and nature are ontological and epistemological givens, prior to all construction or representation. The cyborg model is a powerful reminder that the SUBJECT and SUBJECTIVITY are hybrid creations – part nature, part machine – and that the *non-human* is not inimical to humanity but rather a potential collaborator in new modes of experience with revolutionary potential.

Hayles' work on chaos science, field theory, and digital humanities has done much to transform the idea of the human and provides a new standpoint for a critique of the humanities. From the start, her main concern has been the interface between traditional models of humanist thought and emerging models of scientific understanding that subtend the information age. This has made her vision of the posthuman quite different from that of Latour, **Gilles Deleuze**, and other French philosophers, in large measure because she is more interested in "informational pattern" than in "material instantiation"; indeed "embodiment in a biological substrate" may well be "seen as an accident of history" (*How We Became* 2). For Hayles, the posthuman is essentially a hybrid formation – technological adaptations of the human body, or "virtual embodiments" – that confirms the tendency (from Heidegger on) to regard human development as coextensive with the development of tools and other technologies (see also Hayles' *How We Think*). Unlike the "zones of indistinction" that posthumanism frequently posits as the space of confrontation between the human and the non-human, Hayles posits, in the domain of digital media, a zone of discursive and technological distinction. But not all posthumanists follow Hayles on her radical journey. **Cary Wolfe**, whose interest in social-systems theory aligns his project with hers, finds her approach negligent of "that thing called 'the human,'" which he believes ought to be regarded "with *greater* specificity, *greater* attention to [human] embodiment, embeddedness, and materiality, and [to] how these in turn shape and are shaped by consciousness" (*What is Posthumanism?* 120).

The first step toward this greater specificity and materiality is a critique of the sciences, human and natural, that can offer it to us. The scientific method, which seeks objectively to know the reality of human experience, is revealed by Latour to be a discourse open to bias and "fracturing" and the temptation to "massage" the facts. The new history of science has led to the radical skepticism that Latour describes in *On the Modern Cult of the Factish Gods* (2010). He traces the words *fact* and *fetish* to the same common root (*facere*, to make) and sees in their convergence a fruitful space for theoretical reflection. The neologism *factish* designates the suspension of "the belief of belief" and "the robust certainty that allows practice to pass into action without the practitioner ever believing in the difference between construction and reality, immanence and transcendence" (x, 22). In a similar way, he renovates the idea of *iconoclasm*, which requires that one know what icon is being smashed and can explain one's motives for smashing it. With *iconoclash*, which "aims at suspending iconoclastic gestures," one "does not know: one hesitates, one is troubled by an action for which there is no way to know, without further enquiry, whether it is destructive or constructive" (x, 68). This emphasis on the ontology of facts has arisen in discussions of affect in phenomenology, as Brian Massumi illustrates in his discussion of "affective fact" (such as a threat), which "will have been real because it was *felt* to be real" (53–4). Massumi differentiates between actual and affective fact by stating that the former must be legitimized by "a normative system for the establishment of publicly recognized fact" (66), while the latter needs no such legitimation. "A doctrine of preemption is instead validated by the general atmosphere of threat. The affective fact is made 'superlatively real'" (55) by this atmosphere, even though the "threat is from the future." The legitimacy of this thing that has not happened yet can only be verified or debunked through a metaphysics of *human* feeling, in which a fact is felt to be true, and the truth of that fact is unbounded by time: "the threat will have been real for all eternity" (63, 53).

Posthumanism undermines subject/object dualism that guarantees the veracity of acts and the autonomy of the subject who "objectifies" the world. The "new question" Latour wants to ask "does not refer back to the subject, to his autonomy, to his ideal of freedom, nor does it link back to the objectification or reification by which we would lose our autonomy ... The old question directed attention toward either the subject or toward outside forces that caused the subject's alienation. The new question takes on things themselves, and it is among these things that it claims to distinguish good from evil" (*We Have Never* 22). By way of actor-network theory, Latour calls into question the very foundation of the social as it has been understood since the seventeenth century. He asks how far one can go "by suspending the common sense hypothesis that the existence of a social realm offers a legitimate frame of reference for the social sciences" (*Reassembling* 12). Actor-network theory focuses on the nature of groups, actions, objects, and facts, as well as the very process by which one performs a "science of the social." His vision seeks to renegotiate the social terms on which we develop our sense of a shared humanity. The conventional ways by which we discuss the social are not exactly wrong, since they seem to have provided "a ready explanation for many puzzling subjects. But the time has come to have a much closer look at the type of aggregates thus assembled and at the ways that they are connected to one another" (22). The actor-network scholar pursues every connection and refrains from letting preconceived notions of the social occlude what empirically exists; she has to "trudge like an ant," but Latour advises her to "pack as little as possible, don't forget to pay your ticket and prepare for delays" (25).

Latour's radical challenge to science and the history of science is part of a larger project that includes the work of Foucault, Georges Canguilhem, and Michel Serres who were involved in a historical project that focused on disorder and disjunction rather than causation, orderly progress, or chronological consistency. Speaking of Canguilhem, one of his mentors, Foucault writes that for him, "marking discontinuities is neither a postulate nor a result, but rather a 'way of doing,' a process which is an integral part of the history of science because it is summoned by the very object which must be treated by it" ("Introduction" 14). The new history of science cannot offer the truth because it refuses to honor the true/false opposition. The historian needs to be both a rationalist and a "philosopher of error": "I mean that it is in starting from error that [Canguilhem] poses ... the philosophical problem of truth and life" (23). This "negative" approach to historiography is in keeping with the general intellectual climate of France in the late 1960s. As **Jacques Rancière**, a student of **Louis Althusser**, recalls, the task at hand was more vital than it might appear. "The urgency of the situation demands that it take risks," he wrote, emphasizing that all aspects of theory and the "production of scientific knowledges" be rethought "without delay" (57–9). His chief concern was that philosophy might miss the opportunity to represent the "class struggle in the sciences" because that struggle had yet to penetrate the laboratory. The "social function of the scientific institution" and its "concomitant modes of selection" betray "the double relationship scientific activity entertains with power and with the masses" (63).

Foucault's genealogical critique of this "double relationship" with social institutions has inspired posthumanist thought in many disciplines. His theorization of the CONSTELLATION POWER/KNOWLEDGE ultimately led to a transformative theory of the *subject of* power/knowledge. (On Foucault, see Poststructuralism 172–5 and Gender Studies 200–1.) His work, which seems to strip humanism of every one of its ideals, became associated more than anyone else's with the notion of the "death of man," of a certain structure of "humanness" that was no longer adequate as a model for human being. What he "killed off" was an IDEALIZATION that routinely blinded itself to its material conditions, its capacities and promise. His most famous text on this theme is "What is an Author?" in which he argues that the author who stands behind and verifies a work is nothing more than a function of that work. "One can say that the author is an ideological product, since we represent him as the opposite of his historically real function. (When a historically given function is represented in a figure that inverts it, one has an ideological production.) The author is therefore the ideological figure by which one marks the manner in which we fear the proliferation of meaning" ("What" 159). The larger context in which Foucault's critique of the author rests is that of "the anthropologico-humanist structure of nineteenth-century thought" in which "man" appeared as the "subject of all knowledge and object of a possible knowledge" (*Religion* 93). These and many other remarks clearly situate Foucault's thought in a posthumanist frame, one that does not assassinate human being so much as bring it out of the light of theological and idealist speculation. As Béatrice Han-Pile puts it, his "rejection of humanism was motivated by his philosophical analyses of the APORIA of the anthropological turn and the analytic of finitude, and that some of the bitterness of the 'death of man' debate was due to the fact that such analyses were grievously misunderstood by his opponents" (120).

The "death of man," like Nietzsche's "death of God," designates a condition of radical decentering, for the idea of the human and the ideal of humanism (the basis for our much-lauded humanities) centered and stabilized what is at bottom a constantly evolving, internally divided creature. But some theorists, notably Stanley Cavell and Gerald Bruns, wonder if we should worry too much about "the vanishing of the human." Indeed, Bruns has his own "futurist fantasy in which one day the experience, or fact, of ceasing to be human would no longer fill people with alarm, or even with dissatisfaction, because nothing would any longer give them 'the idea that living things, human beings could feel'" (56–7; Bruns quotes Cavell; see also

Wolfe, *What is Posthumanism?* ch. 9). Allied with these investigations is the idea that human experience is an instance of the "being of difference" within zones of indistinction that, in posthumanist thought, come to supplant the dialectical and categorical rigidities of metaphysics. Foucault's "Theatrum Philosophicum," a discussion of **Gilles Deleuze**'s theory of difference, announces the stakes of a philosophical posthumanism that yields new ontologies, new grounds for being. Unlike poststructuralists, Deleuze does not simply reject Plato as the origin of a repressive discourse that installs the concept within the Ideal and relegates all things to the shadowy world of inessential existence. Rather, he discovers (in some respects, in Plato's own work) an "anti-Platonism": "it is an element in which the effect of absence is induced in the Platonic series through a new and divergent series," but it is also "an element in which the Platonic series produces a free, floating, and excessive circulation in that other discourse" ("Theatrum" 166). What is important for Deleuze is not the establishment of the Platonic essence or Ideal, but the "delicate sorting operation" that precedes it: for Plato's "singularity" requires the "world of essences in its separation of false simulacra from the multitude of appearances" (i.e., a sorting that discovers the "true" simulacra, the "idol" that becomes elevated, idealized) (167). This is "dethroned para-Platonism," a perverse Platonism in which potentialities and intensities (the Ideal, the Same, the Idol, the Simulacrum, the Appearance) provide a mobile and fluid centering effect: recentering as a multiplied center, as "surfaces at its border." Phantasms exemplify this queer materiality; they form a "series" of ghostly appearances that "topologize the materiality of the body" (168, 170). As Deleuze himself describes them, phantasms are simulacra that "cease to be subterranean rebels and make the most of their effects ... The most concealed becomes the most manifest" (*Logic* 10). In psychological terms, the phantasm is the disorder that rises to the surface, "lateral and spread out from right to left. *Stuttering* has replaced the *gaffe*; the phantasms of the surface have replaced the hallucination of depth; dreams of accelerated gliding replace the painful nightmare of burial and absorption" (30). This form of "anti-dialectical materialism," in which the focus is on the "material forces of nonorganic life" (Cheah 81ff), requires no totalization or closure: only an "uncrossable fissure," the "splitting of the self and the series of signifying points" that refuse to form a unity of subject and object. This very splitting and seriality constitute the event of thought (the "mime") and "incorporeality of the object of thought" (the "problem") (Foucault, "Theatrum" 179).

One effect of this pure difference is the annihilation of the borderline between subject and object, matter and thought, body and spirit. This point is made most persuasively in reflections on aesthetics, which is, strictly speaking, concerned with sensation and the sensible. (On this point, see chapter one, "Rise of Literary Theory" 12–15 and Post-Marxist Theory 273–4.) Deleuze and **Félix Guattari** thus read the fundamentals of being – percept, affect, concept – through an aesthetic lens. "The percept is the landscape before man, in the absence of man" (169). Similarly, the affect is a feeling brought into its non-human aspect: "Affects are precisely these nonhuman becomings of man, just as percepts – including the town – are nonhuman landscapes of nature." The affect is not resemblance, nor is it the "transformation of one into another" but rather "something passing from one to the other. This something can be specified only as sensation, a zone of indetermination, of indiscernibility, as if things, beasts, and persons ... endlessly reach that point that immediately precedes their natural differentiation" (173). The being of sensation "is not the flesh but the compound of nonhuman forces of the cosmos, of man's nonhuman becomings" (183). Beyond conceptualization, percept and affect affirm the human through the constitutive presence of what is *not* human.

This posthumanist vision of vitalism appears to disperse multiples into a singular conception of "interdeterminate" or "indistinct" power, along the lines of Foucault's power/knowledge but outside (beyond or prior to) the confines of a discursive or institutional framework. This space has more affinities with Nietzsche's theory of the will to power and Henri Bergson's theory of intuition than with the idea of a natural world existing prior to language and culture. In any case, Deleuze's contemporary Alain Badiou has criticized him for misunderstanding the relation between the singular and the multiple. "How is it," writes Badiou, "that, for Deleuze, politics is not an autonomous form of thought, a singular section of chaos, one that differs from art, science and philosophy? This point alone bears witness to our divergence, and there is a sense in which everything can be said to follow from it." As something of a Platonist, Badiou wants this autonomy for thought, but he also wants what Deleuze and other postmodern philosophers refuse to postulate: a "metaphysics of the multiple." Badiou cannot abide a mode of multiplicity "beyond the categorical opposition of the One and the Multiple" only because it is ultimately "subordinated to a renewed intuition of the power of the One (as is manifestly the case for the Stoics, for Spinoza, for Nietzsche, for Bergson and for Deleuze)" These thinkers "maintain that the effective intuition of the One ... is that of its immanent creative power, or of the eternal return of its differentiating power as such" ("One" 69–70).

Badiou's discussion of contemporary "situations" as singular multiples has a lot to offer to the posthumanist seeking to understand how the subject constitutes herself in the social field. He takes the idea of non-TOTALITY and derives new ontologies, new modes and ways of being. A Kantian faith in the category of the event, coupled with set theory, allows Badiou to speak of the event in something very close to idealist terms – and this despite his attempt, precisely through the use of mathematics, to incorporate materiality into ontology. In a word, Badiou ontologizes mathematics (via the "matheme" whose truth is, unlike poetry, thought, what is "thinkable").

> Examined from the vantage point of philosophy, both the poem and the matheme are inscribed within the general form of a truth procedure. Mathematics makes truth out of the pure multiple, conceived as the primordial inconsistency of being *qua* being. Poetry makes truth out of the multiple, conceived as a presence at the limits of language. Put otherwise, poetry is the song of language *qua* capacity to make the pure notion of the "there is" [*Il y a*] present in the very effacement of its empirical objectivity. (*Handbook* 22)

Badiou's project is a radical rethinking of being along the lines of Heidegger that brings together problematics from postmodernism, poststructuralism, and post-Marxism and frames them under the aegis of a new meta-question: how does philosophy talk about being human today?

In *Being and Event*, Badiou attempts to answer this question through an examination of the "historical situation," which embodies human being in the form of an *event*. The logic of the event is grounded in Heidegger's ontology; but whereas for Heidegger Da-sein opens being to the world in a simultaneous unconcealment and withdrawal, for Badiou Da-sein is displaced by an event that both includes and excludes it, depending on its status as an element in a "multiple": "it is a process which is opened by an event and which constructs an infinite generic set" (*Infinite* 85). He begins with the concept of the "multiple" in which being finds itself among present and absent elements. If all the possible elements of a multiple belong to it as a "set" (including the element that is constituted by the "full multiple" itself), then it is said to be both presented and represented. If one of the elements is "not registered," is hidden from view or otherwise not available to the multiple, the multiple remains presented but not represented; it is, in Badiou's terminology, abnormal (nature is a "normal" multiple) and singular. Unpresented elements (e.g., a missing family member, a stranger with her back to the camera) have a certain absent causality, in part determining the situation but nowhere in the latter's gaze. A thoroughly "abnormal" multiple – one in which "none of its elements are presented in the situation" – constitutes an *eventa l site*. The site itself, "presented, but 'beneath'" the situation is "not a part of the situation." Nothing intrinsic to the site is presented, but the situation cannot exist without this event underlying it. In a sense, the event is being itself in its being as constituting the situation. It is, as Badiou says, "on the edge of the void, or foundational" (*Being* 174–5). If the event belongs to the situation, thereby constituting its "there is" (*Il y a*), it is counted twice: "once as a presented multiple, and once as a multiple presented in its own presentation" (182). It counts as an event as well as the presentation of itself as event in the situation, and thus "ruptures the site's being 'on-the-edge-of-the-void.'" Badiou also claims that the "event does not belong to the situation" insofar as this interposition does not take place, and "the event, apart from itself, solely presents the elements of its site, which are not presented in the situation" (182). In a sense, then, nothing is presented, which is to say, the void is "subsumed" under the situation, which supports it, as a decisive space, as not presented. The event "addresses" the void, accounts for what is "subtracted" from totality as a support and a foundation.

This is not vitalism, which Badiou believed to be a cunning mode of reaffirming the One, but rather a new conception of the "multiple minus the One," which destabilizes the notion of being (specifically *human* being, Da-sein) and creates the mathemic grounds for an anti-humanist ontology, one that accords with the neo-Heideggerian phenomenologies that crop up in the twenty-first century. The persistent irony of such a project subsists in its Platonic starting point. Of course Badiou *does not* accept the aspect of Plato's thought that holds forth the doctrine of the autonomy of being (e.g., the Idea), "the platonist's ontological thesis that there exist abstract objects." But he does wish to lay claim to "the truth conditions of mathematical sentences (i.e., the matheme)." In a word, Badiou accepts the *semantic* thesis of Platonism, but not the *ontological* thesis (Balaguer). Though opposed to vitalism, Badiou's theory of the multiple shares with postmodernism and posthumanism an interest in the plurivocal nature of human experience, the explicitly *non-autonomous* relation of human being with the world.

Lyotard calls this perspective *paganism*: "the intuition, the idea – in the almost Kantian sense of the term, if I may say so – that is, the idea that no maker of statements, no utterer, is ever autonomous ... To determine paganism then, one needs not only to oppose it to the theory of the model, to give this name to the theory that one finds in Plato, but one must also oppose it to the theory of autonomy." Paganism is a function within a "field of social and political experimentation" and is legible only through a "discourse pragmatics" (31). Legitimacy in such a context, Honi Fern Haber tells us, "resides in the recognition of and respect for the multiplicity and context-dependent nature of language games," each of which is a "sovereign realm" (143).

    This sovereignty is not at all what we find in the Enlightenment narratives of human progress, where it stands for a form of HEGEMONIC power and authority. For the posthumanist, sovereignty is a paradox, as **Giorgio Agamben** describes it, simultaneously "outside and inside the juridical order" (*Homo* 15). It exists not in relation to the rule but rather to the exception, which Giambattista Vico understood in the eighteenth century when he described a good jurist as one who "with sharp judgment, knows how to look into cases and see the ultimate circumstances of facts that merit equitable consideration and exceptions from general rules" (qtd. in Agamben 17). Agamben reasons that the exception, which is a kind of exclusion, is the sign of the rule's suspension: "what is excluded in the exception maintains itself in relation to the rule in the form of the rule's suspension. *The rule applies to the exception in no longer applying, in withdrawing from it*" (17–18). Badiou's thought is a good example of this mode of reasoning, for his "central category of the event corresponds to the structure of the exception" (25). The potentiality of the law to maintain itself in privation – "to apply in no longer applying" (28) – is a kind of *ban* in which exclusion and inclusion collapse into one another. "The ban is the pure form of reference to something in general, which is to say, the simple positing of relation with the nonrelational. In this sense, the ban is identical with the limit form of relation" (29), as it is of "potentiality," which must have "its own consistency and not always disappear immediately into actuality." For Agamben, potentiality cannot become actualized, for it is constituted by the very "*potentiality not to* (do or be)" (45). This suspension of law and power (*potentia, potere*) so brilliantly narrativized in Kafka's *The Trial*, is the domain of the "bare life." Following Walter Benjamin, Agamben describes violence as "situated in a zone in which it is no longer possible to distinguish between exception and rule" (65). The only legible connection between violence and the law appears to be "bare life," which engenders the obscure guilt of being outside the law even as one is the "exception" to it. "The dissolution of legal violence stems," Benjamin writes, "from the guilt of more natural life, which consigns the living, innocent and unhappy, to a retribution that 'expiates' the guilt of mere life – and doubtless also purifies the guilty, not of guilt, however, but of law. For with mere life, the rule of law over the living ceases" (297). This relation to violence is what should, properly speaking, accompany the sacred and the sacrifice; because it no longer does so means that *homo sacer* ("sacred man" or "accursed man") has fallen to the limit of the "mere" or "bare" life. For *homo sacer*, the impossibility of sacrifice is accompanied by a lifting of the taboo on killing the sacred being. Thus the specificity of *homo sacer* is "*the unpunishability of his killing and the ban on his* *sacrifice*" (73). At bottom, the "bare life" is a problem for a biopolitics, for "he who will appear later as the bearer of rights and, according to a curious oxymoron, as the new sovereign subject ... can only be constituted as such through the repetition of the sovereign exception and the isolation of *corpus*, bare life, in himself" (124).

Jacques Derrida approaches some of these same issues by way of Deleuze's concept of *bêtise* (Fr. "beast"), which is "at the heart of philosophy" and opposed to sovereignty understood in its juridical sense. The beast stands for the irreducible power of the "bare life" to stand opposed to power, "never that of someone else because it is always mine or ours, always, then, on the side of what is on 'my side,' of what is close, proper, or similar to me. The similar, the similitude of what resembles me and what I can assimilate because it is on my side" (209). This similitude and resemblance institute a general condition of indistinction, of indiscernibility, because the possibility of *bêtise* ruptures in advance all clear outlines, delineations, and categories. To be human is to have already assimilated the world and therefore to be *almost* indistinguishable from it. "There are clearly many zones of indistinction both ancient and modern," Gerald Bruns reminds us. What distinguishes our own era may well be our explicit theorization of such zones, which has transformed humanism from a divine or existential absolute into an indistinct opening up to (and of) the world. As Bruns notes, in zones of indistinction "the very idea of being human, or anything at all, loses its application." In such zones, creatures of whatever origin are, so to speak, free of their origins, free from the taxonomies that separate them from others – free, in other words, from what Agamben calls 'the anthropological machine': '*Homo sapiens* ... is neither a clearly defined species nor a substance; it is, rather, a machine or device for producing the recognition of the human'" (54, 46; Bruns quotes Agamben, *The Open*, 26). This kind of freedom inspires posthumanism, from cognitive theory to ecocriticism, to explore not only the philosophical integrity of the concept *humanity*, but also the world of objects, environments, and relations in which that concept finds its vitality and its being.

Under separate headings below, I discuss some of the theoretical constellations within the posthuman field. Not all of them will be relevant to the same degree for literary and cultural studies (for example, cognitive studies has begun to take up humanities concerns only since the late 1990s, so it is difficult to tell whether it will develop durable theoretical approaches to literature). In all cases, there is an emphasis on the question of being and on the material object in and of itself. These concerns, often twined together very tightly (as in "thing theory" and material cultural studies), have reintroduced the problem of consciousness and how it knows the world, which accounts for the strong influence of phenomenology, especially Heidegger. They have also returned us to an examination of the body from a new set of "orientations" described and analyzed by what Sara Ahmed calls "queer phenomenology," a "sticky" engagement with the object world that brings consciousness and object together in a way that seeks to obliterate the subject/object distinction. In such modes of thought we find zones of indistinction in which, as Erinn Gilson believes, creativity and sensuous experience find "an obscure domain on the basis of which what is excluded can remain included in a different way and is incorporated in this way only by virtue of its exclusion" (99). The posthumanist interested in phenomenology must concern herself with what cannot be included in thought, in what Georges Bataille calls the "sum of the possibles" (258). Deleuze makes a similar point when he argues, following Leibniz, that such a "sum of the possibles" would be *impossible* for philosophy, for it would then approximate to the abstract quality of chaos. What is required is a screen, which is like "the infinitely refined machine that is the basis of nature," whose function is to "extract differentials that could be integrated in ordered perceptions." These perceptions extend into infinity in the form of the event, in which the origins of sensation, like musical notes, are "monads or prehensions that are filled with joy in themselves, with an intense satisfaction, as they fill up with their perceptions and move from one perception to another. And the notes of the scale are eternal objects, pure Virtualities that are actualized in the origins, but also pure Possibilities that are attained in vibrations or flux" (*Fold* 91).

Deleuze's vitalism, though perhaps not shared by all posthuman theorists, underscores one common theme: the "joy in themselves" of perceptions and objects, which remain, because of our all-too-human gaze, eternal.

Evolutionary Literary Theory

Evolutionary literary theory takes as its starting point the Darwinian interpretation of nature and of the individual's place in it. As Stephen Jay Gould remarks, literary scholars find evolutionary theory useful in large measure because of the "historical *contingency*" (i.e., the unpredictability of evolutionary change) that is central to "any theoretical analysis and understanding of evolution and its actual results" (37). His "macroevolutionary" approach – "a designation of evolutionary phenomenology from the origin of species on up, in contrast with evolutionary change *within* populations of a single species" – appeals to the "literati." Gould has no patience for the "simplistic stereotypes" of scientists and "literary people" (the former resting on "the objective generality of nature's law and the utter insignificance of a practitioner's personality," the latter holding the view that we make "our own way in a subjective and unconstraining world"). The simple fact, for him, is that "literary folk," "from the most snootily arcane to the most vigorously vernacular," are more open to natural contingency (688–9). While Gould does not offer a "pugnacious anti-Darwinian interpretation" (38), he does make available to "literary folk" (readers, writers, scholars) a way of understanding evolutionary theory that is both scientifically grounded and open to the contingencies that literary theory, particularly in the posthumanist moment, locates at the heart of human experience.

One constellation within the larger field of evolutionary theory to emerge in recent years is "cognitive studies," an umbrella term for a host of developments in the human and natural sciences that have altered dramatically our knowledge about the human mind and how thinking, emotions, and consciousness work neurologically. From its beginnings in the work of George Lakoff and Mark Turner in the 1980s, it has expanded rapidly as scientific technology has advanced. It includes a wide range of approaches and methodologies and is by and large governed by standard scientific protocol. Unlike psychoanalysis, whose scientific status rests on an essentially interpretive methodology, the fields of neurobiology and neurochemistry, which are equipped to produce empirical findings using scientific method, have in recent years offered literary and cultural critics ample resources for furthering theoretical investigations of time, memory, affect, motive, and desire in ways that are quite different from other literary approaches, including psychoanalysis. Cognitive and evolutionary scientists of all stripes, since at least the 1980s, have been working at the frontiers of psychology, philosophy, linguistics, bioinformatics, computer programming, and discourse analysis. The study of consciousness and the role of evolution in its development has played a dynamic role in this interdisciplinary theoretical space, where scientists inform the work of humanists and humanists offer the scientists a whole new field of experimental study. Of special importance has been the role that certain artistic forms, preeminently narrative, play in our adaptation to environments. Narrative thinking, writes Nancy Easterlin "arose, presumably, because it facilitated interpretation of events in the environment and consequently promoted functional action ... Thinking in storylike sequences about our lives and those of others not only enables articulation of the links between external events but also facilitates the connection between thought and actions" (47). (On cognitive narratology, see part three of Lisa Zunshine's *Introduction to Cognitive Culture Studies.*)

Our adaptation to reading and interpreting narratives (indeed, any literary form) is a function of a long evolutionary process that is, in crucial ways, unavailable to our investigations. Paul Hernadi follows Steven Pinker and others in arguing for the adaptive function of literature. He speculates on the possibility that "protoliterary experiences of early humans may have enhanced their biological fitness – their ability to survive and reproduce – as individuals and as members of families and societies." Literature provides more than merely literary pleasures, he argues; in fact, such pleasures make the "devotees" of literature "more astute planners and problem solvers, more sensitive and empathetic mind readers, and more reliable cooperators than cospecific rivals" (26). Early forays into evolutionary literary theory, including the work of Gillian Beer and George Levine, were in part a response, as Jonathan Gottschall sees it, to a climate of "aimlessness and low morale in many provinces of the humanities," particularly in literary studies, traceable to "one inescapable truth: in contrast to the gradual, halting, yet undeniable progress of scientific knowledge, literary scholars rarely produce knowledge that can withstand the critiques of the next generation" (xi). Gottschall sees literary studies in the same situation as "the social sciences before the advent of quantitative analysis of mass social phenomena" – that is, literary studies is starting to approach problems that are amenable to quantitative analysis but lacks the tools to raise the questions in a disciplined fashion. Therefore, a "limited and judicious use of quantitative methodology" could confer benefits that have "accrued to other human-related fields" (e.g., history, political science, sociology) (49–50).

The evolutionary literary scholar Joseph Carroll argues that a Darwinian approach to literature would entail an understanding that the "relation between organism and environment is a matrix concept prior to all social, psychological, and semiotic principles," which suggests that the individual as organism enjoys an experience of the world beyond the reach of reason. The mind, he argues, has developed through the "adaptive process of natural selection" in such a way as to evolve "innate psychological structures." If "inclusive fitness" is the regulatory concept for evolution generally, then it becomes an important feature of evolutionary literary interpretation. Carroll describes this approach to literature as "cognitive mapping" (*Literary* 152). The most controversial claim he makes, that a "matrix concept" exists outside of language and culture, effectively dethrones culture in the name of a conception of "nature" in which human beings play a fundamental (if not dominant) role. Brian Boyd makes the case forcefully: "Not everything in human lives is cultural. There is also biology. Human senses, emotions, and thought existed before language, and as a consequence of biological evolution. Though deeply inflected by language, they are not the product of language. Language, on the contrary, is a product of them: if creatures had not evolved to sense, feel, and think, none would ever have evolved to speak" ("Getting" 19). This conclusion presents us with the irony of a deconstructionist maneuver that attempts to overturn the founding presupposition of deconstruction that language produces the world by mediating our experience of it. For Boyd, as for many other evolutionary and cognitive studies thinkers, language is a product of a long process of adaptation to material environments. This suggests a "primordial" source in reality of that which poststructuralism always assumed to be a retrospective postulate: a space outside of and prior to language. At the same time, though, culture is regarded as a significant determinant in human development, for while "an evolutionary view of human nature will often focus on 'universals,' on common features of our brains and behavior, it does not ignore or deny the enormous cultural differences between peoples" (Boyd, *Origin* 20).

Laura Salisbury has recently noted that the relation between genetic adaptation and culture is more intricate and interpenetrating than we might have supposed:

> Evolutionary literary theory argues strongly that genes prescribe trends of evolutionary adaptation that determine regular and analysable modes of human sensory perception and mental development; these, in turn, mould and direct the growth of particular cultural forms. As culture then plays its part in determining which of these prescribing genes will be preserved – which will go on to multiply in succeeding generations – analysing cultural forms will offer insights into the development of a human organism formed and adapted according to its environment. (530)

Here we see an attempt to draw out the "cultural" aspect of "biocultural theory," which at some level must accommodate itself with the idea of the UNIVERSAL. Patrick Colm Hogan's work illustrates a key renovation introduced by cognitive studies, namely, the redefinition of universals and "how they might be explained by reference to broader principles of literature and cognition." His goal is to find a new way of thinking of the human being in terms of a conception of universality that could account for subjective experience and difference. Hogan draws on Lalita Pandit's work on caste in Indian society to distinguish between *hegemonic* universalism, which is not really a universalism at all but a form of absolutism, and *empathic* universalism, which "is based on the assumption that all people share ethical and experiential subjectivity and that universality must both derive from and contribute to this sense of shared subjectivity, with all that it entails in terms of allowing each set of subjective experiences equal weight" (38–9). Hogan's empathic universality, like the contingent forms of the universal put forward by many post-Marxists, furthers human thought and creativity by eschewing presuppositions that ignore the material and biological elements of our human experience. Theoretical approaches that make use of such universalisms are especially sensitive to literary affect. Indeed, the "explanatory framework of affective science," by which Hogan means cognitive and neuroscience, can help us understand "the fundamental, universal properties of narrative" and the function of ideology, which "is always an abstraction of common features from diverse individual cognitive and affective operations" (*Affective* 9–10, 26). Finally it can help us construct a new discourse of human nature that does not hold culture and science at an artificial remove. This discourse, sometimes called "cognitive poetics," strikes a balance between scientific thought about cognition and humanist modes of reflection and interpretation. Alan Richardson draws on Reuven Tsur's *Toward a Theory of Cognitive Poetics* to argue that cognitive poetics is not a reduction of the literary text to "formulations provided by more 'exact' sciences like psychology, phonetics, and acoustics," since the "'human *significance*' of literary texts remains paramount." Rather, cognitive studies enables us to advance literary theories "in consonance with work in 'more basic fields'" which will "help ensure that the 'relating of perceived qualities to literary structures is not arbitrary'" (8).

"Cognitive poetics" and "biocultural criticism" describe a fundamentally "creative enterprise," as opposed to a model that is imposed upon "unsuspecting texts" (Easterlin 38). Most evolutionary literary scholars would concur, I think, though they would insist, as does Carroll, that literary Darwinists have a "scholarly responsibility" to intervene in theoretical debates and "to situate texts and critical histories in the broader context of evolutionary social science" and by so situating them to avail themselves of a much wider array of theoretical resources (*Reading* 30). If culture remains, as Carroll puts it, the "weakest aspect" of biocultural analysis, it is not because evolutionary literary theorists wish to disavow it. He argues, as do many others (e.g., Hogan, Zunshine), that we must get past the limitation that is imposed on our cultural practice by a tendentious division between biology and culture. "Collaboration between people with humanities expertise and people with expertise in scientific methodology will be almost indispensable in taking the next major step toward turning the evolutionary human sciences into a truly comprehensive explanatory framework for all things human" (*Reading* 53). Boyd takes a similar position when he argues that biocultural criticism regards the social aspect of human nature as paramount, for sociality "occurs only within living species, and hence within the biological realm ... Culture occurs only within the social and therefore, again, the biological realm" (*On the Origin* 25). But Carroll is quick to caution us not to succumb to the allure of two extremes: one, that human culture is essentially no different than that of any other animal; and two, that it "has kicked itself loose from human nature and now operates independently of genetically conditioned behavioral dispositions" (*Reading* 43). Culture and nature (human and otherwise) are inseparable, though the reasoning of most of these theorists leads us to imply a priority: first comes nature, then human adaptation to environments, out of which comes language and culture. Culture is therefore "the medium through which we organize those dispositions into systems that regulate public behavior and inform private thoughts. Culture translates human nature into social norms and shared imaginative structures." Unfortunately, contemporary literary theory has failed to "come to terms with the reality of an evolved and adapted human nature" (Carroll et al. 213, 215). Carroll offers as an example the kind of interpretations that biocultural criticism affords in his reading of Oscar Wilde's *Picture of Dorian Gray*, which situates aesthetics and homoeroticism within a biologically grounded human nature: "A Darwinian critique of *Dorian Gray* would acknowledge the way in which all its symbolic figurations – sexual, religious, and philosophical – are culturally and historically conditioned, but it would also identify the way in which those culturally conditioned figurations organize the elemental, biologically grounded dispositions of human nature" (*Reading* 93).

The approach taken by Boyd and Carroll exhibits implicitly – that is to say, in the form of a deep structure of theoretical influences – what Ellen Spolsky wants to put front and center: the congruence of cognitive and poststructuralist methodologies. In her view, the "evolutionary cognitive perspective" is part of a larger deconstructionist critique of representation. Her understanding of how cognitive studies might help us understand "the cultural production of human minds and brains" is based "on an analogy between some elementary facts about the human evolved brain and the post-structuralist view of the situatedness of meaning and of its consequent vulnerability to the displacements and reversals that deconstructionist criticism reveals" (44). Lisa Zunshine and others who take a cognitive approach to the study of literature share this concern with the problem of representation. For Zunshine, the cognitive approach "testifies to the spectacular diversity of venues offered by the parent fields" associated with cognitive studies. In her view, cognitive *literary* analysis "continues beyond the line drawn by cognitive scientists" and introduces, through interpretation, something else, which she calls "noise," that which exists outside the sanctum sanctorum of the laboratory (36–9). She develops a mode of interpretation that is grounded in the "theory of mind" concept of "metarepresentation," which Dan Sperber defines as "a representation of a representation" (qt. in Zunshine 47). She argues that the capacity to perform metarepresentational tasks (like literary criticism) is an adaptive mechanism, for it "allows us to store certain information/representations 'under advisement'" (that is, we can process information we know may be "faulty"). Indeed, the ability to process "local, contingent facts" and information gave an edge to our prehistoric ancestors and may well have evolved into metarepresentational strategies (50–2). We read (and write) novels, therefore, because our cognitive abilities have been adapted by an environment rich in information and representations, images and narratives; and we teach them in an institutional context in which instructor and student alike share a "cognitive adaptation for source-monitoring," that is, a skill in keeping track of narrators and other elements of the text's address to the reader (82). We read because we want to know the world and our enjoyment of this practice is an adaptation developed over a long period of time. Evolutionary and cognitive approaches underscore the paradox of the posthuman, for the all-too-human adaptability of mind to nature is the only way we can hope to overcome the limitations of our humanity.

Object-Oriented Ontologies

The desire for an objective basis of analysis, for a collaboration with natural science, that we see in cognitive studies and evolutionary literary theory is consonant with a general trend in posthumanism to ground theory and practice on a material basis according to an ontology oriented not toward human consciousness but rather toward objects or, to use the term so common in the discourse, toward the *non-human*. "Modernity is often defined in terms of humanism," writes Bruno Latour, "either as a way of saluting the birth of 'man' or as a way of announcing his death. But this habit itself is modern, because it remains asymmetrical. It overlooks the simultaneous birth of 'nonhumanity' – things, or objects, or beasts – and the equally strange beginning of a crossed-out God, relegated to the sidelines" (*We Have Never* 13). This latter claim, as well as the desire to subvert the unique experience of being enjoyed by humanity, testifies to a Nietzschean outlook on human "nature." Nietzsche recognized in the late nineteenth century that the problem of modern humanity was the potential loss of nature and of a "natural" connection to the world. And in this recognition he discovered a foundational *mis*recognition: to be "natural" humanity would have to create its own nature. "Not 'return to nature' – for there has never yet been a natural humanity ... man reaches nature only after a long struggle – he never 'returns' – Nature: i.e., daring to be immoral like nature" (*Will* 73). To some extent, the new object-oriented ontologies, like the anti-humanism of Nietzsche and his successors (principally Foucault), seek a world beyond human perception, beyond the vanities and resentments, the acquisitiveness and greed that spring from idealism and its inversions (i.e., asceticism, tyranny, "public opinion"). Indeed, they seek a world free of humanity's centrality – not a world in which humanity has been extinguished, but rather a world *from the standpoint* of the non-human.

In a sense, the posthumanist relation to the world of objects is a return to the Kantian problem of the *Ding an sich* ("thing in itself"), though this time the ambition is to break through the veil of perception and grasp as *phenomenon* what for Kant was the ungraspable *noumenon*. The return to Kant is mediated by Heidegger, whose own work on objects ("equipment," tools, artworks) revitalizes the Kantian problem by positing a dialectical interplay between being and becoming that hinges on human being (Da-sein) but that also provides provocative flashes of an essence free of Da-sein. Heidegger states the case throughout his work (with respect to art, in "The Origin of the Work of Art"), but his treatment of the topic in "The Question Concerning Technology" has had a profound influence on posthumanist ontology. The "essence of modern technology shows itself in what we call Enframing," "the way in which the real reveals itself as standing-reserve," as "nature orderable as standing-reserve" (24, 23). This Enframing, by which the world of objects stands in its own clearing, like an airliner on the runway, all of whose parts are "on reserve," i.e., "ready for takeoff" (17), raises the pertinent question: "Does this revealing happen somewhere beyond all human doing? No. But neither does it happen exclusively *in* man, or decisively *through* man." Enframing "sets upon man and puts him in position to reveal the real" (24), and this position, as Da-sein, brings other beings into play as unconcealment/withdrawal, for Enframing "not only conceals a former way of revealing, bringing-forth, but it conceals revealing itself and with it" (27).

But what exactly is brought forth and revealed by way of concealment? What is the "phenomenon" understood from the phenomenological point of view? It is not a formal concept, as in Kantian and common usage, but rather "a distinctive way of something being encountered." A phenomenon is the consciousness of encounter, of coming into the purview of "self-showing": "what already shows itself in appearances prior to and always accompanying what we commonly understand as phenomena, though unthematically, can be brought thematically to self-showing. What thus shows itself in itself ("the forms of intuition" [Kant]) are the phenomena of phenomenology" (*Being* 27–8). Through phenomenology, the theme of this self-showing is highlighted, for "ontology is possible only as phenomenology" (31).

The new object-oriented ontologies sustain the critique of metaphysics, dialectics, and dualism that runs from Heidegger through the poststructuralists. They focus on the *non*-human, the object, the array of things – "A storm, a rat, a rock, a lake, a lion, a child, a worker, a gene, a slave, the unconscious, a virus" (Latour, *Pasteurization* 192) – in an attempt to discover the elusive quality of another's essence. A touchstone for this kind of reflection is Thomas Nagel's 1974 essay, "What Is It Like to Be a Bat?" Nagel called for an "objective phenomenology" whose goal would be the perhaps impossible one of describing "the subjective character of experiences in a form comprehensible to beings incapable of having those experiences." What is common to the new theorists of ontology is an enthusiasm for Nagel's belief that we might "begin with humans" (449), an enthusiasm that leads inevitably back to Heidegger's Da-sein. Graham Harman finds this problematic, however, for he believes that many Heideggerians have misread Heidegger, particularly on the function of "tool-being," which for Harman is the very being of being rather than a mere adjunct to technology understood as Enframing (see *Tool* 180ff). In fact, tool-being is what shows itself *in* the Enframing. Like Jane Bennett, whose vital ontology seeks to understand the quivering life of things, Harman sees in the being of objects something of the same "riddle" that fills human being. As opposed to a "literalist" reading of Heidegger, according to which objects are inert presences that come into being only insofar as Da-sein clears the space for them, Harman's reading demonstrates "that objects themselves far from the insipid physical bulks that one imagines, are already aflame with ambiguity, torn by vibrations and insurgencies equaling those found in the most tortured human moods" (19). In his view, an object-oriented ontology would retain the "structure of Heidegger's fundamental dualism [consciousness and object], but would develop it to the point where concrete entities again become a central philosophical problem" (49). In a grand *ricorso*, posthumanist philosophy returns to fundamentals with the hope of transcending human limitations in order to finally know what a bat thinks about.

To be sensitive to the non-human is to be more openly and vulnerably human. The philosopher Ludwig Wittgenstein approached the same problem in quite a different way. After wondering whether a chair thinks, he remarks that "the question *where* the chair talks to itself silently to itself seems to demand an answer. – The reason is: we want to know *how* the chair is supposed to be like a human being; whether, for instance, its head is at the top of the back, and so on" (121). Wittgenstein grasps the central problem: *we want to know* about the object, but why should we demand an answer to the questions we have about bats and chairs? Bruns reads Wittgenstein alongside Kafka and concludes that the desire at work in both writers is to "re-enchant" the world "by causing people in it to cease being human, but only *almost* or *not quite*," which is to say that human beings are "hosts of the inhuman" (39). We might say that we *host* the chair we sit in just as much as the chair upholds our bodies. Posthumanism poses the question of the OTHER (as object) as one that ought to be posed elsewhere: what if we were to inquire about the relations of things in the world from their perspective as objects *for themselves*? Harman's desire to put "concrete entities" back into philosophical inquiry is an attempt to overcome a philosophical tradition that consoles itself with a transcendental idea or forever-veiled presence. Ultimately, his aim is to show how philosophy can think "the absence of Da-sein" (227). "When a gale hammers a seaside cliff," writes Harman in *Guerrilla Metaphysics*, "when stellar rays penetrate a newspaper, these objects are no less guilty than humans of reducing entities to mere shadows of their full selves." The relation between human beings and stellar rays and newspapers, Harman notes, is an inherent quality of things, not an effect of Da-sein. "The fact that humans seem to have more cognitive power than shale or cantaloupe does not justify grounding this difference in a basic ontological dualism" (83).

This resistance to dualistic thinking is really a reversal of priority or privilege, putting the object foremost in the question of being. Not only does this develop Heidegger's "fundamental dualism," it does so in the direction of Maurice Merleau-Ponty's phenomenology of perception. The subject/object problem is, for Merleau-Ponty, resolved in "the flesh," which "is not matter, is not mind, is not substance. To designate it, we should need the old term 'element,' ... a sort of incarnate principle that brings a style of being wherever there is a fragment of being" (139). Subject and object are sutured by a mutual gaze (things see us every bit as much as we see them). Harman, like Alphonso Lingus, develops this idea in terms of object/object relations: how is it that things see *each other*? What is it they see? He believes that their interactions take place at a remote distance, each in their own world. Ian Bogost raises the pertinent question: "if objects recede from one another, forever enclosed in the vacuum of their individual existences, how do they interact?" (65). For the new ontologists, the point is to close this distance, to reflect on the variegated life of things in which human being and the being of the object (a tea cup, a lamp, an étude) are equally vibrant and self-contained, equally joined in the same chorus of existence that can be truly known only in human terms. This brings us back to Nagel's challenge, and the problem of using (as Heidegger did, though in a different way) human being as the port of access to the being of the *other* (as object). But while Heidegger makes Da-sein the condition of all being, the new ontologists want to make Da-sein a *species* of all being. Thus we have "queer" and "alien" phenomenologies, because their presupposition is not (or strives not to be) *homocentric*, and we have "tiny" and "flat" ontologies (see Bogost, ch. 1), because theories of being "tend to be grandiose" and being is simple enough "to be rendered via screen print on a trucker's cap" (Bogost 21). It is not that the "domain of being is small," but rather that ontology, the "phenomena of phenomenology" (Heidegger) ought to be "compact and unornamented." Like tiny ontology, "flat ontology" suggests that "there is no hierarchy of being, and we must thus conclude that *being itself* is an object no different from any other" (21–2). This last claim, which provocatively leaps over Heidegger, lands

Bogost precisely back where phenomenology began (with Edmund Husserl): an apprehension, through consciousness, of the way "the world subjectively takes shape as valid for us and perhaps as given with insight" (Husserl 86). The worst that could be said of the new ontologies is that they glamorize the non-human in an all-too-human fashion. (On Husserl, see Phenomenology and Hermeneutics 142–4.)

The new ontologies, then, continue a phenomenological tradition inaugurated by Heidegger, a tradition of questioning the dualism of subject/object and the radical displacement of the former into the field of the latter. It is a familiar dialectical entwinement, one that submits an essentially dialectical movement of deconstruction to the detour of phenomenology, in which movement, space, and temporality take on new meanings outside the logic of CENTER, structure, PRESENCE, and absence. In this way, the new ontologies do aim to "get outside the text," and while they must in the end admit the impassable limit of being human, they find in rhetoric (or *tropology*) a parallel road to the being of the object. Bogost, for example, finds Nagel's "objective phenomenology" untenable and posits an "alien phenomenology" that acknowledges "the subjective character of experiences," which makes it impossible for it to recuperate objects fully. "In a literal sense, *the only way to perform alien phenomenology is by analogy*: the bat, for example, operates like a submarine [via sonar]. The redness hues the fire" (64). This metaphorism is meant to take us closer than Kant or Heidegger to the *Ding an sich* of the object by virtue of our peculiarly human capacity to use language. Bogost, who has a background in computer engineering and software design, selects a good many illustrations from that highly specialized technological domain. For example, he shows how LCD displays "metaphorize" what they represent, so that one object is connected to another through the analogic relation of their being-in-the-world. One variation of this relation Bogost calls "phenomenal daisy chains" that are "built of speculations on speculations as we seep farther and farther into the weird relations between objects" (81). Despite the vertiginous character of this analogic or tropological method – "what of the [LCD] sensor's impression of the dog's impression of the grass?" (81) – it nonetheless make us aware of new relations to the world of things and beings that do not require human mediation.

The Deleuzean strain in this kind of thinking leads ultimately to the idea of the assemblage to explain the coherence of things around something other than themselves as well as the absence of a transcendental principle of structure or of ideal form that can enforce coherence. This is particularly the case for Bennett, who speaks of cultural forms as "powerful material assemblages with resistant force" (1). Like Latour and **Gilles Deleuze**, the philosopher Baruch Spinoza grounds a return to what Bennett calls "thing-power," which reorganizes human experience on non-human lines. Thus, one moral of the "onto-story" is that "we are also nonhuman and that things, too, are vital players in the world." This story is meant to "generate a more subtle awareness of the complicated web of dissonant connections between bodies, and … enable wiser interventions into that ecology" (4). Like Bruns, Bennett makes the claim that human beings are "hosts" of the non-human; they are themselves "composed of vital materials" and their power is a "thing-power." The "vital materialist" does not ignore the technological world of machines and components, of commodities and objects, but rather grants them all the same life force and is therefore ethically obliged to promote "healthy and enabling instrumentalizations" (11–12). Her vision of the non-human human bears some resemblance to Adorno's concept of non-identity and the method of negative dialectics, the latter being, in her view, "the pedagogy inside Adorno's materialism" (14). This pedagogy is oriented toward non-conceptual knowledge, that which is beyond concepts or exists as the excluded term of the concept dialectically understood. In such a decentered world, in which "thing-power" is distributed across human and non-human actants and operators, the only things that can provide coherence are assemblages, which are "ad hoc groupings of diverse elements, of vibrant materials of all sorts" (23). As a formation, the assemblage is affective and dynamic, decentered and amorphous; Bennett uses the example of a power grid, "a material cluster of charged parts that have indeed affiliated, remaining in sufficient proximity and coordination to produce distinctive effects" (24). She is interested in reconfiguring agents and operators within a restructured material domain, which raises all sorts of questions about the ethical, moral, and legal responsibilities each being and thing bears for every other thing and being. With the example of a blackout, she runs up against the ethical crux of this vibrant ontology, for while it would give her pleasure "to assert that deregulation and corporate greed are the real culprits in the blackout, the most [she] can honestly affirm is that corporations are one of the sites at which human efforts at reform can be applied, that corporate regulation is one place where intentions might initiate a cascade of effects" (37). Such are the problems of "distributed agency," which can only be accommodated by a complete renovation of corporate law and a new ethics of social articulation. (On the assemblage, see Postmodernism 137.)

Ontology thus raises the question of ethics in a new light: to what do we attribute blame or praise in a world of desubjectivized assemblages? Or, to save the subject, is there a position from which the subject can "take responsibility" for actions if Bennett and Bogost are right? What, for example, do we make of a radical particularization that concentrates power in surprising and sudden ways, open-ended and contingent, but yet concentrated in sectors where certain "flows" (i.e., money and other incentives) converge and are exploited? Is there a kind of agency and action in the world that is not governed by human being or human consciousness? Is there a "congregational" logic of things (or *beings*), as Bennett suggests, that directs all things, including *human* things, to cohere, in a purposeful, if not permanent and strategic, way? And if there is such a logic, how do we make moral and ethical judgments? How do we assess the value of non-human things in legal and moral systems that were founded on the sovereignty of the human subject? These questions are especially pertinent for those who study the being of animals. And if we change our approach, the question is just as urgent: how do we make new values to reflect our changed attitude toward the non-human thing and toward things as such? In some cases, in Bogost's work for example, the ethical question is not raised, for his interest, like Harman's, is ontological, the being of things themselves.

Closely allied to these new ontologies are various forms of materialist analysis that have emerged since the 1990s, loosely regarded as the "new materialism." Many of the thinkers working in this field follow Foucault, Latour, Deleuze, Henri Bergson, Nietzsche, Spinoza, and a host of other philosophers in an attempt to reach the same goal as the object-oriented ontologist: to know the non-human and to see the human in a new non-human light (i.e., as an object among other objects). Bill Brown's approach to "thing theory" is similar to Harman's approach to "tool-being," in that he seeks to clarify the relation between being and object and between different beings and different objects. However, he is as much indebted to C. S. Peirce and pragmatism (and to the realist and naturalist traditions of US literature) as he is to Heidegger. In his reading of Henry James, for example, he arrives at the conclusion that "human relationships become the medium for expressing things, for apprehending the intensity of their *being*, for recognizing that the being of things lies no more in the details of their mere physicality than does the being of humans" (*Sense* 155). Thing theory, then, is about how things are *expressed* and *recognized*, how they become real *for human consciousness*. "Temporalized as the before and after of the object, thingness amounts to a latency (the not yet formed or the not yet formable) and to an excess (what remains physically or metaphysically irreducible to objects" (21). The dialectical interplay of thing/object is instantaneous, and we must therefore read in stages what comes together as a complex manifold every instant, for "the thing seems to name the object, just as it is, even as it names some other thing" ("Thing" 5). The issue for Brown is not about the status of things for human beings or for society, but rather about the "claims on your attention and on your action [that] are made on behalf of things" (9). This position seems to concede both the reality of things and the impossibility of knowing that reality outside of our temporalized "versions" of the thing under the guise of the object. But at the same time, under the influence of Heidegger, Lacan, and Latour, thing theorists like Brown regard the "thing" as an unknowable kernel of the REAL and the "thingly" (i.e., object-like) aspect of the material object as both a screen for this unknowable kernel but also a discourse *about* it and the dimension of the real in which it dwells. The analysis of things in their dual character as being a name for an object and for its "thingness" resembles, on some points, the methodologies of material cultural studies (see, for example, Boradkar), though the latter is more interested in cultural semiotics than in the philosophical issues that concern the new ontologists.

Elizabeth Grosz, a proponent of the new materialism, positions her argument slantwise to this line of development. She argues that we need to look outside the philosophical tradition for a new understanding of subjectivity and our relation to a world of objects, for that tradition is largely concerned with subjectivity as "the realm of agency and freedom" only insofar as it coincides with "the attainment of reason, rights, and recognition: that is, only through the operation of forces – social, cultural, or identificatory – outside the subject" ("Feminism" 140). Grosz aligns herself with a posthumanist position when she argues that subjectivity itself is altered by a new centrality of matter (objects, things). Bypassing the necessity of linking freedom to a narrative or act of emancipation, Grosz hopes to take critique in a new and perhaps newly productive direction. Like Agamben, she is interested in developing the "concept of life, bare life, where freedom is conceived not only or primarily as the elimination of constraint or coercion but more positively as the condition of, or capacity for, action in life" (140).

New ontologies from the Heideggerian school (Bogost, Harman) to the vitalist (Deleuze, Bennett, Grosz) make possible not only a greater understanding of humanity and human subjectivity, but also of the bodies we inhabit. Theorists such as Lauren Berlant and Sara Ahmed extend the investigations of the new ontologists in order to address problems of affect, sexuality, and embodied identity. Berlant defines the "object of desire" as a "cluster of promises we want someone or something to make to us and make possible for us." These promises can be found in any number of things: a person, a material object, an idea, any kind of sensate experience. She argues that "all attachments are optimistic." This does not mean that they bestow positive affect upon the subject; one may very well dread the return to scenes of physical or emotional trauma. "But," Berlant explains, "the surrender to the return to the scene where the object hovers in its potentialities is the operation of optimism as an affective form. In optimism, the subject leans toward promises contained within the present moment of the encounter with their object." (93). This clarification allows her to define cruel optimism as "a relation of attachment to compromised conditions of possibility whose realization is discovered either to be *im*possible, sheer fantasy, or *too* possible, and toxic" (94). Even though a person's attachment to an object might be self-harming or *cruel*, it is so attached to the manner in which she understands her life and the surrounding world that shedding this attachment could prove to be devastatingly, permanently injurious. Cruel optimism and attachment are part of a "rhetorical indirection." They allow thought to comprehend "strange temporalities," which emerge when the object enables the consciousness that intends it, that attaches itself to it, thus "disabling" the subject by virtue of this attachment (95). It is in just this way that, for Ahmed, "orientations matter," for in our projections and relations, we take into our bodies the contact points between the body and the object world. "For a life to count as a good life, Ahmed avers in "Happy Objects," "it must return the debt of its life by taking on the direction promised as a social good, which means imagining one's futurity in terms of reaching certain points along a life course. The promise of happiness thus directs life in some ways rather than others" (41). Ahmed further states that people as well as objects make the promise of happiness, for "happiness is not only promised by certain objects, it is also what we promise to give to others as an expression of love" (41–2).

The relation between objects and affect is a function of our orientation to them. In *Queer Phenomenology* (2006), Ahmed takes the idea of orientation in a number of directions: personal and sexual, geographical, historical, phenomenological. "The concept of 'orientation' allows us … to rethink the phenomenality of space – that is, how space is dependent on bodily inhabitance" (6). This inhabitance involves "orientation devices" which extend the body into space and that "creates new folds, or new contours of what we could call livable or inhabitable space" (11). The echo of Merleau-Ponty in the word "fold" indicates a willingness to see the body as *enfolded* with and in space, as penetrating and penetrated by space. Orientations to objects in most cases follow a line, for orientation "*acquires its direction only by taking a certain point of view as given*" (14). There is a temporal dimension to this spatial conception of "social investment," for if "orientation is a matter of how we reside, or how we clear space that is familiar, then orientations also take time and require giving up time" (17, 20). Her theory of orientation proves especially useful for reexamining queer identity in a postcolonial context in which the "orient" is both the colonialist ideal (Ahmed notes that her mother is white and English, her father

Pakistani) and the directionality of intentions and desire, of objects toward one another. "Queer objects" may not be able to "come into view," in part because their desire and their relation to other queer objects is not legible in a HETERONORMATIVE environment (91). There is more than just a *sexual* politics involved here. "The politics of mobility," Ahmed writes, "of who gets to move with ease across the lines that divide spaces, can be redescribed as the politics of who gets to be at home and who gets to extend their bodies into inhabitable spaces, as spaces that are inhabitable as they extend the surfaces of such bodies" (142). The body is not only the space on which power is written on the subject, as **Judith Butler** and others have argued, it is also the limit at which all forms of power must reach an accommodation. Posthumanist ontologies recognize this border status of the body, which traces its outline as an object in the congregation of other objects to which it by rights belongs.

Disability Studies

The problem of mobile bodies, of inhabiting spaces, arises in a fundamental way in disability studies, an interdisciplinary field rooted in sociology and political activism and that has in recent years become more prominent in the humanities. Disability studies has had the dual effect of alerting us to the deeply ingrained fear of and unease about the disabled body in every sector of culture, while at the same time showing how that very body is a vital part of our collective human experience. Indeed, as many disability theorists point out, at one point or another, through genetic defect, accident or other trauma, and the processes of aging, we will *all* experience disability. Yet these same thinkers come up against a general resistance to considering disability as anything other than an "exception." But if **Giorgio Agamben** is right, it is by virtue of the exception that law or rule (i.e., the able body as the norm) exists *as a mechanism of exclusion*, for the exception is excluded for being "beyond" the law; in its "bare life," the exceptional existence of the disabled body is one for which the law is suspended. Yet this very suspension gives the law its substance. "Law is made of nothing but what it manages to capture inside itself through the inclusive exclusion of the *exceptio*: it nourishes itself on this exception and is a dead letter without it" (*Homo* 27). This "threshold of indistinction" is the place of sovereignty, which must to some degree disavow the role played by the *exceptio* through a biopolitics driven by "its constant need to redefine the threshold in life that distinguishes and separates what is inside from what is outside" (131). Agamben articulates here a key posthumanist PROBLEMATIC (the dualism inside/outside) in a way that helps us understand the position of the disabled body in the constitution of norms about the "able" body.

The figure of the disabled body is in some ways a *monstrous* exception, evidence of which we see in countless images and descriptions from literature, journalism, pictorial art, and film. One example, from Marx's *Capital*, will illustrate how tightly woven are the disabled body and the law that excludes it. At several points Marx speaks of labor power as being in a "crippled state" and of "the division of labour in society as a whole" suffering a "crippling of body and mind" (277, 484; see also 486). Manufacture exacerbates this process and "seizes labour-power by its very roots," converting "the labourer into a crippled monstrosity" (481). In a curious way, Marx's rhetoric doubles back on itself, for while he appears to invoke disability as the mark of exclusion – "[c]rippled as they are . . . these poor devils are worth so little outside their old trade" (568) – he also appears to use this imagery to unveil the politics of exclusion, to lay bare for critique the material constraints of norm-generating exceptions. Marx, of course, is not interested in the disabled body *as such* but in using the rhetoric of disability to underscore the extent to which life under capitalism is a *reduction* in our humanity, in our sense of being, in and of ourselves, universal and free.

Modern attempts to pursue this kind of critique of the "exceptional" disabled body began in the 1970s among sociologists. In the UK, we see the rise of a controversial "social model of disability" in which disability is seen not as a product of "individual failings," which was developed, as Shelley Tremain points out, to counter the biomedical model, according to which disability is "an intrinsic deficit or personal flaw" (9). The social model holds that disability is socially created and hence a social problem; it "looks to fundamental political and cultural changes to generate solutions" (Barnes et al. 4–5). However, as Tremain and others have noted, the social model is, in essence, a form of juridico-discursive power, of the sort Foucault describes: it creates normative categories for disability that enable both exclusion and regulation (the latter concealing the norm-generating power of the former). At the core of the social model is a distinction between *disability* and *impairment*. Bill Hughes describes the formation of this distinction as a result of the rejection, by sociologists, of the idea that disabilities are "natural 'abnormalities'" and that "the science of pathology [lies] at the aetiological core of disability." The social model separates the biological and social aspects of disability. Thus, the *social condition* of disability was decoupled from the *bodily impairment* that underlies it. In this way, the "ontological essence of disability was transformed from a physical or mental deficit into a matter of exclusion and discrimination" (64). The problem is that impairment becomes a purely biological phenomenon, a form of "biological dysfunction" given over to the "authority of the medical gaze" (67). By creating what is essentially a *discursive* category (disability), the social model apportioned a purely discursive responsibility to the state, but left the actual material disability (impairment) in the hands of the biomedical establishment. Tremain notes that the social model denies the existence of a causal relation between the two conditions. As a result, according to the social model, "impairment neither equals disability nor causes it" (9). (On the social model, see the essays in Gartner and Joe, and Shakespeare.)

In such a climate, the stigmatization of disability arises precisely because the impaired body is already detached from the discourse of its disability and ready to be made into a marker of difference, in which, according to Erving Goffman, "the person with a stigma is not quite human" (6). The stigma arises not so much for being disabled but for failing to support and realize a bodily norm. In fact, the greater the deviation from the norm, "the more wonderfully [the stigmatized person] may have to express possession of the standard subjective self if he is to convince others that he possesses it." The normative power of the able body is generated by the anxiety of the stigmatized and disabled person who feels compelled to provide a model "of what an ordinary person is supposed to feel about himself" (116). There are a variety of affective responses to stigmatization, which for Lerita Coleman is a "consequence of social comparison" (142), and the most insidious are linked to the maintenance of "the status quo through social control" (148). Two examples, one from the 1980s and 1990s, illustrate the mode of juridico-discursive power by which this social control operates, for the stigma of disability is a matter of coercive categorization and regulation, of the body being reintroduced to the medical model in an age of biopower. In 1982 doctors in Bloomington, Indiana allowed a baby born with Down Syndrome to die of starvation, because it could not, in the doctor's words, sustain "a minimally adequate quality of life" (qtd. in Hentoff 264). This decision touched off a fierce debate about the "quality of life" and who had the right to measure it. Francis Crick, a Nobel laureate in medicine and biology, weighed in with this opinion: "No newborn infant should be declared human until it has passed certain tests regarding its genetic endowment and … if it fails these tests, it forfeits the right to live" (qtd. in Hentoff 267). Nat Hentoff's essay, "Awful Privacy of Baby Doe," is an impassioned denunciation of the medical establishment and the arrogant doctors who took the attitude exhibited by Crick as a professional policy. As Hentoff demonstrates, the fundamental questions of privacy, of the disposition of the body, of the right to life were often raised by doctors "in chambers," as it were, without conducting a dialogue with the parents. The horrors of a medical model gone wrong are illustrated by the testimony of doctors who routinely let disabled babies die without intervening to save them. Those who did survive, because either parents or doctors fought against this policy, spoke eloquently on the subject. In response to the use of the word "vegetable" in *Newsweek* to describe severely handicapped newborns, Sondra Diamond, severely disabled by burns, writes, "Instead of changing the law to make it legal to weed out us 'vegetables,' let us change the laws so that we may receive quality medical care, education, and freedom to live as full and productive lives as our potentials allow" (qtd. in Hentoff 274).

In the cases described by Hentoff, the families of the disabled infants were held hostage to a medical establishment that quantified human life. And while there has been some improvement since the early 1980s, it has come at the cost of a new kind of difficulty, one posed by *too much information* and not enough resources to interpret it. This problem is discussed with intelligence and wit by Michael Bérubé in his memoir, *Life As We Know It: A Father, A Family and an Exceptional Child* (1998). Bérubé's book is not simply an account of how he and his wife handled the reality of their son's Down Syndrome; it is also an analysis of the medical discourse on Down and on disability in general from the point of view of a concerned (and theoretically inclined) parent who is confronting the "social apparatus of 'disability'" (13–14). Bérubé describes the conflict between medical information one can easily obtain online and the social policies that affect disabled people. In this respect his experience differs dramatically from, say, that of Baby Jane Doe's parents. But in both cases the crucial issues arise: what is normal? what is healthy? what is the role of medical science in ethical decisions over the life and death of another human being? Bérubé's personal account of the "dialectics of disability," by which the self confronts the norm of the "able" body, illustrates the "development trap" parents fall into when they seek a norm against which to measure their child's progress (or "delays") (116).

What is so profoundly evident in these examples is the focus on the body itself and on the emotional lives of disabled people. The contradictions that Hentoff and Bérubé uncover in their analyses point to the central problem with a model that attempts to separate the condition of disability from the impaired body. The "somatic turn" that Hughes describes has enabled an advance beyond the constraints of the social model (and, residually within it, of the medical model) precisely by bringing the body back into the social discussion and by rendering the concept of disability less abstract. Hughes' laconic formulation – "*Impairment is social and disability embodied*" (66) – sums up the entwinement of these hitherto separated and discrete categories. His argument indexes the influence of feminism and gender studies, fields that provide models of critique and analysis and enable disability studies scholars, at least since the mid-1980s, to reframe the central questions of disability – questions about the body, representation, race, and sexuality – in ways that recognize the interpenetration of impairment and disability. Foucault's work has been particularly helpful in this task of recognition, especially his essays on governmentality, which posit a new model of power that refuses the repressive mechanisms of juridico-discursive forms of regulation and control. In this new model, "the exercise of power ... is a total structure of actions brought to bear upon possible actions; it incites, it induces, it seduces." Most important, it is "a way of acting upon an acting subject or acting subjects by virtue of their acting or being capable of action" ("Subject" 220).

Robert McRuer's theorization of queer disability is an attempt to show how Foucault's model of power might change perceptions of queer and disabled people. Within the commodifying logic of identity theory, there may well be no defense better than offense: "instead of simply producing ourselves as blank commodities and objects that erase entirely the history of their production, we might produce commodities (including ourselves) that bear the mark of queer labor and that thus hint at alternative values" (175). One such value is articulated in "crip experience" and "crip theory," the latter resisting the delimitation of "the kinds of bodies and abilities that are acceptable or that will bring about change" (31). Crip theory thus takes the same oppositional stance to a normative discourse of the body that "queer theory" takes to similarly normative discourses about sexuality. Both occupy regions in which categories, dualisms, and other forms of juridico-discursive control have trouble gaining purchase, particularly in order to solidify and regulate social identity (and thus social responsibilities). As **Lennard Davis** points out, disability is "an amorphous identity with porous boundaries" and for that reason it has had less success than other "legitimized groups" (e.g., Latino/as and African Americans), who have been "reluctant to admit disability into the multicultural arena" (36). To some extent, this difficulty is shared by gay and lesbian individuals, whose identity might also be regarded as amorphous and porous, though the Foucauldian reading of such sexual identities tends to celebrate these very characteristics as evidence of a refusal to be coerced into adopting heteronormative behaviors and attitudes. But the disabled person is not violating a norm of behavior or attitude; nor can she be said to violate a religious or cultural prohibition. Indeed, "even within the disability rights movement itself, notions about who falls into the category of the 'disabled' are unclear" (e.g., many deaf activists see themselves not as disabled but as a linguistic minority) (37). What is at stake is the "able" body, the "normal" body, so perhaps it is justified for the deaf activist to see deafness not as a *bodily* issue but a *linguistic* one (that is, a cultural one).

Of course, Davis and other theorists – for example, H.-Dirksen L. Bauman, whose critique of Derrida reminds us that "audism" (the privileging of speech) is rarely legible in the way that racism and sexism are – regard this kind of thinking as indicative of how "ableism" at large tends to work. "The fact is," Davis writes, "disability disturbs people who think of themselves as nondisabled" (38). And this disturbance, which does not always manifest itself consciously, has led to a kind of mass disavowal of disability *as such*; the result is a lag in the kind of social progress we have seen elsewhere in Western societies (e.g., civil rights, equal rights for women, gay marriage, and so on). Marginalized and ignored, the disabled remain behind in almost every measurable way. "Legal decisions filled with ableist language and attitudes [remember Marx's "crippled monstrosity"] are handed down without anyone batting an eyelid." Academic and activist research on disability and identity has had, Davis argues, the counter-productive effect, at least in the "popular imagination," of relegating disability "to a lower status in a pecking order of abuses" (150). Drawing on Tobin Siebers' work on narcissism, Davis explores the tendency of psychoanalysts to regard disabled people as narcissists who "inherently view themselves as 'exceptions.'" Such tendencies "carry over into the judicial realm," where judges often see "the disabled plaintiff as first and foremost narcissistic and egoistic" (124–5). They see someone with a personal problem, not a legitimate claim on the law. The idea of a "narcissistic demand for exceptions," made by employees and others who seek to be more humanely accommodated in social contexts, leads to the behavior Davis describes as "bending over backwards" on the part of employers, governments, institutions, and so on. Where Goffman sees an overcompensation on the part of the disabled person (i.e., trying harder to express one's "standard subject self" and thereby console others about the status of the norm), Davis discerns the inverse of this overcompensation in the inability of the non-disabled to recognize disability *as such*.

What we see here is not so much a concerted attempt to disenfranchise a particular social group as a zone of indistinction in which the disabled subject is not recognizable; nor is the legal system sure of its own standing in law when confronted with what it cannot or will not rule on (e.g., refusing the childish narcissistic demand). Davis draws our attention to the way lawyers and judges respond to the explicit announcement of the exception that, in a primordial sense, suspends the law and defines it. The disabled person is not just a challenge to the statutes that prevent him from moving freely in society but a challenge to the very "exceptionality" that grounds the law itself. "From the point of view of sovereignty," writes Agamben, "*only bare life is authentically possible.*" In the "zone of indiscernibility" formed by the *ban* on the disabled body, sovereignty – in Davis's analysis, the legal system – must resist the appearance of being challenged by the very exception that has already established the legitimacy of sovereign law. Agamben tells us that the ban is an "originary juridico-political relation," and this applies both to the "formal structure of sovereignty" but also its "substantial character, since what the ban holds together is precisely bare life and sovereign power" (*Homo* 106). The disabled person, as *homo sacer*, endures just this kind of estrangement from the world of enfranchised subjects, and therefore endures a "life that may be killed but not sacrificed" (107). Davis's analysis of the "pecking order of abuses" in the legal system illustrates the baroque and seemingly arbitrary mechanism by which differential exceptions are created that sustain current legal statutes at the same time that the law refuses to recognize the bare facts of disabled bodies. In this case, the law does not cover bare life, but adjudicates the relation of such a life to the other bodies of exception (e.g., gendered, racialized, sacralized, queered). Davis calls this web of juridico-discursive motives and prejudices "intersectionality," a state in which "individuals who fall into the intersection of two categories of oppression will, because of their membership in the weaker class, be sent to the margins of the stronger class" (154). The problem is not simply that the legal system is insensitive to disabled people with "diminished capacities"; it lies in the invisibility of the role the disabled play in legitimizing legal and social norms. Legal authorities are simply "unaware, for the most part, of the way that ableism is built into the social, physical, and ideological environment" (155). They are unaware of it because the exception instills in them the "naturalness" of a norm.

Davis's critique of normative standards for able and disabled bodies has contributed much to raising awareness about the largely unacknowledged contradictions and prejudice about disability. Rosemarie Garland-Thomson believes that a transformed feminism has much to offer this critique.

> A feminist disability theory denaturalizes disability by unseating the dominant assumption that disability is something that is wrong with someone. By this I mean, of course, that it mobilizes feminism's highly developed and complex critique of gender, class, race, ethnicity, and sexuality as exclusionary and oppressive systems rather than as the natural and appropriate order of things. (6)

Garland-Thomson suggests that the critical paradigm of queer theory, as put forward by **Eve Kosofsky Sedgwick**, would be a good model for a feminist critique in the construction of "'a universalizing view' of disability that will replace an often persisting 'minoritizing view'" (5). Another important figure for feminist disability studies scholars is **Judith Butler**, whose theory of the body, its relation to power and subjection, has deeply informed feminism and gender studies. However, Ellen Samuels wonders if Butler's theory of the body would be adequate if the inquiry really is to "foreground (dis)ability" and the existence of a disabled body (60). Samuels calls for a "rigorous critical scrutiny" of the tactic that (con)fuses the category "(dis)abled" and the category "sex/gender," for these terms refer to "very different realms of social and bodily existence." The bottom line is that, however helpful Butler's work might be, it is "en-abled by its own reliance upon a stable, functional body that is able to walk, talk, give birth, see and be seen" (64–5). Part of the trouble is that we have historically seen a *correspondence* between disability and *femininity*, which tends to blur the differences between the two. Another part is a perception that Butler's work evinces "a certain disinterest on her part regarding those aspects of the body which are firmly rooted in the physical realm" (67). The ambivalence about Butler, summed up in the subheading announcing Samuel's conclusion – "Can't think with her, can't think without her" (72) – is of a piece with the zone of indistinction that encompasses both the disabled body and the discourse about it.

Nor is Foucault immune to the critique of theory that reveals it to be, like every other facet of culture, incapable of grasping the disabled body. His examination of the "docile body" of modernity reveals beneath its surface the "able body." "The new docile body," writes Tobin Siebers, "replaces the able body … The docile body requires supports and constraints, its every movement based on a calculation." Foucault is rightly praised for work that unveils "structures of exclusion," but "it has never been remarked that he describes what has been excluded as purer and fitter conceptions of the body and mind" ("Disability" 175). In short, Foucault's picture does not register with the realities of disability. The problem for theory is the "harsh realities of the body," which drive the tendency, too easy in Siebers' view, "to mythologize disability as advantage. Disabled bodies are so unusual and bend the rules of representation to such extremes that they must mean something extraordinary" (178).

The problems outlined here have to do in part with the failure of identity theory to grapple with the reality of disabled bodies. "The dismodern era," writes Davis, "ushers in the concept that difference is what all of us have in common" (26). In response to *dismodernity*, contemporary disability studies needs to make explicit what is implicit in the history of human culture: that the disabled body is required dialectically to constitute the norm and has done so since antiquity. Nowhere is this more evident than in what has come to be known as "disability aesthetics." Michael Davidson, for example, has called for a "poetics – as much as a politics – of disability," which would theorize "the way poetry defamiliarizes not only language but the body normalized *within* language." Such a poetics could "unsettle the thematics of embodiment" that characterizes so much cultural production since the 1960s. Davidson asks what would happen if we were to read this poetics of embodiment "for its dependence on ableist models" while at the same time recognizing its innovations and subversions (118–19). A disability poetics would look critically not only at how ableist models function unconsciously in language but also at how the disabled body is communicated and offered up to understanding through critique. Bauman similarly posits a "viewer oriented phenomenological criticism" that would do justice to poetry in sign language and thereby move away from the "formalized 'text-as-object' toward the 'text-as-event' that takes place somewhere between the poet and the audience" (362). Literary critics such as David T. Mitchell and Sharon L. Snyder are doing the kind of work feminists did in the 1960s and 1970s: rereading the canon from a fresh perspective. In their view, literature betrays a "discursive tendency" either to use disability as a "stock feature of characterization" (i.e., as a "narrative prosthesis") or to exploit it "as a metaphorical signifier of social and individual collapse" (47). Literary narratives thus use the disabled body as a sign of the unknowable real, not only in terms of reality as such (i.e., the reality of material objects) but also the unknowable real of *human being*. Mitchell and Snyder take a Lacanian position when they describe disability as "the *hard kernel* or recalcitrant corporeal matter that cannot be deconstructed away by the textual operations of even the most canny narratives or philosophical idealisms" (49). The metaphorization of the disabled body offers narrative "one thing it cannot possess – an anchor in materiality" (63). At the same time the deviant body is marked textually, and this textual mark serves as a mark of difference *as such*. There are "myriad inroads" (e.g., gender, race, class, sexuality, ethnicity, religion, and so on) by which the writer might describe the anomalous, "and disability services this narrative appetite for difference as often as any other constructed category of deviance" (55).

In *Disability Aesthetics* Siebers argues that the disabled body is the site *par excellence* of the aesthetic relation to the world, which is not surprising, given that aesthetics derives from the Greek αἰσθητός, "sensible, perceptible," and has since at least the eighteenth century been associated with the philosophical project of grounding reason in lived experience. In the modern period, aesthetics "is the human activity most identifiable with the human because it defines the process by which human beings attempt to modify themselves, by which they imagine their feelings, forms and futures in radically different ways" (3). We do more things with our bodies today, evidently, but Siebers contradicts himself in a deliberately astonishing way, for he shows that the disabled body, either by chance or design, has been at the vital core of art from the beginning. One need only call to mind the blind, club-footed Oedipus, but then, if we think back further, we find blind Polyphemus in Homer's *Odyssey*, perhaps the first time disability was used to mark otherness in what we might call (preserving our own uniqueness) the modern sense. Siebers points to the armless Venus de Milo and many other works of art and literature that depict disability and is reluctant to regard these representations solely in terms of prosthesis or metaphoric appropriation. In his view, disability "does not express defect, degeneration, or deviancy in modern art. Rather, it enlarges our vision of human variation and difference, and puts forward perspectives that test presuppositions dear to the history of aesthetics" (*Disability* 3). Since human feeling is "central to aesthetic history," the affective dimension of disability is bound to prove powerful, both in terms of the emotions depicted in art and those elicited from the viewer and reader. This understanding of the disabled body in art both redefines and revalues art *and* disability by taking a more inclusive perspective on what it means to be human. The disabled body is, in this sense, the sign of the *posthuman* body, one that refuses to be consigned to the space of an ideal perfection. Siebers sees just this refusal in the artist Paul McCarthy's "chaotic, almost feral, bodily performances" (11–12) and in the fascinating and obscure works of Judith Scott, institutionalized from a young age, who made sculptures using materials (e.g., string, twigs, forks, scraps of paper, fabric) that she had "pilfered." Though Scott has no connection to the art world, "her primary materials mimic modern art's dependence on found art" (17). More fundamentally, the body itself becomes motive and material for aesthetic experience. In an examination of traumatic injury, Siebers makes the point that the marks or scars that serve as physical signs of disability can be "potent for the imagination" because "every disability is technically invisible until it becomes visible under the pressure of social convention, which means that the appearance of disability is often linked to violence and prejudice" (129).

Hence, the injured body, like the disabled body generally, is, for better or worse, tightly woven into the larger social body. The emphasis on corporeality, on the body as a screen or text, situates disability studies in a posthumanist dialogue about what it means to be human, to be an *embodied* human being. By redefining disability and the situation of the disabled body in the world at large, disability studies scholars expand the parameters of the human by retrieving from obscurity and ignominy a vital part of human experience. The burden for disability studies today is to be even more inclusive, to open the discussion more fully to include urgent questions of race, class, sexuality, mental illness (the invisible disability), and the especially vexed question of an environment (both private and public spaces) that has only recently been RETERRITORIALIZED (via ramps, motorized doors, and other features) to accommodate those who move around on wheels. In the posthuman era, the disabled body is, like any other, a body in the world. Its difference is one we all share, in one form or another, at one time or another. Disability is the future.

Ecocriticism

Ecocriticism designates a number of related fields, including environmental theory and literary criticism, environmental justice studies, ecofeminism, sustainability studies, animal studies, and what we might call inter-species studies. In all of these areas, we see another valence of the posthumanist critique of the relation between humans and nature and between humans and non-humans. From Marx's analysis of "species-being" and Darwin's unveiling of the human as animal, we have evolved complex ways of talking about the natural and built environments in which we live and work. The Frankfurt School critique of modernity, like many twenty-first century environmentalist groups, held humanity responsible for the transformations in nature that have alienated us from the "natural" ground of our being. For Max Horkheimer and Theodor Adorno, the relation to nature under capitalism is characterized by "domination of nature by human beings, domination of nature within human beings, and, in both of these forms of domination, the domination of some human beings by others" (11). By the 1960s, the ecology movement shifted the focus from a critique of domination to a commitment to preservation; with this shift came renewed interest in naturalist writers such as Edwin Muir and Gary Snyder and in Martin Heidegger's reflections on the relation between *earth* and *world* (see Garrard 34–6). What differentiates ecocriticism from other "contemporary literary and cultural theories," according to Greg Garrard, is just this "close relationship with the science of ecology." And while literary scholars may not be expected to master the science, "they must nevertheless transgress disciplinary boundaries and develop their own 'ecological literacy' as far as possible" (5). The term *ecology* was coined by German zoologist Ernst Haeckel (Gr. *oikos*, "house, dwelling" [*OED*]). It has since come to designate what Neil Evernden calls a "subversive science," whose basic premise is "interrelatedness." Evernden believes that this "genuinely radical" premise is misrecognized as "casual connectedness," which implies a random determined environment in which discrete entities interact. What ecology means for him, though, is *ecosystem*, "a genuine *intermingling* of parts" in which "there are no discrete entities." This interrelatedness defies the fundamental dualisms that authorize the modern scientific method; and while ecology originates as "a normal reductionist science," it has developed into counter-knowledge that undermines "not only the growth addict and the chronic developer, but science itself" (93).

What Evernden describes is a posthumanist system of knowledge not unlike the systems theory approach described by **Cary Wolfe**, one that is indebted to the sociology of Niklas Luhmann and the philosophy of Stanley Cavell (both are prominent figures in the emerging posthumanist canon). And while he does not address ecology or ecocriticism in *What is Posthumanism?* (2010), Wolfe's description of systems theory calls to mind the ecosystems Evernden describes.

> All systems carry out their operations and maintain their autopoeisis [i.e., self-creation] by deploying a constitutive distinction, and a code based on it, that in principle could be otherwise. This means that there is a paradoxical identity between the two sides of the system's constitutive distinction, because the distinction between both sides is a product of only one side. (222)

Wolfe's example of this asymmetry is the legal system, which gets to define what is *illegal*. We can say the same thing about the ecosystem, that it too is the product of only one side, *nature*, and that this systemic condition confronts human beings with their own singular distinction, for while we are an intricate part of the ecosystem (i.e., in our capacity as a species among other species, occupying an ecological niche), our reflection on it as well as our ability to alter it (e.g., global warming) makes our own experience with the system unique. Cows may emit a tremendous about of methane and in that way alter the environment and, also in that way, stand alongside human beings. But cows do not reflect either on their own contributions or on the system in which their existence forms a more or less vital component. And because they do not reflect on their environment, they have no need to disavow their existence within it. But human beings do, or at least their systems do. No system, Wolfe argues, following Luhmann, "can acknowledge this paradoxical identity of difference – which is also in another sense simply the contingency – of its own constitutive distinction *and* at the same time use that distinction to carry out its own operations. It must remain 'blind' to the very paradox of the distinction that links it to its own environment" (222). For Luhmann, the "connection with the reality of the external world is established by the blind spot of the cognitive operation. Reality is what one does not perceive when one perceives it" (qtd. in Wolfe 223). This is what happens in ecocriticism, especially by the 1980s, as poststructuralist and emergent posthumanist theory exploit this blind spot in order to find the reality that we have not yet perceived. Such discoveries, Luhmann argues, are made by "second-order observations" ("observations of observations") that are at one and the same time "first-order observations" (i.e., one can observe on the first-order the world in which second-order observations are taking place) (see 60ff). "The proposition that a second-order observer is always also a first-order observer rephrases the familiar insight that the world cannot be observed from the outside" (56). Luhmann is interested in the conundrum thrown up by the "second-order observation," which is "at once a highly improbable evolutionary fact and entirely normal occurrence" (63). This is a vital insight because it appears that "modern society imbued all of its functional systems with second-order observation and itself ceased to provide a stable counterbalance." Thus, "the concept of the world had to be altered" (92).

I am suggesting here that this alteration is precisely what goes on in the "second-order observations" of ecocriticism, which accepts the paradox of humanity being somehow outside of nature and accepts as well the idea that the world is conceived "along the lines of a Husserlian metaphor, as an unreachable horizon that retreats further with each operation, without ever holding out the prospect of an outside" (Luhmann 92). Ecocriticism attempts to reach not the natural *as such* but the systems that subtend this unreachable horizon, and not just natural systems, but those historical, scientific, and aesthetic formations (from oral traditions to systems theory) that (re)present the environment for us. It should be noted that this generalization applies largely to academic ecocriticism, and not to those who are dedicated to saving real trees and real endangered species, who may in fact regard ecocriticism with much the same skepticism the Irish countryman reserved for the city-bred poet, W. B. Yeats, who sought to teach him about the world of faery. The point is that ecocritics, by taking as their object of critique literary and cultural texts (works of literature, of course, but also music, painting, sculpture, and other art forms), are exemplary second-order observers whose theoretical reflections inspire others, for example environmental activists whose own first-order observations may be of non-human "zero-order" observers. We can therefore speak of ecocriticism as yet another new phenomenology, one that adds, as Glen Love does, the "working of the body and brain to the power of place, bringing philosophy and cognitive and life sciences into the mix" (93).

The posthumanist orientation toward nature and the environment is grounded in classical and Romantic idealist conceptions that it has only in recent decades managed to deconstruct or otherwise abandon, in favor of more materialist conceptions of nature (i.e., materialist in the Marxian sense but also in the Foucauldian/Deleuzean sense of the material reality of discursive effects). As Garrard puts it, since "the Romantic movement's poetic responses to the Industrial Revolution, pastoral has decisively shaped our constructions of nature" (37). Of course there is a long history of writing about nature, from the classical pastoral tradition, particularly in Latin, to seventeenth- and eighteenth-century topographical poetry (e.g., Alexander Pope's "Windsor Forest"); but most ecocritics see Romanticism as the standpoint that had to be transcended if nature was not to remain forever veiled by IDEALIZATIONS. The Nature of William Wordsworth and Percy Bysshe Shelley, of William Blake and Edmund Burke, is shot through with divinity and fosters a form of reciprocity into which the individual enters and enjoys an "unremitting interchange," as Shelley puts it in "Mont Blanc." This view of nature persisted throughout the nineteenth century, despite Darwinian ideas that threatened to unveil "nature red in tooth and claw" (Tennyson). Indeed, an idealized and stylized Nature serves as the life-world of the pre-Raphaelite poets and painters and is still legible in modernist poetry by Yeats. A common motif throughout this literary tradition is the identification of nature with the *feminine* (i.e., earthy materiality versus the masculine ideal of abstract reason). A good example of this is the "uniquely American 'pastoral impulse'" that Annette Kolodny describes, one that is grounded in "a yearning to know and to respond to the landscape as feminine" (175). In some cases, as in the naturalist novel, nature is itself rendered as an abstraction, an inexorable force or a physical necessity (in terms both of climate and geography and of human nature, i.e., heredity). From an aesthetic point of view, nature is an artificial ecology, one that uses the signifiers of the "natural" to create an idealized representation of nature. The politics and poetics of these representations are a major preoccupation of the ecocritic, for aesthetics makes clear that the representation of nature is a *removal* from nature, a critical second-order perspective on it and within it (first-order as opposed to "zero-order"), but one that is already *unnatural* in the sense that it ceases in advance to correspond with the original.

In a sense, the Romantic poets knew this already, and it is not for nothing that Kant before them took the "givenness" of nature as a template for understanding the autonomy of the art object. Nature has, paradoxically, always been understood as a profoundly creative force. The Romantics also understood the terrifying dimension of nature and developed a sense of the sublime rooted in its awe-inspiring power:

> Your snows and streams
> Ungovernable, and your terrifying winds
> That howl so dismally for him who treads
> Companionless your awful solitudes!
> (Wordsworth, *Prelude*, VI.219–20)

Wordsworth puts into verse the sublime effect that Edmund Burke had theorized some thirty years before. "The passion caused by the great and sublime in *nature*," writes Burke, "when those causes operate most powerfully, is astonishment; and astonishment is that state of the soul, in which all its motions are suspended, with some degree of terror. In this case, the mind is so entirely filled with its object, that it cannot entertain any other, nor by consequence reason on that object which employs it" (95–6). While some contemporary theorists, like **Jean-François Lyotard**, have elaborated on this Romantic sublime, ecocriticism has largely bypassed it in its efforts at de-idealizing the natural world. In this effort, paradoxically enough, Wordsworth has played a decisive role, despite his tendency to idealize nature, for he recognizes the interpenetration of nature and human consciousness:

> Therefore am I still
> A lover of the meadows and the woods,
> And mountains; and of all that we behold
> From this green earth; of all the mighty world
> Of eye, and ear, – both what they half create,
> And what perceive; well pleased to recognise
> In nature and the language of the sense,
> The anchor of my purest thoughts, the nurse,
> The guide, the guardian of my heart, and soul
> Of all my moral being.
> ("Tintern Abbey" ll. 102–11)

In a sense, "nature writing" – particularly in the work of Gary Snyder, Rachel Carson, Wendell Berry, and Barry Lopez – is an attempt to connect directly to nature, to feel Wordsworth's "wise passiveness." Contemporary nature writers, are, as Scott Slovic notes, "constantly probing, traumatizing, thrilling, and soothing their own minds – and by extension those of their readers – in quest not only of consciousness itself, but of an *understanding* of consciousness." Slovic goes further than Wordsworth and the Romantics, who contained their reflections on nature within the perceptual/creative matrix of a purely human understanding, and argues that both nature and our reflections contribute to our understanding of both the "self and non-self" (352).

Slovic hits upon a dominant concern within the posthumanist field, the idea that subject/object, self/non-self, human/non-human dualisms need to be overcome. From the 1980s, this longstanding PROBLEMATIC has been rethought using the tools of poststructuralism to get (quite literally) "outside the text." According to Sueellen Campbell, poststructuralist theory and "deep ecology" "share two basic tactics for revealing the flaws of old ideas and building new ones. One is largely polemical – to overturn old hierarchies, to take value from the once dominant and give it the weak." The other has to do with calling into question the dualistic concepts "on which the old hierarchies are built." Campbell argues that these "oppositions come under scrutiny, are revealed as artificial, biased, and oversimple, and are then somehow restructured" (127–8). Contemporary ecocriticism illustrates the discombobulating effect of these dualisms – i.e., we are inside our homes while nature is outside; and we are *outside* when we are *in* nature – which makes it impossible to claim in good faith that one has "captured" nature in language (or paint, or stone), for what we capture, as William Howarth explains, is our *consciousness* of nature.

> We know nature through images and orders, a process that makes the question of truth in science and literature inescapable, and whether we find validity through data or metaphor, the two modes of analysis are parallel. Ecocriticism observes in nature and culture the ubiquity of signs, indicators of value that shape form and meaning. Ecology leads us to recognize that life speaks. (77)

The idea that "life speaks" resonates throughout the ecocritical field, and serves as an antidote to the Worthsworthian formula of speaking *for* life. We might say, following **Lawrence Buell**, that this line of thought, rooted in Heideggerian phenomenology, is primarily concerned with "the project of reorienting literary-critical thinking toward more serious engagement with nonhuman nature" (90). Buell notes that this same tendency also points the way toward evolutionary literary criticism and cognitive studies, particularly in the work of Joseph Carroll, and is at least a partial response to the "call for literary critics and humanists generally to attain greater science literacy" (92).

Buell believes that a second wave of ecocriticism – or, as he prefers to call it, environmental criticism – began in the 1990s and sought to go beyond "the first wave's characteristic limitations of genre, geography, and historical epoch." The agenda of environmental criticism encompasses "the whole sweep of Western literary history from antiquity to the present," taking root all over the world (93; see also Nixon, ch. 8). As a result new issues arise having to do with indigenous perspectives on nature, with the relation of gender to nature, with the role of the non-human, particularly animals, and with the idea of environmental justice. The standpoint of ecocriticism, as we have seen, regards nature as a holistic system that can be known, but not by scientific reduction to empirical facts. This way of knowing is described in Barry Lopez's *Arctic Dreams*: "If we are to devise an enlightened plan for human activity in the Arctic, we need a more particularized understanding of the land itself not a more refined mathematical knowledge, but a deeper understanding of its nature, as if it were, itself, another sort of civilization we had to reach some agreement with" (11). What we see in Lopez's work, as well as in that of indigenous writers like Simon Ortiz, is a kind of *ricorso* that takes us back to traditional and indigenous *local* conceptions of the natural world, but in a way that allows us to move forward in the present with a renewed respect for the environment in which we are to see ourselves as caretakers and not masters. Ortiz's own sense of himself as an artist is bound up with his commitment to and connection with a particular place. "I write about the experience of native people ... That means that my poems and stories have to do with the environmental setting of Acoma [New Mexico], and all of the Americas, where indigenous native people live ... When I write, I write as an Indian, or native person, concerned with his environmental circumstances and what we have to do to fight for a good kind of life" (qtd. in Adamson and Stein 158). The "environmental circumstances" that Ortiz insists upon are both ordinary in the sheer fact of their *being there*, but also extraordinary in their spiritual manifestations. Native peoples – "old Indian ghosts," the Quapaw and the Waccamaw – become, in the desacralized space of indigenous lands, "billboard words / in this crummy town" ("Passing Through Little Rock" ll. 1–5). One needs to cross over, to climb "the next hill" and move through the trees and "come out the other side"

> and see a clean river,
> the whole earth new
> and hear the noise it makes
> at birth.
>
> (ll. 10–16)

For Ortiz, the environment is not an issue or a problem; it is the core of aesthetic, religious, and social life.

A different set of concerns lies behind the feminist critique of nature. As feminists have known from the start, there is nothing "natural" about femininity, nor is nature inherently feminine in any way that is not inscribed upon it by masculinist conceptions of nature as "mere matter," free of any taint of rationality or abstraction. As mere matter, woman is "natural" yet, as **Luce Irigaray** has shown, she has no essence. Nature, like the idealized inessential figure of woman, makes possible a wide range of self-serving idealizations by virtue of its reflective capacity (something Wordsworth understood well). Beginning in the 1970s, according to Catriona Sandilands, a form of cultural feminism arose in critical response to this tendency and, in part, embraced the very idealizations of nature that correspond to woman as "earth mother":

> Women would find, or perhaps create, their true identity in spaces carefully separated from the distorting influences of patriarchy. New relations to nature were an integral part of this culture; women's "special" knowledges of reproduction and their experiences of mediating between nature and culture were part of their difference from men and thus needed to be discovered and freed. (10)

Sandilands claims that "feminist discourses on spirituality and theology" (11) played a vital role in ecofeminist theory, which hinges on the way spirituality shapes political contexts and modes of critical reflection. Ecofeminism departs from cultural feminism at large when it transfers "cultural feminist narratives of the historical oppression of women to ideas on nature" (16). Sandilands is no doubt right to say that ecofeminism is a result of converging strands within feminism at large, anchored by the central critique of the nature/culture dualism that, as Karen Warren points out, is at the root of the domination of women and of nature. Warren forcefully attacks the patriarchal language of business, politics, and the academy for reinforcing this relation of dominance and implicitly indicts cultural feminism for using language in the same way: "Language which feminizes nature in a (patriarchal) culture where women are viewed as subordinate and inferior reinforces and authorizes the domination of nature: 'Mother Nature' is raped, mastered, conquered, mined – her secrets are 'penetrated' and her 'womb' is to be put into service of the 'man of science'" (Warren 12).

At the center of ecofeminism, particularly of the activist kind represented by Warren, is a concern for social justice that links the fight for the environment with a fight for human rights. "There is a clear and profound relationship between militarism, environmental degradation, and sexism. Any commitment to social justice and nonviolence that does not address the structures of male domination of women is incomplete" (114). The ecofeminist critique of nature, like the critique of the role of the non-human in animal studies, focuses on the ethics of our relation to the environment and to all those who find their place in it. As Mei Mei Evans argues, nature must not remain "the province of white heterosexual masculinity" because the FORECLOSURE of nature has had "material consequences" (183) – and not just for women who have suffered the indignity of being identified with mere mute nature, but for myriad other groups who have borne the brunt of environmental politics at the local, national, and international level. Cheryll Glotfelty believes that ecocriticism and environmental justice movements need to extend there warrant beyond a largely Western and white constituency. "It will become a multi-ethnic movement when stronger connections are made between the environment and issues of social justice, and when a diversity of voices are encouraged to contribute to the discussion" (xxv). Buell agrees, for he has noted, at least since the turn of the twenty-first century, an increase in what he calls "extensionist thinking," by which we acknowledge and reflect on our responsibility to the environment and to its non-human inhabitants. The ethical implications are considerable, for environmental justice must ultimately consider the question, "What qualifies an entity for moral consideration." What, Buell wonders, are the criteria: "higher-order animal intelligence" or the capacity to suffer or some other "interest." The question behind extensionist thought is, *what is being extended?* "Is it rights," he asks. "A kind of utopian parliament of all beings?" (226).

The way that Buell frames these questions presuppose the rejection of anthropocentric ethics, which leads, he warns, into a thicket of controversy over alternatives that explore "nonanthropocentric or ecosystem-first ethics." This is especially true of "the idea of cross-species fraternity," which is vulnerable to attack for being yet another form of "ecofascism" that lumps non-Europeans together with non-humans (227–8). Yet in the twenty-first century, many posthumanist scholars are moving toward just this kind of non-anthropocentric ethics as they revise our way of thinking about how humans and non-humans interact. This is especially the case in animal studies, which focuses on the ontology of the non-human. As **Bruno Latour** has said, the birth of humanity is also the birth of the non-human, only we have misrecognized the latter in our need to know ourselves better, often employing the non-human as a foil in the process. The animal studies perspective is an acknowledgment of this birth. But even as we acknowledge the non-human *other*, we reinscribe the very problematic dualism (self/other, human/non-human) that posthumanism seeks to overturn. This may be why Wolfe believes that we should avoid creating a "super-interdiscipline" called *animal studies*. Instead, we should approach the question of animals and non-human being through our "disciplinary specificity." The "question of the animal" therefore needs to be a *specific* question within a multi- or transdisciplinary field. Moreover, this questioning ought to take place within a larger critique of the "fundamental repression that underlies most ethical and political discourse: repressing the question of nonhuman subjectivity, taking it for granted that the subject is always already human" (*Animal* 1). Wolfe criticizes some theorists, like Stanley Cavell, for allowing "a kind of humanism, a palpable nostalgia for the human," to slip in "through the back door to severely circumscribe the ethical force" of reflection on the nonhuman (*Animal* 48). Ron Broglio approaches these issues from a direction quite different from Wolfe's systems-theory model, but makes a similar point. He takes a phenomenological approach that focuses on ethics and ontology, on "our being and comportment in our world and on this earth" (xviii). He asserts that "animal phenomenology challenges humanism and its scaffolding of mastery," but he is also quick to note that there is no animal-specific phenomenology (though he instances **Donna Haraway**'s *When Species Meet*, which focuses on understanding a dog's life). But even though the question of the being of animals threatens to reaffirm the divide between human and non-human, it is worth asking, if only as an "opening gambit in what culture calls 'the animal'" (xxii–xxiii). Broglio's phenomenological approach leads him to the same point at which Maurice Merleau-Ponty arrived in the mid-twentieth century: *the other gazes back at us.* "When the animal looks back," Broglio writes, "the hegemony of human vision becomes confounded" by the animal's "radical otherness," its proximate materiality, for an "actual encounter with an animal means physical proximity and (near) contact with the flesh of the animal Other" (58–60). The point about flesh is an important one for it marks the surface of the animal, a surface which is, as Broglio argues, "an overlooked site of productive meaning" (81). Surfaces mediate the inside/outside dichotomy, typically serving as the hinge for discerning what is inside (beneath or behind the surface) and what is outside (on, or on the other side of, the surface). The surface is not unlike the elemental concept of Flesh in Merleau-Ponty or the metaphor in Ian Bogost's "alien phenomenology." (On Merleau-Ponty, see Phenomenology and Hermeneutics 146–7.) It is the skin of the animal, which maintains the integrity of its "inside" but is also a screen upon which the human gaze mediates on that inside from a perspective "outside" the animal. "The animal surface is contrasted with and co-opted by the human, who uses his own reflexive interiority (that is, 'thinking') to divide the animal surface into categories and traits of interest" (83).

What I think Broglio and other scholars focusing on non-human ontology are looking for is a way to use the surface of the object (thing, animal, *other*) as the outside that is also inside, as the only conceivable proximity of human being to non-human being. **Giorgio Agamben** sees this possibility in terms of a "caesura between the human and the animal [that] passes first of all within man." But if this is so, then we need to formulate the question of posthumanism in yet another way. Agamben points to the presence in humanity of "a body and a soul, of a living thing and a *logos*, of a natural (or animal) element and supernatural or social divine element." We need to think through "what results from the incongruity of these two elements, and investigate not the metaphysical mystery of conjunction, but rather the practical and political mystery of separation" (*Open* 16). Humanness could thus be understood as a constitutive disjunction, a necessary but fruitful separation of the human from what is animal in her and the human from the non-human world. Reflecting on this disjunction is required if we are to grasp the full dimension of our own humanity and to escape the temptation to fall back into a hierarchical way of structuring the caesura – that is to say, of *re*placing the other within us and the nature that is outside of us. From religion to philosophy, from ethics to law we are "drawn and suspended in the difference between man and animal" (22). **Elizabeth Grosz** makes a similar point when she claims that "the animal prepares and enables the world of human art to fill itself with qualities: the qualities of materiality, nature and the real" (*Becoming* 187). This does not mean that animals inspire us but that the condition *animal* (i.e., animal being) is part and parcel of our artistic aspirations and projects. This idea forces us to rethink the role of *other animals*, "both in human self-understanding" and "in the evolutionary movement in which the human is in the process of self-overcoming, that is, in the process of becoming human. The animal becomes not that against which we define ourselves but that through which we come to our limits" (170). The link between the animal and the human, in short, is already a function of being human, and this "animal becoming," the nearness to materiality of all sorts, is the precondition for art.

The question of the non-human has been posed in many ways by posthumanists seeking a new orientation toward humanity. Whether we speak, as do Broglio and Grosz, of the mediating point between the human and the non-human – either phenomenological or material – or if we speak of inter-species relations, as Donna Haraway does, we are formulating the same kind of questions: what is our humanity and how do we best define if for ourselves? What is the role of discourse and technology in this quest for definition? Does the cyborg model of human adaptability put forward by Haraway – a "hybrid creature, composed of organism and machine" (1) – have more to offer us in an advanced technological era than phenomenological attempts to understand what bats think about? As is the case in almost all contemporary theoretical fields, posthumanism does not require a single answer to the question, but moves forward on the assumption that the project of investigating what it means to be human will require many different forms of the same persistent question: what lies on the other side of our human experience?

We might say, in closing, that this question is really at the back of all modern literary theory, which has persisted in phrasing it again and again for over a hundred years. We might go farther and say that this question is at the back of all of philosophy. For as posthumanist theorists have tirelessly demonstrated, only through human experience can we reach what lies on the other side. But then, in a *ricorso* whose intricate temporality we can thank Nietzsche and Heidegger for uncovering, we will find that we have learned only about ourselves. We may become more sensitive to the non-human *other* and more watchful of the disabled body; we may become more careful of our environment and more eagerly explore the hidden potentialities of our own cognition. If we remain, as Nietzsche believed, "all-too-human," the emphasis falls more readily now on the "all" (the "extensionist thinking" that leads us beyond our humanity and incorporates the world into our sense of ourselves as human) rather than the "too" (which, for Nietzsche, connoted all that was weak and despicable in human nature). We are "all in," as the new phenomenologists and ontologists might say, and that includes the dog, the doorway, the vapor over the swamps, the young girl's half-formed idea, the model car, the ringing phone, the bacteria in the sponge, a Thelonius Monk solo, a mouse, a doctor, a nuclear bomb, a philosophical system, a motorcycle, my favorite aunt, my other, myself.

Works Cited

Adamson, Joni and Rachel Stein. "Environmental Justice: A Roundtable Discussion." *Interdisciplinary Studies in Literature and Environment* 7.2 (Summer 2000): 155–70.

Agamben, Giorgio. *Homo Sacer: Sovereign Power and Bare Life*. Trans. Daniel Heller-Roazen. Stanford: Stanford University Press, 1998.

Agamben, Giorgio. *The Open: Man and Animal*. Trans. Kevin Attell. Stanford: Stanford University Press, 2004.

Ahmed, Sara. "Happy Objects." In *The Affect Theory Reader*. Ed. Melissa Gregg and Gregory J. Seigworth. Durham, NC: Duke University Press, 2010. 29–51.

Ahmed, Sara. *Queer Phenomenology: Orientations, Objects, Others*. Durham, NC: Duke University Press, 2006.

Badiou, Alain. *Being and Event*. Trans. Oliver Feltham. New York: Continuum, 2005.

Badiou, Alain. *Handbook of Inaesthetics*. Trans. Alberto Toscano. Stanford: Stanford University Press, 2005.

Badiou, Alain. *Infinite Thought: Truth and the Return to Philosophy*. Ed. and trans. Oliver Feltham and Justin Clemens. New York: Continuum, 2003.

Badiou, Alain. "One, Multiple, Multiplicities." *Theoretical Writings*. Ed. and trans. Ray Brassier and Alberto Toscano. London: Continuum, 2004. 68–82.

Barnes, Colin, Mike Oliver, and Len Barton. "Introduction." In *Disability Studies Today*. Ed. Colin Barnes, Mike Oliver, and Len Barton. Cambridge: Polity, 2002. 1–17.

Bataille, Georges. *Eroticism, Death and Sensuality*. 1962. Trans. Mary Dalwood. San Francisco: City Lights Books, 1986.

Bauman, H.-Dirksen L. "Toward a Poetics of Vision, Space, and the Body: Sign Language and Literary Theory." In *The Disability Studies Reader*. Ed. Lennard Davis. New York: Routledge, 2006. 355–66.

Benjamin, Walter. *Reflections: Essays, Aphorisms and Autobiographical Writing*. 1978. Ed. Peter Demetz. Trans. Edmund Jephcott. New York: Schocken, 1986.

Bennett, Jane. *Vibrant Matter: A Political Ecology of Things*. Durham, NC: Duke University Press, 2010.

Berlant, Lauren. "Cruel Optimism." In *The Affect Theory Reader*. Ed. Melissa Gregg and Gregory J. Seigworth. Durham, NC: Duke University Press, 2010. 93–117.

Bérubé, Michael. *Life As We Know It: A Father, A Family and an Exceptional Child*. New York: Vintage, 1998.

Bogost, Ian. *Alien Phenomenology, Or What It's Like To Be a Thing*. Minneapolis: University of Minnesota Press, 2012.

Boradkar, Prasad. *Designing Things: A Critical Introduction to the Culture of Objects*. New York: Berg, 2010.

Boyd, Brian. "Getting It All Wrong: Bioculture Critiques Cultural Critique." *American Scholar* 75.4 (Autumn 2006): 18–30.

Boyd, Brian. *On the Origin of Stories: Evolution, Cognition and Fiction*. Cambridge, MA: Belknap Press of Harvard University Press, 2009.

Broglio, Ron. *Surface Encounters: Thinking with Animals and Art*. Minneapolis: University of Minnesota Press, 2011.

Brown, Bill. *A Sense of Things: The Object Matter of American Literature*. Chicago: University of Chicago Press, 2003.

Brown, Bill. "Thing Theory." In *Things*. Ed. Bill Brown. Chicago: University of Chicago Press, 2004.

Bruns, Gerald L. *On Ceasing To Be Human*. Stanford: Stanford University Press, 2011.

Buell, Lawrence. "Ecocriticism: Some Emerging Trends." *Qui Parle* 19.2 (Spring/Summer 2011): 87–115.

Buell, Lawrence. *Writing for an Endangered World*. Cambridge, MA; London, UK: The Belknap Press of Harvard University Press, 2001.

Burke, Edmund. *A Philosophical Enquiry into the Origin of Our Ideas of the Sublime and Beautiful*. 5th ed. London: J. Dodsley, 1767.

Campbell, Sueellen. "The Land and Language of Desire: Where Deep Ecology and Post-Structuralism Meet." In *The Ecocriticism Reader: Landmarks in Literary Ecology*. Ed. Cheryll Glotfelty and Harold Fromm. Athens: University of Georgia Press, 1996. 124–36.

Carroll, Joseph. *Literary Darwinism: Evolution, Human Nature and Literature*. New York: Routledge, 2004.

Carroll, Joseph. *Reading Human Nature: Literary Darwinism in Theory and Practice*. Albany: State University of New York Press, 2011.

Carroll, Joseph, Jonathan Gottschall, John Johnson, and Daniel Kruger. "Imagining Human Nature." In *Evolution, Literature, and Film: A Reader*. Ed. Brian Boyd, Joseph Carroll, and Jonathan Gottschall. New York: Columbia University Press, 2010. 211–23.

Cheah, Pheng. "Non-Dialectical Materialism." In *New Materialism: Ontology, Agency, and Politics*. Ed. Diana Coole and Samantha Frost. Durham, NC: Duke University Press, 2010. 70–91.

Coleman, Lerita M. "Stigma: An Enigma Demystified." In *The Disability Studies Reader*. Ed. Lennard Davis. New York: Routledge, 2006. 141–52.

Davidson, Michael. *Concerto for the Left Hand: Disability and the Defamiliar Body*. Ann Arbor: University of Michigan Press, 2008.

Davis, Lennard. *Bending Over Backwards: Disability, Dismodernism, and Other Difficult Positions*. New York: New York University Press, 2002.

Deleuze, Gilles. *The Fold: Leibniz and the Baroque*. 1993. Trans. Tom Conley. London: Continuum, 2006.

Deleuze, Gilles. *The Logic of Sense*. 1969. Trans. Mark Lester. London: Continuum, 2004.

Deleuze, Gilles and Félix Guattari. "Percept, Affect, and Concept." In *What is Philosophy?* Trans. Hugh Tomlinson and Graham Burchell. New York: Columbia University Press, 1994. 163–99.

Derrida, Jacques. *The Beast and the Sovereign*. Trans. Geoffrey Bennington. Chicago: University of Chicago Press, 2009.

Easterlin, Nancy. *A Biocultural Approach to Literary Theory and Interpretation*. Baltimore: Johns Hopkins University Press, 2012.

Evans, Mei Mei. "'Nature' and Environmental Justice." In *The Environmental Justice Reader: Politics, Poetics and Pedagogy*. Ed. Joni Adamson, Mei Mei Evans, and Rachel Stein. Tucson: University of Arizona Press, 2002. 181–93.

Evernden, Neil. "Beyond Ecology: Self, Place and the Pathetic Fallacy." In *The Ecocriticism Reader: Landmarks in Literary Ecology*. Ed. Cheryll Glotfelty and Harold Fromm. Athens: University of Georgia Press, 1996. 92–104.

Foucault, Michel. "Introduction." *The Normal and the Pathological*. By Georges Canguilhem. 1943. Trans. Carolyn R. Fawcett and Robert S. Cohen. New York: Zone Books, 1989. 7–24.

Foucault, Michel. *Religion and Culture*. Ed. J. R. Carrette. New York: Routledge, 1999.

Foucault, Michel. "The Subject and Power." In *Michel Foucault: Beyond Structuralism and Hermeneutics*. Ed. Herbert L. Dreyfus and Paul Rabinow. Chicago: University of Chicago Press, 1984. 208–26.

Foucault, Michel. "Theatrum Philosophicum." In *Language, Counter-Memory, Practice: Selected Essays and Interviews*. Ed. Donald F. Bouchard. Trans. Donald F. Bouchard and Sherry Simon. Ithaca: Cornell University Press, 1977. 165–96.

Foucault, Michel. "What is an Author?" In *Textual Strategies: Perspectives in Post-Structuralist Criticism*. Ed. and trans. Josué Harari. Ithaca: Cornell University Press, 1979. 141–60.

Freud, Sigmund. *Civilization and Its Discontents*. Trans. James Strachey. New York: Norton, 1989.

Freud, Sigmund. *Future of an Illusion*. Ed. Todd Defresne. Trans. Gregory C. Richter. Toronto: Broadview Press, 2012.

Garland-Thomson, Rosemarie. "Integrating Disability, Transforming Feminist Theory." *NWSA Journal* 14.3 (Autumn 2002): 1–32.

Garrard, Greg. *Ecocriticism*. 2004. 2nd ed. London and New York: Routledge, 2011.

Gartner, Alan and Tom Joe, eds. *Images of the Disabled, Disabling Images*. New York: Praeger, 1987.

Gilson, Erinn Cunniff. "Zones of Indiscernibility: The Life of a Concept from Deleuze to Agamben." *Philosophy Today* 51 (2007): 98–106.

Glotfelty, Cheryll. "Introduction." In *The Ecocriticism Reader: Landmarks in Literary Ecology*. Ed. Cheryll Glotfelty and Harold Fromm. Athens: University of Georgia Press, 1996. xv–xxxvii.

Godwin, William. *Enquiry Concerning Political Justice, and Its Influence on Morals and Happiness*. 1793. 2nd ed. Vol. 1. London: G. G. and J. Robinson, 1796.

Goffman, Erving. *Stigma: Notes on the Management of Spoiled Identity*. New York: Simon and Shuster, 1963.

Gottschall, Jonathan. *Literature, Science, and a New Humanities*. New York: Palgrave Macmillan, 2008.

Gould, Stephen Jay. *The Structure of Evolutionary Theory*. Cambridge, MA: Harvard University Press, 2002.

Grosz, Elizabeth. *Becoming Undone: Darwinian Reflections on Life, Politics and Art*. Durham, NC: Duke University Press, 2011.

Grosz, Elizabeth. "Feminism, Materialism and Freedom." Ed. Stacy Alaimo and Susan Hekman. Bloomington: Indiana University Press, 2008. 139–57.

Haber, Honi Fern. "Lyotard and the Problems of Pagan Politics." *Philosophy Today* 39.2 (Summer 1995): 142–56.

Han-Pile, Béatrice. "The 'Death of Man': Foucault and Anti-Humanism." In *Foucault and Philosophy*. Ed. Timothy O'Leary and Christopher Falzon. Oxford: Wiley-Blackwell, 2010. 118–42.

Haraway, Donna. *Simians, Cyborgs, and Women: The Reinvention of Nature*. New York: Routledge, 1991.

Harman, Graham. *Guerrilla Metaphysics: Phenomenology and the Carpentry of Things*. Chicago: Open Court, 2005.

Harman, Graham. *Tool Being: Heidegger and the Metaphysics of Objects*. Chicago: Open Court, 2002.

Hayles, N. Katherine. *How We Became Posthuman: Virtual Bodies in Cybernetics, Literature, and Informatics*. Chicago: University of Chicago Press, 1999.

Hayles, N. Katherine. *How We Think: Digital Media and Contemporary Technogenesis*. Chicago: University of Chicago Press, 2012.

Heidegger, Martin. *Being and Time*. Trans. Joan Stambaugh. Albany: State University of New York Press, 1996.

Heidegger, Martin. "Letter on Humanism." In *Basic Writings*. 2nd rev. and expanded ed. Ed. David Farrell Krell. New York: HarperCollins, 1993. 213–66.

Heidegger, Martin. *The Question Concerning Technology and Other Essays*. Trans. William Lovitt. New York: Garland, 1977.

Hentoff, Nat. "The Awful Privacy of Baby Doe." *The Nat Hentoff Reader*. Boston: De Capo Press, 2001. 263–85.

Hernadi, Paul. "Why is Literature: A Coevolutionary Perspective on Imaginative Worldmaking." *Poetics Today* 22.1 (Spring 2002): 22–42.

Hogan, Patrick Colm. *Affective Narratology: The Emotional Structure of Stories*. Lincoln: University of Nebraska Press, 2011.

Hogan, Patrick Colm. "Literary Universals." In *Introduction to Cognitive Cultural Studies*. Ed. Lisa Zunshine. Baltimore: Johns Hopkins University Press, 2010. 37–60.

Horkheimer, Max and Theodor Adorno. *Dialectic of Enlightenment: Philosophical Fragments*. 1947. Ed. Gunzelin Schmid Noerr. Trans. Edmund Jephcott. Stanford: Stanford University Press, 2002.

Howarth, William. "Some Principles of Ecocriticism." In *The Ecocriticism Reader: Landmarks in Literary Ecology*. Ed. Cheryll Glotfelty and Harold Fromm. Athens: University of Georgia Press, 1996. 69–91.

Hughes, Bill. "Disability and the Body." In *Disability Studies Today*. Ed. Colin Barnes, Mike Oliver, and Len Barton. Cambridge: Polity, 2002. 58–76.

Husserl, Edmund. "Phenomenology." In *Psychological and Transcendental Phenomenology and the Confrontation with Heidegger*. 1927–1931. Ed. and trans. Thomas Sheehan and Richard E. Palmer. Dordrecht: Kluwer, 1997. 80–198.

Kolodny, Annette. "Unearthing Herstory: An Introduction." In *The Ecocriticism Reader: Landmarks in Literary Ecology*. Ed. Cheryll Glotfelty and Harold Fromm. Athens: University of Georgia Press, 1996. 170–81.

Latour, Bruno. *On the Modern Cult of the Factish Gods*. Trans. Catherine Porter and Heather MacLean. Durham, NC: Duke University Press, 2010.

Latour, Bruno. *The Pasteurization of France*. Trans. Alan Sheridan and John Law. Cambridge, MA: Harvard University Press, 1988.

Latour, Bruno. *Reassembling the Social: An Introduction to Actor-Network Theory*. Oxford: Oxford University Press, 2005.

Latour, Bruno. *We Have Never Been Modern*. 1991. Trans. Catherine Porter. Cambridge, MA: Harvard University Press, 1993.

Lopez, Barry. *Arctic Dreams*. New York: Scribner, 1986.

Love, Glen A. *Practical Ecocriticism: Literature, Biology and the Environment*. Charlottesville: University of Virginia Press, 2003.

Luhmann, Niklas. *Art as a Social System*. Trans. Eva M. Knodt. Stanford: Stanford University Press, 2000.

Lyotard, Jean-François. *The Inhuman: Reflections on Time*. Trans. Geoffrey Bennington and Rachel Bow. Cambridge: Polity Press, 1991.

Marx, Karl. *Capital: A Critique of Political Economy.* Vol. 1. Trans. Ben Fowkes. New York: Vintage Books, 1977.

Massumi, Brian. "The Future Birth of the Affective Fact: The Political Ontology of Threat." In *The Affect Theory Reader.* Ed. Melissa Gregg and Gregory J. Seigworth. Durham, NC: Duke University Press, 2010. 52–70.

McRuer, Robert. *Crip Theory: Cultural Signs of Queerness and Disability.* New York: New York University Press, 2006.

Merleau-Ponty, Maurice. "The Intertwining – The Chiasm." In *The Visible and the Invisible.* Ed. Claude Lefort. Trans. Alphonso Lingis. Evanston, IL: Northwestern University Press, 1968. 130–55.

Mitchell, David T. and Sharon L. Snyder. *Narrative Prosthesis: Disability and the Dependencies of Discourse.* Ann Arbor: University of Michigan Press, 2000.

Nagel, Thomas. "What Is It Like to Be a Bat?" *Philosophical Review* 83.4 (1974): 435–50.

Nietzsche, Friedrich. *The Gay Science.* Trans. Walter Kaufmann. New York: Vintage, 1974.

Nietzsche, Friedrich. *Thus Spoke Zarathustra.* Trans. Graham Parkes. Oxford: Oxford University Press, 2005.

Nietzsche, Friedrich. *The Will to Power.* Ed. Walter Kaufmann. Trans. Walter Kaufmann and R. J. Hollingdale. New York: Viking, 1968.

Nixon, Rob. *Slow Violence and the Environmentalism of the Poor.* Cambridge, MA: Harvard University Press, 2011.

Ortiz, Simon. "Passing Through Little Rock." In *Woven Stone.* Tucson: University of Arizona Press, 1992. 98.

Rancière, Jacques. *Althusser's Lesson.* Trans. Emiliano Battista. New York: Continuum, 2011.

Richardson, Alan. "Studies in Literature and Cognition: A Field Map." In *The Work of Fiction: Cognition, Culture, and Complexity.* Alan Richardson and Ellen Spolsky. Aldershot: Ashgate, 2004. 1–25.

Salisbury, Laura. "Cognitive Studies." In *The Encyclopedia of Literary and Cultural Studies.* Vol. 2. Ed. Robert Eaglestone. Oxford: Wiley-Blackwell, 2011.

Samuels, Ellen. "Critical Divides: Judith Butler's Body Theory and the Question of Disability." *NWSA Journal* 14.3 (Autumn 2002): 58–76.

Sandilands, Catriona. *The Good-Natured Feminist: Ecofeminism and the Quest for Democracy.* Minneapolis: University of Minnesota Press, 1999.

Shakespeare, Tom., ed. *The Disability Reader: A Social Science Perspective.* New York: Cassell, 1998.

Siebers, Tobin. *Disability Aesthetics.* Ann Arbor University of Michigan Press, 2010.

Siebers, Tobin. "Disability in Theory: From Social Constructionism to the Realism of the Body." In *The Disability Studies Reader.* Ed. Lennard Davis. New York: Routledge, 2006. 173–84.

Slovic, Scott. "Nature Writing and Environmental Psychology: The Interiority of Outdoor Experience." In *The Ecocriticism Reader: Landmarks in Literary Ecology.* Ed. Cheryll Glotfelty and Harold Fromm. Athens: University of Georgia Press, 1996. 351–70.

Spolsky, Ellen. "Darwin and Derrida: Cognitive Literary Theory as a Species of Post-Structuralism." *Poetics Today* 22.1 (Spring 2002): 43–62.

Tremain, Shelley. "Foucault, Governmentality, and Critical Disability Theory: An Introduction." In *Foucault and the Government of Disability.* Ed. Shelley Tremain. Ann Arbor: University of Michigan Press, 2005. 1–24.

Warren, Karen J. *Ecofeminism: Women, Culture, Nature.* Bloomington: Indiana University Press, 1997.

Wittgenstein, Ludwig. *Philosophical Investigations.* Rev. 4th ed. Ed. P. M. S. Hacker and Joachim Schulte. Trans. G. E. M. Anscombe, P. M. S. Hacker, and Joachim Schulte. Oxford: Wiley-Blackwell, 2009.

Wolfe, Cary. *Animal Rites: American Culture, the Discourse of Species and Posthumanist Theory*. Chicago: University of Chicago Press, 2003.

Wolfe, Cary. *What is Posthumanism?* Minneapolis: University of Minnesota Press, 2010.

Wordsworth, William and Samuel Taylor Coleridge. *Lyrical Ballads*. 1800. 2nd ed. London: Longman, 2007.

Zunshine, Lisa, ed. *Introduction to Cognitive Cultural Studies*. Baltimore: Johns Hopkins University Press, 2010.

3

Key Figures in Literary Theory

All shuffle there; all cough in ink;
All wear the carpet with their shoes;
All think what other people think;
All know the man their neighbour knows.
Lord, what would they say
Did their Catullus walk that way?
                    W. B. Yeats, "The Scholars"

Theodor Adorno (1903–69)

Theodor Adorno was born Theodor Ludwig Wiesengrund in Frankfurt, Germany, later taking on his mother's maiden name. His father was a Jewish convert to Protestantism and his mother a Catholic, though it would be his Jewish background that would prove decisive in his intellectual development. He was a highly gifted student, studying Kant and Husserl at an early age. He attended the University of Frankfurt, where he received the doctorate in philosophy in 1924. He was also a musician and composer. In the mid-1920s, he traveled to Vienna, where he studied with the composer Alban Berg and became a devotee of Arnold Schoenberg, the great modernist composer whose work had influenced Berg and, according to some critics, inspired some of the innovations in Adorno's philosophy.

Adorno began his academic career with a dissertation on the Danish philosopher Søren Kierkegaard, published in 1933. At this time, he was attached to the Institute for Social Research, which had been established ten years earlier. However, the Institute's work was disrupted by the rise to power of Hitler's National Socialist movement. Like so many other Jewish intellectuals at this time, Adorno went into

The Literary Theory Handbook, First Edition. Gregory Castle.
© 2013 John Wiley & Sons, Ltd. Published 2013 by John Wiley & Sons, Ltd.

exile, first at Oxford, later in the United States. He was affiliated with Princeton University in the period 1938–41, then followed the Institute to Geneva and New York and finally to Los Angeles, where he became co-director with Max Horkheimer. His first major publication, with Horkheimer, was *The Dialectic of Enlightenment* (1944), a penetrating critique of the Enlightenment tradition of philosophy and literature and its consequences for contemporary culture, including the rise of the "culture industry," totalitarianism, and the commodification of art and AESTHETICS under capitalism. In 1958, he became the director of the Institute, and the ten years that followed, until his death in 1969, were the most productive of his career. In this period, he wrote his most important philosophical works, including *Negative Dialectics* (1966), *Minima Moralia* (1966), and *Aesthetic Theory* (1970). In these works, Adorno critiqued the German idealist tradition from Kant to Heidegger and offered a powerful new alternative to it, one that resisted the seduction of identitarian thought, which led to the loss of authentic subjectivity and, ultimately, to an instrumentalized and administered society. His concern with the practical social consequences of theory was inherited by his students who became involved in violent protest on the Frankfurt University campus against government emergency laws. During this tumultuous time, while vacationing in Switzerland, Adorno died of a heart attack after mountain climbing.

Selected Bibliography

Adorno, Theodor. *The Adorno Reader*. Ed. Brian O'Connor. Oxford and Malden, MA: Blackwell, 2000.

Adorno, Theodor. *Aesthetic Theory*. Ed. Gretel Adorno and Rolf Tiedemann. Trans. Robert Hullot-Kentor. Minneapolis: University of Minnesota Press, 1997.

Adorno, Theodor (with Max Horkheimer). *The Dialectic of Enlightenment*. Trans. John Cumming. New York: Herder and Herder, 1972.

Adorno, Theodor. *Minima Moralia: Reflections from Damaged Life*. Trans. E. F. N. Jephcott. London: Verso, 1974.

Adorno, Theodor. *Negative Dialectics*. Trans. E. B. Ashton. New York: Seabury Press, 1973.

Adorno, Theodor. *Prisms*. Trans. Samuel and Shierry Weber. Cambridge, MA: MIT Press, 1981.

Giorgio Agamben (1942–)

Giorgio Agamben was born in Rome and educated at the University of Rome where he studied political thought. He attended lectures by Heidegger in the 1960s. He was a fellow at the Warburg Institute, University of London, in the 1970s and has taught at a number of European universities, including the European Graduate School in Saas-Fee, Switzerland, where he holds the Baruch Spinoza Chair. He also teaches at the University of Paris VIII and the University of Macerata in Italy. Agamben began publishing in the 1970s and these early works show a wide-ranging interest in literature, politics, religion, and culture. In *Stanzas* (1977), he drew on psychoanalysis to develop a theory of *phantasms*, the lost or obscure object of desire. In the 1980s, he focused on the critique of history and the concept of negativity. His *Language and Death: The Place of Negativity* continues a line of thought that can be traced back at least to Georges Bataille in that it tries to account for the function of the negative and the role of death, the ultimate negation, in our social and ethical systems. He begins to move more fully into an ethical and political philosophy with *The Coming Community* (1990) and *Homo Sacer: Sovereign Power and Bare Life* (1995). The latter's theory of the "exception," exemplified by the "bare life" of the new sacred man, has had a profound impact on literary and cultural studies, as well as in philosophy and political science. *Homo Sacer* was followed by several volumes that carry on its principal argument, including *State of Exception* (2003) and additional volumes on economy and government and the oath. Agamben has also published on poetics, the nature of the witness in *Remnants of Auschwitz* (1998), and on biblical texts. A posthumanist orientation is revealed in *The Open: Man and Animal* (2002). Like many postmodernist and posthumanist theorists, Agamben is interested in rethinking the foundations of Western culture, which has drawn him to foundational languages (Greek, Latin), cultures (classical, medieval), and political structures. Though hard to categorize, Agamben models the twenty-first-century posthumanist philosopher-critic.

Selected Bibliography

Agamben, Giorgio. *The End of the Poem: Studies in Poetics*. Trans. Daniel Heller-Roazen. Stanford: Stanford University Press, 1999.

Agamben, Giorgio. *Homo Sacer: Sovereign Power and Bare Life*. Trans. Daniel Heller-Roazen. Stanford: Stanford University Press, 1998.

Agamben, Giorgio. *Language and Death: The Place of Negativity*. Trans. Karen E. Pinkus. Minneapolis: University of Minnesota Press, 1991.

Agamben, Giorgio. *The Open: Man and Animal*. Trans. Kevin Attell. Stanford: Stanford University Press, 2004.

Agamben, Giorgio. *State of Exception (Homo Sacre II, 1)*. Trans. Kevin Attell. Chicago: University of Chicago Press, 2005.

Louis Althusser (1918–90)

Louis Althusser was born in Algeria and studied at the École Normale Supérieure in Paris. During World War II, he was involved in Catholic youth groups and became radicalized during the Nazi occupation of France. After a short time spent in a German concentration camp for his activities on behalf of the French Communist Party, he took his degree in 1948 and began teaching at the ENS, where he remained until 1980. One of his students in the early years of his tenure at the ENS was **Michel Foucault**, who was inspired by (if not converted to) Marxism under Althusser's tutelage. Althusser's form of "structuralist Marxism" was very much a product of the intellectual environment of France in the 1950s and early 1960s. Rejecting the humanism of so much Marxist theory, but not its empiricism, Althusser insisted on the importance of IDEOLOGY and ideology critique. In *For Marx* (1965), he revised the idea of dialectical contradiction, stressing the condition of OVERDETERMINATION, an intensification of class contradictions at moments of social and economic crisis that leads to either "historical inhibition" or "revolutionary rupture." With Étienne Balibar, Althusser wrote *Reading "Capital"* (1968), a critique of classical economics and a close analysis of Marx's political economy. In this work, Althusser and Balibar reject the theory that Marxism is a species of historicism and put forward a scientific theory of Marx's thought.

The attempt to transform Marxism into a more rigorous science dedicated to the structuralist analysis of ideology is continued in Althusser's most influential work, the collection of essays titled *Lenin and Philosophy* (1971). In "Ideology and Ideological State Apparatuses," Althusser argues that ideology "interpellates" or conscripts SUBJECTS into ideological discourses. Subjects are subjects precisely because of this interpellation. Also in *Lenin and Philosophy*, Althusser reflects on the importance of Freudian and Lacanian psychoanalysis for a Marxist analysis of capitalism. He continued to publish essays throughout the 1970s, but met with an infamous end to his career in 1980. In that year, Althusser murdered his wife and, after confessing to the crime, was committed to a psychiatric hospital where he spent the last ten years of his life. He told the story of the murder in his memoirs, *The Future Lasts a Long Time*.

Selected Bibliography

Althusser, Louis. *Althusser: A Critical Reader*. Ed. Gregory Elliott. Oxford and Cambridge, MA: Blackwell, 1994.
Althusser, Louis. *For Marx*. Trans. Ben Brewster. New York: Pantheon Books, 1969.
Althusser, Louis. *Lenin and Philosophy, and Other Essays*. Trans. Ben Brewster. London: New Left Books, 1971.
Althusser, Louis and Étienne Balibar. *Reading "Capital."* Trans. Ben Brewster. London: New Left Books, 1970.

Mikhail Mikhailovich Bakhtin (1895–1975)

Mikhail Mikhailovich Bakhtin was born in Orel, Russia, and was educated at the University of St. Petersburg. In 1918, he left St. Petersburg, at the height of the Revolution, and settled in Vitebsk, where he worked as a school teacher and started the Bakhtin Circle, whose members combined formalist methods with an interest in genre study (especially prose styles) and the impact of IDEOLOGY on language, discourse, aesthetics, and literature. The writings of key members of this group, including P. N. Medvedev and V. N. Voloshinov, were once considered by scholars to have been written by Bakhtin, but the consensus now is that Medvedev and Voloshinov were responsible for the texts that bear their names. In 1924, Bakhtin moved to Leningrad, where he had difficulties finding employment due to his lack of enthusiasm for Marxism. By 1929, he had the misfortune to draw the attention of Stalin's regime which, in those early years, conducted regular purges of intellectuals. He was accused of associating with the underground Orthodox Church, a charge that has never been substantiated or dismissed, and sentenced to internal exile, first in Kazakhstan (1930–6), where he worked on a collective farm, later in Mordovia (1937–69), where he taught at the Mordov Pedagogical Institute in Saransk. Throughout these years, Bakhtin suffered from poor health and in 1938 had to have one of his legs amputated.

In Leningrad, in the years before his exile, Bakhtin produced his first important work, *Problems of Dostoevsky's Poetics* (1929), which explored the structures of novelistic prose and introduced the concept of DIALOGISM to describe the polyphonic and dynamic totality of language possibilities in a given discourse or text. In the 1930s and 1940s, Bakhtin introduced two other concepts: HETEROGLOSSIA, a discourse "environment" characterized by polyphony, by multiple languages, dialects, jargons, and other discursive forms; and the CARNIVALESQUE, a mode of subversive representation based on the inversion of hierarchies. Also during this time, he began studying the *Bildungsroman*, but most of this work was lost when his publisher's stock was destroyed by the Germans. Due to a shortage of cigarette paper, Bakhtin was forced to use the pages of the prospectus to roll cigarettes. Fragments of the work were published in *Speech Acts and Other Late Essays* (1979).

After Stalin's death in 1953, Bakhtin's work attracted more notice by scholars and by the late 1950s he was a well-known and respected figure among the Soviet intellectual elite as well as among European circles familiar with Russian Formalism. In 1973, the essays on the novel written in the 1930s were published, and they solidified his reputation in the Soviet Union. Lionized and widely influential, Bakhtin died in 1975. These essays, translated into English as *The Dialogic Imagination* (1981), are Bakhtin's most important contribution to poststructuralism and the theory of the novel.

Selected Bibliography

Bakhtin, M. M. *The Bakhtin Reader: Selected Writings of Bakhtin, Medvedev, and Voloshinov.* Ed. Pam Morris. London: E. Arnold, 1994.

Bakhtin, M. M. *The Dialogic Imagination.* Ed. Michael Holquist. Trans. Caryl Emerson and Michael Holquist. Austin: University of Austin Press, 1981.

Bakhtin, M. M. *Problems of Dostoevsky's Poetics.* Trans. Caryl Emerson. Minneapolis: University of Minnesota Press, 1984.

Bakhtin, M. M. *Rabelais and His World.* Trans. Hélène Iswolsky. Cambridge, MA: MIT Press, 1968.

Roland Barthes (1915–80)

Roland Barthes was born in Cherbourg, northern France, but after his father's death in World War I, his mother relocated to Bayonne. In 1924, the family moved to Paris, where Barthes studied classics, grammar, and philology at the Sorbonne, receiving degrees in 1939 and 1943. He taught at a number of lycées in Biarritz, Bayonne, and

Paris, and, in the late 1940s, at the French Institute in Bucharest and the University of Alexandria in Egypt. In the 1950s, he worked for the Direction Générale des Affaires Culturelles and held a research post with the Centre National de la Recherche Scientifique. His academic appointments include director of studies at École Pratique des Hautes Études (1960–76), and chair of the department of literary semiology at the Collège de France (1976–80).

Barthes' early work emphasized SEMIOLOGY and structural linguistics. *Writing Degree Zero* (1953) introduced the concept of *écriture*, the "written" quality of language, while *Elements of Semiology* (1964) and *S/Z* (1970) focused on the structuralist analysis of literary texts. Barthes' unique mode of structuralist analysis was applied to a host of texts, including works by the Marquis de Sade and St. Ignatius of Loyola. In *Mythologies* (1958), he applied structuralist and semiological methods to a wide array of non-literary cultural texts, from wrestling and food to fashion and striptease. In 1966, he published the groundbreaking essay, "Introduction to the Structural Analysis of Narrative." Though grounded in structuralism and semiology, Barthes' work frequently challenged the limits of these fields. His most celebrated essay, "The Death of the Author" (1968), announced that the reader, the "modern scriptor," had overturned the traditional authority of author. In works like *The Pleasure of the Text* (1973), he transcended the limitations of structuralism and became a pioneer of poststructuralism. His later essays continued this new trend in poststructuralist analysis. His last work, *Camera Lucida* (1980), explored the communicative potential of photography, bringing to bear on that medium his unique brand of poststructuralist semiology. In that same year, Barthes was killed in a street accident in Paris. A memoir, *Incidents*, appeared posthumously in 1983.

Selected Bibliography

Barthes, Roland. *A Barthes Reader*. Ed. Susan Sontag. New York: Hill and Wang, 1982.

Barthes, Roland. *Image-Music-Text*. Trans. Stephen Heath. New York: Hill and Wang, 1977.

Barthes, Roland. *Mythologies*. Selected and trans. Annette Lavers. New York: Hill and Wang, 1972.

Barthes, Roland. *The Pleasure of the Text*. Trans. Richard Miller. New York: Hill and Wang, 1975.

Barthes, Roland. *Writing Degree Zero and Elements of Semiology*. Trans. Annette Lavers and Colin Smith. New York: Hill and Wang, 1968.

Stafford, Andy. *Roland Barthes, Phenomenon and Myth: An Intellectual Biography*. Edinburgh: Edinburgh University Press, 1998.

Jean Baudrillard (1929–2007)

Jean Baudrillard was born in Reims, France, and studied German at the Sorbonne University in Paris. He went on to teach German at the lycée level (1958–66) and later worked as a translator and critic. Until 1987, he taught at the University of Paris X (Nanterre) at various levels. He then served as scientific director at the Institut de Recherche et d'Information Socio-Économique at the University of Paris

IX (Dauphine). From 2001 until his death, he was associated with the European Graduate School in Saas-Fee, Switzerland.

Baudrillard's work emerges at the intersection of SEMIOLOGY and the post-Marxism of the French avant-garde. His first major work, *The System of Objects* (1968), with its emphasis on collecting, advertising, and consumption, argues that objects structure social life by signifying status and position within a general system of objectified relations. Important works of this period include *For a Critique of the Political Economy of the Sign* (1972) and *The Mirror of Production* (1973), which refine Marxian analysis of cultural discourse by thinking of the "signifying economies" that accompany production and dictate consumption. In later works like *Simulations* (1981), which gained him academic acclaim and a certain degree of celebrity, Baudrillard defined postmodern signifying economies in terms of "hyperreality" in which SIMULATIONS of the real displace reality. His most famous example is Disneyland, which exists in order to disguise the fact that it is itself the "real" America. His work in the 1990s continued this examination of postmodern culture, especially in America. Perhaps his most controversial book is *The Gulf War Did Not Take Place* (1991), which argues that both sides of the conflict generated computer simulations that became the basis for "actual" events. His later work, particularly the multi-volume *Cool Memories* (1995–2000), touches on a multitude of contemporary topics, from cats to **Foucault**, and call to mind the fecund imagination of **Roland Barthes**. Though much criticized for his "fatal" criticism, which some critics see as thinly disguised nostalgia for referentiality, Baudrillard's work has contributed much to our understanding of the way signs and simulations function in media-saturated societies.

Selected Bibliography

Baudrillard, Jean. *Baudrillard: A Critical Reader*. Ed. Douglas Kellner. Oxford and Cambridge, MA: Blackwell, 1994.

Baudrillard, Jean. *For a Critique of the Political Economy of the Sign*. Trans. Charles Levin. St. Louis: Telos Press, 1981.

Baudrillard, Jean. *The Gulf War Did Not Take Place*. Trans. Paul Patton. Bloomington and Indianapolis: Indiana University Press; Sydney: Power Publications, 1994.

Baudrillard, Jean. *Simulations*. Trans. Paul Foss, Paul Patton, and Philip Beitchman. New York: Semiotext(e), 1983.

Walter Benjamin (1892–1940)

Walter Benjamin was born in Berlin and studied philosophy in Bern, Switzerland, receiving his doctorate in 1919, though his *Habilitationsschrift* (a second thesis required for a professorship at a university), *The Origin of German Tragic Drama*, was rejected by the University of Frankfurt because of its unconventional use of quotation as a compositional method. It was published in 1928 and was the only book-length study he published in his lifetime. Benjamin became a freelance critic and translator and was associated with the theorists of the Frankfurt Institute for Social Research. He was especially close to **Theodor Adorno**, who disagreed with some of his ideas but formed a lasting intellectual bond with him. He was also close to the playwright Bertolt Brecht, who shared his skepticism about orthodox Marxism. Benjamin practiced a form of CULTURAL MATERIALISM that was strongly influenced by Surrealism, mysticism, and a "messianic" vision of history.

After Hitler and the National Socialists took power in Germany in 1933, Benjamin fled to Paris, where he found a congenial environment for his idiosyncratic method of cultural analysis. His reflections on the Parisian "arcades," indoor markets that extended for blocks and that contained a multitude of separate businesses, were meant to constitute his *magnum opus*, but they were not published in his lifetime. In another of his posthumously published works, *Charles Baudelaire: Lyric Poet of High Capitalism* (1969), Benjamin elaborated on the important concept of the *flâneur*, that modernist figure *par excellence*, at home in the city, moving among an endless array of spectacles and commodities. Adorno, who corresponded with Benjamin from 1928 until his death, was fascinated with this project, but he was also frustrated with his friend's optimism with respect to commodity culture.

Events ultimately caught up with Benjamin. As the Nazis closed in on Paris in 1939, he fled to the Spanish frontier, hoping to make it to the United States. Weakened because of heart trouble and in despair that he could not obtain a visa to enter Spain, Benjamin committed suicide. With the devoted attention of Adorno, Hannah Arendt, and others, Benjamin's arcades project and his numerous essays were finally published.

Selected Bibliography

Benjamin, Walter. *The Arcades Project*. Trans. Howard Eiland and Kevin McLaughlin. Cambridge, MA and London: Belknap Press, 1999.

Benjamin, Walter. *Selected Writings*. Ed. Marcus Bullock and Michael W. Jennings. 4 vols. Cambridge, MA: Belknap Press of Harvard University Press, 1996.

Homi Bhabha (1949–)

Homi Bhabha was born in Bombay, India, a member of the ancient Parsi community there. He studied at the University of Bombay and completed his doctorate at Oxford University. He has held teaching positions at several English universities and at Princeton University, the University of Pennsylvania, and the University of Chicago. He is now Anne F. Rothenberg Professor of the Humanities at Harvard University.

Bhabha's analysis of colonial experience is grounded in the work of **Frantz Fanon**, especially his theories of racial difference and mimicry, **Jacques Derrida, Michel Foucault**, and **Jacques Lacan**. His first major work, an edited volume of essays, *Nation and Narration*, brought together a wide variety of theorists who challenged the Enlightenment conception of nationalism and nationality and questioned the possibility of an ESSENTIALIST or UNIVERSALIST idea of the nation. Bhabha's contribution to the debate, "DissemiNation: Time, Narrative, and the Margins of the Modern Nation," used the tools of poststructuralism, specifically Foucault's theories of power and discourse, to critique the Enlightenment tradition of historicism and to develop a theory of *emergence* to account for the wide variety of nations and nationalist movements. *The Location of Culture*, a collection of Bhabha's essays from the 1980s and early 1990s, was an immense success and has remained influential in postcolonial studies. Bhabha advanced the concepts of HYBRIDITY and MIMICRY, which refer to the conditions of AMBIVALENCE that characterize colonial experience and colonial discourse. In the act of mimicry, the colonial subject inhabits and revises the "colonialist script," using it to express anti-colonial sentiments, even to serve as the rallying cry of insurrection. In the decade since the publication of *The Location of Culture*, Bhabha has written on vernacular cosmopolitanism and the ethical dimensions of narration in a transnational context.

Selected Bibliography

Bhabha, Homi K. *The Location of Culture*. London and New York: Routledge, 1994.
Bhabha, Homi K., ed. *Nation and Narration*. London: Routledge, 1990.
Bhabha, Homi K. "Unsatisfied: Notes on Vernacular Cosmopolitanism." In *Postcolonial Discourses: An Anthology*. Ed. Gregory Castle. Oxford: Blackwell, 2001. 38–52.

Pierre Bourdieu (1930–2002)

Pierre Bourdieu was born in Denguin, a village in the Pyrenées in southern France, and attended school at the École Normale Supérieure in Paris, excelling at rugby and philosophy. Like **Jacques Derrida**, a fellow student at the ENS, Bourdieu studied the phenomenology of Merleau-Ponty, Heidegger, and Husserl. After a short stint in Algeria, serving in the French Army, he lectured at the University of Algiers (1959–60). He began his anthropological study of Berber culture at this time. The 1960s found him teaching at the University of Paris and the University of Lille and, from 1968, directing the Centre de Sociologie Européenne.

Bourdieu's early work in anthropology and sociology focused on education and social environment. A study of the Kabylia people in Algeria, *Outline of a Theory of Practice*, was published in 1972. He developed the concept of HABITUS, or "socialized subjectivity," to describe the personal adaptations and motivations, attitudes, and modes of perception that arise as a result of individuals interacting in complex modern societies. He combined empirical methodologies with a theoretical framework that owes much to poststructuralism to form a hybrid theoretical approach to complex cultural fields. His first major work, *Distinction* (1979), argues that social life is marked by the levels of distinction that attach to the individual by virtue of his or her manipulation of habitus within the wider social field. The broad theoretical implications and a "practical logics" are explored in *The Logic of Practice* (1980). Later works, like *The Field of Cultural Production*, explore the sociology of AESTHETICS, a form of reflexive analysis that regards the work of art as embedded within social fields and the systems dependent upon them. Bourdieu's work has influenced a broad array of disciplines, including literature, anthropology, sociology, discourse theory, philosophy, and aesthetics.

Selected Bibliography

Bourdieu, Pierre. *Bourdieu: A Critical Reader*. Ed. Richard Shusterman. Oxford and Malden, MA: Blackwell, 1999.

Bourdieu, Pierre. *Distinction: A Social Critique of the Judgment of Taste*. Trans. Richard Nice. London: Routledge and Kegan Paul, 1984.

Bourdieu, Pierre. *The Field of Cultural Production: Essays on Art and Literature*. Ed. Randal Johnson. New York: Columbia University Press, 1993.

Bourdieu, Pierre. *The Logic of Practice*. Trans. Richard Nice. Stanford: Stanford University Press, 1990.

Lawrence Buell (1939–)

Lawrence Buell was educated at Princeton University and Cornell University, receiving his doctorate from the latter. He is currently the Powell M. Cabot Professor of American Literature at Harvard University, where he is also a faculty associate of the Center for the Environment. Buell began his scholarly career with a study of American transcendentalism and an edited volume of the work of Elizabeth Barstow Stoddard, a little-known nineteenth-century American writer. He continued this line of scholarly work with *New England Literary Culture*, which explores the professionalization of literary culture in New England from the Revolutionary era to the late nineteenth century. Buell's interest in the American transcendentalists grounds him in a tradition of writing about nature and the environment that is both localist and idealist, qualities that characterize his own reflections on environments. By the mid-1990s, with the publication of *The Environmental Imagination: Thoreau, Nature Writing, and the Formation of American Culture*, Buell was a leading figure in the emergent field of ecocriticism, which he prefers to call environmental criticism. His next book, *Writing for an Endangered World* (2001), established an "ecoglobalist" perspective, with reflections on place, modernization, fiction, and the city and the concept of "nonanthropocentric ethics." The emphasis on space is continued in *The Future of Environmental Criticism* (2005), which is something of a manifesto that traces the history of ecocriticism and the emergence of an emphasis on environmental justice. The combination of local treatment of the American scene – exemplified in a volume edited by Buell and Wai Chee Dimock, *Shades of the Planet* – and a globalist standpoint redefines our notions of place, landscape, geography, environment, and ecology. The "ecoglobalist affects" he discusses in his contribution to *Shades of the Planet* are the signs of an environment, even a historical environment, *talking back*.

Selected Bibliography

Buell, Lawrence. "Ecocriticism: Some Emerging Trends." *Qui Parle* 19.2 (Spring/Summer 2011): 87–115.

Buell, Lawrence. *The Environmental Imagination: Thoreau, Nature Writing, and the Formation of American Culture*. Cambridge, MA: Harvard University Press, 1995.

Buell, Lawrence. *The Future of Environmental Criticism*. Oxford: Wiley-Blackwell, 2005.
Buell, Lawrence. *Writing for an Endangered World*. Cambridge, MA: Belknap Press of Harvard University Press, 2001.

Judith Butler (1956–)

Judith Butler was born in Cleveland, Ohio, and studied at Bennington College and Yale University, where she completed her doctorate in philosophy in 1984. She is currently Chancellor's Professor of Rhetoric and Comparative Literature at the University of California at Berkeley. She published her dissertation as *Subjects of Desire: Hegelian Reflections in Twentieth-Century France* in 1987. Butler made her reputation in the 1990s with two important works on gender and sexuality. *Gender Trouble* (1990) critiqued the norm of compulsory heterosexuality and argued that IDENTITY was a function not of ESSENTIALIST gender roles or characteristics but rather of PERFORMATIVITY, which challenges the very notion of a subject. This argument was pursued further in *Bodies that Matter* (1993), which analyzes the status of sex as a regulatory social norm, with particular emphasis on how this norm is inscribed on the body, how it in fact animates and "materializes" the body.

Butler's later work, especially *Excitable Speech: A Politics of the Performative* (1997), indicates the decisive role that public language – her chief example is "hate speech" – plays in constituting the performative element of social life. In the *Psychic Life of Power* (1997), she pursued the idea that social power is internalized in an ambivalent form of subjection that is also the ground of the subject as such. At the turn of the twenty-first century, Butler collaborated with Ernesto Laclau and **Slavoj Žižek** to produce a collection of essays on problems in critical theory, *Contingency, Hegemony, Universality* (2000). Butler's contributions address, among other things, the possibilities of "contingent universals" that could avoid the absolutism of Enlightenment traditions of critical thinking but that could also galvanize and consolidate movements for social change. Late work, like *Precarious Life* (2004) and *Frames of War* (2009), examines the ethics of mourning in the wake of the attacks on the World Trade Center and the Pentagon in 2001. Her brand of critical theory welds Hegelian methods and concepts to the themes of contemporary violence, mass mediation, and identity politics.

Selected Bibliography

Butler, Judith. *Bodies that Matter: On the Discursive Limits of "Sex."* New York: Routledge, 1993.
Butler, Judith. *Excitable Speech: A Politics of the Performative*. New York: Routledge, 1997.
Butler, Judith. *Gender Trouble: Feminism and the Subversion of Identity*. New York: Routledge, 1990.
Butler, Judith. *The Judith Butler Reader*. Ed. Sara Salih. Oxford and Malden, MA: Blackwell, 2004.
Butler, Judith. *The Psychic Life of Power: Theories of Subjection*. Stanford: Stanford University Press, 1997.

Hélène Cixous (1937–)

Hélène Cixous was born in Oran, Algeria. She studied in France and completed her doctorate in 1968. In the next year she published her dissertation, *The Exile of James Joyce*. A year after the student uprisings in May 1968, Cixous was put in charge of developing curriculum for the new experimental University of Paris VIII (Vincennes). Along with Tzvetan Todorov and Gérard Genette, Cixous started *Poétique*, a journal for new criticism and theory. Here peers and colleagues throughout the 1960s and 1970s were, among others, **Michel Foucault, Jacques Derrida, Roland Barthes**, and **Julia Kristeva**. Cixous' literary theory was boldly innovative, as were her fiction and drama. In all of her writings, she resists the patriarchal power behind Western philosophical and theoretical traditions. "The Laugh of the Medusa" (1975) and *Three Steps on the Ladder of Writing* (1990) articulate her critique of these traditions and advocate an alternative discourse form, ÉCRITURE FÉMININE (feminine writing, writing the body). *The Newly Born Woman* (1975), written with Catherine Clément, reconsiders the Freudian scenario in which the little girl seduces her father and suggests that it needs to be rewritten in terms of women seeking new representational forms based on their own "libidinal economies." Throughout the 1970s and 1980s, Cixous created innovative fictions like *The Book of Promethea* (1983), which shows the influence in her writing of Ukraine-born Brazilian novelist Clarise Lispector. Cixous' dramatic work also underwent a shift at this time after meeting Ariane Mnouchkine, experimental director at the Théâtre du Soleil to which she contributed several plays, including *The Terrible but Unfinished Story of Norodom Sihanouk, King of Cambodia* (produced in 1985), which explored the nature of power, responsibility, and memory. Cixous continues to write fiction and theory. In 2000, she published a collection of memoirs, *Daydreams of the Wild Woman*.

Selected Bibliography

Cixous, Hélène. *"Coming to Writing" and Other Essays*. Ed. Deborah Jenson. Trans. Sarah Cornell, Deborah Jenson, Ann Liddle, Susan Sellers. Cambridge, MA: Harvard University Press, 1992.
Cixous, Hélène. *The Hélène Cixous Reader*. Ed. Susan Sellers. New York: Routledge, 1994.
Cixous, Hélène. *Three Steps on the Ladder of Writing*. Trans. Susan Sellers. New York: Columbia University Press, 1993.
Cixous, Hélène and Catherine Clément. *The Newly Born Woman*. Trans. Betsy Wing. Minneapolis: University of Minnesota Press, 1986.

Lennard Davis (1949–)

Lennard Davis was born in the Bronx, New York, to deaf parents, a circumstance that would ultimately alter the direction of his academic career. He attended Columbia University where he studied with **Edward Said** and Steven Marcus, and received his doctorate in comparative literature in 1976. In addition to his work at Columbia, he was a special student at the Columbia Psychoanalytic Training Clinic at the École Pratique des Hautes Études in Paris, where he attended a year-long seminar directed by **Roland Barthes**. He has taught at a number of universities including SUNY Binghamton and the University of Illinois at Chicago, where he is a Professor in the Departments of English and Disability and Human Development and a Professor of Medical Education in the College of Medicine. The multiple roles Davis plays places him in the unique position of being able to participate in the many debates on disability and the disabled body that extend beyond the discipline of literary studies. His first book, *Factual Fictions* (1983), focuses on the role played by journalism, criminality, and IDEOLOGY in the development of fictional techniques. This line of thought is continued in studies on ideology and fiction and leftist politics in literary and academic settings. His first book in disability studies, *Enforcing Normalcy* (1995), was groundbreaking not only for its challenge to normative thinking about the disabled body, but also for its focus on deafness. The first edition of his well-nigh exhaustive edited collection, *The Disability Studies Reader* (1997), brought together the many strands of discourse on disability, from the sociological to the poststructuralist (a third edition was brought out in 2010). The book that solidified his position in disability was *Bending Over Backwards* (2002), a study that introduced the concept of *dismodernism* and argued for a paradigm shift in how we think about disability. The new directions in disability studies, many of which he pioneered, are represented in *Disability and Social Theory*, co-edited with Dan Goodley and Bill Hughes. In addition to these works in disability theory, Davis has also written a history of obsession and a memoir, *My Sense of Silence: Memoirs of a Childhood with Deafness* (2000).

Selected Bibliography

Davis, Lennard. *Bending Over Backwards: Disability, Dismodernism, and other Difficult Positions*. New York: New York University Press, 2002.

Davis, Lennard. *Enforcing Normalcy: Disability, Deafness, and the Body*. London and New York: Verso, 1995.

Davis, Lennard. *My Sense of Silence: Memoirs of a Childhood with Deafness*. Urbana: University of Illinois Press, 2000.

Davis, Lennard. *Resisting Novels: Ideology and Fiction*. New York: Methuen, 1987.

Davis, Lennard, ed. *The Disability Studies Reader*. New York: Routledge, 2010.

Teresa de Lauretis (1939–)

Teresa de Lauretis was born and educated in Italy, receiving her doctorate from Bocconi University, Milan. She taught widely in the United States and Europe before settling at the University of California, Santa Cruz, where she is a professor of the history of consciousness. She wrote books in Italian on the novelist Italo Svevo and the semiotician and novelist Umberto Eco. Her first theoretical work in English, *Alice Doesn't: Feminism, Semiotics, Cinema* (1984), established her as a major figure in both feminism and film studies. In this volume, she critiques the male gaze, using Lacanian psychoanalysis to formulate a conception of feminist gazing that "looks back" at the male subject, whose voyeuristic perspective characterizes Western art and culture. *Technologies of Gender* (1987), her most influential work, counters **Michel Foucault**'s tendency to distinguish bodies and pleasure from the "discourse of sexuality" with a theory of the body that situates it and its desire wholly in socio-historical contexts. In the 1990s, she published important studies of lesbian sexuality and queer theory and in 2008 published *Freud's Drive*, a study of psychoanalysis, literature, and film.

Selected Bibliography

De Lauretis, Teresa. *Alice Doesn't: Feminism, Semiotics, Cinema*. Bloomington: Indiana University Press, 1984.
De Lauretis, Teresa. *Freud's Drive: Psychoanalysis, Literature and Film*. New York: Palgrave Macmillan, 2008.
De Lauretis, Teresa. *The Practice of Love: Lesbian Sexuality and Perverse Desire*. Bloomington: Indiana University Press, 1994.
De Lauretis, Teresa. *Technologies of Gender: Essays on Theory, Film, and Fiction*. Bloomington: Indiana University Press, 1987.

Gilles Deleuze (1925–95) and Félix Guattari (1930–92)

Postmodern philosophers Gilles Deleuze and Félix Guattari have had a significant impact on literary theory writing together, and both have forged distinctive projects on their own. Their work converges on the problem of the subject and the limits of subjectivity in capitalist societies, and they both advocate new models of desire and modes of mapping social spaces. Gilles Deleuze was born and educated in Paris and studied philosophy at the Sorbonne. He taught the history of philosophy at the Sorbonne and worked at the Centre National de la Recherche Scientifique (1960–4). At the behest of **Michel Foucault**, he moved to the experimental University of Paris VIII (Vincennes), where he remained until he retired in 1987. His earliest works were philosophical critiques of Nietzsche, Spinoza, Bergson, and Kant, and studies of Kafka, Proust, and other literary figures. In 1968, he published *Difference and Repetition*, which put forward an affirmative Nietzschean conception of difference as "(non)being," which escapes the annihilation of dialectical closure.

Félix Guattari was born in Villeneuve-les-Sablons, France, and gravitated to the study of psychiatry as a young man of twenty. He practiced a form of psychiatry influenced by philosophy, linguistics, literature, and Lacanian psychoanalysis. Along with his collaborator, Jean Oury, he performed research and trained students in a private clinic, La Borde, at Cour-Cheverny. He wrote widely on philosophical questions but also on environmentalism and postmodern ethics. His collection of early writings, *Chaosophy*, and his later collection, *Chaosmosis*, continue the radical critique of capitalism and psychoanalysis he inaugurated with Deleuze.

In May 1968, in the midst of student protests and rioting, the two men met at Vincennes. In the next few years they developed the material that became *Anti-Oedipus* (1977) and *A Thousand Plateaus* (1983), which together constitute one of the most controversial and complex critiques of capitalist culture and its links to psychoanalysis. Crucial to their understanding of the social body and social spaces are innovative concepts like TERRITORIALIZATION, which refers to the ways bodies and spaces are inscribed or demarcated by social, political, and cultural networks of power. DETERRITORIALIZATION and RETERRITORIALIZATION are processes which erase or reconstruct, respectively, the limits and boundaries of the social space. The social space is envisioned as a "body without organs" traversed by "desiring machines." This vision combines vitalism with a machinic principle of structure. In place of the Freudian model of SUBJECTIVITY, based on the Oedipus complex, is the "anti-Oedipal" condition of schizophrenia, in which desire is the free and fluid expression of "desiring machines" along the surface of a "body without organs." These formulations have been influential in postmodernist politics and aesthetics. Deleuze and Guattari also published *Kafka: Toward a Minor Literature* (1975), which explores the subversive and emancipatory potential of an "assemblage" within a dominant tradition, a minor literature constituted as a "Kafka-machine."

Selected Bibliography

Deleuze, Gilles. *Difference and Repetition*. Trans. Paul Patton. London: Athlone Press, 1994.

Deleuze, Gilles and Felix Guattari. *Anti-Oedipus: Capitalism and Schizophrenia*. Trans. Robert Hurley, Mark Seem, and Helen R. Lane. Minneapolis: University of Minnesota Press, 1983.

Deleuze, Gilles and Felix Guattari. *A Thousand Plateaus: Capitalism and Schizophrenia*. Trans. Brian Massumi. London: Athlone Press, 1988.

Deleuze, Gilles and Felix Guattari. *Kafka: Toward a Minor Literature*. Trans. Dana Polan. Minneapolis: University of Minnesota Press, 1986.

Guattari, Félix. *Chaosmosis: An Ethico-Aesthetic Paradigm*. Trans. Paul Bains and Julian Pefanis. Indianapolis: Indiana University Press, 1995.

Paul de Man (1919–83)

Paul de Man was born in Antwerp, Belgium, and came of age during a time of invasion and occupation by Nazi forces. His father, Henrik de Man, was a well-known intellectual in Belgium and Germany. During the war and for a time afterwards, De Man worked in journalism and publishing. He found his way to the United States just after the war and received his doctorate from Harvard in the late 1950s. He began teaching at Yale University in 1970, where he held the position of Sterling Professor of the Humanities at the time of his death.

Like many European theorists of his generation, De Man was steeped in the phenomenological tradition of philosophy and literary criticism. He met **Jacques Derrida** at a symposium on structuralism at the Johns Hopkins University Humanities Center in 1966. De Man came to be known as one of the founders of the Yale school of deconstruction. Although De Man's style was quite different from Derrida's, the two shared similar methods and objects of study. His preferred subjects were AESTHETICS, rhetoric, Romantic literature, especially the work of Jean-Jacques Rousseau, and Nietzsche's philosophy. In his first major work, *Blindness and Insight* (1971), he argues that criticism, due to a gap between its theoretical assumptions and its practice, is blind to its own insights. Blindness of the sort that De Man investigates often develops when rhetorical statements are mistaken for literal ones, and vice versa. In *Allegories of Reading* (1979), he uses this deconstructionist mode of analysis to explore the works of Rousseau, Nietzsche, Rilke, and Proust. In this volume, De Man emphasizes the vertiginous possibilities offered to the critic when confronted with a text that will not let the reader clearly decide between literal and figural (or rhetorical) readings. These two volumes of essays established De Man as a formidable and influential critic, despite his tendency to write essays rather than monographs. In his posthumously published *Aesthetic Ideology* (1996), he furthers his critique against UNIVERSALIST and idealist conceptions of aesthetics by applying his deconstructionist method of rhetorical analysis to the works of Kant, Hegel, and Schiller.

In 1987, four years after De Man's death, a Belgian researcher uncovered important information about De Man's wartime journalism, which includes at least one article, "Les Juifs dans la littérature actuelle," in which De Man takes an anti-Semitic position when he argues that European literature will survive negative Jewish influence. The reaction among critics and scholars was complex and ambivalent, in part because it was difficult to reconcile such attitudes with De Man's brilliant academic career. De Man's life, tempered after death by the irony of his own past, exemplifies the very problematic nature of language and experience that his work strove to understand.

Selected Bibliography

De Man, Paul. *Aesthetic Ideology.* Ed. Andrzej Warminski. Minneapolis: University of Minnesota Press, 1996.

De Man, Paul. *Allegories of Reading: Figural Language in Rousseau, Nietzsche, Rilke, and Proust.* New Haven: Yale University Press, 1979.

De Man, Paul. *Blindness and Insight: Essays in the Rhetoric of Contemporary Criticism.* New York: Oxford University Press, 1971.

De Man, Paul. *The Resistance to Theory.* Minneapolis: University of Minnesota Press, 1986.

Jacques Derrida (1930–2004)

Jacques Derrida was born in El Biar, Algeria, where his early education was interrupted when Algerian officials, acting on orders of the collaborationist Vichy government, expelled him from his lycée because he was Jewish. In 1949, he moved to France and shortly thereafter failed his first attempt to enroll in the École Normale Supérieure in Paris. He entered in 1952. While working toward his doctorate, he studied with **Michel Foucault** and **Louis Althusser**. He wrote a dissertation on the work of the phenomenologist Edmund Husserl, published in 2003. For two years in the late 1950s, he taught the children of soldiers in lieu of military service in Algeria, where the French Army was fighting against native Algerian forces. In 1960, he began teaching at the Sorbonne and in 1964 moved to the École Normale Supérieure, where he remained until 1984. After 1966, the year he presented "Structure, Sign and Play in the Discourse of the Humanities" at Johns Hopkins University, Derrida was a regular speaker in forums worldwide and a visiting professor at many US universities. *Of Grammatology*, together with two volumes of essays, all published in 1967, established Derrida as the leading proponent of the deconstructionist approach in literary theory in France. By the mid-1970s, English translations produced the same effect in the English-speaking world. In the 1970s, his reputation grew rapidly and widely throughout the US academy as his books were translated into English. This early work is concerned primarily with problems in philosophy and linguistics, but Derrida's deconstructionist critique of the problems of origin, ESSENCE, and PRESENCE caught the attention of critics and scholars who had become frustrated with the limitations of New Criticism and structuralism.

Margins of Philosophy (1972), a collection of essays, and *Disseminations* (1972), a meditation on Plato and Stéphane Mallarmé, solidified Derrida's reputation. In the mid-1970s, Derrida found himself in a public debate with analytical philosophy, a debate that produced *Limited Inc* (1977). In the 1980s, he wrote several major works, including *The Post Card* (1980), numerous essays on James Joyce and Heidegger, and a memoir for his friend, **Paul de Man**. In the 1990s, he published *Specters of Marx* (1993) and explored problems in psychoanalysis and ethics. Of particular interest at this time was a series of books on the economies of the "gift" and the ethics of giving: *Given Time* (1992), *On the Name* (1995), and *The Gift of Death* (1995). In the last decade of his life, Derrida remained focused on ethics and memory, writing his *Adieu to Emmanuel Levinas* in 1997 and *The Work of Mourning* in 2001.

Selected Bibliography

Derrida, Jacques. *Dissemination*. Trans. Barbara Johnson. Chicago: University of Chicago Press, 1981.

Derrida, Jacques. *Margins of Philosophy*. Trans. Alan Bass. Chicago: University of Chicago Press, 1982.

Derrida, Jacques. *Of Grammatology*. Trans. Gayatri Chakravorty Spivak. Baltimore: Johns Hopkins University Press, 1976.

Derrida, Jacques. *Psyche: Inventions of the Other*. Ed. Peggy Kamuf and Elizabeth Rottenberg. Stanford: Stanford University Press, 2007.

Derrida, Jacques. *Specters of Marx: The State of the Debt, the Work of Mourning and the New International*. Trans. Peggy Kamuf. New York: Routledge, 1994.

Derrida, Jacques. *Writing and Difference*. Trans. Alan Bass. Chicago: University of Chicago Press, 1978.

Terry Eagleton (1943–)

Terry Eagleton was born in Salford, England, and educated at Cambridge University. While at Cambridge, he was a student of **Raymond Williams**, the most important Marxist critic of the 1960s and one of the founders of British cultural studies. Eagleton earned his doctoral degree at twenty-one and became a tutor of English at Wadham College, Oxford University. He has proven to be Williams' successor not only in Marxist literary theory but also, especially since the 1990s, in cultural studies.

Eagleton's early works were devoted to literature and society, with a focus on Shakespeare and the Brontës. His *Myths of Power* (1975) was a tour de force Marxist reading of the Brontës' works that made his reputation as a theorist. At this time, he also published important works on Marxist theory, including *Criticism and Ideology* (1976). In the 1980s, he produced monographs on a number of literary and theoretical figures, notably **Walter Benjamin** and Samuel Richardson. He also published his most widely read book, *Literary Theory: An Introduction* (1983). No simple primer, *Literary Theory* begins by examining critically the concept of literature and the institutional setting in which it is taught. It then offers historically grounded surveys of the major theoretical fields, concluding with an appeal for "political criticism." In 1999, Eagleton published an authorative study of the Kantian aesthetic regime, *The Ideology of the Aesthetic*, which was followed by two volumes of essays on Irish literature and culture, *Heathcliff and the Great Hunger* (1995) and *Crazy John and the Bishop* (1998), both of which bear the distinct hallmarks of Williams and the English Marxist tradition. In the twenty-first century, Eagleton continues to write on a broad array of topics, including questions of faith, tragedy, literary theory, and the "idea of culture," and he continues to explore the relevance of Marxist theory.

Selected Bibliography

Eagleton, Terry. *Criticism and Ideology: A Study in Marxist Literary Theory*. London: New Left Books; Atlantic Highlands, NJ: Humanities Press, 1976.
Eagleton, Terry. *The Idea of Culture*. Oxford and Malden, MA: Blackwell, 2000.
Eagleton, Terry. *The Ideology of the Aesthetic*. Oxford and Cambridge, MA: Blackwell, 1990.
Eagleton, Terry. *Literary Theory: An Introduction*. 2nd ed. Minneapolis: University of Minnesota Press, 1983, 1996.

Frantz Fanon (1925–61)

Frantz Fanon was born in Martinique, in the French Caribbean, and studied at a lycée in Fort-de-France, where one of his teachers was Aimé Césaire. During World War II, he served with the French Army in North Africa. He was wounded in 1944 and received the Croix de Guerre. After the war, he returned briefly to Martinique, where he worked on the parliamentary campaign of his former teacher, Césaire. Fanon left for France, where he studied psychiatry in Paris and Lyons. At this time, he composed his first book, *Black Skin, White Masks* (1952), an investigation of

COLONIALISM from the perspective of race consciousness and race relations. In 1952, Fanon began practicing psychiatry in Algeria, at Blida-Joinville hospital, where he was director of the psychiatric ward. The war between French colonial forces and the National Liberation Front (FLN) began in 1954. By 1956, Fanon had resigned and begun his work with the liberation movement. He traveled all over North and Saharan Africa, visiting guerilla camps and training medical personnel. He also hid insurgents in his home. In the last few years of his life, in addition to writing several books, he worked as an ambassador of the provisional Algerian government to Ghana, edited a journal in Tunisia, and set up the first African psychiatric clinic. He died of leukemia in Washington, DC, but was buried in Algeria.

Fanon's work is largely concerned with African colonialism and the Algerian independence movement. *Toward the African Revolution*, published posthumously, brought together his shorter works published in FLN newspapers. Other essays on Algeria and the Algerian "national psyche" were compiled in *A Dying Colonialism* (1959). His most important work, a neo-Hegelian critique of colonialism, *The Wretched of the Earth* (1961), was also his last. Unlike the essay collections, this volume presented an integrated study of spontaneity and colonial violence, national consciousness, nationalist parties and leaders, the native intellectual, and the psychological trauma exacted by colonial wars. He was as critical of the nationalist bourgeoisie that inherited the privileges of the European colonizers as he was of the colonizers themselves. He understood that anti-colonial resistance could only succeed if the people were given the tools to "re-create" themselves as human beings. If necessary, they must do this through violence. The recognition and theorization of this hard necessity earned Fanon some criticism, but by and large his work and life have proven a positive inspiration for liberation groups worldwide and a valuable theoretical resource for postcolonial studies.

Selected Bibliography

Fanon, Frantz. *Black Skin, White Masks*. Trans. Charles Lam Markmann. London: Pluto, 1986.

Fanon, Frantz. *Toward the African Revolution: Political Essays*. Trans. Haakon Chevalier. Harmondsworth: Penguin, 1970.

Fanon, Frantz. *The Wretched of the Earth*. Trans. Constance Farrington. New York: Grove Weidenfeld, 1963.

Gordon, Lewis R., T. Denean Sharpley-Whiting, and Renée T. White, eds. *Fanon: A Critical Reader*. Oxford and Cambridge, MA: Blackwell, 1996.

Stanley Fish (1938–)

Stanley Fish was born in Providence, Rhode Island, and educated at the University of Pennsylvania and Yale University. He has taught at the University of California at Berkeley, Johns Hopkins University, Duke University, and the University of Illinois, Chicago. He currently teaches humanities and law at Florida International University.

Fish's early professional life was spent teaching medieval and seventeenth-century literature. His first major work, *Surprised by Sin* (1967), advanced a then unique argument about the reader of *Paradise Lost*, who is seduced by Milton's language into experiencing Satan's temptation of Adam and Eve. Fish's "affective stylistics," which stresses the reader's response to a literary text, departed from the formalism of the New Critics. His next book, *Self-Consuming Artifact* (1972), overcame some of the limitations of affective stylistics and offered a new theory of interpretive communities, cohorts of readers who agree, in principle, on a specific set of conventions and strategies. *Is There a Text in This Class?* (1980) brings together essays from the 1970s along with new material that contrasts his early conceptions of affective stylistics with his later formulations of reader response and interpretive communities. These later texts show the influence of **Wolfgang Iser** and Roman Ingarden, who were developing similar projects in Europe at this time.

During the 1980s and 1990s, Fish turned his attention to matters of law and legal theory, rhetoric, ethics, and the professionalization of literary studies. His interest in pragmatism and logic made him a formidable and often amusing interlocutor. Fish considered himself an anti-foundationalist, and his attacks on postmodernism were eloquent reminders that principles and standards are inevitable in human society and that the important issue is not protesting their existence but in constructing smart and tolerable ones. In 1989, Fish published *Doing What Comes Naturally*, a seminal work in the critical legal studies movement. This was followed by his controversial volume on the First Amendment, *There's No Such Thing as Free Speech: And It's a Good Thing, Too* (1994). From the mid-1990s, Fish's career settled into legal studies and administration. He served as Dean of Arts and Sciences at the University of Illinois, Chicago (1999–2004). He continues to write on language, television, politics, liberalism, and the law.

Selected Bibliography

Fish, Stanley. *Doing What Comes Naturally: Change, Rhetoric, and the Practice of Theory in Literary and Legal Studies*. Durham, NC: Duke University Press, 1989.

Fish, Stanley. *Is There a Text in This Class? The Authority of Interpretive Communities*. Cambridge, MA: Harvard University Press, 1980.

Fish, Stanley. *Professional Correctness: Literary Studies and Political Change*. New York: Clarendon Press, 1995.

Fish, Stanley. *The Stanley Fish Reader*. Ed. H. Aram Veeser. Malden MA: Blackwell, 1999.

Fish, Stanley. *Surprised by Sin: The Reader in Paradise Lost*. 2nd ed. Cambridge, MA: Harvard University Press, 1967, 1998.

Michel Foucault (1926–84)

Michel Foucault was born and educated in Poitiers, France, then sent to the prestigious Lycée Henry IV in Paris. He entered the École Normale Supérieure in 1946. At the ENS and later at the Sorbonne, Foucault came into contact with leading intellectuals of the day, including Jean Hippolyte and **Louis Althusser**, and became a communist (though he left the Party in 1953); he remained deeply committed to radical politics for the rest of his life. In 1952, he received his diploma in psychopathology from the University of Paris. After teaching briefly at the ENS and the University of Lille, Foucault spent three years at the University of Uppsala (1955–8), then one year directing the French Institute in Hamburg. His doctoral dissertation was published as *Madness and Civilization* in 1961. In the next five years, he published *The Birth of the Clinic* (1963) and *The Order of Things* (1966). These early texts exemplify the ARCHAEOLOGICAL method of history and sociology presented systematically in *The Archaeology of Knowledge* (1969). Foucault was not interested in traditional historiographic methods that relied on cause and effect and chronological temporality. Drawing on the "anti-historicism" of Nietzschean GENEALOGY, he developed a new "anti-historical" historical method.

Whether he studied medicine, psychiatry, economics, grammar, biology, or education, Foucault was interested in analyzing the discursive pathways by which POWER circulates within DISCURSIVE FORMATIONS and traditions. His conception of power is an elaboration of the Nietzschean "will to power" that, in his early writings, was linked to mechanisms of social control – exemplified by the analysis of social control in *Discipline and Punish* (1975) – while in the later writings, it was seen as constituting forms of "governmentality." For Foucault power is a social function, *power/knowledge*, a term that makes explicit the link between domination and discourse. In *The History of Sexuality* (1976), Foucault turned to the discourse on sex and sexuality, the "care of the self," and a new theory of the relation between the subject, identity formation, and the regime of biopower and biopolitics. Foucault gradually came to reject his own early position that the subject was in thrall to social discourses and began to theorize new forms of positive social agency (e.g., governmentality), of action *within and with* power. This work was cut short by Foucault's death in 1984, of an AIDS-related neurological disorder.

Selected Bibliography

Foucault, Michel. *The Archaeology of Knowledge and the Discourse on Language*. Trans. A. M. Sheridan Smith. New York: Pantheon Books, 1972.

Foucault, Michel. *Discipline and Punish: The Birth of the Prison*. Trans. Alan Sheridan. New York: Vintage, 1979, 1977.

Foucault, Michel. *The Foucault Reader*. Ed. Paul Rabinow. New York: Pantheon Books, 1984.

Foucault, Michel. *The History of Sexuality*. 3 vols. Trans. Robert Hurley. New York: Pantheon Books, 1978–88.

Foucault, Michel. *The Order of Things: An Archaeology of the Human Sciences*. New York: Vintage, 1994.

Henry Louis Gates (1950–)

Henry Louis Gates was born in Keyser, West Virginia, and attended Yale University and Cambridge University. He completed his doctoral degree in 1979, the first black person ever to receive one from Cambridge. While at Cambridge, Gates became friends with the Nigerian playwright Wole Soyinka, who tutored him in the cultural traditions and language of the Yoruba tribe. After teaching at Cornell University and Yale, he joined the faculty at Harvard University, where he currently serves as the W. E. B. Du Bois Professor of the Humanities.

Gates studied widely in African American, African, and Caribbean cultures and literatures. He made his reputation with the republication of Harriet E. Wilson's *Our Nig*, the first novel published in the United States by an African American. His reputation was confirmed with the publication of two studies in black literary theory: *Figures in Black* (1987), a reconsideration of the nativist strand of influence in African American literature, and *The Signifying Monkey* (1988), an in-depth study of a native black rhetorical tradition of "Signifyin(g)" rooted in the mythologies and storytelling practices of West Africa. These works established Gates as a major figure in African American studies. His other major work at this time, an edited volume of essays, "*Race*," *Writing, and Difference* (1986), brought together a number of established theorists, including **Jacques Derrida**, **Homi Bhabha**, and **Gayatri Chakravorty Spivak**. Many of the essays explored the intersection of poststructuralism and historicist theories of race and racial difference.

In the 1990s, Gates edited several important anthologies on African American writers and co-edited (with Nellie Y. McKay) the *Norton Anthology of African American Literature* (1997). In 1999, Gates and Kwame Anthony Appiah published, in conjunction with Microsoft, *Encarta Africana 2000*, an electronic resource on all things African. Also at this time, Gates wrote *Wonders of the African World* (1999), the companion to a BBC/PBS series. In recent years, he has published numerous biographical studies and works on African American history.

Selected Bibliography

Gates, Henry Louis. *Figures in Black: Words, Signs and the "Racial" Self*. New York: Oxford University Press, 1987.

Gates, Henry Louis. *Life Upon These Shores: Looking at African American History, 1513–2008*. New York: Knopf, 2011.

Gates, Henry Louis, ed. "*Race*," *Writing, and Difference*. Chicago: University of Chicago Press, 1986.

Gates, Henry Louis. *The Signifying Monkey: A Theory of Afro-American Literary Criticism*. New York: Oxford University Press, 1988.

Gates, Henry Louis. *Thirteen Ways of Looking at a Black Man*. New York: Random House, 1997.

Sandra Gilbert (1936–) and Susan Gubar (1944–)

The collaboration of Sandra Gilbert and Susan Gubar constitutes a cornerstone of feminist literary theory in the United States. Sandra Gilbert was born in New York City and was educated at Cornell and New York University. She received her doctorate from Columbia University in 1968. After teaching at a number of schools, she took a position in 1975 at the University of California at Davis where she remained, save for four years at Princeton University, until she retired.

Susan Gubar was born in Brooklyn, New York, and was educated at the City University of New York and the University of Michigan. She received her doctorate from the University of Iowa in 1972. Within a year, Gubar joined the faculty of Indiana University, retiring as Distinguished Professor of English and Women's Studies.

The two women met at Indiana University, where they designed a course on the feminist literary tradition and began a collaboration that would yield, in 1979, *The Madwoman in the Attic.* This was a groundbreaking work in literary criticism, but also a compelling revision of literary history. Gilbert and Gubar argued that women's writing in the nineteenth century constituted a feminist tradition of resistance to PATRIARCHAL culture. This argument is extended in their three-volume study of twentieth-century women writers, *No Man's Land* (1988–94). In these volumes, they argue that modernist and postmodernist literature is comprehensible historically only if feminism and writing by women are considered seriously as influences in literary traditions and CANONS. Through the 1980s and 1990s, they edited many volumes together, including the *Norton Anthology of Literature by Women* (1985) and *The Female Imagination and the Modernist Aesthetic* (1986). They have also written a satire on the profession of teaching and canon formation, *Masterpiece Theatre: An Academic Melodrama* (1995).

Each of these women has been productive on her own as well. Gubar has published works in cultural studies, including *Racechanges* (1997), an analysis of "cross-racial masquerade." She has also published a volume on contemporary poetry, *Poetry After Auschwitz* (2003). In 2011, she edited *True Confessions: Feminist Professors Tell Stories Out of School.* While battling ovarian cancer, Gubar published *Memoir of a Debulked Woman: Enduring Ovarian Cancer* (2012). Gilbert, a past president of the Modern Language Association, has written a study on the American poet H.D. and a memoir recounting her husband's death from cancer. She also published numerous books of poetry, including *Ghost Volcano* (1995), *Belongings* (2005), and *Kissing the Bread: New and Selected Poems, 1969–1999.*

Selected Bibliography

Gilbert, Sandra and Susan Gubar, eds. *The Female Imagination and the Modernist Aesthetic.* New York: Gordon and Breach, 1986.

Gilbert, Sandra and Susan Gubar. *The Madwoman in the Attic: The Woman Writer and the Nineteenth-Century Literary Imagination.* 2nd ed. New Haven and London: Yale University Press, 1979, 2000.

Gilbert, Sandra and Susan Gubar. *No Man's Land: The Place of the Woman Writer in the Twentieth Century.* 3 vols. New Haven: Yale University Press, 1988–94.

Stephen Greenblatt (1943–)

Stephen Greenblatt was born in Cambridge, Massachusetts. He studied at Yale University and Cambridge University, receiving his doctorate from Yale in 1969. He began teaching at the University of California at Berkeley that year and remained there until 1997, when he moved to Harvard University. In 2000, he became Cogan University Professor of the Humanities.

In his early years at Berkeley, Greenblatt was influenced by **Raymond Williams** and attended seminars given by **Michel Foucault**. The very different approaches to literary history and social theory represented by these theorists combined in Greenblatt's work to produce a nuanced style of close reading sensitive to the impact made on texts by social and historical forces. His third book, *Renaissance Self-Fashioning* (1980), drew on Foucault's ARCHAEOLOGICAL method of historical writing to describe the various ways that social power determines the subject and the representation of SUBJECTIVITY. It was widely read and is regarded as a leading example of the New Historicism then emerging out of Renaissance studies. The New Historicist method was popularized in the pages of *Representations*, a journal co-founded by Greenblatt.

Greenblatt refined his new approach to mapping social power and its literary effects in *Shakespearean Negotiations* (1988). In addition to his editorial responsibilities with *Representations*, Greenblatt edited numerous volumes of essays. He also continued to produce scholarly studies of early modern literatures. Together with Catherine Gallagher, Greenblatt revisited the theoretical problems of New Historicism in *Practicing New Historicism* (2000). This text both situates New Historicism in the academic and social contexts of the late 1970s and 1980s and offers virtuoso readings by acknowledged masters in the field. In 2004, Greenblatt made the headlines again with a new biography of Shakespeare, *Will in the World*, which was shortlisted for the National Book Award. In recent years, he has turned his attention to cultural studies, co-editing *Cultural Mobility: A Manifesto* (2010).

Selected Bibliography

Gallagher, Catherine and Stephen Greenblatt. *Practicing New Historicism*. Chicago: University of Chicago Press, 2000.

Greenblatt, Stephen. *Greenblatt Reader*. Ed. Michael Payne and Stephen Greenblatt. Oxford: Blackwell, 2005.

Greenblatt, Stephen. *Learning to Curse: Essays in Early Modern Culture*. New York: Routledge, 1990.

Greenblatt, Stephen. *Renaissance Self-Fashioning: From More to Shakespeare*. Chicago: University of Chicago Press, 1980.

Greenblatt, Stephen et al., eds. *Cultural Mobility: A Manifesto*. Cambridge: Cambridge University Press, 2010.

Elizabeth Grosz (1952–)

Elizabeth Grosz was born in Sydney, Australia. She received her doctorate in philosophy at the University of Sydney in 1978 and taught there until 1991. She also taught at Monash University in Melbourne and was Director of the Institute of Critical and Cultural Studies. She has had visiting professor posts in numerous US universities, including Johns Hopkins University, the University of California at Irvine, and Rutgers University. She is currently Jean Fox O'Barr Professor in Interdisciplinary Feminist Studies at Duke University. Grosz was among the first feminist philosophers to focus on the body. Her early work investigates French feminism and **Jacques Lacan** and includes *Volatile Bodies: Toward a Corporeal Feminism* (1994), in which she begins her exploration of a new materiality that she will ultimately link back to the French philosopher Henri Bergson. The issues raised in this text were pursued further in the next two, *Space, Time and Perversion* (1995), which considers the politics of bodies, and *Architecture from the Outside* (2001). These studies redefine materialist analysis in order to encompass aspects of social and personal space that are not often registered in Marxist or cultural studies approaches. This interest in the spatial dimension of the body and biopolitics has led to reflections on time and politics and includes *Time Travels: Feminism, Nature, Power* (2005), which exemplifies a posthumanist feminism. In *Becoming Undone* (2011), Grosz explores the categories *human* and *inhuman* from the perspective of Darwin, Bergson, and Deleuze and reflects on feminism and the role of animals in art. Grosz is one of the most prominent feminist philosophers whose work continues to shape our sense of what it means to be human and what the materiality of human and inhuman bodies means politically and aesthetically.

Selected Bibliography

Grosz, Elizabeth. *Becoming Undone: Darwinian Reflections on Life, Politics and Art.* Durham, NC: Duke University Press, 2011.

Grosz, Elizabeth. *Jacques Lacan: A Feminist Introduction.* London and New York: Routledge, 1990.

Grosz, Elizabeth. *Sexual Subversions: Three French Feminists.* Sydney and Boston: Allen and Unwin, 1989.

Grosz, Elizabeth. *Time Travels: Feminism, Nature, Power.* Durham, NC: Duke University Press, 2005.

Grosz, Elizabeth. *Volatile Bodies: Toward a Corporeal Feminism.* Bloomington: Indiana University Press, 1994.

Stuart Hall (1932–)

Stuart Hall was born in Kingston, Jamaica, and moved to England in 1951, where he became a Rhodes Scholar at Oxford University. In the 1950s and early 1960s, Hall was active in socialist movements and, together with Charles Taylor and others, founded a journal of art and criticism, *Universities and New Left Review*, which later became the *New Left Review*. After the publication of his first book, *The Popular Arts* (1965), Hall was invited to join the Centre for Contemporary Cultural Studies at the University of Birmingham in 1964. By 1968, he had taken over as director. Hall's work during these years included a study of the SEMIOTICS of television in 1973 and a work written in collaboration with other members of the Centre,

Policing the Crisis (1978). This volume draws from Antonio Gramsci's interpretation of Marxism to argue that the racist representation of violent street crime by the British press in the 1970s masked economic and social crises.

Hall moved to the Open University in 1979, and the next year he published an important essay, "Cultural Studies: Two Paradigms," that sketched the history of and theoretical influences on British cultural studies and suggested that there were two models from which to choose: culturalist and structuralist. Throughout the 1980s, Hall edited a number of volumes on cultural studies, sociology, the modern state, modernity, and Marxism. He also published *The Hard Road to Renewal* (1988), a study of Margaret Thatcher's years as prime minister and the effects of those years on the British left. Hall's work on DIASPORIC IDENTITIES and immigration continues to influence our understanding of the global ramifications of the modern multicultural state. Many of these issues are addressed in a collection of essays by and about Hall, *Critical Dialogues in Cultural Studies* (1996), and in the collection dedicated to him, *Without Guarantees: In Honour of Stuart Hall* (2000).

Selected Bibliography

Gilroy, Paul, Lawrence Grossberg, and Angela McRobbie, eds. *Without Guarantees: In Honour of Stuart Hall*. London: Verso, 2000.

Hall, Stuart. *Critical Dialogues in Cultural Studies*. Ed. David Morley and Kuan-Hsing Chen. London and New York: Routledge, 1996.

Hall, Stuart. "Cultural Studies: Two Paradigms." *Media, Culture and Society* 2 (1980): 57–72.

Hall, Stuart. *The Hard Road to Renewal: Thatcherism and the Crisis of the Left*. London and New York: Verso, 1988.

Hall, Stuart et al. *Policing the Crisis: Mugging, the State and Law and Order*. New York: Holmes and Meier, 1978.

Donna Haraway (1944–)

Donna Haraway was born in Denver, Colorado, and studied zoology and philosophy at Colorado College. After a brief period as a Fulbright scholar studying evolutionary theory in Paris, she studied biology at Yale University, where she received her doctorate in 1972. After teaching at the University of Hawaii and Johns Hopkins University, Haraway joined the faculty of the History of Consciousness at the University of California, Santa Cruz, in 1980.

Haraway's interdisciplinary studies of technology and gender have had a powerful impact on cultural studies, postmodernism, and feminism. Her first book, *Crystals, Fabrics and Fields* (1976), based on her dissertation, concerned the way metaphors are used to describe organic development in biology. In her second book, *Primate Visions*, she began to explore the representation of gender and race in modern science. Haraway's cultural studies approach to science and its representations challenges our presuppositions about science, gender, nature, and humanity. "A Manifesto for Cyborgs" (1985) and *Simians, Cyborgs, and Women* (1991) counter idealist conceptions of human beings with a vision of the *cyborg*, a new model for describing the relationship in postmodernity between nature and science. Haraway argues that this vision is especially valuable for socialism and radical feminism, for the cyborg model opens SUBJECTIVITY to hybrid collaborations with the non-human (animal, technological) world.

Modest_Witness@Second_Millennium (1997) continues Haraway's exploration of posthumanist science. In this volume, she examines how genetic research creates the body as a kind of "hypertext" that requires a new form of "technoscience" to map and understand. In recent years, she has written *The Companion Species Manifesto* (2003) and *When Species Meet* (2008), important studies in an emergent field of animal studies.

Selected Bibliography

Haraway, Donna. *The Haraway Reader*. New York and London: Routledge, 2004.
Haraway, Donna. *Modest_Witness@Second_Millennium.FemaleMan_Meets_OncoMouse:Feminism and Technoscience*. With paintings by Lynn M. Randolph. New York: Routledge, 1997.
Haraway, Donna. *Simians, Cyborgs, and Women: The Reinvention of Nature*. New York: Routledge, 1991.

N. Katherine Hayles (1943–)

N. Katherine Hayles was born in Saint Louis, Missouri. She studied chemistry at the Rochester Institute of Technology and received an MA in chemistry from the California Institute of Technology in 1969. She spent several years working as a research chemist and consultant for Xerox and elsewhere before taking an MA degree at Michigan State University in 1970. She received her doctorate in literature from the University of Rochester in 1977. She has taught at a number of US universities, including the University of California at Los Angeles and Dartmouth College, and is currently Professor and Director of Graduate Studies at Duke University. From the start, her main concern has been the interface between traditional models of humanist thought and the emerging models of scientific understanding that formed the informational substratum of the information age. Both *The Cosmic Web* (1984) and *Chaos Bound* (1990) argue that the late twentieth century has witnessed a paradigm shift, from a Cartesian–Newtonian paradigm to one dominated by chaos theory and field theory. Her readings of literature indicate that the humanities has been moving in a similar direction. By the turn of the century, her focus had shifted to cybernetics and "virtual bodies," the subject of *How We Became Posthuman* (1999). She was also becoming more involved in theorizing digital media, both in traditional monograph form, as in *My Mother Was a Computer: Digital Subjects and Literary Texts* (2005), and in experimental formats, such as the ebook *Writing*

Machines (2002) and *Nanoculture: Implications of the New Technoscience*, an edited volume that accompanied an exhibit on nanotechnology at the Los Angeles County Museum of Art, 2003–4. For Hayles, the posthuman is essentially a hybrid formation, a *cyborg* that is holistically connected to virtual and digital technologies. Her commitment to "electronic literature" is grounded in a theory of "technogenesis" (human beings coevolve with technology) and its relation to the digital, the focus of *How We Think* (2012). Hayles' work offers an alternative to the "zones of indistinction" that posthumanism frequently posits as the space of confrontation between the human and the non-human.

Selected Bibliography

Hayles, N. Katherine. *Chaos Bound: Orderly Disorder in Contemporary Literature and Science*. Ithaca: Cornell University Press, 1990.

Hayles, N. Katherine. *The Cosmic Web: Scientific Field Models and Literary Strategies in the Twentieth Century*. Ithaca: Cornell University Press, 1984.

Hayles, N. Katherine. *How We Became Posthuman: Virtual Bodies in Cybernetics, Literature, and Informatics*. Chicago: University of Chicago Press, 1999.

Hayles, N. Katherine. *How We Think: Digital Media and Contemporary Technogenesis*. Chicago: University of Chicago Press, 2012.

Hayles, N. Katherine. *Writing Machines*. Cambridge, MA: MIT Press, 2002.

bell hooks (1952–)

bell hooks (née Gloria Watkins) was born in Hopkinsville, Kentucky, and was educated at Stanford University and the University of Wisconsin. She received her doctorate from the University of California, Santa Cruz, in 1983. After teaching at Yale University and Oberlin College, hooks began teaching at the City College of New York, where she was a Distinguished Professor of English. She is currently Distinguished Professor in Residence in Appalachian Studies at Berea College.

In her first book, *Ain't I a Woman* (1981), hooks argues that sexism and racism have the same cause – white PATRIARCHY – against which feminists and anti-racist groups need to forge a shared position. The point is carried further in her most influential book, *Feminist Theory: From Margin to Center* (1984), in which hooks systematically critiques mainstream European and US feminism for neglecting the issue of racism and for refusing to see sexism as its corollary. She urges feminists to take up these issues if they hope to make substantial social changes. Throughout the 1980s and 1990s, hooks published many volumes on issues concerning race, gender, representation, and art. In *Talking Back* (1989) and *Black Looks* (1992), hooks emphasizes education as both an institutional impediment and a possible site of resistance to institutional power. She explores the margins of gender and sexual IDENTITY in *Outlaw Culture* (1994) and examines the interplay of sex and class in film in *Reel to Real* (1996). For hooks, the nature and direction of theory should tend towards a "passionate politics," a point she argues in *Feminism is for Everybody* (2000). Since the 1990s, she has written two memoirs and other books on a variety of topics, including love, self-esteem, and education among African Americans (*Rock My Soul* and *Teaching Community*, both in 2003) and black masculinity (*We Real Cool*, in 2004). *Feminist Theory* was issued in a second edition in 2002, testifying to its continuing relevance. Since 2003, she has written extensively on pedagogy, particularly the *practice* of teaching, including *Teaching Critical Thinking: Practical Wisdom* (2010), a collection of practical essays on a broad array of social and cultural topics.

Selected Bibliography

hooks, bell. *Black Looks: Race and Representation*. Boston: South End Press, 1992.

hooks, bell. *Feminist Theory: From Margin to Center*. Cambridge, MA: South End Press, 1984, 2002.

hooks, bell. *Outlaw Culture: Resisting Representations*. New York: Routledge, 1994.

hooks, bell. *Talking Back: Thinking Feminism, Thinking Black*. Boston: South End Press, 1989.

hooks, bell. *Teaching Critical Thinking: Practical Wisdom*. New York and London: Routledge, 2010.

Luce Irigaray (1930–)

Luce Irigaray was born in Belgium and was educated at the University of Louvain and the University of Paris, from which she received an MA (her second) in psychology (1961), followed by a diploma in psychotherapy (1962) and a doctorate in linguistics (1968). For two years, Irigaray worked for the Fonds National de la Recherche Scientifique in Belgium, and in 1964 she began working for the Centre National de la Recherche Scientifique in Paris, where she served as Director of Research. Throughout the 1960s, she trained as a psychoanalyst and was a member of **Jacques Lacan**'s École Freudienne de Paris. In the late 1960s, she began teaching at the University of Paris VIII (Vincennes). Upon publication of her dissertation (for a second doctorate), *Speculum of the Other Woman* (1974), Irigaray was dismissed from her position at the University of Paris (and from Lacan's École Freudienne de Paris), largely due to Lacan's disapproval of her work. She has, since the 1980s, taught abroad, at the University of Rotterdam (where she chaired the Department of Philosophy) and in England, at the Universities of Nottingham, Bristol, and Liverpool.

In *Speculum*, Irigaray argues that Western philosophy and psychoanalysis regard women as mere reflecting surfaces on which masculine IDENTITY constitutes itself in a DIALECTICAL relation of dominance. In *This Sex Which Is Not One* (1977), she experimented with an innovative mode of ÉCRITURE FÉMININE, which eschews the PHALLOGOCENTRIC standards of psychoanalysis, philosophy, and literature. In her subsequent works, Irigaray pursued questions of DIFFERENCE and ALTERITY, especially as it concerned gender and sexual identity. In the 1990s, she worked with the Commission for Equal Opportunities for the region of Emilia-Romagna in Italy, producing a report on the status of rights for women, *Democracy begins Between the Two* (1994). She also wrote many books exploring the ethical implications of gender difference, including *Je, Tu, Nous* (1990), a collection of essays on civil rights and biological difference, and *An Ethics of Sexual Difference* (1993), a study of the ethical tradition in philosophy and an elaboration of her own ethical vision. She also produced new works on philosophy, psychoanalytic method, and language, as well as a series of works on the role of the elements in the sensual life of philosophers, including *Marine Lover of Friedrich Nietzsche* (1991). In 2002, drawing on Eastern philosophy and yoga, she revisited, in *Between East and West: From Singularity to Community* (2002), the questions of gender and sexual difference that had first secured her reputation as a feminist philosopher.

Selected Bibliography

Irigaray, Luce. *An Ethics of Sexual Difference*. Trans. Carolyn Burke and Gillian C. Gill. Ithaca: Cornell University Press, 1993.

Irigaray, Luce. *Between East and West: From Singularity to Community*. New York: Columbia University Press, 2002.

Irigaray, Luce. *Je, Tu, Nous: Toward a Culture of Difference*. Trans. Alison Martin. New York: Routledge, 1993.

Irigaray, Luce. *Speculum of the Other Woman*. Trans. Gillian C. Gill. Ithaca: Cornell University Press, 1985.

Irigaray, Luce. *This Sex Which Is Not One*. Trans. Catherine Porter. Ithaca: Cornell University Press, 1985.

Wolfgang Iser (1926–2007)

Wolfgang Iser was born in Marienberg, Germany, and educated at the University of Heidelberg, where he received his doctorate in 1950. In the 1960s, he was involved in founding the experimental University of Konstanz. Ultimately, Konstanz would become closely associated with the reader-response theory of Iser and the reception theory of Hans Robert Jauss. In addition to teaching at Konstanz, Iser held a long-standing appointment at the University of California, Irvine. His academic career began in earnest with the publication of *The Implied Reader* (1974), a work of literary criticism, and *The Act of Reading* (1978), a meditation on the theoretical principles of what came to be known as reader-response theory. Iser's work explores the problems faced by readers when confronted with literary texts. Following in the footsteps of Roman Ingarden, whose phenomenology of reading was well known by the Konstanz theorists, Iser argued that the literary work was the result of the reader's engagement with the text. The very process of taming the semantic and SEMIOTIC possibilities of the text awakens in the reader a profound understanding of what it means to confront an alien consciousness.

Throughout the late 1970s and 1980s, Iser wrote on Walter Pater's AESTHETICS, Shakespeare, and Laurence Sterne. At this time, he was also studying certain theoretical and critical implications of reader-response theory, specifically the process of self-discovery that it entails. In *Prospecting* (1989) and *The Fictive and the Imaginary* (1993), he developed a conception of "literary anthropology," a mode of fieldwork in which readers use the literary work as a basis for "staging" their own responses to being human. His later thought focused on interpretation and how "to do" theory. He remains an influential theorist for those studying the status of the reader and the affective dimension of human experience made available by the reading process.

Selected Bibliography

Iser, Wolfgang. *The Act of Reading: A Theory of Aesthetic Response*. Baltimore: Johns Hopkins University Press, 1978.

Iser, Wolfgang. *The Fictive and the Imaginary: Charting Literary Anthropology*. Baltimore: Johns Hopkins University Press, 1993.

Iser, Wolfgang. *The Implied Reader: Patterns of Communication in Prose Fiction from Bunyan to Beckett*. Baltimore: Johns Hopkins University Press, 1974.

Iser, Wolfgang. *Prospecting: From Reader Response to Literary Anthropology*. Baltimore: Johns Hopkins University Press, 1989.

Iser, Wolfgang. *The Range of Interpretation*. New York: Columbia University Press, 2000.

Fredric Jameson (1934–)

Fredric Jameson was born in Cleveland, Ohio, and educated at Haverford College and Yale University. He received his doctorate in 1959 from Yale and began teaching at Harvard University. In 1967 he moved to the University of California, San Diego, where he taught French and comparative literature. In 1976 he returned to Yale as a professor of French, and remained until 1983. In that year, he moved to the University of California, Santa Cruz, where he taught in the History of Consciousness program. In 1986, he was named William A. Lane, Jr. Professor of Comparative Literature at Duke University, where he continues to teach.

His first book, *Sartre: The Origins of a Style* (1961), focused on the politics and ethics of existential philosophy and their relation to the problem of style. His next two works, *Marxism and Form* (1971) and *The Prison House of Language* (1972), are steeped in Marxism and the Russian formalist tradition. His first major work, *The Political Unconscious* (1981), is a Marxist analysis of the early modernist novel that stresses the ways in which ideological MASTER NARRATIVES operate at an unconscious level in the text. Following **Louis Althusser**'s theories of IDEOLOGY and structural causality, Jameson regards the novel as the purveyor of ideological codes that can only be grasped by the critic capable of reading the text's "political unconscious." Jameson's renown as a theorist came from his application of "post-Marxist" methodology to postmodern cultural texts. In *Postmodernism, or, The Cultural Logic of Late Capitalism*, he inaugurated a materialist critique of the postmodern in literature, architecture, and the arts. The collection of essays by the same name, published in 1991, established Jameson as a leading theorist of postmodernism. Much of his work in the 1990s was dedicated to the critique of postmodernism and its relation to modernity; of special note is *A Singular Modernity* (2002), a study of modernity and literary modernism. Jameson continues to work with Marxist theory, and his later works include a study of utopian desire in science fiction, a commentary on *Capital*, and a study of DIALECTICS.

Selected Bibliography

Jameson, Fredric. *The Ideologies of Theory: Essays 1971–1986*. 2 vols. Minneapolis: University of Minnesota Press, 1988.

Jameson, Fredric. *The Political Unconscious: Narrative as a Socially Symbolic Act*. Ithaca: Cornell University Press, 1981.

Jameson, Fredric. *Postmodernism, or, The Cultural Logic of Late Capitalism*. Durham, NC: Duke University Press, 1991.

Jameson, Fredric. *A Singular Modernity: Essay on the Ontology of the Present*. London: Verso, 2002.

Jameson, Fredric. *Valences of the Dialectic*. London and New York: Verso, 2009.

Julia Kristeva (1941–)

Julia Kristeva was born in Sliven, Bulgaria, and studied at the University of Sofia before moving to Paris in 1966. She studied linguistics and semiotics at the University of Paris VII (Denis Diderot) and the École des Hautes Études en Sciences Sociales, from which she received a doctorate in linguistics in 1973. In 1974, she became a permanent visiting professor in the department of French at Columbia University (a position she also enjoyed, after 1992, at the University of Toronto) and began her long career at the University of Paris VII. In 1992, she became Director of the École Doctorale at Paris VII and is currently professor of literature and linguistics. In addition to her academic appointments, Kristeva has, since 1979, maintained a career in psychoanalysis.

Kristeva's innovative combination of SEMIOTICS, literary theory, and psychoanalysis – "semanalysis" as she puts it – exemplifies the interdisciplinary nature of poststructuralism. Her early linguistics and semiotics research found an audience among readers of the journal *Tel Quel*, whose editorial board she joined in 1969. In these years, she collaborated with **Roland Barthes** and Philippe Sollers (whom she later married). In 1974, she published her doctoral dissertation as *Revolution in Poetic Language*, a study of semiotic poetics and nineteenth-century experimental poetry. Her most important early work involved an investigation of the semiotic *khora*, a pre-Oedipal space prior to signifying systems and the patriarchal system of gender differentiation. Kristeva's work in the 1970s focused on linguistics and semiotics, though *About Chinese Women* (1977) looks ahead to her later psychoanalytic works. In the same year, *Polylogue*, a collection of her early essays on semiotics and the novel, appeared and, with some modifications, was translated as *Desire in Language* (1980). In *Powers of Horror* (1980), she introduced the concept of "abjection," a condition resulting from the need, in patriarchal societies, to regard the maternal body as a threat to the development of normative SUBJECTIVITY.

Throughout the 1980s and 1990s, Kristeva wrote on psychoanalysis, social alienation, nationalism, Proust, and a host of other topics. She also wrote fiction, with her *roman à clef*, *The Samurai*, attracting critical attention. Important mid-period works include *Tales of Love* (1983) and *Black Sun* (1987), a study of depression and melancholy, and *Intimate Revolt* (2002), a study of psychoanalysis and literature. In *New Maladies of the Soul* (1995), she brought together her essays from the previous two decades. In 1998, Kristeva collaborated with Catherine Clément on *The Feminine and the Sacred* and, since 2000, she has written on Melanie Klein, Hannah Arendt, and Colette. She has also published studies on art and problems in psychoanalysis, including *Hatred and Forgiveness* (2010).

Selected Bibliography

Kristeva, Julia. *Desire in Language: A Semiotic Approach to Literature and Art*. Ed. Leon S. Roudiez. Trans. Thomas Gora, Alice Jardine, and Leon S. Roudiez. New York: Columbia University Press, 1980.

Kristeva, Julia. *New Maladies of the Soul*. Trans. Ross Guberman. New York: Columbia University Press, 1995.

Kristeva, Julia. *Powers of Horror: An Essay on Abjection*. Trans. Leon S. Roudiez. New York: Columbia University Press, 1982.

Kristeva, Julia. *Revolution in Poetic Language*. Trans. Margaret Waller. New York: Columbia University Press, 1984.

Kristeva, Julia. *Tales of Love*. Trans. Leon S. Roudiez. New York: Columbia University Press, 1987.

Jacques Lacan (1901–81)

Jacques Lacan was born in Paris and educated in Jesuit schools before beginning his studies in medicine and psychiatry at the Faculté de Médecine de Paris. He started his clinical training in 1927, working on "automatism" and personality disorders. He received his doctorate in 1932 with a thesis on paranoid psychoses and the possibilities of combining psychiatry with psychoanalysis. Two years later, he joined the Psychoanalytic Society of Paris and began undergoing psychoanalysis. During World War II, he protested the brutality of the Nazi occupiers of France by ceasing all professional work. In the decades following the war, he developed an interest in structuralism and linguistics, believing that these sciences shed light on the workings of the unconscious. His unorthodox theories of clinical practice led to his break from the International Psychoanalytical Association in 1953. In the same year, at a congress in Rome, Lacan read his most important early essay, "Function and Field of Speech in Psychoanalysis," which argues that SUBJECTIVITY and the unconscious were fundamentally determined by linguistic structures, specifically, linguistic *difference*.

For the next ten years or so, Lacan devoted his time to a project often referred to as a "return to Freud." As he readily admits, his discovery of the importance of structure and language in the unconscious was actually a working out of discoveries Freud himself had made without the benefit of the Saussurean linguistics necessary to understand them. The essays of this period, collected in *Écrits* (1966), form the basis of his early reputation, though his seminars, beginning in 1954, account for the lion's share of his work on Freudian theory. In *Écrits*, Lacan postulates a structural theory of language that permeates the ego's relations with the world, that indeed constructs the ego as a subjectivity *in* the world. Lacan articulates this formation as a process in which the SUBJECT becomes constituted by her ascension to the SYMBOLIC order of language, law, and representation. In the Symbolic, desire displaces demand and institutes "lack" as the foundation of subjectivity. He also posited an IMAGINARY order, characterized by narcissistic desire and fantasy, and an order of the REAL, the domain of unmediated, undifferentiated existence. The Real is wholly external to the Symbolic and Imaginary orders, the unrepresentable ground of human experience.

In the early 1970s, Lacan and members of the École Freudienne de Paris, which Lacan had formed in 1964, published *Feminine Sexuality* (1973). Since the early 1980s, translations of Lacan's seminars on psychoanalytic theory have steadily appeared, many of which were not published in any form in his lifetime. The seminars, particularly those on the symptom and methodology, confirm the originality and critical power of his "return to Freud."

Selected Bibliography

Fink, Bruce. *Lacan to the Letter: Reading Écrits Closely*. Minneapolis: University of Minnesota Press, 2004.

Lacan, Jacques. *Écrits: The First Complete Edition in English*. Trans. Bruce Fink. New York: Norton, 2006.

Lacan, Jacques. *Feminine Sexuality: Jacques Lacan and the École Freudienne*. Ed. Juliet Mitchell and Jacqueline Rose. Trans. Jacqueline Rose. New York and London: Norton; New York: Pantheon Books, 1985.

Lacan, Jacques. *The Four Fundamental Concepts of Psycho-Analysis*. Ed. Jacques-Alain Miller. Trans. Alan Sheridan. New York: Norton, 1978.

Lacan, Jacques. *The Other Side of Psychoanalysis* [*The Seminar of Jacques Lacan*, Book XVII]. Trans. Russell Grigg. New York: Norton, 2007.

Lacan, Jacques. *The Seminar of Jacques Lacan*. Ed. Jacques-Alain Miller. Trans. John Forrester. 2 vols. Cambridge: Cambridge University Press, 1988.

Bruno Latour (1947–)

Bruno Latour was born in Beaune, in the Burgundy region of France, to a family of wine merchants and growers. He studied philosophy, biblical exegesis, and anthropology at the Université de Bourgogne. He was deeply influenced by the philosopher and historian of science Michel Serres who, like **Michel Foucault**, was rethinking how science works and how we tell the history of scientific innovations. Latour taught at École des Mines de Paris (associated with the Centre de Sociologie de l'Innovation) from 1982 to 2006 and is now professor at the Institut d'Études Politiques de Paris (Sciences Po), where he also served for five years as vice-president of research. His career, like some other posthumanists, embraces philosophical critique and scientific method, which makes the *use* of science in his work a highly self-critical one. Latour did some ethnographic fieldwork in Côte d'Ivoire and in a neuroendocrinology laboratory, the latter resulting in *Laboratory Life: The Construction of Scientific Facts* (with Steve Woolgar, 1979). This volume was an early entry in the field of science and technology. It focused on "actor-network theory" (ANT), which brings SEMIOTIC systems into material embodiment as *social* networks. This was followed by such studies as *Aramis: Or, The Love of Technology* (1993), a "field study" of a French subway system. *Reassembling the Social* (2005), Latour's Clarendon lectures at Oxford on management studies, illustrates how ANT allows both the "redistribution of the local" and connects local sites into systems. A critical history of medicine and the socialization of the physician, *The Pasteurization of France* (1984), led to a more broad-based critique of modernity and the role of the human in it. *We Have Never Been Modern* (1991) takes on a range of philosophical, scientific, and political issues from the standpoint of an anti-"post-post-postmodernist" who claims that we have not reached the era of the "modern," much less that of the postmodern. Latour's challenge to sociology and the presumptions of modern science found expression in *On the Modern Cult of the Factish Gods* (1996). Late works like *Politics of Nature* (2004) explore the idea of "political ecology," a part of the larger ANT problematic that Latour explored the next year in *Reassembling the Social*. A response to the questions raised by *We Have Never Been Modern*, particularly the question of how to define our experience if "the modern" is not the model for it, is proffered in *An Inquiry into Modes of Existence* (2013). With Peter Weibel, he has written in connection with the ZKM Center for Arts and Media in Karlsruhe, Germany. Like other posthumanists interested in systems theory and chaos theory, Latour works within new scientific paradigms, in part as a standpoint for a critique of where we *have been*.

Selected Bibliography

Latour, Bruno. *Aramis: Or, The Love of Technology*. Trans. Catherine Porter. Cambridge, MA: Harvard University Press, 1996.

Latour, Bruno. *An Inquiry into Modes of Existence*. Trans. Catherine Porter. Cambridge, MA: Harvard University Press, 2013.

Latour, Bruno. *On the Modern Cult of the Factish Gods*. Trans. Catherine Porter and Heather MacLean. Durham, NC: Duke University Press, 2010.

Latour, Bruno. *Reassembling the Social: An Introduction to Actor-Network Theory*. Oxford: Oxford University Press, 2005.

Latour, Bruno. *We Have Never Been Modern*. Trans. Catherine Porter. Cambridge, MA: Harvard University Press, 1993.

Jean-François Lyotard (1924–98)

Jean-François Lyotard was born in Vincennes, France, and studied philosophy and literature at the Sorbonne. After passing his *agrégation* in philosophy in 1950, he began teaching in a lycée in French-occupied Algeria. He became radicalized in the mid-1950s and joined the socialist collective Socialisme ou Barbarie. By the early 1960s, he was lecturing at the Sorbonne, attending **Jacques Lacan**'s seminars, and, later in the decade, teaching at the University of Paris X (Nanterre) as well as serving as Director of Research at the Centre National de la Recherche Scientifique. In 1971, Lyotard received his doctorate and began teaching at the University of Paris VII (Vincennes), where he remained until his retirement in 1987. Throughout the late 1980s and 1990s, he lectured and taught all over the world and was a regular visiting professor at the University of California, Irvine.

After publishing a book on phenomenology in 1954, Lyotard devoted much of his time to political journalism and Marxist essays on philosophical topics, publishing many of them in the *Socialisme ou Barbarie* journal, which was deeply concerned with the nationalist struggle in Algeria. The group's ambivalence over the possibility of a socialist revolution, together with the outcome of the War of Independence, which did not issue in a socialist state, led Lyotard to abandon revolutionary socialism and orthodox Marxism. In 1971 he published his doctoral thesis as *Discours, figure*. This text is a response to Lacan's seminars and to structuralism in general. Throughout the 1970s Lyotard continued to explore psychoanalytic questions, often alongside Marxist themes, as in *Dérive à partir de Marx et Freud* (1973). His most important work of this period was *Libidinal Economy* (1974), an innovative critique of philosophy and Marxism from the perspective of Freud's theory of desire. Lyotard's reputation as a postmodernist was secured with *The Postmodern Condition* (1979), a study of Western knowledge and its transmission that focused on new forms of information analysis, especially game theory and pragmatics. His famous formulation of the postmodern as that which, in the modern, resists representation has been widely adapted by theorists of postmodernity. Throughout the 1980s, he turned his attention to AESTHETICS, specifically the concept of the sublime, and to philosophical ethics. His work on the latter produced *Le Différend* (1983), which argues that social and cultural discourses often perpetuate a situation of incommensurability in which it is impossible to guarantee agreement in matters of justice, aesthetics, and moral philosophy. The *différend* marks this impossibility by naming the irreducible DIFFERENCE that defines it. Lyotard's theory of the postmodern was developed throughout the 1980s and early 1990s, issuing in two important essay collections, *The Postmodern Explained to Children* (1986) and *Toward the Postmodern* (1993). His late work on aesthetics, temporality, and the question of what it means to be human are collected in *The Inhuman: Reflections on Time* (1991). The last decade of his life saw a renewed interest in Kant's aesthetics and the publication, in 1994, of *Lessons on the Analytic of the Sublime*. In this text, as in so many of his works at this time, Lyotard reminds us of postmodernity's lingering indebtedness to Enlightenment philosophy.

Selected Bibliography

Lyotard, Jean-François. *The Differend: Phrases in Dispute*. Trans. Georges Van Den Abbeele. Minneapolis: University of Minnesota Press, 1988.

Lyotard, Jean-François. *The Inhuman: Reflections on Time*. Trans. Geoffrey Bennington and Rachel Bow. Cambridge: Polity Press, 1991.

Lyotard, Jean-François. *Libidinal Economy*. Trans. Iain Hamilton Grant. Bloomington and Indianapolis: Indiana University Press, 1993.

Lyotard, Jean-François. *The Postmodern Condition: A Report on Knowledge*. Trans. Geoff Bennington and Brian Massumi. Minneapolis: University of Minnesota Press, 1984.

Lyotard, Jean-François. *Toward the Postmodern*. Ed. Robert Harvey and Mark S. Roberts. Atlantic Highlands, NJ: Humanities Press, 1993.

J. Hillis Miller (1928–)

J. Hillis Miller was born in Newport News, Virginia, and studied at Oberlin College and Harvard University, where he received his doctorate in 1952. He taught for nearly twenty years at Johns Hopkins University, then taught at Yale University, where he held the Frederick W. Hilles Chair in English and Comparative Literature. In 1986, he left Yale for the University of California, Irvine, where he is currently Distinguished Research Professor of English and Comparative Literature.

Miller's early work, especially *Charles Dickens: The World of His Novels* (1958), grew out of his interest in the phenomenology of Georges Poulet. Over the next ten years, he studied nineteenth-century literary traditions, producing *The Disappearance of God* (1963) and *Poets of Reality* (1965), texts which examine how the "here and now" serves to ground literary vision in the absence of God. Through the late 1960s and 1970s, Miller continued to write about literature but from a poststructuralist perspective, and in the mid-1970s he wrote two articles – "Ariadne's Thread" and "The Critic as Host" – which both defended and brilliantly exemplified the deconstructionist method. He followed up these influential essays with *Fiction and Repetition* (1982), an important study of the novel that drew on Nietzschean and Deleuzean theories of DIF-FERENCE and repetition to describe the two modes of repetition (unifying and differential) that construct novelistic narrative. In the 1980s, Miller began to explore a linguistically based "ethics of reading," arguing that our compulsion to read enabled the development of an ethical sensibility. In 1990, Miller consolidated his position on the ethics of reading with three collections of essays, *Tropes, Parables, Performatives*, *Versions of Pygmalion*, and *Victorian Subjects*. These texts, with their emphasis on literature as a performative act involving the reader as collaborator, confirmed his reputation as a major innovator in deconstructionist and reader-response theories. In 1992, he published *Ariadne's Thread*, which explored further his earlier ideas about labyrinthine narratives in conjunction with his new performative theory of ethical reading. His work of the late 1990s tended toward studies of literature and speech act theory, including *Speech Acts in Literature* (2001). He also published a study of **Derrida** in 2009. More than any other poststructuralist critic, Miller has taught us the myriad possibilities of an ethics of reading grounded in the openness of the text.

Selected Bibliography

Miller, J. Hillis. *Ariadne's Thread: Story Lines*. New Haven: Yale University Press, 1992.

Miller, J. Hillis. *The Ethics of Reading: Kant, de Man, Eliot, Trollope, James and Benjamin*. New York: Columbia University Press, 1987.

Miller, J. Hillis. *Fiction and Repetition*. Cambridge, MA: Harvard University Press, 1982.

Miller, J. Hillis. *The J. Hillis Miller Reader*. Ed. Julian Wolfreys. Stanford: Stanford University Press, 2005.

Miller, J. Hillis. *Speech Acts in Literature*. Stanford: Stanford University Press, 2001.

Miller, J. Hillis. *Tropes, Parables, Performatives: Essays on Twentieth-Century Literature*. New York: Harvester Wheatsheaf, 1990.

Antonio Negri (1933–)

Antonio Negri was born in Padua, Italy, and educated at the University of Padua, where he rapidly became a professor in the field of "state theory," which has a long tradition in the Italian academy and includes the study of juridical and constitutional theory, a subject on which Negri frequently wrote. He was part of the editorial group of the journal *Quaderni Rossi* and was involved in radical political movements from the early 1950s, including, by the 1970s, the Organized Workers Autonomy movement. He began writing on Marx, the state, and revolutionary resistance in the 1970s. The kidnapping and murder in 1978 of Aldo Moro, former prime minister of Italy, brought the terrorist group Brigate Rosse (Red Brigades) to worldwide attention. In 1979, Negri, rumored to be the "mastermind" of the Red Brigades, was indicted on charges of murder connected with the Moro affair. He fled to France, where he was befriended by **Michel Foucault, Jacques Derrida**, and **Gilles Deleuze**. Ultimately, his thirty-year sentence was reduced to thirteen years, and he returned to Italy to serve it out. In 1983, he was elected to the Italian legislature, representing the Radical Party, and claimed parliamentary immunity, which led to his temporary release (after four and a half years' incarceration) and his flight back to France. Once in Paris, he started teaching at the University of Paris VII (Denis) and the Collège International de Philosophie, founded by Derrida. In the 1990s, he co-founded the journal *Futur Antérieur*. He was imprisoned again from 1997 to 2003.

Like Antonio Gramsci, another Italian Marxist who spent years behind bars, Negri used his time in prison to write. After his first imprisonment, he published *The Savage Anomaly* (1981), a study of Baruch Spinoza, a key figure for many post-Marxists. His earliest works are on the state and on radical politics, particularly the Autonomy Movement. Some of the work from this era appears in *Labor of Dionysus* (1994), which is otherwise co-written with Michael Hardt (a professor at Duke University). One of his most important theoretical works, *Marx Beyond Marx*, was written during his first exile in France and is a close consideration of the *Grundrisse*, an early manuscript by Marx that contains important theoretical reflections on social and theoretical practice. By the late 1980s, Negri was writing again about the modern state and reflecting, in *The Politics of Subversion* (1989), on late capitalism and postmodernism. In 1997, Negri followed his early study of Spinoza with *Subversive Spinoza* and a volume on Descartes. Beginning in 2000, Negri started a collaboration with Michael Hardt that has produced four major volumes, including *Labor of Dionysus: A Critique of the State-Form* (1994) and *Empire* (2000), heralded by many as a transformational study of the age of globalization. They followed up with *Multitude: War and Democracy in the Age of Empire* (2004) and *Commonwealth* (2009).

Selected Bibliography

Hardt, Michael and Antonio Negri. *Empire*. Cambridge, MA and London: Harvard University Press, 2000.

Hardt, Michael and Antonio Negri. *Labor of Dionysus: A Critique of the State-Form*. Minneapolis: University of Minnesota Press, 1994.

Hardt, Michael and Antonio Negri. *Multitude: War and Democracy in the Age of Empire*. New York: Penguin, 2004.

Negri, Antonio. *Marx Beyond Marx: Lessons on the Grundrisse*. Ed. Jim Fleming. Trans. Harry Cleaver, Michael Ryan, and Maurizio Vianno. South Hadley, MA: Bergin and Garvey, 1984.

Negri, Antonio. *Political Descartes: Reason, Ideology and the Bourgeois Project*. London: Verso, 2007.

Negri, Antonio. *The Politics of Subversion: A Manifesto for the Twenty-First Century*. Trans. James Newell. Cambridge: Polity Press, 1989.

Jacques Rancière (1940–)

Jacques Rancière was born in Algiers, Algeria, and studied at the École Normale Supérieure in Paris under **Louis Althusser**. He began teaching at the University of Paris (VIII) in 1969 and stayed there until 2000, and remains a professor emeritus. He is also on the faculty of the European Graduate School in Saas-Fee, Switzerland. Rancière is of the same generation as **Gilles Deleuze** and Alain Badiou, who were involved in various ways in the radical political scene in Paris in the 1960s. Like many of his generation, Rancière's positions are often hard to place in the usual theoretical categories; he shares ideas and concepts with poststructuralists, postmodernists, and post-Marxists, but it may be that his radical critique of politics and AESTHETICS places him among the posthumanists.

His first major publication was a joint volume, with Althusser and Étienne Balibar, *Lire de Capital* (1968). But that same year, in May 1968, Rancière broke with Althusser because he thought that his mentor's structuralism had led him to underestimate the power of the individual and tended to perpetuate repressive capitalist social structures (i.e., the university system). His next book, *Althusser's Lesson* (1974), argued that educators like his own mentor tended to reaffirm and protect existing pedagogical practices and educational institutions by assuming an asymmetrical relation between students (ignorant) and teachers (knowledgeable). He continued this critique in the social histories of the 1980s, including *The Ignorant Schoolmaster* (1987). The

1990s saw a shift to political reflection, particularly on the "poetics of knowledge" in history and on the direction of political critique. *Disagreement: Politics and Philosophy* (1995) suggests that political rationality is really a rationality of *disagreement* that philosophy misrecognizes. Some critics have noted a shift from politics to aesthetics after 1995, but it might be more accurate to say that the two themes become dialectically entwined. This is especially the case in *The Politics of Aesthetics* (2000), in which Rancière returns to the origin of aesthetics in sensation and offers new strategies of "distributing the sensible." The argument is picked up in *Aesthetics and Its Discontents* (2004), which critiques the Kantian "aesthetic regime" and the anti-modernist aesthetics of Alain Badiou and **Jean-François Lyotard**. Politics and aesthetics are again explicitly conjoined in *The Emancipated Spectator* (2008), in the sense that a revamped notion of our engagement with art leads to forms of social emancipation. His most recent work, *Dissensus: On Politics and Aesthetics* (2010), introduces the term *dissensus* to mark the intervention in political consensus (which can often be led by elite interests) of new subjects and new points of view.

Selected Bibliography

Rancière, Jacques. *Aesthetics and Its Discontents*. Trans. Steven Corcoran. Cambridge: Polity Press, 2009.

Rancière, Jacques. *Althusser's Lesson*. Trans. Emiliano Battista. London and New York: Continuum, 2011.

Rancière, Jacques. *Dissensus: On Politics and Aesthetics*. Ed. and trans. Steven Corcoran. London and New York: Continuum, 2010.

Rancière, Jacques. *The Ignorant Schoolmaster: Five Lessons in Intellectual Emancipation*. Trans. Kristin Ross. Stanford: Stanford University Press, 1991.

Rancière, Jacques. *The Politics of Aesthetics: The Distribution of the Sensible*. Trans. Gabriel Rockhill. London and New York: Continuum, 2009.

Edward Said (1935–2003)

Edward Said was born in Jerusalem, British Occupied Palestine, and moved with his family to Cairo after the 1947 partition by Israel. He was educated in Cairo and the United States, studying piano briefly at the Juilliard School of Music. He received his BA degree from Princeton University and his doctorate from Harvard University in 1964 and began his career at Columbia University, where he was teaching at the time of his death. He held visiting professorships at a number of institutions, including Yale University and Stanford University. His dissertation was published in 1966 under the title *Joseph Conrad and the Fiction of Autobiography*. His next book, *Beginnings* (1975), showed the influence of **Michel Foucault** and poststructuralist theories of discourse. In the years following the Arab–Israel war in 1967, Said turned increasingly to a study of COLONIALISM and the discourse of empire. His seminal study, *Orientalism* (1978), was the first major work to respond to the troubles in the Middle East. In this volume, he analyzes a vast structure of knowledge and power dedicated to representing and controlling the Orient. His critique of the binomial logic of "us and them" that subtends Orientalist discourse was a foundational work for the emergent field of postcolonial studies and a powerful influence on **Homi Bhabha** and **Gayatri Chakravorty Spivak**.

In the 1980s, Said turned increasingly to the study of Palestine, challenging Western media stereotypes of the Middle East in *Covering Islam* (1981) and *After the Last Sky* (1986). He also elaborated on his theory of "secular criticism" in *The World, the Text and the Critic* (1983), which explores the cultural and political stakes of criticism and included the much-discussed essay, "Traveling Theory," a reflection on the globalization of theoretical discourse. Said wrote on a wide variety of topics through the 1980s and 1990s, with many of his essays, including those on Jane Austen's representation of colonial economies, appearing in an important collection, *Culture and Imperialism* (1993). He continued to write about his involvement with the Palestine Liberation Organization, with which he was affiliated throughout his career. He was also interested in the role of the intellectual and wrote many essays on the particular problems of intellectuals in colonial and postcolonial societies. In 1999, he published a memoir, *Out of Place*, that recounts the privileged yet traumatic upbringing he experienced in Palestine and Cairo, his involvement with Palestinian causes, and his long academic career in the United States. In the last years of his life, he published collections of his essays and interviews on the Middle East peace process and other issues in contemporary politics. One of Said's last works, published the year after his death, *Humanism and Democratic Criticism* (2004), sums up his humanistic vision and reiterates the need for public intellectuals. Few literary theorists have been as passionately and consistently dedicated to the values of secularism and the free exchange of ideas.

Selected Bibliography

Said, Edward W. *Beginnings: Intentions and Method.* New York: Columbia University Press, 1975.

Said, Edward W. *Culture and Imperialism.* New York: Knopf, 1993.

Said, Edward W. *Humanism and Democratic Criticism.* New York: Columbia University Press, 2004.

Said, Edward W. *Orientalism.* New York: Pantheon Books, 1978.

Said, Edward W. *The World, the Text and the Critic.* Cambridge, MA: Harvard University Press, 1983.

Eve Kosofsky Sedgwick (1950–2009)

Eve Kosofsky Sedgwick was born in Dayton, Ohio, and was educated at Cornell University and Yale University, where she received her doctorate in 1975. She taught at a number of institutions, including Boston University, Dartmouth College, and Duke University, where she was the Newman Ivey White Professor of English. At the time of her death, she was Distinguished Professor at the Graduate Center of the City University of New York.

Sedgwick's early work was instrumental in establishing a theoretical vocabulary for queer theory. Of crucial importance was the concept of HOMOSOCIAL DESIRE, which she introduced in her first book, *Between Men* (1985). Drawing on the work of Gayle Rubin and René Girard, Sedgwick constructed a theory of "triangular desire" or the relation in which a woman serves as the conduit for a homosocial bond between men. *Epistemology of the Closet* (1990), a pioneering study of homosexuality in literature, solidified her position as the leading queer theorist. In the early 1990s, she continued to pursue questions of queer IDENTITY in literature, causing something of a scandal at the Modern Language Association meeting in 1989 with her essay "Jane Austen and the Masturbating Girl." She also co-edited important essay collections, including *Performativity and Performance* (1995) and *Shame and Its Sister: A Silvan Tomkins Reader* (1995). The latter marks Sedgwick's interest in the work of Tomkins and his theories of innate primal affects, which she used to refine her own conception of "queer PERFORMATIVITY" in *Touching Feeling: Affect, Pedagogy, Performativity* (2003).

In addition to her groundbreaking theoretical work, Sedgwick published a book of poems, *Fat Art, Thin Art* (1994), and an account of her experience with depression while recovering from breast cancer, *A Dialogue on Love* (1999). An experimental mélange of generic elements, her memoir seeks to understand the significance of therapy and the power of self-exploration.

Upon her death, in 2009, Duke University decided to close down the Q Series, co-edited by Sedgwick, which specialized in queer theory and began with Sedgwick's *Tendencies* (1993) and finished with a volume of her essays, *The Weather in Proust* (2011).

Selected Bibliography

Sedgwick, Eve Kosofsky. *Between Men: English Literature and Male Homosocial Desire*. New York: Columbia University Press, 1985.

Sedgwick, Eve Kosofsky. *Epistemology of the Closet*. Berkeley: University of California Press, 1990.

Sedgwick, Eve Kosofsky. *Tendencies*. Durham, NC: Duke University Press, 1993.

Sedgwick, Eve Kosofsky. *Touching Feeling: Affect, Pedagogy, Performativity*. Durham, NC: Duke University Press, 2003.

Elaine Showalter (1941–)

Elaine Showalter was born in Cambridge, Massachusetts, and educated at Bryn Mawr College, Brandeis University, and the University of California at Davis in 1970. After teaching at a variety of institutions, including high school and adult education, she landed at Princeton University, where she is Avalon Foundation Professor Emerita. She has chaired the department of English at Princeton and served as president of the Modern Language Association (1997). In a refreshing change from the usual academic curriculum vitae, she has been actively involved in writing for the popular press, with articles in *People*, *Vogue*, *New Statesman*, the *London Review of Books*, and other periodicals, and appears as a regular guest on television talk shows.

Showalter was one of the leading figures in US feminism in the 1970s. She coined the term "gynocriticism," which refers to a mode of criticism with a feminist standpoint. Her second and most influential work, *A Literature of Their Own* (1976), rewrote the literary history of the novel and developed a compelling alternative to the PATRIARCHAL tradition in fiction. Her theory of "the female aesthetic," influenced by French feminism, especially the work of **Hélène Cixous**, argues for a vision of literary art in which language and narrative resist the constraints of patriarchal traditions. Showalter turned to cultural history in *The Female Malady* (1985), in which she critiqued the medical establishment, particularly psychiatry, and its attempt to define and control women by "medicalizing" personality traits and behaviors that violate heterosexual masculinist norms. Her next two books were elaborations on this critique. *Sexual Anarchy* (1990) continued her interest in the cultural history of women's experience, focusing on the psychology of gender in the 1890s. In *Hystories* (1997), Showalter continued the argument advanced in *Sexual Anarchy* but went beyond the limits of her critique of gender to focus on chronic fatigue syndrome, Gulf War syndrome, recovered memory, satanic ritual abuse, and alien abduction. Her work in the twenty-first century has so far focused on pedagogy, feminist history, and the academic novel.

Selected Bibliography

Showalter, Elaine. *The Female Malady: Women, Madness and English Culture, 1830–1980.* New York: Pantheon Books, 1985.

Showalter, Elaine. *Hystories: Hysterical Epidemics and Modern Culture.* New York: Columbia University Press, 1997.

Showalter, Elaine. *A Literature of Their Own: British Women Novelists from Brontë to Lessing.* 2nd expanded ed. Princeton: Princeton University Press, 1999.

Showalter, Elaine. *Sexual Anarchy: Gender and Culture at the Fin de Siècle.* New York: Viking, 1990.

Gayatri Chakravorty Spivak (1942–)

Gayatri Chakravorty Spivak was born in Calcutta, West Bengal, and educated at the University of Calcutta. She then moved to the United States, where she studied comparative literature with **Paul de Man** at Cornell University. She began teaching at the University of Iowa in 1965, receiving her doctorate two years later. She has taught at a variety of institutions, including Brown University, the University of Texas, Austin, the University of Pittsburgh, and Emory University. She is currently University Professor at Columbia University.

Spivak published her dissertation on Yeats, *Myself Must I Remake: The Life and Poetry of W. B. Yeats*, in 1974, followed by a translation of **Jacques Derrida**'s *Of Grammatology* (1976). Throughout the late 1970s and 1980s, Spivak published *In Other Worlds* (1987) and a number of important essays, including "Can the Subaltern Speak?" (1988). These essays combined an interest in deconstruction and Marxism with a defiant resistance to PATRIARCHAL structures of knowledge and power. Of special importance was her attention to the problems of gender and SUB-ALTERN identity and the development of a feminist perspective sensitive to the political and cultural conditions of colonial and postcolonial societies. She also contributed a critical edge to the revisionist historiography coming out of the Subaltern Studies Group at this time. These works established her as something of a celebrity, much sought after by interviewers. Her early interviews are collected in *The Post-Colonial Critic* (1990).

Throughout the 1990s, Spivak pursued diverse interests within postcolonial theory. Of special note is her work on pedagogy in *Outside In the Teaching Machine* (1993) and other texts, in which she reflects on the responsibilities of educators in multicultural societies, both Western and postcolonial. Some of her work in this period was taken up and reframed in *A Critique of Postcolonial Reason* (1999). In 2000, she delivered the Wellek Library Lectures, published as *Death of a Discipline* (2003), in which she argues for a new conception of comparative literature, a "transnational cultural studies" that transcends traditional notions of nation and national boundary. Spivak continues the critique of postcolonial knowledge in her rereading of Friedrich Schiller and Immanuel Kant in *An Aesthetic Education in the Age of Globalization* (2012).

Selected Bibliography

Spivak, Gayatri Chakravorty. *An Aesthetic Education in the Age of Globalization*. Cambridge, MA: Harvard University Press, 2012.

Spivak, Gayatri Chakravorty. "Can the Subaltern Speak?" In *Marxism and the Interpretation of Culture*. Ed. Cary Nelson and Lawrence Grossberg. Urbana: University of Illinois Press, 1988. 271–313.

Spivak, Gayatri Chakravorty. *A Critique of Postcolonial Reason: Toward a History of the Vanishing Moment*. Cambridge, MA and London: Harvard University Press, 1999.

Spivak, Gayatri Chakravorty. *In Other Worlds: Essays in Cultural Politics*. New York: Methuen, 1987.

Spivak, Gayatri Chakravorty. *The Post-Colonial Critic: Interviews, Strategies, Dialogues*. Ed. Sarah Harasym. New York: Routledge, 1990.

Raymond Williams (1921–88)

Raymond Williams was born in Llanvihangel Crucorney, a small village in Wales. He entered Trinity College, Cambridge University, in 1939, but within two years was serving as a tank commander during the war. He returned to Cambridge and received his MA in 1946. He began teaching at Oxford University as an extra-mural tutor in literature, mostly in adult education. In 1961, he became a Fellow at Jesus College, Oxford, only to return to Cambridge as a Reader in 1967. By 1974 he was Professor of Drama, a position he held until 1983.

Williams' earliest works were on modern drama, then he turned to literary and cultural history and published *Culture and Society: 1780–1950* (1958) and *The Long Revolution* (1961). These volumes placed Williams squarely in a tradition of British CULTURAL MATERIALISM. *Culture and Society* reconsidered CANONICAL literary and cultural works in terms of their role in the development of "culture," which he understood in Gramscian terms as a complex web of IDEOLOGICAL articulations and "structures of feeling." In *The Long Revolution*, he critiqued the concept of organicism that had shaped the conservative tradition of social theory that began with Edmund Burke. Of special importance was his analysis of English educational institutions and the role they play in the creation and preservation of culture. Williams was also instrumental in developing programs in communications. His *Communications* (1967) became a textbook for new academic programs throughout the UK and the US.

These works form the basis of Williams' contribution to British cultural studies and cultural materialism. His work in the 1970s, beginning with *The English Novel from Dickens to Lawrence* (1970), continued the emphasis on cultural and literary history. This study was one of the first to submit the English novel tradition to a sustained materialist analysis. *The Country and the City* (1973), a penetrating analysis of the English pastoral tradition, highlights the political realities of both the country and the city. Other major works include *Keywords* (1985), an in-depth glossary of terms in cultural analysis, and *Marxism and Literature* (1977), one of the first general studies of Marxism and its uses for literary criticism. His later work focused on the popular media and the problems in cultural materialism. His last book, *The Politics of Modernism*, published the year after his death, explored the problematic relationship between radical politics and modernism. Evidence of his continuing relevance for literary and cultural theory is the new revised edition of *Keywords* (2005).

Selected Bibliography

Williams, Raymond. *Culture and Society: 1780–1950*. Rpt. New York: Columbia University Press, 1983.

Williams, Raymond. *The Long Revolution*. New York: Columbia University Press; London: Chatto and Windus, 1961.

Williams, Raymond. *Marxism and Literature*. Oxford: Oxford University Press, 1977.

Williams, Raymond. *The Politics of Modernism: Against the New Conformists*. Ed. Tony Pinkney. London and New York: Verso, 1989.

Williams, Raymond. *The Raymond Williams Reader*. Ed. John Higgins. Oxford and Malden, MA: Blackwell, 2001.

Cary Wolfe (1959–)

Cary Wolfe was born in North Carolina and educated at the University of North Carolina, at Chapel Hill, and Duke University, where he received his doctorate in 1990. He has taught at Indiana University, the University of Albany (SUNY), and Rice University, where he is presently Bruce and Elizabeth Dunlevie Professor and chair of the Department of English. He began publishing in the early 1990s on American ideology in writers like Ralph Waldo Emerson and Ezra Pound and co-edited (with Bill Rasch) a special issue of *Cultural Critique* on "The Politics of Systems and Environments" (1993), which was brought out in 2000 as *Observing Complexity: Systems Theory and Postmodernity*. These projects mark Wolfe's entrance into the field of the posthuman, scholars of which are often drawn to systems theory. His next major work was *Critical Environments* (1998), which focused on pragmatics and systems theory, with an emphasis on *autopoiesis*, the idea that systems are self-generating and self-regulating, and on the relation between systems theory and postmodernists like **Michel Foucault** and **Gilles Deleuze**. *Animal Rites* (2003) critiques the tendency among some theorists, like Stanley Cavell, to allow a nostalgic humanism to undermine their work on the non-human. Also in 2003, he edited *Zoontologies: The Question of the Animal*, which featured essays by Judith Roof, **Jacques Derrida**, and Alphonso Lingis, the latter a philosopher whose critique of phenomenology includes a new approach to ethics and ethical imperatives that might come from non-human subjects. Wolfe's *What is Posthumanism?* (2010) is in some ways a synthesis of all these developments, including systems theory, pragmatism, postmodernism, animal studies, and the problem of ethics and the non-human. He continues to work with issues in posthumanism, including new material on biopolitics, biophilosophy, and the idea of species difference. Wolfe's work characterizes the scholarly profile of the posthumanist whose starting point is a critique of the human.

Selected Bibliography

Wolfe, Cary. *Animal Rites: American Culture, the Discourse of Species and Posthumanist Theory*. Chicago: University of Chicago Press, 2003.

Wolfe, Cary. *Critical Environments: Postmodern Theory and the Pragmatics of the "Outside."* Minneapolis and London: University of Minnesota Press, 1998.

Wolfe, Cary. *What is Posthumanism?* Minneapolis: University of Minnesota Press, 2010.

Wolfe, Cary, ed. *Zoontologies: The Question of the Animal*. Minneapolis and London: University of Minnesota Press, 2003.

Slavoj Žižek (1949–)

Slavoj Žižek was born in Ljubljana, Slovenia, and studied philosophy at the University of Llubljana, where he received his doctorate. He also studied psychoanalysis at the University of Paris and underwent analysis by Jacques Alain

Miller, **Jacques Lacan**'s son-in-law. In 1979, he became a researcher at the Institute for Sociology and Philosophy, at the University of Llubljana. He has lectured widely and served as a visiting professor in many US and European universities. In the 1980s, he was active in Slovenian politics, running for the presidency of the Republic of Slovenia in 1990. In addition to his duties at the Institute of Sociology, Žižek teaches at the European Graduate School in Saas-Fee, Switzerland.

Žižek is one of the most provocative and original thinkers, and has written on a wide array of topics. From the beginning of his career, he has worked within two very different theoretical traditions: Hegelian critical theory and Lacanian psychoanalysis. Following the lead of early theorists like Herbert Marcuse, he applied psychoanalytic theory to social and cultural phenomena. In the space of two years, he published *The Sublime Object of Ideology* (1989), a study of Marx and Hegel from a Lacanian perspective, and *Looking Awry* (1991), a Lacanian reading of a wide variety of subjects, including detective fiction, the films of Alfred Hitchcock, pornography, politics, and postmodernism. These texts established Žižek as one of the most influential Lacanian theorists. *Tarrying with the Negative* (1993) uses Lacanian theories to understand the power and variety of contemporary ideologies. His study of the Lacanian "Thing" – the unknowable REAL object that serves as the magnetic center for unconscious thoughts – within a context of Eastern European nationalism was a signally important application of psychoanalysis to social phenomena. In the 1990s, he wrote and edited numerous volumes on psychoanalysis, and several works on the German Romantic critic F. W. J. von Schelling. In *Plague of Fantasies* (1997), he explored the breakdown of the centered psychological SUBJECT in the COMMODI-FIED space of fantasy. Since 2000, Žižek has turned his attention once again to Hegel and political theory. He co-authored (with **Judith Butler** and Ernesto Laclau) *Contingency, Hegemony, Universality* (2000). In the wake of the attacks on the World Trade Center in 2001, Žižek has written on the occupation of Iraq, notably in *Welcome to the Desert of the Real!* (2002). Also at this time, Žižek edited *Lacan: The Silent Partners*, contributed essays on Lacan and Alain Badiou to the website *Lacanian Ink*, and put out a video, *The Pervert's Guide to Cinema*. Among his many books since 2000 are *Violence: Six Sideways Reflections* (2008), *The Monstrosity of Christ: Paradox or Dialectic?* (2009), and his 1,000-page opus, *Less Than Nothing: Hegel and the Shadow of Dialectical Materialism* (2012).

Selected Bibliography

Žižek, Slavoj. *Enjoy Your Symptom! Jacques Lacan in Hollywood and Out*. New York: Routledge, 1992.

Žižek, Slavoj. *Less Than Nothing: Hegel and the Shadow of Dialectical Materialism*. London and New York: Verso, 2012.

Žižek, Slavoj. *Looking Awry: An Introduction to Jacques Lacan through Popular Culture*. Cambridge, MA: MIT Press, 1991.

Žižek, Slavoj. *The Monstrosity of Christ: Paradox or Dialectic?* Cambridge, MA: MIT Press, 2009.

Žižek, Slavoj. *The Sublime Object of Ideology*. London and New York: Verso, 1989.

Žižek, Slavoj. *Tarrying with the Negative: Kant, Hegel, and the Critique of Ideology*. Durham, NC: Duke University Press, 1993.

4

Reading with Literary Theory

Nor dare she trust a larger lay,
But rather loosens from the lip
Short swallow-flights of song, that dip
Their wings in tears, and skim away.

Tennyson, *In Memoriam*

In what follows, I offer a few short sample readings that use different theoretical methods and techniques. These heuristic writings are meant to illustrate (a) how one might talk about literature using theory and (b) how different theories work together. These analyses are intended to exemplify the kinds of questions that a particular theory might ask of a particular text. Though crafted in their present short form for pedagogical purposes, they give a fair sense of the variety of approaches to a single text. I have tried whenever possible to give an indication of how theories are combined in critical practice. The reader is invited to argue different points and to arrive at different conclusions.

Readers who are beginning to use theory in their analysis of literary and cultural texts are not usually expected to do the kind of archival research demanded by New Historicism or to have the background in philosophy that distinguishes so many theorists of deconstruction and poststructuralism. Nor are readers expected to have mastered technical knowledge of psychoanalysis or formalism. But they are expected to keep an open mind and to experiment with the tools that they have at their disposal. They can also be expected to use their own resources, garnered from work in the classroom and the library, to build on the research that theorists have done. What the reader brings to her own analyses of literary texts is a degree of curiosity about how theory might open up avenues of interpretation and a willingness to

The Literary Theory Handbook, First Edition. Gregory Castle.
© 2013 John Wiley & Sons, Ltd. Published 2013 by John Wiley & Sons, Ltd.

acquire a modest background in the theory in question. The *Literary Theory Handbook* provides a starting point for this kind of work.

In addition to these sample readings, which do not cover all the theories, concepts, and ideas considered in the *Handbook*, the reader will find throughout chapter two, "The Scope of Literary Theory," brief considerations of literary texts, film, and other artworks. I have listed the more substantial sections below.

- On contemporary art and installations, see Post-Marxist Theory; Postmodernism
- On memorial art, see Trauma Studies
- On poetry, see Trauma Studies; Posthumanism
- On fiction, see African American Studies; Theory of the Novel; Postcolonial Studies
- On aesthetics, see chapter two, "2 Ideology/Philosophy/History/Aesthetics."

William Shakespeare, *The Tempest*

*Reader Response * New Historicism * Postcolonial Studies*

The Tempest was Shakespeare's last romance, written in 1611, and in it he meditates on the problems of power and "right rule." Readers (or spectators) of the play will regard the treatment of these issues in different ways, depending on the circumstances and conditions of their own experience. Reader-response theory attempts to understand just these differences. Seventeenth-century readers would have understood the political point of *The Tempest* according to the "horizon" of their own experience and the specific nature of their "interpretive communities." They might see Prospero as a symbol of social harmony, civil justice, and dynastic succession. However, for modern readers schooled in the history of COLONIALISM and imperial expansion, Prospero is an oppressive colonist, using magic to mask social and political power. Similarly, while Shakespeare's own contemporaries might have regarded Caliban as an inhuman barbarian (or, at best, an early form of the Romantic "noble savage"), a modern reader is more likely to regard him sympathetically as the subject of colonial oppression and dispossession, of the inequality and discrimination at the heart of European power.

Reader-response theory requires the reader of a literary text to make decisions about the significance of character, action, theme, and symbol. It assumes that the reader completes the text at hand, not by discovering "hidden" meanings but by interpreting gaps, contradictions, and ambiguities. Consider the following lines spoken by Caliban to Stephano, one of the men planning a revolt against Prospero:

> Why, as I told thee, 'tis a custom with him
> I' th' afternoon to sleep. There thou mayst brain him,
> Having first seized his books; or with a log
> Batter his skull, or paunch him with a stake,
> Or cut his weasand with thy knife. Remember

> First to possess his books, for without them
> He's but a sot, as I am, nor hath not
> One spirit to command. They all do hate him
> As rootedly as I. Burn but his books. (3.2.82–90)

It is difficult for a modern reader not to discern a certain resourcefulness behind Caliban's barbarism, evidence of the extent to which he has learned the language of his oppressor. "You taught me language," he tells Prospero, "and my profit on 't / Is I know how to curse" (1.2.364–5). But he knows more than how to curse. In the above-quoted passage, the savage beast becomes the strategist, aware of Prospero's weaknesses (his afternoon nap) but also aware that his books of magic are the signs of his social authority. Readers are led to regard Caliban not as a dangerous threat to social order but rather as a victim of that order. But they are also led to regard Prospero, without his books, as no better than Caliban: "without them / He's but a sot, as I am." The reader of *The Tempest* must fill in gaps that have been created not only by language (what exactly do "books" signify?) but by the "aesthetic distance" between the play's historical context and the modern reader.

The problem for the New Historicist critic is to determine the "historicity" of the text, the precise relation between the elements of the play and the historical context in which it is embedded. Of particular importance for *The Tempest* is the New World, where early settlers were engaged in Indian wars, and Ireland, which had experienced a major crisis in 1607 when the indigenous aristocracy fled to the Continent (the "flight of the earls"), displaced by a huge influx of English "planters" into Ulster, Ireland's northern province. In addition to the colonial subtext is another, which would have been more readily grasped by Shakespeare's contemporaries: the problem of proper governance and the right of succession, especially with respect to the new Stuart regime. The play is framed by comic scenes of monarchical infighting between the mutinous nobility (Sebastian and Antonio) and the enlightened guardians of civil harmony (Prospero and Gonzalo). This drama of internecine struggle is mirrored by the farcical plot among Stephano, Trinculo, and Caliban to kill Prospero and take over the island (see 2.1.1–53). The comical struggles that surround Prospero reflect dissatisfaction with the absolutism of James I, who ascended the throne in 1603 and whose relations with Parliament were contentious. The important question is whether Shakespeare is defending the new king, and thus the Stuart line of succession, or if he is questioning not only his right to rule but also his policies of conquest. The inverse problem is also important: to what extent does Shakespeare's play exemplify the TEXTUALITY of history? For the New Historicist critic, interpreting *The Tempest* as a commentary on colonial expansion and monarchial absolutism amounts to opening up history itself to interpretation. Indeed, it calls into question the possibility of a singular, irrefutable historical account.

The masque in Act 4, which celebrates Ferdinand and Miranda's engagement, solidifies power within a recognizable European tradition by which marriage consolidates and legitimizes political power. From a feminist perspective, then, *The Tempest* illustrates the crisis at the heart of monarchical rule: the sexual division of labor represented by the young couple's engagement. Ferdinand will continue holding the same PATRIARCHAL power Prospero wields in a way that both mystifies and intensifies the inequalities at its basis. One could read this play as an allegory not only of sovereignty and its legitimation (in line with New Historicism and Marxist and post-Marxist approaches), but also of the passage from a feudal to a modern economy, a passage enabled by the IMPERIALIST designs of European powers that, by this time, were laying claim to the New World.

These perspectives raise the question of whether this power, entailing as it does the oppression of native peoples, constitutes a "right to rule." For postcolonial studies, the issue is not proper governance or the right to rule within a context of orderly succession. The issue is rather one of colonial dispossession and the SOCIAL CON-STRUCTION of Caliban, represented as an abject, animal-like slave, as racially OTHER with respect to Europeans. Caliban thus becomes a screen on which the conquering Europeans project their own desire. "When thou didst not, savage, / Know thine own meaning, but wouldst gabble like / A thing most brutish, I endowed thy purposes / With words that made them known" (1.2.358–61). Miranda speaks here, but she speaks for Prospero and for the West when she tells Caliban that his own "gabble" has been made "known" because she has taught him language. It is typical for the European colonizer to hear only silence from native peoples and to take them seriously only when they have accepted the language and culture of the colonizer. Miranda sums up this new political dispensation (which is really a "righting" of the old one, like the wrecked ship miraculously righted at the end) by seeing it as if it were new: "O brave new world / That has such people in 't!" (182–3). However, the civil unity that Miranda misreads has been achieved not only at her expense (she has been successfully married off), but mostly at Caliban's. In a final gesture, Ariel and Caliban are freed, but only Caliban is "claimed" by his master – "This thing of darkness I / Acknowledge mine" (5.1.275–6) – but in such a way as to suggest that Caliban's existence as an Other is essential to Prospero's identity as colonial ruler. For the modern reader, Shakespeare's play thus appears to critique the European colonial order at the very point in history when it was first gaining legitimacy by constructing an Other that requires conquest and conversion.

John Keats, "Ode on a Grecian Urn"

*Structuralism and Formalism * New Criticism * Hermeneutics * Deconstruction*

John Keats' "Ode on a Grecian Urn" is one of the most famous and most puzzling Romantic poems. It is an example of a form known as *ekphrasis*, the representation in a literary work of an artistic work in another medium. A reading of the poem following Roman Jakobson's formalist theory would note how ekphrasis determines the formal structure of *addresser* and *addressee* and how the interaction of *context* and *code* determines meaning. The opening line – "Thou still unravish'd bride of quietness" – clearly indicates an addressee, presumably the urn, and an addresser, the "I" implied by the use of "thou." The scene of ekphrastic meditation splits this formal mode of address, directing a part of its *message* to the urn and another part to the reader. The poem is further complicated by an ekphrastic structure that doubles its referential ground: on one level, the poem represents an urn, but on another level, the urn serves as a reference point for another representation (i.e., what is inscribed upon it). The speaker's question about a ground for these representations – "What leaf-fring'd legend haunts about thy shape / Of deities or mortals, or of both…?" – leads not to any definitive answer but to a litany of more questions. And it is unclear whether these questions are addressed to the reader or to the urn itself. The speaker's address to the urn in the second stanza is a rhetorical set-piece, a vividly painted scene of potential vibrancy awakened in the poet's imagination by the urn's silent history:

> Heard melodies are sweet, but those unheard
>> Are sweeter; therefore, ye soft pipes, play on;
> Not to the sensual ear, but, more endear'd,
>> Pipe to the spirit ditties of no tone:
> Fair youth, beneath the trees, thou canst not leave
>> Thy song, nor ever can those trees be bare;
>>> Bold Lover, never, never canst thou kiss,
> Though winning near the goal – yet, do not grieve;
>> She cannot fade, though thou has not thy bliss,
>> For ever wilt thou love, and she be fair!

Keats' stanza form in this ode is a ten-line structure, the first four lines rhyming *abab*, the second six alternating in one form or another, as here *cdeced* – very much like a Petrarchan sonnet. The poet calls upon the formal limitations of this sonnet-like stanza to perform the same function as the urn itself: to capture a moment of longing and desire. The stanza is shot through with negatives – "unheard," "not," "no tone," "canst not," "nor ever," "never, never canst thou," "do not," "cannot," "not thy bliss." The cumulative effect of these negations is to cancel out the picture otherwise painted of fair youths and fair girls "winning near the goal." NEGATION structures a verbal form of painting: it simulates the stasis of action in representation. The poet's selection of metaphors (i.e., substitutions for ideas) – melodies, soft pipes, ditties – is "projected," as Jacobson would say, onto the level of metonymy (i.e., the world of extension, time, contiguity), which is also the level of cancellations and prohibitions. The poetic function, then, is precisely this invocation of metaphors that must be cancelled, in order to reproduce the effect of a "painted scene." This function is, indeed, the poem's message: immortality lies in the representation of immortality.

A New Critical reading of Keats' poem might focus on rhetorical figures, especially irony, PARADOX, and AMBIVALENCE, which give the poem its powerful but tentative formal unities. It opens on a significant ambivalence: the urn is referred to as a "bride of quietness," the "foster-child of silence," but also as a "Sylvan historian." Moreover, what the historian of silence tells us is ambivalently associated with "deities or mortals, or … both." The poem hangs on this ambivalence, because it creates the rhetorical grounds for the questions that conclude the first stanza. The poem's formal structure concentrates and intensifies verbal, prosodic, and rhetorical symmetries; this is especially the case in the second and third stanzas, where negations and ecstatic repetitions symbolize the contrapuntal energies unleashed in the process of artistic creation. The tension of opposites is resolved or reconciled in the unity of an aesthetic object (an urn, a poem). The persistently unanswered questions in the fourth stanza – "Who are these coming for the sacrifice?" – remind the reader of the fundamental strangeness of this artifact: it sends a message, but the original context (and addresser) is missing. Keats' poem transforms this puzzling message into a new context, harmonizing an authentic but lost meaning with a new meaning derived by the modern poet meditating on eternity and concluding, with Blake, that "eternity is in love with the productions of time." "Beauty is truth, truth beauty," the urn offers as its final, nearly neoclassical message; it is all we need to know.

In a sense, Keats' poem is an attempt to hear what the urn has to tell him, the central concern of hermeneutic criticism, in which the artifact makes possible not only a connection with a past world (ancient Greece) but also a measure of self-understanding (the poet's desire for a certain kind of suspended desire). The message, then, is not about abstract beauty and truth; it is about a specific moment in an ancient time that the poet, in his own temporal moment, can access by virtue of a mode of interpretation that is also a mode of listening to the "soft pipes" of the past.

The harmony of this message is undermined somewhat by an image of the "Cold Pastoral," another ekphrastic doubling that splits the pastoral into a scene on the urn and the speaker's (and reader's) more distanced, "cooler" perspective meditating upon it. This short phrase reflects an aspect of the poem's ambivalence that a post-structuralist would call "undecidability." The speaker (or reader) cannot decide with authority how to interpret the phrase. The most powerful example of this undecid-ability occurs in the last lines – "'Beauty is truth, truth beauty' – that is all / Ye know on earth, and all ye need to know." This appears to be a message of startling simplic-ity and power, though it is a matter of fierce critical debate just what exactly the urn says (in part because in some editions the internal quotation marks enclose the last two lines, rather than the opening phrase of the penultimate one). This raises an important question: who or what speaks the quoted words about beauty and truth? This question signals an APORIA, a point at which contradiction expresses itself as an unsolvable puzzle, an incomprehensible script, an allegorical or coded message. The speaker reminds us that the urn's story is a fiction, a series of images, "with brede / Of marble men and maidens overwrought." Keats' ekphrastic meditation on a "painted scene" is thus a representation of a representation. On this view, a poststructuralist reading of "Ode on a Grecian Urn" is redundant, since the poem is already deconstructing itself, drawing the reader's attention to its formal contradic-tions, its mirroring, and its ekphrastic doubling.

Charlotte Brontë, *Jane Eyre*; Jean Rhys, *Wide Sargasso Sea*

Feminist Theory * *New Historicism* * *Postcolonial Studies* * *Ethnic and Indigenous Studies* * *Posthumanism*

Charlotte Brontë's *Jane Eyre* offers the reader numerous avenues for interpretation. Most prominent since its publication in 1847 have been readings that focus on the representation of women. Feminist theory, particularly that form of it that emphasizes issues of social and sexual equality, has found a rich resource, even a foundational text, in *Jane Eyre*. As a *Bildungsroman*, *Jane Eyre* records a young woman's self-formation, her struggle to harmonize her own desire with the demands placed on her by society. This struggle takes many different forms: reason versus passion, self versus society, self-fulfillment versus social duty, passive obedience versus active rebellion, self-mastery versus slavery, wife versus concubine. The polarized nature of these conflicts is symptomatic of the image we have of Jane and that she has of herself: a *divided self*, a SUBJECT torn between responsibilities to herself and to society. This self-division is reflected in her chosen occupation of governess, one of the few positions open to single women of modest means; but this role is ambiguous (she is both part of the household and an employee in it) and therefore stands for the uncertain and confusing status of women in Victorian society.

In the end, however, it is not clear if Jane ever effectively transcends or repairs her divided selfhood. Her desire for liberty – "I desired liberty; for liberty I gasped; for liberty I uttered a prayer" – is dampened and finally set aside in an unrelenting DIA-LECTIC of diminished choices. "I abandoned it and framed a humbler supplication; for change, stimulus: that petition, too, seemed swept off into vague space: 'Then,' I cried, half desperate, 'grant me at least a new servitude!'" (72). Jane's desire for a "new servitude" is to some degree a capitulation to the very PATRIARCHAL social order that restricts her life options to begin with. But it is also a sign of Jane's AGENCY, of her willful acceptance of social responsibility. Jane's powerful feelings for Rochester – "He stood between me and every thought of religion, as an eclipse inter-venes between man and the broad sun" (234) – signal her enslavement to patriarchal authority. Indeed, Jane frequently uses the language of slavery to describe her rela-tionship with Rochester. His Gothic intensity and energy "were more than beautiful to me," she notes: "they were full of an interest, an influence that quite mastered me" (149). However, it is possible to argue that Jane appropriates the language of slavery to assert her own authority and AUTONOMY. When Rochester makes an implicit com-parison between her and "'the grand Turk's whole seraglio; gazelle-eyes, houri forms and all!,'" Jane responds in mutinous terms: "'I'll be preparing myself to go out as a missionary to preach liberty to them that are enslaved – your harem inmates amongst the rest.'" She adds that Rochester will find himself "fettered amongst our hands" and forced to "sign[] a charter, the most liberal that despot ever yet conferred'" (229–30). *Jane Eyre* is an AMBIVALENT text, unable decisively to assert Jane's depend-ence or independence.

As I have suggested above, Jane's ambivalence is partly a function of her position in Rochester's household. A Marxist or New Historicist approach might focus on the socio-historical grounds for this ambivalence. In *Jane Eyre*, Brontë famously indicts institutions like Lowood School, dedicated to producing "proper" young ladies the best of whom, like Jane, go on to become governesses for the upper classes, teaching their students the same skills they themselves have learned. Jane attends a school popu-lated by orphans and unwanted children and is fortunate enough to succeed and go on to teach herself. In the opening decades of the nineteenth century, the time frame of *Jane Eyre*, there was no formal system of education available for women. After the formation of the national school system in the 1830s, there were some improvements. By the mid-1840s, when Brontë was writing, primary and some secondary education was fairly widely available. By setting her novel in the recent past, Brontë was able dramatically to point up the paucity of educational and occupational opportunities for women. Jane's relationship with her long-lost cousin, St. John Rivers, underscores another historical context in the novel. Rivers is a minister, and his Calvinism emphasizes both the social importance of religion, especially its missionary programs, and the severity of his religious authority. "'I am not a pagan,'" he tells Jane, "'but a Christian philosopher – a follower of the sect of Jesus. As His disciple I adopt His pure, His merciful, His benignant doctrines. I advocate them: I am sworn to spread them'" (320). His advocacy is very much a part of the patriarchal social order that limits Jane to subservient roles. Moreover, Rivers' insistence that she learn Hindustani in preparation to join him on a mission to India situates her within a specific historical context: the consolidation of British colonial power in India. That Jane resists the passive historical role foisted upon her is testimony not only to her strength of character, to her unwillingness to be conscripted into a colonialist enterprise, but also to Brontë's dissatisfaction with Protestant missionary activities. By depicting Jane's challenge to the limited agency offered to her by male authority figures (Rochester and Rivers), Brontë undermines the historical authority of the church and the aristocracy. Though Jane's job as a schoolmistress, which she enters into while staying with her cousin, and her subsequent marriage to Rochester limit the efficacy of her challenge, her negotiation of these positions, together with her critique of patriarchy, calls into question the univocal authority of a historical narrative that subordinates women to male power.

Edward Said has argued that novels like Jane Austen's *Mansfield Park*, when subjected to critical examination, reveal the colonialist substructure of early nineteenth-century British society. A similar critical exposé is possible with *Jane Eyre*, for Rochester's fortune is derived from plantations he controls as a result of his marriage to Bertha Mason, a West Indian Creole (i.e., a European born in the Caribbean). On this view, Brontë's novel indirectly depicts the social impact of COLONIALISM on the English upper classes, specifically the way that colonial fortunes enabled those classes to maintain their social and cultural privileges. In *Jane Eyre*, Bertha is the "mad woman in the attic," a literal prisoner but also a powerful symbol for the colonial OTHERNESS that Rochester attempts to repress by locking her up. It is clear from Rochester's account of his marriage that he has been tricked into marrying a woman of mixed race. To Jane he speaks of "'vile discoveries'" and the "'treachery of concealment'"; her nature is "'wholly alien to mine,'" he confesses, "'her tastes obnoxious to me; her cast of mind common, low, narrow, and singularly incapable of being led to anything higher, expanded to anything larger.... What a pigmy intellect she had – and what giant propensities!'" (261). Rochester's language identifies Bertha as *racially* Other; her "alien" nature and "pigmy" intellect, her sexual openness and fondness for alcohol, were at that time qualities typically associated with SUBALTERN peoples. Moreover, the contrast with Jane identifies Jane herself as a version of the emblematic "English lady," the symbol of English values, of what colonialism and Christian missionary work are meant to instill in the barbaric peoples of Africa, India, and the Caribbean. The rebellion that Jane threatens to instigate should Rochester try to entrap her in a harem-like subservience testifies to her unwillingness to be identified as a colonized Other. But her subsequent marriage to him undermines her rebellious intentions by suggesting that, in the end, Jane is complicit in a colonial social order. Once again, Jane's (and Brontë's) ambivalence challenges the MASTER NARRATIVE of historical destiny according to which Europe takes upon itself the authority to rule the subaltern races of the world.

The postcolonial critique of *Jane Eyre* is deepened and extended when read alongside Jean Rhys' *Wide Sargasso Sea*, a novel that tells the repressed story of the colonized Other, Bertha Mason (whose real name, we discover, is Antoinette). Set mostly in the Caribbean, Rhys' novel attempts not only to give substance to Bertha's character, but also to reveal the precise nature of Rochester's involvement in the plantation system in the West Indies. Rhys' intertextual critique of *Jane Eyre* dovetails with an ethnic studies approach that emphasizes problems of race and miscegenation. *Wide Sargasso Sea* avoids the kind of character assassination we see in *Jane Eyre* and tackles the problem of Antoinette's racial heritage through a more or less straightforward exposition of her background. In a powerful scene, Rochester confronts Daniel Cosway, the man he believes to be Antoinette's brother, and becomes increasingly hysterical in his dealings with his wife. He is drawn to Antoinette's sensuality, but at the same time repelled by the otherness that she represents. She is soon associated in his mind with an unfriendly native environment. Just before Antoinette tells her mother's story, Rochester thinks, "the feeling of something unknown and hostile was very strong." Then he tells her, "'I feel very much a stranger here ... I feel that this place is my enemy and on your side'" (78). He tries to efface this otherness (he renames her "Bertha"), but Antoinette is surrounded by women who remind him of it. Amelia, a young servant, represents an object of forbidden desire – the purely racial Other – on whom Rochester is able to displace his desire for the equally forbidden Antoinette. Christophine is a more troubling figure, for she is a self-reliant, independent native woman, a practitioner of *obeah*, an Afro-Caribbean form of shamanism that is used as a weapon of resistance to the colonial authority that Rochester represents. When Antoinette asks Christophine to use *obeah* to make Rochester love her, she is attempting to use native resources to overcome her husband's European prejudices. Christophine warns her against this strategy. "'So you believe in that tim-tim story about obeah, you hear when you so high? All that foolishness and folly. Too besides, that is not for *béké* [white person]. Bad, bad trouble come when *béké* meddle with that'" (67–8). As a Creole, however, Antoinette is neither Afro-Caribbean nor *béké*, so it is unclear how she ought to understand Christophine's words. Her fall into madness is a psychic response, a turning inward and away from a social world in which she is neither native nor European, but rather a "white nigger" caught in the middle of a colonial DIALECTIC. Her mother was "driven" mad in a very similar way. But this madness is not a sign of "a pigmy intellect" or of "giant propensities," as Brontë has Rochester claim in *Jane Eyre*. It is rather a response to a profound sense of ALIENATION and displacement. By the time Antoinette arrives in England, she succumbs to what Brontë herself called "moral madness" but she more closely resembles the Afro-Caribbean *zombi*, "a dead person who seems to be alive or a living person who is dead" (64). A feminist or gender critique thus reaches the very limits of what it means to be human. For a posthumanist, these novels might well be read as part of a broader critique of the *humanism* that ostensibly lies behind the civilized world of privilege that Rochester represents. We see a systematic mode of dehumanization (epitomized by Bertha in her attic cage) that is graphically reinforced by images of disfigurement and disability – even

St. John Rivers, presented with the opportunity of accompanying Jane to India as friends, uses the language of disability to refuse to offer such a "mutilated sacrifice." When Jane and Rochester are reunited, after the fire at Thornfield in which Bertha perishes, he loses a hand and becomes partially blinded. It is to this "reduced" man that Jane offers her services as a helpmate. Brontë uses disability here as a kind of narrative prosthesis that allegorizes Rochester's transition from Byronic hero to ruined man: his "mutilated limb" signifies more than disability. For Jane accepts him, not by bearing with his "infirmities" or overlooking his "deficiencies," as Rochester surmises; her acceptance is based on reading these infirmities as signs of a change in his moral character. Unlike the "lightning-struck chestnut-tree," to which Rochester compares himself, Jane sees a man who is "green and vigorous" whose strength can serve as a "prop" to those around him. This idea of disability as a moral prop (see, for example, Tiny Tim in Dickens' *A Christmas Carol*) is so common in literature as to be almost invisible; bringing disability to light *as disability* is an important facet of the posthumanist movement.

Works Cited

Brontë, Charlotte. *Jane Eyre*. Ed. Richard J. Dunn. 3rd ed. New York: Norton, 2001.
Rhys, Jean. *Wide Sargasso Sea*. New York: Norton, 1999.

Joseph Conrad, *Heart of Darkness*; Chinua Achebe, *Things Fall Apart*

*Narrative Theory * Theory of the Novel * Psychoanalysis * New Historicism
* Ethnic and Indigenous Studies * Postcolonial Studies*

Joseph Conrad's *Heart of Darkness* (1899) was written at a time when the late Victorian imperial romance was at the height of its popularity. Unlike other such tales of the era, like Rider Haggard's *She* (1887), Conrad's novella is less interested in imperial adventures than in the study of IMPERIALISM as it is manifested in character. From the point of view of narrative theory, specifically the theory of the novel, Conrad's choice constitutes a hybrid form in which the emergent "psychological novel," pioneered by Henry James, combines with the more conventional romance narrative. His story concerns Charlie Marlow, an Englishman employed by a company with a concession to hunt ivory in the Congo, a possession of King Leopold of Belgium. His job is to retrieve Kurtz, a renegade trader. Conrad complicates the propulsive, paratactic movement of the romance narrative by heightening certain elements of the narration itself, especially Marlow's meditations on barbarism, civilization, human nature, and the importance of self-knowledge.

The story opens with an unnamed narrator who describes a group of unidentified people on the deck of "the *Nellie*, a cruising yawl," listening to a story told by Marlow. The unnamed narrator has command of our attention for about eight paragraphs and in this short space establishes that Marlow's stories are not typical: "to him the meaning of an episode was not inside like a kernel but outside, enveloping the tale which brought it out only as a glow brings out a haze, in the likeness of one of these misty halos that sometimes are made visible by the spectral illumination of moonshine" (9). Having served the purpose of establishing Marlow as an unreliable narrator, the unnamed narrator all but disappears, save for a brief resurgence a page or so later to supply one more telling detail about the storyteller: "he had the pose of a Buddha preaching in European clothes and without a lotus-flower" (10). The kind of expectations set up by the romance narrative are gratified by this reference to Marlow's "Eastern" character, but his story seems to bog down in lengthy descriptions of COLONIAL administrators and his own commentary on the difference between Europeans and Africans. Several times he meditates on the nature of storytelling and insists that no one can communicate the "truth" about lived experience. In one of the rare moments when Marlow directly addresses his listeners on the *Nellie*, he tries to communicate to them (and, indirectly, to the reader) this very impossibility. "'Do you see anything? It seems to me I am trying to tell you a dream … No, it is impossible; it is impossible to convey the life-sensation of any given epoch of one's existence – that which makes its truth, its meaning – its subtle and penetrating essence'" (30). With this statement, the reader is warned not to expect the kind of revelations typically found in romance narratives. The only message conveyed by Marlow's narration is an impression of his experience, not *the truth* of it, much less the truth of anything beyond it. In this way, Marlow's story – non-linear, digressive, overtly figural – achieves a kind of *expressive form*, shaping itself to the storyteller's "hazy" sense of the truth of his own experience.

Narrative theory alerts us to other possible motifs, including journeying, questing, and wandering – all of which can add nuances to a reading focused on Marlow's impressionistic storytelling. More than one reader has been struck by the quest motif and the irony of substituting Kurtz, the renegade from reason and civilization, for the more exalted object of such narratives. The quest motif can also be regarded from the point of view of psychoanalysis. Thus Marlow embarks on a metaphorical journey into the unconscious, both his own and his culture's. According to Freud, the unconscious contains traces of ancient prehistoric human experience, precisely the quality that most persistently attracts Marlow's notice about the Congo: "'Going up river was like traveling back to the earliest beginnings of the world, when vegetation rioted on the earth and the big trees were kings'" (35). Passages like this invite us to see this journey as an exploration of the unconscious. Marlow's language – lushly modified with vaguely sinister adjectives and adverbs repeated in an incantatory style – gives us a sense of a strange, unearthly landscape: it is inscrutable, abominable, impalpable, ominous, timeless. Moreover, as Marlow himself suggests, his experience is like a dream, "'that commingling of absurdity, surprise, and bewilderment in a tremor of struggling revolt, that notion of being captured by the incredible which is of the very essence of dreams'" (30). He regards his own memories of the past "'in the shape of an unrestful and noisy dream'" (36).

If the Congo symbolizes the unconscious, the elements that make up the landscape – the river, the jungle, the native inhabitants – symbolize repressed material ("latent content") that is transformed through "dream-work" into the "manifest content." Certainly there is a sense that the jungle withholds something from Marlow, something he suspects he may have repressed: "'I saw a face amongst the leaves on the level with my own, looking at me very fierce and steady ... I made out, deep in the tangled gloom, naked breasts, arms, legs, glaring eyes'" (46). What is it that Marlow (that humanity) represses? His own OTHERNESS, perhaps, which is projected onto the African natives as *their* birthright but also as part of non-human nature. Marlow thinks he understands his glimpse into the unconscious; he sees that what he (and humanity) represses is his own "'remote kinship'" with "'this wild and passionate uproar'" (38). A psychoanalytic reading draws out the relation between the European and the native *other*, whose indigenous "belonging" is so radically different from familiar modes of sociality that Marlow can only draw back in horror at the thought of a shared humanity. Here we see not only the recognition of the *other*, but also limitations of Enlightenment humanism.

Modern editions of *Heart of Darkness* often provide just the sort of context that makes New Historicist readings possible. Conrad had himself made a journey up the Congo working as a merchant marine, and there were a number of people who had an interest in exposing King Leopold's practice of awarding concessions to adventurers. Roger Casement, an Irishman serving as British consul in Africa, investigated conditions in the Congo in the 1890s and delivered a highly critical report to the British Parliament in 1903. Conrad's novel is not simply further evidence of what Casement discovered; it is a fictional version of the same anti-colonialist discourse. Casement criticized colonialist efforts to compel natives to harvest india rubber and regarded the atrocities in the region as a direct result of these efforts. This compulsion is nowhere more graphically expressed than in Marlow's impressions of the same colonial context: "'Six black men advanced in a file, toiling up the path.... Black rags were wound round their loins.... I could see every rib, the joints of their limbs were like knots in a rope; each had an iron collar on his neck.... They passed me within six inches, without a glance, with that complete, deathlike indifference of unhappy savages'" (19). Marlow's account of atrocities in the Congo joins Casement's as part of a larger discourse on African colonialism. Certainly the story's impressionistic manner and dream-like logic lend themselves to interpretations that extend beyond the Congo. For example, the Boer War (1899–1902) was being conducted during the same period Conrad was revising his serialized version of *Heart of Darkness*. This was not a popular war, especially among Liberal politicians and the intelligentsia, so it is conceivable that Conrad's critique of European imperialism is meant to indict British interests elsewhere in Africa. There is something almost allegorical (and thus transportable) about Conrad's historical vision, a feature that is brilliantly confirmed in Francis Ford Coppola's appropriation of the narrative structure of *Heart of Darkness* for his haunting portrayal of the Vietnam War in *Apocalypse Now*.

For a postcolonial critic like Chinua Achebe, Conrad's novel is not a critique of colonialism but a symptom of it. Achebe's famous critical response to *Heart of Darkness*, "An Image of Africa" (1971), accuses Conrad of racism and of effectively silencing the African natives in his representation of the Congo. To be sure, Conrad's representations of Africans are problematic; by and large, they are rendered as SUBALTERN SUBJECTS, threatened by colonial violence and enslavement. There are very few instances in which an African speaks; one famously says, "'Mistah Kutz – he dead,'" "'in a tone of scathing contempt'" (68–9). There are no occasions on which Africans are presented as members of peaceful, organized, communicative societies. Too often, they are associated with "'a complaining clamor, modulated in savage discord'" or a "'tumult of angry and warlike yells'" (41, 47). To the Europeans in *Heart of Darkness*, the sound of drums is part of this general incomprehensible clamor produced by an insidious natural environment. Over against this silence, this wordless clamor, we have Marlow's obsession with Kurtz, his presence and authority guaranteed by the gift of his voice: "'He was very little more than a voice. And I heard – him – it – this – voice – other voices – all of them were so little more than voices'" (48). Achebe takes issue with this repression of the African voice in his essay as well as in his most famous novel, *Things Fall Apart* (1959). Though Achebe's novel is written in a recognizably realist style, it is an "appropriated" style, borrowed and modified for the purposes of COLONIAL MIMICRY. It is shot through with Ibo phrases, names, and proverbs that block any easy facility with realist conventions and at the same time communicates to the Western reader something of the materiality of Ibo culture. Narrative style is simple and direct, in contrast to the complex frame-narration of *Heart of Darkness*, and the skeptical impressionism that suffuses Conrad's story is utterly missing from Achebe's. *Things Fall Apart* is told from the perspective of a self-assured, traditional culture whose proverbs "are the palmoil with which words are eaten" (7). In contrast to the angry discord Marlow hears, Achebe's characters hear familiar and comforting sounds: the air is "message-laden" with the sound of drums, a part of "the living village": "It was like the pulsation of its heart. It throbbed in the air, in the sunshine, and even in the trees, and filled the village with excitement" (120, 44).

The traditional world articulated by these meaningful drums begins to deteriorate with the encroachment of Christian missionaries on tribal lands. Okonkwo, the protagonist, values the traditions of his own culture, but he is also a victim of one of its most serious taboos. He kills a neighbor's son accidentally and receives the ultimate punishment. "It was a crime against the earth goddess to kill a clansman, and a man who committed it must flee from the land" (124). From his position in exile with his mother's kinsmen, Okonkwo grows increasingly disturbed about the influence of the Christian missionaries and ultimately becomes involved in a violent and impetuous act of anti-colonial resistance. Upon hearing of Okonkwo's suicide, the white District Commissioner "changed instantaneously" from the "resolute administrator … to the student of primitive customs" (207). The novel ends with the Commissioner meditating on the "reasonable paragraph" that Okonkwo's story will fill in his book, "*The Pacification of the Primitive Tribes of the Lower Niger.*" These words, the echo of a white man's colonial desire, conclude Achebe's novel and reinforce what the reader already knows: the people of Umuofia will never be the same again. Achebe's message is one that **Frantz Fanon** had himself conveyed just a few years earlier: only when the West recognizes the humanity of primitive "savages" can it begin to undo the dehumanizing legacy of colonialism.

Works Cited

Achebe, Chinua. *Things Fall Apart.* New York: Anchor, 1994.
Conrad, Joseph. *Heart of Darkness.* Ed. Robert Kimbrough. 3rd ed. New York: Norton, 1988.

Virginia Woolf, *To the Lighthouse*

*Feminist Theory * Gender Studies * Psychoanalysis * Deconstruction*

Virginia Woolf's *To the Lighthouse* presents a challenge to feminism and to those who study gendered identity. Mrs. Ramsay is in many ways typical of Woolf's protagonists: middle class, married and somewhat matronly, strong willed, imaginative but not quite artistic, socially confident but AMBIVALENT in deeply ingrained and deeply hidden ways about her own needs and desires. She is beautiful and possesses an almost childlike wonder about the people in her life. "Her simplicity fathomed what clever people falsified" (29), the narrator tells us, and it is this simplicity that makes it possible for her to get at "the still space that lies about the heart of things" (105). As her young house guest, Lily Briscoe, observes, she has the artist's power to transform the world through aesthetic vision. "In the midst of chaos there was shape; this eternal passing and flowing (she looked at the clouds going and the leaves shaking) was struck into stability. Life stand still here, Mrs. Ramsay said" (161). At the same time, Mrs. Ramsay is devoted to her philosopher husband and longs for her children to marry and lead exemplary conventional lives. Her attitude towards her husband's line of work – his students are always studying "the influence of something upon somebody" (12) – reveals a gulf between his rationalist sensibility and her own intuitiveness and maternal solicitude. One can read Mrs. Ramsay as a complacent middle-class woman who has sacrificed her own creative energies in order to support her husband's career. But it is also possible to regard her without recourse to stereotypes about housewives. Her desire to bring people together for a meal or a marriage signals not complicity with PATRIARCHAL authority but an assertion of an alternative to the ALIENATING effects of the rationality that characterizes that authority. "They all sat separate. And the whole of the effort of merging and flowing and creating rested on her. Again she felt, as a fact without hostility, the sterility of men" (83). Mrs. Ramsay's power, as the artist Lily knows best, lies in her ability to create – not simply the maternal power to reproduce, but the human power to create social bonds within a community.

Woolf's concern for personal relationships – a concern that characterized the Bloomsbury group of writers gathered around Woolf and her sister – invites psychoanalytic readings of a novel so obviously indebted to the Oedipus and castration complexes. The story opens with James, the Ramsays' youngest child, at his mother's feet, both of them posing for Lily. Meanwhile, Mr. Ramsay storms about the house and yard declaiming that there will be no trip to the lighthouse, a journey James very much wants to take. The weather will be fine, his mother murmurs, but his father contradicts her, "it won't be fine" (4). The bond with the mother is looked upon jealously by the powerful father who symbolically withholds the PHALLUS/lighthouse, the means by which James can win his mother's heart but also the sign of his ascension to the SYMBOLIC order. This threat of castration should initiate the normative process of development in which the male child learns to identify with the father and to transfer his desire to a more appropriate love object. Ten years later we discover the outcome of James' development. He is sixteen now, and his mother is dead. He has clearly not resolved the Oedipal conflicts that had surfaced so long before. "He had always kept this old symbol of taking a knife and striking his father to the heart" (184). The imagery is appropriate, especially when we recall that the narrator frequently refers to Mr. Ramsay's presence as an "arid scimitar," a reference to his ability to use reason, the *sine qua non* of the Symbolic order, to dismantle reality into its constituent parts. His son appropriates this same image in order to do away with what it represents: the relentless tearing apart of the world under the illusion of understanding its secrets. That James may be moving towards resolution is suggested by his dissociation of his father – "an old man, very sad, reading his book" – from the tyrannical authority that he once wielded: "that fierce sudden black-winged harpy, with its talons and its beak all cold and hard.... That he would kill, that he would strike to the heart" (184). It is odd that he would associate this authority with a "harpy," a legendary creature with the body of a vulture and the head and breasts of a woman. Perhaps for James male authority and power are a distortion of some primal femininity that he associates with his mother, a most unharpy-like woman. This aligns with a Lacanian reading of Woman as the screen on which men project their desires and from which they receive their sense of masculine identity. The arrival at the lighthouse suggests that the tyrant has been dispatched, the mother is no longer a screen or a threat or an object of desire, and the phallus can now be handed on to James without his father fearing for his own position. "There!" his sister, Cam, thinks, as they land. "You've got it at last. For she knew that this was what James had been wanting.... His father had praised him" (206). The scene ends with Mr. Ramsay standing in the bow of the boat "as if he were saying, 'There is no God'" (207). For James, the father is no longer a god-like tyrant, and there appears to be no longer any obstacle to James identifying with him.

The reader may well wonder about Cam's own relation to her father, and to some degree we get a glimmer of it in the final paragraphs in which Lily Briscoe completes her abstract portrait of Mrs. Ramsay and James from ten years before. In a sense, Lily deconstructs the novel's Oedipal dynamic, the severing and disarticulating power of castrating reason in an artistic context that exploits a quite opposite power of knitting together, of rearticulating and unifying in an IMAGINARY register what is forestalled at the level of the Symbolic. In Mr. Ramsay's rationalist view, a line is a division and demarcation, knife-like and phallic, not at all like a dome or a triangle or a wedge (images associated with Mrs. Ramsay). It is also the "bar" that separates binomial opposites (man/woman, adult/child, inside/outside, picture/frame, reality/image). The line is decisive, but it cuts two ways, for the same line that cleaves apart and separates can also cleave things to each other. The moment James lands at the lighthouse, Lily, echoing Cam, says, "It is finished." She has finally harmonized the "nervous lines" she had laid down earlier (158). Now a single line centers and balances her vision: "With a sudden intensity, as if she saw it clear for a second, she drew a line there, in the centre. It was done; it was finished.... I have had my vision" (209). Lily's creative inspiration puts "under erasure" the other sense of the line, cancels it but leaves it legible as a constituent element of her vision. The same line that draws distinctions (e.g., between genders), that places woman "below the bar" (in the manner of **Jacques Lacan**'s algorithms in which the signified "slides under" the signifier), can also eliminate the bar by transforming it into a space for "merging and flowing and creating."

Work Cited

Woolf, Virginia. *To the Lighthouse*. New York: Harcourt Brace Jovanovich, 1989.

Zora Neale Hurston, *Their Eyes Were Watching God*

*Feminist Theory * African American Studies * Narrative Theory * Trauma Studies*

For a feminist critic, Zora Neale Hurston's *Their Eyes Were Watching God* (1937) represents a landmark achievement, for it offers the perspective of an independent-minded black woman, Janie Crawford, who tells the story of her life and loves. Though now regarded as one of the most acclaimed works of the Harlem Renaissance, the book was neglected after its first publication, only to be rediscovered and promoted over forty years later by Alice Walker. One of the things that impressed Walker was Hurston's representation of Janie and the women in her life on their own terms and in their own language. Her uncompromising depiction of a black woman's self-formation was a direct challenge to both the prejudices of white readers and the literary standards of black male writers. Just before her first marriage, Janie's grandmother, Nanny, tells the story of her escape from slavery and the violent circumstances of her granddaughter's birth: "'Dat school teacher had done hid her [Janie's mother] in de woods all night long, and he had done raped mah baby and run on off just before day'" (19). A legacy of slavery and sexual violence does not prevent Janie from exploring her own sexuality and eagerly awaiting the day when she might discover the joys of marriage. At first, she experiences a rush of delight at the thought: "She saw a dust-bearing bee sink into the sanctum of a bloom; the thousand sister-calyxes arch to meet the love embrace and the ecstatic shiver of the tree from root to tiniest branch creaming in every blossom and frothing with delight. So this was a marriage!" (11). However, after her first marriage to Logan Killicks, a local man with a bit of property, she has another revelation: "She knew now that marriage did not make love. Janie's first dream was dead, so she became a woman" (25). Her second husband, Joe Starks, is more ambitious and exciting, a vibrant force behind a new town founded by black people. But Janie soon discovers she is meant to be a silent and passive wife among men who do not understand the desires of women. To her husband and his friends she says, "'how surprised y'all is goin' tuh be if you ever find out you don't know half as much 'bout [womenfolks] as you think you do'" (75).

A feminist reading of *Their Eyes Were Watching God* inevitably dovetails with approaches that emphasize themes in African American studies, particularly passing and the idea of Signifyin(g) put forward by **Henry Louis Gates**. Hurston addresses the issue of race as inextricably bound up with gender IDENTITY, and constructs the relationship between Janie and Tea Cake, her third husband, around the same PROBLEMATIC that we find in Nella Larson's *Passing*: the identity and self-formation of light-skinned black women. Janie's friend Mrs. Turner makes note of her "coffee-and-cream complexion and her luxurious hair" but cannot "forgive her for marrying a man as dark as Tea Cake" (140). Unlike Larson's protagonist, Janie embraces blackness, primarily in the form of the carefree, exciting, and unpredictable Tea Cake. With him she seeks to affirm a particular vision of being black, one that she formed in the wake of her disappointments with Logan and Joe. She did not want to be the kind of black woman who marries for social status. When she longs for love and desire to enter her relationship with Logan, her Nanny exclaims, "'Lawd have mussy! Dat's de very prong all us black women gits hung on. Dis love! Dat's just whut's got us uh pullin' and uh haulin' and sweatin' and doin' from can't see in de mornin' till can't see at night'" (23). Janie defies her grandmother's wisdom and seeks to define love and marriage for herself. Though life with Tea Cake is rough, Janie feels a "self-crushing love" (128) for him in large measure because she can speak her mind with him. When things go badly for them it is not the result of an accident, nor a loss of love. A dog bite infects Tea Cake with rabies and during one of his "fits of gagging and choking" (177) Janie kills him in self-defense. This traumatic event has the ironic effect of liberating Janie. The scenes of her trial vividly underscore the difficulties of giving an account of one's own experience of trauma. Issues of race complicate not only her trial, but also her life in the aftermath of it. She is acquitted of murder, though some people believe that her light-skinned appearance rather than Tea Cake's condition was the cause. "'Well, you know whut dey say,'" she overhears one man say to another, "'"uh white man and uh nigger woman is de freest thing on earth." Dey do as dey please'" (189). But what these men do not realize is how strongly Janie had identified, through her intense love, with a black man. "Of course he wasn't dead," she thinks to herself. "He could never be dead until she herself had finished feeling and thinking." Janie's appeal lies in her will to overcome trauma and recover her own future: "She pulled in her horizon like a great fish-net.... So much of life in its meshes!" (193).

Janie's traumatic experience is framed in a plurivocal, dialogic context in which dialectic becomes a form of Signifyin(g), a vernacular use of English that throws into relief the self-consciously rhetorical performance of the characters. Far from representing an uneducated perspective, Hurston is able, through the Signifyin(g) tactic, to convey something of the "vernacular cosmopolitanism" that, as **Homi Bhabha** styles it, signals the vital survival of communities in their dialogic free-dom. Hurston is able to achieve her extraordinary effects through a variation of third-person perspective (or "voice"), *free indirect style*. The bulk of the novel is narrated this way, with point of view shifting from an omniscient voice to one that sounds a lot like Janie. Describing her in her Jacksonville boarding house, the narrator concludes, "But, don't care how firm your determination is, you can't keep turning round in one place like a horse grinding sugar cane. So Janie took to sitting over the room...." (118). The third-person point of view is here permeated by Janie's sensibility, though there is no trace of the dialectal forms Hurston uses when she records speech. Free indirect discourse gives the reader access to Janie's consciousness without surrendering the context of communal intimacy from which it emerges. Hurston studied anthropology under Franz Boas and possessed a sensitive and intuitive ear for folklore, especially the performances of "mule-talkers" and "big picture talkers" who used "a side of the world for a canvas" (54). Lengthy portions of *Their Eyes Were Watching God* are given over to speakers whose linguistic style signals social belonging. A notable example is Nanny's story in chapter two. A formalist approach to narrative might concentrate on *skaz*, a technique for rendering precisely the speech characteristics of an oral storyteller. In the examples quoted above, *skaz* calls our attention to the individualized teller, as opposed to the omniscient narrator. This narrative polyphony, which **M. M. Bakhtin** called HETEROGLOSSIA, reinforces the community of speakers surrounding Janie and creates a dynamic, DIALOGIC space in which her own voice can be discovered, heard, and appreciated.

Work Cited

Hurston, Zora Neale. *Their Eyes Were Watching God*. New York: HarperPerennial, 1998.

Samuel Beckett, *Endgame*

*Critical Theory * Marxist Theory * Post-Marxist Theory * Postmodernism * Posthumanism*

Samuel Beckett's *Endgame* (1958) has been praised as an unflinching commentary on the human condition in the wake of World War II and the horrors of the Holocaust. From a perspective informed by critical theory, Beckett's play critiques the UNIVERSAL values of Enlightenment humanism, which are exposed as self-serving mystifications that rationalize and instrumentalize the practices of social life. **Theodor Adorno,** who found Beckett to be one of the few "authentic" artists in the modern era, famously noted that "[t]o write poetry after Auschwitz is barbaric." However, he also praised artists like Beckett, who were able to wring poetry out of the desolation, despair, and dehumanization that is native to an instrumentalized and administered society. For critical theorists, as for post-Marxists and posthumanists, Beckett's view of the world calls into question our traditional notions of humanism and the value of human life. *Endgame* is a glimpse into a world where the dignity and majesty of humanity – its ideals, aspirations, philosophies and discoveries, its spirituality and high-mindedness – are stripped away. Dreams of a benign humanism are mercilessly pilloried by Hamm: "Use your head, can't you, use your head, you're on earth, there's no cure for that!" (53). The reduction of human existence to a disease and human aspirations to a mundane concern for the epiphenomena of material social conditions is dramatized in spare stage settings and a small random collection of objects – ladder, alarm clock, toy dog, telescope – that serve primarily to underscore the utter lack of a meaningful human social context. This new condition is symbolized by the views afforded by two windows: a "zero" world in which the earth and the sea (the "without") lack light and living inhabitants. As Clov puts it, "the earth is extinguished though I never saw it lit" (81). Despite this dismal outlook, he and Hamm manage to remain together (for "the dialogue," Hamm claims), barely maintaining the belief that "we're getting on" (14), that "something is taking its course" (11), that they might someday "mean something" (32).

The impoverished human condition Beckett dramatizes invites a Marxist reading in which the relationship between Hamm and Clov allegorizes the class struggle between capitalists and the proletariat. Hamm's mistreatment of Clov in this reading would signify the capitalist's dehumanizing domination of his workers. Their complementary deformities – Clov cannot sit, Hamm cannot stand or see – comically render the unceasing labor of the worker and the insulation from labor of the capitalist class. Hamm's insistence on being in the precise center of the room signifies both his tyrannical power and Clov's servile submission to that power. Both capitalist and worker are represented as estranged from the human values of work and reduced to mindless functionaries: "Every man his speciality" (10). This is certainly a plausible, if "vulgar," reading, which lacks the kind of nuance that would capture the ways in which Beckett's characters are entirely caught up in the dehumanized social world of which they appear to mourn the loss. We could instead read *Endgame* in terms of the post-Marxist critique of HEGEMONY, in which case the relationship between Hamm and Clov indexes not class struggle but rather the power of IDEOLOGY to achieve a non-coercive form of consensus. On this reading, Hamm's authority over Clov is ideological; it is not a function of brute force (his physical disabilities preclude it) but rather of a process whereby Hamm convinces Clov that his view of the world is the most reasonable, even natural one. As he looks out the window, Clov tells Hamm: "I warn you. I'm going to look at this filth since it's an order. But it's the last time" (78). Of course, it is not the last time, because he has already offered up his consent to a "one-dimensional world."

In some respects, a Marxist reading is foreclosed by the lack of any clear historical context. Beckett's play is precisely about this lack of context, this lack of any meaningful historical consciousness. Hamm and Clov thus allegorize the "postmodern condition," which is characterized by immobility, passivity, incompleteness, lack of desire and of affect: "Is it not time for my pain-killer?" Hamm asks (7). It is a *general* condition, as Hamm reminds Clov: "One day you'll be blind like me" (36). This thematic insistence on postmodern meaninglessness is reflected in the play's deconstruction of dramaturgy. Dialogue is desultory, repetitive, fragmented, often monosyllabic. There is no "point," no rising action, no action at all, really, aside from Clov's attempt to kill a rat (which takes place off-stage). There are no complications, no crisis, no dénouement, no decisive conclusion, no patterns of significance. *Endgame* opens with a parody of Calvary: "Finished, it's finished, nearly finished, it must be nearly finished" (1). These lines both cite the Passion of Christ, a foundational MASTER NARRATIVE of Western culture, and announce its inadequacy as a meaningful narrative legitimation of contemporary society. They signal the impossibility of finishing or, worse, the probability that things are already finished. In any case, it is the outcome of what **Jean-François Lyotard** calls *delegitimation*, the process by which master narratives lose their power to authorize social, political, and cultural discourses. All that is left are dreams – "What dreams! What forests!" (3) – and the ineffectual invocation of nature goddesses: "Flora! Pomona!" (39). The past is reduced to "yesterday" (15), "that bloody awful day, long ago, before this bloody awful day. I use the words you taught me" (43–4). Tradition is fragmented and misquoted, as with the echo of Shakespeare's *Richard III*: "My kingdom for a nightman" (23). The delegitimation of master narratives and other forms of cultural authority does not mean the end of stories, however, for it is precisely stories, paltry though they may be, that bind these characters together. Aimless, episodic anecdotes of a barely remembered life constitute a precarious bond, a social contract for a "post-human" era. "[W]e are obliged to each other," Hamm says at the conclusion of the play, caught up in an interminable endgame, whose outcome is implicit in its beginnings: "old endgame lost of old, play and lose and have done with losing" (82). In Beckett's postmodern universe, the "old endgame" is reduced to a "little turn.... right round the world! ... Hug the walls then back to the center again" (25). There are no grand strategies, no winning or losing, nothing really but "getting on."

Work Cited

Beckett, Samuel. *Endgame and Act without Words*. New York: Grove Press, 1958.

Salman Rushdie, *Midnight's Children*

*Postcolonial Studies * Postmodernism * Theory of the Novel * Ethnic and Indigenous Studies * Transnationalism*

Salman Rushdie's *Midnight's Children* (1980), one of the most influential postcolonial novels, is a sprawling narrative told by Saleem Sinai. It begins with his grandfather in 1915, in the princely state of Kashmir, and proceeds through the major events of Indian history, beginning with the Amritsar massacre of 1919 then moving to Bombay and the creation of the Indian state (and the simultaneous partitioning of Pakistan), the Indo-Pakistan war, and the creation of Bangladesh out of East Pakistan. From a postcolonial studies point of view, Rushdie's treatment of these historical events constitutes a revisionist critique of COLONIALIST and nationalist visions of India. He embraces the idea that "there are as many versions of India as Indians" (323). One version is offered up by Dr. Narlikar, who invents a concrete tetrapod to be used in land reclamation. (Bombay was erected on land reclaimed from the sea.) These lingam-like structures prompt him to meditate on the "old dark priapic forces of ancient, procreative India" (209). Dr. Narlikar is able to sustain in his imagination, simultaneously, a precolonial conception of India and a vision of a project that will help usher India into modernity. The category of the transnational can help us understand the nature of this entry into modernity, for we see not only a transition from an imperial territory to an independent state, but also at the same time the fracturing of that new state along largely secular lines. The new Indian state is *traversed* by new national borders, and the new nation-states that emerge, India and Pakistan, take their place in a new globalized geopolitical environment in which they play multiple roles (regionally and internationally). Rushdie's novel, by focusing on the interplay between the globalizing forces of decolonization and neo-imperialism and the localizing forces of culture and tradition, underscores the complexity of transnational identities and histories.

In creating his postcolonial fable, Rushdie draws on a wide range of native cultural forms – including Vedic texts, Bollywood films, the *Arabian Nights*, pop songs and magic shows, advertisements for wise men like Lord Khusro Khusrovani, and on and on – and on Western narratives, including the multigenerational saga form favored by novelists, including D. H. Lawrence and John Forsythe, and the *Bildungsroman*. In Rushdie's version, the narrative dynamics of the European *Bildungsroman* – a representation of the bourgeois SUBJECT's harmonious self-formation – undergo a convulsive reorganization. Rather than occupy its own AUTONOMOUS narrative space, Saleem's *Bildung* unfolds within a dense historical and familial context. He is "buffeted by too much history" (37). Saleem is born at midnight, August 15, 1947, the very moment of India's independence. His ability to connect telepathically, via his hypersensitive nose, with the hundreds of other children born at midnight, all of whom also possess magical gifts, links his development to that of the new Indian nation. The "children of midnight were also the children *of the time*," writes Saleem. "[F]athered, you understand, by history" (137). His narrative is a "long-winded autobiography" (548).

Rushdie's postmodernist critique of history takes the form of anonymous letters fashioned from newspaper cut-outs, which Saleem uses to gratify his desire for love and vengeance: "Cutting up history to fit my nefarious purpose" (311). This instance of *citation* is joined by many others in which Saleem creates a network of INTERTEXTUAL references, or nodal points, which offer the reader alternative modes of constructing the narrative logic of the text. A good example is Aadam Aziz, Saleem's grandfather, who signals an intertextual relation with E. M. Forster's *Passage to India*. Forster's protagonist, Aziz, is not only a doctor but a Muslim, and shares many of Aadam's attitudes. For example, Aadam IDEALIZES the "Kashmiri girl" (33), echoing Forster's Aziz who waxes eloquent on the independence of Indian women. This and other intertextual connections to colonialist literature suggest to the reader a buried history of colonial and postcolonial India. Intertextuality also contributes to the METAFICTIONAL quality of Rushdie's text. Through ludic strategies of digression, repetition, summary, and prolepsis, the narrator draws the reader's attention to the artifice of narrative, "laying bare" the devices by which the text is created as a work of art. Saleem himself refers to his "miracle-laden omniscience" (177), a phrase that captures well the quality of Rushdie's *magic realism*. In this regard, *Midnight's Children* resembles Gabriel García Márquez's *One Hundred Years of Solitude*, another novel with a strong postmodern orientation towards magical, anti-realistic representation. Some postcolonial critics condemn Rushdie's use of postmodernist techniques of representation, claiming they are signs of a commitment to European intellectual values. Others would claim that these same techniques make possible a strategy of "writing for resistance" that we find in many postcolonial texts. Saleem himself provides a wonderful conceit, in the Snakes and Ladders game, for a narrative PERFORMANCE that negotiates between magic realism and historical mimesis. "[I]mplicit in the game is the unchanging twoness of things, the duality of up against down, good against evil; the solid rationality of ladders balances the occult sinuosities of the serpent" (167). Snakes and Ladders vividly models the HYBRID nature of postcolonial life and offers a profoundly *anti*-narrative model for representing human experience: the interminable up-and-down of a MANICHAEAN dualism and the "sinuous" path of resistance to dualities of all kinds. In this case, Rushdie's postcolonial HISTORICISM – his "chutnification of history" – complements a postmodern critique of history, for both are combating the influence of deterministic MASTER NARRATIVES.

Colonial and postcolonial SUBJECTS come of age in an environment in which identity is fractured along national, religious, and ethnic lines. Saleem is born on the hour of independence and lives to see his family claim Pakistan as its home. Can ethnic identities survive the breakdown of traditional geographical, linguistic, and cultural boundaries? Can they survive the militancy of "language marchers" who use language as a litmus test for national autonomy? There is also the question of Saleem's patrimony. A disgruntled family retainer had switched Amina Sinai's baby for another (Shiva, named for the Hindu deity who is both destroyer and transformer). Saleem, it turns out, is the son of a low-caste Hindu woman and an Englishman. Due to the "accidents" of history, Saleem embodies the multiplicity of India, with its "infinity of alternative realities" (389). Negotiating a plurality of identities, some illusory, complicates self-formation, but it also suggests new modes of collectivity. One of the consequences of his *Bildung*-plot, entangled as it is with the history of the nation, is that his own racial and ethnic identity is HYBRIDIZED. Saleem's hybrid condition is dramatized by his ability to be a "receptor" for all of midnight's children: "I decided to form … a gang which was spread over the length and breadth of the country, and whose headquarters were behind my eyebrows" (247). These children are the outcasts of history; they represent the historical realities of migrancy and DIASPORA, the geopolitical consequences of colonialism and decolonization. They are also to some extent an adumbration of the posthumanist condition, which is marked here by the extraordinary receptivity to new modes of community. Rushdie conveys this condition as both redemptive and destructive (in the figures of Saleem and Shiva), which points to a complex interplay between nation-states and a global realm that Michael Hardt and **Antonio Negri** call Empire. We see, then, in Rushdie's novel, the passage of sovereignty from the traditional nation-state to the new global empire, which continues to dominate the world, even though imperialism has been left behind. Like other postcolonial novelists, Rushdie reminds us of the "contingent universality" of the postcolonial condition.

Work Cited

Rushdie, Salman. *Midnight's Children*. New York: Penguin, 1991.

Recommendations for Further Reading

African American Studies

Baker, Houston. *Afro-American Poetics: Revisions of Harlem and the Black Aesthetic*. Madison: University of Wisconsin Press, 1988.

Bobo, Jacqueline, ed. *Black Feminist Cultural Criticism*. Oxford: Blackwell, 2001.

Ervin, Hazel Arnett, ed. *African American Literary Criticism, 1773 to 2000*. New York: Twayne, 1999.

Gates, Henry Louis, ed. *"Race," Writing, and Difference*. Chicago: University of Chicago Press, 1986.

Spillers, Hortense J. *Black, White, and In Color: Essays on American Literature and Culture*. Chicago and London: University of Chicago Press, 2003.

Chicago School Neo-Aristotelian Theory

Booth, Wayne. *The Essential Wayne Booth*. Ed. Walter Jost. Chicago: University of Chicago Press, 2006.

Crane, R. S., ed. *Critics and Criticism: Ancient and Modern*. Chicago: University of Chicago Press, 1952.

Olson, Elder, ed. *Aristotle's Poetics and English Literature: A Collection of Critical Essays*. Chicago: University of Chicago Press, 1965.

Phelan, James and Peter J. Rabinowitz. *Understanding Narrative*. Ed. James Phelan and Peter J. Rabinowitz. Columbus: Ohio State University Press, 1994.

The Literary Theory Handbook, First Edition. Gregory Castle.
© 2013 John Wiley & Sons, Ltd. Published 2013 by John Wiley & Sons, Ltd.

Critical Theory

Arato, Andrew and Eike Gebhardt, eds. *The Essential Frankfurt School Reader*. 2nd ed. New York: Continuum, 1993.

Benhabib, Seyla and Drucilla Cornell, eds. *Feminism as Critique: Essays on the Politics of Gender in Late-Capitalist Societies*. Cambridge: Polity, 1987.

Bernstein, Jay, ed. *The Frankfurt School: Critical Assessments*. 6 vols. London and New York: Routledge, 1994.

Habermas, Jürgen. *The Philosophical Discourse of Modernity: Twelve Lectures*. Trans. Frederick Lawrence. Cambridge, MA: MIT Press, 1987.

Kellner, Douglas. *Critical Theory, Marxism and Modernity*. Baltimore: Johns Hopkins University Press, 1989.

Tallack, Douglas, ed. *Critical Theory: A Reader*. New York: Harvester Wheatsheaf, 1995.

Cultural Studies

Bennett, Tony, Graham Martin, Colin Mercer, and Janet Woollacott, eds. *Culture, Ideology and Social Process: A Reader*. London: Batsford, 1981.

Bérubé, Michael, ed. *The Aesthetics of Cultural Studies*. Oxford: Blackwell, 2005.

Brantlinger, Patrick. *Crusoe's Footprints: Cultural Studies in Britain and America*. New York: Routledge, 1990.

Grossberg, Lawrence, Cary Nelson, and Paula A. Treichler, eds. *Cultural Studies*. New York and London: Routledge, 1992.

Ryan, Michael, ed. *Cultural Studies: An Anthology*. Oxford: Blackwell, 2008.

Warren, Catherine A. and Mary Douglas, eds. *American Cultural Studies*. Urbana: University of Illinois Press, 2002.

Williams, Raymond. *New Keywords: A Revised Vocabulary of Culture and Society*. Ed. Tony Bennett, Lawrence Grossberg, and Meaghan Morris. Oxford: Blackwell, 2005.

Deconstruction

Cohen, Tom, ed. *Jacques Derrida and the Humanities: A Critical Reader*. Cambridge: Cambridge University Press, 2001.

Culler, Jonathan. *On Deconstruction: Theory and Criticism After Structuralism*. Ithaca: Cornell University Press, 1982.

Holland, Nancy J., ed. *Feminist Interpretations of Jacques Derrida*. University Park, PA: Pennsylvania State University Press, 1997.

Norris, Christopher. *Deconstruction: Theory and Practice*. 3rd ed. London and New York: Routledge, 2002.

Wood, David, ed. *Derrida: A Critical Reader*. Oxford and Cambridge, MA: Blackwell, 1992.

Ethnic and Indigenous Studies

Anderson, Wanni W. and Robert G. Lee, eds. *Displacements and Diasporas: Asians in the Americas*. New Brunswick, NJ: Rutgers University Press, 2005.

Flores, Juan and Renato Rosaldo, eds. *A Companion to Latina/o Studies*. Oxford: Wiley-Blackwell, 2007.

Goldberg, David Theo and John Solomos, eds. *A Companion to Racial and Ethnic Studies*. Oxford: Blackwell, 2002.

Moraga, Cherríe and Gloria Anzaldúa, eds. *This Bridge Called My Back: Writings by Radical Women of Color*. 2nd ed. New York: Kitchen Table, Women of Color Press, 1983.

Sadowski-Smith, Claudia, ed. *Globalization on the Line: Culture, Capital, and Citizenship at US Borders*. New York: Palgrave, 2002.

Susser, Ida and Thomas C. Patterson, eds. *Cultural Diversity in the United States: A Critical Reader*. Oxford: Blackwell, 2001.

Vizenor, Gerald, ed. *Narrative Chance: Postmodern Discourse on Native American Indian Literatures*. Albuquerque: University of New Mexico Press, 1989.

Wu, Jean Yu-wen Shen and Thomas C. Chen, eds. *Asian American Studies Now: A Critical Reader*. New Brunswick, NJ: Rutgers University Press, 2010.

Feminist Theory

Butler, Judith and Joan W. Scott, eds. *Feminists Theorize the Political*. New York: Routledge, 1992.

Collins, Patricia Hill. *Black Feminist Thought: Knowledge, Consciousness, and the Politics of Empowerment*. 2nd ed. New York and London: Routledge, 2000.

Cudd, Ann E. and Robin O. Andreasen, eds. *Feminist Theory: A Philosophical Anthology*. Oxford: Blackwell, 2005.

Ferguson, Margaret and Jennifer Wicke, eds. *Feminism and Postmodernism*. Durham, NC: Duke University Press, 1994.

Moi, Toril. *Sexual/Textual Politics: Feminist Literary Theory*. 2nd ed. London and New York: Routledge, 2002.

Orr, Catherine M., Anne Braithwaite, and Diane Lichtenstein, eds. *Rethinking Women's and Gender Studies*. New York: Routledge, 2012.

Formalism and Structuralism

Culler, Jonathan. *Structuralist Poetics: Structuralism, Linguistics and the Study of Literature*. Ithaca: Cornell University Press, 1976.

Dosse, François. *History of Structuralism*. 2 vols. Trans. Deborah Glassman. Minneapolis: University of Minnesota Press, 1997.

Hawkes, Terence. *Structuralism and Semiotics*. Berkeley: University of California Press, 1977.

Jameson, Fredric. *The Prison-House of Language: A Critical Account of Structuralism and Russian Formalism*. Princeton: Princeton University Press, 1972.

O'Toole, L. M. and Ann Shukman, eds. *Russian Poetics in Translation*. Vol. 4: *Formalist Theory*. Trans. L. M. O'Toole and Ann Shukman. Oxford: Holdan Books, 1977.

Scholes, Robert. *Structuralism in Literature: An Introduction*. New Haven: Yale University Press, 1974.

Gender Studies

Adams, Rachel and David Savran, eds. *The Masculinity Studies Reader*. Oxford: Blackwell, 2002.

Doan, Laura, ed. *The Lesbian Postmodern*. New York: Columbia University Press, 1994.
Essed, Philomena, David Theo Goldberg, and Audrey Kobayashi, eds. *A Companion to Gender Studies*. Malden, MA and Oxford: Blackwell, 2005.
Goldberg, Jonathan, ed. *Queering the Renaissance*. Durham, NC: Duke University Press, 1994.
Turner, William B. *A Genealogy of Queer Theory*. Philadelphia: Temple University Press, 2000.
Williams, Christine L. and Arlene Stein, eds. *Sexuality and Gender*. Oxford: Blackwell, 2002.

Marxist and Post-Marxist Theory

Eagleton, Terry and Drew Milne, eds. *Marxist Literary Theory: A Reader*. Oxford and Cambridge, MA: Blackwell, 1996.
Goldstein, Phillip. *Post-Marxist Theory: An Introduction*. Albany: SUNY Press, 2005.
Harvey, David. *A Companion to Marx's Capital*. London and New York: Verso, 2010.
Mandel, Ernest. *Late Capitalism*. Trans. Joris De Bres. London: Verso, 1978.
Nelson, Cary and Lawrence Grossberg, eds. *Marxism and the Interpretation of Culture*. Urbana: University of Illinois Press, 1988.
Sim, Stuart. *Post-Marxism: An Intellectual History*. New York and London: Routledge, 2000.
Solomon, Maynard, ed. *Marxism and Art*. New York: Knopf, 1973.
Williams, Raymond. *Marxism and Literature*. Oxford: Oxford University Press, 1977.

Narrative Theory/Narratology

Abbott, H. Porter. *The Cambridge Introduction to Narrative*. 2nd ed. Cambridge: Cambridge University Press, 2008.
Fludernik, Monika. *An Introduction to Narratology*. Oxford and New York: Routledge, 2009.
Mitchell, W. J. T., ed. *On Narrative*. Chicago: University of Chicago Press, 1981.
Phelan, James and Peter Rabinowitz, eds. *A Companion to Narrative Theory*. Oxford: Blackwell, 2005.
Prince, Gerald. *A Dictionary of Narratology*. Lincoln: University of Nebraska Press, 2003.

New Criticism

Burke, Kenneth. *Counter-Statement*. 2nd ed. Los Altos, CA: Hermes Publications, 1953.
Jancovich, Mark. *The Cultural Politics of the New Criticism*. Cambridge: Cambridge University Press, 1993.
Ransom, John Crow. *The New Criticism*. Norfolk, CT: New Directions, 1941.
Spurlin, William J. and Michael Fisher, eds. *The New Criticism and Contemporary Literary Theory: Connections and Continuities*. New York and London: Garland Publishing, 1995.
Wellek, Rene and Austin Warren. *Theory of Literature*. London: Cape, 1949.

New Historicism/Cultural Poetics

Brannigan, John. *New Historicism and Cultural Materialism*. New York: St. Martin's Press, 1998.

Fox-Genovese, Elizabeth and Elisabeth Lasch-Quinn, eds. *Reconstructing History: The Emergence of a New Historical Society*. New York and London: Routledge, 1999.

Gallagher, Catherine and Stephen Greenblatt. *Practicing New Historicism*. Chicago: University of Chicago Press, 2000.

Ryan, Kiernan, ed. *New Historicism and Cultural Materialism: A Reader*. London and New York: Arnold, 1996.

Veeser, H. Aram, ed. *The New Historicism Reader*. New York: Routledge, 1994.

Phenomenology and Hermeneutics

Dreyfus, Hubert L. and Mark A. Wrathall, eds. *A Companion to Phenomenology and Existentialism*. Oxford: Wiley-Blackwell, 2006.

Glendinning, Simon. *In the Name of Phenomenology*. London and New York: Routledge, 2008.

Holub, Robert. "Phenomenology." In *The Cambridge History of Literary Criticism*. Vol. 8: *From Formalism to Poststructuralism*. Ed. Raman Selden. Cambridge and New York: Cambridge University Press, 1995. 289–318.

Husserl, Edmund. "Phenomenology." In *Psychological and Transcendental Phenomenology and the Confrontation with Heidegger (1927–1931)*. Ed. and trans. Thomas Sheehan and Richard E. Palmer. Dordrecht, Netherlands: Kluwer Academic Publishers, 1997. 80–198.

Ricoeur, Paul. *Hermeneutics and the Human Sciences: Essays on Language, Action and Interpretation*. Ed. and trans. John B. Thompson. Cambridge and New York: Cambridge University Press, 1981.

Postcolonial Studies

Ashcroft, W. D., Gareth Griffiths, and Helen Tiffin. *The Postcolonial Studies Reader*. 2nd ed. London and New York: Routledge, 2006.

Castle, Gregory, ed. *Postcolonial Discourses: An Anthology*. Oxford: Blackwell, 2001.

Guha, Ranajit and Gayatri Spivak, eds. *Selected Subaltern Studies*. Delhi and New York: Oxford University Press, 1988.

Lazarus, Neil, ed. *The Cambridge Companion to Postcolonial Literary Studies*. Cambridge: Cambridge University Press, 2004.

Loomba, Ania. *Colonialism/Postcolonialism*. 2nd ed. London: Routledge, 2002.

Quayson, Ato, ed. *The Cambridge History of Postcolonial Literature*. 2 vols. Cambridge: Cambridge University Press, 2012.

Williams, Patrick and Laura Chrisman, eds. *Colonial Discourse and Post-Colonial Theory: A Reader*. New York: Columbia University Press, 1994.

Young, Robert J. C. *Postcolonialism: An Historical Introduction*. Oxford: Blackwell, 2001.

Posthumanism

Adamson, Joni, Mei Mei Evans, and Rachel Stein, eds. *The Environmental Justice Reader: Politics, Poetics and Pedagogy*. Tucson: University of Arizona Press, 2002.

Badmington, Neil, ed. *Posthumanism*. New York: Palgrave, 2000.

Boyd, Brian, Joseph Carroll, and Jonathan Gottschall, eds. *Evolution, Literature, and Film: A Reader*. New York: Columbia University Press, 2010.

Brown, Bill, ed. *Things*. Chicago: University of Chicago Press, 2004.

Davis, Lennard, ed. *The Disability Studies Reader*. New York: Routledge, 2010.

Garland-Thomson, Rosemarie, ed. *Re-Presenting Disability: Activism and Agency in the Museum*. London and New York: Routledge, 2010.

Garrard, Greg. *Ecocriticism*. 2nd ed. London and New York: Routledge, 2011.

Glotfelty, Cheryll and Harold Fromm, eds. *The Ecocriticism Reader: Landmarks in Literary Ecology*. Athens: University of Georgia Press, 1996.

Gottschall, Jonathan and David Sloan Wilson, eds. *The Literary Animal: Evolution and the Nature of Narrative*. Evanston, IL: Northwestern University Press, 2005.

Richardson, Alan and Ellen Spolsky, eds. *The Work of Fiction: Cognition, Culture, and Complexity*. Aldershot and Burlington, VT: Ashgate, 2004.

Zunshine, Lisa, ed. *Introduction to Cognitive Cultural Studies*. Baltimore: Johns Hopkins University Press, 2010.

Postmodernism

Connor, Steve. *Postmodernist Culture: An Introduction to Theories of the Contemporary*. 2nd ed. Oxford: Blackwell, 1997.

Docherty, Thomas, ed. *Postmodernism: A Reader*. New York. Harvester Wheatsheaf, 1993.

Hassan, Ihab. *The Dismemberment of Orpheus: Toward a Postmodern Literature*. 2nd ed. Madison: University of Wisconsin Press, 1982.

Kaplan, Ann, ed. *Postmodernism and Its Discontents: Theories, Practices*. London and New York: Verso, 1988.

Lucy, Niall. *Postmodern Literary Theory: An Introduction*. Oxford: Blackwell, 1997.

Malpas, Simon. *The Postmodern*. London and New York: Routledge, 2005.

Natoli, Joseph and Linda Hutcheon, eds. *A Postmodern Reader*. Albany: SUNY Press, 1993.

Poststructuralism

Belsey, Catherine. *Poststructuralism: A Very Short Introduction*. Oxford: Oxford University Press, 2002.

Harari, Josué, ed. *Textual Strategies: Perspectives in Post-Structuralist Criticism*. Ithaca: Cornell University Press, 1979.

Lotringer, Sylvère and Sande Cohen. *French Theory in America*. New York and London: Routledge, 2001.

Macksey, Richard and Eugenio Donato, eds. *The Structuralist Controversy: The Languages of Criticism and the Sciences of Man*. Baltimore: Johns Hopkins University Press, 1972.

Sarup, Madan. *Poststructuralism and Postmodernism*. 2nd ed. Athens: University of Georgia Press, 1993.

Psychoanalysis

Bowie, Malcolm. *Psychoanalysis and the Future of Theory*. Oxford and Cambridge, MA: Blackwell, 1994.

Evans, Dylan. *An Introductory Dictionary of Lacanian Psychoanalysis*. London and New York: Routledge, 1996.

Felman, Shoshana. *Literature and Psychoanalysis: The Question of Reading: Otherwise*. Baltimore and London: Johns Hopkins University Press, 1982.

Greenberg, Jay R. and Stephen A. Mitchell. *Object Relations in Psychoanalytic Theory*. Cambridge, MA: Harvard University Press, 1983.

Khanna, Ranjana. *Dark Continents: Psychoanalysis and Colonialism*. Durham, NC and London: Duke University Press, 2003.

Mitchell, Juliet. *Psychoanalysis and Feminism*. New York: Vintage Books, 1975.

Rabaté, Jean-Michel. *The Cambridge Companion to Lacan*. Cambridge: Cambridge University Press, 2003.

Sarup, Madan. *Jacques Lacan*. New York and London: Harvester Wheatsheaf, 1992.

Vice, Sue, ed. *Psychoanalytic Criticism: A Reader*. Cambridge: Polity, 1996.

Reader-Response Theory

Jauss, Hans Robert. *Toward An Aesthetic of Reception*. Trans. Timothy Bahti. Minneapolis: University of Minnesota Press, 1982.

Machor, James L. and Philip Goldstein, eds. *Reception Study: From Literary Theory to Cultural Studies*. New York: Routledge, 2001.

Tompkins, Jane, ed. *Reader-Response Criticism: From Formalism to Post-Structuralism*. Baltimore: Johns Hopkins University Press, 1980.

Theory of the Novel

Casanova, Pascale. *The World Republic of Letters*. Trans. M. B. DeBevoise. Cambridge, MA: Harvard University Press, 2004.

De Groot, Jerome. *The Historical Novel*. London and New York: Routledge, 2010.

McKeon, Michael, ed. *Theory of the Novel: A Historical Approach*. Baltimore: Johns Hopkins University Press, 2000.

Moretti, Franco. *The Novel*. 2 vols. Princeton: Princeton University Press, 2006.

Parker, David. *Ethics, Theory and the Novel*. Cambridge and New York: Cambridge University Press, 1994.

Scholes, Robert. *Fabulation and Metafiction*. Urbana: University of Illinois Press, 1979.

Watt, Ian. *The Rise of the Novel*. Berkeley: University of California Press, 1957.

Transnationalism

Cheah, Pheng and Bruce Robbins, eds. *Cosmopolitics: Thinking and Feeling Beyond the Nation*. Minneapolis: University of Minnesota Press, 1998.

Held, David and Anthony G. McGrew, eds. *Globalization Theory: Approaches and Controversies*. Cambridge: Polity, 2007.

Krishna, Sankaran, ed. *Globalization and Postcolonialism: Hegemony and Resistance in the Twenty-First Century*. Lanham: Rowman and Littlefield, 2009.

Levitt, Peggy, ed. *The Transnational Studies Reader: Intersections and Innovations*. New York and London: Routledge, 2008.

Mandaville, Peter and Terrence Lyons, eds. *Politics from Afar: Transnational Diasporas and Networks*. New York: Columbia University Press, 2012.

Palumbo-Liu, David, Bruce Robbins, and Nirvana Tanoukhi, eds. *Immanuel Wallerstein and the Problem of the World: System, Scale, Culture*. Durham, NC: Duke University Press, 2011.

Trauma Theory

Caruth, Cathy, ed. *Trauma: Explorations in Memory*. Baltimore and London: Johns Hopkins University Press, 1995.

Felman, Shoshana and Dori Laub. *Testimony: Crisis of Witnessing in Literature, Psychoanalysis, and History*. New York: Routledge, 1992.

Hirsch, Marianne and Irene Kacandes, eds. *Teaching the Representation of the Holocaust*. New York: MLA, 2004.

Miller, Nancy K. and Jason Tougaw, eds. *Extremities: Trauma, Testimony, and Community*. Urbana: University of Illinois Press, 2002.

Ringel, Shoshana and Jerrold R. Brandell, eds. *Trauma: Contemporary Directions in Theory, Practice, and Research*. Thousand Oaks, CA: Sage, 2012.

Encyclopedias, Histories, and Introductions

Baldic, Chris. *Criticism and Literary Theory 1890 to the Present*. London and New York: Longman, 1996.

The Cambridge History of Literary Criticism. 9 vols. Cambridge and New York: Cambridge University Press, 1989–2001.

Cassedy, Steven. *Flight from Eden: The Origins of Modern Literary Criticism and Theory*. Berkeley: University of California Press, 1990.

Eagleton, Terry. *Literary Theory: An Introduction*. 2nd ed. Minneapolis: University of Minnesota Press, 1983, 1996.

Graff, Gerald. *Professing Literature: An Institutional History*. Chicago: University of Chicago Press, 1987.

Greenblatt, Stephen and Giles Gunn, eds. *Redrawing the Boundaries: The Transformation of English and American Literary Studies*. New York: MLA, 1992.

Greene, Roland et al., eds. *The Princeton Encyclopedia of Poetry and Poetics*. 4th ed. Princeton: Princeton University Press, 2012.

Groden, Michael, Martin Kreiswirth, and Imre Szeman, eds. *The Johns Hopkins Guide to Literary Theory and Criticism*. 2nd ed. Baltimore: Johns Hopkins University Press, 2005.

Kaplan, Charles and William Davis Anderson, eds. *Criticism: Major Statements*. 4th ed. Boston: Bedford/St. Martin's Press, 2000.

Kritzman, Lawrence D., ed. *The Columbia History of Twentieth-Century French Thought*. New York: Columbia University Press, 2006.

Leitch, Vincent et al., eds. *The Norton Anthology of Theory and Criticism*. New York: Norton, 2001.

Lentricchia, Frank and Thomas McLaughlin, eds. *Critical Terms for Literary Study*. Chicago: University of Chicago Press, 1995.

Macksey, Richard and Eugenio Donato, eds. *The Structuralist Controversy: The Languages of Criticism and the Sciences of Man*. Baltimore: Johns Hopkins University Press, 1972.

Murray, Chris, ed. *Encyclopedia of Literary Critics and Criticism*. 2 vols. London: Fitzroy Dearborn, 1999.

Newton, K. M., ed. *Theory Into Practice: A Reader in Modern Literary Criticism*. Basingstoke: Macmillan, 1992.

Richter, David H., ed. *Falling Into Theory: Conflicting Views on Reading Literature*. 2nd ed. Boston: Bedford/St. Martin's Press, 2000.

Rivkin, Julie and Michael Ryan, eds. *Literary Theory: An Anthology*. 2nd ed. Oxford: Wiley-Blackwell, 2004.

Ryan, Michael, Gregory Castle, Robert Eaglestone, and M. Keith Booker, eds. *The Encyclopedia of Literary and Cultural Theory*. 3 vols. Oxford: Wiley-Blackwell, 2011.

Schreibman, Susan, Raymond George Siemens, and John Unsworth, eds. *A Companion to Digital Humanities*. Oxford: Blackwell, 2004.

Stanford Encyclopedia of Philosophy. Ed. Edward N. Zalta. http://plato.stanford.edu/

Wellek, René. *A History of Modern Criticism*. 8 vols. New Haven: Yale University Press, 1955–92.

Williams, Raymond. *Keywords: A Vocabulary of Culture and Society*. Rev. ed. New York: Oxford University Press, 1983.

Wimsatt, William K. and Cleanth Brooks. *Literary Criticism: A Short History*. 2 vols. Chicago: University of Chicago Press, 1957, 1978.

Glossary

Note. Terms that designate a movement or major trend covered in chapter two, "The Scope of Literary Theory" (e.g., poststructuralism, deconstruction, psychoanalysis, and so on) are not included in this glossary. Terms in small caps within the definitions below have their own entries. As elsewhere in this *Guide*, boldface indicates that additional discussions of the theorist in question can be found in chapter three, "Key Figures in Literary Theory." The index will direct readers to further discussion of these terms as well as to those terms of a highly specialized nature (e.g., those found in psychoanalytic theory).

AESTHETIC THEORY, AESTHETICS.   Generally, these terms refer to theories of artistic value, production, and judgment. Theories of aesthetics began with Aristotle's *Poetics*, and most philosophers to follow him have written on the subject. The Enlightenment aesthetics of writers like Edmund Burke and Immanuel Kant identify *beauty* and the *sublime* as the two chief aesthetic responses. A Kantian tradition in aesthetics predominated in the nineteenth and twentieth centuries. In recent years, postmodernists like **Jean-François Lyotard** have championed an aesthetics that locates the sublime experience in "perpetual negation," the unrepresentable difference of language and pure *figurality*.

AESTHETICISM.   Typically used to designate a movement, associated with Charles Baudelaire, Théophile Gautier, and Oscar Wilde, *aestheticism* celebrates "art for art's sake." It privileges beauty above all things and insists on the AUTONOMY of art. Within the *aesthete* movement there coexisted a trend towards *décadence*, which regards the perverse and the decayed, the malformed and merely natural, as themselves objects of beauty. Both *aestheticism* and *décadence* are retreats from realism and naturalism and from the sentimental moralizing attendant upon both. See AESTHETIC THEORY.

The Literary Theory Handbook, First Edition. Gregory Castle.
© 2013 John Wiley & Sons, Ltd. Published 2013 by John Wiley & Sons, Ltd.

AGENCY.   This term typically refers to the actions of a subject free of social domination and of forms of consensus that narrow choices and effectively weaken or limit action. To have *agency* is to have social power; to lack it is to be ignored or subjugated by others who possess it. An *agent* is the subject of action, one who performs the action, and in whom *agency* is the absolute freedom to act. *Agency* can be manifested in a number of ways, but is most often confronted as a problem in theories of the subject and of gender. See PERFORMANCE.

ALIENATION.   A multifaceted term, with wide currency in literary and cultural theory. The general concept stems from the Marxist notion that workers cannot enjoy the fruits of their labor and are thus alienated from the objective world they help to create. In many cases, this term is used with a psychological emphasis and denotes experiences of anomie, disconnection, and isolation.

ALTERITY. See OTHER.

AMBIVALENCE.   This term derives from psychoanalysis and refers to the unstable nature of IDENTITY when the norms governing sexual choice do not function predictably. In general, it refers to the failure of language or DISCOURSE to settle on a single definitive meaning. Rhetorically, *ambivalence* resembles *irony*, which marks a gap between a thing said and a thing done or between intention and effect. Cf. TOTALITY and UNIVERSALITY.

APORIA.   From the Greek, *a-byssos*, without depth or bottom. Typically, this term refers to textual instances of contradiction or of uncertainty about meaning; it also refers to an unsolvable puzzle, a gap or ellipsis. Many poststructuralists hold that language itself, by virtue of its quality of DIFFERENCE, is *aporetic*.

ARCHAEOLOGY.   Associated with **Michel Foucault**, *archaeology* is a mode of analysis in which discourse is described as a function of an archive (or DISCOURSE FORMATION). It entails an array of protocols for specifying discourses as practices within the archive, but it does not establish origins or definitions. *Archaeology* eschews conventional historical methodologies and focuses on ruptures and discontinuities in order to come to an understanding of the emergence of statements and events in the archive. Cf. GENEALOGY.

ARTICULATION. This term is used in three different ways. In one sense, it means to make clear and distinct, as in "articulating a position"; it also means to assemble at the joints (as in a skeleton). In a third sense, common in Marxism, especially after **Louis Althusser**, the term refers to the combination of and connections between elements in the social field. Thus a particular IDEOLOGY *articulates* the various productive forces and cultural components according to the needs of a particular class. For cultural studies, theory produces an *articulated* discourse which seeks to unify with productive social forces. In both cases, *dis-* and *rearticulation* are the starting point of any new theory or social practice. Cf. ASSEMBLAGE, CONSTELLATION.

ASSEMBLAGE. In the work of **Gilles Deleuze and Félix Guattari**, this term designates a contingent consolidation of structural elements in a complex system as well as a flexible, multidirectional *valence* through which power (money, commands, information, verdicts, knowledge) flows and that can be redirected in order to optimize results. An *assemblage* is meant to combat the dominance of the ego and the marketplace and of DIALECTICS generally; it frequently takes a *rhizomatic* form (i.e., destructured, horizontal, dispersive, and exclusive) rather than an *arboreal* form (i.e., hiearchical, ranked, organized, and inclusive).

AUTONOMY, AUTONOMOUS.   These terms refer to the sovereign character of states and to the freedom from influence and oppression of social and cultural institutions. They also refer to the possibility of grounding subjectivity or aesthetic production beyond the influence of social, political, and cultural forces. The bourgeois SUBJECT is often described as *autonomous* in this sense. Some theorists speak of a process of *autonomization* by which the illusion of *autonomy* is maintained in both theory and practice.

BASE/SUPERSTRUCTURE.   In classical Marxism, *base* refers to the modes of production, while *superstructure* refers to the aggregate of social, cultural, political, and commercial institutions and practices that are supported by the base. The precise nature of the relationship varies from school to school within Marxism. A mechanistic relationship would yield a predictable superstructure, which is clearly not the case. Post-Marxist theories of *structural causality* are concerned with IDEOLOGICAL determinations within the *superstructure* itself rather than with direct expressions of economic forces deriving from the *base*. See CULTURAL MATERIALISM and HISTORICAL MATERIALISM.

CANON.   A term first used to designate an authoritative body of sacred texts and legal statutes within the Roman Catholic Church. In literary studies, the term *canon* is used to designate the most important texts in a particular literary tradition. In recent years, the very idea of a literary *canon* has been called into question, in part because it is thought to exclude women and ethnic minorities. The so-called "canon wars" of the 1980s and 1990s were a sign of deep cultural division, especially in the United States and Britain.

CARNIVALESQUE.   Associated with the work of **M. M. Bakhtin**, the *carnivalesque* designates a subversion of social norms in ritual spectacles, comic overturnings, and scatological representations. Linked to the early Christian notion of *carnival*, a time of feasting and merriment before the sacrifices of Lent. See also DIALOGISM and HETEROGLOSSIA.

CENTER, DECENTERED.   Associated with **Jacques Derrida**'s critique of structuralism, the "center" refers to the idea that forms and structures are oriented and stabilized by something that exists outside of the structure itself. The "center," in this metaphysical sense, is a paradox, for it is at the "heart of things" but beyond the influence of the things it "centers" and forms into a coherent structure. To "decenter" a structure is to reveal the mythic character of the center and indict the ideology behind the myth. In postcolonial studies, the imperial *center* is often referred to as the *metropole* or *metropolis* and is contrasted to the colonial *periphery*.

COLONIAL DISCOURSE.   A discursive form of DOMINATION. *Colonial discourse* consists of all those texts, documents, art works, and other means of expression that relate directly and indirectly to colonial rule. *Colonial discourse* is the object of certain forms of discourse analysis, for example ORIENTALISM. See also MIMICRY.

COLONIALISM. Colonialism is the process whereby imperial states acquire new territories and exploit them for land, raw materials, and human labor. *Administered colonies* like India were in large part driven by commerce in native produce, but they were also major centers of imperial power. The colonial bureaucracy was large and offered advancement to Europeans, but it also created the need for native civil servants. By contrast, *settler colonies* involve the extensive settlement of Europeans, either through the establishment of penal colonies, as in Australia, or through the appropriation of arable land, as in Ireland, the Caribbean, and parts of Africa. *Decolonization* is a period of intense social contradiction and conflict that typically ends in an anti-colonial resistance and the creation of independent nations. *Neocolonialism* refers to the continuation of European exploitation of former colonies and implies, on the part of those colonies, either economic helplessness or collusion. Due to its geographical and cultural proximity to the center of empire, Ireland is sometimes called a *metrocolony*. See METROPOLITAN.

COLONIAL MIMICRY. See MIMICRY.

COMMODITY, COMMODIFICATION. A commodity is a product of human labor, created under capitalist conditions; such a product acquires its character as a commodity only in the process of exchange. What ever *use-value* a product may possess becomes, in the process of exchange, a "repository" for exchange value, which is the *social* form of its value. The commodity thus bears the stamp of a social relation, and a value that appears abstracted from use-value. When the commodity is exchanged for money in order to buy other commodities, which are consumed in use, the process of exchange comes to a halt; when money is exchanged for a commodity, which is subsequently sold for more money, a process of endless circulation transforms money into capital. Only a commodity can be converted into capital. The term *commodification* refers to this process. The variant *commoditize* has recently be used to refer to the similarity of goods in the marketplace that possess an equivalent value (e.g., table salt or hydrogen peroxide); *commoditization* produces an undifferentiated market for such goods.

CONCEPT. In idealist philosophy the term *concept* designates the transcendent locus of meaning or being, and the origin and terminus of any particular thing. The concept implies the perfect form or being of things. Terms like UNIVERSALITY and TOTALITY all belong to *conceptual* thinking, as do abstractions like Truth and Beauty, Justice and the Good. Concepts can be empirical (in nature), logical (in the pure sciences like mathematics), and metaphysical (in philosophy and religion). Non-conceptual thinking, such as negative theology or negative DIALECTICS, does not so much give up the concept as challenge its sovereignty over knowledge. A Kantian tradition of AESTHETICS posits an indeterminate concept to preserve the universality of aesthetic judgment.

CONSTELLATION. A mode of philosophical reflection in which the SUBJECT arranges the experiences of multiple perceptions (texts, ideas, phenomena) in such a way as to draw out a general idea or truth. A *constellation* is subjective in the sense that it is a function not of the quality of the experiences but of the critic's understanding of their true idea. It is also provisional: it *might* reveal an idea. Cf. ARTICULATION, ASSEMBLAGE.

CONTEXT, CONTEXTUALIZE.   In literary theory, *context* is the socio-historical milieu within which a text is written, published, and read; to *contextualize* is a way of reading that seeks out the specifics of the work's milieu in order to form a more nuanced and complex sense of the world it expresses.

COUNTER-HEGEMONY.   See HEGEMONY.

CREOLE, CREOLIZATION.   See HYBRIDITY.

CULTURAL MATERIALISM.   A mode of analysis that focuses on how ideas, beliefs, and IDEOLOGIES are formed by material conditions, by constraints imposed by social, cultural, and political policies and forces. *Cultural materialism* holds that social and cultural artifacts are sites of ideological conflict; in such artifacts, the reader can discern the figural expression of social contradictions. It is grounded in the Marxist theory of materialism according to which the modes of production and material conditions are chiefly responsible for determining social, cultural, and political institutions and practices. See BASE/SUPERSTRUCTURE and DIALECTICS. Cf. HISTORICAL MATERIALISM.

CULTURAL POETICS.   Often used to describe the methodologies of cultural criticism in New Historicism and textualist anthropology. Sometimes referred to as *poetics of culture*, this perspective calls into question the objectivity or scientific status that anthropology and other disciplines claim for their representations. It argues that all representations of culture are determined by the same linguistic constraints and freedoms that govern aesthetic discourse.

DECOLONIZATION.   See COLONIALISM.

DETERMINATION.   In philosophy, a concept *determines* an instance of any thing it covers (e.g., any ball under the concept "ball") by virtue of universal elements (e.g., a ball is determined as ball because it is a spherical orb and thus conforms to a crucial element of the concept). In Marxist thinking, determination refers to the role of productive forces (the *base*) in causing and/or furthering the development of social, political, and cultural institutions and trends (the *superstructure*). *Overdetermination* refers to an intensification of class contradictions which can lead (as Lenin said of Russia) to revolution. See HISTORICAL MATERIALISM and NEGATION.

DETERRITORIALIZATION.   See TERRITORIALIZATION.

DIACHRONY/SYNCHRONY.   *Diachrony* is a temporal progression moving in sequence, typically chronologically, within a system. Cf. *synchrony*, a spatial dimension extending in all possible directions from any single point; it thus designates the totality of a system. The former tends to be associated with traditional history and the logic of causality, the latter with atemporal or spatial representations that do not heed causality, sequence, or priority.

DIALECTICS, DIALECTICAL MATERIALISM.   These terms refer both to a kind of process and to a mode of analysis. The former goes back to Plato and the Socratic dialogues, in which logical propositions are formulated through the give-and-take of discussion. Hegel made famous the idea of an interplay between thesis and antithesis that yielded a new synthesis; in the Hegelian sense, the antithetical term (the "negative") is itself negated ("negation of the negation") in a process that both annihilates and preserves it. The Hegelian term for this dialectical consummation is *Aufhebung,* which is typically translated as *sublation.* Over against the Hegelian idealist and logical dialectical forms, Marxian dialectics emerges first and foremost in social and political practice, as in the dialectics of class struggle. *Dialectical materialism* is a variation of HISTORICAL MATERIALISM developed by Marxist theorists like Georgi Plekhanov; the former differs from Marx's own view of history, which is the history of human material production and the transformations of the modes of production, by arguing that nature itself is governed by dialectical laws. See NEGATION.

DIALOGISM.   The dynamic totality of linguistic possibilities that condition individual utterances within social or cultural discourses; dialogism also designates the polyphonic effects of this totality. *Dialogized discourse* is open to, and stratified by, multiple historical and social contexts, a condition **M. M. Bakhtin** called HETEROGLOSSIA. See INTERTEXTUALITY.

DIASPORA, DIASPORIC IDENTITIES.   See HYBRIDITY.

DIFFERENCE, *DIFFÉRANCE.*   A principle according to which language makes meaning by virtue of the *difference* between signs within a system rather than the similarity between a sign and its external referent. *Difference* in this sense evolved from **Jacques Derrida**'s notion of *différance,* which combines the meanings "to defer" and "to differ." It has come to have a general application in the study of gender, sexuality, race, and other topics. See SIGN and PLAY.

DISCOURSE.   Refers primarily to SIGNIFYING SYSTEMS, typically linguistic, within the limits of a particular field of study or knowledge (e.g., medical discourse, literary discourse). For some formalist theorists, *discourse* signifies a linguistic system constituting a dynamic totality. **Michel Foucault** has proposed the idea of the DISCOURSE FORMATION, a term which refers to the aggregate of statements made about a given idea (madness, sexuality, punishment). For **M. M. Bakhtin**, the term discourse designates the concrete totality of languages used in social and literary contexts. See COLONIAL DISCOURSE, MASTER NARRATIVE, ORIENTALISM, and SOCIAL FIELD.

DISCOURSE FORMATION.   Associated with the work of **Michel Foucault**, this term refers to a field of statements and textual "events" that reflect relations of social and cultural power. Many such formations are structured hierarchically and reinforce established traditions and dominant IDEOLOGIES. They are characterized also by the creation of rules of exclusion and, to this extent, are self-regulating systems. The unity or coherence of *discourse formations* is dependent not on the unity or coherence of particular ideas but rather on their emergence and transformation within the formation. *Discursive practices* are those textual and linguistic enunciations that enforce these rules in a specific, disciplined fashion. They can, however, be exploited for subversive purposes, as in COLONIAL MIMICRY and in Foucault's own analytical methods, ARCHAEOLOGY and GENEALOGY. See DISCOURSE and SOCIAL FIELD.

DOMINATION.   In Marxist theory, this term refers to a social condition in which power is exerted over others by material (i.e., military or police) force. Cf. HEGEMONY, which can take the form of domination or consensus.

ÉCRITURE FÉMININE.   A form of strategic ESSENTIALISM, which revalues women's bodies and identities outside of hegemonic discursive practices. It is an acknowledgment of the body as the mystical or spiritual ground for a specifically female *essence*, and thus as the origin and legitimation of a new form of writing. Literally, "feminine writing," it is typically translated as "writing the body."

EPISTEME, EPISTEMIC. These terms refer to epochs or eras, specifically with the philosophical orientation of an era. *Episteme* is from the Greek for "knowledge" and forms the basis for the word "epistemology" (the study of knowledge, of how we know the world). For example, the postmodern episteme is characterized by forms of knowledge (informatics, cybernetics, and so on) radically different from a previous *episteme*. The term *epistemic* is often used to refer to how the knowledge formations of a particular era are used (e.g., colonial discourse is a form of *epistemic violence*).

ESSENCE, ESSENTIAL, ESSENTIALISM.   The essence of a thing is what is inherent, indivisible, immutable about it, what it must possess in order to be *a thing*. It is the chief assumption behind biological theories of race and gender and it drives certain theories of literature and culture that rest on moral and ethical premises. Such theories are often referred to as *essentialist*. Opposed concepts include PERFORMATIVITY, SOCIAL CONSTRUCTION and ÉCRITURE FÉMININE.

FABULATION.   See METAFICTION.

FORECLOSURE. Used by **Jacques Lacan** to describe the psychic state of schizophrenia, in which the subject is utterly cut off from the SYMBOLIC ORDER and "the name-of-the-Father." Language disorders like aphasia are a sign of foreclosure, and in such disorders language use becomes decoupled from perception and sensation, and ultimately becomes the object of intense emotional investments ("cathexes"). **Judith Butler**, among others, has developed models of discourse and identity based on foreclosure that circumvent dominant male subjectivity and the Freudian model of Oedipal desire. See JOUISSANCE.

FORMATION. See DISCOURSE FORMATION.

GENEALOGY.   *Genealogy* is the term Friedrich Nietzsche used to describe his critique of morality, which focused on the interpretation of moral practices rather than on the discovery of an origin for moral ideas or a "moral sense." **Michel Foucault** elaborated on this idea in his work on punishment, sexuality, mental health, and the SUBJECT. *Genealogy* for Foucault is concerned not with natural or divine origins or with chronological, sequential, or causal development over time but rather with the specific points of emergence or transformation or interpretation of POWER. *Genealogies* are forms of "anti-science" that arise out of the convergence of traditional knowledge and local memories in order to establish the grounds for a form of historical understanding that is critical and tactical.

GLOBAL, GLOBALIZATION.   These terms encompass a number of theories concerning the international extension of political, technological, and economic capital, in association with a form of cultural imperialism that seeks a UNIVERSALIZED consumer culture. A *globalized* economy or a global culture is one in which difference is minimized and standardization the norm. Theories of globalization often include a critique of the nation-state, which sustains its separate identity on the basis of geographic, racial, ethnic, linguistic, and/or religious criteria. Connected to this critique is a general resistance to imperialism as a world system (i.e., the idea of the nation and the creation of most nations was a function of imperial IDEOLOGY and policy). See MULTICULTURALISM.

HABITUS.   According to **Pierre Bourdieu**, *habitus* is a form of social subjectivity in conformity with the immanent laws of a particular SOCIAL FIELD. These laws are not arbitrary or externally applied but are rather the result of the aggregate of practices, habits, beliefs, and general knowledge that individuals acquire living in specific social environments. The *habitus* can be fluid and unpredictable, but it is a bounded state. The ability successfully to manipulate *habitus* guarantees the individual social *distinction*.

HEGEMONY. The process by which a particular class achieves social, political, and cultural legitimacy, either through direct DOMINATION (e.g., military and police force) or through modes of consensus that are more or less non-coercive. *Ideological hegemony* is the form typically taken by social power in modern societies, in which general consent is achieved through the subtle coercions of IDEOLOGY. In Marxist thought, the term has been used (e.g., by V. I. Lenin) to designate the power and autonomy of the working class; later theorists have used the term *counter-hegemony* to refer to a critique of the hegemonic power of a dominant class.

HETEROGLOSSIA.   A condition of language, determined by DIALOGISM, that is open to multiple historical and social determinations. Associated with **M. M. Bakhtin**, this term typically refers to the linguistic stratification of discourses characterized by the inclusion of diverse dialects, ideolects, jargons, and other speech forms.

HETERONOMY.   This term is often used in theory to refer to a force or influence that intervenes from the outside, e.g., an external law or mode of DOMINATION. In Kant, it refers to actions made under pressure by forces outside the realm of reason or of ethical law (i.e., outside the realm of *freedom*).

HETERONORMATIVITY.   This term, frequently used in gender studies, refers to a society, institution, or discourse in which heterosexuality is the norm. *Heteronormativity* can be expressed in a variety of ways, from violent coercion ("gaybashing") to unwritten rules of etiquette. A heteronormative society typically outlaws gay marriage and, in some case, homosexuality itself. A related idea, *compulsory heterosexuality*, is often used to refer to a dominant mode of this norm.

HISTORICAL MATERIALISM.   A theory of history that holds that all human events are affected in material ways by the economic sphere of society (i.e., the modes of production in classical Marxism). History is therefore the history of *determinations* made by productive forces. Of course, such determinations are complex, especially in advanced industrial societies. For post-Marxists, the most important *determinations* occur at the superstructural level (i.e., media, social and cultural institutions, ideologies); for them, the relationship is not deterministic or mechanistic but HEGEMONIC. See BASE/SUPERSTRUCTURE, DETERMINATION, and NEGATION. Cf. DIALECTICAL MATERIALISM.

HISTORICISM.   A view of history and historiography according to which social, cultural, philosophical, and religious values have meaning only when grasped as part of the historical moment in which they arise. For some philosophers of history, it refers to the laws of development that characterize historical processes. In some cases, as in Marxist *historicism*, history is understood as functioning according to a theory of HISTORICAL MATERIALISM.

HOMOSOCIAL.   This concept emerged out of the work of Gayle Rubin and **Eve Kosofsky Sedgwick**. It designates a social relationship in which a woman, real or figurative, serves as a conduit for the desire, social or sexual, of two men. To varying degrees, the desire of men for other men is thus sublimated and recast as the competition between men for a woman. Women thus become tokens in an exchange that really has nothing to do with them. At a certain extreme, *homosocial desire* can manifest itself as *homophobia*.

HYBRIDITY, HYBRIDIZATION.   The term hybridity became widely used in postcolonial studies to describe the multitude of subject positions and identities in colonial and, especially, postcolonial societies. **Homi Bhabha** describes it as an "affect" of COLONIAL MIMICRY, in which the subject is doubled in a transgressive rewriting of colonial discourse. It has also come into common usage when speaking of intellectual and artistic practices that cross disciplinary lines or use concepts and ideas from multiple disciplines. *Hybrid identities* are typically discussed in the context of colonial and postcolonial historical formations and, in these contexts, IDENTITY is driven and riven by IDEOLOGY. *Hybridity* also refers to a pluralized identity, open to contingency and change, to linguistic, ethnic, and racial merger. *Diasporic identities* entail a relationship between an individual and a homeland mediated by experiences of slavery, exile, desertion, expulsion, or emigration. These identities may be formed and nourished in enclaves or they may develop along cosmopolitan, multiracial, and multilingual lines. The term *Creole* designates a different form of hybridity and has a long and complex history. In the Caribbean colonies, it came to refer to any person, native, African, or European, who had been born (or "seasoned") in the region. In linguistics, it is used to describe a new indigenous language formed by mixing several other languages. *Creolization*, whether it refers to the process of acclimation to a foreign environment or to linguistic, ethnic, and racial mixing, constitutes a common form of hybrid social and cultural development. See SUBJECT.

IDEALIZE, IDEALISM.   A practice in which something (an object, place, concept, or person) is represented in its most highly evolved and perfected (*ideal*) form. *Idealization* is a form of symbolic representation, whereby the *ideal* of a thing is substituted for the thing itself. *Idealizations* are often invested with a value that has little to do with the thing represented, as when an emergent nation symbolizes its sovereignty as a stylized and perfected woman. A related term comes from psychoanalysis; the *ego-ideal* is what one thinks oneself to be: the *ideal* form of oneself. *Idealizations* generally are fantasy constructions, but they can have a profound impact on personal, social, and cultural life.

IDENTITY. A term that traditionally has designated the distinct and stable "personality" or "character" of an individual, both as it is conceived by others in social environments and as it is conceived by the individual herself. *Identity* is often spoken of in terms of its SOCIAL CONSTRUCTION or its gender and sexual determinations. Important for many theorists is the relationship between *identity* and IDEOLOGY. *Self-identity* refers to the awareness of one's own identity as a stable and singular entity. In metaphysical philosophy, it refers to the possibility of a thing according perfectly with its idea, of the sublation of difference within absolute sameness. *Non-identity* is a term from NEGATIVE DIALECTICS that names the other of *identity* and by so doing offers an alternative to dialectics. Non-identity as such is always a refusal of dialectical closure. This kind of FORECLOSURE, in Lacanian terms, is a condition of psychosis: a schizophrenic (non-)identity. See PRESENCE and NEGATION.

IDEOLOGY. In Marxist theory, a set of beliefs, laws, statutes, principles, practices, and traditions proclaimed by a dominant class in order to rule other classes. Some theorists believe that *ideology* is an "unscientific" point of view, a form of "false consciousness" because it obscures the reality of historical processes. But *ideology* can also refer to *any* set of beliefs, laws, statutes, and the like; thus, we can speak of "working-class ideology" or "socialist ideology." Some theorists hold that *ideology* is precisely the process of representing ideas and beliefs in SIGNIFYING SYSTEMS, of making meaning in a social context. **Louis Althusser**'s influential conception emphasizes the idea of *ideological state apparatuses* (e.g., bureaucracies, schools, universities, the police and military) and the production of *ideology* as an all-encompassing social demand on individuals. See BASE/SUPERSTRUCTURE, HEGEMONY.

IMAGINARY, SYMBOLIC, REAL. Orders of reality proposed by **Jacques Lacan**. The *Symbolic* designates the realm of law, language, reason, metaphysics, the PHALLUS, and so on. The *Imaginary* is the order of fantasy, of pre-Oedipal merger (mother and child bond) and lack of differentiation, JOUISSANCE, DIFFÉRANCE. Some theorists argue that the *Imaginary* is, in fundamental ways, a misrecognition of the *Symbolic*. The *Real* designates what cannot be designated, what cannot be thought or known via the *Symbolic* or the *Imaginary*. But its persistence, as in the Freudian unconscious, can be felt as symptoms in the *Symbolic* and, more effectively, the *Imaginary* order.

IMMANENCE/TRANSCENDENCE. These terms refer to the disposition of "essence" with respect to an object or idea. A *transcendent idea* lies outside the object or ideal it "covers" (usually through conceptual means); thus, as Plato might have it, the concept "good" is transcendent if its true form lies beyond any particular instance of "the good." Similarly, an object's essence lies in a transcendent idea of it. *Immanence* refers to the idea that essence lies within the object and is defined by its internal logic and actuality, which Aristotle called *entelechy*.

IMPERIALISM. If COLONIALISM refers to the administration of foreign territories, *imperialism* refers to the social and political objectives of colonialism and the economic and political consequences of competition with other European states. It also specifies a phase of capitalist development in which markets and labor shift to peripheral territories. *Imperialism* also designates a complex matrix of cultural codes and practices grounded in the social, political, and economic realities of colonialism. *Neo-imperialism* designates the continuation of these codes and practices after the imperial era, a situation which leaves the postcolony in a familiar state of dependency. Often used interchangeably with NEOCOLONIALISM.

INTENTIONALITY.   In the New Criticism, *intentionality* refers primarily to the author's intentions with respect to a work's meaning; in phenomenology, it refers to the mechanism by which consciousness grasps the world by *intending* it, by grasping the in-tension of the object *in the world*.

INTERDISCIPLINARY.   This term refers to research and creative expression that crosses disciplinary boundaries as established in universities and other social and cultural institutions. Poststructuralism, a movement that grew out of multiple interconnected disciplines (like linguistics, anthropology, philosophy, sociology, semiotics, feminism), is inherently interdisciplinary. Interdisciplinarity is the condition of HYBRID theoretical formations.

INTERTEXTUALITY.   A theory of textual reference which holds that the relationship between texts within and between DISCURSIVE FORMATIONS is partly determined by citations and allusions. For **M. M. Bakhtin**, *intertextuality* is the inevitable result of DIALOGIZED HETEROGLOSSIA, of languages stratified and coded with a multitude of dialects, jargons, and other speech forms. Building on Bakhtin, other theorists have linked stratified and dialogized language to the desiring subject (the reader, the writer). Still others have regarded *intertextuality* as a form of auto-critique, of discourse policing itself, of plagiarism, cannibalism, and other forms of consumption. This term should not be confused with *influence* or standard forms of scholarly reference, for they imply a level of INTENTIONALITY not typically associated with *intertextuality*.

JOUISSANCE.   This French noun, often left untranslated, has only near equivalents in English. From the verb *jouir*, to enjoy, *jouissance* designates a range of experiences: religious ecstasy, sexual pleasure, meditation, and poetic imagination. In **Jacques Lacan**'s writings, *jouissance* designates a relation to the unknown and inexpressible aspects of unconscious experience and desire, as well as to death. *Jouissance* is therefore that which is *not* known, that which is beyond knowledge, beyond the SUBJECT of knowledge. In its aesthetic manifestations, *jouissance* is the IMAGINARY misrecognition of the SYMBOLIC, the pleasure taken in the subject's FORECLOSURE of the Symbolic and the "Law of the Father."

LOGOCENTRISM.   This term refers to the primacy, in Western cultures, of *logos* (literarily, "word"), specifically of discourses characterized by reason, logic, and rationality. Often modified as PHALLOGOCENTRISM to emphasize the underlying PATRIARCHAL and masculinist authority of such discourses.

MANICHAEISM.   In its ancient Persian religious context, *Manichaeism* refers to the division of the world into good and evil forces that battle for the possession of humanity. In literary and cultural theory, it designates a binary relation of power characterized by ESSENTIAL difference (e.g., primitive/civilized, male/female, nature/culture), polarization, and inequality. Abdul JanMohamed coined the term "Manichean allegory" to express the relations of power between colonizer and colonized.

MASTER NARRATIVE, GRAND NARRATIVE.   Popularized by **Jean-François Lyotard**, this term refers to the authoritative or foundational narratives of Western societies, specifically the narratives of emancipation and knowledge. Such narratives serve to *legitimate* the power of dominant social classes; their failure results in a process Lyotard calls *delegitimation*. The term is commonly used to refer to any dominant discourse, but especially those that lend themselves to narrative treatment (e.g., Homeric return, Christian Providence, Hegelian world Spirit, Marxist class struggle). See DISCOURSE, METADISCOURSE.

MATERIALISM.   See CULTURAL MATERIALISM and DIALECTICS.

MEDIATION.   This terms designates the practices and discourses that come between human consciousness or experience and the object world. An *immediate* relation to the world implies the identity of subject and object, while a *mediated* one affirms the contingent nature of consciousness, that is, it affirms the fact that consciousness is always separate from and determined by outside forces. For critical theory, *mediation* is a crucial concept in the analysis of IDEOLOGY and the social and cultural institutions that give it material shape and force.

METADISCOURSE.   Any discourse that comments upon or governs another discourse. For example, *metalinguistics* would refer to a technical discourse that reflected upon the way linguistics is discussed and its findings presented. See METAFICTION.

METAFICTION.   A quality of postmodern fiction whereby narrative reflects upon its own status as fictional. It can take the form of structural self-reflection (Linda Hutcheon's "narcissistic narrative") or a "laying bare" of the devices by which novelists traditionally achieve their effects. A related term is Robert Schole's *fabulation*, which refers to the complex patterns and arrangements of language and image often found in postmodern and contemporary fiction. See METADISCOURSE.

METANARRATIVE.   See MASTER NARRATIVE.

METROCOLONY.   See METROPOLITAN, COLONIALISM.

METROPOLE, METROPOLITAN.   The first term refers to an imperial capital (e.g., New York, London, Paris, Amsterdam), while the second designates the characteristic attitudes and IDEOLOGY of imperial culture. The *metropolitan center* connects to the colonies on the periphery of the empire. A *metrocolony* is a large, and largely urban, colony in close proximity to the *metropole*. Ireland is a classic example. See CENTER, COLONIALISM.

MIMESIS.   This term is used throughout the humanities and sciences to refer to imitation, "holding a mirror up to nature" (Shakespeare, *Hamlet*). The mirror of mimesis is said to produce a faithful and exact copy of the world. *Literary realism* is a mimetic mode of narrative that uses language to re-present the physical contours and setting, the personages, the temporalities, and the languages of daily life. Evocative and proximate, it relies on conventions, on a "contract" with the reader (one that frequently presupposes normative social, cultural and political conditions). Realism in the plastic arts accomplishes this re-presentation in ways that are tactile and sensual, that rely on vision and touch. *Mimesis* and *realism* are not meant to disclose the Real, which is a term **Jacques Lacan** uses to designate that which cannot be represented and thus cannot be imitated.

MIMICRY.   This term is frequently used in a general sense to designate forms of imitation, parody or social construction. In postcolonial theory, it used to designate a critical relation to colonial discourse. **Frantz Fanon** argued that colonized people, forced to abandon traditional notions of selfhood and national identity, learn to *mimic* their colonial masters. **Homi Bhabha** modified the concept to emphasize its critical and productive potential. *Colonial mimicry* entails an act of subverting COLONIAL DISCOURSE by exploiting the AMBIVALENCE at its heart, its unstable, contradictory, non-identical potentiality. It results in HYBRID IDENTITIES. See SOCIAL CONSTRUCTION and PERFORMANCE.

MODERNISM, MODERNIZATION.   See MODERNITY.

MODERNITY.   This term designates a period after the decline of feudalism in which we see the rise of secular science, technology, and rational philosophy. It embraces the Renaissance, the Enlightenment, the nineteenth-century Age of Progress, and the triumphs of the early twentieth century. It is grounded in secularism, humanism, and an openness to innovation in all spheres. Key features of *modernity* include industrial capitalism, the nation-state, the development of governmental bureaucracies, the development and refinement of educational systems, and the emergence of the SUBJECT as sovereign and self-identical. *Modernization* refers to the material processes that ensure scientific and technological advancement. It refers also to a condition of rapid and pervasive social and cultural development. *Postmodernity*, in historical terms, begins with or shortly after World War II. It is at the same time a general critique of *modernity* and the articulation of radically new ways of seeing and knowing the world. Technology plays a decisive role in many theories of postmodernity. On *modernism*, see chapter one, "The Rise of Literary Theory" 18–23.

MULTICULTURALISM.   *Multiculturalism* refers both to a state IDEOLOGY (as in the UK and some aspects of the US) regarding race, immigration, and related issues and to a description of transnational society. In the latter more neutral sense, *multiculturalism* is a condition that follows upon patterns of immigration, travel, diplomacy, warfare, and population displacements that spring from the near-total *globalization* of capitalism. See GLOBALIZATION.

NEGATION, NEGATIVE.   In dialectical logic, the negative (antithetical) position is sublated (taken up, annulled, transformed) in the thesis (the "positive term"), thus creating a new term (synthesis) that will logically attract its own negation. In Hegelian philosophy, this is known as *negation of the negation*. The process of *negation* is a necessary and constitutive one for all syntheses; it does not designate the absence of elements. This form of *negation* should not be confused with "negative" in the mathematical sense of subtraction or in the moral/ethical sense of "not good." The term *determinate negation* refers to the process by which negation *determines* the outcome of the dialectical interplay. *Negative dialectics* seeks to subvert the classical *negation of the negation* by safeguarding the negative, or its remnant, as the *non-identical* outside the limits of dialectical closure (*Aufhebung*; sublation). See DIALECTICS, HISTORICAL DETERMINISM.

NEGATIVE.   See NEGATION.

NEGATIVE DIALECTICS.   See CONCEPT and NEGATION.

NEOCOLONIALISM.   See COLONIALISM.

NON-IDENTITY.   See IDENTITY.

ONTOLOGY.   The study of the nature of being (Greek *onto-* "being"), often associated with a belief in PRESENCE, in the absolute fullness of things, absolute SELF-IDENTITY. For Heidegger, phenomenology was the sole means of grasping being for analysis and study. *Object-oriented ontologies* seek to grasp the being or "thingness" of the object that eludes idealist theories of being.

ORIENTALISM.   Associated with the work of **Edward Said**, this term refers to the authoritative discourses on the East (or Orient) produced by the West (or Occident). These discourses include historical, linguistic, philological, and literary works and operate on latent and manifest levels. See DISCOURSE and COLONIAL DISCOURSE.

ORTHODOXY.   Rooted in the concept *doxa*, which means "opinion," *orthodoxy* has come to mean definitive or established truth, typically that of an institutional authority (e.g., the Roman Catholic Church). *Heterodoxy* indicates a deviance from "true opinion," while *paradox* refers to a situation in which contrary opinions appear to be true at the same time. In logic, a *paradox* is a contradictory statement. The New Criticism privileged *paradox* as one of the chief elements of poetry.

OTHER, OTHERNESS.   Terms in widespread use that designate a variety of positions opposed to the *same* or the *self-same*. So, logically, x is not y, so y is the *other* against the "same" that is x. Sticking with logic, if we say x is x, we have achieved self-identity and the "sublation" of the *other*. In this sense (established by Aristotle, modernized by Hegel), the *other* refers to the negative pole of a dialectic. Ethical philosophy treats the *other* in a similar fashion, as the receiver of actions and attitudes; in some cases (e.g., in Emmanuel Levinas), the other is the necessary silhouette that establishes the outlines of the self. From Lacanian psychoanalysis, we get the sense of the *other* as the unconscious (Other) which speaks through the Symbolic. The "object-cause of desire" in **Jacques Lacan**, *objet petit a*, means the "other object" or object of the "big Other." The psychoanalytic dynamic is akin to the Hegelian. For example, the "woman as other" refers to a situation in which a woman becomes a mere surface from which the male subject receives back his own vision of himself, which is generated from the unconscious (Other). Postcolonial theorists, in some cases influenced by psychoanalysis, have developed dialectical theories of the *other* based on racial, ethnic, and cultural difference. Theorists will often use the term *alterity* in a sense roughly synonymous with *otherness*, though etymologically, the meaning of "change, alteration" is discernible from 1270 (*OED*).

Note. In the *Handbook,* I use *other* (lowercase and italicized) to refer to the other in the logical or Hegelian sense (i.e., negative term of the dialectic) and Other when I want to refer specifically to Lacan's Other (i.e., the unconscious in the Symbolic order).

OVERDETERMINATION.   See DETERMINATION.

PARADIGMATIC/SYNTAGMATIC.   *Paradigmatic* refers to the aggregate of relations among elements in a given SYNCHRONIC system. *Syntagmatic* refers to the combinations and relations of elements within DIACHRONIC sequences (e.g., sentences, narratives).

PARADOX.   See ORTHODOXY.

PATRIARCHY.   A social formation in which the father, or a father figure, is the supreme authority. More commonly, the term refers to complex societies in which social and cultural institutions are created and ruled by men, and in which women are accorded inferior or secondary status. *Patriarchal* societies are legitimated and sustained by political, psychological, and philosophical conceptions of the superiority of the PHALLUS and male subjectivity.

PERFORMANCE, PERFORMATIVITY.   These terms refer to a specific form of SOCIAL CONSTRUCTION THEORY, the idea that IDENTITY is a function of the *performance* of gender and sexuality. **Judith Butler** usefully distinguishes between *performance* (the enactment of normative gender and sexual roles) and *performativity* (the subversion of these roles in a critical restaging of identity). See AGENCY.

PHALLUS, PHALLOGOCENTRISM.   *Phallus* refers to the abstract idea of male or PATRIARCHAL power. *Phallocentrism* refers to masculine and patriarchal foundations of Western thought. A common variant, *phallogocentrism,* emphasizes that language and reason (*logos*) are implicated in a *phallic* economy of knowledge and power. See LOGOCENTRISM.

PLAY.   In deconstruction, *play* refers to the relationships of DIFFERENCE that obtain within linguistic systems. Without a stable center in such systems, and without a predictable relationship between SIGNIFIER and SIGNIFIED, the signifying elements of the system (i.e., the signifiers) enter into *play,* free of any MIMETIC or referential connection to the external world. *Play* occurs by virtue of the arbitrary relationship between words and what they signify; we can never be sure, therefore, that our discourse refers to what we think it does. Opposed to the free *play* of the signifier is the idea of pure PRESENCE.

POETICS OF CULTURE.   See CULTURAL POETICS.

POINT DE CAPITON.   In Lacanian theory, this term, which roughly translates as "upholstery pin" or, more generally, "nodal point," refers to certain signifiers that halt the PLAY of signification, thereby creating more or less stable meaning. These points are provisional and subject to AMBIVALENCE and, in some cases, an excess of meaning (as, for example, when the shark in *Jaws,* as **Slavoj Žižek** has pointed out, serves to consolidate the exorbitant signs of our anxiety and fears).

POSTMODERNITY.   See MODERNITY.

POWER.   A commonly used term, *power* can mean many things. In **Michel Foucault**'s usage, dependent on Nietzsche's *will to power*, power is a non-hierarchical expression of "dynamic quanta." This position has been attacked as a form of "negative theology" or metaphysical absolutism that reinscribes the very absolute authority it seeks, through appeal to an undifferentiated force that is absolutely unmeasurable. Foucault's term *power* can be harnessed by social forces as DOMINATION, which can take the form of physical or epistemic violence. **Gayatri Chakravorty Spivak** has analyzed COLONIAL DISCOURSE as a form of epistemic violence. A related term is Foucault's *power/knowledge*, which refers to the way in which discourses (e.g., of medicine, of punishment, of economics) not only represent power but exercise it through mechanisms of exclusion, regulation, prescription, and identification. For theorists like **Gilles Deleuze** and **Félix Guattari**, the roots and locations of *power* are amorphous, unpredictable, *rhizomatic* (like crabgrass). **Giorgio Agamben** has theorized the concept of *potere* in terms of potentiality.

POWER/KNOWLEDGE.   See POWER.

PRESENCE.   A philosophical concept that refers to Being as such, to the essence of a thing, to the present material reality of objects but also a transcendental reality (or Being), outside the realm of signifiers. These conceptions of *presence* provide the foundation for science, morality, AESTHETICS, religion, even language itself. **Jacques Derrida**'s deconstructionist project was inaugurated with a critique of *presence* as a stable reference in linguistic and philosophical statements. Cf. PLAY.

PRIMITIVISM.   A form of COLONIAL DISCOURSE dependent upon a MANICHEAN distinction between civilization and savagery. It derives from scientific, historical, anthropological, philological, sociological, and imaginative texts whose common denominator is a vision of *primitive* peoples as childlike, feminine, irrational, superstitious, violent, garrulous, and genetically inferior. As part of the ideological structure of colonialism, *primitivism* played an important role in establishing the inhumanity of non-Western peoples, thus making it easier to subjugate, exploit, and exterminate them. Interest in *primitivism* was an important part of modernist literature and art. See COLONIALISM and ORIENTALISM.

PROBLEMATIC.   In Hegelian Marxism (especially in **Louis Althusser**), this terms refers to the ideological context for the framing of theoretical questions about a given theme, concept, text, tradition, or practice. A *problematic*, then, is a set of questions that CONSTELLATE around a concept, e.g., the subject. The *problematic of the subject* would thus consist in a far-reaching investigation and critique. It is often used imprecisely as an adjective, to signal that something is complicated or challenging.

REAL.   See IMAGINARY.

REIFICATION.   In Marxist theory, *reification* refers to a process by which social practices are converted into abstractions and objectified, thus distorting the real nature of social conditions and forestalling the development of class consciousness.

In this sense, see COMMODIFICATION. It is often regarded as a form of *depersonalization*. In logic, it is used to refer to a process by which abstractions are treated as if they were concrete material realities.

RETERRITORIALIZATION.   See TERRITORIALIZATION.

RHIZOME.   See ASSEMBLAGE and POWER.

SELF-IDENTITY.   See IDENTITY.

SEMIOLOGY, SEMIOTICS.   Both terms refer to the science of signs and signification. *Semiotics* is associated with the work of Charles Sanders Peirce and emphasizes reference and representation, while *semiology* is associated with the work of Ferdinand de Saussure and emphasizes difference. The terms are often used interchangeably, though the more common term in Continental European theory is *semiotics*. Some poststructuralist theorists (like **Julia Kristeva**) use it in tandem with other theoretical models to craft innovative, non-conventional strategies for analyzing signifying systems.

SETTLER COLONY.   See COLONIALISM.

SIGN, SIGNIFIER, SIGNIFIED.   In Saussurean linguistics, *signifier* refers to a word or sound-image within a linguistic system and *signified* refers to a concept that the signifier designates. Taken together, the two elements constitute a *sign*, which is itself arbitrary in its relation to external reality. A *signifying system* is one in which *signs*, linguistic or otherwise, constitute a single formation in which rules of enunciation and exclusion define the limits of the system. *Transcendental signifier* is the name given by some critics to a metaphysical *Sign* (e.g., God, Reason, the PHALLUS) that legitimates specific *signifying systems* (e.g., metaphysical philosophy, psychoanalysis). The *transcendental signified* is that to which the transcendental signifier refers (e.g., the *phallus* refers to SYMBOLIC authority of the "name-of-the-Father"). See POINT DE CAPITON.

SIGNIFYING SYSTEM.   See SIGN.

SIMULATION, SIMULACRA.   Associated with the work of **Jean Baudrillard**, these terms refer to the idea that "signs of the real" substitute for reality. The "orders of simulation" extend from simple mimetic copies (i.e., exact representations of an external referent) to copies that have no referent at all, that create the illusion of reference and, thus, of reality.

SOCIAL CONSTRUCTIONISM.   This term refers to a process by which material forces emanating from social and cultural institutions *construct* individual IDENTITY and SUBJECTIVITY. It stands in opposition to ESSENTIALISM, which assumes that race, gender, and other features of identity are innate, non-contingent, beyond the influence of material social forces. To construct an identity, personal or national, is a matter of making choices from a wide array of models and combining choices in startling ways. This is most evident in the sphere of gender and sexual identity. See ÉCRITURE FÉMININE.

SOCIAL FIELD.   As used by **Pierre Bourdieu** this term refers to two forms of "social hierarchization": one that encompasses the modes of material and ideological domination while another encompasses cultural and symbolic production, which has its own forms of domination. Cf. DISCURSIVE FORMATION and HABITUS.

SOCIAL FORMATION. A term in Marxist theory, *social formation* refers to the totality of productive forces (at the level of the base) and superstructural components (i.e., class relations, IDEOLOGY, culture, and the like). A dominant social formation is one that has achieved ideological HEGEMONY. See BASE/SUPERSTRUCTURE.

SUBALTERN, SUBALTERN SUBJECT. These terms refer to social groups – e.g., migrants, shantytown dwellers, displaced tribes, refugees, untouchable castes, the homeless – that either do not possess or are prevented from possessing class consciousness and who are in any case prevented from mobilizing as organized groups. In this limited sense, *subalternity* refers to many but not all strata of colonized peoples. The Subaltern Studies Group introduced the current critical meaning, but the term is grounded in the idea of *subject races*, a term put forward by Lord Cromer in 1907 to refer to non-European peoples. The colonialist frame of reference that envisioned subaltern races could do so only because it was supported by a MANICHEAN IDEOLOGY of racial DIFFERENCE. For Antonio Gramsci, the term refers to individuals or groups subordinated to a dominant class in a capitalist system. See SUBJECT.

SUBJECT, SUBJECTIVITY. These terms typically refer to Western traditions of citizenship, selfhood, and consciousness. The *subject* of modern Western societies is often referred to as the *subject of knowledge* (i.e., of a specific epistemological framework) or the *universal subject* (i.e., absolute and sovereign, the norm in all cases). For many theorists, the *subject* is at the mercy of social forces that determine it, more or less completely, through norms, regulations, and other modes of social repression; this is a condition of *subjection*. For some theorists (e.g., Hegelians), the subject *subjects* herself to a dialectic of being in which the subject is born of a struggle with the *other*. SUBJECTIVITY is the goal of this struggle, the condition of being a *subject*, specifically the condition of self-identity (i.e., self-awareness), and the ability not only to recognize oneself as a *subject* (agent or citizen) and to regulate one's actions accordingly but also to recognize the role of the *other* as part of this condition of self-identity. To be capable of conscious action and social and historical AGENCY, the *subject* must occupy a recognizable and legitimate *subject position* within a specific social context. In a Lacanian framework, the role of language in the Symbolic order, in which subjects find their position, ties agency to one's position as a *speaking subject*. See IDENTITY and SUBALTERN.

SUBJECT POSITION. See SUBJECT.

SUBLATION. See DIALECTICS.

SUPERSTRUCTURE. See BASE/SUPERSTRUCTURE.

SUPPLEMENT, SUPPLEMENTATION. In the special sense given it by **Jacques Derrida**, this term refers to the ambivalence of language understood both as an addition to the full PRESENCE of the world of objects and as a substitute for that presence which is thus deferred indefinitely in the free PLAY of SIGNS as *supplements*.

SYMBOLIC. See IMAGINARY.

SYNCHRONY. See DIACHRONY.

SYNTAGMATIC. See PARADIGMATIC.

TELOS, TELEOLOGY.   *Telos* means end or termination. *Teleology* is typically used with reference to natural processes (i.e., the *telos* of an oak tree is contained in the acorn). This sense derives from the idea of "final cause" in classical philosophy. *Teleological* also refers to a form of HISTORICAL DETERMINISM in which the endpoint of history justifies and legitimizes in advance the means of attaining it; Hegel's theory of history is "determined" by the world Spirit that drives it and that constitutes its being as a process of becoming towards an end, its Idea. *Teleology* also applies to historical materialism in the Marxist sense, in which the end is a communist society, with the proletariat organized as a ruling class.

TERRITORIALIZATION.   Associated with the work of **Gilles Deleuze** and **Félix Guattari**, *territorialization* refers to the demarcation of social and cultural spaces by principles of law and rationality (i.e., the SYMBOLIC). To *deterritorialize* is to remove these demarcations, while to *reterritorialize* is to inscribe new demarcations in place of the old. These processes are associated with the imposition of dominant ideologies, especially fascism and COLONIALISM.

TEXT, TEXTUALITY.   In literary theory, a *text* is not simply a book. It is rather a complex, unstable, and unpredictable site, where a number of operations take place: the reader's engagement with the author's words, the PLAY of DIFFERENCES in the language apart from any authorial (or readerly) intent, the INTERTEXTUAL connections with other *texts*, the DETERMINATIONS of social and cultural institutions and traditions. *Textuality* refers to this multivalent aspect of *texts*, to this quality of playfulness and instability. *Textualism*, especially in fields like history and anthropology, refers to the fact that one's consciousness of the world is MEDIATED by written texts.

TOTALITY, TOTALIZE.   *Totality* refers to a structural concept of perfect fullness, inclusion, or completeness. In philosophy, it refers to the fullness of a concept. To *totalize* is to represent a complex entity or unfinished process as if it were a complete and unified object. Because totalizing visions always come at the expense of other visions, to *totalize* is, paradoxically, to exclude. To *totalize* is not necessarily to cover universally all instances of a concept or idea, but to constrain the development of and focus attention on a given number of them. In classical Marxism, *totality* refers to the aggregate of social relations that constitute a SOCIAL FORMATION; yet this same totality is known primarily by the contradictions that call it into question. Thus, *totality* requires contradiction; we could even say, following some post-Marxists, that contradiction founds the social *totality*, which means that *totality* encompasses and nourishes every threat to it. Cf. UNIVERSALITY.

TRANSCENDENCE.   See IMMANENCE.

TRANSCENDENTAL SIGNIFIER/SIGNIFIED.   See SIGN.

UNIVERSAL SUBJECT.   See SUBJECT.

UNIVERSALITY.   A term that refers to the absolute condition of all instances of a concept under its idea (e.g., that all balls are round yields a universal trait for the idea *ball*). We often speak of values and ideas as "universal" (e.g., humanism, liberalism, democracy, freedom, goodness; the latter would be an ethical *universal*). Our modern notions of the term derive either from the logical and mathematic universals of the classical philosophers or the metaphysical universals of Kant and the German Idealists. Cultural and historical universals in the Enlightenment era were, paradoxically, provincial ideas magnified to cover all times and places. Structuralist anthropology, however, has discovered some evidence of cultural universals in language use, kinship systems, religious ceremonies, and the rituals of day-to-day life. Contemporary theorists have developed new variations, e.g., *contingent universals*, that serve to galvanize support for specific strategic ends. See SUBJECT and cf. TOTALITY.

Index

The Literary Theory Handbook, First Edition. Gregory Castle.
© 2013 John Wiley & Sons, Ltd. Published 2013 by John Wiley & Sons, Ltd.

Printed and bound by CPI Group (UK) Ltd, Croydon, CR0 4YY